# POLITICS IN A HALF MADE SOCIETY TRINIDAD AND TOBAGO, 1925-2001

# POLITICS IN A HALF MADE SOCIETY
# TRINIDAD AND TOBAGO, 1925-2001

Kirk Peter Meighoo

Ian Randle Publishers
*Kingston*

James Currey Publishers
*Oxford*

Marcus Wiener Publishers
*Princeton*

First published in Jamaica, 2003 by
Ian Randle Publishers
11 Cunningham Avenue
Box 686, Kingston 6



ISBN 976-637-079-6 paperback

A catalogue record of this book is available from the National Library of Jamaica.

First published in the United Kingdom, 2003 by
James Currey Publishers
73 Botley Road
Oxford, OX2 OBS

British Library Cataloguing in Publication Data

Meighoo, Kirk Peter
Politics in a half made society: Trinidad and Tobago, 1925-2001
1. Trinidad and Tobago - Politics and government
I. Title
320.9'72983

ISBN 0-85255-873-2 paperback

First published in the United States, 2003 by
Markus Wiener Publishers
231 Nassau Street
Princeton, NJ 08542

Library of Congress Cataloging-in-Publication Data

Meighoo, Kirk Peter.
Politics in a "half made society": Trinidad and Tobago, 1925-2002/
Kirk Peter Meighoo.
p. cm.
Includes bibliographical references and index.
ISBN 1-55876-306-6 (hardcover : alk. paper) -- ISBN 1-55876-307-4
(pbk. : alk. paper)
1. Trinidad and Tobago--Politics and government--20th century. 1.
Title.
F2121.M45 2003
972.983'03--dc21

Cover image by Christopher Cozier
Cover design by Christopher Cozier & Juliet Ali
Book design by Shelly-Gail Cooper

Set in Plantin 10pt

Printed and bound in the United States of America

*To my wife, Mona, whom I love very much*

# *Contents*

**Appendices**

# *Illustrations*

**Figure**

# Tables

# Abbreviations

| | |
|---|---|
| ACDC | Action Committee of Democratic Citizens |
| ACS | Association of Caribbean States |
| AES | Annual Economic Survey |
| app. | appendix |
| ASD | Annual Statistical Digest |
| ATSFESWTU | All Trinidad Sugar Estates and Factory Workers Trade Union |
| ATS&GWTU | All Trinidad Sugar and General Workers' Trade Union |
| BECWHRP | British Empire Citizens' and Workers' Home Rule Party |
| BLP | Barbados Labour Party |
| BP | British Petroleum |
| bus. sec. | business section |
| BWIA | British West Indies Airways |
| CBTT | Central Bank of Trinidad and Tobago |
| CCN | Caribbean Communications Network |
| CES | Centre for Ethnic Studies |
| CI | Caribbean Insight |
| CIL | Caribbean Ispat Ltd. |
| CL | Caribbean Life |
| CLS | Committee for Labour Solidarity |
| COLA | Cost of Living Allowance |
| COTT | The Colony of Trinidad and Tobago |
| CPTU | Council of Progressive Trade Unions |
| CSP | Caribbean Socialist Party |
| CWU | Communication Workers Union |
| DAC | Democratic Action Congress |
| DEWD | Department of Environmental Works and Development |
| DLP | Democratic Labour Party |
| DPP | Director of Public Prosecutions |
| EBC | Elections and Boundaries Commission |
| EB | Economic Bulletin |
| ESC | Emancipation Support Committee |
| FERTRIN | Fertiliser Company of Trinidad and Tobago |
| GOTT | Government of Trinidad and Tobago |
| GORTT | Government of the Republic of Trinidad and Tobago |
| ICFTU | Island-wide Cane Farmers Trade Union |
| ICN | International Communications Network |

| | |
|---|---|
| IDB | Inter-American Development Bank |
| IFS | International Financial Statistics |
| ILO | International Labour Organization |
| IMF | International Monetary Fund |
| IRO | Inter-Religious Organiation |
| ISA | Industrial Stabilisation Act |
| ISCOTT | Iron and Steel Company of Trinidad and Tobago |
| JTUM | Joint Trade Union Movement |
| LARRCR | Latin American Regional Reports: Caribbean Region |
| LNG | Liquefied Natural Gas |
| LRC | Legislative Reform Committee |
| MATT | Media Association of Trinidad and Tobago |
| MOTION | Movement for Social Transformation |
| MUP | Movement for Unity and Progress |
| NAEAP | National Association for the Empowerment of African People |
| NAR | National Alliance for Reconstruction |
| NATT | National Alliance of Trinidad and Tobago |
| NATUC | National Trade Union Centre |
| NDP | National Democratic Party |
| NFL | National Federation of Labour |
| NJAC | National Joint Action Committee |
| NGC | National Gas Company |
| NTT | News from Trinidad and Tobago |
| NUFF | National Union of Freedom Fighters |
| NUGFW | National Union of Government and Federated Workers |
| NWRHA | North West Regional Health Authority |
| ONR | Organisation of National Reconstruction |
| OWTU | Oilfields Workers Trade Union |
| PASU | Party Administrative Support Unit |
| PCS | Potash Corporation of Saskatchewan |
| PDP | People's Democratic Party |
| PEG | Political Education Group |
| PEM | Political Education Movement |
| PEP | People's Empowerment Party |
| PETROTRIN | Petroleum Company of Trinidad and Tobago |
| PNM | People's National Movement |
| PNP | People's National Party (Jamaica) |
| POPPG | Party of Political Progress Groups |

| | |
|---|---|
| PPG | People's Progress Group |
| PPM | People's Progressive Movement |
| PPP | People's Progressive Party (Guyana) |
| PSA | Public Services Association |
| QEB | Quarterly Economic Bulletin |
| repr. | reprint |
| SARA | St Augustine Research Associates |
| SDMS | Sanatan Dharma Maha Sabha |
| SDR | Special Drawing Right |
| sec. | Section |
| SOPO | Summit of People's Organisations |
| suppl. | Supplement |
| SWWTU | Seamen and Waterfront Workers Trade Union |
| tcf | trillion cubic feet |
| TE | Trinidad Express |
| TECA | Teachers Education and Cultural Association |
| TG | Trinidad Guardian |
| THA | Tobago House of Assembly |
| TIDCO | Tourism and Industrial Development Corporation |
| TIWU | Transport and Industrial Workers Union |
| TLP | Trinidad Labour Party |
| TRINTOC | Trinidad and Tobago Oil Company |
| TRINTOMAR | Trinidad and Tobago Marine Petroleum Company |
| TSTT | Telecommunications Service of Trinidad and Tobago |
| TTLC | Trinidad and Tobago Labour Congress |
| TTMC | Trinidad and Tobago Methanol Company |
| TTR | Trinidad and Tobago Review |
| TTT | Trinidad and Tobago Television |
| TTUC | Trinidad and Tobago Urea Company |
| TTUTA | Trinidad and Tobago Unified Teachers' Association |
| TTYB | Trinidad and Tobago Year Book |
| TUC | Trades Union Congress |
| TUC and SP | Trades Union Council and Socialist Party |
| TWA | Trinidad Workingmen's Association |
| UF | United Front |
| ULF | United Labour Front |
| UNC | United National Congress |
| UNDP | United Nations Development Program |

| | |
|---|---|
| UPP | United People's Party |
| URP | Unemployment Relief Programme |
| UWI | University of the West Indies |
| VAT | Value Added Tax |
| WASA | Water and Sewerage Authority |
| WFP | Workers and Farmers Party |
| WIFLP | West Indian Federal Labour Party |

# Acknowledgements

The bulk of this book is a slight reworking of my PhD thesis in the Department of Politics at the University of Hull, England, where I was Wilberforce Scholar from 1997-2000. I thank the West India Committee/Caribbean Council for Europe, the Overseas Research Student Committee of Vice-Chancellors and Principals of the Universities of the United Kingdom, the University of Hull's Scholarships Committee and the Faculty of Social Sciences, and BP Amoco for funding my research and maintenance during that period.

The staff at the libraries and research and information divisions of the Central Statistical Office, Port of Spain (particularly Sandra Loregnarde); the West Indiana Division, University of the West Indies, St Augustine (particularly Bertrianna Gransaull); Central Bank Library, Port of Spain, Trinidad and Tobago (particularly Marilyn Jaggernauth); the Elections and Boundaries Commission (particularly Dave Danpaul); the Office of the Prime Minister, Port of Spain (particularly Dr Roodal Moonilal); the Ministry of Energy, Port of Spain; the Office of the Attorney-General, Port of Spain; the Tourism and Industrial Development Corporation, Port of Spain; Market Facts and Opinions (particularly Feisal Muradali and Kimlin Philip); and the Brynmor Jones Library, University of Hull, were all generous in their assistance. Special thanks must also be given to Paul Sutton and Ivar Oxaal for giving me unrestricted access to their well-built personal collections, without which this study would have been much poorer.

Professor Norman Girvan must also be thanked for encouraging me to pursue my doctoral research at the University of Hull. I also thank Ivar Oxaal, Lloyd Best, Brinsley Samaroo, and Kevin Yelvington for their interest, encouragement, and friendship. In addition, I express my appreciation to Daniel Miller, Bridget Brereton, Gad Heuman, David Scott, Gert Oostinde, Robin Cohen, and Bob Norton for commenting on proposals and draft manuscripts sent to them at various stages.

After obtaining my doctorate, I returned to Trinidad and Tobago where I updated and revised my original thesis. For this period, I must thank Dr Kris Rampersad, Editor of the *Sunday Guardian*, and Lloyd Best of the *Trinidad and Tobago Review*, for inviting me to work out my ideas and share information in various national and popular media, and for providing me with regular public space to do so.

Finally, I must thank my wife, Mona, who has been a great companion to me during the years that this book has been with me. In our first year of marriage, she unfortunately has had to share me with the demands of this book. Nevertheless, she has provided me with much help, especially in the final stages.

Thanks also to the following organisations which gave permission for their photographs to be used in this publication:
The Main Library of the University of the West Indies, St Augustine
Information Division, Office of the Prime Minister, Trinidad and Tobago
The *Trinidad Guardian*
The Trinidad and Tobago Institute of the West Indies
To these persons, and to any others whom I have forgotten to mention, I am grateful.

# Introduction

This study is about politics in Trinidad and Tobago from 1925 to 2001. The original intention of the author had been to theorise about the political, economic, and social transformations that have been occurring in Trinidad and Tobago, especially over the decades since Independence. However, it was found that there was insufficient information available to enable the proper formulation of such a theory. While gathering data and evidence, the author became convinced that simply establishing the facts of the period and presenting them in a coherent whole, as plainly as possible, was more important than the original theoretical project envisaged.

As a result, this study has in essence updated, revised, and extended leading Trinidadian political scientist Selwyn Ryan's seminal *Race and Nationalism in Trinidad and Tobago*,[1] which analysed the country's transition to nationhood and the problems it faced in the first decade of Independence. The present study consolidates research done since that book's publication and fills in the numerous and significant gaps with original research. The outcome, it is hoped, is a coherent and accurate account of the historical operation of politics in Trinidad and Tobago that allows one to perceive a sufficiently detailed sense of the evolving whole, and provides a broad and sturdy base for further scholarship – empirical, comparative, and theoretical.

For readers perhaps unfamiliar with Trinidad and Tobago, the following information might be useful. Trinidad and Tobago is a twin-island state composed of the two southernmost islands in the Caribbean archipelago. The island of Trinidad lies at the mouth of the Orinoco River and at its closest point is 11 kilometres from Venezuela (see Maps 1.1 and 1.2).

### *Map 1.1. Central America and the Caribbean*

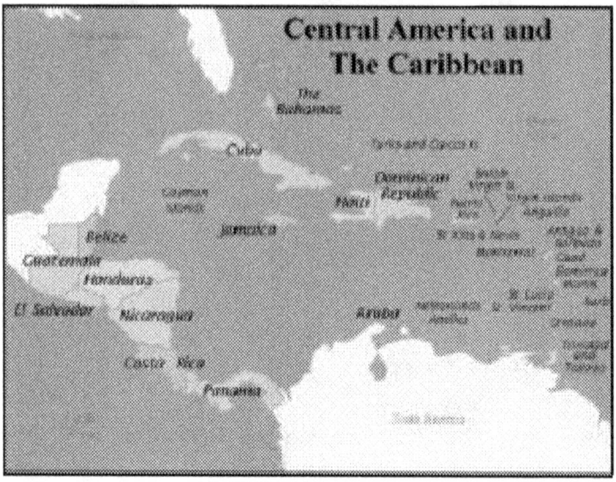

*Source*: *Mindscape World Atlas MPC* 1995 (converted to greyscale by the author)

### *Map 1.2. Trinidad and Tobago*

*Source*: *Mindscape World Atlas MPC* 1995 (converted to greyscale by the author)

Trinidad and Tobago's combined area is 5,123 square kilometres, of which Tobago comprises 303.1 square kilometres. The population in 1999 was estimated at 1.29 million and, according to the 1990 Census was ethnically composed of Indians (40.3 per cent), Africans (39.6 per cent), Mixed (18.4 per cent), White/Caucasian (0.6 per cent), Chinese (0.4 per cent), Other Ethnic Group (0.2 per cent), Syrian/Lebanese (0.1 per cent), and Not Stated (0.4 per cent). Today it is officially an English-speaking country, with a local West Indian English dialect in widespread use. Since the middle of the twentieth century – coinciding with the advent of mass schooling in English – an inconsequential number of persons remain fluent in their ancestral languages.

Trinidad and Tobago were separate colonies at their modern founding, with significant differences in society, politics, and economy. Particularly, Tobago has not had any strong Catholic, Hindu, or Islamic presence, unlike Trinidad. And neither has Tobago any oil deposits. Geologically, Tobago is part of the Caribbean archipelago, while Trinidad is connected to the South American continent.

The two islands were fully unified into a single colony in 1899, and achieved Independence from Great Britain in 1962. Since 1961 it has operated a Westminster-derived system of parliamentary democracy, with its own characteristics evolved from past practice. It became a Republic in 1976. In the *Human Development Report 2001,* Trinidad and Tobago ranked 49th out of a total of 162 countries in Human Development, placing it first in the category of Medium Human Development.[2] Life expectancy was estimated at 74.1 years, literacy at 93.5 per cent of persons 15 and above, the combined primary, secondary and tertiary gross enrolment ratio at 65 per cent, and GDP per capita at US$8,176. Its Human Development Index ranking is four places higher than its GDP ranking. Trinidad and Tobago's Human Poverty Index was ranked fifth among developing countries, with 7.9 per cent of the population estimated to experience deprivation in health, knowledge, and a decent standard of living. It ranks immediately below Chile and Cuba, and immediately above Panama and Jordan. In 1998 its urban population was estimated at 73.2 per cent. Trinidad and Tobago was ranked 41st out of 72 countries in its Technology Achievement Index, placing it the fourth highest Dynamic Adopter of Technology. It falls immediately below South Africa and Thailand, and immediately above Panama and Brazil.

Trinidad and Tobago's GDP measured at US$6.4 billion at current market prices, with services comprising 50.7 per cent, industry 47.5 per cent, and agriculture 1.8 per cent. Notably, Trinidad and Tobago produces oil and gas, and the petroleum sector accounted for about 27 per cent of GDP at factor cost in 1998. Trinidad and Tobago's GDP per capita in 1999 ranked 53rd by the Untied Nations Development Program (UNDP). In 2000 the Central Bank of Trinidad and Tobago estimated the unemployment rate at 12.8 per cent.[3]

## PERSPECTIVE OF THE STUDY

Perhaps to the disappointment of some, no established theoretical framework as such has been used in this study, and no theory has been tested. The author used a descriptive, historical narrative approach in presenting and analysing data, as is appropriate in presenting such a factually-based overview. Unlike Ryan's pivotal text, whose 'principal aim' was 'to explore the influence . . . [of] cultural and ethnic diversity . . . on the struggle for political and social reform and to suggest explanations for the failure of the programme of radical decolonization',[4] the author of the present work has not employed a central hypothesis and has avoided political suggestions. An open-ended, eclectic approach has been taken, for a number of reasons. Firstly, an openness to data as wide as practicable allowed a more comprehensive and accurate picture of the period and its dynamics to emerge, without the investigative limitations imposed by an hypothesis. Secondly, it is the author's opinion that theorising on Trinidad and Tobago's political development (except at the most general level) is premature: on the one hand, because of the insufficiency and impreciseness of the existing empirical material upon which such theory can be soundly constructed; and, on the other hand, because of the author's conviction that Trinidad and Tobago remains an unsettled society which has been in fundamental flux for most of the period under study. Thirdly, the author sympathises with James Manor's argument in *Rethinking Third World Politics* that paradigm-building and its implicit agenda-setting have undermined understanding of 'how things actually work in Third World political systems', and that 'attempts at prescription . . . [have impeded] attempts to comprehend what is taking place' in these countries.[5] Manor and his cohorts have favoured 'thick description' over 'parsimonious models' in order to arrive at 'the most sophisticated possible understanding of how things actually work.'[6] This study presents such a 'thick description' of politics in Trinidad and Tobago.

Two important political studies dealing with Trinidad and Tobago have used a similar descriptive approach: *Black Intellectuals Come to Power* by Ivar Oxaal and *The Growth of the Modern West Indies* by Gordon Lewis.[7] As did the researchers in those studies, the present author acknowledges that 'invisible rubrics, theoretical issues, and concepts . . . have guided this narrative'[8] but maintains that concentrating on them would have distracted and diverted from the task of 'thick description' (which is a demanding art itself).

The author does consider it important, however, to elaborate in this introduction two main sets of ideas guiding his perspective. First, the study displays many assumptions, predispositions, and arguments of classical conservatism as outlined by Jerry Z. Muller in his essay, 'What is Conservative Social and Political Thought?'[9] The general outlook includes an emphasis on human imperfection; an insistence on the limits of human knowledge and an attitude of 'epistemological modesty'; a critique of 'theory'; a mindfulness toward unanticipated consequences, latent functions, and the functional interdependence of social elements; a respect for the order of institutions; an appreciation of custom, habit, prejudice, and 'second nature'; sensitivity to historical and particular contexts, and scepticism towards universalism; 'anti-contractualism'; an 'anti-humanitarianism' that is conscious of the sometimes perverse outcomes of well-intentioned actions; an acceptance of the necessity of trade-offs, costs, and limits, not uncommonly expressed in an ironic or tragic mode; scepticism towards written constitutions, as opposed to the informal, sub-political, and inherited norms and mores of a society; the need for individual or socially imposed restraint and identity and, hence, scepticism regarding projects intended to liberate the individual from existing sources of social and cultural authority; the legitimacy of a level of inequality and the need for elites, cultural, political, and economic; and the occasional need for 'veiling' as opposed to transparency.

In addition to these philosophical tendencies, more specifically the author's comprehension of Trinidad and Tobago has been strongly guided by the understanding of Sir Vidia Naipaul, Trinidad-born writer and Nobel Laureate. Naipaul sees Trinidad and Tobago as a 'half-made society', a term he coined in a 1970 essay on the Black Power movement in Trinidad and Tobago and used again, in a 1974 essay on Joseph Conrad, to describe many of the countries in which he is intellectually interested.[10] This seemingly harsh and dismissive-sounding term implicitly rejects the assumption that societies, justly labelled, necessarily emerge from a given collection of people living together, or that any two societies function equally well in their contexts. In particular, the author understands Naipaul's term as highlighting the fact that some societies, such as Trinidad and Tobago, have not yet established enduring, meaningful standards of their own. They are societies still in formation and unmade, without a firm foundation (intellectual, cultural, political, military, and/or economic), and in which solidity is elusive.

Many readers may find it difficult to accept such a concept or may confuse it with the idea of a 'developing' society. To explain it, one must articulate the idea more explicitly than Sir Vidia does. (Accordingly, one risks interpreting his idea incorrectly.) The opposite of a 'half-made society' (I suppose, a 'full' society) is not a 'developed' society or a rich society. It is a society with a full range of social groups and statuses, and relatively full, largely self-generated economic, military, political, aesthetic, artistic, moral, and intellectual traditions. Such a society might have existed

200, 500, or 1,000 years ago, or might endure that far ahead. It is suggested that a society that maintains its existence for so long does so because it is full and strong enough to persist in all, or most of, these areas, despite the necessary changes. Examples of countries which one could consider 'fully formed,' are England, France, China, and Japan. Politics in these societies have a certain depth not found in Trinidad and Tobago, for example.

A 'half-made society' is not necessarily a poor society. Trinidad is an excellent example of a half-made society because of its newness – both in terms of political independence and in terms of settlement. Canada, despite its wealth, might also be called a 'half-made society'. (One might be tempted to include the United States here, too.) On the other hand, societies such as Nigeria or Fiji, for example, do not suffer from the same problems of newness as Trinidad and Canada. Nigeria arguably contains 'full' societies – with strong, binding traditions – incorporated within its borders, but they are not fully integrated with one another in the modern nation-state. It, therefore, faces a distinct problem. Alternatively, societies such as Turkey, India, or Iran should not be considered 'half-made' but decaying from earlier grandeur and now falling apart, unable to maintain their positions in contemporary economic, military, moral, and intellectual contexts. Their problems might be ones of regeneration.

To further explore this idea of 'half-made' and 'full' societies would take one into territory that might not be able to be quickly crossed. And it would detract from the main purpose of the book, which is to examine the politics of a particular society.

While the concept of a 'half-made society' certainly does not describe Trinidad and Tobago entirely, it captures an important, perhaps even fundamental, historical quality that one can recognise in the empirical material presented in this study. In many ways, this book is a chronicle of the challenges that have faced the cumulative historical attempts to establish effective and durable political institutions (that is, institutions of overarching national authority) in one such half-formed society.

## RESEARCH QUESTIONS

The major research question asked in this study was: what have been the main political challenges faced by the various governments of Trinidad and Tobago between 1925 and 2001? Subsidiary questions, indirectly explored, were: have there been distinctive problems, programmes, goals, methods, and themes transcending particular governments and oppositions? How far have racial and ethnic concerns dominated politics in Trinidad and Tobago? How did Prime Minister Eric Williams survive in office for five terms? How did the three subsequent Prime Ministers fail to win a second term? How did Basdeo Panday break this trend?

With respect to the major research question, 'main political challenges' refers to significant parliamentary, extra-parliamentary, legal, and extra-legal attempts to remove the government from power or office; actions that have resulted, by accident or design, in significant loss of electoral or parliamentary support for the government; and actions that have affected or attempted to affect government's policies, programmes, or goals. The author has considered it important to elaborate in detail by whom, on what issues, by what methods, for what reasons, at what times, and in what context and fora these challenges occurred.

It is important for the author to describe the view of politics taken in this study. Politics is seen as having a formal, institutional level – the official constitution of authority, including the constitution, Parliament, political parties, government, Opposition, and so on. Influencing that level is a sub-formal level – such as pressure groups, influential individuals, personal rivalries, controversial social, cultural, and economic issues, racial fears, protests, public opinions, attitudes, fears, sociological and psychological factors, race relations, ideologies, social movements, opposition parties. This influence can sometimes be unpredictable. It can be overwhelming in some instances. Yet at other times, its influence can be less important than one might expect, or less important than one might think it ought to be. This study, it should be emphasised, will focus on the formal level of politics, that is the institutional expression of politics. The study is de-limited in such a way that 'sub-formal' aspects, public policy and administration, constitutional changes, development policy, and economic policy will be examined only when they demonstrably have affected the administration of government programmes, elections, and political survival. If this study is successful, the weaknesses resulting from this method may therefore imply the weaknesses of formal politics in the twin-island state. It will also show how far 'non-political' phenomena have influenced formal politics.

With regard to the major research question, 'various governments' refers to the Crown Colony government from 1925 to 1956 (with legislative and executive councils headed by a governor appointed by the British government), and after 1956 (when an elected Chief Minister headed the legislative and executive councils) the administrations formed after general elections. Between 1925 and 1956 six Legislative Council elections were held and eight governors administered the colony. Since self-government in 1956 to 2001, there have been ten governments: five headed by Eric Williams from 1956–81, one by George Chambers from 1981–6, one by A.N.R. Robinson from 1986–91, one by Patrick Manning from 1991–5, and two by Basdeo Panday from 1995–2001.

Throughout the study, ethnic terms have been employed according to their vernacular usage in Trinidad and Tobago. The terms 'African', 'Negro', 'black', and 'Afro-Creole' are used to mean persons who identify themselves and/or are identified as being of African descent. Unless otherwise stated, such persons are citizens of Trinidad and Tobago. The terms 'Indian' and 'East Indian' are used to mean persons who are of Asian Indian descent and unless otherwise specified, are citizens of Trinidad and Tobago. 'Syrian', 'Syrian/Lebanese', 'Portuguese', and 'Chinese' refer to citizens of Trinidad and Tobago so descended, unless otherwise specified. 'Local white' and 'French Creole' are terms used to identify light-skinned persons of mainly European descent who are citizens of Trinidad and Tobago. 'British', however, does not refer to British-descended citizens of Trinidad and Tobago. The term 'Creole' is generally used to refer to the non-Indian population and culture of Trinidad and Tobago.

The study is organised historically/chronologically, from 1925 to 2001, with the greatest emphasis placed on the relatively under-researched 1986–2001 period, and a short chapter looking at the 1925–53 period, the first 28 years of electoral politics in Trinidad and Tobago. The study's main limitation has been the broad time-frame which has prohibited deeper investigation into some of the more important and complex issue areas and events. In addition, some information gaps have remained, often due to a lack of sources. In some cases this was due to the impossibility of the author's access due to circumstantial constraints, in other cases because authoritative sources and material were non-existent. In such instances, less than authoritative sources have been used, such as newspapers and secondary reports.

## EXISTING LITERATURE

After the completion of the manuscript, three books were published relevant to this study: the autobiography of Alloy Lequay (2001), a biography of Eric Williams by Ken Boodhoo (2002), and a thorough study of Trinidad and Tobago's foreign policy by former Minister of Foreign Affairs, Sahadeo Basdeo, and Graeme Mount (2001). Unfortunately, it was not possible to incorporate into this study the important material found in these works.

As a whole, the body of secondary material on politics in Trinidad and Tobago displays significant weaknesses. This includes the absence of sustained work and investigation, that has resulted in few published books and a patchy smattering of articles located in sundry journals with a less than systematic coverage of events and issue areas. Another major deficiency has been the empirical and factual failings of the material that does exist. Furthermore, the individual studies that make up the literature on Trinidad and Tobago politics seem to be largely disengaged from one another, with reference rarely being made to other researchers' work either in the text or in the bibliographies (when they are compiled). Through empirically-detailed, information-intensive 'thick description' and systematic investigation, this study seeks to fill some of the more important gaps.

Partly because Great Britain had acquired Trinidad and Tobago much later than it did its first West Indian colonies, relatively little had been written in English on Trinidad and Tobago.[11] Apart from comprehensive histories, academic study of politics in these islands began with Charles Reis's study of constitution and government in Trinidad (the first edition was published in 1915), followed 37 years later by Hewan Craig's study of the Legislative Council of Trinidad and Tobago.[12] Political study of Trinidad and Tobago in the colonial period usually took place within larger contexts, either the West Indies as a whole or the colonies of the British Empire.[13] As the short-lived Federation of the West Indies (1958–62) came into being, Trinidad and Tobago's politics were placed more firmly in the context of developments in the West Indies. The studies during the Federal period mainly focused on constitutional developments towards self-government and displayed a concern with the colony's political sociology and the gradually diminishing influence of the British.[14]

The University of the West Indies (UWI) (established in Mona, Jamaica in 1947) instituted its Faculty of Social Sciences at the Mona Campus in 1960, with a Department of Government teaching politics courses to undergraduates for the first time in the West Indies.[15] In 1966, the Faculty of Social Sciences at the St Augustine campus in Trinidad was founded.[16] Between the establishment of the two campus faculties, Jamaica and Trinidad and Tobago separately achieved independence in August 1962. These developments greatly stimulated political studies in the West Indies by West Indians.

Caribbean-wide studies continued to be published, despite the break-up of the Federation of the West Indies. Radical nationalists based at UWI developed the Plantation Thesis which had argued that the structural heritage of colonial plantation slavery continued to determine international and national economic, class, ethnic, and political relations, privileging metropolitan over local interests. Although the thesis exerted a strong influence in West Indian political science,[17] serious development of the model was carried out by economists and sociologists.[18]

In 1974 the Caribbean Community (CARICOM) was established out of the Caribbean Free Trade Area (formed in 1967), prompting political studies on the regional integration movement, which deliberately avoided moves toward closer political union, and instead concerned itself with economic and 'functional' co-operation.[19] By the 1980s, the political concerns expressed in the Plantation Thesis became expressed more diffusely, without a necessary commitment either to the theory's explanation of causes or to its recommended solution of at least partial disengagement from the capitalist world-system. At the same time, progress in regional integration seemed to be halted. The Caribbean-wide studies that were published in the 1980s continued to be concerned with the dominance of international over national interests and were stimulated by the failures of the socialist governments in Jamaica,[20] Guyana,[21] and Grenada[22]; the emergence of a strong anti-Communist US foreign policy under the Reagan Administration, embodied by the US invasion of Grenada in 1983; and the emergence of IMF and World Bank-sponsored structural adjustment programmes in the region.[23] By the 1990s there also emerged a concern with the development of democracy in the region[24] while regionally published undergraduate-level teaching texts were developed with a focus on comparative political institutions and administrative systems.[25] Ryan has also recently published a book that has examined comparatively the experience of Westminster-derived government in the Commonwealth Caribbean.[26]

Since independence, however, serious study of politics in Trinidad and Tobago has taken place within a national rather than regional context. The most important text published has been Selwyn Ryan's *Race and Nationalism in Trinidad and Tobago*.[27] That study, as indicated above, provided a political-historical overview of the transition to nationhood and the problems faced in the first decade of independence, while having as its principal aims the exploration of the country's cultural and ethnic diversity on the struggle for political and social reform and the suggestion of explanations of the failure of the programme of radical decolonisation.[28] Despite its empirical gaps (in particular through its less than systematic account of post-Independence politics, perhaps most notable in its omission of the 1966 elections), that book remains the most complete study published of the process of politics in Trinidad and Tobago. Professor Ryan has continued with great vigour his project of chronicling the political life of Trinidad and Tobago, providing a valuable resource for researchers beginning to explore politics in the country.[29] Many of these publications have been collections or slight re-workings of previously published newspaper columns (which he has been writing weekly since the 1970s), journal articles, and opinion polls (which he began on a national basis in 1976).[30] However, weaknesses found in his first study – the concentration on racial and ethnic issues above all else and a parsimoniousness with regard to facts – have been combined with his studies' increasing reliance on racially-categorised opinion poll data. This turn has necessitated academic supplementation even more urgently. In particular, his studies' habitually incomplete data on elections, the limited analysis of general election results (especially in comparison to analysis of his opinion poll data), and the almost total neglect of local government elections are shortcomings that need to be corrected.

Information gaps have been partially filled by such studies as those done on parliamentary and constitutional developments,[31] on particular general elections,[32] on the 1990 attempted coup,[33] on the black power movement of 1970,[34] on figures from the union movement and from politics,[35] on the labour movement,[36] on the opposition Democratic Labour Party,[37] on the National Union of Freedom Fighters,[38] on dissident political groups of the unemployed,[39] on the women's movement,[40] on the 'power elite,'[41] and on public policy and politics.[42]

This material has added useful information, but at best they provide a discontinuous and not fully consistent account of politics in the period under study. It should be noted, however, that Hamid Ghany's locally-published biography of Kamaluddin Mohammed, Cabinet Minister (1956–86), of the People's National Movement (PNM) stands out, if not for its interpretation, then certainly for the impressive amount of primary research in government, Colonial Office and other authoritative records covering a considerable period.[43] Malik also provided much valuable information on the largely neglected period of the 1960s.[44]

Most political research on Trinidad and Tobago – including Ryan's – has concerned itself with conceptual issues, such as the development of nationalism and democracy, the role of ethnicity and class in Trinidad and Tobago's politics, and the nature of government and the state. An enduring, classic study of the independence movement in Trinidad and Tobago was undertaken by Ivar Oxaal,[45] who along with Wendell Bell[46] and Charles Moskos[47] intensively examined the peculiar historical development of West Indian nationalisms while placing them in the context of 'the spread and development of the democratic revolution through time and space from the eighteenth-century Atlantic community to the twentieth-century global society.'[48] A concern with the development of West Indian nationalism is also at the heart of Lewis's enterprise, which remains equally enlightening to this day.[49] Unfortunately, this insightful body of work was not followed up to examine the developments in Trinidad and Tobago democracy since Independence. Since then, a study by Magid has been published examining the development of what he called 'urban nationalism' in the period 1895–1903,[50] but it was not well received on account of its interpretative and empirical failings.[51] Anthropologist Thomas Hylland Eriksen has subsequently taken up the Trinidad and Tobago example (together with that of Mauritius) to examine the wider phenomenon of nationalism, but his theorisation is situated in the context of work on 'identity politics'.[52]

Working nationalism into questions of identity fits in with the most prevalent and enduring theme in the study of politics in Trinidad and Tobago: politics as an expression of ethnic competition. This approach to political study spills over to and from anthropology and sociology. It is the persistent theme in Ryan's work. Besides his work, there are a about a dozen of these studies published that can be justifiably called political studies.[53] The claims of the various works are not identical, however. Vera Rubin and Yogendra Malik stand out as the most coolly analytical of these scholars,[54] while Ralph Premdas represents the polemical and emotional extreme. Premdas's work, which has been building up to a critical mass, has significant weaknesses, particularly its curtness with evidence and data in what this author considers to be his haste to construct an ethnic conflict theory for politics in Trinidad and Tobago.

Ethnic competition undoubtedly is a major feature of politics in Trinidad and Tobago, but other researchers have understood this rivalry to be complicated, modified, and sometimes by-passed by political motivations based on class and other interests. The theorist operating most consistently from this perspective has been Percy Hintzen who has been developing a view which sees race as one of the tools that local elites have used to secure their political control and domination.[55] Others also have considered analytically ethnic and class motivations in Trinidad and Tobago politics.[56]

A few researchers have attempted to develop theories of the state or the government or both in Trinidad and Tobago, but since the early 1980s this body of work has attenuated. A common theme among this work has been the determination or limitation of national politics by the political economy of the international system.[57] During the Williams era, the development of a 'presidential' or authoritarian style was commonly linked to the country's structural situation. Updating this last point about domestic politics, Maingot has linked Trinidad and Tobago's racially divided politics to the requirements of global capitalism.[58]

Because so few books have been published on Trinidad and Tobago politics, MacDonald's singular study is worthy of mention.[59] In that work, he explains the relative success of democracy in Trinidad and Tobago by tracing the evolution of the country's democratic-minded middle class (multi-racial in nature), its sizeable state sector in the economy, oil industry, and its accepted, yet controlled, foreign investment.[60] Although the study stretches from the colonial era to 1983, adding a period not found in Ryan's first book, Ryan's later works have eclipsed it.

These theoretical, conceptual, and interpretative studies have undoubtedly contributed to a greater understanding of politics in Trinidad and Tobago. However, there are common flaws in them. One is that, since 1972, Ryan's body of work has of necessity been the main authority cited by these theorists. His weaknesses and gaps, though remedied in part by the original research done in these other studies, have not been adequately redressed by them. Accordingly, theorising has proceeded on an incomplete and faulty empirical base. Another weakness, most especially seen in the work on nationalism and in the (loosely Marxist-derived) theorising about the state, is that such theory has been overtaken by subsequent developments, sometimes in less than a decade. This particular vulnerability of theory is general and has been noted by Manor.[61] Especially in a newly settled, rapidly evolving country such as Trinidad and Tobago, it is arguable that anything more than an extremely general theory will not stand the test of time.

It must be admitted that, in this respect, ethnic interpretations have been the most durable. However, the existing literature's inattention to data, its haste to conclude and recommend, and its intent to reduce Trinidad and Tobago's political reality to a simple, clear, and solvable framework (through power-sharing, consociationalism, or other recognition of cultural and ethnic pluralism) at times bypasses the actual operation of politics. Simple ethnic models not infrequently exaggerate objective political reality, such as with Premdas's overly ethnic view of the split in the National Alliance for Reconstruction (NAR).[62] These models often do not account for important facts such as the entrenchment in the 1971–81 period of the Afro-Creole led PNM and the fall in support for the Indian-led Democratic Labour Party (DLP) and United Labour Front (ULF), even though the Indian population increased in economic, cultural, and numerical strength during this time.

To remedy the weaknesses of the literature on Trinidad and Tobago's politics, it seems that the first necessary task is the carrying out of further solid, empirically-based, systematic, and durable research. This perhaps modest task is what the present study seeks to accomplish.

## RESEARCH DESIGN

To achieve the ends of this study, a reconstruction of political events has been attempted, mainly through the examination of written documentation. The research procedure has been fairly standard, with no substantial methodological innovation. Perhaps notable, however, is the extent to which the author has used official statistics (especially from the Central Statistical Office, the Central Bank, and the Elections and Boundaries Commission), public relations documents, memoirs, autobiographies, biographies, and speeches of major political personalities.[63] The other sources – local newspapers, official government reports, pamphlets, bulletins, monthly reports, and interviews – are typical in the field. The more diligent attempt at their systematic investigation is perhaps what is distinctive in this study. Regarding interviews, a total of 19 persons who played important roles in politics, both in the past and at present, were interviewed specifically for this dissertation.[64] These personalities included the contemporary Prime Minister, the two living former Prime Ministers (who led different political parties and at the time of interview were the President and the Leader of Opposition), and five current and former Cabinet Ministers (see Appendix E). The interview data were rarely used directly in the study, but they did provide valuable backgrounds against which were placed information gathered from other sources.

The seven substantive chapters of the study provide a detailed historical reconstruction of politics from 1925 to 2001. They are grouped into a prelude briefly covering the period 1925-53 (chapter one), and three parts: 1953–81 (chapters two and three), 1981–91 (chapters four and five), and 1991–2001 (chapters six and seven).

The prelude outlines the establishment and development of electoral politics in Trinidad and Tobago between 1925 and 1953. The period was marked by constitutional advance toward self-government but an absence of a nationally organised political movement.

This leads to Part One, which focuses on the long reign of Eric Williams and the PNM from 1956 to 1981. Chapter two follows the entrance of Eric Williams onto the political stage of Trinidad and Tobago in 1954 to the achievement of national independence in 1962 under the governance of the PNM, the country's first nationally organised party, which Williams led. Chapter three looks at the peculiar challenges faced by Williams and the PNM from 1962 to 1981, including a collapsed parliamentary opposition, vigorous subversive extra-parliamentary protest movements, and the structural transformation of the Trinidad and Tobago economy occasioned by the over twenty-fold increase in oil prices over the period. The era ends with the death of Williams while in office.

Part Two examines the rapid rise and quicker fall of the NAR party and government from 1981–1991. Chapter four looks at the performance of the post-Williams administration under George Chambers from 1981–6, that ended in the first defeat in a general elections for the PNM. Chambers was faced with three major challenges in office: succeeding a charismatic political icon who had mastered the Trinidad and Tobago political environment, managing a more than 50 per cent drop in oil prices, and fighting off a newly invigorated and consolidated political opposition, the NAR. He failed all three. Chapter five reviews the NAR administration (1986–91), the party's split during its second year in office, the popular resistance to its policies of structural adjustment, the attempted coup of 1990, and the party's failure to secure a second term in 1991 despite the enthusiastic and unprecedented electoral mandate it received in 1986.

Part Three looks at the move towards political stalemate in 2001, after a cross-party consensus on structural adjustment, and the emergence of parity in the political forces with the coming to power in 1995 of Basdeo Panday, the country's first Indian Prime Minister. Chapter six examines the 1992–5 PNM administration under the leadership of Patrick Manning in the context of a newly emerging political, social, and economic context: the stabilising of three major political parties, the newly confident Indian presence in the country's cultural mainstream, and the emergence from economic recession with a significantly transformed economy. In Chapter seven the two administrations of the United National Congress (UNC) are analysed. On the one hand, it was one of the country's most important governments, in terms of its reforming zeal and its ability to win a second term of office. On the other hand, the intense opposition against it eventually effected the unprecedented collapse of the government just eight months after resuming its second term in 2001. The UNC governments, with threadbare majorities, unexpectedly pushed the independence model of self-government to its extremes, highlighting the problems of legally constituted authority in Trinidad and Tobago: the division of powers and responsibilities of the President, the Prime Minister, the Courts and the Judiciary, the Tobago House of Assembly, and the Constitution itself. In questioning their powers, their limitations were reached. At the same time the country reached a political stalemate, that, at the time of writing, persists, even if in muted form.

The Conclusion summarises the findings in relation to the main and subsidiary research questions and discusses the impact, implications, and recommendations for further study. At the end of this study are appendices that provide a detailed chronology of the period 1921–2001; election statistics from 1925 to 2001; maps showing the distribution of legislative council and parliamentary seats from 1956 to 2001; selected economic indicators from 1970–2000; outlines of the structure of government from 1925 to 2001; the regional distribution of legislative council and parliamentary constituencies from 1925 to 2001; and a list of persons interviewed.

*Prelude to Self-Government*

# One

## THE ESTABLISHMENT OF ELECTORAL POLITICS, 1925-53: 'WE ARE ALL INDIVIDUALS'

In this chapter, we outline the establishment and development of electoral politics in Trinidad and Tobago. During the period 1925–53, it should be noted, government was firmly in the hands of Great Britain. The labour disturbances of 1937 could not in any reasonable way be seen to have threatened Britain's political power over the colony. They did, however, contribute to greater questioning among some members of the society about the British rule in Trinidad and Tobago; and by no means were the answers uniformly against the British. The Moyne Royal Commission, appointed in the wake of the labour riots, recommended the introduction of universal adult suffrage which, in turn, propelled limited agitation toward self-government and home rule.

In particular, we note the conditions and pressures (both institutional and social) under which electoral politics operated and performed. Three Orders-in-Council – in 1924, 1945, and 1950 – were passed during the period covered in this chapter, each Order increasing the proportion of elected members in the

Legislative Council, bestowing upon the elected members greater responsibility, and extending the franchise. Perhaps the most notable aspect of political organisation during this period was the absence of nationally organised political parties. Instead political aspirants contested seats as independents or as members of loosely-organised and short-lived parties organised around one of many interests and groups – regionally, ethnically, labour, and ideologically based. These beginnings constitute a sort of 'ground zero' for politics in Trinidad and Tobago and most clearly support the idea of Trinidad and Tobago as a 'half-made society'.

It would do us well to note that Trinidad, in particular, is among the most recently settled of West Indian islands. On July 31, 1498, during his third voyage, Christopher Columbus sighted the island, christened it 'Trinidad', and claimed it for Spain. But almost 300 years later in 1783, the population of Trinidad comprised only 126 whites, 259 free coloured, 310 slaves and 2,032 Amerindians (Caribs and Arawaks).[1] That year, on November 24, the Cedula of Population was issued by King Charles III from Madrid to encourage the settlement of Roman Catholic French West Indian planters and their slaves. By 1797 the population was composed of 2,151 whites; 4,476 free coloureds; 10,009 slaves; and 1,082 Indians.[2] On February 18 that year, during the French Revolutionary Wars, the Spanish Governor surrendered the island to the British. The opening up and settlement of Trinidad continued under British sovereignty with the migration from older and more populated West Indian islands (especially Grenada, Barbados, and St Vincent, continuing to the present day) following the British abolition of slavery in 1838[3] there came the importation of 143,949 Indian indentured labourers between 1845 and 1917; and the smaller, but socially significant immigration of 866 French and German labourers between 1839 and 1840; 1,309 free blacks from the US between 1839 and 1847; liberated Africans (3,383 from Sierra Leone and 3,198 from St. Helena between 1841 and 1861); 1,298 Madeirans, beginning in 1848; 2,500 indentured Chinese labourers between 1853 and 1866; and Syrians and Lebanese at the beginning of the 20th century.[4] Even before the abolition of slavery and the introduction of indentured labour, it could be said that 'society in Trinidad was perhaps more like that of a typical frontier colony, with its mixture of nationalities and races, than any of the newly ceded islands [in the British West Indies]'.[5] In contrast to Barbados and Jamaica, for example, the less than fully effective imprint of British dominance in Trinidad can be seen today in the great abundance of Amerindian place names (Tunapuna, Chaguaramas, Chaguanas, Naparima, Tacarigua, Cunupia, Guayaguayare), and the fewer number of Spanish names (San Fernando, Rio Claro, Sangre Grande) and French names (Blanchisseuse, Grande Rivière). English place names are found mainly in the names of Counties (the administrative units), and in only a few towns that the British renamed (Princes Town, Port of Spain, St Joseph).

Tobago, on the other hand, followed more closely the pattern of development in the other British West Indian islands. (With regard to place names, in Tobago there are English, French, Spanish, and even Courlandish[6] names but no Amerindian ones. This reflects the sparse pre-Columbian settlement of the island.) Tobago was economically under-exploited, as colonial powers fought for possession of the island from 1626 to 1803, the year the British held the island once and for all. In 1771, Tobago's population was 5,084. White men numbered 243; slaves 4,716; and runaways 125. Uninterrupted British rule, however, did not help Tobago to become much more populous or profitable. Due to Tobago's financial troubles, on January 1, 1889 Tobago was joined to Trinidad to form the single colony of Trinidad and Tobago. On January 1, 1899, Tobago became a ward of the colony, giving up her separate Financial Board.[7]

Largely due to economic development in Trinidad right up to 1964, except for seven years between 1944 and 1955, Trinidad and Tobago experienced annual net immigration.[8] From only 2,727 in 1783 (2,032 of which were Amerindians), Trinidad's population had grown to 17,718 by 1797. In 1851, there were 68,600 inhabitants. Between 1851 and 1881, the population more than doubled, and by 1911 it more than doubled again (see Table 2.1).

***Table 1.1. Population of Trinidad and Tobago, 1851–1921***

| Trinidad | | Tobago | |
|---|---|---|---|
| 1851 | 68,600 | 1891 | 18,253 |
| 1861 | 84,438 | 1901 | 18,751 |
| 1871 | 109,638 | 1911 | 20,749 |
| 1881 | 153,128 | 1921 | 23,390 |
| 1891 | 200,028 | | |
| 1901 | 255,148 | | |
| 1911 | 312,790 | | |
| 1921 | 342,523 | | |

*Source*: *Census of the Colony of Trinidad and Tobago* (1923)

Even up to 1921, only 50.9 per cent of the population were classified by the Census as having a nationality of 'Trinidad' or 'Tobago' (see Table 2.2).[9]

***Table 1.2 Population of Trinidad and Tobago by Nationality, 1921***

| | | | |
|---|---|---|---|
| Trinidad | 159,236 | | 43.5% |
| Trinidad, Indian Parents (both) | 81,837 | | 22.4% |
| Trinidad, Indian Father | 1,580 | | 0.4% |
| Trinidad, Indian Mother | 649 | | 0.2% |
| Tobago | 27,051 | | 7.4% |
| Barbados | 16,744 | | 4.6% |
| St Vincent | 10,113 | | 2.8% |
| Grenada | 12,838 | | 3.5% |
| Antigua | 701 | | 0.2% |
| St Kitts and Nevis | 1,486 | | 0.4% |
| Other British West Indies | 4,529 | | 1.2% |
| British North America | 633 | | 0.2% |
| British North America of Indian Parents | 157 | | 0.0% |
| Other British Colonies | 633 | | 0.2% |
| SUB-TOTAL | | 318,187 | 87.0% |
| India | 37,341 | | 10.2% |
| United Kingdom | 1,389 | | 0.4% |
| Naturalised British Subjects | 193 | | 0.1% |
| SUB-TOTAL | | 357,110 | 97.6% |
| Foreign West Indies | 1,094 | | 0.3% |
| Foreign West Indies, Indian Parents | 77 | | 0.0% |
| France | 152 | | 0.0% |
| Spain | 50 | | 0.0% |
| Portugal and Colonies | 517 | | 0.1% |

| | | | |
|---|---|---|---|
| Germany | 20 | | 0.0% |
| Italy | 59 | | 0.0% |
| Austria-Hungary | 9 | | 0.0% |
| Holland | 27 | | 0.0% |
| Denmark | 19 | | 0.0% |
| Sweden and Norway | 10 | | 0.0% |
| United States of America | | | 0.1% |
| | 294 | | |
| Venezuela | 4,135 | | 1.1% |
| South America | 523 | | 0.1% |
| China | 1,334 | | 0.4% |
| Africa | 177 | | 0.0% |
| Arabia | 108 | | 0.0% |
| Not described (or born at Sea) | 198 | | 0.1% |
| Total Foreign | 8,803 | | 2.4% |
| GRAND TOTAL | | 365,913 | 100.0% |

*Source: Census of the Colony of Trinidad and Tobago (1923)*

From 1797 to 1925, unlike the other British West Indian colonies, Trinidad had been directly ruled by Britain. Deriving from the fact that the free population of Trinidad was either French or Spanish (and overwhelmingly coloured) and from the influence of the anti-slavery movement in parliament (which desired that Trinidad be a model colony for the older self-governing West India Islands regarding the amelioration and gradual abolition of slavery), Trinidad was administered as a 'crown colony'. This was a significant departure from the West Indian norm of Crown-appointed governor, nominated council and popular Assembly. There would be no elected representation of free men (effectively meaning planter-domination, and non-British, at that) in government, despite British reservations about despotism and tyranny. In accordance with His Majesty's Prerogatives in consequence of the Capitulation, the governor governed in the absence of any other authority in the colony (not without protest from the planters).[10] The governor presided over a Council of Advice, then a Council of Government, and finally an Executive and Legislative Council, all to advise but not to control. Membership in these councils consisted of *ex officio* civil servants and unofficial members nominated from 'the most respectable of the inhabitants of the island'. As the system developed in the nineteenth century, political reformists based in Trinidad's capital, Port of Spain, in the north of the island (and, to a lesser extent, in the Borough of

San Fernando in the south), revived agitation for representative government, without success.[11]

Soon after the victory of the Entente Powers in the Great War (1914–1918) and the extension of suffrage in Britain, Parliamentary Under-Secretary of State for the Colonies, Major E.F.L. Wood, assisted by W. Ormsby-Gore and R.A. Wiseman, toured Jamaica, St Kitts, Antigua, Dominica, St Lucia, St Vincent, Barbados, Grenada, Trinidad, and British Guiana from December 13, 1921 to February 14, 1922 on behalf of Winston Churchill (Secretary of State for the colonies) to make enquiries 'for the bestowal of a measure of representative government'.[12] Major Wood recommended the introduction of elected members. He recommended that they form a majority of the unofficial members (i.e. non-civil servants) in the various Legislative Councils, and that a two-stage process be inaugurated in which the unofficial members would first form a minority, and later a majority of council members.[13] While for most other islands (including Tobago), the introduction of elected elements represented a restoration of earlier rights, in Trinidad it was a first under British rule.[14]

Notably, the Report singled out Trinidad

> *as the one community which appeared largely to lack any homogeneous public opinion. Socially, it is divided into all kinds of groups which have very few relations with one another. There is a considerable French Creole element largely engaged in cacao-growing, French-speaking and preserving its own tradition. There is a Spanish element which is reinforced continually by intercourse with Venezuela. Above all, the Colony possesses a very considerable East Indian element, roughly 130,000 people out of a total population of 360,000, largely illiterate, speaking some five or six different languages, and living a life of its own. And lastly, in addition to the African and coloured element, there is an appreciable number of Chinese, mostly engaged in the retail trades. With a population so constituted, Trinidad is exceptionally cosmopolitan. It is the only one of the West Indian islands which contains mining enterprises on any substantial scale, and considerable capital has been embarked in asphalt and oil development by outside corporations. It is, accordingly, important that no action should be taken which would disturb the confidence felt by such capital in the stability of the local Government.*[15]

Not all in the colony agreed with Major Wood. The Trinidad Chamber of Commerce,[16] the Agricultural Society, and a Deputation of East Indians[17] opposed any change to the crown colony system. On the other hand, the Legislative Reform Committee, the Trinidad Workingmen's Association,[18] and the East Indian National Congress favoured the introduction of elected members.[19] The East Indian National Congress advocated the introduction of communal representation, which the other two organisations (in addition to a 'Deputation of East Indians') opposed.

Major Wood agreed with 'the weight of official opinion' that a 'measure of representation, subject to adequate safeguards' was desirable.[20] It is significant to note his concluding remarks concerning his recommendations:

> *It will be seen from the above that I have not adopted the system of the election of members by particular interests or any system of communal representation. We came to the conclusion that the objections to the first were insuperable on the ground of the difficulties of determining what the constituency would be and of drawing the line between bodies which should, or should not, be represented .... As regards communal representation, apart from the objection that this arrangement would be opposed by the chief advocates of constitutional change, there would again be great difficulty in deciding what the constituencies were to be, and, moreover, it would accentuate and perpetuate the differences which, in order to produce a homogeneous community, it should be the object of statesmanship to remove. The East Indians are an important element in the community, and it would be a great misfortune if they were encouraged to stand aside from the main current of political life instead of sharing in it and assisting to guide its course. Finally, if a concession of this kind were granted to the East Indians, there would be no logical reason for withholding it from persons of French, Spanish or Chinese descent, a situation which would become impossible. By retaining the system of nomination by the Crown, it will always be possible to secure representatives on the Council of races or important interests not otherwise adequately represented by direct election.*[21]

The Trinidad and Tobago Order-in-Council reconstituting the Legislative Council in 1924 largely followed Major Wood's recommendations. It provided for an unofficial membership increased from 11 to 13 members, seven of whom were to be elected and six nominated. Concomitantly, the number of Official Council members was increased from ten to 12, and the Governor retained an original and casting vote in order to ensure an Official majority.[22] The official (i.e. civil servant) members in 1925 were the Attorney-General, Colonial Secretary, Treasurer, Solicitor-General, Inspector-General of the Constabulary and Commandant of the Local Forces, Director of Public Works, Surgeon-General, Protector of Immigrants and Director of Labour Exchange, Collector of Customs, Director of Agriculture, General Manager of Railways, and Director of Education.[23]

The seven seats were to represent the city of Port of Spain, the five counties of St George, Caroni, Victoria, St Patrick, the Eastern Counties (St Andrew, St David, Nariva, and Mayaro), and the Ward of Tobago (see Appendix F). The electorate represented by each seat was quite divergent, the largest being Port of Spain (with a total electorate of 7,230) and the smallest St Patrick (with 1,405). The Council was to have a life of three years.[24]

Even in this reformed system, it should be noted that the governor, as president of both Executive and Legislative Councils, remained the key authority, as he would in such a Crown Colony where there was no relevant preceding tradition of government. As Hewan Craig explains,

> *The Governor was President of the Council and its Chairman when the Council was in Committee. In speaking, members were required to address themselves to him. He was rarely addressed as "Mr. President" or "Mr. Chairman" by the members of the Council, who called him "Sir" or "Your Excellency". It might be said that in Council he remained the Governor, with all the power and prestige of his office, and that the unofficial members addressed him as such, rather than as the president of a legislative body.*
>
> *The singular importance attaching to the post of Governor in a crown colony [was] evident from Colonial Regulation 105, which [described] him as "The single and supreme authority responsible to, and representative of, His Majesty"....*
>
> *He [was] by virtue of his Commission, and the Letters Patent or Order in Council constituting his office, entitled to the obedience and assistance of all military, air force, and civil officers, although, except on special appointment by the King, he [was] not invested the command of His Majesty's regular forces in the colony. In addition to the legislative authority with which he [was] endowed, he [was empowered], subject to certain conditions, [to] dispose*

> *of Crown lands, and [was empowered to] appoint, dismiss, or suspend public officers. The Governor [could] also grant to any offender convicted of any crime or offence in the colony, a pardon, either free or subject to lawful conditions, or any remission of the sentence passed, or any respite of the execution of such sentence, for whatever period he [thought] fit ....*
>
> *All nominated official and unofficial members of the Trinidad Legislative Council were appointed by the governor, subject to the approval of the Secretary of State, and the governor [could have suspended] any such members from membership of the Council ....*
>
> *As the King's representative, he ... [took] precedence of all persons in the colony. He [was] the leader of society and invitations to Government House, as the official residence [was] styled, [were] cherished privileges. Subject to the complications introduced by distinctions of colour in a mixed society like that of Trinidad, standards of social prominence ... [were] set by the degree of association with the Governor and his family and official entourage. All classes [regarded] him with respect and the less privileged especially [saw] in him a being to whom nothing [was] impossible and [petitioned] his aid in issues of all kinds, a tendency reinforced in Trinidad by the long tradition of crown colony rule with the large powers which it [conferred] on the governor.*[25]

A local franchise committee determined that, subject to income, property, and residence qualifications, the vote be extended to men over 21 years of age and women over 30, as in Great Britain. In addition, the registering officer had to be satisfied that the voter could understand spoken English.[26] As a result, the electorate was tiny. In the first General Elections of February 7, 1925, only 21,794 voters were registered.

The property qualifications for members, though not exorbitant, did 'ensure that the elected members would in the main be drawn from much the same classes as the nominated members'.[27] Members also had to be male. Only five of the seven seats were contested, with a mere 6,832 persons voting (see Appendix B).[28] The next three elections were similarly low-keyed: in the elections of March 3, 1928 only three seats were contested; on January 28, 1933 four seats; and on January 4, 1938, only two. Not once in these elections did more than 18 per cent of the total registered electorate vote.[29] Cumulatively, in the four general elections between 1925 and 1938, exactly half of the seats were uncontested.

Perhaps related to the limited franchise and the pre-eminence of the governor, there was another notable aspect of the emerging Trinidad and Tobago political system: candidates acted independently, without wider loyalties. Candidates at various times did present themselves as 'Socialists', 'Independents', 'Independent Socialists', 'Unionists', and even 'capitalists'. Craig notes, 'As the divisions taken between 1929 and 1934 show, the nominated members tended to vote together more often than did the elected members, but there was no consistent alignment of nominated members on one side and elected members on the other.'[30] Community standing and a candidate's ability to command personal loyalty seemed to be the basis of electoral success.[31] Sir Vidia Naipaul famously noted, 'Nationalism was impossible in Trinidad. ... There were no parties, only individuals.'[32]

Captain Arthur Andrew Cipriani (b.1875) of the Trinidad Workingmen's Association (TWA), renamed the Trinidad Labour Party (TLP) in August 1934 (Reddock 1994, 133), was an exceptional figure of the period who 'for many years [had been] the only elected member who showed persistent opposition to the government.'[33] He was a French Creole of Corsican descent who had served with the West India Regiment in the Great War. He defeated Major Randolph Rust in the 1925 election for the Port of Spain seat. Until his death in 1945, Cipriani was consistently returned unopposed. (This absence of political challenge is notable for a capital city.) He was the period's leading political figure, presenting himself as the champion of the 'barefoot man' in the Legislative Council. Cipriani also served continuously in the Port of Spain City Council from 1926 to 1941, eight of these years as Mayor.[34] The TWA/TLP's strongest showing in the Council, however, amounted to three loosely aligned members – Cipriani, Timothy Roodal (Victoria), and Sarran Teelucksingh (Chaguanas).[35] They campaigned as 'Socialists'.

*Arthur Andrew Cipriani.*

In the four elections, the largest voter turnout of 11,128 (43.4 per cent of the electorate in the contested seats) occurred in 1933 (see Appendix B). That election was the first given front page coverage. A sort of party 'rivalry' occurred in 1933. The 'Independent Socialists', led by Teelucksingh, complained about the 'dictatorship' of Cipriani, and campaigned against the 'Socialists' who were supported by the TWA. The *Trinidad Guardian* headline of January 29, 1933 read '"Cipriani" Defeat in General Elections'. In fact, only one of the two 'Socialists' who had fought a contested seat was defeated (Cipriani's Port of Spain seat was uncontested). Additionally, Teelucksingh was the only one of the three 'Independent Socialists' returned (one lost to a 'Socialist', the other to an independent).

The year 1931 was politically significant since Charles Henry Pierre – an independent who was returned to the Eastern Counties seat unopposed – became the first 'elected' member appointed to the Executive Council.

Teelucksingh and Cipriani had fallen out in 1933 over the divorce question. That question, and the debates on the labour disturbances of 1937, were identified by Hewan Craig as the most important issues in the Council's history in that period.[36] No lasting political consequences resulted from the controversy over the divorce bill, but for fully a year this issue greatly agitated public opinion by highlighting, inflaming, and articulating racial, religious, social, and economic divisions in the colony. Also, in both debates, Cipriani emerged on the more conservative side, supporting the Catholic Church against divorce in 1931, and opposing the Trinidad labour riots of June 19 to July 6, 1937, in which Tubal Uriah 'Buzz' Butler was the dominant figure. Butler was a Grenadian small-church preacher and labour leader who emigrated to Trinidad at the age of 26. He had broken with the TLP in July 1936 to found his British Empire Workers and Citizens Home Rule Party (BEWCHRP). Riots broke out as authorities tried to arrest him on a charge of sedition. Two policemen and 12 civilians were killed in the unrest; nine policemen and volunteers, and 50 civilians were wounded.[37] Butler was incarcerated from September 9, 1937 until May 1939. In the 1938 elections, two pro-Butler candidates (C.C. Abidh in Caroni and Adrian Cola Rienzi in Victoria) called themselves 'Unionists'. Only Rienzi was successful. When Britain declared war against Germany in September 1939, Butler was re-arrested and detained for the duration of the war as a security risk under the Defense Regulations.

*Tubal Uriah 'Buzz' Butler*

The governor, Sir Murchison Fletcher, resigned officially on grounds of ill-health on December 24, 1937. In fact, Governor Fletcher was asked by the Prime Minister, Neville Chamberlain, on the recommendation of Secretary of State, W. Ormsby-

Gore, to demit office for his inconsistent support of the employers over the workers.[38] Fletcher was replaced as governor by Major Sir Hubert W. Young.

Similar labour disturbances occurred throughout the West Indies, and in 1938 a West India Royal Commission – composed of Walter Edward, Baron Moyne (Chairman); Sir Reginald Edward Stubbs; Dame Rachel Eleanor Crowdy; Sir Walter McLennan Citrine; Sir Percy Graham Mackinnon; Ralph Assheton; Mary Georgina Blacklock; Frank Leonard Engledow; Hubert Douglas Henderson; and Morgan Jones – was appointed 'to investigate social and economic conditions in Barbados, British Guiana, British Honduras, Jamaica, the Leeward Islands, Trinidad and Tobago, and the Windward Islands, and matters connected therewith, and to make recommendations.'[39]

In 1941, following the Report's general constitutional recommendations, Trinidad and Tobago implemented the next stage of constitutional advance by changing the composition of the Legislative Council. Nine official members were removed from the Legislative Council, leaving only the Colonial Secretary, the Attorney General, and the Financial Secretary. In addition, Port of Spain and Victoria were given one extra representative each (see Appendix F).[40] Elections were held for the additional Port of Spain seat on June 26, 1941 and for Victoria on June 28.[41]

In 1945 a new Constitution was established. It provided for an Executive Council and Legislative Council, over which presided the governor, and for a Public Service Commission. Under the new constitution, the elected and non-elected elements were evenly balanced, numbering nine each. The governor held his original and casting votes, and was granted reserve powers. These powers were exercisable with the consent of the Executive Council, but in the event of their refusing to give such consent, with the approval of the Secretary of State in Great Britain. The composition of the Executive Council (still only with advisory powers, and not responsible to the legislature) changed only insofar as the governor began appointing elected members in 1931. By 1940, it became standard for the governor to appoint an unofficial majority in the Council (three nominated unofficials and two elected members). By 1944, governors normally appointed one nominated and four elected members (Appendix E)[42]. The governor retained his original and casting vote, giving the non-elected element (governor, three *ex-officio*, one nominated unofficial Legislative Council member) a guaranteed majority of one, despite the unofficial's relative independence from the government.

Increasing the elected members' participation in the policy process was the aim of the reform. But it was not felt that Trinidad and Tobago was ready for self-government. There was not only the argument about the colony's political inexperience. The governor's guaranteed dominance in the Executive Council followed the consideration by the West India Commission that the islands would continue to need substantial funds from His Majesty's government and therefore the continuance of substantial control by the crown was necessary to properly align power with responsibility. (Ayearst 1960: 68–9). The term of both Councils was to be five years.

Perhaps more important than all of these reforms was the institution of universal suffrage (with some residence qualifications) for all adults 21 years and over, following the recommendation of the Moyne Commission of 1938. Under universal adult franchise, 46 per cent of the population were registered to vote in 1946, as opposed to 6.6 per cent in 1938.[43] This provision was introduced on August 3, 1945, after some controversy regarding the English language qualification.[44] However, Council members were required to read and write English, but income qualifications were lowered, and women were allowed to become members.[45]

As the constitutional framework advanced towards greater participation, the local society seemed to be organising itself into more numerous and diverse groups, multiplying since Major Wood's visit 26 years earlier. Evidence of this could be seen from the variety of often conflicting interests and organisations – representing working class, racial, professional, populist, socialist, and regional interests – who made their representations to the Franchise Committee of 1941–44 and would express later their dissatisfaction with the resulting 1945 Constitution.[46]

The numerous groups reflected the significant social, cultural, and economic developments since the 1930s when, among other things, the lower classes seem to have discarded Cipriani's relatively organised and institutionally-focused politics.[47] Negro pride received a boost in 1935 in reaction against the Italian invasion of Abyssinia, and elsewhere with the triumphs of the American boxer Joe Louis;[48] middle-class activists in Port of Spain began to promote the folk arts – with their strong non-European, non-Christian roots – and to develop a 'native' dance, music and literature;[49] and the art forms of calypso and steel band, and the establishment of Negro participation in West Indian cricket (most famously noted by C.L.R. James)[50] were significant developments in the popular culture of the lower classes. Among Indians, the nationalist movement in India stimulated a great deal of pride, while in 1945 the Centenary of Indian Arrival was celebrated in Skinner

Park, San Fernando. Soon to follow was an efflorescence of Indian music, film, radio broadcasts, and Muslim and Hindu school building.[51] Also of great importance in the period was the widespread prosperity and influx of new ideas, lifestyles and opportunities (legal and illegal) occasioned by the establishment of American military bases in Chaguaramas and Wallerfield as part of the Anglo-American Bases Agreement of 1941.[52]

*C.L.R. James in conversation with Mr Jeff Stollmeyer.*

In this variegated, emerging environment in 1946, after the end of World War II, Trinidad and Tobago held its first elections under universal adult suffrage on July 1. Port of Spain and Victoria were divided into two single-member constituencies, providing a total of nine elected seats (see Appendix F). Of the 259,512 eligible voters, an unremarkable 52.9 per cent turned out (see Appendix B), despite a heavy promotional and educational campaign by the government.[53] All seats were contested: 20 candidates represented political parties, and 21 ran as independents. According to Dr John LaGuerre, of the 42 originally nominated candidates, 16 were Negroes, 13 East Indians, 7 of European origin, and 6 of mixed descent.[54] This might be compared with the 1946 census figures in Table 1.3.

***Table 1.3. Population of Trinidad and Tobago by Race, 1946***

| | | | | |
|---|---|---|---|---|
| White | | | 15,283 | 2.7% |
| Black | | | 261,485 | 46.9% |
| East Indian | | | 195,747 | 35.1% |
| Syrian | | | 889 | 0.2% |
| Chinese | | | 5,641 | 1.0% |
| Mixed or Coloured | Total | | 78,775 | 14.1% |
| | Indian Creole | 8,406 | 1.5% | |
| | Chinese Creole | 3,673 | 0.7% | |
| | Other | 66,696 | 12.0% | |
| Carib | | | 26 | 0.0% |
| Not Stated | | | 124 | 0.0% |
| TOTAL | | | 557,970 | 100.0% |

Source: *Central Bureau of Statistics (1949)*

The parties that contested the elections were the United Front (UF), the Progressive Democratic Party (PDP), the Trinidad Labour Party (TLP), the Trades Union Council and Socialist Party (TUC and SP), and the British Empire Citizens' and Workers' Home Rule Party (BECWHRP), led by T.U.B. Butler, who had been released from prison at the end of the war in 1945.[55] Four of the seven members returned under limited franchise in 1938 contested the 1946 elections: Sarran Teelucksingh (Caroni), Edward Vernon Wharton (Eastern Counties), Timothy Roodal (St Patrick), and George de Nobriga (Tobago). Only Roodal was returned in 1946.

Peculiarly, he contested on both a TLP and BECWHRP ticket. His dual candidacy was reported without comment in the *Trinidad Guardian*.[56] This illustrates the fact that despite the greater presence of political parties in the elections of 1946, their authority and longevity was limited. The official report by the newly constituted Supervisor of Elections did not anywhere indicate party affiliations of candidates.[57] In general, the parties that existed at this time did not have clearly defined programmes, aims, or enforced constitutions. The absence of responsible government perhaps reinforced this loose organisation. By both habit and structure then, 'parties' were often electoral alliances formed by independent-minded candidates who sought additional votes. Of all the parties in 1946, only the Butler Party and the TLP survived beyond two elections. But not even these parties could claim exclusive allegiance from their members.

Besides the St Patrick seat, the BECWHRP secured the Tobago and St George seats; the UF won North Port of Spain, South Port of Spain, and San Fernando; the TUC and SP won Caroni and the Eastern Counties; and Victoria was won by an independent candidate, Ranjit Kumar.[58]

Although party candidates won the most seats in the elections, the greatest number of votes went to independent candidates. Betraying the weakness of the parties, none of the party leaders won their seats. Butler lost to Albert Gomes (b.1911) in Port of Spain,[59] while John Kelshall of the UF and John Rojas of the TUC and SP lost in St Patrick.

In addition to the first elections with universal adult suffrage, 1946 saw the first general elections for seats in the newly established County Councils, also recommended by the 1938 Royal Commission. The County Councils were established as advisory bodies to consider the needs of their respective districts and to make recommendations thereon. They replaced the Local Road Boards in Chaguanas, Manzanilla, Naparima, St Ann's and Diego Martin, and Tacarigua.

The original County Council ordinance of 1945 was replaced on April 18, 1946. It provided for seven county councils with 36 wards in all: Tobago was divided into seven; St George and St David/St Andrew six each; Victoria five; and Caroni, St Patrick, and Nariva/Mayaro four each. Unusually, each ward had two representatives (see Appendix E).[60]

Elections were held on October 28, 1946 (see Appendix B). Party affiliation of candidates was not noted in any of the official or newspaper reports. There were 154 candidates; ten returned unopposed to five seats (three in Tobago, one in St George, and one in St Andrew St David).[61] Voter turnout was 36.8 per cent, prompting the *Trinidad Guardian* headline to read 'Trinidad Shows Little Interest in County Elections'.[62]

In the Legislative Council, in accordance with the established pattern of the previous years, even the elected party candidates acted as independents. The party groupings that were formed at the time of the elections did not endure.[63] Governor Sir Bede Clifford appointed four elected members to the Executive Council, drawn from three different parties.[64] Four of the remaining five – affiliated to the same 'labour' parties as their Executive Council colleagues – formed a loosely aligned 'Parliamentary

Opposition Group' (Ranjit Kumar apparently was not part of this bloc.) This was the first opposition bloc to have emerged in the Legislative Council. Previously, such opposition had been limited to Captain Cipriani. With the extension of the franchise and the reduction of the financial qualifications required for membership of the Council, the government's opponents in the legislature became more numerous. The members of the opposition bloc contended that the constitutional limitations on the powers of the elected members, which made it impossible for them to secure a majority on any measure without official or nominated support, forced them into the role of a permanent opposition (Craig 1952: 155).

Interestingly, Governor Clifford expressed in a public speech in July 1943 the view that members of the legislature were members of the government and should take their share of any blame laid on the government. In that year Captain Cipriani, who was appointed to the Executive Council in 1941, resigned. It was believed that Cipriani frequently found himself in opposition to decisions taken in the Council. After his resignation he explained that he did not like the atmosphere of the Executive Council (Craig 1952: 146-7).

Governor Sir John Shaw, who began his duties in 1947, took a seemingly more liberal view than his predecessor. In March 1948, Governor Shaw announced to the Legislative Council that unofficial members of the legislature whether elected or nominated, whether members of the Executive Council or not, were 'absolutely and unequivocally free', not only to hold their own opinions but to express them in public should they wish to do so, and to vote in the Legislative Council on any matter before it according to their own free will. Members of the Executive Council, while in the best possible position to appreciate the reasons underlying policy and decisions of all sorts, might disagree with the reasons and dissent form the policy according to their own deliberate judgement, but 'the responsibility for the ultimate decision, whatever it may be, rests with the Governor'. In spite of this statement, however, Governor Shaw found it necessary the following month to request the resignation of Timothy Roodal from the Executive Council on the grounds that he was at odds with the administration on so many points and had so frequently absented himself from meetings of the Executive Council that his continued membership of the Council could no longer be regarded as acceptable. After Roodal's resignation, he joined the 'opposition' in the Legislative Council (Craig 1952: 150, 156). Inside and outside the Councils the original parties collapsed, and personalities formed new alliances, never seeming stronger than the immediate opportunities with which candidates might be presented.[65]

It seems that the independence of members was highly valued in the political system of the time. In the by-election of July 1945 to fill the vacancy created by the death of Cipriani, for example, Louis Gilman Thomas assured his audience that 'he would not be dictated to by any parties or cliques.'[66] Others believed that belonging to a party was to be 'partisan'.[67] Even Roy Joseph, UF member for San Fernando in the 1946 Executive Council argued, 'We are different beings and we cannot all unite on every point; we have to act as we see things and not as any individual would like us to see them.'[68]

Notably, Albert Gomes,[69] echoing Major Wood's concerns of 1922, had declared in the *Sunday Guardian*, July 7, 1946,

> *We have not yet reached the stage where political impulse is guided by cognate considerations. As a people, we have not yet crystallised into that hard mould of objective opinion which guarantees stable development to a country. The pattern of our population in terms of loyalty to fundamental patriotic motifs is confused and chaotic . . . . Unless we can produce in the next five years a fusion of the disparate and extraneous loyalties that now bedevil us, then the progress of Trinidad as a cohesive organism is a mere fantastic notion of the idealists in our midst. Our position, as revealed by the election, is not a happy one . . . . Our political talent as displayed in the elections seems much too fluid and unstable to earn us the right to more ample political opportunities. We have not yet begun to think politically . . . . The national groups in Trinidad will continue to hark back to former loyalties so long as Trinidad offers them no more than the day-to-day agony of eking out an existence.*[70]

*A group of West Indian dignitaries (Albert Gomes in the centre of the front row) gathered outside Walker's Art Studio, St. John's Antigua, December 6, 1955.*

It was acknowledged that Trinidad and Tobago's constitutional structure – in particular, the system of nomination of Executive Council members by the governor, irrespective of party, and the non-recognition of a leader of the Opposition – encouraged its weak party organisations. This led a number of members to interpret the Legislative Council as a generally unified body. For example, in 1925, in the first Council with an elected element, member of Legislative Council T.M. Kelshall twice rebutted the idea that there was any fundamental opposition between unofficial and official members, protesting, 'The idea seems to be gaining ground that some of us on this side of the House are *de facto* in opposition . . . . I am not a member of the Opposition; I am proud to be a member of the Government – on the Unofficial side.'[71]

Dissenting voices, on the other hand, were easily outvoted. Even in the 1945 it was impossible for the elected members to form an effective majority in the Legislative Council due to their limited numbers, the limited powers granted to elected members, and the veto powers given to the governor.[72] In 1947, in response to a motion by Roy Joseph, the governor appointed a 20-member constitutional committee under the chairmanship of nominated member Sir Lennox O'Reilly to recommend further constitutional reform. The following year they submitted their report along with four minority reports attached and accompanied by several memoranda both for and against. The legislature accepted the majority report of the Reform Committee. All six of the nominated members of the Legislative Council voted in favour of the resolution urging acceptance of the majority report. Only two of the nine elected members supported the resolution. Two others were not present at the time of the voting and the remaining five voted against the resolution (Craig 1952: 159). After the Secretary of State discussed the proposal in England with Trinidad and Tobago Legislative Council members and Governor Sir John Shaw, separately, the outline for the new constitution was presented to the governor in 1949.[73] The new arrangements were embodied in three constitutional documents, Letters Patent of March 16, 1950, the Trinidad and Tobago (Constitution) Order in Council of March 31, 1950, and Instructions of the same date.

The resulting Trinidad and Tobago (Constitution) Order-in-Council came into force on April 20, 1950. The new Legislative Council doubled the number of elective seats to 18 and reduced the number of nominated unofficials to five, while the three *ex officio* members remained unchanged.[74] There was to be a more equitable division of the population between the constituencies, which were previously based on county boundaries.[75] Each constituency would have approximately 30,000 electors. Accordingly, Port of Spain was divided into three seats, St George into five, and Victoria, the Eastern Counties, St Patrick, and Caroni were divided into two. San Fernando and Tobago remained with one seat each (see Appendix F).

The governor no longer presided over the Legislative Council, but would appoint a Speaker, with neither an original nor casting vote, from outside the Council to do so. The new Executive Council comprised five elected and one nominated unofficial, in addition to the three Crown Officials and the governor, who remained President of the Executive Council. The elected members were to be elected by the Legislative Council from among the elected members by secret ballot, while the governor appointed the nominated member from among the nominated members of the Legislative Council (see Appendix E). The elected members of the Executive Council could also be removed by a two-thirds majority of the elected members of the Legislative Council, also in a secret ballot. Significantly, the Executive Council had its role elevated from a purely advisory body to the 'chief instrument of policy', in which the governor only had a casting vote. In addition, all five elected members in the Executive Council were granted limited ministerial responsibility, and were each associated with the administrative work of particular government departments. Importantly, an elected member would be chosen as leader whom the governor would consult on the allocation of portfolios. The elected members were in a clear majority, and could control the Executive Council, subject to the governor's reserve powers, if they voted together. Further, the former Executive Council could only be summoned on the governor's authority. The new Executive Council could be summoned on the written request of five of its members. It was the most advanced constitution in the British West Indies at the time, even ahead of Jamaica, whose Executive Council had a non-elected majority of one (Craig 1952: 160).[76] The old Legislature was dissolved on August 30, 1950, a year earlier than it was scheduled, to accommodate the new constitution.[77]

Together with the increase in governmental responsibility, however, emerged an electoral contest more confused than in 1946. With 18 elected seats instead of nine, it was like throwing petrol onto a fire: 141 candidates contested the elections on September 18, 1950 – 91 independents, 50 with party affiliations (see Appendix B).[78] The parties contesting were the Butler

Party (formed in 1950), the Political Progress Group (PPG) led by Albert Gomes (formerly of the UF), the Caribbean Socialist Party (CSP) led by Dr Patrick Solomon (also formerly of the UF), the TLP, and the TUC. Again, the party affiliations followed the loose Trinidadian pattern. Tobago was successfully contested by A.P.T. James on both a CSP and Butler Party ticket, while two candidates claiming affiliation to the CSP unsuccessfully contested the Port of Spain East seat.[79]

Voter turnout was 70.1 per cent, the highest yet seen. Butler's Party captured seven seats (counting A.P.T. James), independents six, the PPG two, the TLP two, and the CSP one (not counting James). All nine of the elected members in 1946 contested in 1950. Six were returned.[80] Overall, the number of unsuccessful candidates was so great that a *Trinidad Guardian* headline read, 'Number of Lost Deposits May Be Empire Record'.[81]

*Dr. Patrick Solomon*

After the elections, Bhadase Maraj (independent member for Tunapuna) and A.P.T. James announced that they would support Butler in the Legislative Council.[82] Although Butler commanded the support of the largest number of members, his support only numbered eight in a council of 26. The Legislative Council did not vote Butler or any of his supporters to the Executive Council. The Independents Roy Joseph, Norman Tang, and Ajodasingh, PPG leader Albert Gomes, and CSP member Victor Bryan were instead elected ministers.[83] Gomes was the leading elected member of the Executive, holding the most prestigious post of Minister of Industry, Labour, and Commerce. Parties and allegiances continued to split and recombine. The most important combinations were the People's Democratic Party (PDP) – formed in 1953 under the leadership of Bhadase Maraj, bringing together all seven Indian MLCs (Maraj, Ajodasingh, four of Butler's MLCs, and Simbhoonath Capildeo from the CSP)[84] – and the Party of Political Progress Groups (POPPG), led by Albert Gomes, emerging from his People's Progressive Group (PPG).

In 1953, general elections for the County Councils were held. In accordance with the ordinance passed in the previous year, the County Councils were granted executive powers, and were to discharge a wide array of functions under Roads, Health, and Finance and General Purpose Committees.[85]

Contesting in the elections were 273 candidates, and the voter turnout was 47.3 per cent (see Appendix B). Though the number of contestants increased, party affiliations were again not recognised in official reports, and only anecdotally in newspaper reports.[86] The *Trinidad Guardian* headline read, 'Titled Lady, M.L.C. and Pastor Among New Councillors: Trinidad, Tobago Have Quiet Day At County Polls.'[87]

The diverse, immigrant, developing, and colonial society of Trinidad and Tobago was generally considered much behind the political development of Jamaica and Barbados, in particular. In contrast to Trinidad and Tobago, Jamaica's People's National Party (PNP) (founded in 1938) and the Barbados Labour Party (founded in 1942) were widely respected in the West Indies and abroad for their national organisation and programmes.[88] As responsible government progressed in Trinidad and Tobago, there had been no comparable organisation ready to lead the country to self-government and independence.

# *Part 1*

## *The Long Reign of Eric Williams, 1956-81*

# Two

# THE COMING TO POWER OF ERIC WILLIAMS, 1954-62: 'PNM AGAINST THE REST'

*Dr Eric Williams*

In this chapter, we follow the entrance of Dr Eric Eustace Williams (1911–1981) on the political stage of Trinidad and Tobago in 1954 through to the achievement of national independence in 1962 under the governance of the People's National Movement (PNM), led by Williams. The PNM, founded in 1956, was the first political party in the country's history to put up candidates for every available legislative seat. Williams fervently sought to prevail over the political tradition of independent candidates by introducing the concept of party discipline and programme, and to portray himself as a national, as opposed to sectional or racial, leader. The PNM's precarious victory in 1956 prompted the opposition groups to organise themselves more nationally, stimulating the PNM in turn to establish itself more vigorously as the pre-eminent political organisation in the country. By Independence on August 31, 1962, after a contentious six-year period of settling in, the PNM had won two general elections and was in firm control of government.

## 'I AM GOING TO LET DOWN MY BUCKET RIGHT HERE': DR ERIC WILLIAMS, 1954–5

Dissatisfaction with the 1950 Constitution led, on November 26, 1954, to the passing of a motion by the member for Port of Spain East, Aubrey James (elected as a TLP member), for the establishment of a Select Committee on Constitutional Reform. Earlier, Albert Gomes had rejected the original motion in April 1954 on the grounds that it would postpone the coming general elections, due after the scheduled dissolution of the Council on September 26, 1955. The passing of James's motion (by a vote of 18–5) on April 15, 1955, led to the extension of the Legislature and the setting of the election date to July 26, 1956, at the latest.[1]

The Butler Party and the PDP objected to the postponement of elections, arguing that elections should occur before constitutional changes were introduced.[2] Shortly after the decision had been taken in the House on the motion, PDP leader Bhadase Maraj promptly resigned his Tunapuna seat and won the resulting by-election on June 13, 1955 handsomely.[3] It was speculated that Gomes, in collusion with the Colonial Office, had intended to use the time granted by the postponement to rebuild his political machinery in order to prevent the possibility of a PDP victory in the 1955 elections, which seemed a likely occurrence at the time. There is the opinion also that the Colonial Office did not want to have to negotiate with a new government in the final Federation talks, which were due in February 1956, and that they feared that an Indian-led government would not be co-operative.[4] This perception could have been justified by events on December 12, 1954 when four of the seven Indian members of the Legislative Council voted against a motion to accept the 1953 Federal scheme, while the three others (including the Executive Council member, Ajodasingh, who was told that he would have to resign his portfolio if he voted against the plan) abstained.[5]

Despite these concerns, the postponement of the general elections had other vital, unintentional consequences. At each stage, it cleared the way – through a combination of accident and ambition – for the political emergence of Dr Eric Williams, one of the island's leading intellectuals who by then had a poor relationship with his employers. Born on September 25, 1911, the son of a Post Office official and the eldest of 12 children, Williams left

Trinidad to take up the prestigious Island Scholarship in 1932. He received his PhD in History from Oxford in 1938 (making a decisive break from the Island Scholarship convention of pursuing medicine or law), authored the path-breaking *Capitalism and Slavery* (1944) and *The Negro in the Caribbean* (1945), lectured as Assistant Professor of Social and Political Science at Howard University from 1939 to 1948 and, in 1944, was appointed to the Anglo-American Caribbean Commission, eventually holding third rank as Deputy Chairman of the Caribbean Research Council and Head of the Research Branch of the Secretariat.[6] In 1948, Williams had returned to Trinidad as the Commission's Deputy Chairman of the Caribbean Research Council. As head of research, he directed conferences and special studies on trade statistics, industrial development, timbers, fisheries, housing, trade promotion, education, and small scale farming.[7]

Once settled in Trinidad, Williams set about popularising his historical work with its unbending themes of West Indian nationalism and Negro progressivism. He had accepted the presidency of the Caribbean Historical Society in 1948, initiated publication of a *Caribbean Historical Review* (in print from 1949 to 1953), published a weekly series of 40 articles in the *Trinidad Guardian* (in 1950), presented a series of lectures in Port of Spain and San Fernando, contracted by the University College of the West Indies and was consulted by Minister Gomes on problems of the sugar preference agreement and trade. At his home in the elite residential district on Lady Chancellor Road in Port of Spain, he held evening adult seminars, attracting a number of persons who would become his most active supporters when he prepared to enter politics. One such group based in San Fernando, calling itself *Bachacs* (a biting species of ant in Trinidad), would later be instrumental in founding the PNM, and three of its members – Winston Mahabir, Gerard Montano, Donald Granado – became Ministers in the first PNM Government.[8]

His most significant support, arguably, came from the Teachers Education and Cultural Association (TECA), a group of young teachers organised in the 1940s as an alternative to the official teachers' union. TECA members considered themselves more socially conscious and militant than their peers, held deep grievances against the dual Church-State system of education with its attendant racial and religious discrimination, and attempted to make a cultural contribution to their communities through the organisation of study groups, music festivals, and a book shop on Park

Street in Port of Spain.[9] In 1951, the TECA published Williams's *Education in the British West Indies*, a proposal for a West Indian University, rejected six years earlier by the Caribbean Commission, in which TECA head, DeWilton Rogers, extolled Williams as 'the philosopher of West Indian Nationalism'.[10] Impressively, the publication boasted a forward by the distinguished American philosopher, educator and psychologist, John Dewey.

Williams's relationship with his employers had long been uneasy, and on May 22, 1954 he had been placed on one year's probation. The following month he wrote to the leader of the People's National Party of Jamaica, Norman Manley (who had been a member of the British section of the Anglo-American Caribbean Commission), 'I am persecuted because of my writings; I think, therefore, that I should write some more.'[11]

Williams organised an adult education series of public lectures, principally at the Trinidad Public Library in Port of Spain.[12] In September 1954, he gave five scrupulously detailed addresses on West Indian economics, literature, agriculture, and education. In November he gave another three.[13] Despite their historical and technical detail, they aroused much passion. The highlight of that campaign grew out of the address of November 5, 1954 in which Williams quoted from Aristotle's *Politics* to defend his advocacy of state control of education: an issue which touched long-standing, highly sensitive questions about the power of the Catholic Church in British Trinidad, local white elitism, discrimination against aspiring blacks, and the racial and social implications of democratic advance.[14] In the audience, a tall, striking, black figure, the Reverend Dom Basil Matthews, a Benedictine Monk, local Catholic educator of note, and PhD holder himself from Fordham University, had taken issue with Dr Williams's position during questioning time. On November 9, Dom Basil retorted with his own public lecture, equally learned but more philosophically attuned to Catholic doctrine. On November 17, Williams gave a rejoinder lecture, about which the *Trinidad Guardian* of November 19, 1954 reported:

> *Hundreds were storming the gates of the Public Library long before Dr. Williams was due. ... When Dr. Williams arrived he had difficulty in getting through the hundreds who were pleading for admission to the already crowded Library. Some even suggested to Dr. Williams at the gates that he transfer the lecture to the Grand Stand at the Savannah or to Woodford Square.*[15]

After the lecture, Williams invited voluntary organisations to meet with him to discuss the formation of a non-partisan Committee for Education in Citizenship.[16] Emboldened by his success, on November 24, 1954 – six months after receiving his notice of year-long probation – Williams wrote to the Caribbean Commission a bold but carefully-worded memorandum,[17] in effect leaving them with only two options: promoting him to Secretary-General (the position which he felt he deserved) or firing him. Williams later wrote, 'There was never at any time in my mind the slightest doubt as to which course the Commission would elect to adopt.'[18] Two days later, the Legislative Council passed a motion by Aubrey James seeking constitutional reform.[19]

In the first months of 1955, members of the TECA had quietly formed the Political Education Group (PEG), whose initial purpose chiefly was to promote Dr Williams's personal candidacy for public office.[20] From January to May 1955, Williams intensified his public campaign by organising four concurrently running public lecture series at the Public Library, giving occasional lectures to various interest groups, and writing a few pieces in the *Trinidad Guardian.*[21] Meanwhile, on January 17, 1955, Governor Sir Hubert Rance appointed Ashford Sinanan (member for Naparima, elected on a Butlerite ticket) to chair a 35-member Constitutional Reform Committee – comprising all members of the Legislative Council and 11 other eminent persons. By April 15, 1955, the date of the next elections was officially pushed ahead to July 26, 1956.[22]

Six weeks later, on May 26, 1955, the Caribbean Commission had officially informed Williams that on June 21 his contract would not be renewed. On that day, after long discussions with his friends, Drs Winston Mahabir, Elton C. Richardson, and Ibbit Mosaheb, he made a decision to form and lead a new political party. The party would gather support through Williams's public education programme, and it was decided that on the night of the day of his departure from the Commission – eight days after Bhadase Maraj would win the by-election in Tunapuna – he would give a public lecture in Woodford Square, Port of Spain, immediately opposite the Red House (Trinidad and Tobago's legislature), under the auspices of the Political Education Movement (PEM), the new organisation formed by the TECA.[23]

In that lecture, 'My Relations with the Caribbean Commission, 1943–1955,' Williams proclaimed,

> *I stand before you tonight ... the representative of a principle, a cause and a defeat. The principle is the principle of intellectual freedom. The cause is the cause of the West Indian people. The defeat is the defeat of the policy of appointing local men to high office . . . .*
> *What has happened to me could not have happened in Puerto Rico, Surinam, Jamaica, the Gold Coast, Nigeria, which have either achieved self government or will achieve it in the very near future. It can happen only in Trinidad and Tobago, politically the most backward area in the Caribbean, except for those monuments of backwardness, Martinique and Guadeloupe. Whether it is Queen's Royal College or the Government Training College, the Police Band or the Post Office, our local men have either to be content with a bone as a substitute for meat or have to seek outside of Trinidad what they are not allowed to find in Trinidad . . . .*
> *I was born here, and here I stay, with the people of Trinidad and Tobago, who educated me free of charge for nine years at Queen's Royal College and for five years at Oxford, who have made me whatever I am and who have been or might be at any time the victims of the very pressures which I have been fighting against for 12 years . . . .*
> *I am going to let down my bucket where I am, now, right here with you in the British West Indies.*[24]

Up to October 8, 1955, Williams delivered this lecture along with four others: 'Economic Problems of Trinidad and Tobago', 'Constitution Reform in Trinidad and Tobago', 'The Historical Background of Race Relations in the Caribbean', and 'The Case for Party Politics in the Caribbean', all published by the Political Education Movement. The lectures presented the standards that would guide him through his entire political career: independence, industrial development, Westminster-type constitutionalism, the end of racial discrimination, and the need for disciplined, articulate, principled, national political parties. He consistently opposed his brand of politics to the 'Trinidad bacchanal[25] in the Legislative Council' allegedly practised by the existing politicians.[26]

Oxaal rightly observes,

> *[Williams] had verve and flair; he had that all-important quality identified by Vidia Naipaul as the personal trait which Trinidadians most highly value* – style. *With his dignified bearing, sharp tongue, his ever-present trinity of props – hearing aid, dark glasses and cigaret drooping from his lips – 'The Doc' was a sharply-etched, unique public personality . . . . It is idle to speculate about the course of the island's development if Williams like so many*

> *other gifted West Indian intellectuals, had not returned home, but had pursued a career in Britain or the United States. It seems unlikely, however, that any other man then contemplating a political career in Trinidad would have had such an electric effect on the Creole masses or would have wielded so much power as an elected politician as did Williams.*[27]

Williams delivered his lengthy and meticulously documented addresses to mass audiences[28] in Woodford Square in Port of Spain, Harris Promenade in San Fernando, Auzonville Savannah in Tunapuna, the Couva Car Park, Frisco Junction in Point Fortin, the Casbah Club in Fyzabad, The Arima Race Stand, St Andrew's High School in Sangre Grande, the Scarborough Community Centre in Tobago, the Barataria AME Church, Holy Cross FS Church in Cantaro, the Princes Town Triangle, the Chaguanas Market, Sam's Club in Palo Seco, and the Gasparillo Community Centre.[29] This degree of national political mobilisation had been unprecedented. Williams had argued that the 'most damning criticism of the present government is that it has taken no steps whatsoever to promote the political education of the people.'[30] On July 19, 1955, he famously declared:

> *One recent critic of mine has said that the audience at my lectures is an 'uncultured mob'; I hope the doctors, lawyers, dentists, civil servants, housewives and workers in the audience have noted this. Only on Sunday another one grumbled that it is hardly possible that improvement will come from the quantity rather than the quality of the audiences I seem now to be courting . . . A third critic got very angry at the fact that I do not keep my discussions to university circles. He is quite wrong. I do . . . Now that I have resigned my position at Howard University in the USA, the only university in which I shall lecture in future is the University of Woodford Square and its several branches throughout the length and breadth of Trinidad and Tobago.*[31]

That speech, on constitutional reform, was the climax of the campaign. At its conclusion, Williams invited the public to endorse his recommendations, transferring power over ministers to the chief minister from the governor and the Legislative Council, and achieving a wholly elected Legislative Chamber through the introduction of a bicameral legislature with a wholly nominated Senate.[32] Williams's petition had bypassed – intentionally, no doubt – the Constitutional Reform Committee which had sat from January 17 to July 8, 1955, and completed its exercise on September 3.[33] On October 6, 1955, Williams presented the freshly arrived Governor Beetham, a fellow Oxonian, with six bound volumes containing 27,811 signatures (almost one-tenth of the electorate in 1950) endorsing his constitutional reforms, together with a resolution and an open letter, supported by 19,595 signatures, to the Trinidad and Tobago delegation attending the West Indies Federal negotiations in February 1956.[34] There were critics, of course. Philip Rogers of the West Indian Department in the Colonial Office responded to Williams's lecture on constitutional reform sent to him by Governor Beetham,

> *I have read the whole of Dr. Williams's lecture, without pleasure. It represents almost a case for a psychiatrist. Dr. Williams is an able scholar, but unfortunately he has not grown, but become smaller with the years. Like Mr. Wallace, it surprises me that an audience can be collected for this kind of thing.*[35]

During the gathering of signatures, fortune had again smiled on Williams, as on August 30, 1955 the elections had been pushed forward once again, to September 26, 1956 at the latest.[36] After submitting the petition to Governor Beetham, Williams went abroad on a two-month trip. In addition to the work done for the International Confederation of Free Trade Unions in Geneva and the International Labour Organisation (ILO) in Brussels,[37] Williams had travelled to Paris, London, and Jamaica to meet Aimé Césaire, George Padmore, C.L.R. James, Arthur Lewis, Madame Pandit (the Indian High Commissioner in London), and Norman Manley. Williams had also addressed a meeting of MPs and others in the British House of Commons on Federation, and discussed the issue with the then governor of Jamaica, Sir Hugh Foot. Williams returned to Trinidad on December 18 and resumed another lecture tour, speaking on Federation. During the series, he proclaimed on January 3, 1956 in the *Trinidad Guardian*,

> *Our policy in this matter has been simple, straight forward and honest. We cannot agree to inheriting the prejudices and antagonisms of others, we will not be compromised by them, we decline, for the sake of winning an election, to participate in deals, arrangements or alliances with parties or individuals which we have every reason to believe, from the past history of Trinidad and Tobago, are as dangerous as shifting sands.*[38]

Following through on January 15, 1956, Williams oversaw the inauguration of his own political party, the People's National Movement.[39]

## 'THE PNM AGAINST THE REST': THE CAMPAIGN OF 1956

At the PNM's inaugural meeting were passed the party's two founding documents. The first was the party's constitution, unusual not only because nothing similar had existed in Trinidad and Tobago before but also because of its stringent discipline, by Trinidad and Tobago standards.[40] Modelled largely on the PNP of Jamaica, it outlined a clear democratic structure, moving up hierarchically through Party Groups, Constituency Groups, the General Council of the Party, and ultimately the Annual Convention. Unusually, the Political Leader was not to conduct party business. Instead it would be directed by a Party Chairman. Also included in the manifesto were regulations on the control of party funds and membership contributions, and sanctions against indiscipline, which included nomination to groups contrary to the Movement, the making of unendorsed public pronouncements, resignation from bodies without official notice, and voting against party directives. Affiliation to an organisation 'inconsistent with the Movement', also, precluded membership in the PNM.[41]

'The People's Charter: A Statement of Fundamental Principles' was the party's second document. In it the party proclaimed that it was 'not another of the transitory and artificial combinations to which [voters] have grown accustomed in election years'; it would 'stand or fall by [its] programme'. It called for immediate self-government in internal affairs, a British Caribbean Federation with Dominion Status in not more than five years, elimination of graft, corruption and dishonesty from public life, elimination of racial and other forms of discrimination, the promotion of interracial solidarity, and the 'promotion of political education of the people'. Its social principles were modern and progressive, following guidelines set by major international organisations such as the ILO and the United Nations and, in the area of economics, it advocated an industrialisation programme based on the ideas of Arthur Lewis. Interestingly, the party concluded by promising 'no paradise, offer[ing] no millennium. It [made] no idiotic promise to [voters] that [they will] not have to work any more or that pennies will drop from heaven.' They promised responsibility, fairness, 'and a chance for you to hold your head high and for your children to hold theirs higher among the peoples of the world.'[42] PNM stood for Political Education, Nationalism, and Morality in Public Affairs.

On January 24, 1956 – exactly eight months before the general elections – the PNM was publicly launched at a rally of 'several thousands' in Woodford Square.[43] Between January 24 and June 14, according to his method, Williams held 52 different meetings all over the country, speaking on the Bandung Conference, political trends in 1956, the voter and the vote, and the restatement of PNM's fundamental principles. To this he added lectures to various different trade unions and voluntary societies, even travelling to Barbados and Grenada. Williams expressed pride in his decision never to lower his tone during these addresses, even as he lectured on 'Europe, America and the Caribbean', 'The Development of a Caribbean Nationalism', and 'Caribbean Agriculture in Historical Perspective' to even the remotest and most isolated districts, to people with little or no schooling.[44]

During the tour, in addition to the Federal negotiations, on February 20 the County Council elections were held (see Appendix B). The voter turnout was 56.7 per cent, and the *Guardian* reported heavy polling. There were 231 candidates, but the PNM did not contest. The POPPG won three seats, the Butler Party four, and the candidates supported by Bhadase Maraj fourteen.[45] One hundred and three candidates lost their deposit of $30. In contrast to the newspaper report, the Supervisor of Elections did not record party affiliation of candidates, noting, 'As before there was no great political activity in this election, but there were signs that political activity was increasing.'[46] On May 26, 1956, the Legislative Council was dissolved, with the elections set for September.

On July 14, 1956, the *PNM Weekly* was launched with Williams (then unemployed) as editor. Its circulation rose from ten to twelve thousand, peaking at 20,000 for the August 9 issue which included the PNM Manifesto, advocating 'first and foremost constitution reform, a bicameral legislature and the Cabinet system.' The quality of the paper was generally very high, and included a tribute in its August 30 issue by Barbadian novelist George Lamming – already widely acclaimed for his novels *In the Castle of My Skin* and *The Emigrants* – who wondered 'what strange conversion, what magic, took place in Trinidad between 1950 and 1954.'[47] In its third issue, the party boldly challenged the assertion that

> *no party in Trinidad and Tobago can hope to win a majority. But as a mere matter of interest, why not? Marin has his in Puerto Rico, Nkrumah in the Gold Coast, Manley in Jamaica, Adams in Barbados, Bird in Antigua,*

> *Bradshaw in St. Kitts. Why not the PNM in Trinidad and Tobago? Only the voters can ensure that. And if the answer should be, as the parliamentary jargon goes, in the negative, so what? If not now, then in five years time; if not then, ten years time. The PNM has time on its side, youth on its side. It can wait. The PNM formally rejects the nettle. Its goal is the organisation of a proper party in Trinidad and Tobago; it will arrive at this goal by political education of the people. There is no immediate hurry. If Trinidad and Tobago have not perished in the past 6 years from the sacrifice of principle to expediency, they will never die. The PNM will not lose its way in the bush.*[48]

Meanwhile, on June 1, 1956 the new constitution had been passed in the Legislative Council, to take effect after the next elections. In the new arrangements, a chief minister would be elected by the Legislative Council and would lead both the Legislative and Executive Councils. The Speaker, who now had a casting vote, would be elected by the Council, and could be chosen from outside. The financial secretary would be replaced by a minister of finance drawn from the Legislative Council, thus reducing the number of Official members to two. The number of elected representatives was increased to 24, while the nominated element remained at five. Representative seats were added to all regions except for the under-populated Eastern Counties and Tobago (see Appendix F)

In addition to the governor, the chief minister, and the two *ex officio* members, the Executive Council was to be composed of seven other ministers, elected by the Legislative Council from the elected members, whose portfolios would be allocated by the governor after consultation with the chief minister. No nominated members would be part of the Executive (see Appendix E). It also provided for four persons from any of the elected members of the Legislative Council (not Speaker, deputy speaker, or a member of the Executive Council) to act as parliamentary secretaries.[49] The Butler party had submitted a minority report which called for the removal of all the nominated members, while Roy Joseph, Minister of Education, added a critical rider proclaiming that the position of chief minister would be farcical without a proper party system. Governor Beetham, however, had been pleased with the result, particularly for its flexibility: if a majority party were elected, they could break through the constraints of the system; if no party captured a majority – and this was what was expected – the system was designed to function accordingly. Beetham had expressed fears that a constitution which assumed the existence of parties would result in 'either the emergence of parties inherently racial in outlook or make-up, or the development of an innately unstable government and legislature' due to the unlikelihood of the emergence of strong majorities.[50]

Three weeks later, on July 28–9, 1956 the PNM held its first Annual Convention, the party's highest authority. Present was Puerto Rico-based Professor Gordon Lewis (married to a Trinidadian) who had praised the party for refusing to underestimate the intelligence of the average West Indian.[51] The day after the convention, the PNM presented its candidates for 14 seats; on August 14, eight more were selected. The party had even chartered a plane to canvas in Tobago on August 17th to 19th to secure the candidacy of A.N.R. Robinson there.[52] By the time of the elections, the PNM had been the only party to contest all 24 seats, the first time a party had ever done so in Trinidad and Tobago's history.[53] The PNM shunned all the old politicians, with the exception of Dr Patrick Solomon (formerly of the UF and CSP), whose 1948 Minority Report on Constitution Reform was praised by Williams as an enduring contribution to the movement for self-government.[54] The PNM was able to attract some respected persons who had not hitherto been involved in local politics at the national level. Party chairman and candidate for Tunapuna was famed cricketer Learie Constantine. Dr Winston Mahabir, like Dr Solomon, was notable for the fact that, like Williams, he was also an Island Scholar.[55] Assistant General Secretary and candidate for St Joseph, Kamaluddin Mohammed had been elected in 1953 councillor for the Ward of St Ann's in the St George County Council, and was famous for being the country's leading promoter of Indian popular culture, particularly through his weekly radio programme 'Indian Talent on Parade'.[56] The party then embarked on its nationwide series of election meetings – 157 between July 30 and September 23. During this time two major lectures were presented at Woodford Square: 'Two Worlds in Conflict' on August 14, and on September 6, 'An Evening with Hansard'. The latter speech was an attack on the antics of the Legislative Council members, made all the more hilarious by its verbatim quotes.[57]

The PNM's organisation and focus profoundly affected the normally haphazard political scene.[58] One aspect was that the PNM had been considered by many to be a 'Negro' party, Trinidad and Tobago's first.[59] The PNM, or perhaps more precisely, Dr Eric Williams, magnetically pulled the respectable brown middle classes – notoriously fearful of colour contamination as they aimed ever upwards[60] – and the religiously ecstatic, small church oriented black lower classes.[61] Not unnaturally, this achievement provoked a deep response on both sides, arousing the fear of the Indians and the whites, most notably, while it stimulated Negro enthusiasm. In this environment, accusations of racism flew all around.[62]

The PNM's aggressive campaign for leadership of all the groups of the two islands, while proclaiming in its manifesto its advocacy of secular education, its lack of prejudice towards illegitimacy and birth control, and racial integration in social relations[63] provoked further reactions, again most notably from the Indians and the hierarchy of the powerful Roman Catholic Church.[64]

Interestingly, however, the Indians and whites who together made up 37.8 per cent of the population in 1946 (or Hindus and Catholics, who together totalled over 57 per cent of the population, see Table 2.1) did not make common cause against the PNM, seemingly content to remain as separate interests.[65]

***Table 2.1. Population of Trinidad and Tobago by Religion, 1946***

| | | |
|---|---|---|
| Roman Catholic | 192,500 | 34.5% |
| Anglican | 135,312 | 24.3% |
| Hindu | 126,345 | 22.6% |
| Moslem | 32,615 | 5.8% |
| Presbyterian | 20,074 | 3.6% |
| All Others | 51,124 | 9.2% |
| All Religions | 557,970 | 100.0% |

Source: *Central Bureau of Statistics (1949)*

The Hindus had 'their own' political party, the People's Democratic Party, whose political leader, Bhadase Maraj, was also the president of the Sanatan Dharma Maha Sabha (SDMS), formed in 1952. The Catholic Church chose not to specifically align themselves with any candidates, although political parties (including the POPPG) and independents (including Minister of Education Roy Joseph) publicly sided with them.[66]

Interestingly, however, Henry Hudson-Phillips, a leading member of Gomes's POPPG, published an open letter in the *Trinidad Guardian* in which he called for 'an honourable coalition between the POPPG and the PNM'.[67] This was to prevent the tragic 'emergence of a weak ministry' which might jeopardise the success of Federation and lose the confidence of the foreign investors who had already expressed interest in the colony.[68] Williams immediately rejected the call, with characteristic sarcasm, and declared that in the elections it will be 'PNM against the Rest'.[69] The POPPG had declared that Hudson-Phillips's letter had been forwarded without the party's knowledge and that the party could not ally with the PNM since they 'differ[ed] diametrically on basic principles'.[70] The following week, Hudson-Phillips tendered a public apology.[71]

Also notable were the charges of totalitarianism commonly levied against the PNM because of their zeal for party discipline and nationalism.[72] The Catholic Church, with philosophical sophistication (compromised at times by an exaggerated anxiety), articulated this critique through at least eight 'Official Statements to the Catholic Voter', numerous editorials in its weekly *Catholic News*, articles in the *Trinidad Guardian*,[73] proclamations at religious observances, and even on the hustings itself.[74] It was their argument that party directives, in general, opposed the exercise of personal responsibility, which was the duty of every Catholic. Archbishop Finbar Ryan urged Catholics, 'Vote for a candidate, for a man or woman – and not a party. The candidate's race, colour, religion, social status or party membership must not be considered the reason for giving him a vote. Each voter is bound to vote for the candidate whom, all things considered, he or she believes, in the sight of God, is most likely to serve the interests of the country and its people.'[75]

Not only would the Catholics and Hindus remain apart, so would the five socialist, labour, and Marxist groups – the West Indian Independence Party, the Butler Party, the Caribbean National Labour Party, the Caribbean People's Democratic Party, and the Trinidad Labour Party alliance with the National Democratic Party – contesting on left-wing platforms.[76]

Not only were the parties fragmented, political affiliations remained fluid. Of the 16 incumbents in the Legislative Council who contested the 1956 elections, only six did so with the same party or independent affiliation as in 1950. Regardless of the party affiliations, however, the individual ambitions remained, with almost all the incumbents contesting again. In total, there were 129 candidates vying for 24 seats: 89 representing political parties, and 39 independents.

Not surprisingly in this context, the belief persisted that no party would be able win a majority of seats. The *Trinidad Guardian* also wondered whether parties could exercise effective control over their politicians.[77] Independent candidate for St George West, Abraham Sinanan, argued that party politics could not work in the absence of a fully elected chamber and responsible government.[78]

The *Trinidad Guardian*, in an article headlined 'Coalition!', noted that, with the exception of the PNM, all the parties were predisposed, with some conditions and reservations, to forming a coalition government.[79] Weaker parties were actively seeking alliances.[80] Albert Gomes, too, in a triumphant 'return' to Woodford Square[81] predicted that no single party would be able to form the government. He expected in 1956 a coalition government by 'the cream of the crop' since 'people saw the need for men of experience, men who passed through the mill to carry the country forward.'[82] Deprecating the PNM, he added, 'The new nine day wonder was the cultured man, the arty man and the intellectual. This was the new fad.'[83] The *Trinidad Guardian*'s Political Observer forecast a coalition of five parties controlling government, led by the PDP, in an 11-seat coalition against the PNM.[84] The *Trinidad Guardian* also reported that the Butler Party candidate for Pointe-à-Pierre in south Trinidad had assessed that 'there was definitely no chance of any one party being able to form the government as a result of this election' but there could be some hope of PNM and the Butler Party forming a coalition 'to get rid of the greater enemy.'[85]

Norman Manley, too, Chief Minister of Jamaica since 1955, and leader of the West Indian Federal Labour Party (WIFLP),[86] had expressed his reservations about the state of politics in Trinidad and Tobago during his visit to observe the elections.[87] The *Trinidad Guardian* reported,

> *The Chief Minister pointed out that it was 'quite impossible' to make a decision on which local party will join the Federal Party, in advance of the local general election, as there were several parties all claiming to be Socialist. He remarked that the multiplicity of parties was making a joke of party politics. He explained that in waiting for the political situation in Trinidad to be settled, he was being careful not to do anything that would savour of political interference at this time.*[88]

Governor Beetham, as well, maintained his scepticism and on September 15, 1956, nine days before the elections, he had sent to the Secretary of

State for the Colonies, the Commander-in-Chief for America and the West Indies, and the Officer in Charge of Troops in Jamaica, a Top Secret Inward Telegram that read, in part,

> 1. *So far election campaign has been accompanied by surprisingly little lawlessness. I mistrust this unnatural calm and believe it may well be due to complete confidence in victory of supporters of the Williams party, the mass of whom are negroes.*
> 2. *Present indications are that this party will not (repeat not) achieve anything like overwhelming victory expected and practicability of results to this volatile section of population at the end of long and exciting day may lead to spontaneous disorders particularly in Port-of-Spain.*[89]

Accordingly, a request was made for a visit by one of HM ships at Pointe-à-Pierre on September 22, and at Port of Spain on the next day, to leave on September 25 'if all is quiet'.[90] There was no need for the vessel, however, as the elections occurred without serious incident.[91]

The elections of September 24, 1956 returned 13 seats to the PNM, five to the PDP, and two each to the Butler Party, TLP–NDP, and Independent candidates. The turnout rate had been 80 per cent, the highest ever seen in the Colony up to that time (see Appendix B).

The PNM had captured all ten seats along the conurbation in the north spilling out from Port of Spain — from Chaguaramas to the borough of Arima, the two seats in the borough of San Fernando in the south and, perhaps surprisingly, the rustic constituency of Nariva/Mayaro in the extreme south-east, previously held by Stephen C. Maharaj of the Butler Party (see Appendices C and F). The party had narrowly lost three additional seats (St Andrew/St David in the north-east and Tobago to the TLP–NDP, and Ortoire/Moruga in the south to the Butler Party) to candidates obtaining less than 50 per cent of the votes cast. Winning the majority of elected seats was not the only aspect of their victory. Presenting itself as a new type of party, they defeated six of the incumbents, including three of the five ministers of the 1950 government. Norman Tang (independent) was defeated by Dr. Solomon in Port of Spain South, Roy Joseph (independent) by Dr. Mahabir in San Fernando West, and, most surprisingly, Albert Gomes (POPPG) by the young PNM trade unionist Ulric Lee in Port of Spain North.[92] In addition, the PNM fully secured the capital city, unlike the ruling parties in Jamaica, Barbados, or Guyana, for example.[93] The success of the

PNM impelled the Supervisor of Elections to document the party affiliations of candidates for the first time in his official report.[94]

However, the PNM did not dominate completely. Eight of the incumbents did win seats. Two others, Simbhoonath Capildeo (Caroni South, PDP) and Lionel Seukeran (Naparima, independent) had unsuccessfully contested seats before. The PNM polled less than 40 per cent of the total votes cast. Five of their victories were won by less than 1,500 votes (Table 3.2).

***Table 2.2. Marginal Victories of the PNM, 1956 General Elections***

| CONSTITUENCY | WINNER | MARGIN OF VICTORY | CLOSEST DEFEATED CANDIDATE |
|---|---|---|---|
| St Joseph | Kamaluddin Mohammed | 109 | Chanka Maharaj (Ind.) |
| Tunapuna | Learie Nicholas Constantine | 179 | Surajpat Mathura (PDP) |
| Nariva/Mayaro | Victor Lionel Campbell | 626 | Ramprasad Bhoolai (PDP) |
| San Fernando West | Winston Mahabir | 988 | Roy Joseph (Ind.) |
| San Fernando East | Albert Gerard Montano | 1348 | Edward Adolphus Lee (Butler Party) |
| Port of Spain – North | Ulric Lee | 1458 | Albert Gomes (POPPG) |

Source: *COTT 1958*

One other seat (St George East, in the north) was secured with a minority of 40.7 per cent. The party performed most poorly in the three constituencies in the oil belt of St. Patrick county (the southern peninsula) securing only 13.8 per cent of the total votes cast. In the eastern counties of Nariva/Mayaro and St Andrew/St David, too, the PNM polled only 24.2 per cent.[95] Indeed, if all of the non-PNM candidates had grouped together, and the same results were obtained, the PNM would have secured only 11 seats, as predicted by the *Trinidad Guardian*.

Most importantly, the PNM did not win enough seats to secure a majority in the 31-member Legislative Council, which included five nominated members and two officials. The day after the elections, on September 25,

1956, Governor Beetham sent for Williams to discuss the formation of a government. The Governor had assured Williams that the two official members would vote with the government but that, according to the terms of the 1956 Constitution, he could not accede to Williams's request that two nominated unofficial members be appointed by the PNM and that the other three be appointed after consultation with him. After one month of negotiations, the Secretary of State for the Colonies directed the governor to grant the PNM their request, indicating that the emergence of a majority party must modify the earlier principles of nomination as had occurred 'in one or two other colonial territories with advanced constitutions', in particular the colony of Malaya.[96] In addition to securing the nominated members, Williams had won the significant right to advise rather than to recommend to the Governor the portfolios allocated to his ministers.[97] On October 26, 1956, the Legislative Council sat for the first time under the new arrangements. To add to their victory, Williams and his seven ministers were elected with 19 votes each, four more than the number of PNM members of Council, with nine abstentions and two blank ballots.[98] Certainly, this had been no slight victory for the PNM, and the party celebrated with its supporters in Woodford Square immediately after the sitting.[99] The first hurdle was cleared with great success as the PNM became the first party government in Trinidad and Tobago.

## 'OPPOSITION FOR SO': THE RISE OF THE DLP, 1957–60

Having secured leadership of government, the PNM faced the task of implementing its programme, and staying in power. Williams later remarked about this period, 'the first five years were years of hard work.'[100] His deputy, Patrick Solomon, seems to have agreed.[101]

The first and foremost goal of the 1956-61 term, as expressed by Williams, was full internal self-government and the elimination of colonialism.[102] This was achieved through constitutional reform in 1959 and 1961. Other major tasks included presenting its first Five Year Development Plan in 1957, increasing development expenditure in Tobago from 1957, reorganisation of the public service in 1959, reforming the education system in 1959–60, reorganising town and country planning in 1960, taking over the telephone company in 1958-60 and public transportation in 1961, and renegotiating from 1957–60 the 1941 Anglo-

American Bases Agreement in order to reclaim Chaguaramas, chosen as the site for West Indian Federal Capital.

Some difficulties in the implementation of the PNM programme resulted from problems within the party itself, such as Williams's dissatisfaction with Solomon as Minister of Education,[103] or the party's unfamiliarity with the Council, in the first year especially, which had made them vulnerable to many attacks from the opposition, most of whom were seasoned Council members.[104] Perhaps the most important challenge was political rather than governmental. This came from the formation of the Democratic Labour Party (DLP), with the support of nine opposition members.[105] The formation of the party was motivated by a visit, on May 17, 1957 from Jamaica of Sir Alexander Bustamante, leader of the opposition Jamaica Labour Party, who was expecting to form a federal political party to counter the West Indian Federation Labour Party (WIFLP), led by his cousin, Norman Manley.[106] On May 23, 1957, the Trinidad unit of the federal DLP was launched, with the PDP, TLP and POPPG declaring affiliation. Two months later, on July 18, 1957, the parties dissolved themselves to form the DLP of Trinidad and Tobago.[107] The development – widely interpreted as a maturation of the political system – was welcomed by many, including the PNM Government who had provided the DLP with office space, salary for a secretary, and recognised the Leader of the Opposition in its Estimates and salary scales.[108]

Although the DLP's deep flaw – its opportunistic basis of alliance – seemed quite apparent from the start, the party offered itself as a more truly 'democratic' (seeming to mean less centralised, less personality-centred, and less rule-bound[109] than the PNM), free enterprise oriented, and multi-racial alternative to the PNM.[110] But, with some exceptions,[111] its politics in the Legislative Council on the whole seemed to be negative: its tactics included obstructionism, walkouts, and time-consuming allegations of corruption.[112] In addition, their performance was peppered with internal party squabbling – sometimes quite ugly – played out in the Council.[113]

Significantly, the DLP opposed the PNM's insistence on the reclamation of Chaguaramas from the Americans. The PNM made the demand in order to implement the Standing Federal Committee's recommendation on May 17, 1957 (the same day as Bustamante's visit to Trinidad) that Chaguaramas be made the site of the West Indian Federal Capital.[114] This required the renegotiation of the 1941 Anglo-American Bases Agreement, which had granted the United States a 99-year lease on the site. On August 7, 1957,

Williams had introduced the issue in the Legislative Council to DLP opposition.

In the face of the opposition, Williams embarked on a crusade over Chaguaramas, passing a motion at the PNM Annual Convention on September 29, 1957, soliciting support from Canada, India, Ceylon, and Pakistan in July and August 1958, writing articles in the new PNM organ *The Nation* (under the editorship of C.L.R. James), and conducting a series of public lectures, the most famous being 'From Slavery to Chaguaramas' delivered in Arima on June 17, 1959.[115] The UK and the USA were not the only targets of Williams's campaign. He attacked the West Indian Federal Government as well, as the Federal Prime Minister, Sir Grantley Adams, who had accepted public assurances made by the American and British Governments and announced in the House of Representative on June 16, 1958 that the West Indies would be prepared to review the situation in 'say ten years time'.[116]

***Clockwise from top left:*** *Mr. Norman Manley; Victor Bryan; Sir Grantley Adams, Prime Minister of The West Indies (1958-62); Sculpture of the late C.L.R. James.*

In the meanwhile, the DLP introduced two separate motions of no confidence, partly over the Chaguaramas issue, the first on September 9, 1957, and the second on February 21 to 28, 1958.[117] The DLP were able to claim its biggest victory over on the PNM on March 25, 1958 in the West Indian Federal Parliament elections. Trinidad and Tobago had been divided into ten seats, and the DLP won six (see Appendices B and F).[118] This was the first national test of the PNM's electoral strength after the 1956 elections, and the first ever for the DLP.[119] The PNM had campaigned on its intellectualism and launched some savagely comic attacks on the DLP.[120] The DLP, however, put up well-known candidates for election: three candidates defeated in the 1956 elections (Albert Gomes, Roy Joseph, and Surajpat Mathura), two Trinidad and Tobago members of the Legislative Council (Ashford Sinanan and Victor Bryan), and one newcomer, Mohammed Shah. The PNM were greatly disappointed, as they believed that the 1956 elections had buried the 'old era' politicians.[121] Indeed, Ashford Sinanan was the Opposition Leader in the Federal House of Representatives. To add to the indignity, the West Indian Federal Governor-General, Lord Hailes, overruled one of the PNM Government's two recommendations for the Senate, in order to bring balance to what would have been a disproportionately WIFLP-dominated Senate in the Federal Parliament.[122]

*Inauguration of the Legislature of the West Indies by H.R.H. The Princess Margaret at the Governor-General's House, Trinidad. Lord Hailes is seated next to the Princess and his wife Lady Hailes is seated at extreme right. April 22, 1958.*

The DLP's electoral success continued with the two by-elections in Point-à-Pierre and St Andrew/St David to replace Sinanan and Bryan. On February 16, 1959, almost one year after the Federal elections, the DLP added to its victories by winning control of five of the seven County Councils (see Appendix B).[123] The PNM were totally shut out of Caroni, while the DLP had at least one seat in every Council, even though they had not put up a full slate of candidates.

In the Municipal Elections, the PNM continued to prevail but faced some notable setbacks: in the elections of November 1 and 3, 1956, Louis Philip Rostant, a French Creole, beat the PNM candidate in Port of Spain North and went on to become mayor that year. In the 1959 Municipal Elections, a DLP candidate, (Alphonso Hadeed, of Middle Eastern descent) defeated the PNM candidate, again in the Port of Spain North constituency.[124]

Shifting the DLP–PNM balance further, the Colonial Office seemed to show uncommon support for the DLP after the Federal elections. F.E. Brassington, Honorary Secretary of the DLP, 1957–60, noted,

> *From the very first flush of DLP poll successes the Colonial Office had recognised the integral part which our Party had to play in [Trinidad and Tobago] . . . Colonial Office officials present for the . . . . inauguration of the Federation in [April] 1958, made it a point to seek out DLP politicians and Party officials and consult them especially with regard to Constitutional advance.*[125]

The most significant displays of Colonial Office support for the DLP resulted in the 'Cabinet crisis' of June 25 to July 8, 1959 and the breakdown of the constitutional talks in London of October 27 to November 25, 1959.[126] On both occasions, constitutional reform had been delayed by the Colonial Office who argued that 'if the PNM were not successful in the next elections [they] could not bind the victorious party to implement a policy which they had opposed.'[127] This was forwarded even though the opposition's proposals had already been considered according to parliamentary convention. The 'Cabinet crisis' was resolved, and a Cabinet system of government was introduced in 1959, changing the title of Chief Minister to Premier, giving him, instead of the Legislative Council, the power to form the government.[128] However, the disputes on wider constitutional reform had been left unresolved.

## 'THE BANKRUPTCY WHICH I DEFY': MAKING THE PNM'S WILL PREVAIL, 1960-62

In the face of electoral defeat, and with both its constitution reforms and Chaguaramas demands in limbo, the PNM began a serious effort of popular mobilisation to make its political will prevail. The first attempt in April 1958, less than a month after its Federal Elections defeat, was the most controversial. Addressing a crowd at Woodford Square on 'The Danger Facing Trinidad and the West Indian Nation', Williams launched into an unrestrained attack against the backward, rural, Indian 'wave of illiteracy' swamping the PNM's urban strongholds;[129] he called the Indians a 'hostile and recalcitrant minority', prostituting the name of India for selfish and reactionary ends; he chastised Victor Bryan for becoming a 'lickspittle' of Bhadase Maraj; he accused the DLP of mere power-seeking and 'keep[ing] the country down in the ditch in which they find themselves'; the whites for wanting to 'preserve the old aristocracy of the skin'; the Church for '[abusing] the confessional for propaganda purposes'; the 'venal press' for carrying on 'its vendetta against the PNM,' and even non-voters who by staying home allowed the DLP to win.[130]

The speech offended many, including the non-African government ministers and party executives, who registered their complaints to Williams. He, however, felt no need to retract or re-phrase his address, and repeated it in San Fernando in their presence.[131] Alexander Bustamante branded Williams's speech as vulgar and unbecoming.[132] At the next sitting of the legislature, DLP member Lionel Seukeran (Naparima) introduced a motion of censure against the Chief Minister for his 'derogatory attack on the Indian Community'.[133] Mahabir writes that Williams had been led to believe that his three non-Negro Ministers – Montano, Kamal Mohammed, and himself – were going to support the motion, but 'in the interest of national peace' the three instead persuaded the opposition to drop the charges.[134]

By the time of the next PNM Annual Convention, meeting on October 17, 1958, it was decided that the PNM had to 'go to the Party. The party left to fend for itself two years and nine months, becomes automatically and necessarily the number one priority from October 1958.'[135] Plans for the establishment of a permanent headquarters, improved liaison between the party and government, a reorganised Central Office, the transformation of the party press, the extension of party education in weekend schools, and the keeping of party record books were some of the priorities listed. A noteworthy extension of this initiative had been the appointment of C.L.R. James to edit a new party newspaper, *The Nation*, launched on December 6, 1958.[136] Williams lavished high praise on the paper and its editor, right up to his March 11, 1960 'Address to the Fourth Annual Party Convention', calling it 'the textbook of Independence . . . . [giving the PNM] what it did not have before, a public-relations voice in the outside world.'[137]

In that same address, Williams defiantly declared, 'The war of Independence in on.' The culmination of this activity was reached at 11:00 a.m. on April 22, 1960, the date and time that the PNM had adopted in September 1957 for the independence of the West Indian Federation. A rally was organised in Woodford Square where, in conclusion to a stirring address by Williams, were burned in a bonfire 'seven deadly sins'; the existing constitutions of Trinidad and Tobago and the West Indies; the 1941 Anglo-American Bases Agreement, the report of the 1956 Federal Capital Site Commission recommending against Trinidad; the Telephone Ordinance; the Democratic Party's 'racial statement'; and the *Trinidad Guardian*. Afterwards, a memorial on independence was read and the crowd marched peacefully around the Port of Spain Savannah, in the rain, while small delegations presented copies of the memorial at the Governor's Residence and the American Consulate.[138]

*Shaking hands with Sir Grantley Adams (left) is Mr. H. Macmillan, Prime Minister of England, during his visit to the UCWI's St. Augustine Campus in March 1961. Standing between them is Mr. A.N.R. Robinson*

The demonstration coincided with a decisive change in the British Government's attitude toward its colonies. In early 1960, British Prime Minister Harold MacMillan (elected in October 1959) ended his tour of Africa proclaiming that 'the wind of change', i.e. the growth of national consciousness, was a political fact of which British government policy had to take account.[139] The fortunes of the PNM became bright once again. The dispute over the new constitutional proposals was solved during Secretary of State Iain MacLeod's visit to the West Indies from June 7 to 19, 1960, personally settling the matter in Trinidad. The new constitution provided for full internal self-government within the framework of the Federation of the West Indies. It provided for a Prime Minister heading a Cabinet of 12 ministers. The post of Attorney-General (the last remaining *ex-officio* position) became a political post and the governor became more or less a merely formal head of the state, required to act on the advice of the prime minister. A bicameral Legislature was established, with a fully elected Lower House composed of 30 members. The wholly nominated 21 member Senate would be composed of 12 prime ministerial appointees, seven appointees of the governor to represent special interests, and two from the leader of the Opposition (see Appendix E). They would have powers to debate but not decide, and up to two could be appointed as ministers of government by the prime minister.[140] Williams's 1955 constitutional reforms were thus realised by his PNM Government. The Constitution was to take effect immediately after the elections on December 4, 1961.[141]

In addition to the solution to the dispute over the constitution there came the renegotiation of the Bases Agreement. After some communication between London and Port of Spain, a conference had been convened in Tobago from September 28 to December 9. It concluded with the United States agreeing to renegotiate its lease, ceding 21,000 acres by 1962, committing itself to aid and training projects (including the development of a College of Arts and Sciences at the Trinidad branch of the University College of the West Indies) and agreeing to a review of the situation in 1968.[142]

More fortune was showered on the PNM as the DLP had started to disintegrate. The process, perhaps naturally resulted from the DLP's inaugural ceremony on September 1, 1957 that had avoided the question of party leadership. Victor Bryan (member of Council for the eastern county of St Andrew/St David, formerly of the TLP) had been elected provisional chairman of the party and was also made provisional leader of the Federal Labour Party. The latter appointment was made after the intervention of the Federal DLP's life leader, Alexander Bustamante, who, like WIFLP leader Norman Manley, did not contest the Federal Elections.[143] These one-year provisional appointments were ostensibly designed to allow time for the party to organise itself, while avoiding early leadership squabbles. Leaving the positions open, however, only encouraged the rivalries that were easily predictable, given the collection of political chiefs in the party.[144] On January 8, 1958, five and a half months after the founding of the Trinidad and Tobago DLP, Bhadase Maraj (member of Council for Caroni North in central Trinidad, formerly of the PDP) was unanimously elected leader of its parliamentary wing. The following week, Ashford Sinanan (member of Council for Pointe-à-Pierre in central/southern Trinidad, also formerly of the PDP) was chosen by Bustamante to become Federal Prime Minister if the DLP won the Federal elections.[145]

After the Federal victory, however, Victor Bryan led a manoeuvre to oust Bhadase Maraj, feeling that Maraj, as a rural Hindu, would be a hindrance in the Trinidad and Tobago 1961 general elections, which the DLP felt it could win. Bryan was thwarted, however, and after the 1959 County Council elections he declared himself an independent in the Federal Parliament.[146] Meanwhile, Gomes (Federal member for St George West in north Trinidad, formerly of the POPPG) launched an attack – using his *Trinidad Guardian* columns and his parliamentary privilege – on Bustamante's anti-Federalism and his single-minded rivalry with his cousin Norman Manley. Bustamante resigned from the federal party over the issue. This, in turn, led to conflict between Gomes and Sinanan, who had been a firm Bustamante supporter.[147]

Adding to the troubles, Bhadase Maraj became sick and bedridden, and addicted to pethidine, in 1959.[148] Parliamentary leadership passed, without any institutionalised process, first to A.P.T. James (member of Council for Tobago, formerly of the TLP), who was unable to command the support of his colleagues, and then to Simbhoonath Capildeo (member of Council for Caroni South, formerly of the PDP).[149] During this confusion, Simbhoonath Capildeo's younger brother Rudranath had been positioning himself to enter the party. Rudranath Capildeo, like Williams, was an Island scholar (of 1938) from Queen's Royal College. He received his Ph.D. in physics from London University, and returned to Trinidad from 1958 to

1959 on the invitation of Williams, to accept the position of Principal of the newly established Trinidad Polytechnic in St James.[150]

Dr Rudranath Capildeo seemed to many an ideal solution to the leadership problems of the DLP: a man who could be considered Williams's intellectual equal, thereby attracting more non-Indian votes.[151] After some intrigue and irregularities, Capildeo had displaced Bhadase Maraj on March 29, 1960 at a confused party convention.[152]

*Dr Rudranath Capildeo*

Brassington, Albert Gomes and Romalho Gomes (the two Gomes were unrelated), although initially supporting Capildeo, had been piqued by his violation of past procedure and his subsequent declaration that he would begin the DLP *de novo*, rewriting the party constitution and disregarding the structures, executive members, programmes, strategies and constitutional negotiating teams already in place.[153] Adding insult to injury, soon after his leadership coup Dr Capildeo had left Trinidad to resume teaching at the University of London. The dissident Port of Spain-based faction, following proper legal procedure, called a conference at Queen's Hall in April 1960, expelled Dr Capildeo, Sinanan and others, elected Albert Gomes as leader, and moved to organise for the coming Arima Borough by-elections. As a counter, on the day of the by-election a message from Dr Capildeo had been published in the press announcing that the DLP were not contesting any seats that day. The Gomes-Brassington faction had lost the by-elections (reportedly by only a small difference in votes) and subsequently left the party. In June 1960, Albert Gomes and Brassington addressed a rally in Woodford Square denouncing the Capildeo-led DLP. Rudranath Capildeo was now the unchallenged, and absent, leader of a fractured party.[154]

*Clockwise from top left: Albert Gomes; Roy Joseph; Ashford Sinanan, A.N.R. Robinson.*

At a speech delivered on May 30, 1960, Williams commented,

> *Here we face a great tragedy, the tragedy of Trinidad and Tobago – that there is no opposition, there is none in sight, no opposition that is, which agreed on fundamentals, agreed on the national outlook, can present to the national community an alternative set of proposals, an alternative programme for the achievement of our material aim.*
>
> *Opposition there is, opposition galore – but it is opposition for so . . . .*
>
> *These moral anarchists, these enemies of democracy, will sell their country down the Gulf of Paria, in order to achieve the prominence of Quisling and the notoriety of Judas Iscariot . . . .*

> *[The PNM's perspectives] spring from an objective analysis, contradiction of which I defy, of the bankruptcy in every sphere of West Indian colonialism – whether it be the political, the constitutional, the economic, the social, the intellectual, the cultural, the moral.*[155]

As the general elections of 1961 approached, the PNM introduced its controversial Representation of the People Bill, debated on January 20, 1961, proposing to modernise the electoral system of Trinidad and Tobago by instituting permanent registration, identification cards, voting machines, and a revised procedure for demarcating the new electoral boundaries. The DLP reacted strongly against these measures, claiming that the reforms attempted to disenfranchise illiterate, rural, Indian voters by intimidating them with 'complex' application procedures, to rig elections through manipulation of the voting machines, to allow non-national Afro-West Indians to vote in Trinidad and Tobago, and to gerrymander constituencies to ensure a PNM majority in light of the DLP's electoral victories in 1958 and 1959. The DLP proposed 118 amendments to the 1961 Representation of the People Bill, but the party failed to achieve any of its objectives.[156] Stephen Maharaj's Minority Report of the Boundaries Commission presented a delimitation of constituencies differing considerably from the majority report, along with detailed instances of deviation from the principles for guidance set out by the Order in Council.[157]

The elections of December 4, 1961 have been considered the most tense in the country's history, with race seeming to dominate the campaigns.[158] Williams had highlighted the Negro-white tensions with his phrase 'Massa Day Done', introduced on December 20, 1960 when he reported in Woodford Square on the renegotiation of the Bases Agreement at the Tobago Conference, and later expanded to an entire speech, delivered on March 22, 1962 and published as a pamphlet.[159]

Indian-Negro tensions manifested themselves as early as January 1961 when DLP meetings were broken up by PNM supporters. In November the DLP complained that they were not protected by the Negro-dominated police.[160] Because of the alleged harassment, the DLP felt it necessary to suspend all public meetings for the three weeks before the elections. At the same time, the government refused to grant free air time to the party on the state-owned radio station.[161] Also exacerbating the tension was Dr Capildeo's reputation for making intemperate and unbalanced statements,[162] starting with his first statement read in the Legislative Council on April 8, 1960. His most infamous remark was made on October 15, 1961, at a meeting held in front of the governor's residence in Port of Spain, in order to (unsuccessfully) deter molestation from PNM supporters. Capildeo lost his temper and announced to his supporters, 'You will be called to arms. Wherever the PNM holds a meeting, you will have to break it up.'[163] Indeed, violence did break out in some areas and on November 22, minister of Home Affairs, Patrick Solomon, declared limited States of Emergency in St Augustine, Barataria, Caroni East and Chaguanas, with the police conducting armed house-to-house searches for ammunition. The searches turned up nothing.[164]

The election results returned the PNM in a sweeping victory, firmly entrenching their position in government with an unprecedented two-thirds majority (see Appendix B). They captured 57 per cent of the ballots cast, and won 20 seats. In addition to the 13 seats of 1956, the PNM gained two additional seats in the northern conurbation of the country and made genuine gains by winning two seats in St Patrick, the Toco/Manzanilla seat in the extreme northeast, and both Tobago seats.[165] The La Brea seat in St Patrick was won by Alexander C. Alexis, who formerly had held the seat as an independent but had joined the PNM by 1961.[166]

The DLP secured 42 per cent of the votes and ten seats. Compared to the 11 non-PNM seats in 1956, the DLP lost significant ground to the PNM. It kept all five PDP seats; retained the two southern seats of Naparima and Princes Town; kept one seat in the east; gained one extra by the increase in the number of constituencies in Central Trinidad, the Hindu heartland; and kept two seats in the deep south (see Appendices C and F). The DLP contested the results by submitting an election petition, basing its case mainly on the inaccurate operation of the voting machines. The case was lost by a two to one decision in March 1962. In protest, the party boycotted the opening of Trinidad and Tobago's first parliament on December 29, 1961.[167]

The turnout for the elections was the highest ever in Trinidad's history, 88.1 per cent. The PNM and DLP together polled 98.6 per cent of the ballots cast. Only two other parties (the Butler Party and the African National Congress) and two independents contested, all losing their deposits.[168] Only 69 candidates contested the elections. Both successful parties securely won every seat with a majority of over 1,500 votes, except for the DLP in Fyzabad, where victory was secured by a small margin of 126. The election results seemed to show the establishment of a two-party system in Trinidad and Tobago, with the PNM dominant (see Appendix B).[169]

The next major step in the PNM's programme for the country was the movement towards independence. On September 19, 1961, Jamaica had voted by referendum to quit the Federation and pursue independence alone.[170] After various discussions among the Colonial Office, the Federation of the West Indies, its new advisor Arthur Lewis, and the remaining nine territorial governments, the PNM government decided to withdraw Trinidad and Tobago from the Federation. Without Jamaica, Trinidad and Tobago would have had to provide almost 75 per cent of the Federal budget while being allotted less than half of the seats in a Federal structure which it had consistently criticised as being too weak. A resolution was adopted by the PNM's General Council on January 15, 1962 stating that Trinidad and Tobago would

> *reject unequivocally any participation in the proposed Federation of the Eastern Caribbean and proceed forthwith to National Independence, without prejudice to the future association in a Unitary State of the people of Trinidad and Tobago with any Territory of the Eastern Caribbean whose people may so desire and on terms to be mutually agreed.*[171]

This resolution caused the British Government to terminate the Federation and grant independence on an individual territorial basis.[172]

*'Whitehall', Office of the Prime Minister of Trinidad and Tobago situated on the Western side of the Queen's Park Savannah, Port of Spain, Trinidad. The now-forgotten Federation of the West Indies flags flying outside.*

The PNM then proceeded to draft an Independence Constitution.[173] The DLP, however, objected to the whole procedure – from the publication of the draft constitution on February 19, 1962 (upon which the public was invited to make comment) on the grounds that the Opposition, representing 40 per cent of the population, should have been made part of the process, to the Queen's Hall Conference held between April 25 and 27, 1962 in which presentations were made by 75 organisations and individuals, where the DLP walked out over objections to the 'limited' format,[174] to the Joint Select Committee of Parliament (convened from May 9 to 16, 1962 to consider the public comments) in which the DLP were included but voted down 16 to nine.[175] The DLP's objections, consistently overruled by the PNM, were motivated by a desire to establish a greater role for the Opposition in providing a check on executive power and in the protection of minorities' interests.

In the meantime, the county councillors were required to demit office on February 28, 1962. In order to accommodate the provisions of the expected independence constitution, on February 16 and 20 a bill to extend indefinitely the term of office of the councillors was passed in the House of Representatives and in the Senate. When Senators expressed anxiety about signing a 'blank cheque' to the government, Attorney General Senator George Richards replied that since elections 'would probably occur in two months or so', it was 'hardly necessary to include a clause setting a time limit to this bill'. The last county council elections had been held in 1959, with the DLP gaining overwhelming control. The last municipal elections had been held on November 1, 1960 in Arima; November 1, 1961 in San Fernando and November 3, 1961 in Port of Spain.[176]

On May 11, 1962, a draft constitution was accepted in the Lower House. Interestingly, during the debate Williams argued at length against a proposal by the Indian Association that Trinidad be ethnically partitioned along Cypriot lines. He refuted in detail the arguments that Indians were discriminated against. Testifying to its significance almost 40 years after it was first written, Williams had quoted from Major Wood's 1922 Report, which had led to the establishment of electoral politics in Trinidad and Tobago, arguing that '[communal representation] would accentuate and perpetuate the differences which in order to produce a homogenous society it should be the object of statesmanship to remove'.[177]

The amended draft was taken to London for the Independence Conference at Marlborough House on May 28, 1962. The DLP, unsatisfied, increased its demands for a moratorium on independence, proportional representation in the police force, a constitutional provision for consultation between the prime minister and the leader of the Opposition on major appointments and on all issues of national importance, a larger share for the DLP in the appointment of senators, and a provision for a two-thirds majority for adopting any legislative measure in the Senate. Emphasising the racial nature of the dispute, the Indian Association and the Sanatan Dharma Maha Sabha (SDMS) had gone to the conference to protest against the proposed constitution. The Indian Association again raised its call for partition if proportional representation was not implemented.[178] The PNM, however, were adamant that they would not concede to 'government by the Opposition', but were not opposed to developing consultation as a conventional practice. On the whole, it seems as though they were supported by the Colonial Office.[179] On June 8, having made preparations to invite Secretary of State Reginald Maudling to intervene and abate the racial tensions, Williams approached Capildeo, at tea break and suggested that he would

> *raise with the opposition the general question of national integration and national unity with specific reference to (a) Nehru's Integration Committee in India, (b) the promotion of the national culture, (c) the working out of a campaign code on elections, (d) fair employment practices without discrimination on grounds of race, political affiliation, etc.* (Williams 1969, 285)

Capildeo agreed, and the date for Independence was set on August 31, 1962, allowing Williams to attend the Commonwealth Prime Minister's Conference in September.[180] In the final Trinidad and Tobago (Constitution) Order-in-Council 1962, the 30 entrenched provisions (i.e. requiring a two-thirds majority in both Houses) in the Report of the Joint Select Committee had been expanded to 14 ordinarily entrenched and 25 specially entrenched provisions (i.e. requiring a three-quarters majority in the Lower House and a two-thirds majority in the Upper House). The number of Opposition senators had increased to four in an enlarged 24-member Senate (see Appendix E). Up to two senators were allowed to be nominated by the prime minister as members of the Cabinet. In addition, the Report of the London Conference included a commitment by the prime minister to honour the convention of consultation with the leader of the Opposition on all appropriate occasions, including the appointment of the chairmanship of the Election and Boundaries Commission.[181] The PNM had become firmly established as the governing party of an independent Trinidad and Tobago, dominating its politics.

*Dr Eric Williams and H.R.H. The Princess Royal stand by the eastern side of the entrance of the Red House on August 30, 1962, midnight, watching the lowering of the Union Jack at the Independence ceremony.*

Williams and the PNM had prevailed over the independent political tradition with party politics; vanquished the old politicians; established a Cabinet system of government, a bicameral legislature, and a liberal, non-racial constitution; secured American withdrawal from Chaguaramas; arrived at a Concordat on education with the Catholic Church; negotiated independence with the British government and with the parliamentary opposition; and secured an unprecedented two-thirds majority in parliament. These achievements in the PNM's first six years were made out of a combination of political shrewdness, determination, toughness, aggression, luck, and circumstance, sometimes at the cost of antagonism and bitterness, particularly in terms of African-Indian relations. With an impressive force of will, Williams had pushed Trinidad and Tobago into a new era.

*Opening of the first Parliament of independent Trinidad and Tobago, 1962.*

# Three

## POLITICS IN THE INDEPENDENCE PERIOD, 1962-81: 'RIGHT BACK TO 1956'

*Governor-General Sir Solomon Hochoy swears in Dr Eric Williams, the first Prime Minister of Trinidad and Tobago.*

In this chapter, we look at the peculiar challenges faced by Williams and the People's National Movement from 1962 to 1981. Parliamentary Opposition, after having been decisively defeated by the time of Independence in 1962, collapsed through splits and non-participation. Meanwhile there had developed a vigorous and popular extra-parliamentary opposition to the Williams government. This movement, centred in the trade union movement and at the University of the West Indies, appealed to anti-imperialist, youth, socialist, 'cultural nationalist' (particularly pro-African), and other anti-establishment sentiments current at the time. Despite the numerous protest marches, an army mutiny in 1970, and a No-Vote campaign in 1971, the PNM maintained its firm hold on government, without significant departures from the norms of liberal democracy. However, in 1973 Williams announced his frustration with the situation in Trinidad and Tobago and declared his intention to retire. He reversed his decision as the oil shock of 1973–74, together with further constitutional reform, provided a renewed opportunity to build the strong, secure, and independent state (in terms of both government and economy) that he had envisaged since 1956. Despite the continuous extra-parliamentary opposition, the new generation of opposition parties that emerged in 1976, and the challenge posed in 1980–81 by a break-away faction of the party, the PNM maintained its two-thirds majority right up to Williams's death in 1981. Williams was continuously challenged during his long period in office and, not without difficulty, he prevailed over the diversiform, disorganised, and fragmentary opposition at every juncture.

## 'DON'T STOP THE CARNIVAL': UNCONVENTIONAL POLITICS, 1962–73

*Dr Eric Williams on the 'Meet the People' tour, 1963-4.*

In the first decade of independence, the PNM advanced its programme for building the modern Trinidad and Tobago state, summarised by Sutton as 'the development and implementation of a foreign policy; the development of a sense of national community; public service reform; and reform of the economy by way of development planning, regulation of labour and capital, and tripartite consultation.'[1] Specifically, the PNM presented in 1963 its

*Second Five Year Development Plan, 1964–68*,[2] started the reorganisation of the public service in 1964, and instituted that same year a wide-ranging community development programme highlighted by the 'Best Village' competition and the 'Special Works' programmes for the unemployed.[3] In the financial sector it passed the Central Bank and Banking Acts of 1964 and the controversial Finance Act of 1966 which increased taxes on businesses in order to prevent the 'leaking' of income earned in Trinidad and Tobago. In 1965 the government passed perhaps its most socially important piece of legislation, the Education Act, placing the entire school system and its curriculum under closer government control in order to rationalise the process of expansion.[4]

Near the end of the party's term, in the January 21, 1966 edition of *The Nation*, Williams reflected on the party's achievements in office: 'It has been Ten Years of hard and relentless work, dedicated always to the public welfare, to political dignity and stability, to the national community, to the political education of our educated democracy'.[5]

While the PNM made impressive achievements in government, the opposition was falling apart, reverting to the individualism, factionalism, and bacchanal that the PNM thought it had destroyed in 1956. In January 1963, following his decisive failure to become prime minister in 1961, and his failure to secure specific safeguards in the 1962 Independence Constitution for the protection of minorities, Dr Capildeo accepted a teaching post at the University of London. He replaced his tutor, Professor Stevenson, who had died. Constitutional rules or requirements concerning leadership meant little in the DLP and so Capildeo decided to retain his post as party leader, running the party from London and returning to Trinidad in the academic recess periods. He was able to retain his position in parliament as Leader of the Opposition as he was granted a special leave of absence by the Speaker of the House, Arnold Thomasos, PNM MP for Arima.[6]

Absurdly, in March 1963, Capildeo gave the DLP – founded in 1957 on an anti-socialist platform – a new creed of 'Democratic Socialism.' Tired of his antics, the (nominated) DLP executive called for Dr Capildeo to resign. As a compromise, in the Christmas recess of 1963 Dr Capildeo appointed Stephen Maharaj (a former member of the Butler Party) as Leader of Opposition in parliament, while retaining leadership of the party. Still unsatisfied, in January (after Dr Capildeo had returned to London) the executive attempted to install Maharaj as party leader as well. In retaliation, Capildeo dismissed the entire executive. On January 13, 1964, three MPs – Dr Montgomery Forrester, party chairman; Peter Farquhar, editor of the party paper; and Tajmool Hosein (two Negroes and one Muslim, newly elected in 1961) – resigned from the DLP, reducing the party's parliamentary strength to seven (all with Hindu backgrounds). On March 27, 1964, the three ex-DLP MPs formed the Liberal Party of Trinidad and Tobago, giving parliament an additional opposition party.[7]

In 1965 another split occurred in the DLP as a result of the government's Industrial Stabilisation Act (ISA), introduced on March 18, during a State of Emergency. The ISA had been precipitated by a number of events. Strike activity had increased greatly from the late 1950s (see Figure 4.1), as a strong section of the trade union leadership began to actively oppose the PNM which, in the 1961 elections, had received notable support from the national Trades Union Congress (TUC).[8]

***Figure 3.1. Man-Days Lost:***
***Workers Involved and Work Stoppages, 1955-1964***

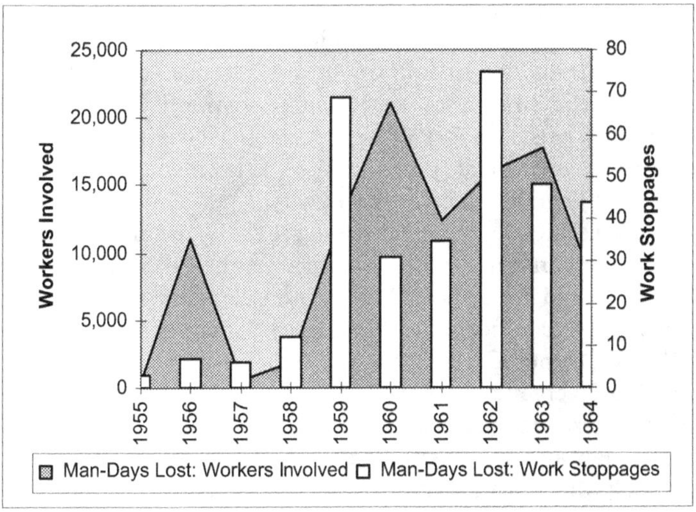

*Created by the author from CBTT (1993)*

George Weekes – elected to the Presidency of the Oilfields Workers' Trade Union (OWTU)[9] on June 25, 1962, and a great admirer of Butler – had become a central figure opposed to the PNM and its policies.[10] The antagonism between the government and the radical trade union leadership was highlighted by the February 1963 OWTU strike against British Petroleum.[11] In response, on April 5, 1963, the government announced in parliament that it had decided to set up an inquiry into the oil industry and another inquiry into subversive activity in the country.[12] The trade union movement eventually split in two when the TUC (also led by Weekes) boycotted tripartite talks with the government in October 1964.[13]

In the sugar industry, Bhadase Maraj's leadership of the All-Trinidad Sugar Estates and Factory Workers' Trade Union (ATSEFWTU)[14] was being challenged by an ally of Weekes, Krishna Gowandan, who from February 21 to March 8, 1965 led a strike that spread throughout the entire industry. The TUC had passed a resolution in support of the Gowandan-led movement and, at the same time, two other strikes were occurring, while one other action had been threatened.[15]

On March 9, 1965, the government had declared a State of Emergency in the sugar belt of Caroni, against the advice of DLP leader of the opposition Stephen Maharaj. On March 22, the State of Emergency had been extended to Barataria in order to place the visiting C.L.R. James under house arrest.[16]

Three days after the initial declaration of the emergency, legislation restricting strike action was introduced in parliament and on March 18 the report of the Commission of Enquiry into subversive activities was tabled. Also tabled at the March 18 sitting of parliament was the Industrial Stabilisation Bill, based on Australian legislation, seeking to regulate labour disputes through compulsory recognition, settlement of disputes by an Industrial Court, and a ban on strike activity.[17]

The legislation had been criticised greatly by the radical trade unions. Despite Maharaj's instructions to vote against the bill in Parliament, only three DLP MPs, and none of the DLP senators (including Thomas Bleasdell, DLP public relations officer, and Mrs Lucky Samaroo, the party treasurer) did so.[18] The Governor-General, Sir Solomon Hochoy, assented to the ISA on March 20. Divergence over the ISA had grouped the DLP into centrist (led by Vernon Jamadar), radical (led by Maharaj), and conservative (led by Ashford Sinanan and L.F. Seukeran) factions. In June 1965, the rivalry reached a peak when the conservative faction outmanoeuvred Maharaj, who had attempted to replace the current DLP senators with C.L.R. James, A.C. Rienzi, and Clive Phil. They thwarted his move by advising the Governor-General to install Simbhoonath Capildeo (Dr Capildeo's elder brother) as leader of the opposition.

Not until the July 1965 academic recess did Dr Capildeo make any

*Vernon Jamadar speaking on the 'No Vote' campaign in 1971.*

intervention and, when he did, it was highly erratic. He denounced the ISA, accused his brother of being the main case of trouble in the DLP and even accused him of sending a hired killer after him. He applauded the PNM for the stability and progress the party had brought to the country; and accused James, Maharaj, and Rienzi of hatching a 'plot' and attempting to 'make a deal' with him by offering him the prime ministership of the country.[19]

As a result, the DLP split again: Maharaj (with George Weekes, C.L.R. James, and others) formed the Workers and Farmers Party (WFP) on August 8, 1965.[20] Simbhoonath Capildeo joined the Liberal Party, and Lionel Seukeran declared himself an independent. By 1966, the parliamentary opposition was comprised of ten members: four DLP, four Liberal, one WFP, and one Independent. The two-party system did not survive the term.

The next general elections were held on November 7, 1966. Thirty-six seats were contested, in accordance with the newly passed constitutional provision prescribing one seat for every 12,000 electors.[21] Following the disintegration of the DLP in parliament, 154 candidates contested, in contrast to the sixty-nine candidates contesting in 1961. The PNM, DLP, the Liberals, and the WFP put up candidates for every seat except in Tobago West where the WFP did not contest.[22] Three other parties contested, including the Butler Party and the PDP, in addition to six independents.[23] With the greatly increased number of candidates, it was perhaps not surprising that the PNM and DLP received a smaller share of the vote than they did in 1961 (Appendix B).

In contrast to the increase in candidates, there were 30,964 fewer voters than in 1961, and a significantly lower turnout rate of 65.8 per cent. However, the proportional distribution of the seats was exactly the same as in 1961: the PNM won two-thirds of the seats and the DLP one-third, in the same geographical areas (see Appendix C). In addition to the 20 seats in 1961, the PNM gained an extra three seats in the northern conurbation. It also made a real gain in the deep south by taking the marginal constituency of Fyzabad from the DLP, turning its loss in 1961 by 126 votes into a small victory of 365 votes.[24] The DLP offset its Fyzabad loss by gaining three seats as a result of the increasing population in the south (see Appendices C and F). The Liberals did not capture any seats, and all the WFP candidates lost their deposits. Even Bhadase Maraj lost the St Augustine seat to the DLP's minor candidate, John McKenzie Bharath, with 943 votes compared to 5,230. Apart from the PNM, only the DLP would contest general elections again and only in a severely fractured form.[25]

The DLP continued on its long process of decay, almost completely nullifying its political relevance. The party's decision to shun the radical trade union movement seemed to be vindicated by the poor showing of the WFP at the elections, and the DLP continued to blame the voting machines for their defeat, calling the elections a 'big fraud'.[26] In protest, Dr Capildeo ordered the party to 'maintain silence' in parliament as a strategy of non-cooperation designed to embarrass the government by making a mockery of the two-party system.[27]

Dr Capildeo had given a promise to stay in the country in the new parliament, no matter what the result. However, in April 1967 he was granted by the party a two-year leave of absence to work on a textbook, *Vector Algebra and Mechanics: Theory, Problems, and Solutions*.[28] In December 1967, the Speaker of the House refused Capildeo's request for further leave and declared Capildeo's Chaguanas seat vacant. In the by-election of January 1968, the DLP conducted a no-vote campaign as an act of protest.[29] Forty-three per cent of the electorate voted. The seat was won by Bhadase Maraj who had by then recovered from his drug addiction and fought as an independent. Maraj severely criticised the DLP for its policy of silence and for giving the PNM an opportunity to secure a two-thirds working majority, even with a PNM MP as Speaker.[30]

The DLP was forced to abandon its non-cooperation strategy. On June 24, 1968, the party contested the municipal and county elections, the first held since the local government elections of 1959-61.[31] The turnout was low, 34.9 per cent in the seats that were contested, lower than in the County Council elections of 1946. In this less than ideal context, the PNM demonstrated its dominance of the political scene once again. The PNM were returned unopposed in 14 seats: ten in Port of Spain, one in San Fernando, and three in St George. It secured a total of 68 seats and controlled all three municipalities and four of the seven County Councils: St George, St Andrew-St David, Nariva-Mayaro, and Tobago. The DLP secured 28 seats and controlled the Caroni, Victoria, and St Patrick County Councils (see Appendix B). Twenty-eight persons lost their deposit.[32]

Opposition to the PNM outside the institutions of government was growing more vocal. The failure of the parliamentary opposition to articulate a coherent position and ally itself in the ISA controversy of 1965 perhaps encouraged the growth of 'unconventional politics', expressed by a wide array of extra-parliamentary groups drawing from a variety of radical anti-establishment, socialist, and black nationalist perspectives, with an almost complete disregard for the formal processes of government.[33]

By making strike action illegal, the ISA had calmed considerably the industrial relations climate.[34] The radical trade union movement had been further energised with the election of Joe Young to the leadership of the Transport and Industrial Workers Union (TIWU) based in north Trinidad. Both Young and Weekes led marches and demonstrations in 1967 and 1968 in defiance of the ISA.[35]

In 1968, the National Joint Action Committee (NJAC) had emerged out of the Guild of Undergraduates at the University of the West Indies (UWI) under the presidency of Geddes Granger. Granger encouraged the Guild to make links with community organisations, trade unions, and other 'people's organisations' through a radicalising outreach and education programme. On February 26, 1969, NJAC was formally launched to protest against the recent arrest of West Indian students at Sir George Williams University in Montreal, Canada. They blocked the Canadian Governor-General, Roland Michener, from entering the UWI campus, demonstrated against Canadian imperialism and, more generally, against 'racism at home and abroad'.[36]

Other important organisations were founded around the same time as NJAC. *The Trinidad Express* started publication in June 1967 as the only locally owned daily newspaper then in circulation, sympathising with local viewpoints in an unprecedented way, and providing the country with a second daily newspaper;[37] the Tapia House Group was founded by UWI economics lecturer Lloyd Best on November 14, 1968, definitively ending the New World Group (founded in 1962); a rival paper, *Moko*, had been formed in October of the same year by UWI history lecturer James Millette, former Chairman of the defunct New World Group. In addition, there had been a host of smaller ephemeral community, youth, cultural, religious, and other groups from the middle and lower classes throughout the country, inspired by the radical ideas current at the time.[38] In May 1969, many of these cultural, university, political and trade union groups joined together – including NJAC, George Weekes, OWTU lawyer and ex-WFP candidate Basdeo Panday[39] – to confront the police in solidarity with TIWU transport workers who had been striking for three weeks, protesting against a ruling of the Industrial Court.[40]

What became known as the 'Black Power Revolution' began during the Carnival celebrations on February 9, 1970, where a masquerade band called 'Pinetoppers' had caused a stir by portraying revolutionary heroes such as Fidel Castro, Stokely Carmichael, and Malcom X in its band, 'The Truth about Africa'.[41] On February 26, 1970, one year after their first meeting, the NJAC led a march in Port of Spain demonstrating against racism at home and abroad, the Canadian 'imperialist' banks, and then made the famous entry into the Roman Catholic Cathedral of the Immaculate Conception (for which the leaders were later charged). On March 4 they renamed Woodford Square – out of political use for years – the 'People's Parliament' and led a 10,000-strong march from Port of Spain to Shanty Town on the eastern edge. On March 12, under the banner 'Indians and Africans Unite Now', a much longer march was organised from Port of Spain to Caroni; and the marches continued, occasionally resulting in vandalism and destruction of property.[42]

On March 23, Dr Williams had addressed the nation in a television broadcast declaring, 'I am for Black Power'.[43] He sympathised with the demands of the youthful demonstrators and stressed that the demands were 'entirely legitimate and in the interest of the community as a whole'. He reminded his audience that the PNM had been addressing these concerns continuously in programmes to remove racial discrimination, provide opportunities for education, localise decision making, promote small businesses, and restrict alien landholdings, while he expressed sympathy with the marchers' frustration at the slow pace of change. In response, the prime minister announced the introduction of a special 5 per cent levy 'devoted exclusively to providing jobs in all counties and municipalities, including training facilities for various skills which the country requires' and the establishment of the country's first locally owned commercial bank. He further emphasised, 'the Government remains ready to give serious and sympathetic study to any concrete proposals that may be formulated,' and that six such approaches to dialogue had already been made. He continued,

> *Our young people are a part of the general world malaise, seeking something new and something better, and seeking it with a sense of urgency. They are restless, frustrated, possibly a little exuberant. But let there be no misunderstanding about this. It is a horse of a different colour if what is involved is arson and molotov cocktails. In that case, the law will have to take its course.*[44]

Despite Williams's plea for more constructive approaches, marches continued to be the main expression of the movement, and the police increased their efforts to keep the crowds under control. On April 6, a young demonstrator was shot and killed by the police, rallying more persons to the marches. Quite unexpectedly, and adding to the atmosphere of disarray, on April 13, 1970, Deputy Prime Minister, Deputy Leader of the PNM, and Member of Parliament for Tobago East, A.N.R. Robinson, announced his resignation from the Cabinet in a speech critical of the PNM government given to the Seamen and Waterfront Workers Trade Union.[45] Meanwhile, on April 18, sugar workers went on strike at Brechin Castle in central Trinidad. The OWTU, TIWU, and NJAC planned actions to express their solidarity with the sugar workers and there had been rumours of a general strike. Almost ten years to the day after the PNM's March for Independence, on April 21, 1970, a State of Emergency was declared and 15 Black Power leaders were arrested. Small skirmishes with the police, fires and alarms occurred in Port of Spain but were controlled in a matter of hours. However, one 750-member section of the Trinidad Defence Force, led by the young Raffique Shah and Rex Lasalle, in broad sympathy with the Black Power movement, mutinied at the Teteron barracks, taking hostages. The rebels were contained by a Coast Guard ship off Chaguaramas, and after five days of negotiations, on April 25, the hostages were surrendered. Five people were killed in the mutiny.[46]

During this time Williams delivered three further nation-wide broadcasts, on May 3, May 10, and June 30.[47] Williams again emphasised, 'Let me make no bones about it: I identify myself fully with [Black Power's] constructive aspect.'[48] He announced a number of measures to effect 'within the limits of the Constitution' a widespread programme of social, economic and political National

Reconstruction, essentially speeding up, rededicating, and extending already-existing programmes of the PNM, such as the Third Five-Year Plan and constitutional reform.[49] In keeping with his stress on order, Williams further emphasised that the fate of mutineers would be determined by the Courts. On May 10, 1970, Williams announced a major Cabinet reshuffle, for which he secured the resignation, 'by Parliamentary convention', of three ministers (including the two local white Cabinet members, John O'Halloran and Gerard Montano),[50] and three senators, in order to bring in 'new men and the ideas they can offer'.

To secure the forces of law and order, a new Ministry of National Security, with Williams at the head, was also announced in May.[51] On August 7, 1970, the government introduced the draft National Security Act 1970 (Public Order Bill) which would require permission to be granted for marches, impose penalties for the incitements to racial hatred or violence, prohibit quasi-military organisations, and empower the police to search premises and seize firearms. The bill was circulated for public comment. A.N.R. Robinson, with his newly formed group, the Action Committee of Democratic Citizens (ACDC), was prominent in leading opinion against the legislation. The bill was withdrawn on September 13, 1970. As a matter of principle, Attorney-General Karl Hudson-Phillips[52] offered his resignation over the affair, but the Prime Minister refused it.[53]

On November 19, the State of Emergency was lifted, all except five political prisoners were released from custody, and another Cabinet reshuffle had been announced.[54] Continuing the process of rededication, from November 27 to 29, 1970, the PNM had convened a Special Convention to approve 'PNM's Perspectives in the World of the Seventies', later known as 'The Chaguaramas Declaration – Perspectives for The New Society (People's Charter 1956, Revised).'[55] It was a major re-statement of the party's role in helping 'the West Indian people to acquire economic as well as political power, . . . to make their own culture, to participate fully in both the political and economic process, and to become true men instead of what one critic has savagely called us – mimics.'[56]

Meanwhile, the Democratic Labour Party had also undergone a process of renewal. In July 1969, Vernon Jamadar was able to capture the leadership from Dr Capildeo.[57] PNM founding member Dr Elton Richardson[58] and UWI lecturer Dr Krishna Bahadoorsingh were brought in as Deputy Political Leaders. Less than two weeks after the State of Emergency was lifted, on December 1, 1970, the DLP had moved a vote of no confidence in the government.[59] In December 1970, the DLP formed an alliance with the ACDC to contest the coming elections, with Robinson as the coalition leader. On March 6, 1971, the PNM published a draft election manifesto and on March 28 presented its 36 candidates in Woodford Square. At a public meeting in Arima on April 22, Williams announced the date of elections as May 24, 1971 (instead of November 1971 when they were due).[60]

On May 9, four days before nomination day, Robinson declared at a rally in the Queen's Park Savannah that he would neither contest the elections nor support any party or candidate who did. The DLP members were upset by Robinson's move because they felt that the ACDC–DLP coalition could have finally toppled Williams. The two factions split acrimoniously. Robinson claimed that he had fulfilled the ACDC-DLP promise to boycott the elections if the government did not introduce electoral reform – including the removal of voting machines, the lowering of the voting age from 21 to 18; the provision of equal media time for all political parties, and the re-drawing of constituency boundaries under an independent Electoral Boundaries Commission. Williams called Robinson a 'half-wit' and poked fun at his failed alliance.[61] Significantly, United Revolutionary Organisations (emerging out of *Moko* in February 1970), NJAC, and Tapia House, had quickly declared their refusal to contest. Instead, a No-Vote campaign had been launched to pressure the government to embark on electoral reforms before elections were held.

The 1971 elections proceeded as planned, with only the marginal Democratic Liberation Party (led by Bhadase Maraj), African National Congress (led by John Broomes), and two independents contesting the PNM.[62] On nomination day, May 14, eight seats were publicly declared for the PNM, as they were uncontested at the close of nomination proceedings. Fifty-eight candidates contested in the remaining seats. The PNM won all 36 seats, with only 33.1 per cent of the electorate in the contested seats voting. The PNM alone polled 84.1 per cent of all votes cast (see Appendix B).[63]

In the local government elections held on November 1 that same year, the boycott was stronger: 74 seats were uncontested. Overall, the PNM secured 90 seats and controlled all municipal and county councils (see Appendix B).[64] Parliamentary non-cooperation was virtually complete, to the point of nihilism.

The extra-parliamentary opposition continued after the elections, reaching a new extreme in late 1971 with the emergence of an armed 'revolutionary' group calling itself the National Union of Freedom Fighters

(NUFF).[65] The group was led by Guy Harewood, the son of Jack Harewood, Government director of statistics and head of the economics research department at UWI. Many who joined NUFF were from similar backgrounds. Members of the organisation were involved in bank robberies and some non-fatal shoot-outs, idealistically trying to inspire a general resistance.[66] At the same time, labour militancy had been increasing once again: on September 11, 1971, the radical Council of Progressive Trade Unions was formed (breaking away from the main trade union body), and in that year alone there were 71 work stoppages involving 18,367 workers (one in every 18).[67] During the labour unrest, on October 19, 1971 the government called a State of Emergency once again.[68]

Critics called for the government to 'step down',[69] to which Williams replied,

> *Imagine last year this same man [Robinson] opposed the creation of the State of Emergency and now he wants the Governor General to declare a State of Emergency .... We got our vote. What do you want us to do? Stop a race because one horse did not go? ... [The lack of an opposition is nothing new, since] for 18 months [the DLP] said nothing and on occasions walked out to leave us to carry on.*[70]

Williams formed a government without an opposition, forcing the Governor-General to declare the position of Leader of the Opposition vacant, leaving the Upper House without Opposition Senators. To overcome this problem, the government indicated, by way of the Speech from the Throne on June 18, 1971, that it would 'adopt four types of measures to ensure that alternative views . . . [were] heard and respected': publishing proposed legislation for comment by the public; introducing legislation in the Senate first, wherever possible; further enlisting the assistance of the Senate in Joint Committees of both Houses; and appointing a member from the Senate to head the Public Accounts Committee to ensure the strictest possible control over government expenditures by parliament.[71] Another problem posed by the lack of an opposition was that the Joint Select Committee could not be formed to consider constitutional reform. Accordingly, it was announced in the Throne speech that a ten-member Constitution Commission composed of prominent citizens (under the chairmanship of Sir Hugh Wooding, a former Chief Justice of Trinidad and Tobago) would be formed in its place.[72]

Faced with the nihilistic anarchy of political opposition in Trinidad, the PNM continued its assertion of constitutional order. In his address to the PNM's Annual Convention held on September 29 to October 1, 1972, Williams commented,

> *Our 14th Annual Convention finds our Party, the People's National Movement, in continuing control of the Government of Trinidad and Tobago. This control, looking at the situation as objectively as possible, is likely to continue. I have come to this conclusion after an analysis of the forces, and interests in opposition to the PNM.*
>
> *First there are the political parties and their leaders. Notwithstanding all their predictions of doom, the country has not collapsed since the elections in May last year. Notwithstanding their persistent efforts at home and abroad to smear and denigrate our Police Service, we have no police state. Despite all their talk of repressive laws, they say what they like, meet as they like, the only problem being that it would appear that they cannot get people to come out to them. Their civil disobedience campaign proposal has had no impact. They spend their time belabouring one another. The electorate can see all this for itself without any interference from the PNM and will draw the inevitable conclusion that they are accustomed to draw for 15 years: if this is the sort of way these people behave in opposition, what can one expect of them if they ever form the government?*[73]

Williams declared, 'I couldn't care less whether we use voting machines, sewing machines, computers, ballot box, Indian ballot box, cardboard box, soap box, show of hands, voice vote or acclamation. As far as I am concerned, 'same Khaki pants' . . . . They ask for constitutional reform, they will get constitutional reform. They want electoral reform, they will get electoral reform. They say they want reduction of the voting age, they will get reduction of the voting age'.[74] About an unnamed Indian 'self-styled party', Williams quipped, 'This is another example of what I have repeatedly indicated to the population of Trinidad and Tobago, that political ambition ... should be made of sterner stuff.'[75]

In dealing with the protesters of 1970, he remarked, 'It was a very simple strategy: give them rope and they will hang themselves. But more important than that, you would be able to see who is who, who were really subversive, who were just exuberant and following for the most part what many regarded as a fashion parade.'[76]

Williams went on to justly, if harshly, ridicule the inconsistent press, the University radicals paid with public taxes, and the prominent businessmen seeking their narrow self-interest by opposing state participation in the economy and the unemployment levy. He continued:

> *What we have to face here in this country and try to understand is the peculiarities of our national psychology. Whilst a few people make a big fuss in certain quarters about a Commission of Inquiry into a football fracas, nobody turns up for a Commission of Inquiry into a matter like the Postal Services on which there has been continuing agitation for years. They don't turn up, for that matter, for a Commission of Inquiry into the abuse of beauty contests on which complaint after complaint has been made over the years. A few agitate about the La Basse, and then when the Government seeks to stop rummaging at the La Basse sometimes the same people shed crocodile tears over the number of persons who make their living out of the La Basse . . . .*
>
> *There is loud-mouth agitation for Constitution Reform attacking the powers of the Prime Minister, challenging the constitutional provisions on the declaration of emergencies and the temporary suspension of human rights, calling for the abolition of the Senate or for giving the Senate greater powers and selecting its members differently, for the substitution of a Republic for the Monarchy, for the change in the powers of the position of the Governor-General, for all sorts of things. You appoint a Commission, nobody attends in any substantial numbers, and those who attend do so merely to use the Commission for their own party propaganda.*[77]

Williams's frustration, expressed above, was perhaps aggravated in 1973 by the campaigning in the PNM party elections. From July to September 1973, Williams and Karl Hudson-Phillips were embroiled in a public exchange of sometimes heated words, resulting in Hudson-Phillips's resignation from the Deputy Chairmanship of the PNM and from Cabinet on September 12, 1973.[78]

At the 15th Annual PNM Party Convention on September 28, 1973, during which his term as Political Leader had ended, Williams announced that he had taken no steps to seek re-election, detailing in considerable length the frustrations prompting his decision.[79]

Williams lamented that the Caribbean region had become weaker with independence, rather than stronger, by providing tiny, weak states in which foreign governments or their armies, multinational corporations, and international criminals could operate. He was forced to accept that his vision of the integration of the entire Caribbean – Anglophone, Francophone, Hispanic, Dutch – 'beyond any possibility of doubt . . . [would] not be achieved in the foreseeable future.'[80]

In Trinidad and Tobago he deplored the persistent individualism with its attendant lack of perspective, indiscipline and irresponsibility:

> *When the PNM came on the scene in 1956, we encountered a society in which individualism was rampant, and this was best reflected in the large number of individual candidates for election or in the temporary coalition of a number of individuals to form a Party without a coherent programme. We set out deliberately to establish a disciplined Party with a coherent programme and to organise a national movement. Today, 17 years later, the disease of individualism is more pronounced than ever, and such national movement as there is does not go beyond the increased participation in Carnival and the general desire to migrate. Is there a polio epidemic? Irregardless, as you would say, the individual must be free to play his carnival. Is there an armed search for outlaws in the hills? Irregardless, the individual's hunting season must not be interfered with. Does the Government wish to protect your child by immunisation against communicable diseases? Irregardless, the parents must be free to ignore this or to leave it till the very last minute.*[81]

The list went on and on. This irresponsibility combined with 'our own capacity for sensationalism and self-denigration' and a ready willingness to adopt an exaggerated sense of crises was most tragically reflected in the 'guerrilla' movement, which had no clear enemy or programme, unlike the successful guerrilla movements in other places:

> *It is not that the development is of no significance and can be treated casually. But one gets the distinct impression [of] exaggeration and ... aggravation especially at the level of political opposition forces . . . .*
>
> *If, as I have read, the goal is to move the country from crippling dependence to true socialist independence and a 'drastic change in the economic system under which the country operates', I am not sure that those who preach this know what they mean, appreciate the results in other countries or can justify their claim that the road to all this is violence.*[82]

The 'peculiar national psychology' of dramatic complaint about a problem, equally vehement complaint about solutions proposed, the shiftless refusal to participate in formulating solutions, and the ready disregard for almost every existing, agreed upon, ordered, prioritised positive programme – whether it be in health, education, or economic transformation – in favour of disorderly lobbying, entreaty, and intrigue particularly bothered him. He noted, 'Exactly what the PNM laughed at unmercifully and condemned at its birth in 1956, to the plaudits of the population, the same population is now demanding and advocating.'[83]

Williams also bemoaned that he had been criticised for refusing to choose a successor:[84] 'In many countries of the world, this decision of mine would be cause for the warmest commendation. Here in Trinidad it is the cause of condemnation. It is yet another indication of the extent to which the people themselves practise politics dominated by personalities.'[85]

The party, too, lacked direction in constitution reform, and refused to take seriously its 1956 pledge for morality in public affairs, including cleaning up instances of personal corruption and the ultimately divisive use of patronage.[86] Emphasising his own morality, Williams respectfully returned to the five donor governments the foreign awards conferred on him as Prime Minister, took vacation leave (for the first time in 17 years), declared his assets to the Party Chairman (TT$234,769, an extremely modest, and probably accurate figure), and made arrangements to purchase a private house to which he would retire with his daughter.[87]

Williams summarised,

> *One of America's more popular writers has recently written a book dealing with the American Virgin Islands in respect of tourism, in the course of which he pokes a lot of fun at the Virgin Island politicians. The title of the book is 'Don't Stop the Carnival'. For my own part I don't wish to stop the carnival. I merely seek not to be caught up in it.*[88]

He suggested that December 31, 1973 would be the date of his departure, and that the party should choose its successor in the meanwhile.[89]

The reaction in the country was characteristically mixed: some PNM party groups, the major Christian, Hindu and Muslim religious leaders (who had in 1970 formed the Inter-Religious Organisation [IRO]), the *Guardian* and the *Express* asked him to stay; other PNM party groups (notably organised around Hudson-Phillips), the Democratic Action Congress (DAC), Tapia, and the weekly tabloid *The Bomb*,[90] accepted or even welcomed Williams's decision; and yet others expressed cynicism.[91] On December 2, 1973, Lloyd Best, leader of Tapia, argued that Williams's move had been a ploy to fool the gullible, to raise the ante, and to scare the cowards. He continued,

> *men who have had the rank to change the rules and bend the course of history do not go out like a squib . . . . Williams is simply not going any place . . . . Men of Williams's stature can only die in faith and hope, their gaze transfixed by wide horizons . . . . To the practised poker-player it means that Williams is playing by the golden rule which says that the only card which counts is the last and final one. Stalin, goes the legend, dominated the table because, apart from anything else, he could wait forever.*[92]

## 'RIGHT BACK TO 1956': THE PNM AGAINST THE REST, 1973-81

From October 7 to December 2, 1973, the PNM took the necessary steps to elect a new political leader. On October 9, Errol Mahabir indicated that he was not going to seek nomination; on October 12 Kamaluddin Mohammed wrote to the General Secretary, Nicholas Simonette, a letter stating that he would stand for election only if it was certain that Williams would not return. Mohammed ended up not signing any nomination papers. George Chambers's St Ann's constituency group led efforts to persuade Williams to return. Only Karl Hudson-Phillips led a forceful campaign for party leadership. On November 18, the General Council received from the 476 party groups 224 nominations for Hudson-Phillips, 26 nominations for Mohammed, 9 invalid nominations, 40 messages with no nominations, and 177 non-responses.[93]

However, at the next meeting on December 2, a motion was passed to form a delegation to visit Williams to ask him to continue in office 'at least until all necessary steps have been taken to implement the proposed new constitution for Trinidad and Tobago' with 348 in favour, 61 against, and 14 abstentions.[94] By 5:00 pm, Williams had returned. Karl Hudson-Phillips had criticised the action as did Irwin Merrit, Ferdi Ferreira (PNM foundation member) and Ivan Williams (Chairman of Dr Williams's constituency organisation and head of a number of state organisations) – close confidants of Dr Williams who had tried to dissuade him from delivering his initial resignation speech.[95]

In Williams's reply to the Convention resolution asking him to stay on, he stressed that any new prime minister would have to seek a mandate from the voters 'almost immediately'. This would frustrate the process of constitutional reform, which was urgent. He added, 'I have no desire, whatsoever, to hold on to what is called 'power'. I feel no attraction, whatsoever, for what is called the 'prestige of the office involved'. Your resolution that I continue in office . . . will disrupt my plans and interrupt my personal work.'[96]

In addition to the need for constitutional reform, Williams mentioned 'world economic uncertainties'. This likely referred to the Yom Kippur War which broke out on October 6, 1973, eight days after Williams's resignation speech. As an oil producer, Trinidad and Tobago would gain immensely. In January 1973 Amoco paid approximately US$0.50 tax and royalty per barrel of oil; in December 1973 it was paying US$4.69, and as new prices and taxes posted by Trinidad and Tobago took effect from January 1, 1974 this was practically to double again.[97] Williams must have recognised the possibilities available to the country under such circumstances. On December 20, 1973, Williams began a series of six radio and television broadcasts (continuing on January 1 and 17, February 14, May 8, and June 27) updating the country on international developments related to oil and the profound impact they might have on Trinidad, a tiny producer.[98]

By the time of the 1974 PNM Annual Convention, Williams had revived his hopes, declaring, 'We of the PNM find ourselves in 1974 on a development road that leads in a straight line right back to the People's Charter of 1956.'[99] The essential linkage of constitutional reform, West Indian unity, industrial development, the raising of social standards, and independence, proclaimed in the 1956 People's Charter and consistently pursued with each PNM administration, could be pursued in 1974 in a way not possible before with the 'heaven-sent opportunity arising out of the energy situation'. Williams continued, 'It may be said that we have had to wait a long time for this . . . . We simply could not have done it before, the current was against us. We bought out Shell in 1974;[100] which of you here would say that we could have done it ten years before?'[101] As ever, Williams also warned that foreign interference and Trinidad and Tobago's individualistic tendencies threatened any potential gains. He was confident, though, that the PNM could consolidate economic independence for Trinidad and Tobago, slowly but surely.

Around the same time, on January 22, 1974 the Constitutional Commission had reported to parliament.[102] After almost one year's discussion, the Commission's report and Draft Constitution together with a Minority report by Mitra Sinanan were laid in the House of Representatives in December 1974 by the Prime Minister. Over two sittings, on December 13 and 17, Williams launched a seven-hour attack on the Commission's report.[103] One of the major points of disagreement was the Commission's recommendation for proportional representation.[104] Williams had opposed proportional representation in the 1970s with the same resolve as his opposition to communal representation in the 1950s and 1960s. In April 1973, Williams had published in the Commonwealth journal, *The Round Table*, 'Proportional Representation in Trinidad and Tobago: The Case Against', and the PNM had reprinted that same month a number of his articles and addresses in a booklet titled *PR: To Dissolve the Present PNM Majorities*.[105] Williams rooted his argument in the understanding that the origins of proportional representation in Britain in 1857 was explicitly 'to dissolve the present majority and to create all sort of minority parties'.[106] It was the opposite of what Trinidad and Tobago needed. His basic argument was that proportional representation would create a weaker state. Earlier, in his resignation speech, Williams had argued, 'I believe, however, that in seeking to avoid the abuse of power by the executive, we should not fall into the equally dangerous error of reducing the effectiveness of the executive.'[107] In Trinidad and Tobago's political climate, the coalitions that would result from such a system would be disastrous, he argued, giving examples of the PNM's inclusion of the PDP and the DLP members in Federal, foreign relations, and sports programmes in the 1950s and 1960s. As Williams argued in Parliament,

> *it would lead to total confusion, it would lead to a constant trading of votes, bargaining of this, that and the other, and you are going to get no more legislation that is in the interest of the people which they claim to be their principal motive. A Government with a majority in this House can govern; it can carry its measures. I do not see why the President, whom we think should be elected by a simple majority of the Assembly reflecting the voting patterns in the country as a whole, should have the power to override the people's representatives and refuse to assent to a bill and send it back to them for their reconsideration. He could not do that as Governor-General. Obviously, the Queen could not. And why should the President do that? There are ways and means of doing things without referring back. This is part of the deliberate effort to break down the centralizing tendencies in this county. It has gone too far.*[108]

A Joint Select Committee of Parliament was established on June 16, 1975 to draft a new constitution. On February 20, 1976 its report was laid before the House of Representatives, with a Minority Report by Senator Denis Solomon (of Tapia). Governor-General Sir Ellis Clarke signed the proclamation on August 1, 1976. The Constitution provided for a Republic headed by a President, elected by a simple majority of an Electoral College composed of all 67 members of both Houses of Parliament;[109] an increase in the number of senators to 31 (see Appendix E), the removal of restrictions on the number of senators allowed to be appointed as ministers of government by the prime minister; the creation of an Integrity Commission, an office of Ombudsman, and two public accounts committees (the new second committee would be normally chaired by a member of the opposition in the senate and was to consider the accounts and financial reports of all state-controlled enterprises); and with respect to elections, the creation of a single

Election and Boundaries Commission, the lowering of the voting age from 21 to 18 and the re-introduction of the ballot box.[110] It had been fairly uncontroversial, although some Commissioners expressed dissatisfaction at the number of major recommendations that were disregarded.[111] Republican status would officially be effected on September 24, 1976.

These two developments – the increase in oil prices and constitutional reform – provided the base for a strong economy and a strong government upon which Williams could build a strong, independent Trinidad and Tobago state. In the first half of 1976, Williams wrote in a supplement to the *Washington Star*, an article entitled 'Oil as the Basis of Economic Development and Political Stability', arguing,

> *Amid all the ferment in the Caribbean area, perhaps unprecedented in territorial scope, ideological content and political intensity, Trinidad and Tobago purses the even tenor of its economic ways. The key to it all is its hydrocarbon resources . . . .*
>
> *Trinidad and Tobago is even less dependent on tourism activities than it has previously been, and it has never relied on tourism to the extent of some of its Caribbean colleagues . . . .*
>
> *To the extent that our country can continue along its present lines of orthodox economic planning, subordinating ideological considerations to economic realities, non-interference with human rights and fundamental freedoms except in so far as obviously subversive activities are involved, maintenance of law and order without recourse to repression . . . then it would be possible for our small country to be thankful for the small mercies which have come its way in the past two years.*[112]

On September 13, 1976, the first proper general elections were held in ten years (if one discounts the 1971 elections with its boycott, 26 per cent turnout, and No-Vote campaign). Eleven political parties along with five independents put up a total of 269 candidates, approximately 15 for every two seats (see Appendix B). More than a year before the elections, on October 3, 1975, Williams remarked in his speech to the PNM Annual Convention, 'If economically '56 is virtually prehistory in '75, psychologically and politically we are back in '56 all over again.'[113]

As in 1956, all political parties except the PNM were fluid. The Democratic Action Congress (DAC) and the United Labour Front (ULF) attempted a merger, and Vernon Jamadar had invited James Millette and later A.N.R. Robinson to lead the Social Democratic Labour Party, but the efforts were unsuccessful.[114] Besides the PNM, only three parties – the United

Labour Front (ULF), Democratic Action Congress (DAC), and the Tapia House Movement[115] – lasted long enough to contest the general elections in 1981, after which they dissolved. Six party leaders lost their deposits.

The old DLP had split into two factions. The first was the Democratic Liberation Party, the new name give to the party that remained after Alloy Lequay beat Vernon Jamadar in the December 1972 party elections. In February 1976, Alloy Lequay, Simbhoonath Capildeo, John Brooms, and Charles Clarke, of the United Democratic Labour Party were appointed opposition senators by the UPP. By the 1976 elections, Simbhoonath Capildeo took over leadership of the party. In the 1976 elections, J.R.F. Richardson (Point Fortin), Peter Farquhar (Port of Spain Central), and Satnarine Maharai (Chaguanas) were candidates.

In December 1973, after an unsuccessful court battle over the right to use the DLP symbol, Vernon Jamadar established the Social Democratic Labour Party.[116] Former DLP member Frank Brassington was SDLP candidate for St Joseph. Neither party won any seats. Both Jamadar and Lequay fought the Siparia seat. They were roundly defeated by newcomer (and former mutineer) Raffique Shah of the ULF. After 16 years of decay, the DLP had finally died.

A.N.R. Robinson led the DAC, which had evolved from the ACDC after its split with the DLP in 1971. Tapia started its involvement in conventional politics through the appointment by the UPP of Tapia members Lloyd Best, Hamlet Joseph, and Ivan Laughlin, as opposition senators on October 15, 1974, up to February 1976.[117] Though quite different in character, both the DAC and Tapia could be considered reformist in nature, with some radical liberal positions.

The newest political presence was the ULF. The group was formed on February 18, 1975 at a rally of the radical trade unions, OWTU, ATSEFWTU, TIWU, and the Islandwide Cane Farmers Trade Union (ICFTU) in Skinner Park, San Fernando.[118]

After the bus strike of May 1969, some unions became more defiant and more radicalised. From 1966 to 1970, no strikes were officially recorded. However, from 1971 to 1976 there were an unprecedented 397 work stoppages, resulting in 163,557 man-days lost (see Figure 3.2). These amounts exceeded the total number of stoppages and man-days lost from 1955 to 1965.[119] Under no term of government was the level of strike activity higher. The PNM passed the Industrial Relations Act in 1972, to replace the failed Industrial Stabilisation Act of 1965. In this Act, however, the government was forced to concede the right to strike to the unions.

***Figure 3.2. Man-Days Lost: Workers Involved and Work Stoppages, 1971-1976***

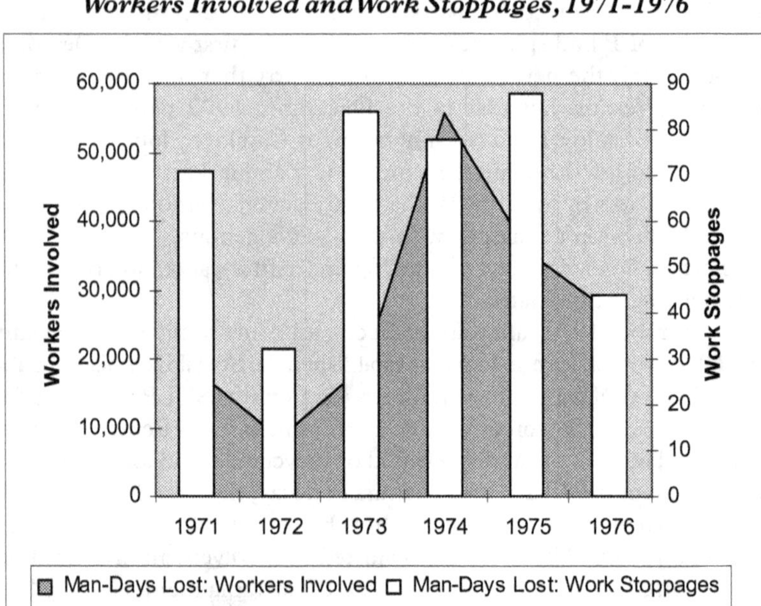


*Created by the author from CBTT (1993)*

During the PNM's unfettered rule of government from 1971 to 1976, it passed a number of laws to increase government's monitoring of subversive activity. This included a ban on 'subversive literature' (later lifted); the declaration of (politically) undesirable immigrants, and barring such individuals as Trinidad-born US Black Power advocate Stokely Carmichael from entering the country; the Sedition Act; the Firearms Act; and the Summary Offences (Amendment) Act which required permission from the Commissioner of Police to hold public marches and demonstrations. It was this last piece of legislation that the ULF defied on March 18, 1975 with their professedly religious march (which was not prohibited by the Act). The march was for 'peace, bread, and justice' and involved left-leaning religious leaders along with the radical trade unions.[120] The march was prematurely stopped by the police who exercised force uncommonly displayed in Trinidad with tear gas. No persons died, 29 were arrested. The march was subsequently referred to as 'Bloody Tuesday'.[121]

The ICFTU was formed by Raffique Shah, one of the leaders of the 1970 Teteron mutiny, as a rival organisation to the pro-PNM Trinidad Island-wide Canefarmers Association.[122] Meanwhile, in the ATSEFWTU, the death of Bhadase Maraj on October 21, 1971 left a leadership void in the Indian-dominated sugar union. By September 1974, senator Basdeo Panday, a trade unions legal advisor with links to the OWTU and former WFP candidate for Naparima, had taken control of the union by outmanoeuvering the union's old leadership and securing guaranteed work for the sugar workers.[123] George Weekes and Joe Young of the OWTU and TIWU continued to be active in the radical section of the labour movement.

On March 28, 1976, after some debate on the merits of conventional political involvement, the ULF was launched as a political party.[124] Its focus was class-based but it did not attach itself to any particular ideology. Many tendencies existed within its ranks. The party included in its membership various fringe radical political groups such as the United National Independence Party led by James Millette, the New Beginning Movement, the National Movement for the True Independence of Trinidad and Tobago, the National Liberation Movement, Students for Change, the Union of Democratic Students, the United Revolutionary Organisation, and the (demilitarised) NUFF.[125] The party had not made clear who was its political leader. It preached collective leadership. However, Panday had emerged as the natural leader. Yet it was decided that, should the party win the election, the prime minister would be low-keyed labour lawyer Allan Alexander – who eventually lost his seat in Point Fortin to Cyril Rogers of the PNM by a vote of 5,802 to 2,580.[126] Apart from Basdeo Panday, who received only 326 votes in Naparima South in 1966, the ULF presented an entirely new slate of candidates. Adding to its problems was the fact that the party was denied broadcast time on the national media which was government owned.

Perhaps the most unexpected aspect of the 1976 elections was Dr Williams's odd, perhaps shrewd, campaign for the PNM. On May 12, 1976, he had rebuked the PNM membership and its General Secretary, Nicholas Simonette, for not understanding that the 'majority of PNM incumbents' would be unacceptable to the electorate, who had showed its 'total indifference to the traditional electioneering and its disdain for political parties.'[127] Williams called the antics of the party's political aspirants 'simply pathetic', and declared that he had

> *not the slightest intention of encumbering himself, yet again, with these traditional party millstones, unable to speak properly, knowing nothing of*

*basic issues facing country and world, incapable for higher responsibilities which ultimately fall on the Political Leader's shoulders, unable – unbelievable though it sounds – even to seek to assist their constituents in difficulty who further turn to the Political Leader and interfere with his attention to his formal, public, national responsibilities.*[128]

Williams called for more women and more young people on the party's slate, and chastised the party for ignoring his request that it enforce public declarations of assets by all MPs, cabinet ministers, statutory board members, public servants and state board members higher than the grade of Administrative Officer V, along with their families. He demanded that all MPs submit a dated and signed letter to authorise payment of 7½ per cent of their salaries to the Party Secretary and another undated and signed letter of resignation addressed to the Speaker of the House of Representatives to be given to the political leader.

The speech riled some party members. In Woodford Square on July 5, Hudson-Phillips, Ferreira, and Simonette organised a meeting criticising Williams's latest move. In the end, the five ex-ministers whom Williams called 'millstones' were retained by the party, but Williams refused to speak on their campaign platforms.[129]

Despite the new personalities and unorthodox campaigns of 1976, the election result did not depart radically from that of 1966. Most notable was the DAC's victory in Tobago. But even with this loss, the PNM retained a two-thirds majority. In comparison to the 1966 elections, the PNM gained by taking Pointe-à-Pierre in the south and Nariva in the east, both with pluralities of 48 per cent and 39.2 per cent, respectively. The PNM took advantage of the opposition discord. The ULF were boxed into five southern and five central constituencies (see Appendices C and F). However, the ULF decisively removed the DLP figures, and replaced them with new political personalities.

As in 1966, the increase in candidates was ironically accompanied by a decrease in voters. The turnout rate was only 55.8 per cent, significantly lower than the rates in all other general elections, except those held in 1971 and in the 1925–1946 period (see Appendix B).[130]

By 1966, Williams had decisively defeated – and outlived – the old politicians. Ten years later, after trade union radicalism, a Black Power 'revolution', an army mutiny, a nation-wide no-vote campaign, the emergence of young, new political personalities, parties, and ideas, the PNM maintained the two-thirds majority it secured 1961. In his 'Thank You' speech after the elections Williams remarked,

> *I was rather surprised after all these years looking at commentaries on elections and what people say and don't say when I read that if it hadn't been for – what was it? – a particular motorcade, where, whatever it was, wherever it came from or where the hell it went to – if it hadn't been for that motorcade I wouldn't be here tonight.*[131] *And you all wouldn't be here.*
>
> *I don't know where the devil you would be, following the motorcade, wherever the hell it went to. There is no accounting for the views of these commentators, etc.*
>
> *So at once I looked at the election results, statistics and so on; and then I looked at the obvious thing.*
>
> *We are the only party, my dear friends. I keep telling you this, you know this as well as I. Let's say it once more. Some day it is going to get into the hard heads of these commentators. PNM is the only party in the Caribbean which has uniformly controlled the capital city of the country.*[132]

Williams lampooned the opposition's showing at the polls, their campaigns, and their excuses. He regretted that the PNM weren't tested more, adding

> *It would have been nice to see what would've happened if people could have had the opportunity to vote . . . .*
>
> *[Referring to Lloyd Best:] You have to use a little imagination in terms of size and all the rest of that . . . . You run about the place here saying for 15 years, especially in the last five years, you say PNM this, PNM that, PNM the other, PNM doing that.*
>
> *And then when you finish all you could say is because of a motorcade people get fraid and turned to the very party that took care of them for five years and more. What the hell you think the voters of Trinidad and Tobago are?*[133]

Two local government elections were fought during this term of office, on April 25, 1977 and April 21, 1980. In the context of very low voter turnouts, the results emphasised the PNM's dominance in the political scene (see Appendix B).[134] In 1977, the PNM were uncontested in 25 seats; in 1980 the number rose to 31.[135] By 1980 complete supremacy in local government was achieved as the PNM controlled all 11 municipal and county councils (see Appendix F).

Williams's last term in office also witnessed a remarkable economic transformation, occasioned by the rise in oil prices (see Appendix D). Between 1970 and 1980, the price per barrel of oil rose over 22 times to US$28.70 (see Figure 3.3). Government revenues rose accordingly, almost 20 times to

TT$6,226.4 million (see Figure 3.4). Incredibly, net official foreign reserves expanded from its low point in 1973 to nearly 100 times that level in 1980, from TT$67.1 million to TT$6,336.7 million (see Figure 3.5). With these developments, real GDP rose by over two-thirds during the period at a rate of 5.3 per cent per annum from TT$1,643.7 million in 1970 to TT$2,748.4 million in 1980 (see Figure 3.6). In the 1978 Budget, presented in December 1977, Williams declared, 'The Trinidad and Tobago Government is a billionaire.'[136]

***Figure 3.3. Crude Prices Per Barrel, 1970-1980 (US$)***

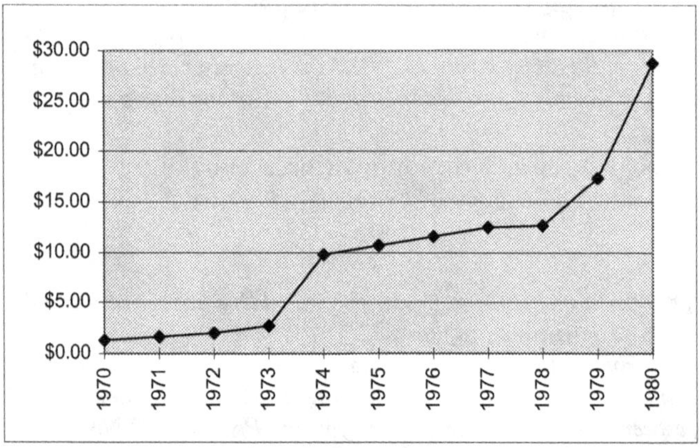

*Created by author from CBTT (1993)*

***Figure 3.4 Government Revenues, 1970-80 (TT$M)***

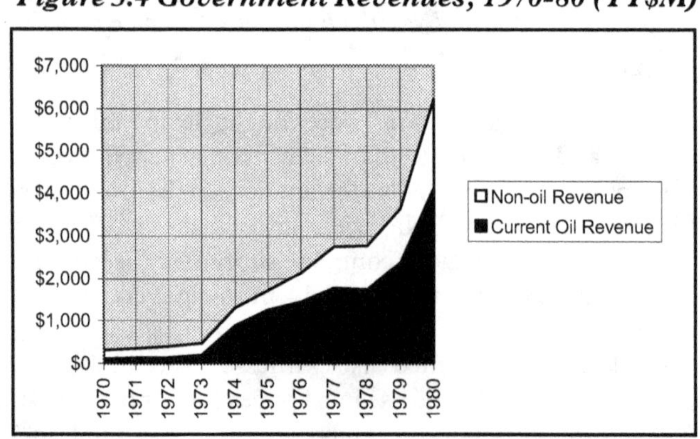


*Created by author from CBTT (1993)*

***Figure 3.5 Net Official Foreign Reserves, 1970-80 (TT$M)***

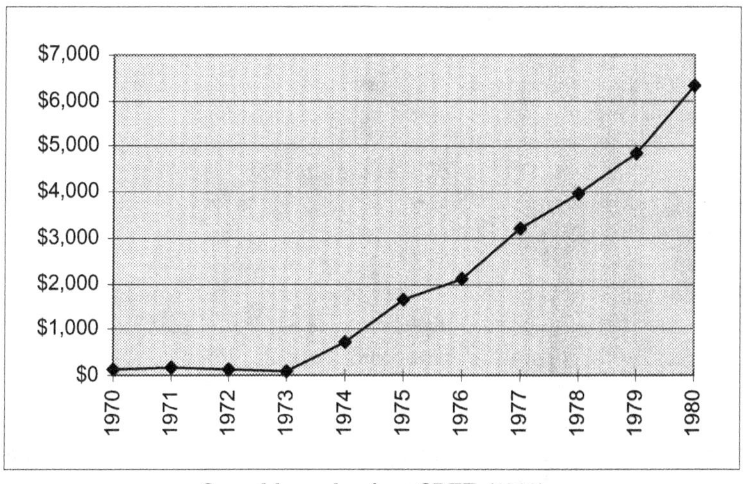


*Created by author from CBTT (1993)*

***Figure 3.6. GDP at Constant 1970 Prices, 1970-80 (TT$M)***

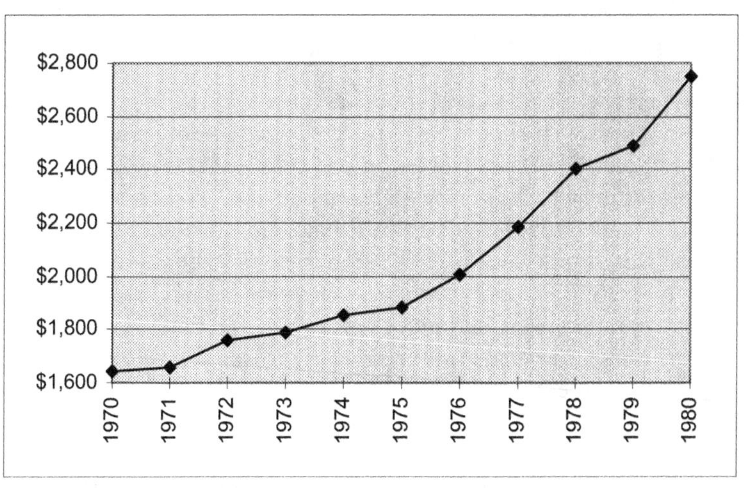


*Created by author from CBTT (1993)*

With these increased revenues, government expenditure climbed almost 14 times, from TT$390.1 million in 1970 to TT$5,446.3 million in 1980. Williams stressed that the windfall should be used productively. As early as in his January 1, 1974 radio and television broadcast, he stressed,

> *we must not behave as if we just have a windfall. We must use the additional revenue to accelerate the restructuring of our economy. We must have something concrete and tangible to show when the crisis is all over – a new petrochemical complex, the realisation of Point Lisas, one or more new planes, a substantial number of additional jobs in new spheres of economic activity.*[137]

Government engaged in large capital expenditures, which had risen more than 21 times from 1970 to 1980 (from TT$109.7M to TT$2,331.3M). In total, gross capital formation expanded from 25.9 per cent of real GDP to 64.6 per cent during the period. The most notable area in which this investment was directed was the heavy industrial programme – ammonia, methanol, nitrogen, urea, and steel production – centred in the 860-hectare Point Lisas Estate in Couva, south Trinidad.

In addition, the government had established 47 special Funds for Long-Term Development – begun in 1974, and kept separately from the general Consolidated Fund – totalling an estimated TT$4,401.8 million in 1980 (compared to total government expenditure of TT$5,446.3 million in that year).[138]

The government had taken a much larger role in the life of Trinidad and Tobago's economy during this period. Government expenditure as a proportion of real GDP rose from 13.1 per cent in 1970 to 21.1 per cent in 1980.[139] In addition was the great expansion of the state's direct involvement in the economy. In 1972 the Trinidad and Tobago Government held shares in 35 companies, with a book value of TT$82mn. By 1983, the value of its portfolio had risen to TT$2,000 million in 66 companies. They included holding companies; manufacturing companies in such varied fields as agri-products, metals, fertilisers and petroleum products; and service companies offering financial, management (hospitals), maintenance (schools), road building (secondary roads), real estate and solid waste disposal expertise.[140]

The (at least superficially) strong economy was combined with what some observers have called the development of a 'presidential' style of rule, not only in Williams's personal predisposition, but through the powers granted in both the Independence and Republican Constitutions, which gave the prime minister veto over the appointments of over 200 heads and deputy heads in the Civil Service.[141] This combination seemed to embolden Williams to more aggressively defend, even assert, the State's independence in the face of foreign governments, multinational companies, the trade union movement, the radical left, and the local private sector, each time in the name of the small citizens of Trinidad and Tobago.[142]

For the general population, the material standard of living undoubtedly rose during the period. Real average weekly earnings rose 22.8 per cent between 1971 and 1980, beating the overall price increase of 328 per cent over the same period.[143] Most importantly, unemployment – one of the country's most intractable economic problems – had fallen from a high of 15.4 per cent in 1973 to 9.9 per cent in 1980, the lowest recorded rate in Trinidad and Tobago's history, and the first time that the rate fell below 10 per cent (see Figure 3.7).

***Figure 3.7. Unemployment, 1970-80***

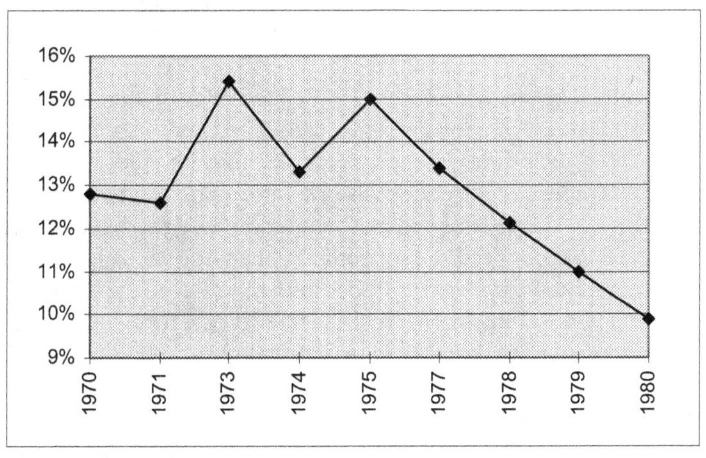


*Created by author from CBTT (1993)*
Note: *data unavailable for 1972 and 1976*

With the general prosperity came much extravagance, illustrated by the numerous stories of weekend shopping flights to Miami, and so on. Imports during the period rose from TT$684.9 million to TT$2,380.4 million in constant 1970 prices, or from 41.7 per cent to 86.6 per cent of real GDP.[144] MacDonald has spoken of a process of 'middle classisation', with the *Times*

(London) in 1978 remarking on the country's consumer 'revolution', and *Business Latin America*, commenting in 1980 that 'Trinidadians seem to have an unlimited appetite for consumer goods'.[145] One of the political results of this exuberance was an increase in corruption. The most notable allegation was the 'DC-9 scandal', erupting in July 1980 and involving John O'Halloran, one of the local white PNM ministers who resigned in the aftermath of the Black Power marches. He was afterward employed in the state sector.[146]

The climate of PNM dominance and economic prosperity did not restrain the political 'bacchanal.' The 1976–81 parliament may have been the most confused of all Trinidad and Tobago's parliaments. On one side, the ULF was rocked by bitter in-fighting dividing the MPs into two shifting camps. Between August 9, 1977 and March 31, 1978, the ULF had changed its nominee for leader of the opposition from Panday (MP for Couva North) to Shah (MP for Siparia) and then back to Panday, eventually ending up with Panday's faction outnumbering and decisively defeating Shah's supporters through a local government by-election on September 26, 1978 in Siparia – by a vote of 1,591 to 185.[147] The two DAC MPs split as well, with Dr Winston Murray (MP for Tobago West) suspended from the party at the end of March 1978.[148]

Meanwhile, also on March 31, 1978, Hector McLean, PNM MP for Arouca and minister of Works, Transport, and Communications, had crossed the floor to the opposition benches, declaring that he would not resign his seat despite attempts to claim otherwise via his undated signed letter.[149] With the loss of the PNM MP, this led to speculation that the five 'millstones' – who had not been appointed to any ministerial positions – might also resign, splitting parliament between the PNM and the rest of the opposition, 18 seats on each side. The PNM had hurriedly drafted a constitutional amendment compelling a member of parliament to vacate his seat if he should resign or be expelled from his party. Williams secured the cooperation of Panday in drafting the proposed amendment. McLean and the Tobago members joined with the four Shah supporters in early April, asking the President to remove Panday from the leadership of the opposition once more. However, their request had been dismissed because of the members' disagreement on naming a replacement. The constitutional amendment was passed at the end of April but was not used as the Standing Orders of Parliament did not recognise the existence of political parties.[150]

Further disruption occurred in the PNM with the suspension of Karl Hudson-Phillips and Ferdi Ferreira from the party in March 1980. Both of them publicly criticised Williams's 1979 Annual Convention address, which was based on the imagery of calypsonian Black Stalin's Roadmarch song (that is, the most popular calypso at Carnival) titled, 'Caribbean Man', as 'totally irrelevant'.[151] On April 19, 1980, two days before the local government elections, Hudson-Phillips launched the Organisation of National Reconstruction (ONR), involving such former PNM members as Ferreira and former PNM General Secretary and Senator, Nicholas Simonette. Attacks on corruption and inefficiency had been among the ONR's strongest platforms, and Hudson-Phillips was formally expelled from the PNM. The ONR was subsequently launched as a political party on November 30, 1980 and held its inaugural meeting on February 1, 1981. On March 15, 1981, an opinion poll conducted by Selwyn Ryan's St Augustine Research Associates (SARA) had indicated that the ONR's support exceeded that of the PNM by one percentage point (29 per cent to 28 per cent).[152]

At the same time Tobago was moving away from the PNM. Though the issue of secession was raised in the 1976 elections, all candidates advocating independence lost their deposits.[153] Tobagonians were not willing to proclaim independence, but they desired more autonomy. In his 1976 post-election 'Thank You' speech, Williams's bitterness and indignation were only barely hidden by his dismissive attitude:

> *Nothing new and nothing much .... It is part of a general malaise over the world, ... part of a particular Caribbean madness resulting from all the flotsam and jetsam brought to the Caribbean over a century.*
>
> *They want to go off on their own small island, . . . I am not one to bother.*
>
> *. . . I said it in Tobago, 'If you want to go, go. We are not holding you. I am not going to send any Coast Guard or ship or army there to hold them back. What for? They want to go, go!' . . .*
>
> *It's a financial matter; what terms do we agree on without bitterness, without any emotion? All they have to tell me is what it is they want and how to do it. I appoint somebody to do it. I have more important things to do.*[154]

Williams went so far as to dismantle the Ministry of Tobago Affairs in his Government of 1976, a move which affronted many Tobagonians. In January 1977, A.N.R. Robinson, DAC MP for Tobago East, moved a resolution calling for 'internal self-government' for Tobago.[155] On February 11, 1977, the House unanimously agreed to an amended version of the resolution and a Joint Select Committee had been established to consider the question.[156] During the local government elections of April 1977, the PNM secured control of the Tobago County Council by winning seven seats against the DAC's four.[157] In July of the following year, the Committee's report, cited as House Paper No. 6 of 1978, was submitted and ratified by both Houses of Parliament that same month. It was not until November 1979 that the legislation drafted by Senior Counsel Lionel Seemungal was submitted. Further delay occurred as the PNM government claimed that Seemungal had gone beyond his brief, leaving Parliament but two options: to reject the proposals or to grant full independence to Tobago. In early 1980, a re-drafted Tobago (Internal Self-Government) Bill was published for public comment. On September 12, 1980, the Bill was debated in the House of Representatives; Robinson voted against the bill and the ULF walked out. The Bill was passed with the support of Tobago West MP, Winston Murray. As enacted, it provided for a 15-member (12 elected and three appointed) Tobago House of Assembly (THA) charged with implementing in Tobago government policy in respect of finance, economic planning and development, and the provision of various local services.[158] The term of office for the THA members would last for four years.

The THA's first elections, held on November 24, 1980, brought out 66.2 per cent of the registered electorate, a much higher percentage than in the Trinidad county council elections (see Appendix B). The DAC received support from Panday's ULF faction and Tapia. The three were brought together in September–October 1980 by the San Fernando-based Borough Action Team, chaired by Alloy Lequay, and by independent efforts of Tapia to forge an alliance of opposition parties.[159] In the 1977 county council elections, the PNM won seven of the 11 seats in Tobago. In the THA elections, the DAC defeated the PNM eight to four. The PNM held the capital, Scarborough, and three nearby areas falling within the parliamentary constituency of Tobago West. A.N.R. Robinson, who had resigned his parliamentary seat to contest the Tobago elections, was installed as the THA's first Chairman.[160]

Critics continued to maintain that the PNM, Williams, and 'the system' had lost any legitimacy it once may have had. Indeed, the PNM had declared a significant number of States of Emergency since coming to power. Attorney General Selwyn Richardson defended the government reportedly by arguing, 'we have a mandate to rule even if it means 5, 50, 500 States of Emergency'.[161] The UWI political scientist Carl Parris pointed to the fact that between June 1973 and December 1979, no fewer than 11 Commissions of Inquiry were conducted.[162] In addition, nurses and teachers, who 'belonged to that faction of organised labour which earlier was labelled as conservative [i.e. PNM supporters]' had begun to march against the government.[163]

It is difficult to judge to what extent these events perturbed Williams. During this period, Williams rarely addressed Parliament. On January 25,

1981, he delivered the feature address at the PNM's 25th Anniversary celebration. In the speech, Dr Williams noted the steady social, economic and political progress made by the PNM on the one hand, and the constant, irresponsible criticism of its various political opponents on the other. He retorted,

> *To say that nothing has been done in over 25 years and five general elections suggests that something, at least one thing, does work – PNM's appeal to the electorate . . . .*
>
> *Here we stand after 25 years, to report on our stewardship, to establish our readiness and fitness to continue the struggle on which we embarked 25 years ago, then as now against the rest, then as now with powerful vested interests against us, then as now with the mightiest force in the country in our support, ready to go at the word of command, keeping our powder dry until we see the whites of their eyes, confident in the continued support of the Lord God of Hosts who will rule, as he has ruled so often in our 25 years. Great is the PNM and it will continue to prevail.*[164]

Williams died exactly nine weeks later, unexpectedly, from a diabetic coma. Almost no one knew that Williams was even diabetic.

For 25 years, through a combination of skill, determination, and fortune,

*The casket of Dr Eric Williams, 1981*

Williams and the PNM consistently prevailed over the disorder of Trinidad and Tobago politics, both within parliament and outside of it. This would not be repeated in the remainder of the century. While the PNM under Williams was able to consistently emerge on top of the anarchic opposition, it was never able to bring fundamental order to the conduct of politics in the country, which, it could be argued, was the goal of William's project of Political Education, Nationalism, and Morality in Public Affairs. What cannot be meaningfully documented in the public record, and is much harder to objectively evaluate, is the reality that Williams also governed with a ruthlessness, some would add a pettiness, that not only demoralised his opposition, but resulted in the end of relations (at least) with virtually all of his major and important supporters: C.L.R. James, Winston Mahabir, Sir Learie Constantine, Patrick Solomon, A.N.R. Robinson, Karl Hudson-Phillips, Elton Richardson, Ferdi Ferreira, Nicholas Simonette and other comrades in the party. This extended to the public service as well, with important figures such as J.O'Neil Lewis, Eugenio Moore, Dodderidge Alleyne and Frank Rampersad. It would not be peculiar, however, if his personal cruelty and political success were related.

Within these limitations, Williams had achieved a significant measure of what he had set out to do, leading Trinidad and Tobago through significant political, social, and economic transformation, which included the establishment of a Republican and a liberal-democratic constitution, widespread free public education, heavy industrial development, and a greatly increased standard of living, all within a relatively peaceful and free social and political environment. A relatively strong, independent Trinidad and Tobago state had been created, particularly after the oil shocks and constitutional reform exercise of the 1970s. Williams's death would provide a test for the country to see whether such progress as had undoubtedly occurred under his rule could be solidified, sustained, or improved.

# Part 2

## *Paved with Good Intentions: The Rise and Fall of the National Alliance for Reconstruction, 1981-91*

# Four

## THE FALL OF THE PNM, 1981-6: 'ALL AH WE TIEF'

*George Chambers*

In this chapter, we look at the performance of the Chambers' administration (1981–6) which ended in the first defeat in a general elections for the PNM. George Chambers was faced with three major challenges in office: succeeding a charismatic political icon who had mastered the Trinidad and Tobago political environment, managing a 55.2 per cent drop in oil prices from 1982 to 1986, and fighting off a newly invigorated and consolidated political opposition. He failed all three.

### 'WHAT IS WRONG MUST BE PUT RIGHT': GEORGE CHAMBERS AND THE GENERAL ELECTIONS OF 1981

On March 29, 1981, exactly nine weeks after the PNM had celebrated its Silver Jubilee, and two weeks after the publication of the SARA poll which had indicated the ONR's slight lead over the PNM, at approximately 8:00 pm Eric Williams died in his home, unexpectedly, from a diabetic coma. At 10:00 pm, after a meeting at his home with the PNM Party Chairman, Francis Prevatt, and the three Deputy Leaders (Kamaluddin Mohammed, Errol Mahabir, and George Chambers), President Sir Ellis Clarke decided that Chambers would be appointed as Williams's successor.[1]

A special meeting of the House of Representatives was called the next day, on Monday March 30, 1981, at 3:00 pm. George Chambers – member of parliament for St Ann's since 1966; minister of Agriculture, Lands, and Fisheries; and minister of Industry and Commerce – was sworn in as prime minister. Chambers delivered, on television that evening, his first address as prime minister. He informed the country that all ministers would retain their portfolios and that the Cabinet and Parliament had met as usual, noting the significance of these 'acts of continuity . . . . As the late prime minister himself would have wanted it, the ship of state sails steadily on course.'[2]

On May 9, Chambers was elected as political leader of the PNM, without opposition. In his acceptance speech at the Chaguaramas Convention Centre, Chambers announced a Cabinet reshuffle, as well as a halt to the Caroni Racing Complex and the Malabar Housing Project, two public works projects that had been surrounded by controversy.[3] Chambers declared, 'What is right in the country must be kept right. What is wrong must be put right.' Chambers responded positively to the charges against the government of corruption, on which the ONR had capitalised greatly.[4]

Parliament dissolved on September 24, 1981, and general elections were called for November 9.[5] The elections were perceived by many to be a battle between the ONR and the PNM, although there were at least three other serious parties contesting. The ONR was seen by many to be a party serving the interests of French Creoles and big businessmen, much like the POPPG (whose president, Henry Hudson-Phillips, was Karl Hudson-Phillips's father) in 1956 and the Liberals in 1966, but with a strong law and order tendency, which sometimes hindered its popular reach.[6] This ethnic characterisation was not wholly justified, however. At its inception as a party, the ONR incorporated executive members of Vernon Jamadar's Social Democratic Labour Party, including its Deputy Political Leader, Pariag Sookoo. Indeed, the ONR's Deputy Leader was outspoken Hindu cultural advocate, Surujrattan Rambachan.

Following the style of Hudson-Phillips's splashy PNM election campaign of 1973,[7] the ONR hired Sabo Associates, the US public relations firm that helped Edward Seaga's Jamaica Labour Party win elections in 1980.[8] The ONR exhorted the others to 'clear the coast and let there be a straight fight between the enemy and the ONR.'[9] The PNM seemed particularly threatened by the ONR, with Chambers declaring some weeks before the elections,

'Not a damn seat for them!'[10]

Meanwhile, the other main opposition groups were building a coalition. In the August 28, 1977 issue of *Tapia*, commenting on the removal of Panday as Leader of Opposition by the Shah faction, Lloyd Best argued that

> *the ULF took short cuts with half-ripe organisation and half-arsed ideology . . . . But they could have chosen differently. In 1976 they had the choice to break the PNM monopoly with a UPF [United People's Front] along the lines of India;*[11] *but they preferred backdoor negotiation with A.N.R. Robinson, a tactic exposing their basic pessimism and their congenital deviousness.*[12]

In the same article, Best made the important observation: 'we are dealing essentially with non-competing groups' that were focused on their own particular niches. By February–March 1981 he and *Tapia* colleague Allan Harris had elaborated the theoretical basis of 'a viable coalition politics' – a federal 'party of parties' – arguing,

> *As far as we are concerned in Tapia, Tobago constitutes no less than half the country, constitutionally speaking. Within Trinidad, Caroni-Naparima is no less than half the island, socially and culturally speaking.*
>
> *If these are the constitutional, social and cultural realities then these are the conditions to which the practical politics are forced to relate. These are the only premises from which we can meaningfully bargain about the effective government of a Republic, independent and free.*
>
> *It is the organised rivalry between Caroni-Naparima, Tobago and the rest of the country which will make it possible to govern wisely. It is the bargaining between them which will allow our Cabinet to order priorities between agriculture and industry, between big business and small business, between country and town, between Central Government and County Council. It is indeed only the rivalry between leaders and constituent parties that will make it possible to root out corruption. If the leaders are not constantly looking over one another's shoulders, we will wait forever for integrity legislation. Who would there be to monitor the Doctor?*
>
> *The new government in 1981 would be a much better one if it were a coalition party and not simply a coalition* government.[13]

On March 1, 1981, at a meeting held in Port of Spain, A.N.R. Robinson, chairman of the DAC; Lloyd Best, Chairman of *Tapia*; and Basdeo Panday, political leader of the ULF had reached 'complete accord' on the principles that the DAC, *Tapia*, and the ULF would not contest against each other, but would give maximum support and collaboration to each other in all constituencies, collaborate in a programme of voter registration, and work together more generally in preparation for the elections.[14] The coalition initiated its campaign in July 1981 under the name, Alliance. As with the ULF in 1976, there had been no agreed leading candidate. In addition, Robinson refused to contest the general elections, preferring instead to hold on to the chairmanship of the THA. This uncertainty raised anxieties about an Indian (Panday) becoming prime minister.[15] The absence of a clear leader, in combination with the media savvy of the Port of Spain based ONR (ONR candidate for Tunapuna, Rhona Baptiste, for example, was the wife of Owen Baptiste, editor of the *Trinidad Express* and *People* magazine), probably explains the small amount of press coverage received by the Alliance.[16]

*The crowd surrounds the rostrum at the Alliance presentation of candidates in Tunapuna on November 8, 1891. Speaking, on the podium, is Mr A.N.R. Robinson.*

In the elections, 11 parties and two independents contested, providing 156 candidates (closer in number to the 154 candidates in 1966 than the 269 contesting in 1976). The parties included NJAC, which decided to contest elections for the first time, and the odd revival of the old TLP with its lone candidate, Ranjit Kumar (who had fought against the TLP during his political career in the 1940s and 1950s) (see Appendix B).[17] Voter turnout had improved since 1976, with 415,416 or 56.4 per cent of the electorate casting their ballots.

The most surprising result of the elections was the ONR's failure to capture any seats, although their share of votes cast exceed that of the Alliance (who received 87,572 votes, or 21.1 per cent). The ONR secured fewer votes than the PNM in every constituency except one: Oropouche, contested by ONR Deputy Leader Suruj Rambachan (controversial for his outspoken pro-Hindu views), where their votes exceed the PNM's by 4,072 to 3,079. But the ONR lost to the ULF which secured the constituency with 5,161 votes, giving it a plurality of 40.8 per cent.[18] The ONR's defeat was a great embarrassment for Hudson-Phillips and he subsequently withdrew from active politics.[19]

The PNM, on the other hand, secured 26 seats, its largest majority ever, despite the firm hold of Tobago by the DAC. Interestingly, ten seats were won by pluralities in 1981 as opposed to six in 1976, when there were 113 more candidates contesting. Six of the PNM's seats in 1981 (St Joseph, Nariva, Caroni East, Pointe-à-Pierre, Naparima, Princes Town) were won with less than 50 per cent of the ballots cast, and four of the ULF's (St Augustine, Chaguanas, Tabaquite, Oropouche).[20] The PNM gained its two extra seats, Princes Town and Caroni East, with pluralities of 48.8 per cent and 46.2 per cent, respectively.[21] These PNM seats, one in the south and, for the first time, the other in central Trinidad, were deep in Indian-dominated areas (see Appendices C and F). In fact, at least three PNM constituencies – San Fernando East, Nariva, and Princes Town – had Indian majorities of 53 per cent, 55 per cent, and 60 per cent, respectively.[22] Notably, Satnarine Maharaj, Secretary General of the Hindu SDMS, son-in-law of the late Bhadase Maraj, and Democratic Liberation Party candidate for St Augustine in the 1971 elections, supported the PNM on its platforms in six constituencies. Maharaj was unimpressed with the Alliance, and expressed appreciation for the freedom the SDMS had enjoyed under PNM Governments despite the fact that the SDMS had opposed them openly for 25 years. Maharaj, however, was also in a religious rivalry with the ONR's Suruj Rambachan.[23]

## 'THE FÊTE IS OVER': FACING THE ECONOMIC DOWNTURN, 1982–83

With his mandate from the electorate, Prime Minister Chambers, assuming the new Ministry of Finance and Planning, continued his reformist rhetoric in his Budget Speech of January 18, 1982. Warning of a global recession, inflation, monetary instability, high interest rates, growing unemployment, and 'a wholly unprecedented level of indebtedness', he highlighted the weaknesses of the Trinidad and Tobago economy which the country had to confront – inflation rates between 10 and 22 per cent per year, a domestic budget deficit reaching TT$2,227 million in 1980 (hidden by oil revenues), significant increases in wage rates at the same time as declining productivity, and the inefficiency of producers in the protected domestic market.[24] Outlining the challenges facing the country in the 1980s, he noted,

> *It would be naive for us to believe that petroleum – a non-renewable resource – can insulate us completely from the effects of economic recession; that the pursuit of private interest to which so many of our citizens are dedicated will automatically add up to the well-being of all; that gains in real income and standards of living can be achieved without increasing productivity; that some pre-ordained destiny has decreed that Trinidad and Tobago shall have only the breaks and soft options . . . .*
>
> *Trinidad and Tobago is a fortunate country in many ways, but we can no longer permit our vision to be obscured by selfishness and the pursuit of instant affluence.*
>
> *Perhaps, Mr. Speaker, you would permit me to end in the vernacular by saying that the fete is over and the country must go back to work.*[25]

An important announcement of the Budget had been the return to planning (the revised *Third Five-Year Plan, 1968–73*[26] had been the last of its kind) through the establishment of a broad-based National Economic Planning Commission (NEPC) headed by governor of the Central Bank, William Demas. The government also had invited a joint economic mission from the International Monetary Fund and the World Bank for consultations in the middle of the year.[27]

In June 1983 the World Bank published its report, suggesting strategies for Trinidad and Tobago to successfully manage an 'extended period of readjustment' to a context of softened international oil prices and dwindling national oil reserves, while maintaining 'the progress of the 1970s', which had seen 'rapid increases in real income as well as impressive gains in the provision of basic needs to the poorest.'[28] Soon after, in 1983–4, the NEPC had released its two-volume report, *The Imperatives of Adjustment: Draft Development Plan, 1983–86* (sometimes cited as Report of the Demas Task Force, or the Demas Report), with its recommendations for adaptation to 'a new long-term structural situation which requires profound adjustments by everybody in the country – the public sector, workers at all levels, private sector employers, housewives, farmers and indeed consumers in general.'[29]

The 1984 Budget Speech continued Chambers's pleas for restrained consumer spending. He noted that Trinidad and Tobago had been graduated by the World Bank, without a phase-out lending period, because of (in the Bank's words) Trinidad and Tobago's

> *relatively easy access to international capital markets,... [the] country's social development [being] ... well above the level of most bank borrowers and above, also, the level of some countries already graduated by the Bank, and.... [Trinidad and Tobago's] net foreign reserves, measured as a proportion of the country's annual imports, [being] ... also larger than in most other countries, including the developed ones.*[30]

Despite the government's rhetoric of prudence, the TT$4,401 million available in 1980 in its special long-term development funds, foreign reserves amounting to 19.5 months of imports in 1981, and the peaking of average annual oil prices in 1982 at US$33.50 per barrel,[31] the Chambers administration found itself in economic difficulties as early as 1983. Evidence of imprudence could be seen in the fact that between 1974 and 1979, TT$3,482.4 million had been withdrawn from the special funds, while between 1980 and 1983 total withdrawals amounted to TT$11,586.1 million (see Table 4.1 and Appendix D).

***Table 4.1. Special Funds for Long-Term Development, 1979-83 (TT$ Million)***

| | Withdrawals to 31 December | Balance as at 31 December | Estimated Income for following year | Amount Available for following year | Estimated Expenditure for following year |
|---|---|---|---|---|---|
| 1979 | $ 3,482.40 | $2,391.30 | $2,010.50 | $4,401.80 | $2,737.00 |
| 1983 | $15,068.50 | $ 169.30 | $2,340.60 | $2,340.60 | $2,340.60 |

*Sources*: GORTT (1980, 1983)

Trinidad's 125-year-old petroleum industry[32] had not been able to take full advantage of the price rise in 1982 due to the decline in crude production from its peak in 1978 of 229.6 million barrels per day. Government revenues from oil reached their height in 1981 and thereafter dropped abruptly, 42 per cent from 1981 to 1983 alone.[33]

The government had been able to maintain its level of total revenue in these years by increasing the direct taxation of individuals, which had risen from 16.9 per cent to 36.7 per cent of total direct taxes. The government had also increased indirect taxes, moving them from providing 11.9 per cent to 17.3 per cent of current government revenue between 1981 and 1983. Despite the maintenance of revenue levels with a heavier burden of individual taxation, the government in 1982 had incurred a deficit of TT$2,652.4 million, by far the largest on record (the next largest was TT$135.3 million in 1972). Current expenditure accounted for 86 per cent of the increase, and 68 per cent of the current expenditure increase went to wages and salaries.[34] That year the government conceded to several demands for close to 52,000 public employees, allowing a public sector pay award that helped to more than double its wages and salaries bill from TT$1,342.60 million in 1981 to TT$2,970.6 million in 1982. This action was interpreted by observers to be political as the PNM was looking ahead to the local government elections due the following year.[35]

## 'THE PARTY OF PARTIES': THE RISE OF THE NATIONAL ALLIANCE FOR RECONSTRUCTION

In 1982 the Alliance was formalised into the National Alliance of Trinidad and Tobago (NATT). Its Inaugural Conference was held at the Chaguaramas Convention Centre on November 14. Lloyd Best, the most articulate theoretician of the process of coalition, presented the complete version of his 'party of parties' idea, based on an extremely perceptive model which saw nine ethnic groups at the base of the political system:

1. The Afro-Saxon Community of the East-West Corridor founded on the College Exhibition and Christian churching.

2. The Garveyite Black Power Community, occupying the fringes of Afro-Saxon society in Port of Spain, drawn to Low church-cum-Shango religion.

3. The 'Grenadian' working class in the oilfields, a classic European

Marxist proletariat with nothing to sell but their labour to the multinational oil companies of Shell, Texaco, and BP.

4. The Tobagonians, with the militancy of the Grenadian, the African metaphysic of the Garveyite, and the rural sensibilities of the Hindu.

5. The Hindu in Caroni, involved in both small-scale and plantation agriculture, outside of the Middle Eastern, Christian-Judaic framework, less inclined than the Muslims and the Presbyterians to become involved in the urban world of San Fernando and the East-West Corridor.

6. The Muslims who, though Indian by race and Oriental by origin, moved comparatively easily in the urban environments.

7. The Presbyterian Indians who had made the deliberate decision to join the mainstream of College Exhibition education and Christian churching, functioning as part of the Afro-Saxon community and acquiring, under colonial conditions, 'fitness to rule'.

8. The French Creoles, who give their name collectively to the small white and off-white minorities, driven together by mainstream perceptions, economic interest, their 'high' colour and their 'prestigious' origins outside of the subservient slave and indenture areas of Africa and India; yet they neither acquired 'the habits of a class with power as distinct from a class with only influence,' nor, because of its easy and ready influence on the British coloniser, the drive to education and competence so central to the Presbyterian and Afro-Saxon.

9. The group which does not easily fit into any of the above interests, (post-war) nationalists or (pre-war) internationalist intellectuals, with mixed cultural exposure abroad, mixed race, mixed ethnic origin, or mixed marriages that make easy association with other groups problematic.

Best continued,

*The Afro-Saxons of the East-West Corridor and the Hindus of Caroni, as the two big voting blocs, by virtue of their numbers (about 35% each) are the natural centres of gravity. The Tobagonians by virtue of their insular condition and their physical separation, have formed another centre of gravity – as have the French Creoles, by virtue of their prized class and colour status, in a colonial and continuing colonial situation.*[36]

It was his idea that the PNM was the natural party of the Afro-Saxons, building in 1961 an alliance of Tobagonians, Garveyites, Muslims, Presbyterians, 'Grenadians', and the intellectuals. Since then, he argued, that association had in stages disunited, while in 1982 the Alliance Party of parties had 'almost all the trumps in the present game of power and politics in Trinidad and Tobago'.[37]

In February 1983, the NATT had strengthened its hand by entering into a 'non-aggression pact' with the ONR in order to form an 'Accommodation', each group agreeing not to contest seats in which the other was contesting. On May 10, 1983, leader of the opposition Basdeo Panday had appointed as an opposition senator ONR leader Karl Hudson-Phillips, after an eight-year absence from Parliament.[38] After contentious negotiation, the parties agreed that in the coming local elections the ONR would contest 65 seats and the NATT 47.[39]

*Karl Hudson-Phillips*

The elections were held on August 8, 1983 with a voter turnout of 32.9 per cent, significantly higher than the 19.7 per cent turnout in 1980. The Accommodation won 66 seats to the PNM's 54 and gained control of six of the seven county councils. The PNM retained control of the four municipal councils and the St George County Council (see Appendices B and F).

It was the first defeat of the PNM since the county council elections of 1959. The ULF candidates secured 38 seats and Tapia candidates won two seats for the first time. Significantly, the ONR won ten of its 26 seats in the PNM's urban strongholds: four to the PNM's eight in Port of Spain, three to the PNM's four in Arima, and three to the PNM's six in San Fernando.[40] Robinson remarked that the PNM had come now to 'occupy small pockets and unproductive areas in towns'.[41]

The momentum to definitively cement the alliance had been slowed, however, by the many rivalries – personal, ethnic, regional, ideological – among the groups.[42] From April 13–15, 1984, the Alliance and the Trinidad and Tobago Institute of the West Indies (an independent institution founded by Tapia in 1977 that published the non-partisan *Trinidad and Tobago Review*) organised at the Valsayn Teachers' College a conference titled 'Forging a New Democracy', whose proceedings were published in March 1985.[43] A major victory had been procured by the Alliance-Accommodation in the November 1984 THA elections when the DAC secured 11 seats, as opposed to the PNM's single seat in Buccoo/Lambeau. Voter turnout was as high as 70.1 per cent (see Appendix B).[44]

In October 1983 and April 1985, influential SARA polls had been conducted, with the latter poll showing 70 per cent of the sample dissatisfied with Chambers's performance as prime minister, 54 per cent of the sample agreeing that the ONR-NATT coalition was 'a good thing', and that A.N.R. Robinson would receive by far the greatest amount of votes from the supporters of the coalition, regardless of their race.[45]

On August 30, 1985 the Alliance-Accommodation leaders (except Best who was in Central Africa) flew to Grenada on a private jet owned by the powerful local conglomerate, Neal and Massey (whose CEO, Sydney Knox, had been closely involved in the mediation), to meet Hudson-Phillips, who had been state prosecutor for the Grenadian government in the trial for the 1983 murder of Maurice Bishop and other members of the People's Revolutionary Government. The 'Grenada Accord' was agreed upon, stipulating that the allocation of seats in 1986 would follow a formula based on the results of the 1981 general elections. This meeting also resolved the leadership question as Hudson-Phillips and Panday subsequently accepted

Deputy Leaderships so that A.N.R. Robinson could become political leader.[46] On September 8, 1985, the inaugural convention of the newly formed federal political party, the National Alliance for Reconstruction (NAR),[47] was held. The following day, the federal party was publicly launched at the Queen's Park Savannah. Four months later, on February 14, 1986, the Friday after Carnival, the individual parties of the NAR were dissolved, with the intention to form a unitary party.[48] Up to then, without a constitution for the unitary formation, the party executive had already been nominated to avoid potentially embarrassing fights during the election season. Two documents – *Platform for Democracy*, and in July 1986 the 98-page *Platform for Change: An Agenda for the Future* – attempted to mediate and resolve the various positions within the party. However, these documents and, later, the party's manifesto – written by a team led by the ULF MP for Chaguanas and former lecturer in economics at UWI, Winston Dookeran – were apparently never formally ratified by the party.[49]

*Lloyd Best addressing a campaign meeting of the Alliance, 1981*

On August 7, 1986, Lloyd Best returned from a three-year UNCTAD Evaluation Mission in Central Africa and Haiti and almost immediately expressed dissatisfaction that the Tapia constituency had become marginal to the NAR enterprise – not 'merely' in leadership positions, but more fundamentally in terms of vision and direction.[50] Essentially, Best and his colleagues argued that the NAR had concentrated too much on the winning of office and personal advancement while systematically avoiding the tough issues of economic reconstruction during a time of recession and, most importantly, governing a fragmented society through the interplay of the constituencies that the NAR represented.[51] On August 15, the 'Group of Party Members' in the NAR (former Tapia members) had submitted comments on the *Platform for Change*, describing it as 'an amorphous mass of proposals, many of them little more than half-baked'. It continued, 'Between good intentions and effective implementation there has been, and continues to be, a void . . . .The centrepiece for a manifesto of national reconstruction must . . . be a policy and programme for political reconstruction.'[52]

On September 11, Best had called a meeting of former Tapia members to further articulate his dissent. His report and feature address were published in the press. However, he assured the population and the NAR that his dissent was not meant to be disruptive but constructive.[53] He disdained the view that he was 'rocking the boat'. On September 25, 1986, Lincoln Myers had resigned from the deputy directorship of the Trinidad and Tobago Institute of the West Indies and, along with former Tapia members Beau Tewarie (General Secretary of the NAR), Gloria Henry, Shirley Ann Hussein, and Cecil Rampersad, they offered themselves to be considered as prospective NAR electoral candidates.[54] Best gave his colleagues his blessing, but did not himself become an executive member of the NAR or a contestant in the elections.[55]

Not dissimilarly, the ONR's representation in the NAR had been less than expected. Karl Hudson-Phillips spent much of his time in Grenada after he withdrew, with some bitterness, from the leadership contest. In addition the ONR, as a party, had its representation cut from the 21 it should have received under the 'Grenada Accord' to 13.[56]

Whatever problems were occurring during the NAR's construction, however, seemed to be hidden by the Chambers administration's steady loss of the confidence of the population. Perhaps to rejuvenate the government's image, on February 28, 1985, Prime Minister Chambers announced a major Cabinet re-shuffle, affecting ten of the government's 19 ministers and four parliamentary secretaries.[57] The change was essentially minor, however.

Perhaps at the base of the government's unpopularity at the time was its inability to cope with the acute drop in oil prices in 1986 (46 per cent below the 1985 average), having locked itself into deficit spending, increasingly using its dwindling savings on current expenditure and borrowing at unprecedented levels (see Appendix D). The government's fiscal burdens were made heavier in 1984–5 with the acquisition of the local assets of Texaco (including the Pointe-à-Pierre refinery), that had decided to pull out of Trinidad and Tobago as part of its global restructuring.[58]

By 1986, revenue continued to fall, capital expenditure was progressively cut to 14.8 per cent of total expenditure, foreign exchange had dropped to only 2.9 months' worth of imports (from 19.5 months five years earlier), real GDP continued in its fourth year of successive decline, unemployment rose from an all-time low of 9.9 per cent in 1982 to 17.2 per cent (the highest rate then recorded), and the total debt to GDP ratio had also risen to its hitherto highest levels. In August 1986, Kirpilani's, one of the country's four leading conglomerates, had become one of the 170 companies that officially entered into receivership between 1984 and 1988.[59]

That same month, Robinson had charged, 'For the purposes of winning election the Government has used up Treasury's balances . . . . To put it simply: The whole country is still paying for the PNM election campaign in 1981.'[60] Robinson claimed that this had been a common PNM practice since 1961 and that, as PNM minister of Finance in 1966, he was able to oppose it successfully, until his removal in 1967.[61]

Added to the failing economy was the string of PNM scandals in 1985–86. The first, and one of the more embarrassing, occurred on November 19, 1985 when Millette Engineering Company – headed by PNM Senator, Dr Emrin Millette, and represented by prominent PNM member Robin Montano son of Gerard Montano – seized two floors of furniture and 20 vehicles from the PNM-controlled Port of Spain City Council over an unsettled TT$5.9 million debt.[62]

More seriously, in December 1985 opposition senator, Lincoln Myers, conducted a highly publicised 40-day dawn-till-dusk fast on the steps of the Hall of Justice to call attention to the government's 'lack of accountability'. The fast was immediately motivated by the refusal of a state enterprise to hand over papers to the parliamentary Public Accounts (Enterprises) Committee (of which he was chairman) that were deemed necessary to conduct an inquiry into alleged corruption in the allocation of contracts to build houses for the Corporation. The fast highlighted other issues as well, notably the government's refusal to publish the findings of the Garvin Scott Commission's Drug Report,[63] and the secrecy surrounding the losses of the state-owned Iron and Steel Company of Trinidad and Tobago (ISCOTT) which had been rumoured to be between TT$179 million to TT$365 million per year. To demonstrate its own commitment to public morality, the NAR had promised to publish the Scott Report within its first 90 days if it won elections.[64]

On October 6, 1986, Chairman of the Airports Authority, Selwyn Richardson (PNM Attorney General from 1976-81), resigned over a dispute with the Ministry of Agriculture concerning farming near Piarco airport. Richardson's resignation was given front page coverage in the daily press where he recounted in detail his efforts to root out corruption from the 1976–81 PNM Administration (particularly with former Minister John O'Halloran) and the government's attempts to silence him. On November 16, Richardson was presented as a NAR candidate for Ortoire/Mayaro (where he successfully ran against the PNM candidate, his cousin, Leon Prevatt) and was nicknamed 'Mr. Clean' during the NAR campaign.[65]

Finally, on November 11, 1986, businessman Dennis Davidson, who had been known to keep company with PNM ministers, fled the country to escape arrest by the police who wanted him in connection with a US$100 million 'EC-0'[66] foreign currency racket. The incident reminded the country of John O'Halloran – allegedly a major figure in the 'DC-9 Scandal' involving corruption in the sale of airplanes to the state-owned British West Indian Airways and in scandals surrounding the construction of the Caroni Racing Complex – who was also 'allowed' to leave the country for Canada in 1983 after resigning, under contentious circumstances, from the chairmanship of the Trinidad and Tobago Racing Authority in 1981.[67]

PNM ministers, past and present, such as John Eckstein, Kamaluddin Mohammed, Dr Cuthbert Joseph, and George Chambers himself, defended the government against these allegations, pointing out rightly – even if only weakly at times – that no PNM minister had ever been found guilty of corruption. In August 1986, surprisingly, Lloyd Best criticised the NAR for blaming the country's economic ills on the PNM, arguing that it was yet another way of avoiding the responsibility for both the cause and cure of the country's economic crisis:

> *People have the impertinence to say the PNM wasted the money. The country wanted the PNM to waste the money. The country insisted on it . . . Governments . . . can't waste money unless the populations wish them so to do . . . and the problem in the country is that everybody thinks that everybody else is responsible except them.*[68]

The most infamous statement during the campaign, however, was made by Desmond Cartey, MP for Laventille and Minister of Housing and Resettlement. Cartey had responded to a heckler at a public meeting in his constituency with, 'Who ent tief in Trinidad? All ah we tief.'[69] In an observant article, 'The PNM Could Use a Dose of Dignity', *Trinidad Express* columnist

David Renwick wrote, 'I cannot help wondering whether Mr Cartey would dared have said what he did the other night had Dr Williams been alive.'[70]

Certainly, the PNM had lost much of its intellectual, progressive, and resolute character after the death of Williams. Prime Minister Chambers seemed to be considered an embarrassment by many Trinidadians, who derisively referred to him as 'dummy' or 'duncey' in an inordinate number of jokes about his apparent witlessness.[71] The personal disrespect reached a low in August 1986 when, at a televised football match, the audience 'roundly booed' Chambers as he was called upon to present the trophy to the winning Canadian team.[72]

Also in that month, minister of Works Hugh Francis had re-paved the heavily-used Wrightson Road in Port of Spain. To commemorate its completion, the Minister held a press conference at which he unveiled a monument on which was a marble plaque incised with 'The Hon. Hugh Francis'. The population reacted with disgust at the entire undertaking. Letters to the editors complaining about the incident appeared in the press for the next two months.[73] Contradicting Dr Williams's publicly and widely acknowledged wish that nothing ever be named after him, the Chambers government had named the new twin towers financial complex after Williams and re-named the 'Mount Hope Medical Complex', the 'Eric Williams Medical Complex'. The *Trinidad Guardian* commented on the issue in 'The Pappyshowing[74] of Eric Williams', criticising the use of Williams as 'a prop for people who are still unable to stand on their own . . . . One can just imagine how Dr Williams, noted for blunt, incisive comments, would have reacted.'[75]

The available accounts seem to show that the PNM campaign was disproportionately marked by fear and nervous outbursts. At a speech to the PNM Youth League in July 1986, Chambers indicated that rather than follow Williams's advice to 'wait for the white of their eyes', he would 'shoot you from behind'; that the NAR 'was all part of a grand design to wrest political power from a certain section of the community'; and that a 'political calamity' would follow if a coalition government were elected since 'electoral victory precipitated conflict or "war" in coalitions.'[76] Hugh Francis asked why people in the urban areas of Port of Spain were being asked to change their voting behaviour while people in Caroni were not. Senator Muriel Donawa-McDavidson, minister in the Ministry of Community Development and Local Government, was alleged to have exclaimed to Indian protesters outside of Parliament: 'all yuh have the money, all yuh have the land, all yuh want the government too.'[77] Perhaps as a reaction, in August PNM back-bench MP for Nariva, Hardeo Hardath, complained, 'I do get the feeling of "discrimination" – as if my leaders care not for me, my religion, my race and indeed my constituency. Does Mr Chambers really want or care for Indians in the party, Parliament and Cabinet?'[78]

## 'VOTE THEM OUT, PLEASE': THE GENERAL ELECTIONS OF 1986

On November 9, 1986, the PNM held an elections conference at the Chaguaramas Convention Centre at which it presented its manifesto, its 36 electoral candidates, and announced the date of elections as December 15, 1986. A crew from the state-owned Trinidad and Tobago Television (TTT) had arrived late for the event and 'as a mark of protest' Chambers had refused to speak until TTT removed all its lights and microphones. The PNM had been complaining that they had been treated unfairly by the media, including the state-owned radio and television stations, and the crowd that night booed and pelted the media.[79] With good reason, Lloyd Best agreed that the newspapers in particular were 'scandalously biased,' writing 'as if they have been commissioned to campaign against the ruling party'.[80]

Despite Chambers's claim in his July speech to the Youth League that the changes he would make would make him 'become the most unpopular man in the PNM' when the party's election slate was announced, 28 of the 36 candidates were incumbents. Only eight did not contest in 1986, and they withdrew voluntarily.[81] Indeed, Ministers Hugh Francis and Errol Mahabir (each having strained relations with Chambers) had also planned to retire, but were persuaded to contest one more time.[82]

The following week, on November 16, the NAR presented its candidates in Woodford Square to an audience estimated at 15,000.[83] The group of mostly well-known, well-qualified, well respected candidates from an impressive diversity of party, class, racial, religious, and ideological backgrounds came together under the themes of 'one party', 'one leader', 'one nation', and 'one love'. Twenty-four candidates were contesting elections for the first time, along with nine incumbents (eight were former ULF MPs and Pamela Nicholson was formerly of the DAC) and three former ONR candidates who had been unsuccessful in the 1981 elections. The mixture of new and familiar was appealing. The NAR public relations officer had described the party's campaign as 'theatre politics', creatively employing calypsos (Gypsy's 'Sinking Ship' and Deple's 'Vote Dem Out', were both very effective), stylish platform presentation, and much talked about media advertisements (most famously the 'baby ad', featuring a baby of unclassifiable mixed race with big innocent eyes, over the caption: 'VOTE THEM OUT. Please.'). At the other end had been the ONR's 'A-Team', a group of 30 activists devoted since 1983 to community work in the poorer areas of PNM urban strongholds of north Trinidad, countering the ONR's image as a 'big-shot party'.[84]

That night the 28-page NAR Manifesto, described by Ryan as a 'best-seller', was released.[85] The 16-part manifesto began by acknowledging the importance of the PNM in the 1950s, but it criticised the PNM's failure 'to develop a new sense of purpose, . . . the political will to achieve the genuine liberation of our people', and the concomitant development of a 'clique of individuals, committed to the politics of manipulation and control, determined to cling to office and to power, at whatever cost to the national community.' It outlined 13 critical issues – including jobs, corruption, a bankrupt state, social decay, a lack of accountability, and a lack of patriotism – and offered as evidence of mismanagement details of the government's major cost overruns (spending a combined TT$1,449 million on the Mount Hope Medical Complex, the Hall of Justice, and the Financial Complex, when TT$692 million had been the total of the original contract prices). They chided the government for not allowing the population to 'participate, really participate, in the decisions that affect their lives', producing a 'moral and spiritual crisis', and being unable to transcend the fragments of 'race, class, nation, and party'. They pledged to institute an expansionist economic programme of recovery, increase national demand, make the state sector efficient, and acknowledge a 'valuable role for private foreign capital within national development objectives'. The party called for the population to 'put our country together again' by acknowledging the regional and cultural diversity in a 'new nationalism'. They exhorted voters to remove the PNM and help to 'build a new society founded on the ideals of a civilised democracy in which every individual will be free and equal notwithstanding his social standing, his beliefs nor [*sic*] his political affiliation.' The party promised that 'not demagogy and arrogance but sober statesmanship and reason . . . will determine our style of leadership, not arbitrary pig-headedness but consultation and dialogue . . . will infuse the process of government.'[86] Speaking of the audience at the party's launch of candidates, the NAR's *Trinidad Guardian* supplement claimed,

> *people of every creed and race; from every walk of life, and from every place; man and woman, young and old; all proclaimed their belief in, and commitment to a new Trinidad and Tobago. There was no anger in that crowd; no violence. The dominant theme was hope optimism and patriotism; still present in a people so badly abused and battered by the leadership of the party in power.*
>
> *Their presence and their responses made it overwhelmingly clear that they hold in deep respect, morality, ideals and vision, long discarded by those who have ruled us for the last 3 decades.*[87]

One week before the elections, David Renwick had argued,

> *The NAR, for its part, exudes the image and the promise of the PNM in 1956 – self-confidence, appealing to the educated middle class and stirring the interest and the loyalty of the youth, including the female youth, who are today far better education than their counterparts in the mid-fifties. If the PNM has indeed lost the support of the middle class it should be a very distressed party indeed, because Trinidad and Tobago in the mid–80s is nothing if not a middle-class country, with upper and lower echelons perhaps, but middle class nevertheless.*[88]

The NAR's manifesto allied the party to the current 'sweeping away of decadent beliefs and systems' as had happened with Marcos in the Philippines and Duvalier in Haiti (both in February 1986, when the NAR was launched as a unitary party), and the increased opposition to apartheid in South Africa. Indeed, in the previous year, Panday, as Leader of the Opposition, had boycotted all the state functions in honour of Her Majesty Queen Elizabeth II – who had visited Trinidad and Tobago from November 1–4, 1985 – to protest the British government's refusal to impose meaningful economic sanctions against South Africa. In the House of Representatives on March 12, 1986, Panday also expressed support for protesters who had been beaten by police outside the Queen's Park Oval demonstrating against the English cricket team for the same reason.[89] This heightened protest against apartheid followed the establishment of Emancipation Day as an annual national holiday on August 1, 1985 (replacing Discovery Day), to commemorate the abolition of slavery in 1834.[90]

Notably, on the same day that Panday raised the issue of the cricket protesters, the Sexual Offences Bill was being debated in parliament. This could be considered as the most concrete effect of the emerging women's movement in Trinidad and Tobago up to that point. The bill had caused considerable debate – provoking the verbal opposition of Deputy Prime Minister Kamaluddin Mohammed and dividing the PNM Cabinet – surrounding Clause Four, which had proposed that marital rape be made a criminal offence. In response, Women Working for Social Progress (or Workingwomen, formed in January 1985) had organised the various groups who supported the clause into a Sexual Offences Bill Action Committee, adding considerable momentum to the new social movement. In the wake of the controversy, the government established a Joint Select Committee to further consider the bill. After three months, re-drafted legislation was passed with a modified version of the controversial clause.[91] In late November 1986, Chambers inadvertently outraged this newly articulate feminist opinion when he tactlessly declared, 'I am giving free PNM technical advice; if you want to heckle a meeting, you must have a FAB. All yuh have a FAB? You don't send 18 men to heckle a meeting. After two minutes they want a beer. You must put women to heckle a meeting.'[92] ('FAB' stands for 'Fat Arse Brigade', the uncharitable nickname for the PNM's fervent, mainly African, female supporters, organised in the party's Women's League.)

It seems that, particularly after the presentation of candidates, all but the most cautious observers and participants[93] realised that the PNM could not resist the NAR tide. The PNM itself seemed at times resigned to defeat.[94] Despite a full-page PNM advertisement in the *Trinidad Express* warning quite prophetically, with good reason, at great length and detail, that 'THE FACT IS, THERE IS SURE TO BE A POWER STRUGGLE'.[95] The same paper carried on its front page the results of a SARA survey indicating that

> *a majority of those polled believe that even if there would be confusion following a NAR victory, it is still important to vote the PNM out of power . . . . The majority of the electorate believe that there will be no confusion and factionalism if the NAR were to win the elections and will govern the country better than the PNM.*[96]

On December 13, the NAR's final rally of the campaign attracted to Woodford Square the 'largest crowd ever seen there for a political meeting'.[97] In the elections of December 15, 1986, the NAR achieved a unexpected level of victory, winning in 33 of the 36 constituencies (see Appendices B and C). It was a massive landslide.

The PNM, who had governed the country for 30 years, winning its largest victory just five years prior, fell spectacularly. With the exception of Patrick Manning in San Fernando East, all incumbents – including George

Chambers, Kamaluddin Mohammed, and Errol Mahabir – lost their seats. The three seats that the party did retain – Port of Spain East, Laventille, and San Fernando East – were secured by slim margins of 2,670 votes; 1,251 votes; and 61 votes, respectively.[98]

The PNM's support had fallen in 34 seats compared to the 1981 results,[99] losing in total 34,922 votes. The NAR, on the other hand, from its combined amount of 179,276 votes in 1981, had received an additional 200,753 votes in 1986.[100] In 1981, had the Alliance and the ONR combined their votes, they would have only won 14 seats.[101] As Best had argued, the effect of combining the opposition forces had not been merely cumulative; the 'chemistry' had changed.[102] The *Trinidad and Tobago Review* had noted, 'There was no "swing" away from . . . [the PNM] candidates: . . . a *new* electorate came out to vote in 1986. It unhesitatingly dumped the PNM Government'.[103] Impressed by the results, and perhaps caught in the historical enthusiasm, even Tapia, through the *Trinidad and Tobago Review,* which had consistently expressed scepticism about the NAR's chances for victory, proclaimed that 'history will record that the Second Republic was born in December 1986'.[104]

The Chambers administration could not sustain either the political or economic gains made during the Williams years. Despite the rhetoric about prudence and restraint, and the recommendations of the Demas Report which it commissioned, the Chambers administration did not seem to act decisively enough. With the fall of oil prices in 1982–3 and 1985–6, the massive increase in current expenditure incurred in 1982 drained the government's resources, much of which had been carefully accumulated in special funds during the oil boom. Chambers was seen as an intellectual failure as well, with the many jokes made about his witlessness, on the one hand, and the NAR's seizing of the vanguard position through its rhetoric about new economic management and a new ethnic and social progressiveness, on the other. The NAR spectacularly captured, perhaps even nurtured, the popular mood for change. It was given an unprecedented mandate to govern the country, on the edge of yet another significant transformation.

# *Five*

## THE FALL OF THE NAR, 1987-91: 'BETWEEN GOOD INTENTIONS AND EFFECTIVE IMPLEMENTATION'

In this chapter we review the surprisingly ineffectual National Alliance for Reconstruction (NAR) term in office, 1986–91. The NAR attempted to implement important reforms in the social, economic, and political climate of Trinidad and Tobago, attracting perhaps the widest cross-section and greatest show of popular support ever assembled by any political party in the history of Trinidad and Tobago's politics. However, from almost the beginning the NAR administration mismanaged the inevitable political difficulties that any new, reformist administration might expect to encounter. The first major confrontation resulted from Prime Minister A.N.R. Robinson's disagreement with the appointments made by outgoing President Sir Ellis Clarke in March–April 1987. At about this time the first of numerous internal party quarrels emerged. A climax was reached with the expulsion from the Cabinet of Deputy Prime Minister Basdeo Panday in February 1988 (ending in his expulsion from the party in October 1988), but internal dissent among the remaining members continued right up to the end of the party's term in 1991. At the same time, many non-governmental organisations, community groups, and trade unions mounted myriad protests against the government's structural adjustment policies, peaking in a nation-wide 'Day of Resistance' on March 6, 1989. In the background, social problems such as divorce, mass emigration, and crime escalated during the period. The lowest point was reached when, from July 27 to August 1, 1990, a group of 114 armed members of the fringe radical Black Muslim group, the Jamaat-al-Muslimeen, held Parliament hostage for six days in an unsuccessful attempt to remove the government.

The NAR's major efforts during the term had been directed toward restructuring the Trinidad and Tobago economy to become more export-oriented and private-sector-driven. Evidence of economic success was not readily apparent in 1991 and Prime Minister A.N.R. Robinson had lost the support of many of his members of parliament. In the 1991 general elections the NAR did not win one seat in Trinidad. The PNM, renewed under the leadership of Patrick Manning, secured victory while the NAR break-away party, the United National Congress (UNC), led by Basdeo Panday, emerged as the official opposition.

## 'ROUGH SEAS': THE NAR'S FIRST NINE MONTHS

Six days after its unparalleled electoral victory, on December 21, 1986, the NAR responded with a 'National Assembly for Reconciliation' at the Queen's Park Savannah in Port of Spain that was reportedly attended by an estimated 40,000 people. Reflecting the 'spiritual rebirth' noted by Prime Minister Robinson, the assembly endorsed a National Exercise of Cleaning Up the Environment which was impressively conducted by virtually the 'entire population' on January 17, 1987.[1]

With due ceremony, parliament was opened on January 12, 1987. The Throne Speech delivered by President Sir Ellis Clarke indicated that the government 'would put emphasis on honesty, integrity in public life, responsibility, courage, love and the spirit of compromise'.[2] At one point, reportedly, the proceedings were interrupted by NAR Deputy Leader Basdeo Panday because no copy of the *Bhagvad Gita* was available to swear upon – reminding observers that Hindus had become part of the Government of Trinidad and Tobago for the first time since 1956.[3]

In parliament, the new government sought to keep its campaign pledges to root out corruption in government. In its first 12 weeks, up to the Easter break, the NAR government enacted a number of important pieces of anti-corruption legislation.[4] On January 16, the first sitting after the ceremonial opening, 14 reports from the Auditor-General on the accounts of State bodies were laid in the House of Representatives and referred to the Public Accounts (Enterprises) and Public Accounts Committees. In addition were laid the Prevention of Corruption Bill (debated on March 20) and the Integrity in Public Life Bill (debated from February 20–7). On February 6, the controversial Garvin Scott Drug Report (which had become a strong campaign issue in 1986) was laid and was debated until February 18.[5]

During this early period, a number of Commissions were also formed. Almost immediately upon taking office, senior civil servant Dodderidge Alleyne had been appointed to chair a Finances Committee to examine the financial state of the country which, Robinson claimed, was not known in exact terms. At the same time, a Transfer Committee, chaired by Head of the Civil Service Eugenio Moore had also been appointed with a mandate to ensure a smooth transition to the new regime.[6]

Frank Rampersad, a senior civil servant under the PNM and former Chairman of Caroni Limited and BWIA, had been appointed chairman of a committee established to undertake the reorganisation, restructuring, and rationalisation of State Enterprises.[7] A Commission of Enquiry into projects undertaken by the previous government, chaired by former ULF member Senator Allan Alexander, had also been formed to investigate the 'DC–9' scandal, negotiations with the Tesoro Corporation, the Caroni Racing Complex, the formation of the Point Lisas Industrial Port Development Company and the Iron and Steel Company of Trinidad and Tobago (ISCOTT), the Eric Williams Medical Sciences Complex, importation of narcotics, firearms and ammunition, and involvement in prostitution of women brought in from outside of the country.[8] Giving force to the NAR crusade at this time had been the publication in the *Wall Street Journal* of March 12, 1987 of an embarrassing article implicating former Prime Minister Chambers in a backroom deal in the 1970s with the Tesoro oil company involving a blonde prostitute.

After the Easter break, other reformist action included the issue by the Industrial Development Corporation of a Draft Policy on Investment which welcomed foreign capital and affirmed the role of the private sector; and the revision for the first time in 21 years of the Standing Orders of the House of Representatives.[9]

Regarding social representation, the new government seemed to be more broadly embracing than the previous PNM governments. Although the

Cabinet was reduced to 13 members (from 22 in the 1981–6 Chambers administration), the ideological, ethnic, and regional mixture of former members of the PNM, the Tapia House Movement, the ULF, the DAC, the ONR, and even the DLP, gave it an impressive air of inclusivity.[10] The new President of Trinidad and Tobago, Noor Hassanali,[11] sworn in on March 19, 1987, was a Muslim Indian, as was the Speaker of the House, Nizam Mohammed (MP for Tabaquite, formerly of the ULF), elected on January 12. Basdeo Panday, MP for Couva North, Minister of External Affairs, International Marketing, and Tourism, and former leader of the ULF, had been named Deputy Prime Minister, considerably enhancing Hindu and trade union presence in the government. Ken Gordon, managing editor of the *Trinidad Express* and member of the board of Neal and Massy, one of the country's three remaining large conglomerates, had been appointed Senator and Minister of Industry and Enterprise. At the same time, radical Oilfield Workers' Trade Union (OWTU) president, George Weekes, had been made a Government Senator.[12] Worthy of mention, too, was the award of the Trinity Cross on August 31, 1987 (Trinidad and Tobago's 25th anniversary of Independence) to C.L.R. James – Marxist philosopher, writer, first editor of the PNM's *The Nation*, and co-founder of the WFP for whom in 1966 Panday, Weekes, and Trevor Sudama, NAR MP for Oropouche, contested elections for the first time.[13] In addition, the NAR had lifted the immigration prohibition on leading Black Power advocate, Trinidad-born Kwame Ture (Stokely Carmichael), declared by the PNM Government in 1968.[14]

In addition to the inclusion of previously marginalised personalities, the NAR had legitimised island and ethnic demands. The government had announced that the powers of the THA would be enhanced according to the 1980 Tobago House of Assembly Act, and that TT$27.9 million would be put toward the Scarborough Harbour Development Project (Tobago).[15]

The Foreign Minister of India, Narayan Datt Tiwari, visited Trinidad and Tobago in April 1987 and agreed to establish an Indian Cultural Centre (first suggested by Indira Gandhi who visited the country in 1968). The two countries also signed a cultural agreement.[16] On April 11, 1987, Prime Minister Robinson and External Affairs Minister Panday ran the first lap of the six-day island-wide marathon organised by the Divine Life Society to observe 'Human Dignity Day'. Robinson and Panday carried a torch that would eventually be carried around the entire island of Trinidad, performing the Hindu rite of *pradakshana* – circumambulation of a revered object – and beginning the first ever Caribbean Hindu Conference.[17] Panday also represented the government at the Indian Arrival Day celebrations on May 31, 1987.[18]

In addition, Dr Williams' secular legacy was breached when a new prayer – incorporating the phrase 'one love' – had been introduced into Parliament.[19] Furthermore, Minister of Education Senator Clive Pantin, former ONR member and brother of the Catholic Archbishop, Anthony Pantin, introduced a prayer and the singing of the national anthem at the beginning of each school day.[20]

This new inclusiveness had been expressed 'ideologically' by Dr Brinsley Samaroo, former DAC member, MP for Nariva, Minister in the Office of the Prime Minister, and former lecturer in history at UWI. He sought to elevate the importance of the ancestral cultures of Africa and India in particular, sometimes against the 'cultural imperialism' of Europe and North America as manifested by the very popular television programmes 'Dallas' and 'Dynasty', and the comic strips 'Mandrake' and 'Phantom'. Samaroo posed this cultural approach as a direct challenge to Dr Williams' view that in independence there could be no Mother India, no Mother Africa, no Mother England, no Mother China, no Mother Syria or no Mother Lebanon, only Mother Trinidad and Tobago.[21] Expressing a similar view, Panday's interview with the *Trinidad Express* on the occasion of Trinidad and Tobago's 25th anniversary had been titled, 'We are better off as a society of mixed races.'[22]

Perhaps the most memorable phrase emerging from this initial period was made by the Archbishop of Cape Town, Desmond Tutu, who had visited the country from May 22–3, 1987. At the Jean Pierre Complex in Port of Spain, he described Trinidad and Tobago as a 'Rainbow Country', a phrase which was very well received by the government, the media, and much of the population. The *Trinidad Express* used the phrase as the title of its Silver Jubilee Independence Supplement.[23]

But not surprisingly, perhaps, the NAR also experienced some teething problems at this early stage, when many were in government for the first time. Elaborating the NAR's commitment to 'open government', days after his election in January as Speaker of the House, Nizam Mohammed had indicated that he would combine British and American traditions in order that he not be 'removed from the hurly burly of . . . politics', warning,

> *I intend to be outspoken. When we went to the country during our campaign we said that we were going to have open government and that we*

*were going to have people's participation. I was always opposed to the idea that if someone is a member of a political party, he should enslave himself to the extent that he would compromise strong feelings that he may possess. As a representative of a constituency, I have a very strong moral obligation to those people whom I represent.*[24]

On May 5, 1987, less than a month after the party adopted its unitary constitution on April 11,[25] Mohammed publicly criticised the government at a meeting in Preysal, Couva, for the lack of Department of Environmental Works and Development (DEWD)[26] projects in his constituency of Tabaquite. Mohammed attacked his colleague Dr Carson Charles, former ONR member, MP for St Joseph, and Minister in the Ministry of Works, Settlement and Infrastructure (responsible for DEWD), calling him a 'Johnny-come-lately' to the party.[27]

Before the Easter break, Brinsley Samaroo had been removed from his position largely, it seems, because of his outspokenness about the effects of American and European 'cultural imperialism' and the need for the promotion of African and Indian culture. Journalist David Renwick had congratulated the Prime Minister for his forthright action, and criticised Samaroo for his apparent obsession with 'culture', a word that was used 'no fewer than thirteen times in the course of one conversation'.[28]

At about the same time, Minister of Works, Settlement and Infrastructure, John Humphrey, MP for St Augustine and former ULF MP, complained that his ministry was being sabotaged by its civil servants and accused Permanent Secretary David Punch by name in the House of Representatives.[29] Soon afterwards, Dr Albert Richards, MP for La Brea and Minister of Labour, Employment and Manpower Resources, announced that he was personally unsympathetic to a collective Cabinet decision (the removal of COLA), claiming afterwards that he was given 'clearance' by his Cabinet colleagues to make public his disapproval of the decision.[30]

On June 3, 1987 came the most serious rebellion – at a meeting of the Couva North constituency at the All-Trinidad Sugar and General Workers Trade Union's (ATS&GWTU's)[31] Rienzi Complex, with Minister Panday (MP for the constituency and president of the union) and Minister of Energy, Kelvin Ramnath (MP for Couva South and former ULF member). Prime Minister Robinson apparently had decided to depart from the schedule by preceding Panday's feature address and leaving immediately afterwards. Panday followed Robinson's speech with a highly charged, lengthy oration differentiating the government from the party, criticising the former for changing 'nothing,' and thereby continuing the alienation felt by all the groups in the country who were not in office – making specific reference to the selective availability of information on loans and housing, and the granting of scholarships. Panday asked his constituents 'to join in the struggle which we began 21 years ago [in the WFP] – the struggle for fairness'. He told his audience,

> *if therefore you hear me get up in Parliament and make statements that are apparently derogatory of the government, at a party group meeting or wherever, it is not because I have abandoned the government. It is not because I want to break up the government. That has nothing to do with it. It is because we promised an open government and we must never let one act of discrimination go by, because when you let that happen the second, the third and the fourth will also go by. And you can't do anything later on.*[32]

Reminiscent of Lloyd Best the year before, Panday told his audience, 'I assure you that I am not rocking the boat. On the contrary, I am steadying the ship.'[33]

Playing down the importance of the dissent, Robinson declared at the NAR Annual Conference on July 26, 1987, that the party was nearing the end of the transition period. He outlined a list of 27 points of the government's achievements, assured the party that the NAR had now settled, and that soon the period of recovery and reconstruction would begin.[34] Less than a month later, on August 19, Arthur Sanderson, MP for Fyzabad, publicly complained that he had 'lost confidence' in Joe Pires, the Chairman of the government's National Planning Commission, over the decision to reduce the number of work-days for DEWD workers.[35]

The NAR's lack of cohesion was accompanied by dissent from outside the party. The first area of popular discontent surrounded the 1987 Budget, presented by Prime Minister and Minister of Finance and Economy, A.N.R. Robinson on January 23, 1987. Introduced less than one week after the National Clean-Up campaign, the speech outlined the challenges faced by the country due to its virtually empty treasury, to which Robinson continually called attention. He urged 'every patriotic citizen to rally to the task of national recovery and reconstruction,' invoking the 'new spirit that our people have displayed, with our new commitment, our new patriotism, and our new resolve.'[36]

Accordingly, the government announced that it would suspend the Cost of Living Allowance (COLA) and merit increases which, together with a 5 per cent pay reduction for Ministers of Government, would save the government TT$490.8 million.[37] The trade unions, which had begun to close their organisational and ideological divide in 1982,[38] strongly opposed the proposal and organised a 'National Day of Protest' in Woodford Square.[39] In April 1987, the government compromised by paying a reduced COLA to the lowest levels of public servants and the Prime Minister apologised publicly for having to make the cuts in the first place. The Public Services Association (PSA), however, continued its court action for full restoration to all public servants.[40]

Meanwhile, on February 14, 1987, the UK's Channel Four broadcasted a film titled 'The Gathering Storm' hosted by Jan Mottley, wife of Wendell Mottley, former PNM Minister in the Chambers administration. The programme warned of social unrest in the wake of economic decline, and provoked complaints and enquiries from the Trinidad and Tobago government, members of the public, and Trinidadians resident in the UK.[41]

Soon afterwards, from March 14 to April 19, 1987 (Easter Sunday), Prime Minister Robinson found himself in open conflict with the outgoing president, Sir Ellis Clarke. Retired Appeal Court judge, Noor Hassanali, had been nominated by the government to replace Clarke when Clarke's term of office was completed on March 14. It seems, however, that Clarke had expected that he would be asked to continue as president, and was piqued that he had found out about Hassanali's nomination through the press.[42] On December 31, 1986, without consultation with the new prime minister, Clarke had appointed well-known civil servant James Bain to both the Public and Police Service Commissions; and the day Clarke left office he appointed former Chief Justice, Cecil Kelsick, to the Judicial and Legal Service Commission, both to the great displeasure of Prime Minister Robinson.[43]

On March 27, 1987, Attorney-General Selwyn Richardson (Attorney-General in the 1976–81 PNM administration) introduced a Constitutional (Amendment) Bill which would automatically revoke the appointment of Independent Senators and members of Public Service Commissions retroactive to January 1, 1987 (i.e. presidential appointments made by Clarke before the expiration of his term of office). All things done or purported to be done by the appointees would also be invalidated. Academic commentators (including Selwyn Ryan), the PNM, Tapia, the CPTU, the TTLC, the press, and the general public protested that the bill was 'dangerous', fearing that the constitution would be amended whenever a government felt hampered by it.[44]

On Easter Sunday (April 19, 1987), it was announced in the press that Prime Minister Robinson had been advised by Attorney-General Richardson that the appointments of Bain and Kelsick were null and void due to the lack of proper consultation. However, President Hassanali did not accept letters of resignation sent to him from members of the Public Service Commissions. On June 1, a Presidential Commission, headed by former Chief Justice Sir Isaac Hyatali, had been appointed to undertake a comprehensive review of the 1976 Republican Constitution. Pending the commission's report, no further action was to be taken on the constitutional amendment bill.[45] In the meanwhile, on June 12, 1987, Attorney-General Richardson filed an application in the High Court, which was refused on July 30, 1987. An appeal was filed but not pursued.[46]

Meanwhile, general dissent increased. In May 1987, Tapia House leader Lloyd Best had appeared on a *Trinidad Express* breakfast panel, maintaining his critical stance on the NAR government's performance.[47] These views were consistently elaborated in the Tapia-linked *Trinidad and Tobago Review* which criticised the NAR's 'expansionary adjustment' and its inability to deal with the complex political and economic challenges facing the country.[48]

At street level, the trade unions and the Jamaat-al-Muslimeen, a radical group of recently converted African Muslims, [49] based in Port of Spain, organised a number of demonstrations in July and August. The protests were concentrated in Port of Spain but also occurred in the urban areas of San Fernando (in the south) and Arima (in the east). The largest one, it seems, was staged outside Parliament on August 7, 1987 by an estimated 1,000 protesters blaming the government for the high cost of living, job and wage cuts. Their actions attracted other groups such as farmers' organisations, DEWD workers, and the PNM MP for Port of Spain East, Morris Marshall.[50]

On August 23, 1987, Prime Minister Robinson announced that he would meet representatives of the PSA, the CPTU[51] and the TTLC, as well as the Protective Services and DEWD, exhorting, 'This is the time for planting, not marching.'[52] Robinson expressed amazement that 'all this marching was taking place now and not when the PNM was in power, building massive structures, ruining the country and leaving almost no foreign reserves.'

During this time, the Independence calypso competition had been held. The crown was won for the first time by the calypsonian Cro Cro, who was to emerge as a scathing opponent of the NAR (and later the UNC), articulating an unapologetic pro-African position, described by Trinidadian theologian and cultural critic Burton Sankeralli, not without sympathy, as 'tribal attack'.[53]

Such discontent at such an early stage seemed worthy of remark. Leading Tapia member Allan Harris harshly commented,

> *The easy passage we allowed the National Alliance for Reconstruction speaks volumes about our political innocence. It will not do simply to turn now on the Government in anger. We need to face up squarely to some unflattering realities. What disability was it on our part which prevented us, for fifteen, or even twenty years, from replacing a PNM Government in which we had long ceased to believe?*
>
> *What condition of being and array of circumstances could have brought us, in five short months, to our current state of disaffection with the party we had determined was the long-sought replacement for the People's National Movement and which we then proceeded to sweep into office in the most emphatic and triumphant manner imaginable?*
>
> *We betray in our political behaviour what must be the collective equivalent of the shifting moods of a manic-depressive personality. A major problem of our political constitution must be the state of our collective mind.*[54]

Amidst this controversy, local government elections had been scheduled for September 14, 1987. However, the NAR were not the only party facing trouble at the time. The PNM had been undergoing a troubling transformation. After the general elections defeat, Chambers had resigned as Political Leader of the PNM and Deputy Leader Errol Mahabir announced his retirement from active politics. Patrick Manning had been appointed Leader of the Opposition entitling him to appoint six senators – Augustus Ramrekersingh (significantly, a former Tapia member), Ken Valley, Robin Montano, Donna Prowell, Winston Moore, and Dr Keith Rowley.[55] The senators were fresh entrants to Parliament, forming an essential part of Manning's effort to create a 'new PNM'. In February 1987 Manning had been elected Political Leader of the PNM, defeating Dr Aeneas Willis by 572 votes to 127.[56] In his acceptance speech, Manning advocated a 'purge' of the party's 'undesirable qualities and attitudes', exhorting party members to 'understand clearly that the political life of Trinidad and Tobago is basically in a state of transition'. Manning proclaimed that the PNM was a 'government in exile' – an exile whose purpose was to 'build the new party and to create the new society'.[57] Some of the 'old guard' of the PNM expressed resentment at their marginalisation and what they argued was Manning's unconstitutional, and unwise, attempts to by-pass them.[58] Manning responded in turn, sometimes harshly, calling the dissidents 'stumbling blocks' and a 'recalcitrant minority'.[59] Some questioned whether the party could survive. Although the press welcomed Manning's initiative,[60] the PNM could not easily free itself from blame for the country's dismal financial state. For example, less than one month before the local government elections were held, Frank Barsotti, former permanent secretary in the Ministry of Finance, announced at a panel discussion organised by the Economics Association on August 17, 1987, that the PNM government concentrated on 'regime survival' in the oil-boom years, 'spending money on projects for the primary purpose of staying in power'.[61]

Reflecting on the PNM's disarray, the *Trinidad and Tobago Review* perceptively argued,

> *An enduring dream of many of our citizens has been the achievement by us of a working two-party political system.*
>
> *That our dream remained unfulfilled for so long was probably a consequence of our failure to see that our multiplicity of parties was a political condition directly related to the character of our society. To rescue ourselves from a utopian hankering after a simple, 'Westminster-model', two party system, we were required first to achieve a more sophisticated understanding of the social mould which shapes our politics.*
>
> *Leave aside for the moment whether a two-party system is a goal worth pursuing. The truth that may be emerging is that we are as far away from that goal as ever we have been. What prevailed for years during the reign of the PNM was what may be distilled as a one-and-a-half parliamentary party system. That description excludes the many extra-parliamentary parties. Now, notwithstanding the triumph of the National Alliance for Reconstruction, or perhaps because of it, we seem to be back with a one-and-a-half party system.*[62]

The disorder caused by the NAR's sweeping electoral victory continued to work in its favour. Despite the internal dissent, the NAR had secured a convincing victory in the local government elections, which had a voter turnout of 41 percent, significantly higher than the 32.9 percent voting in the 1983 local government elections (see Appendix B). The NAR gained control of the San Fernando and Arima borough councils (not in PNM control for the first time since 1968), and six county councils. The PNM retained control of the Port of Spain, Point Fortin, and St George councils (see Appendix F).

This would be the last triumph for the NAR in Trinidad, however: the rest of its term would be marked by continuous, even dramatic, political, economic, and social deterioration.

## 'CHANGE AND EXCHANGE': THE EXPULSION OF CLUB 88, 1987–8

The NAR local government victory did not quell the discontent within the party.[63] Karl Hudson-Phillips, appointed chairman of BWIA,[64] acted as Minister without Portfolio while Robinson had been touring North America in October 1987. During this time, Hudson-Phillips had written a Cabinet note criticising the irresponsibility of Minister John Humphrey for warning that social unrest would occur if the government did not release money to his Ministry of Works. The note also criticised Junior Finance Minister Trevor Sudama (MP for Oropouche, former ULF member, member of the 1988 Budget's Co-ordinating Team headed by the Prime Minister, and also member of the two-man political team associated with pre-budget discussions) for publicly declaring that he would not defend the 1988 budget as he had no input into its preparations. Panday and Ramnath were also rebuked.[65]

On November 21, 1987, at the Sugar Industry Labour Welfare Committee awards ceremony, Panday and his former ULF colleagues once again publicly pronounced against the government. Panday had reportedly read his statement earlier in the day to a meeting of the NAR parliamentary arm before leaving the meeting. NAR members, including Basdeo Panday's brother Alderman Subhas Panday, had tried to dissuade the Deputy Leader from delivering the statement, following him to the venue at the Sevilla Club.[66] In the speech, Panday charged that 'the history of discrimination, injustice, and inequality' had continued under the NAR despite all hopes for change. He passionately urged his audience to consider the purpose of forming the NAR and winning elections, and if they were unsatisfied with the results from the party's gaining of office, he urged them to be bold enough to take action. He argued,

> *We are so accustomed to the political monolith that we are unable or afraid to think of another kind of political structure. You either rule like Eric Williams and the PNM, or you do not rule at all. The most troublesome*

*problem in Trinidad and Tobago today is the conflict between those who want change and those who do not. And that has nothing to do with the PNM or the NAR. It is much deeper and wider than that. In fact the conflict crosses party lines.*

*After one year of the new government in office, the line between those who want meaningful change and those who only want exchange is becoming clearer and more distinct. That means the future is easily predictable. There will be a new regrouping of forces which will transcend the distinction of race, colour, and creed. It will be a long, drawn out battle, but in the end the forces of change will succeed. Because history has always been on your side.*[67]

Ryan remarked that Panday, Deputy Prime Minister and Minister of External Affairs and International Trade, sounded 'as if he were still Leader of the Opposition'.[68]

On November 22, 1987, the NAR Parliamentarians issued a press release that called for the Prime Minister to 'use his full powers under the Constitution and the law to achieve discipline, cohesion and teamwork at the level of Cabinet'. On November 26, Robinson called on the entire Cabinet to submit their resignations so that he could 'reorganise the Government in the light of all the circumstances'. Three days later the Cabinet changes were announced. The most important changes included John Humphrey's dismissal from the Cabinet, the stripping of International Marketing and Tourism from Panday's Ministry, Ramnath's move from the Ministry of Energy to Public Utilities, and the inclusion of three new Cabinet members.[69]

The rebellion intensified with the re-shuffle. Even during the swearing in ceremony, Panday and Ramnath refused to shake the hand of the Prime Minister. Panday, Ramnath, and Humphrey continued to complain about 'one-man rule', 'PNM-ism,' the prominent role given to technocrats with long histories of service under PNM governments, not being given reasons for their change of status, and, in the case of Deputy Leader Panday, not being consulted in such matters.[70]

The split in the government had become uglier with the press implicating itself in the disputes. One of the most notable press interventions had been the publication in the *Trinidad Express* on December 15, 1987 of an article titled, 'The ULF Grab for Power' written by an anonymous 'Technocrat'. In his polemic, the technocrat accused, not without justification, the 'former United Labour Front elements', the 'East Indian-owned' weekly papers, and 'East Indian journalists' in the daily press of conducting a 'smear campaign' against 'African technocrats' – Dodderige Alleyne, Eugenio Moore, Trevor

Farrell, and Gordon Draper.[71] He accused the ULF group of 'hypocrisy and ingratitude' when they claimed that it was they who put in the hard work to remove the PNM. 'Technnocrat' warned of the personal, as opposed to communal, motivations for power of the ULF group.[72] The article was reminiscent of another contentious article published in the *Trinidad Express*, titled, 'The Indianisation of the Government', with its super-heading, 'Trinidadians Still Fear Take-over of the State by East Indians.'[73] The articles were more alarming, considering that the Minister of Enterprise and Industry, Senator Ken Gordon (who was firmly on Robinson's side in the dispute), had been the most powerful man behind the *Express* from 1969 until his appointment as Government Senator in 1986.

On December 20, 1987, the NAR National Council appointed a committee chaired by Jaigobin Nanga to 'identify the problems in the party and to determine the causes thereof and to make recommendations for their solution'.[74] The committee met for the first time on December 23, 1987 with 11 members. While it was conducting its investigations, two major incidents occurred. First, on January 31, 1988 a meeting of the dissidents had been called to further articulate their case. Two members of the Nanga Committee had to withdraw because of their attendance at the meeting of dissidents.[75] Then, of great significance, on February 8, 1988 Panday, Ramnath, and Sudama were expelled from the Cabinet.[76]

The *Express* subsequently published an article on February 10, by its editor-in-chief, Owen Baptiste, asking, 'What Is Panday Really Up To?' Panday defiantly responded in the House of Representatives on February 12,

> *It is easier to get some people out of the PNM than to get the PNM out of some people . . . . Not only will I not stand by and see another PNM emerge, but I shall not sit idly by and see my country sold out to Neal and Massy, of whom Mr Baptiste and his former boss (Ken Gordon) are the servants, agents and/or licensees, but more specifically the instruments by which such sale is to be effected.*
>
> *But the saving grace, Mr Speaker, is that not only Mr Baptiste knows of the schemes to sell out our patrimony to Neal and Massy and/or their agents, but the workers know and the other businessmen know too. They both live in fear of the great gobbler. But the workers and the businessmen know I am on their side and no amount of propaganda in the* Daily Express *or elsewhere will change that.*[77]

In early March 1988, after receiving memoranda and hearing testimony from the Prime Minister and 35 members of the House of Representatives and the Senate,[78] the Nanga Committee had submitted its report to the NAR General Council. The Committee report was balanced and wide-ranging, arranged under headings which included 'Operations and Functioning of the Party', 'Relationship Between Party and Government', 'Political Education of Parliamentarians', 'Discipline and Ethics', 'Communications', 'Role and Power of the Transition Team,' 'Indian Cultural Centre,' 'Scarborough Deep Water Harbour', and 'Race Relations'.[79] The report acknowledged merits on both sides of the dispute – on the one hand, that the dissidents failed to air their grievances in an acceptable, disciplined, and constitutional manner and, on the other hand, that there had been real grounds for dissent regarding the marginalisation of an important constituency in the NAR government's making of decisions (specifically regarding the selection of the Cabinet, the appointment of ambassadors, the reassignment of permanent secretaries, major policy decisions, and the firing of Ministers). It accused both sides of a lack of communication and unnecessary aggravation. The party leadership was particularly criticised for failing to take early corrective action and allowing the party to divide from the executive level right down to the constituencies. The Committee recommended that the party seek reconciliation with the dissidents 'with a view to the eventual reinstatement of Mr Panday to the Cabinet', in order 'to truly reflect the political reality of the country'.[80]

The General Council had not reached a final decision on the report and arranged a follow-up meeting for March 17, 1988. On March 16, Panday publicly launched CLUB 88 – the Caucus of Love, Unity, and Brotherhood – to act as a lobby group within the NAR to 'save the party'. The following day, the NAR National Council rejected reconciliation by a vote of 77 to 52 and instead a motion to appoint a disciplinary tribunal was passed. On March 27, the nine-member disciplinary tribunal headed by Anthony Smart (MP for Diego Martin East, and former General Secretary and founder-member of the ONR) had been established to consider 31 charges against Panday, Ramnath, Sudama, Humphrey, and Raymond Pallackdharrysingh (MP for Naparima and Assistant General Secretary of the NAR) for 'serious acts of indiscipline inimical to the interests of the party'.[81]

On April 29, 1988, Panday, still Deputy Leader of the NAR, moved a parliamentary motion of no confidence against Prime Minister Robinson.[82] It was unsuccessful. On May 15 the five members were suspended from party activity in a reportedly disordered and contentious vote of acclamation that had been carried by 100 to 78.[83] Nizam Mohammed, Jensen Fox (MP for Port of Spain North, formerly of the ONR),[84] and member of the Nanga Committee Chan Sookhoo each expressed in the press their disappointment with the suspensions. On the other hand, Prime Minister Robinson indicated his satisfaction that 'the party . . . [had] taken control of its affairs.'[85]

Subsequently, CLUB 88 held a press conference in which Panday called the suspension 'tantamount to expulsion' and accused Robinson of having planned the expulsion of the former ULF elements possibly before the elections, 'so that he could exercise absolute and total control over the party and government'. He continued, 'We feel sorry for him but cannot forgive him for the tragedy which he is inflicting on the nation.' Robinson was accused of trying to fracture the society along racial lines 'so that he could create a political base for himself in Trinidad.'[86]

Relations between the leadership and other NAR members not part of CLUB 88 were also becoming strained. In June 1988, Parliamentary Secretary in the Ministry of Food Production, Marine Exploitation, Forestry and the Environment Eden Shand had been removed from office for making an unauthorised call to the nation to destroy the crops of illegal squatters;[87] in July 1988, President of the Senate Michael Williams voted against the government's Free Zones Bill 1988;[88] and on August 29, 1988, the NAR Port of Spain North constituency, in a hastily organised meeting reportedly attended by only nine out of a possible 94 persons, passed a motion of no confidence against Prime Minister A.N.R. Robinson, calling for fresh elections in three months. The motion was piloted by executive member of the Constituency Council, JD Ramjohn, founding member of both the ONR and the NAR. Jensen Fox, MP, who had been present, abstained from voting.[89] Shortly afterward, members of the NAR executive had persuaded the constituency, including Fox, to pass a retracting motion. However, the constituency of Couva South subsequently passed a similar no-confidence motion, while members in Barataria/San Juan, Tunapuna, Port of Spain South, and Sangre Grande threatened to do the same.[90]

On October 16, 1988, on a rainy day at the Aranguez Triangle one week before Panday's term as Deputy Leader of the NAR was to expire,[91] CLUB 88 held a rally of thousands[92] – including, apparently out of curiosity, Morris Marshall, Kamaluddin Mohammed, John Eckstein, John Donaldson, and Wendell Mottley from the PNM; members of the diplomatic corps; Selwyn Ryan; Acting Minister of Finance and the Economy Selby Wilson; and calypsonian Deple who had performed at the cultural programme that preceded the feature address – seeking a mandate to launch a new political party that would 'reincarnate' the 'original NAR'.[93] On October 23, after much argument and debate, the NAR Annual Conference, with a lone dissenting vote from Senator Amrika Tiwary, ratified the expulsion of Panday, Ramnath, and Humphrey, finalising the split in the government after less than two years in office.[94] It was a tragic failure of the 'One Love' spirit proclaimed during the 1986 campaign.

Reflecting on the political situation before the expulsion, Sunity Maharaj, in the August 1988 edition of the *Trinidad and Tobago Review,* conducted extremely illuminating interviews with Peter Farquhar, Vernon Jamadar, and Kamaluddin Mohammed, revealing uncanny similarities between Trinidad and Tobago's political present and its past. Kamaluddin Mohammed had observed that since the formation of the PNM, opposition parties were 'earlier forms of the NAR'. Maharaj suggested that Basdeo Panday:

> *'look into the mirror of his soul and see if he doesn't find Bhadase Maharaj there. Didn't Bhadase, too, unconditionally deliver the same constituency of interests and hopes to a coalition – that of the DLP? Both men placed the interests of their constituency on the unhallowed altar of office with no safeguards whatsoever . . . . Both succumbed to the manipulation of a view that they weren't fit material for high office.'*

Following Peter Farquhar, Maharaj also argued that both the DLP and the NAR gambled on 'image' rather than allowing the politician to prevail.[95] Robinson (with his Tobago retreat), like Dr Capildeo (with his London retreat), had been acclaimed leader through the manipulation of public and party opinion, while the 'two competitors sat back and allowed it to happen for whatever reason and with whatever calculation.' She surmised that if the DLP had won in 1961, the weakness of Capildeo would have resulted in the DLP ending up the same way that the NAR did.[96] The reason that a weak politician could win elections in the first place, Farquhar maintained, was that people in Trinidad and Tobago have always voted 'not *for* somebody, but *against* somebody . . . . Nobody ever imagines that the person you put in could be worse than the person you are keeping out.' Maharaj concluded, 'The *Middle Passage* [by V.S. Naipaul] still holds true. This is a place where 30 years after the PNM boasted it had brought party politics to the country, there are still no parties, mainly individuals.'[97]

Selwyn Ryan similarly concluded:

> *It is now becoming apparent that the 30 years of stable PNM politics might well have been an interlude, an aberration in our political development and that the tradition of indiscipline and 'jammetry'*[98] *which characterised the politics of the parties in opposition in those years was in fact the norm to which we have now returned.*[99]

## 'PRIME MINISTER ROBINSON HAS BEEN OVERTHROWN': THE ROAD TO THE ATTEMPTED COUP D'ÉTAT, 1989–90

The loss of Panday, Ramnath, Humphrey, and Sudama did not significantly affect the NAR parliamentary majority. However, SARA opinion polls released in the *Trinidad Express* stated that 58 per cent of the population wanted fresh elections and that, broken down by religious group, only between 11 and 21 per cent were satisfied with the NAR's performance, and 56 to 70 per cent expressed outright dissatisfaction with Robinson's performance as Prime Minister.[100]

The NAR, however, dominated the THA elections in November 1988, winning 11 of the 12 seats. Voter participation dropped dramatically, however, to 53.5 per cent (see Appendix B). In this context, the NAR increased its share of the ballots cast to 63.5 per cent, from the DAC's 56.6 per cent in 1984.[101]

In addition to and apart from its internal problems, the NAR faced considerable extra-parliamentary opposition, seemingly from every angle and quarter: trade unions, women's groups, religious bodies, community organisations, and business interests. Much of the criticism was directed at the NAR's economic policies. Trade unions, UWI academics, and community groups saw the measures as being disproportionately harsh on workers, favourable to big businesses (both local and foreign), and generally against the national interest. On the other side, those with pro-market leanings were disappointed with what they considered as the government's slow, hesitant implementation of economic reforms.[102]

Early in its term, the NAR government had made plans to formulate a medium-term, macro-planning framework and established a National Planning Commission, chaired by Prime Minister Robinson, but mostly under the responsibility of the Ministry of Planning and Mobilisation (under Winston Dookeran, MP for Chaguanas and former ULF member). The Commission's various sub-committees met with the private sector, the public sector, the university and the labour movement. Draft documents were made available in July and August 1988 on which the public commented at consultations held throughout the country.[103] The first draft programme explicitly articulated a change from an inward-looking to an outward-looking strategy, fostering a climate 'conducive to investment activity in general and the growth of exports in particular' while at the same time setting out 'to bring the lowest quartile of the population into the mainstream of the economic life of the society in a productive and proactive, rather than passive and dependent relationship'.[104]

As part of this effort, Minister of Enterprise, Industry and Tourism Senator Ken Gordon piloted the government's Free Zones Bill in July 1988. The bill aroused significant opposition, with President of the Senate, Michael Williams, voting with the Opposition and Independent Senators against it.[105] The issue became another rallying point for dissent, even before the bill had been presented in parliament. On May 26, 1988, Workingwomen were central in the formation of the Women Against Free Trade Zones Committee,[106] bringing together individuals and groups to organise broad-based popular opposition to the establishment of Export Processing Zones.[107] The development of the Free Zones was thereby deferred.

The government continued its strategy for reversing the economic decline, and in August 1988 it had announced a number of new measures, including devaluation of the Trinidad and Tobago dollar relative to the US dollar from TT$3.60 to TT$4.25, the introduction of a voluntary termination of employment programme for public servants, and a number of tax increases and public spending cuts.[108] On September 11, 1988, Prime Minister Robinson embarked on a three and a half week trip to Brussels, Cyprus, Paris, Berlin, and London to negotiate access to IMF finance facilities to deal with the country's balance of payments problems, among other things.[109] On November 16, 1988, the government submitted a letter of intent to the IMF requesting a 14-month stand-by arrangement in the amount of Special Drawing Rights (SDR) $99 million.[110] In the 1989 budget speech delivered on December 16, 1988,[111] Robinson announced that Trinidad and Tobago had been degraduated by the World Bank, five years after its graduation, in contrast to its earlier status as net creditor to the World Bank, the Inter-American Development Bank (IDB), and the Caribbean Development Bank, and as soft lender to other Caribbean governments.[112] The 1989 budget was presented as the budget in which the recovery programme would start in earnest, after spending 1987–8 setting the country's 'economic house in order'. Robinson argued that the ability of the country to endure the hardships 'in the midst of apparent political confusion, social disequilibrium and economic crisis would be the true measure of our adulthood as a nation'. Trinidad and Tobago, he declared, had come to the end of the era when the state was seen as a 'tireless mother', and stood at the threshold of another.[113]

Under the initiative of Minister Ken Gordon (who would vacate his position in government in January 1990 to resume his position as CEO of Trinidad Newspapers Ltd., publishers of the *Trinidad Express*),[114] the government had attempted to significantly reduce the burden of the state sector. After the government covered TT$2.5 billion of ISCOTT's losses and debt-servicing, the company – which between 1982 and 1986 had accounted for a loss of TT$1,132.7 million, or 77 per cent of the net loss of the energy-based industries[115] – was leased to the Ispat Group of India in October 1988. In August 1989, Ispat agreed to operate ISCOTT for ten years, and renamed the mill Caribbean Ispat Limited (CIL). Ispat invested TT$17 million in the enterprise and made lease payments of TT$46 million per year. In the following year, 1990, the mill declared a profit for the first time since its start-up in 1981.[116] It was the first major turnaround at Point Lisas. In December 1989, 49 per cent of the state-owned Telephone Company (established in 1968) had been sold to Cable and Wireless of the UK (with the promise of a 20-year monopoly), and the company was re-christened the Telecommunications Service of Trinidad and Tobago (TSTT).[117] In 1988, a foreign bank had been permitted to repurchase previously divested stock in its local subsidiary, reversing the policy of localisation that Robinson himself had piloted as PNM Minister of Finance in 1966.[118]

New foreign investment also started to arrive. In November 1989 Conoco and Pan West, two US oil companies, began construction of a US$95 million gas-processing plant at Point Lisas, to extract propane and butane from natural gas. The plant, Phoenix Park Gas Processors, was the first of its kind in Trinidad and Tobago and began operations on June 15, 1991.[119]

In 1989, the government undertook comprehensive tax reform, achieving 'significant reduction in the rate of corporation tax, coupled with measures to increase business savings and to channel these savings into productive investment,' while introducing in the 1990 budget a Value Added Tax (VAT) of 15 per cent on most consumption items.[120] On March 14, 1990, the government submitted another letter of intent to the IMF requesting another 12-month stand-by arrangement in the amount of SDR $85 million (50 per cent of quota), and possible access to contingency financing up to a maximum amount of SDR $42.5 million.[121] In May 1990, the government repealed the Alien Landholdings Act (introduced in 1921 to limit expatriate ownership, and extended in 1969 to prohibit foreign ownership in business), replacing it with a more friendly Foreign Investment Act. The new Act restricted the legal definition of a foreigner so that investment could be easily undertaken by residents from countries with reciprocity agreements, including citizens of CARICOM countries. The Act also removed restrictions on foreign ownership in private companies, once the investment capital was brought in from abroad.[122]

The reform measures, not surprisingly, provoked trade union and other activists on a number of levels. The non-payment of COLA and the 10 per cent reduction in wages to public servants announced in the 1989 budget came after months of dispute. In July 1988, five months before the 1989 budget was presented, the Industrial Court ruled that the government had to re-instate COLA in addition to a salary increase of 2 per cent. The government, however, warned that timely implementation of the wage award would be precluded by the tight fiscal situation, and appealed the decision.[123] Furthermore, in August 1988, at the same time as the government announced the currency devaluation, it had delayed its payments to public servants.[124] The budget announcement increased the fervour of the trade union protest.

On March 6, 1989, the CPTU and the TTLC had organised a one-day 'general strike', asking workers to stay at home as a protest against the government's economic measures and its 'lack of consultation'. The CPTU claimed that the 'strike united almost the entire population and gave them confidence in their unity and ability to not only say NO to Structural Adjustment, but also to build for themselves a better society.'[125] The PSA claimed that 80 per cent of its members stayed away from work. In contradiction, Reginald Dumas, permanent secretary to the Prime Minister, submitted attendance figures showing that only 29.9 per cent of public servants stayed away from work, except in the Ministry of Education where 85 per cent did not come out on March 7. The Minister of Education, Senator Clive Pantin, submitted his resignation because of the exceptionally low turnout at his Ministry and in the schools. Robinson refused Pantin's resignation.[126] On April 22, the trade unions organised in Port of Spain a 'March Against Hunger', in which Basdeo Panday (president of the ATS&GWTU since 1973) was one of the speakers on the platform.[127] In response to these events, a National Consultation of the private sector, government, and the labour movement had been convened at Chaguaramas on May 2, 1989.[128]

Between March 6, 1989 and July 13, 1990, the CPTU engaged in 17 protests, demonstrations, rallies, marches, and public meetings, and issued 56 public statements on alternative economic strategies, government legislation, privatisation, and strikes, among other things.[129] It was notable that many of the new radical trade union leadership were members of the Committee for Labour Solidarity (CLS) that had been formed in November 1981 from the old Shah faction of the ULF. OWTU President, Errol McLeod, (ULF MP for Oropouche 1976–81) and OWTU Education Officer, David Abdulah (son of Anglican Archbishop Clive Abdulah, and unsuccessful ULF candidate for Tunapuna in 1976, and Government Senator George Weekes (who had supported the 10 per cent pay cut) had been extremely critical of each other's positions on the NAR government, whom the CPTU described as 'anti-worker.'[130]

Meanwhile, ten days after the 'Day of Resistance,' on March 16, CLUB 88 celebrated its one year anniversary at the Rienzi Complex in Couva, adopting the party name, the United National Congress (UNC), with Basdeo Panday named interim political leader. Six weeks later, on May 1, 1989, the UNC won the local government by-election in Guaico/Cumuto in the eastern St Andrew/St David county council, with 1,216 votes for the UNC, 631 for the PNM, and 544 for the NAR.

While the party tried to institutionalise itself, trouble emerged. Party elections were scheduled for July 24, 1990. John Humphrey was contesting the post of Deputy Leader, and it was widely assumed that Basdeo Panday had endorsed Humphrey's candidature, largely in order to promote the image of the UNC as more than an 'Indian party.' During the contest, Humphrey had alleged that 'a high level of racialism ... [was] being demonstrated in the [Indian dominated] United National Congress', with Panday's hitherto right hand man of 15 years, Kelvin Ramnath, implied as a leading figure against Humphrey. To investigate the charges, Dr Selwyn Ryan was appointed by the UNC as a one-man Commission of Inquiry. The Commission turned up no positive evidence.[131] On July 22, 1990, the UNC elected its executive officers at its Inaugural Assembly at the Chaguaramas Convention Centre. Humphrey lost to Dr Allan Mackenzie, Ramnath won the post of General Secretary, and Dr Rampersad Parasaram the Party Chairman.[132]

The radical groups continued to organise. The Movement for Social Transformation (MOTION), convened its founding congress on September 10, 1989, with David Abdulah as political leader. This resulted from a decision on November 12, 1988, in which the CLS had been 'mandated' to mobilise 'in the workplaces among the workers and farmers; in the communities amongst the youth, students, housewives, small business people, self-employed, patriotic intellectuals and professionals' to discuss the draft programme of its new political party.[133] Four months later, on January 4, 1990, partly motivated by early left-wing factionalism in MOTION, the Joint Trade Union Movement (JTUM) was founded (by union leadership which included some of the MOTION executives) and at a Conference of Shop Stewards and Branch Officers, the JTUM was commissioned 'to unite with other sections of the society to deal effectively with the NAR's Economic Policies'.[134] As a result, on February 8, 1990 representatives of 29 organisations – 16 unions, one sports and culture club, the Caribbean Association for Feminist Research and Action, the Writers Association of Trinidad and Tobago, the Jamaat-al-Muslimeen, political organisations, youth groups, and others[135] – convened to form the Summit of People's Organisations (SOPO) to 'mobilise the people' and to 'obtain a mandate from the population to press ahead with our demands and economic alternatives'.[136]

During this time, the NAR were caused further parliamentary embarrassment with the resignation of President of the Senate Michael Williams on March 8, 1990, complaining that, as President, he was unable 'to speak out against upsetting issues such as the Service Commissions and the questionable contract awards by the Central Tenders Board'. Williams further declared that the NAR as a party, distinct from government, should not be afraid to remove the 'whole crew' from the Prime Minister on down.[137]

Meanwhile, the NAR attempted to continue its project of cultural and social inclusion.[138] In October 1989, Minister without Portfolio Dr Bhoe Tewarie had organised a lecture series, 'Let Us Discover Ourselves,' to commemorate (three years early) the 500th anniversary of Columbus's arrival in the Caribbean. Jennifer Franco spoke of the European contribution; Suren Capildeo (son of Simbhoonath Capildeo, nephew of Dr Rudranath Capildeo, and first cousin of V.S. Naipaul) spoke on the Indians; Dr Ralph Henry on the Africans; Peter Harris on the Caribs and Arawaks; Dr Robert Lee on the Chinese; and Annette Rahael on the Syrian-Lebanese people. The lectures were surrounded by controversy as the African spokespersons apparently protested consistently that the other groups did not sufficiently acknowledge the exploitation and oppression of Africans, and other groups expressed feelings of marginalisation by what Franco once referred to as the 'Africanisation' of Trinidad. Capildeo's Indian lecture was prematurely ended as various conflicting spokespersons sought to dominate the microphone during question period.[139]

Another basically well-intentioned NAR initiative that turned sour was the attempt to introduce a National Service Scheme aimed at the population aged twenty-five and under.[140] Both the DAC and Tapia had included similar plans in their 1976 manifestos, on April 3, 1984, the PNM Government had set up a committee to consider its establishment, and national service had been included in the 1986 NAR manifesto. From December 28, 1989, a series of meetings had been held to discuss the proposed scheme, on the initiative of Lincoln Myers, former Tapia member, and Minister of the new Ministry of National Service. Myers argued that national service would help to reverse 'the disintegration of family life; widespread teenage pregnancy; the alarming incidence of crime and drug abuse; random violence in the streets; [and the] growing alienation of . . . youths [who have been] betrayed by so-called exemplars of public trust.'[141] The social situation in the country had indeed deteriorated significantly, as seen in statistics on crime, homicide, suicide, divorce, and migration (see Table 5.1). Boldly underlining this decay, in 1988 a net migration of 44,222 persons had been estimated by the Central Statistical Office, an amount greater than the population of Port of Spain (42,605) recorded in the 1990 census.[142]

***Table 5.1 Indicators of Social Breakdown, 1981-90***

| | **1981** | **1990** |
|---|---|---|
| Total Reports to the Police (excluding offences against traffic laws) | 38,889 | 65,138 |
| Homicide | 33 | 77 |
| Suicide | 59 | 170 |
| Rate of Divorce as a proportion of the number of Marriages | 10.4% | 18.2% |
| Net Migration | -3,168 | -20.172 |

*Sources*: *ASD* (1987; 1997)

Support for national service came from small Hindu groups such as the Hindu Seva Sangh, the Hindu Prachar Kendra, the Hindu Academy (whose Pundit Ramcharan Gosine was a member of the eight-man National Service Committee); Dr Patrick Solomon; Tapia activist Hamlet Joseph; *Trinidad*

*Guardian* and *Trinidad Express* columnists; the Presbyterian (and mainly Indian) Hillview College Students; and the Trinidad and Tobago Cadet Force. On the other side, the SDMS seemed the most vigorously opposed to the plan. At a national consultation organised by the SDMS on March 3, 1990, at which Minister Myers, Basdeo Panday, Patrick Manning, Archbishop Pantin, and Suren Capildeo were guest speakers, two discussants from Grenada, Winston Crowe and Gerry Romain (political prisoners under the 1979–83 People's Revolutionary Government), argued that in Grenada, 'There were no checks and balances to prevent abuse of the system, there was no room for protest. Hence the cover-up of mistreatment, where 11-year-old girls lost their virginity to the deflowering parties'.[143] The fear of 'douglarisation'[144] seemed to be the grounds for the most passionate objections to the scheme, raising in the process many questions about pluralism, nationalism, and racism.[145]

The ambiguous statements about whether the scheme would be, or eventually become, compulsory, residential, and/or gender mixing together with distrust of government statements; and scepticism about whether in fact national service could foster patriotism (the negative case of Guyana was cited as a counter-example) added to fearful rumour and speculation. The Inter-Religious (IRO), columnists with the *Express* and the *Guardian*, the weekly paper the *Bomb* (owned by Satnarine Maharaj, Secretary General of the SDMS), the Muslim Co-ordinating Council, Dr Selwyn Ryan, human rights lawyer Ramesh Lawrence Maharaj, the PNM, and the UNC opposed introduction of national service mainly on the grounds that not enough discussion had occurred to relieve the anxieties of those opposed to it. After much heated exchange in the press and a period of lapse, the National Service Scheme was launched on February 18, 1991 as a voluntary, low-profile programme.[146]

During this period, the NAR also continued its campaign to recover money lost through corruption during the years of PNM rule. On July 5, 1988, the Trinidad and Tobago Government filed a claim of TT$500 million in the Supreme Court of Ontario, Canada, against the estate of former PNM Minister John O'Halloran for breaches of trust and fiduciary obligations between 1968 and 1985.[147] In March 1991, ten years after the death of Eric Williams, TT$29.6 million (Cdn$8 million) was awarded to the Trinidad and Tobago Government.[148] In 1990, the government had been awarded damages of TT$12 million by a New York court in a case against the Tesoro oil company involving the bribery of O'Halloran.[149]

Furthemore, at the 44th session of the General Assembly of the United Nations, the Trinidad and Tobago government, represented by Prime Minister Robinson, submitted for consideration a new agenda item concerning the establishment of an International Criminal Court with jurisdiction over such crimes as illegal trafficking of narcotics across frontiers and other criminal activities. After skilfull manoeuvering, the motion was accepted on December 4, 1989 (Resolution A/Res/44/3a). It was the first successful move toward the establishment of an International Criminal Court in the UN since the Nuremberg trials in 1948. Robinson had been committed to the establishment of an International Criminal Court since his days at Oxford in the 1950s and was a Director of the Foundation for the Establishment of an International Criminal Court from 1972-1987.

On July 23, 1990, Prime Minister Robinson opened an apparently heated debate on the Tesoro Report. Its laying in Parliament some considered to be a breach of parliamentary privilege because of the legally questionable nature of the allegations against former members of the PNM government. At 6:00 pm July 27, the third day of the debate, the Leader of Government Business in the House, Joseph Toney (MP for Toco/Manzanilla) was interrupted by 42 armed members of the Jamaat-al-Muslimeen who had come to 'overthrow' the government.[150]

At the same time, 72 other insurgents took over TTT (the country's only television station at the time) and Radio Trinidad (the country's only privately-owned radio station) on Maraval Road, and drove a car-bomb into the Police Headquarters obliquely across from parliament.[151] The total number of hostages taken, according to one source, was 61.[152] In Parliament, one report counted the prime minister, six Cabinet ministers and ten MPs, along with journalists and public servants, as hostages.[153]

That evening, Imam Abu Bakr,[154] the leader of the Jamaat-al-Muslimeen, delivered two television addresses, one at 7:00 pm (during the 'Panorama' evening news time slot) and the other at 10:30 pm. Bakr announced that a 'coup' had occurred, that 'Prime Minister Robinson had been "overthrown,"' that Robinson and his cabinet were under arrest at gun point at that very moment, and that the prime minister would 'be put on trial'. The Imam indicated that 'the last straw that broke the camel's back' had been the government's announcement on July 25, 1990 that it would use TT$500,000 of the money recovered from the Tesoro and O'Halloran cases to erect a statue to the late Gene Miles, a public servant who died in 1972 and had fought against the so-called 'Gas Station Racket' in 1965.[155] In the later broadcast, Bakr announced himself as 'leader of the revolution', bemoaned the country's lack of medicines which the Jamaat could have supplied the government if it were allowed to, abolished the seven-month old VAT, and called for new elections in 90 days.[156]

During the 10:30 pm broadcast, the TTT signal had been jammed from the army base at Camp Ogden on Long Circular Road, three miles away from parliament. Ministers Myers and Pantin, who were among those members of government not present in parliament at the time, and Army Colonel Ralph Brown were briefly able to let the nation know that the government was still in charge.

That evening, the Anglican Canon Knolly Clarke – a fellow member of SOPO with the Jamaat – had entered parliament to negotiate with Bilaal Abdullah, who had been in charge of the Muslimeen at the Red House. The next morning, eight hostages were released, including three women and MP for Diego Martin Central, Leo Des Vignes, who had been shot in the ankle. Shortly afterwards, Canon Clarke had emerged with Minister Dookeran and a list of demands.

With Dookeran released, a 'Cabinet meeting' was called at Camp Ogden that morning, including Acting President Emmanuel Carter, Minister of Energy Senator Herbert Atwell, Minister of Works, Infrastructure, and Decentralisation Dr Carson Charles, Clive Pantin, Lincoln Myers, Chief of Defence Force Staff Colonel Joseph Theodore, and Anthony Smart.[157] At 10:30 am, shortly after the meeting, acting president declared a state of emergency, with a nation-wide curfew announced soon afterward. In addition to Camp Ogden, the Holiday Inn and the Trinidad Hilton in Port of Spain acted as government secretariats and information centres.

Undoubtedly, to the chagrin of Bakr, the population – including members of SOPO – did not rise up to support his cause. Instead there was widespread looting and destruction of property along the 'east-west corridor' of north Trinidad, from Carenage in the west to Arima in the east.[158]

The army, unlike on April 21, 1970, was firmly on the government's side.[159] On July 29, one person had been rescued from Police Headquarters, on July 30, Radio Trinidad had been recaptured, and on July 31, one Muslimeen member surrendered at TTT.[160]

On the night of Monday July 30, from inside the besieged Red House, Prime Minister Robinson announced on radio to the BBC and to the Caribbean News Agency that he had agreed to a list of six demands that:

*Unloading emergency supplies being brought by plane to Trinidad and Tobago during the 1990 coup.*

1. He step down as Prime Minister
2. Other Ministers sign a statement supporting Winston Dookeran as Prime Minister in an interim government
3. The President act within his authority but on the advice of the interim Prime Minister
4. There be elections in 90 days from the date of signing the agreement
5. A Government of National Unity be formed, involving the heads of parties and including Imam Yasin Abu Bakr, leader of the Islamic insurrection
6. The rebels be granted an insurrection amnesty[161]

Prime Minister Robinson, who had also been shot in the ankle as well as beaten badly in his face, was released on July 31. At 2:15 pm the next day, Emancipation Day, Abu Bakr and the Muslimeen surrendered.[162] Initial government figures had reported 30 killed, 150 wounded, and that TT$200 million would be needed to rehabilitate businesses: 102 business outlets were affected by looting, 20 buildings were destroyed by fire, and 27 were severely damaged.[163] On August 13, Bakr and 111 members of the Jamaat-al-Muslimeen were charged with 22 criminal offences, including treason and murder.[164] It was arguably the lowest point that the country ever reached in its history.

*Prime Minister ANR Robinson recuperating after the 1990 coup*

## THE NAR'S FINAL YEAR, 1990–91

The general population did not support the coup,[165] but NJAC, the CPTU, OWTU, SOPO, and MOTION refused to condemn the Muslimeen and instead saw the episode as a fulfilment of their 'warnings' about the government's structural adjustment policies. (Tapia had no reservations about denouncing the action.) Selwyn Ryan and other commentators called for elections within six months.[166] The NAR had one more year to fulfil its term in office.

On August 10, 1990, in the temporary parliamentary chamber set up at the Central Bank auditorium, the government tabled a motion to extend the state of emergency for another three months. The motion was supported by the opposition PNM, but not by the UNC, who (in addition to noting the irony that Robinson opposed a similar measure in the Black Power crisis of 1970) supported only a one month extension so that local government elections, due in September 1990, could be held before the 1991 general elections.[167] On September 5 the life of the county and municipal councils was extended for one year, after which they would be re-organised into entities known as regional corporations. Panday criticised the move as 'an abuse of parliamentary privilege'. On September 10, Basdeo Panday, whose UNC had a total of six MPs as opposed to the PNM's three, was confirmed by President Hassanali as Leader of the Opposition, giving Panday the power to name six senators – Dr Prakash Persaud, Wade Mark, Robert Amar, Salisha Baksh, Dr Ralph Khan, and Mootilal Moonan.[168] Panday argued that his choices represented the Hindus, Muslims, Christians, labour, business, and women, demonstrating that a UNC Government would include all the major groups in the country.[169] On November 9, 1990, the NAR again extended the state of emergency by one month, this time without the support of either the PNM or the UNC.[170] It is difficult not to imagine that the emergency was greeted with relief by the NAR, who were able to govern without public demonstrations during the period. For example, SOPO had faded by the end of 1990.[171] Similarly, MOTION, which was plagued by internal problems from its launch, witnessed the resignation of six of its 12 executive members on April 24, 1991.[172]

The NAR did not escape, however. On December 16, 1990, a by-election was held in Diego Martin Central to fill the vacancy left by Leo Des Vignes. The PNM, which had been re-organising itself since 1987, showed its resilience as former PNM senator Ken Valley won the seat with 5,278 votes; NAR senator Clive Pantin received 4,201 votes; the UNC's Trevor Belmosa, 675; and NJAC's Aiyegoro Ome ,329.[173] Pantin, who had resigned his positions in the Senate and as Minister of Health in order to contest the seat, subsequently announced that he was quitting politics.[174] The NAR was reduced to 26 MPs.

After the by-elections the NAR experienced further distress. MPs Kenneth Butcher (Barataria/San Juan), Jensen Fox, Theodore Guerra (Port of Spain South),[175] Arthur Sanderson (Fyzabad), and Eden Shand (St Ann's West) publicly questioned Robinson's leadership, with Butcher suggesting that Winston Dookeran replace Robinson. Butcher and Shand, in addition, resigned their junior minister portfolios. Prime Minister Robinson had poorly retorted that these men were having personal problems and were 'mental' cases.[176] In the following month, January 1991, MP for Arima Gloria Pollard declared that she would not be contesting for the NAR in the next elections.[177] A few months later, on July 21, 1991, Shand dramatically cut in two his NAR party card in Parliament and announced his resignation from the party declaring, 'I still hold the view that the political leader is more of a liability than an asset and I do not think it has anything to do with harsh decisions. It has to do with the manner in which the decisions were made.'[178] His announcement was reportedly greeted with thumps of approval from his government colleagues. He declared himself an independent and later stated that he 'was now free'. In the July 26 sitting of parliament, Shand went on to link Robinson to the 'ULF Grab for Power' article published three-and-a-half years earlier, and claimed that Robinson had fired him from his position as parliamentary secretary in June 1988 to give the appearance that Panday's suspension in the previous month had not been racially motivated. Robinson protested that those were not the facts. The NAR's parliamentary support was reduced to 25 MPs (still, however, a two-thirds majority). At a public meeting on Wrightson Road in Port of Spain, Robinson lashed out at 'damn useless' MPs.[179] The fallout continued as Dr Albert Richards officially announced on August 1, 1991 that he was leaving politics and not offering himself for re-election.[180] In October 1991, Arthur Sanderson also resigned from the party.[181] By November 1991, seven leading NAR MPs had declared that they would not contest in 1991. They included Minister of Education Gloria Henry (MP for Arouca South), Minister of Food Production Brinsley Samaroo, and Deputy Speaker Anselm St George (MP for San Fernando East).[182]

The government continued to follow its programmes the best it could against the seemingly continuous opposition – internal, official Opposition, and extra-parliamentary. In terms of its social programme, the government had passed the Domestic Violence Act in 1991 and, symbolically, Prime Minister Robinson visited India and Nigeria in the same year.[183] The major efforts of the NAR Government, however, were directed toward its economic recovery programme. In September 1990, the government published *Restructuring for Economic Independence: Medium Term Macro Planning Framework, 1989-1995*.[184] In the midst of its troubles, the government was given something of a blessing when on August 2, 1990, the day after Bakr surrendered, Iraq invaded Kuwait. This had the effect of raising the average price of oil that year to US$20.60 per barrel, 27.2 per cent higher than the 1989 average and the highest yearly average price since the oil price dropped from its yearly average of US$28.00 in 1985.

The 1991 Budget, presented on December 12, 1990, by new Minister of Finance Selby Wilson (MP for Point Fortin), had been nicknamed the 'Santa Claus Budget' by the NAR during the Diego Martin by-election campaign, and included the removal of the 10 per cent salary cut, payment of TT$10 million in arrears since 1983 to sugar workers, and a promise not to return to the IMF.[185] Patrick Manning sceptically called it a 'Saddam Hussein Budget'.[186] By the end of its term in 1991, the NAR could boast of several important economic developments (see Appendix D).

After seven years of successive decline, real GDP had once again shown positive growth, starting with 1.5 per cent growth in 1990. The efforts at diversification seemed to have borne fruit, with 'other exports' (i.e. other than crude petroleum, petroleum products, fertilisers, methanol, sugar, cocoa, coffee, and citrus) reaching their highest levels ever. (Previously, the highest value recorded was TT$663 million in 1982). Foreign Direct Investment also recovered, peaking at US$148.9 million in 1989, the highest level since 1982 when the value was US$211.0 million. In 1989, the balance of payments deficit was reduced to its lowest level (TT$136.0 million) since 1981, when there had been a surplus of TT$569 million. In addition, in 1991 the fiscal deficit had been put at its lowest level since 1983, when the government had surplus measuring 12.2 per cent of GDP.[187]

The recovery might be explained by the rise in oil prices, however, in which case the achievement would be less significant.[188] Oil prices fluctuated from a low of US$13.40 per barrel in 1988 to US$20.60 per barrel in 1990, and in 1991 current oil revenue reached a seven-year high of TT$2,717 million.

Despite the positive signs, the economic base showed definite weaknesses. Net Official Foreign Reserves were very low, running into a TT$23.8 million deficit in 1988. A year later the total debt to GDP ratio reached its highest level up to that time, 60.4 per cent. Investment, measured in terms of Gross Capital Formation, reached its lowest level ever in 1988, measuring 9.7 per cent of real GDP. (The lowest recorded Gross Capital Formation figures before the 1987–91 period were 17.7 per cent in 1969, and 17 per cent in 1986.) Unemployment, too, was at its highest level ever in 1987.[189]

In addition, although divestment in ISCOTT and TSTT were important, the state enterprise sector had grown from 66 enterprises with a shareholding value of TT$2 billion in 1985 to 87 enterprises with a par value of TT$6.5 billion in 1992.[190]

When the general elections were called for December 16, 1991 (Robinson's birthday),[191] prediction seemed difficult. The election date was announced on November 18, one day after the publication in the *Sunday Express* of a SARA poll which had indicated that the NAR was supported by 33 per cent of the electorate, the PNM by 24 per cent, and the UNC by 12 per cent. A new poll one month later, however, saw support change to 34 per cent for the PNM, 24 per cent for the NAR, and 20 per cent for the UNC. After the second poll, Ryan cautiously predicted that the PNM would win 16 seats, the NAR 11, and the UNC three to five. He declined to speculate about the fate of four seats.[192]

The UNC were experiencing vicious in-fighting between Basdeo Panday and a group of UNC members led by the party's General Secretary, Kelvin Ramnath. In March 1991, Party Chairman Dr Parasaram, a consultant psychiatrist and a pundit, resigned from his post. He accused elements in the UNC of waging an anti-Hindu, anti-Indian campaign against him, in order to appoint an African party chairman.[193] There was much friction between the Executive and the Leader, with each holding parallel meetings in constituencies, and Ramnath setting up an office for himself in the UNC's headquarters at Rienzi Complex in the constituency of Couva South. In Parliament, Ramnath had Siparia MP Govindra Roopnarine on his side as well, pitting two UNC MPs against four. By August 31, 1991, Ramnath and his supporters were replaced in the UNC executive by a 'consensus slate' including John Humphrey (Deputy Political Leader), Trevor Sudama (General Secretary), Wade Mark (Chairman), Huslie Bhaggan (Public Relations Officer), and Dr Prakash Persad (Research Officer).

Despite their removal, Ramnath, Parasaram, and Roopnarine intended to contest the coming elections on a UNC ticket. They had submitted their names in the party's primary elections for candidates for Couva South, Caroni Central, and Oropouche, respectively. At the UNC's November 24, 1991 Congress, the highest authority of the party, Ramnath and 60 others were barred from attendance. A resolution was passed there to suspend the system of primaries, professedly because of the imminence of the general elections, but, at the same time, the resolution would allow the submissions of Ramnath, Parasaram, and Roopnarine to be overridden. They did not contest. Ramesh Lawrence Maharaj was selected to contest Ramnath's constituency of Couva South.[194] Ramnath led his campaign against Panday right up to the General Elections.[195]

In addition to the UNC's internal rivalries, Panday, had on December 10, 1991, filed the first of two writs against the *Trinidad Guardian*, with whom he had had an open feud since he had called a boycott of the paper at the UNC's Inaugural Convention on July 22, 1990.[196]

The rejuvenated PNM 'government in exile' had presented a slate of new candidates[197] and a significant policy shift. At its 28th annual conference on October 9, 1988, Manning's address, 'With the PNM there is Hope: A Major Policy Statement', detailed a shift to a pragmatic outward-looking policy encouraging foreign investment, divestment, and a less dominant state, in the context of 'a stable social and economic climate' that could be produced only by 'a well-structured, highly-organised and well-managed party',[198] This was a significant departure from the PNM policies of the 1970s.

The PNM and the NAR each fielded a full slate of 36 candidates, while the UNC fielded 35.[199] All three parties fielded mainly first-time candidates. Only 15 of the original 33 NAR incumbents presented themselves for re-election. Arthur Sanderson (Fyzabad) and Jensen Fox (Port of Spain North/ St. Ann's West) ran as independents. Four ran as UNC candidates, Basdeo Panday (Couva North), Trevor Sudama (Oropouche), John Humphrey (St Augustine), Raymond Pallackdharrysingh (Caroni Central). The UNC also fielded Shamshuddin Mohammed, former PNM MP from 1966–86, Cabinet Minister from 1971–6 (one of Williams's five 'millstones'), and brother of PNM Deputy Leader Kamaluddin Mohammed, as candidate for Caroni East; and Wade Mark, TTLC executive member and unsuccessful People's Progressive Movement (PPM) candidate for Laventille in 1986.[200] The other 29 UNC candidates were new political personalities.

The results, with a voter turnout of 65.8 per cent (and 54,828 fewer voters than in 1986), shut the NAR out of Trinidad completely, despite its respectable showing in terms of votes. The PNM won 21 seats, the UNC 13, and the NAR two in Tobago (see Appendices B and C). The new PNM recaptured most of its 1966 seats, but did not obtain a two-thirds majority, the first time a government had done so since 1961. It was also the first time since 1956 that the PNM won with less than 50 per cent of the vote. As in 1981, when the ONR were expected to be the PNM's main challengers, Basdeo Panday surprised the political analysts in the Port of Spain-based press by outperforming Robinson's remaining NAR party. Compared to the ULF's eight seats in 1981, the UNC gained one through a boundary change in central Trinidad (see Appendix F), and it 'reclaimed' Princes Town, Fyzabad, Caroni East, and Nariva from the PNM.

On December 21, 1991, A.N.R Robinson resigned from the leadership of the National Alliance for Reconstruction (NAR).[201] The NAR, which had been popularly mandated with such enthusiasm in 1986, was a political failure. Its vision both economic (a private sector-led, outward-oriented strategy) and social (national unity based on a recognition of diversity) – has persisted to the end of our period of study, but it could not bring the vision into reality. The NAR government could control neither itself nor the country, losing almost every significant battle it faced after the September 1987 local government elections, whether the conflict was party indiscipline or social protest. The challenges of the period were exceptionally difficult – economic downturn, the first non-PNM government in office in 30 years – and the party, as Lloyd Best suggested, was not up to the task.

The party leadership obviously had overestimated the commitment of its early supporters and of its MPs. Reflecting on the situation later, Karl Hudson-Phillips remarked,

> *The NAR believed that the inherent value of its programme was sufficient by itself to persuade the population to continue supporting the party. It did not pay attention to the straight politics involved and the manner in which the population had become accustomed to be communicated with, as far as new programmes were concerned, so there was that. And I think when people speak about the style of Mr Robinson's leadership that more than anything else was what they were speaking about.*[202]

Indeed, perhaps more than the party it was the leader who was not up to the task. Before becoming political leader of the NAR, Robinson had disparaged Trinidad as a 'perishing society' with 'calaloo politics.'[203] As Best pointed out, the Tobagonian ethos was distinct from any in Trinidad;[204] and perhaps because of its island base and history, it was much more whole. George 'Umbala' Joseph, radio personality and NAR candidate for Arouca South in 1991, later mused,

> *I know that power stings the hand that wields it, but Robinson was, to my mind, a most misunderstood person: a man who failed to play mas in a carnival country; who simply failed at being a whore in an open air brothel. That was basically his problem; people expect the masman to 'dance de mas', display the costume, not just don the pretty thing and walk across the stage. It must be true what the experts say: 'Tobago people do not know how to play Trinidad mas.'*[205]

It might be interesting to speculate about how Eric Williams would have fared in the 1980s had he been alive. Would he have won the 1981 elections? How would he have handled the economic downturn? Would the country have disintegrated to such a deplorable level if he had retired and accepted a lesser position as Senior Minister Lee Kuan Yew did in Singapore, or accepted a higher position as Head of State, as Sir Seewosagur Ramgoolam did in Mauritius? After Williams died, neither the PNM nor the NAR could successfully prevail over Trinidad and Tobago's anarchic politics. Neither administration won a second mandate, despite the unprecedented strength of their first mandates. Economic recovery and political parity in the 1990s would provide another background for Trinidad and Tobago politics after Eric Williams, with the party system achieving a level of constancy similar to the 1961–71 period.

# *Part 3*
# *Toward Stalemate: Structural Adjustment, Indian Arrival, and Slim Majorities*

# *Six*

## THE FALL OF THE MANNING ADMINISTRATION, 1992-5: 'FATHER OF THE NATION'

In this chapter, we examine the Manning administration (1992–95) in the context of a newly emerging political, social, and economic context. The turbulent, 20-year political situation in 1971–91 with its unsettled political entities – found in Opposition while Williams was alive and in government after his death – stabilised in 1991–2000 with the PNM, UNC, and NAR, each dominating definite bases during the period. Importantly, after the NAR administration, no political party secured a two-thirds majority in Parliament. This at first unnoticed predicament would, by the beginning of the next millennium, become a major political fact of life.

This situation emerged alongside a newly liberalised Trinidad and Tobago economy, cross-party consensus on broad economic strategy, and an accompanying period of unbroken economic growth that began in 1994, and was the outstanding achievement of the Manning administration. Manning's PNM government focused on the economic restructuring of the country: selling off state enterprises, inviting foreign investors to make the natural gas sector viable, reducing the external debt, liberalising the trading and financial sectors, and revitalising Port of Spain. At the same time, the celebration in 1995 of the 150th Anniversary of Indian Arrival focused Indians socially and politically, while the UNC embarked on a serious attempt at building a disciplined and credible national party. Parity was being reached. However, combined with the sometime insupportable blunders of the Prime Minister, Manning's administration – following the same road as Chambers' and Robinson's – could not secure a second consective term.

## SETTING THE POLITICAL CONFIGURATION OF THE 1990s: THE PNM, UNC, AND NAR

*Patrick Manning being sworn in as Prime Minister in 1991 by President Noor Hassanali*

Upon taking office in December 1991, the new, 45 year-old Prime Minister Manning (b. 1946) declared that his administration would lead a 'crusade against unemployment, poverty, and destitution', while he assured his political opponents, 'There will be no vindictiveness, there will be no acrimony.'[1]

On January 17, 1992, Finance Minister Wendell Mottley (former Olympic athlete, former member of the ACDC–DLP, and PNM Minister of Industry, Commerce and Consumer Affairs in 1985–6), heralded the 1992 budget as 'the first bill of the new government in the new parliament'. The speech made clear that the PNM government was not going to ignore the 'imperatives of adjustment', using the title of the 1983 draft plan; that its priority was to see that such adjustment was successful; and that 'the task before us . . . [would not be] easy and . . . [could not] be accomplished in a short time.'[2]

The most pressing concern was identified as the rebuilding of foreign exchange reserves. This, however, was closely related to the servicing of public external debt, achieving sustainable economic growth, and effecting a significant and durable reduction in unemployment. Success in exporting activity was to be made a 'national priority', with the government committed to supporting exporters with a 'full range of technical assistance and extension services for training, product design, market penetration, etc.' It was declared that foreign direct investment would be required to supplement domestic saving, and that the economy needed to be liberalised ('fewer restrictions, barriers and special protectionist devices') in order to make local firms more competitive. Mottley announced that the state would change its role from venture capitalist in energy and energy-related industries, trustee on behalf of the public, and investor of last resort. The PNM government firmly committed itself to a policy of divestment, seeking the 'fullest value' for state assets, the 'widest possible shareholder participation', and pledged that proceeds would not be used for the settlement of salary arrears accumulated by the previous regime. The government promised to continue the tight fiscal policy but would couple it with a more conservative monetary policy than the previous regime did, stressing the need for 'prudent financial management'.[3]

To support its efforts, the government announced that it would draw US$40 million from the World Bank and Japan EXIM-BANK in connection with the Structural Adjustment Loan of 1989, and that it did not plan to take out any major new loans.[4] Despite the positive growth in real GDP in 1990–91, Mottley reminded members that the decade of the 1980s had been characterised as the 'lost decade' for development and that in that decade Trinidad and Tobago had experienced a decline in real income of more than 30 per cent, with an increased incidence of poverty. 'So far,' he added, 'the 1990s do not offer much cause for optimism. There is recession abroad and political turmoil in sensitive areas of the world.' Dr Williams' watchwords, 'Discipline, Production, Tolerance', were invoked to emphasise the long-term challenge that the country faced.[5]

In addition to clarifying the PNM's new style of economic management, Manning had made efforts to address ethnicity – particularly the place of Indians in the society – more directly than did his PNM predecessors, not only because of the political breakthroughs Indians had made under the

NAR government but very likely also as a consequence of his origins in south Trinidad.[6] In choosing government senators and forming the new cabinet, Manning announced that he wanted to redress the ethnic imbalance found in the PNM team, which had included only four Indian PNM members of parliament. Manning also mooted the possibility of an Indo-Trinidadian leading the PNM in the future. However, PNM Party Chairman Lenny Saith had been the only Indian to be made a member of the 14-member Cabinet (as Minister of Planning) via an appointment to the Senate.[7]

Apart from government, the Manning administration established at the University of the West Indies the Centre for Ethnic Studies (headed by Drs. John LaGuerre and Selwyn Ryan) which had produced three major studies: *Ethnicity and Employment Practices in the Public and Private Sectors in Trinidad and Tobago*,[8] *A Study of the Secondary School Population in Trinidad and Tobago: Placement Patterns and Practices, A Research Report*,[9] and *Ethnicity and the Media in Trinidad*.[10] At a symbolic level, in March 1992 the prime minister opened an international conference on Hindi (held in Trinidad and Tobago for the first time) by announcing, 'May this conference be successful and rewarding to you all', in the Hindi language.[11]

However, a review of the first hundred days of the new government brought criticism from the UNC and the press that the only piece of legislation passed had been the budget.[12]

Meanwhile, the UNC had begun to strengthen its electoral machinery, which it identified as a major weakness contributing to its defeat in the 1991 elections. On June 6, 1992, at an Indo-Caribbean Conference at York University in Toronto, Ramesh Lawrence Maharaj, human rights lawyer, UNC MP for Couva South, and opposition Chief Whip in Parliament, pointed out to the audience that in 1991 the combined UNC and NAR votes outnumbered those of the PNM, and that only 7,000 votes had prevented the UNC from capturing the government.[13] In the constituencies of Pointe-à-Pierre, St Joseph, Barataria/San Juan, Ortoire/Mayaro, and Tunapuna, if the UNC had captured 7,131 votes from the 16,083 NAR voters, or from the 38,637 non-voters – if not from the PNM voters themselves – it would have secured 18 seats in 1991 (see Table 6.1). Alternatively, if the UNC and the NAR votes had been combined, not only would the PNM have lost these five seats, it also would have lost San Fernando West, in which the PNM polled 6,934 votes, the UNC 2,073 votes, and the NAR 5,087.[14]

***Table 6.1. Five Narrowest Losses of the UNC, 1991 General Elections***

| CONSTITUENCY | PNM | UNC | NAR | OTHER | REJECTED BALLOTS | % VOTED | MARGIN OF VICTORY |
|---|---|---|---|---|---|---|---|
| Pointe-à-Pierre | 5,580 | 5,388 | 4,131 | 245 | 46 | 67.4% | 192 |
| St Joseph | 5,927 | 4,615 | 3,497 | 185 | 128 | 64.5% | 1,312 |
| Barataria/San Juan | 6,052 | 4,689 | 2,626 | 188 | 64 | 62.0% | 1,363 |
| Ortoire/Mayaro | 7,578 | 6,013 | 2,563 | 0 | 86 | 69.5% | 1,565 |
| Tunapuna | 6,872 | 4,173 | 3,266 | 257 | 114 | 65.3% | 2,699 |
| TOTALS | 32,009 | 24,878 | 16,083 | 875 | 438 | 65.8% | 7,131 |

*Source*: GORTT (1992b)

In March 1992 the UNC established a Constitution Commission chaired by Maharaj to reform the party's constitution 'in order for the necessary Party structures to be put in place to facilitate election victories and to assist the Party in governing the country.'[15]

The NAR, on the other hand, continued its process of abridgement. Robinson apparently had been piqued by the party's defeat. After his resignation from leadership of the party on December 21, 1991, he absented himself from the ceremonial opening of parliament on January 13, 1992 and the three-day budget debate starting on January 17. Pamela Nicholson, NAR MP for Tobago West, also had been absent in the first sittings of the new parliament.[16] Winston Dookeran, NAR candidate, former Minister of Planning and Moblisation, and former Acting Prime Minister– who had been defeated in Chaguanas in 1991 by the little-known UNC candidate, Hulsie Bhaggan (UNC public relations officer), by a vote of 9,259 to 3,206[17] – refused nomination for party leadership, as did former Minister of Finance, Selby Wilson. Karl Hudson-Phillips allowed himself to be nominated on the condition that he would serve as interim leader for six months, but withdrew his candidacy on the eve of the elections. The post was won, without challenge, by 36 year old Dr Carson Charles, former Minister of Works and former MP for St Joseph, a minor figure who had only joined the ONR in February 1986, the same month that the party dissolved itself. Charles, however, announced that he would only hold the position for six months and seek re-election at the NAR's Annual Convention in November 1992.[18]

Local government elections, postponed for one year by the NAR government in September 1990 during the state of emergency, were held on September 28, 1992. The elections attracted a 39.8 per cent voter turnout, slightly lower than the 41 per cent figure for 1987. They gave the PNM an overall majority (50.3 per cent of the vote, in contrast to the 44.8 per cent in the 1991 general elections) and resulted in the PNM's control of ten of the 14 regional and municipal corporations (see Appendix F). The UNC's showing was not totally discreditable.[19] On the eve of the elections, Panday declared that the results would be a 'statement as to whether people believe . . . we are in fact an alternative'.[20] The UNC had not put up candidates for 34 seats, but were able to win just over half of the 105 seats that it did contest. The NAR, on the other hand, contested 118 seats, but were not able to win a single one. They were shut out from Trinidad more resoundingly than had they been the year before (see Appendix B).

Ten weeks after, in the THA elections of December 7, 1992, however, the NAR showed its continuing strength in Tobago. The party held on to its 11 seats with 58.2 per cent of all ballots cast, and the PNM held its single seat with 36.7 per cent. Both parties contested all 12 seats,[21] and the UNC did not participate at all. The difference in party strength was not the only contrast with the Trinidad elections as the number of voters increased from 16,720 in 1988 to 17,660 in 1992.[22] Tobago had developed its own political dynamic.

The results of these elections confirmed the situation established in 1988 in Tobago (or in 1984 if one wanted to describe the DAC victory as a 'NAR' one) and in 1991 in Trinidad: the NAR dominating Tobago, with a small PNM opposition and no UNC presence; and the PNM and the UNC competing in Trinidad, with the NAR not able to make a showing. The persistence of the political entities would characterise the remainder of the decade in a similar way to the 1961–71 PNM–DLP balance that followed the inchoate 1925–61 period.

## STRUCTURAL ADJUSTMENT UNDER THE PNM, 1992–5

Meanwhile, the PNM government fulfilled the process of structural adjustment first outlined in 1983 by the Demas Report, but seriously inaugurated by the Robinson administration: trade and financial liberalisation, divestment of state holdings, increased foreign direct investment, outward orientation, and export diversification.

A Trade Reform Programme, sponsored by the World Bank, was embarked on to improve the institutional and legislative structures facilitating trade between Trinidad and Tobago and the outside world.[23] In implementation of the programme, in 1992 non-oil manufactured items were removed from the import Negative List, import duties were frozen, and existing duties were to be phased out over a three to five year period, significantly moving towards a free and open trading regime. Institutional reform included following the recommendations of a 1986 UNCTAD Report to reduce the number of steps (i.e. documentation and bureaucratic procedures) needed for the arrival and departure of ships from the 81 found in the survey, to 45.[24] To help establish relations between local industries, on the one hand, and overseas markets and investors, on the other, the Industrial Development Corporation, the Tourism Development Authority, and the Export Development Agency were merged in 1994 to create the Tourism and Industrial Development Corporation (TIDCO), mandated to help local businesses create jobs, earn foreign exchange, and attract investment.[25] Among Trinidad and Tobago's efforts to increase its international profile was the first summit meeting of the Association of Caribbean States which had been held in Port of Spain on the 17th and 18th of August, 1995, one year after the organisation was established in Cartagena, Colombia. The summit inaugurated a new level of co-operation among the Caribbean, Central America, Mexico, Colombia and Venezuela and was attended by six heads of state (including President Fidel Castro) and ten heads of government, together with one vice-president and government ministers from eight other member states. Five associate or observer governments were represented at ministerial or official level, and there were delegations from 21 regional and international organisations.[26]

In the financial sphere, on April 7, 1992 the government permitted non-residents to hold foreign exchange accounts in local banks, and 'net exporters' were granted unrestricted use of local foreign currency accounts. Although Mottley had declared that currency liberalisation was 'not within the immediate plans of this administration'[27] in 1993, the government did in fact abolish exchange controls on current and capital transactions and floated the Trinidad and Tobago dollar.[28] On August 1, 1995, money laundering laws came into effect, introducing fines and prison sentences for banks that provided service to persons failing to provide adequate evidence of identity.[29] Impressively, the Trinidad and Tobago dollar was able to maintain its value with only slight depreciation from TT$5.35:US$1.00 in 1993 to TT$5.95:US$1.00 in 1995 (see Appendix D).[30]

In 1995, the government published its *Report on Public Participation in Industrial and Commercial Activities* outlining the PNM's programme of divestment, the most extensive to date.[31] Of the 87 companies that comprised government's portfolio as at January 1992, the Investments Division had reviewed 66 of those Enterprises and submitted recommendations approved by Cabinet in 1994 (see Table 6.2).

***Table 6.2. Divestment Programme as at December 31, 1994***

| | | | |
|---|---|---|---|
| Companies Divested | | | 33 |
| | Completed | 15 | |
| | Being Completed 6 | | |
| | In progress | 5 | |
| | In initial stage | 7 | |
| Companies Liquidated | | | 23 |
| | Completed | 14 | |
| | In Progress | 9 | |
| Companies Restructed/ Merged | | | 8 |
| Compaies to be retained | | | 2 |
| TOTAL | | | 66 |

*Source*: GORTT (1995)

However, according to a Central Bank memorandum, the Manning administration divested 26 companies through full and partial privatisation or liquidation. Fourteen of these divestments occurred in 1994.[32]

The government's 1995 report summarised the divestment process for 18 enterprises as seen in Table 6.3.

***Table 6.3. Summary of the Divestment Process, 1995***

| | |
|---|---|
| Open International bids | 2 |
| Open National bids | 3 |
| Stock Exchange | 4 |
| Employee Buy-Out | 1 |
| Strategic Partner/Stock Exchange | 1 |
| Strategic Partner/Open International Bids | 1 |
| Strategic Partner/Open Bids | 1 |
| Strategic Partner | 1 |
| Strategic Alliance | 1 |
| Open bids | 2 |
| Sold to Lessee | 1 |

*Source*: GORTT (1995)

Interestingly, the NAR was critical of the PNM's divestment process, arguing that the NAR government's proposed National Investment Corporation would have allowed for a larger number of shares to be held by Trinidad and Tobago nationals, expanded the local stock market, satisfied debt to public servants, and increased domestic savings and investment.[33] In a television interview on November 3, 1995, Robinson repeated, 'This was a historic opportunity that this (PNM) Government had to bring the bulk of the population into the mainstream of economic activity and let the ordinary citizen feel that he had a stake in the country by owing [*sic*] shares in what were then the State enterprises .... It meant a judicious mix of foreign investment and domestic participation in business. And this historic moment has been lost.'[34]

The UNC expressed concern over the majority sale of BWIA. On January 6, 1995, on behalf of Tobago hotelier Allan Clovin and broadcasting researcher Peta Bain, Ramesh Lawrence Maharaj filed a constitutional motion to block the sale. It was alleged that the United States Acker Group, with whom the government had signed a sale agreement that same day, were given privileged information and privileged treatment compared to his clients who were Trinidad and Tobago nationals. The UNC had opposed the bill for the majority sale of BWIA on January 20, 1995, but the sale was finalised on February 22.[35]

The divestment programme seemed key in the Manning administration's efforts to service government debt, build up foreign exchange, and to finance the adjustment programme. For instance, in the 1995 budget (presented on November 25, 1994) Minister Mottley announced that the proceeds of divesting state enterprises amounted to TT$544 million, of which TT$329 million were reserved for net external repayments and TT$99 million for net internal repayments.[36] The *Report on Public Sector Participation* had noted that up to the time of publication in 1995, capital receipts from divestment totalled TT$1,154.76 million, with the two largest amounts coming from the sale of the Fertiliser Company of Trinidad and Tobago/Trinidad and Tobago Urea Company (FERTRIN/TTUC) (US$91.47 million) and ISCOTT (US$70.05 million). Of these receipts, it was reported that US$58 million had been utilised for debt repayment (US$23.1 million for foreign debt).[37] Importantly, too, the divestment programme was designed to have a minimal impact on overall levels of unemployment. The divestment of FERTRIN/TTUC, Angostura Holdings, Angostura Bitters, Neal and Massy Holdings Ltd., Polymer (Caribbean) Ltd., Trinidad and Tobago Methanol Company, and Trinidad Cement, Ltd. was reported not to have resulted in any employment loss.[38]

Using data provided by the Divestment Secretariat of Trinidad and Tobago dated August 10, 1997, Maingot has provided different values.[39] These figures show that of 20 companies privatised between 1992 and 1995, TT$459 million had been received by the government. They also show that 14 per cent of the value had been purchased by nationals, and 86 per cent by non-nationals (see Table 6.4).

*Table 6.4. Divestments, 1992–98*

| LOCAL DIVESTMENTS | Date Divested | Value (TT$M) |
|---|---|---|
| Farrell House (1975) Limited (100%) | Nov-92 | 4.8 |
| Trinidad and Tobago Printing and Packaging (100%) | Nov-93 | 11.6 |
| National Fruit Processors (100%) | Apr-93 | 0.2 |
| Angostura Bitters (88.0% preference shares) | Dec-93 | 0.4 |
| Angostura Holdings (0.02% ordinary shares) | Dec-93 | 0.1 |
| Neal and Massy Holdings (3.12% ordinary shares) | Dec-93 | 5.0 |
| National Poultry (18% GOTT) | Jul-94 | 0.1 |
| Polymer (Caribbean) Ltd. (25.5% preference shares) | Jul-94 | 0.3 |
| Shipping Company of Trinidad and Tobago (100%) | Dec-94 | 5.5 |
| Allied Innkeepers (Holiday Inn) | Jun-95 | 2.6 |
| National Flour Mills (20%) | May-95 | 23.6 |
| Reinsurance Company of Trinidad and Tobago Ltd. (TRINRE) | Dec-95 | 10.0 |
| **TOTAL VALUE OF LOCAL DIVESTMENTS** | | 64.2 |

| FOREIGN DIVESTMENTS | Date Divested | Value (TT$M) | Principal Investor |
|---|---|---|---|
| Fertrin/TTUC (100%)[40] | Mar-93 | 132.1 | Arcadian |
| Trinidad and Tobago Methanol (TTMC) (31%) | Jan-94 | 47 | Ferrostaal/Helm |
| Arawak Cement (49%) | Mar-94 | 2.8 | Domestic |
| Trinidad Cement Limited (TCL) (20%) | Aug-94 | 10.8 | CEMEX |
| Petrotrin O2C2/UFC Plant | Aug-94 | 4.4 | Domestic |
| Power Generation Company of TT (49%) | Dec-94 | 107.5 | SEI/Amoco |
| Iron and Steel Company of TT (100%) | Dec-94 | 70.1 | ISPAT |
| BWIA (51.0%) | Jan-95 | 20.1 | Acker Group |
| **TOTAL VALUE OF FOREIGN DIVESTMENTS** | | 394.8 | |

*Source*: Maingot (1998, 21)

Following the NAR's introduction of Cable and Wireless into the local telecommunications service in 1989, in May 1995, the British company, Severn Trent, had been selected as the international partner for the Water and Sewerage Authority (WASA).[41] On December 23, 1994, the Power Generation Company of Trinidad and Tobago was established as a joint venture company out of the partial divestment of the Trinidad and Tobago Electricity Company to the Amoco Business Development Company and

Southern Electrical International. The government retained majority shareholding.[42]

Divestment and rationalisation stimulated investment, largely from outside the country. During its term of office, the NAR government had attempted to renew the declining oil industry, in terms of exploration activity and refining. On June 26, 1991, the NAR had signed a 15-year US$260 million agreement with the IDB for the modernisation of the Trinidad and Tobago Oil Company's (TRINTOC) Pointe-à-Pierre refinery (taken over from Texaco in 1985), and for land and marine crude recovery. When the PNM came to power in December that year, however, the IDB stopped the loan. But in July 1992 it was reinstated because the IDB considered the PNM's rationalisation approach to be superior to that adopted by the previous government.[43] In particular, the Trinidad and Tobago government created a new oil company, the Petroleum Company of Trinidad and Tobago (PETROTRIN) in 1993, incorporating the Trinidad and Tobago Petroleum Company (TRINTOPEC) and TRINTOC, creating the largest of the four state-owned oil and gas companies operating in Trinidad and Tobago.[44] The formation of PETROTRIN was a condition for another US$410 million loan for upgrading the country's refineries and the recovery of heavy oil. In May 1993, the first phase of the refinery upgrade project was completed, as part of a plan to increase the full refining capacity of the Pointe-à-Pierre plant from the existing 100,000 barrels per day to 160,000 by the end of the 1995.[45] In addition to refining, crude oil production picked up briefly in 1994 and 1995 (see Appendix D). In October and November 1995, PETROTRIN received favourable assessments from *Petrovision* and the *Petroleum Economist.*[46]

Meanwhile, foreign investment in the natural gas sector had also been picking up. In January 1992 Amoco, (Trinidad and Tobago's most significant foreign investor, beginning operation in the country in 1961), announced that it would invest US$300 million over ten years to expand the production and marketing of natural gas to further increase its non-oil investments in Trinidad.[47] On September 9, 1993, British Gas and Texaco (who had left Trinidad and Tobago in 1984) agreed to jointly invest US$300 million over twenty years for natural gas production. According to the *Economist Intelligence Unit,*[48] both these investments resulted from the PNM's policy shift after the apparently costly failure of the NAR government's Trinidad and Tobago Marine Petroleum Company (TRINTOMAR). The company, which began production in 1990, was the government's first effort to extract in deep water off the east coast, in an attempt to ensure that the country would not be dependent on a foreign gas supplier, namely Amoco Trinidad. Production levels were well below expectations, however, reportedly due to faulty reserve estimates.[49]

Significant natural gas finds had occurred during the period. In 1992 there were 8.4 trillion cubic feet (tcf) of proven natural gas marine reserves, 4.9 trillion probable and 0.6 trillion possible. In 1995, the figures were 12.3 trillion proven, 3.7 trillion probable, and 1.9 trillion possible.[50] Between May 1994 and April 1995, Amoco Trinidad Oil Co. alone had made new natural gas finds of 3.5 tcf.[51]

In 1992, Cabot LNG Corporation, the largest and oldest liquefied natural gas (LNG) importer in North America, approached the state-owned National Gas Company (NGC) to discuss the possibility of buying gas from Trinidad and Tobago. It was the fourth time that such an idea had been mooted since the first significant discoveries of natural gas in 1968, but this was the first time that a buyer initiated discussions. In February 1993, Amoco, British Gas, Cabot, and the NGC began evaluating the feasibility of building an LNG plant in Point Fortin in St Patrick, the original, now contracting oil-producing area.[52] The study indicated that the project should be about one-third bigger than originally envisaged and would require an investment of US$1 billion. Cabot committed itself to purchasing 60 per cent of the plant's output and Enagas of Spain was brought in to purchase the other 40 per cent. In July 1995, an initial shareholding structure was announced, but was later revised to include Repsol (Enagas's parent company). The final equity structure was Amoco Trinidad (LNG) BV (34 per cent), British Gas Trinidad LNG Limited (26 per cent), Repsol LNG Port of Spain BV (20 per cent), Cabot Trinidad LNG Limited (10 per cent) and NGC Trinidad and Tobago LNG Limited (10 per cent).[53]

Investment in the petrochemical sector – nitrogenous fertilisers, methanol, and ammonia – also began to accelerate. In addition to the March 1993 sale of FERTRIN (51 per cent government-owned) and TTUC (100 per cent government-owned) to Arcadian, the Caribbean Methanol Company – a joint venture between the emerging Trinidadian conglomerate, Caribbean Life (CL) Financial (64.9 per cent) [54], Ferrostaal of Germany (25.1 per cent), and Methanex Corp. of the US (10 per cent) – began in 1991 construction, of the country's second methanol plant, which came on-stream in November 1993. The 500,000 tonnes per year plant was located next to the state-owned Trinidad and Tobago Methanol Company (TTMC) plant at Point Lisas and cost US$200 million. In 1994 Ferrostaal and its partner Helm bought a 31 per cent share in the TTMC for US$47 million, and signed an agreement with the government to construct a third methanol plant at a cost of US$235 million. Also in 1994, a letter of intent was signed by Ferrostaal, Helm, the NGC, the TTMC and the government of Trinidad and Tobago to develop a fourth methanol plant, involving an investment of US$250 million, initially planned for La Brea (also in St Patrick), but later moved to Point Lisas.[55] In June 1995, the Mitsui company of Japan bought a 25.1 per cent stake in TTMC from the government for an undisclosed price, leaving the government a 43.9 per cent share in the company.[56] In December 1994, plans were announced by Farmland Industries of Kansas City (owned by a US farmers' organisation) and the Mississippi Chemical Corporation to build also in La Brea the world's largest ammonia plant at 600,000 tonnes per annum, estimated to cost US$1.8 billion.[57]

There had been not only expansion in petrochemicals but in steel as well. In January 1993, the Nucor Corporation of the US announced that it had chosen Trinidad and Tobago as the site for its first overseas operation, building a US$60 million iron-carbide production plant, with a capacity of 320,000 tonnes per year, processing cheap iron ore from Brazil with Trinidad's cheap natural gas, to be used in Nucor's flat-rolled sheet mills in the US. Also in the sector, on November 3, 1994, Caribbean Ispat Limited announced its plans to purchase its facility, which it had been managing since 1989, and to sell 40 per cent of the share capital to nationals of Trinidad and Tobago.[58]

These major investments, in addition to the Investment Sector Reform Programme embarked upon by the government with assistance from the World Bank, contributed to the great increase in foreign direct investment, which totalled US$1,360.3 million between 1992 and 1995, almost three times the 1987–91 total of US$498.5 million during the NAR administration. Importantly, the government constructed the Brian Lara Promenade in downtown Port of Spain in 1994. This greatly helped to revive the capital, after it had been devastated by the attempted coup and the subsequent looting in 1990.

The positive growth in 1990–91, which was reversed in 1992–93, resumed in 1994. This recovery would be sustained until the end of the decade, accompanied by, and achieved through, some significant changes in economic structure (see Appendix D).

In 1994, real GDP growth reached 5 per cent, the highest rate since 1980, when real GDP growth of 10.4 per cent resulted from the oil shock of 1979–80.[59] Growth in 1994, significantly, was underpinned by oil revenues that amounted to only 25.1 per cent of total revenue, as compared to the last peak of 62.1 per cent in 1981 or to 40 per cent in 1991, the last year real GDP growth occurred. Total government expenditure, too, was 25.8 per cent of GDP at current market prices in 1994, as compared to the last peak of 47.4 per cent in 1982. The government was also able to eliminate its fiscal deficit and emerge in surplus in 1995. Importantly, in 1993 the country recorded a surplus in its external balance of payments, the first since 1981. In the current situation, foreign direct investment played a much larger role in the economy, hitting a high of US$521 million in 1994. (The previous high was US$202.8 million in 1975.) The degree of openness, measured as export and imports divided by GDP, reached a 16-year high of 93 per cent in 1995. Significantly, the value of non-fuel exports exceeded the value of fuel exports in 1994. Foreign reserves, too, had been built up rapidly, multiplying three-and-a-half times in 1993–94.

However, the significantly lower level of investment in the 1980s and 1990s might also be considered part of the structural change as well. Investment, measured as gross capital formation, hit a high of 12.5 per cent of real GDP in 1994, but was still lower than anything before 1986 when the ratio was 17 per cent. (In 1980 the rate of gross capital formation reached a high of 64.6 per cent of real GDP.) There was also very little capital expenditure by government, reaching a low in 1993 of 4.4 per cent of total expenditure at current market prices, from a high of 47.7 per cent in 1981.

Unemployment – a persistent problem – had been brought down to 17.2 per cent in 1995, the same rate as in 1986. This was still a higher figure that any before 1986, however. In addition, growth was accompanied by an unpredictable rate of inflation, and the debt to GDP ratio still remained fairly high.[60]

## THE 1994 BY-ELECTIONS: POLITICAL OPENINGS IN TRINIDAD

In 1994, quite unusually, five by-elections took place. In 1993, UNC Councillor for Curepe, Ivan Roopia, died and a local government by-election was called for May 24, 1994. A local government by-election for PNM-controlled Petit Valley/Cocorite had also been scheduled for the same day. On March 13, 1994, PNM MP for Laventille West and Minister of Public Utilities Morris Marshall died, and the by-election for his parliamentary seat was also scheduled for the same day.[61] Soon after, on April 16, 1994, Cyril Rajaram, PNM MP for Pointe-à-Pierre (which the UNC targeted as a borderline seat) died too. The by-election for that parliamentary seat was scheduled for May 30, 1994.[62] On May 22, two days before the elections, UNC MP for Caroni East, Shamshuddin Mohammed, also passed away.[63]

These elections occurred soon after the PNM government had been forced to announce a 'mini-budget' (Variation of Appropriation) in March 1994, due to a fall in oil prices. The Laventille West, Petit Valley/Cocorite, and Curepe seats were returned to their respective parties. Interestingly, a record ten candidates vied for the Laventille West seat, including a short-lived party organised by the Jamaat-al-Muslimeen (see Table 6.5).[64] However, the Pointe-à-Pierre seat in the House of Representatives, which the PNM won by only 192 votes in 1991, switched hands to the UNC (symbolically on the 149th anniversary of Indian Arrival in Trinidad), giving the opposition an unprecedented 14 seats.

***Table 6.5. By-Election Statistics, 1994***

| Seat | Date | PNM | UNC | NAR |
|---|---|---|---|---|
| Laventille West (House of Representatives) | 24 May 1994 | 3,878 | 348 | 365 |
| | 16 December 1991 | 10,947 | 211 | 2,034 |
| Petit Valley/Cocorite (Diego Martin Corporation) | 24 May 1994 | 826 | 162 | 353 |
| | 28 September 1992 | 1,507 | – | 664 |
| Curepe (Tunapuna/Piarco Corporation) | 24 May 1994 | 638 | 1,573 | 102 |
| | 28 September 1992 | 704 | 1,657 | – |
| Pointe-à-Pierre (House of Representatives) | 30 May 1994 | 4,205 | 7,318 | 868 |
| | 16 December 1991 | 5,580 | 5,388 | 4,131 |

*Sources*: Siewah (1994: 461); Siewah and Arjoonsingh (1998, vol. 1: 325–7), GORTT ([1993b]: 291-2)

The Caroni East by-election was later scheduled for August 22, 1994. The NAR and the UNC attempted to forge a coalition and appeared together on a Joint UNC-NAR Unity Platform at St Helena Junction on July 29, 1994. The alliance was extended to include the small, new (and short-lived) NDP party led by former NAR leader, Dr Carson Charles. The coalition did not last as the NAR objected to the UNC's connections with the Jamaat-al-Muslimeen. Exacerbating the situation, Jamaat member Omowale Muhammed had sent a note to Panday while on the unity platform. The UNC eventually recaptured the seat by itself.[65]

Meanwhile, the NAR continued its Trinidadian demise. In the 1994 by-elections it continued to draw fewer shares of vote while, at the leadership level, more people were leaving. In November 1992, Horace Broomes, public relations officer, quit; on May 27, 1993, political leader Carson Charles quit, replaced by Selby Wilson; and, on October 23, 1994, the entire executive resigned.

## THE CONSOLIDATION OF THE UNC, 1992–95

Unlike the ULF, which had lost electoral support from 1976 to 1981, the UNC was growing stronger. In October 1993 the UNC's Constitution Commission presented the draft of the new constitution to the national executive of the party, the parliamentary caucus of the party, and then to conferences of activists of the party. At one of these conventions, Panday reiterated, 'the UNC had more votes than was necessary in order to win those [borderline] constituencies. Had we been able to bring out those votes on election day the UNC would have had 18 seats, the PNM 16 and NAR 2 seats. And had the NAR not divided our votes in 1991, we would have won 19 seats.'[66] In an interview with *Newsday*[67] on March 26, 1995 Panday confidently maintained that the majority of NAR supporters would switch to the UNC once they realised that the NAR had 'no life in it'.[68]

Populist appeals were made to Indians, by allusion to the recently published 1990 Census data showing that they constituted 40.3 per cent of the population of Trinidad and Tobago, as compared to Africans who made up 39.6 per cent, as well as to the 'masses in the East/West Corridor'. These, Panday argued, were 'coming around to the view that they are not the PNM, but the beasts of burden of the PNM, whose backs are ridden election after election by a small French Creole clique supported by a black managerial elite', while aggressively stating 'the party is not content to be in a position of opposition. We are preparing to take the government, and if we are really to mobilise our forces, we need to strengthen our structure.'[69]

The UNC seriously attempted to present itself as an alternative government, similar to Manning's 'government in exile' strategy in 1987–91, preparing itself to capitalise on the new government's perhaps inevitable mistakes.[70] Internationally, the UNC had gained legitimation through its participation in the Commonwealth delegation that monitored South Africa's first all-race elections held on April 26 to 29, 1994.[71] At home, the UNC required that its MPs of both Houses attend weekly Caucus meetings where policy and strategy for debates were discussed and adopted. It was recognised that 'appropriate disciplinary action against members who broke Party lines was necessary to remove or reduce the perception held by a section of the electorate that the Party did not have the strength to impose discipline on its Parliamentarians',[72] no doubt to prevent damage to the party as had occurred during Panday's fights with Ramnath in 1991, Robinson in 1986–87, and Shah in 1977-78.

A test came with Hulsie Bhaggan, MP for Chaguanas, who became prominent and controversial in 1993 by her deeply taboo-ridden public allegations that a spate of rapes in central Trinidad were carried out against Indian women by African men. In November 1993, Bhaggan was jailed for blocking the north-bound lane of the Uriah Butler Highway, protesting against the poor public works leading to floods in the plains of Central Trinidad. She led UNC MPs Kris Jurai (Nariva) and Mohammed Haniff (Princes Town) in the action, without the authorisation or knowledge of the UNC leadership. Panday publicly expressed disapproval, noting that the demonstration created an impression of irresponsibility within the UNC.[73] On June 24, 1994 Bhaggan supported the PNM government's bill to amend the Corporal Punishment Act, which the UNC had opposed. Despite her assurances that she did not oppose the party in general, Bhaggan was subsequently sidelined by the UNC parliamentary caucus for flouting the party line. She became openly critical of the UNC leadership, charging that there was a 'dictatorship' in the party, and that 'the personal views of a few formed the basis of the party line'. She was particularly critical of Ramesh Lawrence Maharaj. Bhaggan echoed Nizam Mohammed in 1987 and Roy Joseph in 1946, with her statement, 'Trinidad and Tobago has come of age and MPs can't be restricted by party line any more like in the 60s and 70s. The population is educated more than ever before and the populace is now forced to think and form its own opinions. It is therefore the job of the MP to seek out what these views are and bring them to Parliament.'[74] Bhaggan argued for a 'more democratic and meaningful approach' to running the party, and claimed that she had no intention of leaving the UNC voluntarily.[75] Bhaggan, who seemed to gain much sympathy from the Creole-oriented women's organisations and the daily press (she was subsequently given her own newspaper column in the *Trinidad Guardian*), formed the 'Monday Club' within the UNC after she was banned from representing the party, and, on December 11, 1994, founded her own political party, the Movement for Unity and Progress (MUP).[76] Bhaggan was not able to persuade any UNC MPs to join her, although she was joined by Jamal Mohammed, son of the late UNC MP for Caroni East, Shamshuddin Mohammed.[77]

The UNC faced an additional challenge at the end of 1994. After a party meeting at the Rienzi Complex on November 16, 1994, less than a month before the MUP was formed, Panday marched with his supporters to the Couva police station and gave himself up to the police, where he was arrested on five indictable offences: three indecent assault and two rape charges. He was released on TT$75,000 bail. Five days earlier, on November 11, the weekly tabloid *Trinidad and Tobago Mirror*,[78] under the front page headline 'Move to Nail Panday in Court!' reported that a private fund had been set up to retain the services of senior counsel Theodore Guerra (former NAR MP for Port of Spain South) to prosecute Panday. At the Rienzi complex before his arrest, Panday defiantly declared, 'They believed that I would lie down and die on the ground with my feet in the air. Old politicians never die, they become more sexy.' He warned that the UNC would be subjected to 'the worst kind of propaganda, vilification and attack. This (impending arrest) is only the beginning. When the time comes for election, the people will decide if they still want me. And if they don't, I will accept their decision with equanimity. In the meantime, I am standing here waiting to be arrested. I hope Manning does not disappoint me.' Speaking the next day in Tunapuna, Panday linked the charges to collusion among the 'parasitic oligarchy' (defined as the 'small white clique buttressed by a black managerial elite' who monopolise the media, the banks, and the 'lucrative aspects of the import export trade'), the PNM, the 'drug mafia', and Bhaggan's Monday Club (which would soon become the MUP), and stated that his arrest would instead give him the opportunity to expose the collaborators. Panday claimed that the SARA poll of December 1993 and the Oxford Analytica poll of June 1994, which both put the UNC ahead of the PNM, frightened the 'clique' into taking desperate measures. With great ribald humour, he lambasted the sexual assault charges in its details, and in conclusion warned his supporters to 'be prepared for a snap election'.[79]

On December 13, 1994, two out of three charges of indecent assault were dismissed as 'substantially defective' by the Couva district court. Hearing was adjourned on the other indecent assault charge and two rape charges. On January 24, 1995, Panday was re-arrested on two revised charges of indecent assault and was released on bail of TT$30,000. On March 10, 1995, two charges of indecent assault were dismissed for the second time, and their re-laying after being dismissed in December was ruled an abuse of process on the part of the Director of Public Prosecutions (DPP). In April 1995 Panday accordingly filed a suit against the state for damages for malicious prosecution.[80]

On March 26, 1995, the UNC held its National Assembly at which the party formally adopted its new constitution. Notably present and in support of Panday was former rival, Kelvin Ramnath.[81] Severed links had started to be re-forged. Bhaggan was formally expelled from the party on August 13, 1995.[82] The UNC petitioned to have Bhaggan's Chaguanas seat declared vacant, but Deputy Speaker Rupert Griffith (MP for Arima) rejected it, since the standing orders of the House did not provide for the recognition of parties or their leaders.[83] The UNC had its seats reduced to 13 once again. There were other lesser defections from the UNC in 1995. Senator Mumtaz Hosein resigned on September 1995, saying that he had lost confidence in the party leadership. Also, three UNC councillors – Mahendra Ramlogan, Charles Persad, and Sheila Boodoosingh – resigned from the UNC to join the PNM.[84] These defections, however, did not seem to harm the party. In particular, the charges against Panday seemed to boost his support by giving the party opportunity to organise a series of public meetings.[85] In addition, new bonds were being formed. Trinidad-born, former US Congressman and former Chairman of the US Congressional Black Caucus, Mervyn Dymally, who returned to Trinidad in 1993, joined the UNC.[86] Dymally was also friend and cousin of Nicholas Simonette, former PNM Senator and General Secretary, and former ONR founder and executive member. His intervention had helped to broaden the UNC's racial appeal, while providing the party with an excellent link to US political circles.

## 'FATHER OF THE NATION' AND INDIAN ARRIVAL: TOWARD THE SNAP ELECTIONS OF 1995

While the UNC was building up its machinery the Manning administration was making serious political errors. In January 1994 Minister of Industry and Commerce Senator Brian Kuei Tung had resigned, and the Prime Minister expressed his displeasure at the press's critical coverage of the incident.[87] While a relatively isolated event at the time, it would feed more than one year later into a series of events which severely lowered Manning's esteem among much of the population. In April 1995 Manning had dismissed (by fax, reportedly) Alexander Lau, honorary consul in Hong Kong. The prime minister had apparently taken action because, while he was making an official visit to Hong Kong, together with permanent secretary permanent secretary Knowlston Gift, the consul was absent from the colony. Lau protested that he had notified the Minister of Foreign Affairs, Ralph Maraj (MP for San Fernando West) in March that he would be absent from Hong Kong at that time, a fact which Maraj had confirmed. On May 5, Lau threatened to sue the prime minister for wrongful dismissal and defamation, but withdrew the threat after a meeting with Manning. On May 7, 1995, forty-nine year-old Prime Minister Manning delivered a television broadcast in which he declared that he was the 'Father of the Nation' and must therefore speak 'in a certain way'. In the broadcast, he announced that Minister Maraj had been relieved of his duties, three months before the Association of Caribbean States' (ACS) conference in Port of Spain. Maraj, who was moved to the Prime Minister's office as minister without portfolio, was replaced by Gift, who had 'hastily' joined the PNM and replaced Jean Elder in the Senate. No reason was given for the demotion of Maraj (formerly a prominent dramatist and playwright), who told a press conference the next day that he had not been informed about the change until he saw the television broadcast, and that his new responsibilities were unclear. He announced that he was going on leave, adding that he would not be 'humiliated, degraded or emasculated'. Several cabinet ministers expressed concern about the events. Further controversy was added when, on May 17, Gift resigned because of questions asked in the press about the sale of vehicles in 1987 at the end of Gift's three-year term as High Commissioner in Jamaica. On May 19, a cabinet re-shuffle was announced, with the Minister of Information and Public Administration Senator Gordon Draper appointed Minster of Foreign Affairs, in addition to his existing portfolios; Maraj appointed Minster of Public Utilities, a portfolio previously held by Energy Minister Barry Barnes; and other changes in the Ministries of Health, National Security, and Social Development. Maraj gained public and collegial sympathy, while the UNC and the *Express* criticised Manning's actions as essentially erratic, unstable and lacking good judgement.[88]

On June 14, 1995, Panday presented a motion of no confidence against the government and was jeered and heckled by a crowd of a reported 3,000 PNM supporters, including a number of government ministers, as he entered the parliament building. He was also booed by PNM members when he entered the chamber. The motion was lost by 19 votes to 13. Many regarded the PNM defence as excessive (the debate lasted 16 hours with each minister individually praising Manning), since the motion could not have passed in any case. The two NAR members left the chamber before the vote was taken; Pamela Nicholson said she 'did not want to miss a basketball game'.[89]

Meanwhile, the government and the speaker of the House, Occah Seapaul (sister of Ralph Maraj), were crossing swords. The government had earlier tried to persuade Seapaul to resign, following her involvement in a court case in June 1995 connecting her to fraudulent conversion of Trinidad and

Tobago funds through a TT$200,000 bank loan. Seapaul refused, prompting Attorney-General Keith Sobion to present a motion of no confidence in the Speaker. Seapaul, however, ruled that the motion was unconstitutional. In July 1995 government and independent senators, opposed by those of the UNC, passed a bill to amend the constitution to permit the House of Representatives to remove its Speaker by a majority vote.[90] On July 24, the date the amendment was to be presented in the Lower House, Seapaul adjourned the sitting, preventing it from being debated. As Seapaul left Parliament, leader of government business, Trade and Industry minister Ken Valley shouted at Seapaul, 'You can run, but you can't hide.' On July 28, Valley was suspended by the Speaker for six months, despite his apology. He later won a High Court order reinstating him to the House pending hearing of a constitutional motion filed by his lawyers. On August 3, Acting President Emmanuel Carter declared a state of emergency in Port of Spain and Seapaul was placed under house arrest. On August 4 the House approved the constitutional amendment. That day, the prime minister explained the government's actions by alleging that the Speaker had been involved in a 'diabolical conspiracy' to deprive the government of its parliamentary majority by 'improperly suspending government members'. Manning further alleged that Seapaul had planned to suspend on that very day Attorney-General Keith Sobion and Education Minster Augustus Ramrekersingh. He suggested that Seapaul had acted in collusion with the opposition in an attempt to suspend the proceedings of the House indefinitely. The government, Manning argued, 'had to act to save the country from the massive instability and social disruption which most certainly would have followed if the schemers had been allowed to carry out their plan of overthrowing the government inside the parliament.' That day, Ralph Maraj resigned from Cabinet. On August 5, Seapaul agreed to hand over her duties to her deputy, Rupert Griffith (MP for Arima), pending determination in court of a constitutional motion against the government. The state of emergency was lifted on August 7 and Seapaul was released from arrest.[91] The UNC subsequently announced its intention to start impeachment proceedings against Acting President Carter. On August 9, hours after his constituency executive passed a resolution of no-confidence in him, Maraj appeared on a UNC platform. He called the general council of the PNM 'a lynch mob', and described Manning as a 'third-rate tyrant' and a 'petty, insecure dictator'.[92] Although a serious situation, there had been a feeling that the declaration of a State of Emergency was excessive and that Manning's allegation of a 'palace coup' engineered by the Speaker and the opposition was exaggerated. On August 14, Maraj sat among the

Opposition benches, where he received warm greetings from Panday and Ramesh Maharaj. On August 24, Maraj resigned as MP and from the PNM. On October 6, Maraj announced that he had applied to the UNC for membership.[93] By the end of the affair, the PNM was reduced to 18 effective members in an officially 36 member parliament, a by-election was to be held by December 1995 for Maraj's San Fernando West seat, and local government elections were due on December 27, 1995 at the latest.[94]

At the same time as the PNM's troubles with Ralph Maraj and his sister Occah Seapaul were occurring, the country was gearing up for the celebration of the 150th anniversary of Indian Arrival, inadvertently giving the PNM controversies a perhaps disproportionate and undeserved racial dimension. The Indian community had been given a strong boost with the establishment in 1993 of FM 103, a 24-hour Indian-oriented radio station.[95] FM 103 had been started by Dik Henderson (a non-Indian) and Marcel Mahabir in opposition to the belief that 'an Indian radio station . . . [would] never survive.' In its first year, FM 103 immediately became the number one radio station in the country. The impact on local Indian culture was tremendous, bringing Indian culture into the mainstream of everyday life; increasing the total radio audience by 200,000; boosting the popularity of Indian films, local Indian music, and local Indian culture for a new generation of young people; and reviving it among the old. In 1995 one other Indian radio station was created, and the radio station at the government-owned International Communications Network (ICN) had converted its programming to an all-Indian format. By 1998 there were four stations dedicated to full-time Indian programming.[96]

In September 1994 the 'hijab issue' would highlight the place in Trinidad and Tobago of Muslims, 93 per cent of whom were Indian according to 1990 census data.[97] Sumayyah Mohammed, a student at Holy Name Convent in Port of Spain, had been told that she would have to leave the school if she continued to wear her hijab (the Muslim covering for a woman's head and breasts). A similar incident had occurred in 1976 at St George's College in Barataria and, in September 1992, a Muslim girl was refused entry to the sixth form at St Joseph's Convent and was transferred to the all-boys Presentation College in Chaguanas. In the 1994 incident, former PNM Deputy Leader Kamaluddin Mohammed and former President of the Senate/ Acting President Dr Wahid Ali intervened. After dialogue with denominational boards proved unsuccessful, the case was taken to the High Court where the judgement favoured Sumayyah Mohammed.[98]

A further debate occurred on the place of ethnicity in Trinidad and Tobago with the appointment on December 14 and 20, 1994, of a Joint Select Committee of both Houses of Parliament on Public Holidays. The report, laid in parliament on May 1, 1995, recommended that one national holiday be granted in honour of the Spiritual Baptists and another for Indian Arrival Day.[99] The PNM decided against the Spiritual Baptist holiday but accepted the Indian Arrival Day holiday proposal. The latter was named 'Arrival Day', although the holiday in 1995 was called 'Indian Arrival Day' and it replaced Whit Monday, indicating the decline of Christian if not Catholic influence in the country.[100] The UNC, however, argued that the Spiritual Baptists should have been granted their particular day as well, and that 'Indian' should have been included in the Arrival Day holiday title, to lessen the alienation felt by both communities. Indeed, Panday had proposed that in addition to the Spiritual Baptist holiday, a separate Lord Shango Day should be established for the Orisha community on a date of their choice. On Indian Arrival Day, at the SDMS's Lakshmi Girls Hindu College, Panday announced, 'I can tell you now with a great degree of confidence that in 1997, May 30th will be renamed and celebrated as Indian Arrival Day . . . the Spiritual Baptists and the Orishas will have their public holiday . . . and the Sanatan Dharma Maha Sabha will be given the green light to build a Hindu Boys College if they so wish.'[101] Opposition Leader Panday gave two temporary senatorial positions to the Spiritual Baptists so that they could argue their case in the Upper House in June 1995.[102]

Other events also occurred. After Indian Arrival Day, from August 11 to 18, 1995 the UWI's Institute of Social and Economic Research, in association with the National Council for Indian Culture (headed by Hansley Hanoomansingh, DLP MP for Caroni East, 1966–71), organised a high-profile international conference, 'Challenge and Change: the Indian Diaspora in its Historical and Contemporary Contexts'. At this conference, Basdeo Panday presented a paper titled 'Trade Unionism, Politics and Indo-Caribbean Leadership'. On August 31, 1995, Independence Day, Dharmacharya Krishna Persad from the SDMS had refused the nation's highest award, the Trinity Cross, because its name did not reflect the religious diversity of Trinidad and Tobago.[103] Beginning in 1994, the Sewdass Sadhu Shiv Mandir, popularly known as the 'Temple in the Sea', was being rebuilt in Carapichaima and it captured the imagination of many, inspiring a play about its original construction against colonial opposition.[104] Between September and October 1995, statues of the elephant-headed Hindu god Ganesh were reported around the world to be drinking milk from devotees. SDMS Secretary General Satnarine Maharaj announced it as a 'sign that the time has come for Hindus to take their rightful place in society', noting the significance of its occurrence during the 150th anniversary of Indian Arrival in Trinidad and, later, the general elections which were called for November 6, 1995.[105]

In addition to the events surrounding the Indian Arrival, the PNM were faced with an escalation in serious crimes. Although in 1995 there were 61,220 reports to the police of serious and minor crimes and minor offences (a decline from the peak of 68,324 in 1988), the number of serious crimes reported reached an all-time high in 1993 at 19,547 and the number of deaths by homicide also reached at an all-time high in 1994 of 146.[106] Not only was the incidence of crime made into a political issue, but the PNM's handling of the problems at times had been questionable.

In 1994 a notorious drug lord, Dole Chadee, was finally arrested with nine other men for the murder of Hamilton Baboolal and three of his family members on January 10 that year.[107] The main state witness in the trial, Clint Huggins, was receiving death threats; in October 1994 the government announced that Huggins had died. The announcement, however, was later revealed as a hoax to entrap three men allegedly conspiring to kill him. Once again, the government's judgement was questioned.[108] Meanwhile, questions surrounded another event. In July 1994 – subsequent to the prominence given to the murder of two women in Westmoorings, an elite western suburb of Port of Spain – the Trinidad and Tobago state had carried out its first execution since 1979 against convicted murderer Glen Ashby. A 200-page international jurists' report submitted in March 1995, however, found that the execution was illegal and that sufficient evidence existed to cite the Attorney-General Keith Sobion for contempt of court. Ashby was hanged on the Attorney-General's instruction while the Court of Appeal was in session, arguably violating the prisoner's right to due process. The hanging occurred six days before Ashby would have completed five years under sentence, and ten minutes before the receipt of a fax from the Privy Council granting him a stay of execution. Sobion responded that the report was not binding on the government. Subsequently, on March 14, 1995, a constitutional amendment bill was introduced into the Senate aimed at abolishing the right of appeal to the Privy Council on constitutional motions relating to criminal cases. In April, however, Attorney-General Sobion withdrew the bill because of numerous charges that it reduced the constitutional guarantees against infringements by the executive of citizens' rights.[109]

On June 20, 1995, 59 year-old former Attorney-General and Minister of National Security Selwyn Richardson was ambushed and shot six times outside his home in Cascade (a northern suburb of Port of Spain) in what was described as a 'Mafia-style killing'. Thousands of people gathered in Port of Spain to see his funeral cortège, and a two-hour ceremony was attended by the Prime Minister and Acting President. The murder, the 59th for the year, highlighted the problem of escalating crime dramatically.[110] The following weekend, two men suspected of Richardson's murder, Abdul Qadir and Curtis Felix (members of the Jamaat-al-Muslimeen) were found shot dead. At the same time, in July 1995, the government had issued writs against Abu Bakr and other members of the Jamaat for compensation estimated at several million dollars.[111] On September 11, Prime Minister Manning denied in parliament the existence of a police 'death squad', refuting the rumours that surfaced after the shooting near the UWI campus, in disputed circumstances two weeks earlier, of another member of the Jamaat-al-Muslimeen, Abdulla Muhammed Aziz. The UNC, the Coalition for Social Justice and Human Rights, and the Law Association expressed concern at the recent shootings of criminals in questionable circumstances, including escaped murder convict Anthony 'Lizard' Brideglal in April 1994 and Jeffrey Alexander in December 1994.[112] The government responded to the crime situation in August 1995 by announcing the construction, at a cost of TT$5.5 million, of 16 new police posts over the next six months, each staffed by 20 officers.[113]

The PNM were also having trouble negotiating with state employees. In August 1995 workers at PETROTRIN and TRINMAR went on strike initially for four days, but then extended it. The PETROTRIN strike ended after six weeks on September 18 and the TRINMAR strike after nine weeks on October 8, two days after the general elections were announced.[114] In addition, up to 75 per cent of the 35,000 members of the PSA took part in a one-day strike on September 15, to pressure the government into paying salary arrears totalling TT$2 billion, accumulating since the NAR administration.[115]

## THE CAMPAIGN OF 1995

After less than four years in office, Prime Minister Manning announced, on October 6, 1995, that general elections would be held on November 6. This action was unprecedented in an independent Trinidad and Tobago. Parliament had not been due to dissolve until January 13, 1997, and the latest possible date for elections was April 12, 1997.[116] The San Fernando West by-election was thereby pre-empted and the local government elections postponed. The prime minister explained that having 18 members reduced the government's 'flexibility' in conducting its business to 'unacceptable levels' and he therefore sought a new mandate.

Calling early elections did not avoid all party problems, however. On October 9, PNM Deputy Leader and Minister of Finance Wendell Mottley announced that he would not be standing for election. Minister John Eckstein declined to contest as well.[117] On October 14, the PNM presented its slate of candidates, calling them the 'Dream Team' (after the United States' 1992 Olympic basketball team), who would fulfil Manning's ambition to make Trinidad and Tobago 'world class.'[118] The PNM pledged a reduction in corporation and the top rate of income tax (which had been at 38 per cent), more vigorous anti-crime measures, and continuing reduction in unemployment.[119] Only 12 of the 21 PNM MPs stood for re-election. Two deaths and one defection during the term partially contributed to the small number. But there were other problems as well. On October 11, for instance, PNM members from two constituencies held a protest demonstration against the dropping of their sitting members, Ken Collis and Jean Pierre, Ministers of Labour and Sports, respectively.[120]

The PNM seemed to be on the defensive during the campaign, often responding to issues raised by the UNC. Regarding the UNC's proposals for 'national unity' and a 'national front' government, Manning reiterated the PNM's traditional hostility towards coalition government, defiantly declaring that the PNM would 'fight alone, win alone, lose alone, and stand alone'. Manning asked the electorate, 'If not the PNM, who? It is either the PNM or chaos'. He stated, 'The choices facing the population are the opposition and its bacchanal or the oasis in the middle of the desert – the cool calm stability that is the PNM.'[121] Although these statements clearly followed the thought of Eric Williams, Manning's performance as political leader (and his slower and duller wit than Panday's, perhaps) did not elevate the words as effectively. When Panday had invited Manning onto the UNC podium to discuss and debate issues, Manning declared that he would not sit on the seat (literally) prepared for him, because he might catch 'political AIDS'.[122]

On the day that the election date was announced in parliament, Panday arrived late. Upon his entrance, he walked over to Manning, shook his hand and said, 'I just came to say goodbye', bringing laughter from members including Manning.[123] That evening, at a meeting in San Fernando West, reportedly scheduled much in advance for the expected by-election, Panday reminded the audience that three weeks earlier he had held a press conference at which he said that Manning would declare general elections in December 1995. He jabbed, 'It's just that Manning so foolish, anybody could read him like a book.'[124] At the beginning of his address, he declared businessman Kama Maharaj as candidate for the constituency, going on to boast, 'Manning thought he would catch us. He has not caught us. In fact, he only declare the General Elections today. Within twelve hours of him declaring an election, we declare a candidate.'[125]

At that meeting, he outlined the programme that the UNC would consistently stick with: devoting more resources and energy in the fight against crime; concentrating on employment generation; promising to settle public sector pay arrears of TT$2 billion in cash (instead of bonds, as proposed by the PNM government); the establishment of an Equal Opportunities Commission; the formation of a National Steel Orchestra and the promotion of a multi-cultural entertainment and tourist industry; and the standardisation of school textbooks.[126] Perhaps the most important campaign platform was the UNC's pledge to bring about 'national unity', either through coalition or the formation of a 'national front' government comprising all political parties. In an interview with *Newsday* on October 18, Panday proposed constitutional change, using the Wooding Commission report of 1974 as a base, to allow small groups in society to participate in the political decision-making process. Panday argued, 'We think we are a nation pulling in different directions and we feel we have the mechanism to unite us once again.' In a television interview on November 3, he further underlined his view, 'We have not yet become a nation, you know.'[127]

In his October 6 speech, Panday declared that it was 'time to love again' and invited the NAR, labour, business, the unemployed, the homeless, and 'the powerless' to unite with the UNC. Prime Minister Robinson, Winston Dookeran, and Panday attended private meetings trying to revive 'the spirit of 1986' but they did not result in any formal arrangement. On October 15, the day after the PNM presented their own slate, the UNC presented its 34 candidates. Only five of the current 13 UNC parliamentarians were standing in 1995.[128] No candidates were put up in Tobago because, according to Panday in his October 18, 1995 *Newsday* interview, the UNC wanted 'to ensure that our intervention . . . [would] not cause a PNM victory in the sister-island'.[129]

Only five of the 13 UNC incumbents stood for re-election.[130] The UNC slate had a number of former NAR members, including Ganga Singh (Caroni East), Kamla Persad-Bissessar (Siparia), John Humphrey (St Augustine), Basdeo Panday (Couva North), Trevor Sudama (Oropouche), Mervyn Assam (St Joseph), and Rawle Raphael (Arouca North). They also put up former

PNM MPs Hector McLean (Tunapuna) and Ralph Maraj (Naparima). Notable, too, was the presence of Spiritual Baptist Archbishop Barbara Burke (Laventille West), who had described herself as a 'traditional PNM [supporter]'.[131] Panday remarked, 'When I said it was time to love again, a lot of our cynics sniggered and laughed at us. Well, when today you look at the slate of candidates that were presented to you, my brothers and sisters – some from the PNM some from the NAR some from the UNC – you will see that we are, in fact, loving again. You see, when I said it is time to love again, they did not wait for me to finish my sentence; they went and jump into all kinds of things. When I said it is time to love again I meant that this time the loving is going to take place in the House of the Rising Sun, but even more important, it is going to take place on a UNC bed.'[132]

Other NAR members also appeared on UNC platforms, including Winston Dookeran, Clive Pantin, Suruj Rambachan,[133] Tim Gopeesingh, Jennifer Johnson, Dr Raphael Sebastien, Felix Celestine, Dr George Laquis, and Dr Robert Sabga. In addition, much note was taken of a grand fund-raising party thrown in October 1995 for Basdeo Panday in Port of Spain by former PNM minister Brian Kuei Tung.[134] It was very significant to see that Panday – whose base was in Central and South – could be accepted in the capital.

The NAR, on the other hand, got off to a slow start. On April 25, 1995, A.N.R. Robinson declined an offer to lead the party again. He accepted it, however, as late as October 8 (two days after Manning's announcement), when it was officially announced at the NAR's National Council.[135] The party held a conference on October 15 and at its first public meeting on October 21, presented its 19 candidates and campaigning under the theme that the NAR would 'Make the Difference'.[136] Although no formal UNC-NAR arrangement had been reached, 15 of the 17 NAR candidates in Trinidad were fighting in PNM-controlled seats.[137] The six PNM seats that the NAR did not contest were the borderline seats of Pointe-à-Pierre, Barataria/San Juan, St Joseph, Ortoire/Mayaro, and San Fernando West; and the PNM safe seat of Diego Martin Central. By the NAR not contesting those borderline seats, the UNC were given a clear battle with the PNM.

On November 3, the TV6 *Morning Edition* [138] invited Manning, Panday, and Robinson to discuss the coming elections. Manning declined the invitation. The interview was the first time that Panday and Robinson had spoken together in public since the break-up of the NAR in 1988. Both men talked about NAR and its split, the coup, and other issues. They seemed to move from enmity to understanding live on air. At one point Panday intervened, 'That question you asked, do we dream of recreating the euphoria and enthusiasm of 1986, the truth is, I dream of nothing else.' After the interview, reportedly, the two leaders went for breakfast together. Manning, on the other hand, issued libel writs against Robinson, Bakr, and CCN over remarks made during the programme, alleging that he had prior knowledge of the coup.[139]

Panday and the UNC had to overcome strong scepticism, and occasional hostility, toward the possibility of an 'Indian party' and an 'Indian Prime Minister' coming to power in the 20th century.[140] The persistent and absurd comment that Panday did 'not want to be prime minister' perhaps reflected this inability to seriously consider such a possibility.[141]

The major pre-election predictions, as well, were influenced by such scepticism, perhaps similar to the scepticism about the possibility that Williams and the PNM could have won a legislative majority in 1956. On October 29, the *Express* published the SARA poll under the headline, 'PNM Wins'. The poll, conducted during October 16–20, gave the PNM 15 seats, the UNC 14, and the NAR two in Tobago. Regarding the five borderline PNM constituencies, Ryan argued that if nothing changed between then and November 6, they would go to the PNM to make a total of 20. He wrote, 'Fastforwarding the general elections to November 6 was clearly a brilliant though potentially risky stroke on the part of the Prime Minister. He caught *everybody* [including members of his government], other than his closest advisors, by surprise.' Ryan argued that the strategy would have found the UNC unprepared, that potential UNC-NAR unity would be pre-empted, and that the building of a 'party of the centre' (as advocated by Lloyd Best) would not be able to get off the ground. Ryan explained that '50 per cent of those polled thought that the PNM should be given another chance, to govern the country. Thirteen per cent said they were disposed to return the PNM to power because they considered the UNC 'politically illegitimate and unviable'. Thirty-nine per cent, however, wanted to 'give the UNC a chance'. Although 64 per cent of Indo-Trinidadians supported Panday and 64 per cent of Afro-Trinidadians supported Manning, the SARA poll indicated that 41 per cent of the mixed group and 9 per cent of Indo-Trinidadians favoured Manning, while only 8 per cent of the mixed and 4 per cent of the Afro-Trinidadians preferred Panday. Ryan concluded, 'Afro-Trinidadians of all classes and genders would find it difficult to endorse Basdeo Panday as Prime Minister. Manning gets more cross-race and cross-gender support.' His weekly column in the same issue argued, 'It seems clear, however, that while the main text of Panday's message articulated a cross-racial appeal against the parasitic oligarchy and their spokespersons, the sub-text represented an unambiguous communal appeal.' The following week, in part two of the SARA poll, Ryan elaborated, 'Given the small size of the samples and the large margins of error that often manifest themselves in samples of limited size, we hesitate to say unequivocally that the PNM would win the four [Tunapuna, St Joseph, Pointe-à-Pierre, Barataria/San Juan] seats. SARA's judgement, however, which is informed by the known ethnic balances in the four areas, is that the PNM is favoured to hold all four seats.'[142]

On November 5, the *Sunday Guardian* published a poll conducted between October 29 and 31 by the local firm Market Facts and Opinion which also predicted that the PNM would win 20 seats, the UNC 14, and the NAR two. It was argued, 'In the end, the odds are too great to be overcome, and the borderline seats are forecast all to be retained by the incumbents.'[143] The less prestigious papers, however, were not as sceptical about a UNC victory. On November 3 the weekly *Bomb* (owned by Satnarine Maharaj, Secretary General of the SDMS) predicted a tie between the PNM and UNC; the daily *Newsday* on November 5 published a poll conducted by Vishnu Bisram of the North American Caribbean Teachers Association (NACTA) of New York predicting 17 seats for the UNC, 17 seats for the PNM, and two for the NAR, with the PNM receiving four per cent more voter support that the UNC; and the weekly *Mirror* (edited by Raffique Shah) on November 5 stated, 'Washington-based political experts assisting the United National Congress (UNC) in its bid for government are confident that the party will win general elections tomorrow.'[144]

As with the PNM in 1956, the UNC did not gain an outright majority in 1995.[145] It was the first tie in Trinidad and Tobago's history, with the UNC winning 17 seats, the PNM 17, and the NAR two (see Appendices B and C).

Voter turnout was 63.3 per cent, slightly less than the 65.8 per cent who voted in 1991, but because the electorate had grown, the actual number of voters increased by 7,839 over the 1991 amount. Despite the much larger electorate (837,741 in 1995 as opposed to 794,486 in 1991), there had been no revision of the constituency boundaries for the new general elections, as would be customary.

Hulsie Bhaggan and her MUP colleagues lost their deposits, and NJAC did not even contest the elections, citing financial reasons.[146] The NAR lost a spectacular 102,352 votes from 1991 to 1995. The PNM were able to increase their votes over 1991 by 22,209; but the UNC outstripped them by capturing 89,326 more votes. Even in the four borderline seats that the PNM lost, PNM votes increased by a total of 3,745; but they were overwhelmed by the UNC's gain of 12,781 votes (see Appendix B and Table 6.6).[147] Tunapuna –

where the PNM, UNC, and NAR all contested – was the only seat won with less than 50 per cent of ballots cast. It would not be unfair to say that the UNC lost a majority in the 1995 general elections by 244 votes there.

***Table 6.6. Distribution ofVotes in the Five Borderline Constituencies, 1995 General Elections***

| CONSTITUENCY | PNM | UNC | NAR | OTHER | REJECTED BALLOTS | % VOTED | MARGIN OF VICTORY |
|---|---|---|---|---|---|---|---|
| Tunapuna | 7,467 | 7,223 | 368 | 58 | 103 | 67.10% | 244 |
| St Joseph | 6,960 | 7,564 | – | 396 | 130 | 65.60% | 604 |
| Ortoire/Mayaro | 8,201 | 8,944 | – | – | 274 | 69.40% | 743 |
| Barataria/San Juan | 6,666 | 7,611 | – | 105 | 89 | 64.00% | 945 |
| Pointe-à-Pierre | 7,055 | 9,367 | – | 83 | 156 | 69.70% | 2,312 |
| TOTALS | 36,349 | 40,709 | 368 | 642 | 752 | 67.20% | 4,848 |

*Source*: GORTT (1996b)

Not only did the UNC hold the Pointe-à-Pierre seat, it captured Ortoire/Mayaro, St Joseph, and Barataria/San Juan – seats which, since 1961, only the NAR in 1986 had been able to capture from the PNM. The excitement was palpable at the UNC headquarters when the election results were read, while at the PNM camp Manning told his supporters to 'go peacefully to your homes' – another inappropriate, even if well-intentioned, remark that would draw criticism at the highest levels even five years later.[148]

Upon hearing the final results, Panday addressed his audience:

> *As you would have known by now, the results are 17-17-2, 17 for the PNM, 17 to the UNC and 2 to the NAR. That means that there is no single Party in the House at the moment with a clear majority. Why these results have come about? It would appear to me, brothers and sister, that Almighty god [*sic*] moves in mysterious ways, His wonders to perform (*Cheers mixed with Applause).
>
> *As you know, I have always contended and always argue that because of the highly plural nature of our society, the highly divisive and fragmented*

> *nature of our society, no one single group can run Trinidad and Tobago successfully to the exclusion of other groups in the society.* (Applause). *Based upon that analysis, I have argued for the need for a National Front Government. But there were groups in the society who did not want a National Front Government. Groups who say 'we shall fight alone and we shall struggle alone' and apparently they have lost alone. (Laughter and Applause). My brothers, my brothers and sisters, man proposes but God disposes* (Cheers). *And what you want may not be what you get.* (Applause). *And so those who do not want unity, unity will be forced upon them. Because God knows that it is only in unity that you shall be prosperous. Only in unity everyone will have a chance. Only in unity we shall deal with crime. Only in unity we shall deal with our educational problems and high prices. God loves this nation and He is forcing us to unite.*[149]

On November 9 between 4:10 pm and 4:12 pm, Basdeo Panday was sworn in as Prime Minister of Trinidad and Tobago, after securing the support of A.N.R. Robinson, his previous partner in government.[150]

The PNM suffered its second loss in ten years. A combination of the UNC's and Panday's political skill, Manning's political blunders, a rise in Indian consciousness sparked by the 150th anniversary of Indian arrival, and perhaps a dissatisfaction with the economic and social situation (despite the objective improvements) served to dislodge the Manning administration, but not definitively. The UNC was to be the latest administration in a Parliament that changed leadership in every term from 1981 and, from 1991, did not contain a party with a secure two-thirds majority. The new Panday administration, Trinidad and Tobago's first Indian-led government, was to release a new energy and bring a new constituency into leadership of government. Where that would take the country was unforeseen.

# *Seven*

## THE UNC GOVERNMENT, 1995-2001: 'NONE SHALL ESCAPE UNSCATHED'

In this chapter, the UNC administrations of 1995 to 2000 and 2000 to 2001 are examined. It is not unfair to judge the UNC's first term of government as one of the three most important terms of government in Trinidad and Tobago's short history, the other two being the Williams administration of 1956–61 and the Robinson administration of 1986-91. This importance is not only due to its accomplishments (which included the winning of a second term of office) but also to the intense opposition against it, which eventually effected the unprecedented collapse of the government just eight months after resuming its second term in 2001.

In addition to antagonising their opposition, the UNC governments raised notable and eventually fatal opposition from the president and dissident UNC MPs. In a reforming enthusiasm, the Panday governments of 1995-2001 pushed the independence model of self-government to its extremes. Quite unexpectedly, since the end of 1999 in particular, the problems of legally constituted authority in Trinidad and

Tobago became highlighted in an unprecedented way: the country specifically questioned the division of powers and responsibilities of the president, the prime minister, the courts and the judiciary, the Tobago House of Assembly, and the constitution itself. In questioning their powers, their limitations seemed to have been reached.

*President Noor Hassanali swearing in the new Prime Minister, The Right Honourable Mr. Basdeo Panday, the 5th Prime Minister of the Republic of Trinidad and Tobago on November 9, 1995.*

From 1995, the Panday administration tried to bring something new to government, in some measure moving beyond a generic IMF/World Bank-type macro-economic structural adjustment policy to stamp an identifiable character onto the government. In many ways they advanced the NAR's social, political, and economic policy, just as the PNM advanced the NAR's economic programme.

By bringing into government leadership a new constituency – the Hindu Indians of Central Trinidad – the UNC released a fresh energy. Indeed, no government introduced as much legislation into Parliament as the UNC administration of 1995–2000 – 302 bills into the Lower House and 311 in the Upper House, according to the Parliamentary Bill Books. It definitely sought to transform the country. However, as with the other two new administrations of 1956 and 1986, while actively transforming the political, social, economic, and moral environment, it simultaneously generated heated opposition at every turn.

The fundamentals of the UNC's vision were articulated during the campaign of 1995 and sustained throughout the term: a greater emphasis on law and order in society, national unity through the affirmation of cultural plurality, and a results-focused approach to economic and social development.[1]

Equally persistent, however, was the intense opposition to the Panday administration from a number of quarters – the political parties, the president, dissident UNC MPs, the media, the THA, the trade unions, and other groups and interests – variously accusing the government of corruption, bellicosity, racism, and nepotism.[2] Disputes between the government and its various centres of opposition were continuous and overlapping, often with two or three events peaking simultaneously.

Panday's seemingly limitless determination, and great ability, to prevail over his sundry oppositions and to govern (in Panday's lexicon, 'to do my duty' or 'to perform') seemed to be vindicated by his electoral victory on December 11, 2000. His style reminded more than one observer of Eric Williams.[3] Like the PNM, the UNC initially won government with less than 50 per cent of votes and seats, and crystallised hostile opposition around it. As with Williams, Panday's missionary zeal generated both strong enthusiasm and fearful resistance. And again, as with the PNM, the UNC won its second term of office clearly in the face of intense opposition.

However, Panday's hubris was ill-suited to that crisis-plagued administration's unsteady start and dishonourable end, after only eight months. As a result, the country was brought to a critical point in its political history. It was pushed by the enthusiasm of the Panday regimes.

## 'THE GOVERNMENT OF NATIONAL UNITY': CONSOLIDATING THE UNC GOVERNMENT, 1995–7

After the historic elections of November 6, 1995, parties started negotiating support for a prime minister, who was to be formally appointed by President Noor Hassanali.[4] It was the first time in Independence that no clear majority had been elected to government. Manning, still the substantive prime minister, publicly suggested that as leader of the party with the greatest number of votes, he was entitled to form the next government. Manning suspected that 'national unity' – led by anyone – was a guise under which the role of the opposition would be undermined and, curiously, that its 'net effect' would be to divide society.

During the standstill, President Hassanali – in the absence of consultation with the incumbent prime minister, Patrick Manning, and the leader of opposition, Basdeo Panday – held private meetings with Robinson to discuss the formation of the new government.[5] Additionally, Ken Gordon, CEO of CCN and former NAR minister, put Robinson in contact with Manning following a request from a PNM government minister, but Manning apparently delayed meeting with Robinson.[6] Meanwhile, Robinson presented to Panday an agreement on November 8, which was accepted in principle. On November 9, 1995, Panday (b. 1933) was sworn in as prime minister by President Hassanali.[7]

Panday's Inaugural Address to the Nation on November 10 was magnanimous, thanking outgoing Prime Minister Manning and calling on the entire population – including the PNM – to work together for the next five years:

> *Fellow Citizens, Ladies and Gentlemen, my Sisters and Brothers. I thank you most sincerely for the confidence you have reposed in me and the Party which I have the honour to lead, the United National Congress. On behalf of my colleagues and on my own behalf, I accept that honour with great humility, but with an even greater determination to serve all the peoples of Trinidad and Tobago.*
>
> *I want to thank all those who have worked so hard to bring about this moment. I know how many resources, how much energy, sweat, and emotional stress you have invested in this campaign. I ask you to accept your victory with humility and generosity.*
>
> *Trinidad and Tobago is a difficult country to govern because of its highly pluralistic nature, its diversity and its fragmentation. I have always been of the firm conviction that without unity this nation cannot go very far. Our first task, therefore, must be to unite this nation as it has never been united before. We must make sure that every man, woman and child in this beloved land of ours genuinely and sincerely feel that they belong. Our first task is to ensure that every human being who inhabits our land is made to feel wanted, secure and safe, that he or she will not be discriminated against for any reason whatsoever, and that here each and everyone shall truly find an equal place. No one needs feel insecure because of a change of Government. I regard your safety as my most important and immediate task. I have already contacted the security forces and I have been assured of their support in protecting this nation from harm both from within and without.*
>
> *... In keeping with our philosophy, and in keeping with our promise to unite this nation, I have invited all the parties that won seats in the House of Representatives to join with the United National Congress to establish a*

*government of national unity, a national front government, so that together we may confront and win the battle against crime and drugs, unemployment and poverty, the alienation of our youths and our senior citizens, rising prices and the deteriorating public utilities.*[8]

On November 11, 1995, the UNC and the NAR signed a nine-point Heads of Agreement,[9] calling for:

1. parliamentary 'decision-making by consensus'
2. the expeditious introduction of legislation 'to implement the national consensus agreement on Tobago contained in the House Paper No. 6 of 1978'
3. the 'integration' of the 'unity process'
4. the utilisation of the 'human resources' of both parties 'in the formation and continuance of the new government'
5. the establishment of legislative provisions, mechanisms, and a code of conduct to effect 'the principles of Truth, the Rule of Law, Transparency in Public Affairs and Morality and integrity [*sic*] in Public Office'
6. the restructuring of the political system 'to afford representation to sections of the electorate who by reason of non-alignment with major political groupings are denied participation in the governance of the Country'
7. further decentralisation at all levels of government
8. the establishment of mechanisms 'to harness the energy, talents, skills and enterprise of the entire population in the nation-building process'; and
9. mechanisms for conflict resolution between the affected parties.[10]

The PNM, perhaps put in an unwinnable position, rejected the UNC's call to join a national front government, and accused the UNC of offering PNM members bribes to cross the floor.[11] By the opening of Parliament on November 27, Panday had assembled a 21-member cabinet that included Robinson (NAR MP for Tobago East) in the newly-created post of minister extraordinaire, Special Responsibility for Tobago, Adviser to the Prime Minister; Pamela Nicholson (NAR MP for Tobago West) as Minister of Youth Affairs and Sports; former PNM minister, Senator Brian Kuei Tung (not a member of the UNC party) as Minister of Finance; Senator Joseph Theodore (a retired army brigadier, also not a member of the UNC party) as Minister of National Security; Senator Daphne Phillips (a lecturer in sociology from the UWI, also not a member of the UNC) as Minister of Community Development, Culture and Women's Affairs; former PNM minister, Ralph Maraj (MP for Naparima), as Minister of Foreign Affairs; MP for St Joseph Mervyn Assam (formerly of the ONR and the NAR, and former High Commissioner to the United Kingdom) as Minister of Trade and Industry; and MP for Siparia, Kamla Persad-Bissessar (formerly of the NAR), as Attorney-General, the first woman to hold the position.[12] Hector McLean (defeated UNC candidate for Tunapuna in 1995, and former PNM minister, 1971–78) was elected speaker of the house.[13]

The *Express*, the *Guardian*, and its columnists Overand Padmore (PNM minister from 1971–86), Frank Brassington (Honorary Secretary of the DLP from 1957–60), and Allan Harris from Tapia, warmly congratulated Panday as the deserving victor in the elections.[14] Manning argued that he had lost office because the country felt that it was time for an 'Indian Prime Minister'.[15] At the same time, however, there was speculation as to whether the Panday administration would last its entire term.[16] Veteran political columnist and former PNM mayor for Arima (in 1959), Percy Cezaire, wrote in the *Guardian* on November 21, 1995,

> *It will take all of Panday's long experience and well-known political skills to chart a stable course through such choppy waters . . . . Mr Panday and Mr Robinson have been thrown together in a repeat of a political experiment that they both failed at before. However, on this occasion, the role of the Prime Minister is reversed. It may be that Mr Panday may turn out to be much better at keeping them together than Mr Robinson was on the last occasion.*[17]

Panday, who had been known for attacking the 'parasitic oligarchy' while in opposition, further demonstrated his commitment to the principle of national unity by meeting in December 1995 with over 200 representatives from the private sector in preparation for the 1996 budget. Panday informed his audience that the government's prime objective was to solve the unemployment problem, while another main aim was to maintain the country's business climate.[18] On January 10, 1996, Minister Kuei Tung presented a budget that managed to please both the National Trade Union

Centre (NATUC)[19] and the Trinidad and Tobago Chamber of Commerce: the government increased expenditure, reduced the rate of taxation for individuals and businesses at all levels, removed VAT from 12 basic food and household items, announced payment of TT$90 million in cash to approximately 45,000 public servants,[20] and maintained a reasonable level of fiscal balance.[21]

Demonstrating its commitment to recognising 'alienated' groups, on January 26, 1996, the UNC government declared March 30 'Spiritual Baptist Liberation Day', a national holiday replacing Republic Day (held on September 24). PNM Leader Patrick Manning protested the removal of a national holiday (and a legacy of Eric Williams) to accommodate a sectional interest.[22] In addition, 'Arrival Day' was renamed 'Indian Arrival Day'.[23] Against the notion that he would be concerned mainly with the Indians of central Trinidad, in March 1996 Prime Minister Panday embarked on a tour of Beetham Estate, Sea Lots, Laventille, and Tobago, the core areas of the PNM and the NAR.[24] In addition, in May 1996 the UNC government gave a 'hero's welcome', with VIP and dignitary status, to Trinidad-born Black Power advocate Kwame Ture (whom the Williams government declared a prohibited immigrant in 1968). Ture, who was the guest of honour at the Emancipation Support Committee's (ESC)[25] Emancipation celebrations, was also pledged US$1,000 per month from the Trinidad and Tobago government to support his cancer treatment.[26]

Panday, on leave but still titular president of the ATS&GWTU, also marched in Fyzabad on Labour Day (June 19) as he had done for the past 30 years. His presence as Prime Minister, however, made the occasion a first, as no other head of government had done so before, and he was welcomed warmly for two years by Errol McLeod, President of both NATUC[27] and the OWTU, and also former ULF MP for Oropouche who had aligned with Raffique Shah.[28]

Controversy, however, came early in the term. On January 4, 1996, Manning held a meeting of the PNM Arouca South constituency. There he declared that there would be 'heat in the Parliament and heat in the streets of the country after the honeymoon is over'.[29] In the budget debate the following week, Panday alleged that Manning's statements were meant to encourage his supporters to 'resort to violence and violent demonstrations to bring this government down'.[30] Manning denied the allegations, and the *Guardian* published an editorial on January 18, 1996, titled, 'Panday's Alarum', criticising the prime minister for making 'alarmist and unsubstantiated charges against his political foes', and reminding readers of the UNC's links to the Jamaat-al-Muslimeen.[31] Four days later, the *Guardian* published an article, 'Chutney Rising – Panday', which further offended Panday because of its alleged sub-textual suggestion that he was a narrowly 'Indian' prime minister.

This began a feud between the UNC and the media that would continue, often quite with considerable intensity, for the entire term of government. On January 31, 1996, Panday announced that the *Guardian* would no longer be invited to government functions. He alleged that the paper was biased against his government and called for the dismissal of editor-in-chief Jones P. Madeira whom he described as 'a racist, vicious and spiteful'. In February, Ken Gordon, Harold Hoyte of the *Barbados News*, and David de Caires of the *Stabroek News* (Guyana)[32] met with Panday to broker a truce. The ban was lifted and it was agreed that an independent press complaints commission would be established. The *Guardian* management later decided to install an editorial board to guarantee the paper's independence.[33]

On March 10, Attorney-General Ramesh Lawrence Maharaj announced that the government intended to revise the law of libel to 'make it more difficult for the media to misuse and abuse' their freedom. Ken Gordon expressed opposition to the suggestion and, on March 31, the Inter-American Press Association board of directors, meeting in Costa Rica, called on the governments of Trinidad and Tobago, Antigua and Barbuda and the Turks and Caicos Islands to cease 'harassment' of the press. On April 1, Alwin Chow was 'constructively dismissed' by the *Guardian* (owned by Trinidad Publications Ltd., part of the Ansa-McAl conglomerate) and by May, 20 editors, senior journalists, and other contributors had resigned from the paper, including Jones P. Madeira (who officially vacated his post as editor-in-chief on May 2) and former UNC MP, Huslie Bhaggan.[34] On April 10 and 12 the Media Association of Trinidad and Tobago (MATT) held a National Symposium on the Freedom of the Press. Ansa-McAl's chairman, Anthony Sabga, and managing director, Michael Mansoor, were unapologetic. They invited other dissenters to leave as well, pointing to the *Guardian*'s editorial policy that it maintain its independence 'without forgetting that it was part of a conglomerate'.[35]

The fight between the UNC and the press occurred at the same time as much fear (and sometimes indignation) was being expressed by Afro-Trinidadians, in particular by newspaper columnists and calypsonians,[36] about their position under an 'Indian government'. Anxiety had been mounting over the firing of black CEO's at state-owned enterprises, including the NGC, WASA, PETROTRIN, the Point Lisas Development Company, TIDCO, the International Communications Network (ICN), and the National Flour Mills, whose new chairmen were all Indo-Trinidadian.[37] In Parliament in March 1996, PNM MP for Diego Martin Central Ken Valley expressed concern that only one of the 12 boards appointed up to that time had a non-Indian chairman.[38] Also causing anxiety was the UNC's desire to 'depoliticise' and restructure the URP to provide 'support to a wider cross section of the unemployed'.[39] The PNM criticised the government for reducing the number of Unemployment Relief Programme (URP) projects in PNM areas,[40] and implied racist and partisan motives. It should be noted, however, that the Jamaat-al-Muslimeen, the NAR, and even UNC members also complained about the lack of URP projects.[41]

Dissatisfaction with URP allocations led to the NAR National Council, on March 31, 1996, unanimously passing a resolution that 'the covenant entered into known as the Heads of Agreement . . . has been breached by the UNC as demonstrated in the open discrimination shown to NAR members in respect of Unemployment Relief Programme (URP) job placements'. The resolution was passed in the absence of NAR leader A.N.R. Robinson who was out of the country at the time. Seemingly to thwart the discontent, at the NAR's Eighth Annual Conference on April 21, 1996, Robinson re-emphasised his commitment to the UNC–NAR government, recounting the reasons for entering into the arrangement: he rejected suggestions that NAR should have formed for racial reasons a coalition with the PNM; he argued that Manning had a poor record of performance and that he was rejected at the polls; and Manning's remarkable slowness to meet after Robinson had contacted him stood in marked contrast to Panday's willingness to discuss. Robinson argued that the NAR was not an organisation like a trade union, primarily concerned about welfare of its members, but a political party aspiring to lead the country as a whole. Referring to his 'experience of the 1986–1991 NAR government', he emphasised the importance of settling differences internally, and accordingly he 'deliberately' maintained a 'low profile' to ensure the stability of the government as a 'necessary condition of law and order in the country'.[42]

With regard to social policy, in December 1995 the World Bank approved a loan of US$51 million to help finance a basic education project.[43] On the economic front, on May 8, TTMC's second plant was commissioned, increasing the country's installed methanol capacity to 11 per cent of the world's total. The steel mill, CIL, secured a financing package totalling US$84.2 million to upgrade the plant and bring it into line with World Bank environmental standards. In addition, the Amoco oil company announced a new natural gas find on April 9, and on May 22, Prime Minister Panday announced that bidding was open for production-sharing contracts on nine new blocks in the deep waters off the east coast.[44]

The major economic development, however, was the signing on June 20, 1996, of seven agreements covering financial and construction arrangements for the US$1 billion Atlantic LNG project at Point Fortin. The terms included renegotiation of the problematic 1991 gas supply contract, which had committed the NGC to buying gas at a higher price from Amoco than the company could sell it to industries at Point Lisas; a commitment by the Atlantic LNG consortium to spend US$100 million on local inputs; and a commitment of US$8 million in support for a national skills development centre. On April 30, 1996, Energy Minister Senator Finbar Gangar had announced in the Senate that TT$12 billion in new investment had been finalised up to that point in 1996, and that investments totalling TT$10 billion were under consideration.

The UNC's determination to fight crime was highlighted by the beginning of the Dole Chadee murder trial on June 10, 1996. Chadee had been due to stand trial in November 1994, but his lawyers had filed a constitutional motion seeking postponement on the grounds that press publicity precluded his right to a fair trial. On February 19, 1996, the High Court and the Judicial Committee of the Privy Council rejected the motion. The following day, state witness Clint Huggins was murdered after he left his safe house against the advice of the security forces. The state prosecution team then secured the co-operation of one of the nine men charged by offering him life imprisonment. On June 4, parliament passed an amendment to the Legal Profession Act to ensure that the English-based prosecution and defence teams in the trial were entitled to practice in Trinidad and Tobago. Justice Lionel Jones also issued three orders restricting reporting of the proceedings, together with a further three orders banning the media from saying what the first three orders contained. On June 14, *Mirror* editor Ken Ali was jailed for 14 days as a result of a complaint from the head of the defence team about a report in that day's *Mirror* about a 'bombshell witness'. The judge also banned media houses from reporting Ali's sentencing. In addition, *Mirror* reporter Sharmain Baboolal was fined TT$1,000 for a description in the same issue of a minor courtroom incident. The Mirror group and the *Independent* filed constitutional motions in the High Court against the banning orders, and MATT highlighted the issue by organising its first public meeting.[45] In the middle of this affair, the local government elections had been called.

The local government elections postponed by the 1995 general elections were called for June 24, 1996, less than eight months into the UNC–NAR's term in government. The UNC and the NAR furthered their cooperation by dividing constituencies among themselves, and they staged a joint unity platform at Arima on June 21, 1996.[46] Some disagreements occurred, however, and both parties fielded candidates for Chaguaramas/Glencoe in the Diego Martin Regional Corporation and San Juan West/Caledonia in San Juan/Laventille (see Appendix B).[47]

The PNM had been dealt a heavy blow in losing the government, and the repercussions were felt in the local government elections. Previously, on January 5, 1996, two months after the general elections, the PNM had endured a significant loss when Manning's three deputy leaders – Wendell Mottley, Keith Rowley, and Augustus Ramrekersingh – resigned from their posts after failing to persuade Manning to seek re-election. On February 11, 1996, however, Manning's leadership was re-affirmed at the party's general council, which also passed a resolution expressing full confidence in him.[48] While in opposition, the PNM's statements had been mainly negative, even alarmist, regularly making wild claims without substantiation. In April 1996, for example, Manning declared that the government's attacks on the media presaged attacks on the Elections and Boundaries Commission, and that the general elections of November 1995 would be the last free elections in Trinidad and Tobago; later in that month he claimed that the government had plans to place him under 'house arrest'; and in July 1996 he charged the UNC with committing the 'worst racists [*sic*] acts ever perpetrated by any Government in Trinidad and Tobago'.[49]

Interest in the local elections was strong, as 51,075 more people voted in 1996 than in 1992, resulting in a voter turnout of 44.0 per cent, the highest ever for local government elections (see Appendix B).

The results for the UNC and PNM, however, were equivocal. Both sides claimed victory. The two parties controlled seven corporations each, not unlike the even split of seats in parliament.[50] The PNM, however, won 63 seats as opposed to the UNC's 61, despite the UNC's leadership of government. This was the first time that an incumbent government was not able to win a majority of seats in a local government election.

On the other hand, the UNC did have a strong base on which to claim a measure of victory. For one reason, it took over from the PNM three Regional Corporations: Sangre Grande in the extreme northeast, Rio Claro/Mayaro in the extreme southeast, and Siparia (which was tied at four seats each, but won by the UNC by the drawing of lots) in the 'deep south' of St Patrick. The UNC controlled a Municipal Corporation as well, since Chaguanas had been made a Borough in 1991.[51] Significantly, the UNC also were able to poll 22,263 more votes than the PNM. The UNC exceeded their 1992 tally by 64,346. The PNM, too, increased their votes, but by a much smaller margin of 767. Lloyd Best, whose Tapia House Movement was dissolved to form the unitary NAR in 1986, declared that the UNC were becoming 'rampant' and that the PNM needed to court more actively and astutely, as the UNC did, the smaller political constituencies, particularly the Tobagonians.[52]

If none could claim outright victory in the June 24 elections, their aftermath unlocked the political balance in favour of the UNC. First, on August 18, 1996, the PNM general council agreed to a proposal from Manning that the party's elections for leadership positions should be brought forward by a year to take place at a convention on October 13, 1996.[53] Manning was challenged by Tobago-born Dr Keith Rowley – MP for Diego Martin West, former deputy leader, and former Minister of Agriculture (1991–95) – who led a slate of 15 candidates contesting all the party posts. Significantly, Rowley's slate included Kamaluddin Mohammed (PNM Deputy Leader, 1971–87, Minister 1956–86, MP for Barataria 1956–86), Marilyn Gordon (former MP for Arouca and Minister of Sport, Culture and Youth Affairs, 1981–86), and Norma Lewis Phillips (former MP for Diego Martin East and Minister of Health and Environment, 1981–86). This was a significant challenge to Manning, who had 'purged' the PNM of its 'old guard' in 1987. In addition, five of the PNM's 17 MPs, including former deputy Speaker of the House Rupert Griffith, were also on Rowley's slate. Every post was won by the Manning slate, however, whose supporters were alleged to be at the centre of violence and hooliganism at the convention (see Table 7.1).[54]

***Table 7.1. PNM Internal Election Results, 1996***

| | MANNING'S SLATE | | ROWLEY'S SLATE | |
|---|---|---|---|---|
| LEADER | Manning | 448 (62%) | Rowley | 279 (38%) |
| CHAIRMAN | Baboolal | 402 (57%) | Mohammed | 305 (43%) |
| LADY VICE-CHAIRMAN | Lewis-Phillip | 401(56%) | Gordon | 313 (44%) |
| SUBTOTALS | | 1,251 (58%) | | 897 (42%) |
| ALL POSITIONS | | 6,588 (64%) | | 3,667 (36%) |

*Source*: *Trinidad Guardian* (October 20, 1996, p. 9)

After his victory, Manning named as deputy political leaders opposition Chief Whip, Ken Valley, and his campaign manager, Joan Yuille-Williams.[55] The contest, the broadest of its kind,[56] left an unamicable split, revealing what Ryan described as 'sociological' divisions in the PNM: the PNM Women's League and the executive in control of the party groups, on the one hand and the 'reformists' and 'old guard' on the other.[57]

At the same time, the NAR was in decline. In contrast to the UNC and the PNM, the NAR polled 13,167 fewer votes in the 1996 local government election than it did in 1992. NAR leader A.N.R. Robinson, Chairman Anthony Smart, and former Minister Lincoln Myers accused the UNC of undermining the NAR in the elections. In August 1996, the party declared that, as a party, it was not part of the government, only its two MPs were.[58]

However, in November 1996 the UNC fulfilled item two of the 1995 UNC–NAR Heads of Agreement when the constitution was amended to insert the THA Act, No. 40 of 1996. The THA now had constitutional status, unlike any other local government body. The Act was the product of a Joint Select Committee of Parliament, which had modified the original recommendations contained in Senate Paper No. 4 of 1996. On the grounds of maintaining the integrity of the unitary state of Trinidad and Tobago, PNM committee members forced the removal of legislative authority for the THA, entrenchment of the Act in the constitution (thereby requiring a special majority for it to be amended), and the expansion of the Senate from 31 to 37 members to allow senatorial appointment by majority and minority THA leaders. The final draft gave the THA authority over the administration of state lands, towns and country planning, customs and excise, housing, education and statistics. In future budgetary allocations to the THA, the Finance Minister was obliged to consider Tobago's special circumstances (physical separation by sea, isolation from national growth centres, and the impracticability of participation by residents of Tobago in the major educational, cultural, and sporting facilities located in Trinidad), and a Dispute Resolution Commission was to be established to manage relations with the central government.[59]

On December 9, 1996, two weeks after the Act was passed, THA elections were held. A total of 15,034 votes were cast, with the lowest voter turnout ever, 43.9 per cent. Both the PNM and the NAR contested all 12 seats and independents contested three seats. Once again, the UNC did not participate, leaving it to its 'partner in government'. The NAR were able to secure ten seats and 60.1 per cent of the vote, and the PNM kept its seat in Buccoo/Lambeau capturing 33.6 per cent of the total votes cast. A surprise victory came from former NAR senator, Deborah Moore-Miggins,[60] who took away the Bethel/Patience Hill seat from the NAR by contesting as an independent. THA Chief Secretary Lennox Denoon, who was deselected by the NAR, was replaced by Hochoy Charles (member for Moriah/Parlatuvier), chairman of the NAR's Tobago Steering Committee, and THA member since 1980.[61]

Political shifts climaxed in early 1997. Seventy-nine year old President Noor Hassanali was due to retire on the completion of his second term in office in February 1997.[62] On February 7, the government nominated NAR leader A.N.R. Robinson for the presidency. Despite denials by both parties, this was widely regarded as the underlying deal made between the UNC and the NAR in 1995. The PNM objected to Robinson – a founding member and former deputy leader of the PNM, founder and leader of the DAC, leader of the NAR, and a former prime minister – being nominated as president, a post which warrants non-partisanship. Manning wrote, 'a partisan political President was surely not what the framers of our republican Constitution intended, nor does it augur well for the future of democratic traditions which we have been accustomed to since Independence.'[63] As an alternative, Manning, as the leader of the opposition, nominated Justice Anthony Lucky for the post, making the presidential election for the first time in its 20-year history a contest between candidates.

On February 12, two days before the election was due, Vincent Lasse (PNM MP for Point Fortin and former Minister of Housing, 1991–95), declared himself an independent, criticising in his resignation letter Manning's preference for Point Fortin Mayor Francis Bertrand as representative for the area. In less than 24 hours Lasse was sworn in by President Hassanali as a minister in the Office of the Prime Minister.[64] The UNC increased its parliamentary majority by one, and the PNM's seats decreased by one.

In the election of February 14, the PNM suffered another embarrassing defeat. Of the 64 potential votes[65] A.N.R. Robinson had secured 46, and Lucky received only 18. One ballot was spoiled. Therefore, at least three PNM parliamentarians did not vote with the party.[66]

More seriously for the parliamentary balance of power, on February 28, PNM MP for Arima Rupert Griffith, former deputy speaker of the House and a candidate on the Rowley slate, also declared himself an independent, describing the PNM as 'drifting rudderless because of a lack of leadership'. Griffith was also promptly sworn in (by President Robinson) as a minister in the Office of the Prime Minister. With Lasse and Griffith on the government side, the UNC could count on 19 seats, without the NAR's support. The PNM were reduced to 15 members.

Manning attempted to have the Arima and Point Fortin seats declared vacant under the Crossing of the Floor Act. On March 7, 1997, Speaker Hector McLean, rejected Manning's application, invoking the ruling in 1995 that the House could not recognise such requests as it had not adopted a standing order recognising political parties or their leaders.[67] At the end of April 1997, Manning was forced to withdraw a High Court application seeking to appeal the speaker's decision. He was ordered to pay TT$1.2 million dollars in legal costs incurred by the speaker.[68] To raise money, the PNM launched a 'Preservation of Democracy Fund' which, by December 1997, had only reached TT$255,000. In October 1997, Manning was forced to deny reports that prominent businessmen offered to pay off his debt in exchange for his resignation as PNM leader.[69]

The NAR, too, suffered further decline. Upon nomination for the presidency, Robinson resigned both from his Tobago East seat and from party leadership. Former speaker of the House (1987–91), and former ULF member for Tabaquite (1981–86), Nizam Mohammed was appointed to be the interim political leader. Choosing a candidate for the Tobago East by-elections was contentious, however. Dr Morgan Job – a controversial media personality known for his outspoken, perhaps 'free-market individualist' views[70] – had been selected by the NAR's Tobago Steering Committee and sanctioned by the national party to contest the seat. Pamela Nicholson (deputy chair of the Tobago Steering Committee) objected to Job's candidacy and to

Hochoy Charles's dismissal of her advice. On April 14, Nicholson resigned from the NAR and declared herself an independent, still keeping her ministry in government. For three weeks the NAR had no representatives in Parliament, yet the new leader, Nizam Mohammed, declared that he did not view Nicholson's departure as a 'major upheaval'.[71] Nicholson and THA independent, Deborah Moore-Miggins, declared their support for the NAR's rejected candidate, Winford James, who contested the seat as an independent. Panday remained neutral and offered a cabinet post to either James or Job, if either won.

*Arthur NR Robinson being sworn in as President in 1997 by Chief Justice Michael de la Bastide*

The by-election was held on May 5, with Job securing 4,117 votes; the PNM's[72] Hilson Phillips 1,184; and Winford James 860.[73] Hochoy Charles, THA Chief Secretary, consulted with the prime minister and on May 22 instructed Job to contact Panday about a cabinet post. Job was eventually sworn in by President Robinson as Minister of Tobago Affairs. Mohammed, however, declared that Job's swearing in was not authorised by the party and that Job was there on his own.[74] By May 1997, then, the government side of the Lower House was composed of 17 UNC members, three independents, and one member authorised by the Tobago Steering Committee of the NAR. The opposition side was reduced to 15 members.[75]

## THE UNC 'RAMPANT', 1997–99

With the UNC's position seemingly secure, the government more confidently proceeded to elaborate its programme. However, as the government grew bolder, passions for and against it swelled. It seemed that what the government saw as law and order others construed as a sustained 'attack' on 'fundamental freedoms'; what the government construed as 'inclusiveness' was suspected by others to be 'racialism'; and when the government focused on results in its social and economic programme, opponents pointed to lack of transparency, corruption, nepotism, authoritarianism, and bellicosity.[76]

As part of its law and order platform, the government introduced a number of well-publicised programmes to assist the police to fight crime. By the end of 1996, 154 vehicles had been distributed to police stations throughout the country; an E999 rapid response system was introduced, at a cost of TT$55 million; in December 1997, a 'zero tolerance' Law Enforcement Action Plan had been established, combining the military and police forces;[77] a community policing programme (conceptualised in 1991) was established in 1996 to involve police officers in community programmes, with the aim of solving problems before they escalated into criminal activity and to build trust between the public and the police; and in May 1999, a Crime Stoppers programme was introduced, rewarding citizens for information leading to arrests.[78] By July 1999, 1,490 new police officers had been recruited; eleven new police stations had been built, ten were reconstructed and three refurbished.

The government also instituted measures to clean up the police service, including the establishment in May 1996 of the Police Complaints Authority and prosecuting a number of corrupt police officers.[79] A Commission of Inquiry into the operation of Justices of the Peace tabled its report, in October 1997, that led to 436 charges, by April 1999, being brought against ten justices of the peace,[80] 19 bailors, three attorneys-at-law, four police officers, and six others in connection with corrupt bail transactions. A Task Force was established in October 1997 to act on a report that drug dealers and other criminals had been paying employees of the Registrar General's department to falsify and duplicate official certificates and documents and, on February 21, 2000, the Special Investigations Unit began probing for corruption in the Red House.[81]

The Panday administration also entered into several bilateral and multilateral agreements to help its fight against crime. Among them were the Extradition Treaty,[82] Mutual Legal Assistance in Criminal Matters Agreement, and Maritime Counter Drug Operations Agreement signed with the US in 1996; the Mutual Legal Assistance Treaty signed with Canada in 1997; and the Mutual Legal Assistance in Criminal Matters Agreement with Great Britain in 1998. A Counter-Narcotics Task Force had also been established with the assistance of the United States and Great Britain. In particular, cooperation with the US in counter-drugs operation increased dramatically under the UNC government. The US government was reported to have donated four specialised counter narcotics vessels in 1996, and in 1998 two 82-foot cutters and four aircraft. Also in 1998, outgoing US Ambassador Brian Donnelly signed a Letter of Agreement committing US$500,000 – ten times the amount allocated to Trinidad and Tobago in 1996 – to assist in counter-narcotics activity.[83]

The commitment to the centrality of law and order was seen in the government's 1998–99 budget, titled 'A Platform for Progress: Security For All', which had allocated to the Ministry of National Security TT$1,107 million, the second largest allocation to any ministry or department.[84] This commitment was in keeping with Panday's frequent references to Singapore as a model for Trinidad and Tobago.[85]

These measures, however, were not without problems. For instance, it was alleged that the contracts for provisioning the police with vehicles were given to UNC financiers. In response, on November 6, 1997, the Prime Minister, the Attorney-General, the National Security Minister, and the head of the civil service met with Manning, who had requested a meeting with Panday to discuss the establishment of an independent inquiry into the contract for the purchase of police jeeps, and other allegations of corruption. One hundred Chrysler Cherokee jeeps at a cost of TT$16 million had been provided to the police service by the recently formed Platinum Motors, whose director Ishwar Galbaransingh (a former financier of the PNM) had also been recently appointed chairman of TIDCO. Manning walked out of the meeting, however, saying that he believed it was a 'trap,' since he had wanted to meet with Panday alone. One week earlier Manning had told a public meeting that the government was 'looking for an opportunity to lock . . . [him] up'. The government appointed former High Court judge, Justice Jim Davis, to make an official enquiry, but it did not substantiate Manning's allegations.[86]

In addition, the government's close co-operation with the US government was seen as compromising national sovereignty. In particular, the popularly named 'Shiprider Agreement' was attacked because it allowed qualified officers of either country to board vessels authorised by the other country to carry out drug interdiction operations. From February to May 1997, Prime Minister Owen Arthur of Barbados created a controversy in Trinidad and Tobago by criticising the 1996 agreement as 'imperialistic', gathering the support of UWI academics, trade unions, NGOs, the PNM, and sections of the press. However, by May 10, 1997, Barbados and Jamaica had signed similar agreements, just before meeting with President Clinton at the first CARICOM–US Summit.[87]

Protest would be raised at more obvious legislation such as the amendment of the Summary Offences Act, requiring longer notice given to police before a demonstration was organised and increasing the penalty for violation from a maximum of one-year imprisonment to two years and from a TT$2,000 fine to TT$10,000;[88] the Domestic Violence (Amendment) Bill, passed on June 22, 1999, which had provoked two weeks of debate finally resulting in an amendment to Clause 23 that opposition and independent senators feared gave too much power to the police, who were empowered by it to enter, without a warrant, premises where they had reason to believe that domestic violence was taking place;[89] and requests by the Attorney-General to introduce the death penalty for rape and for drug trafficking, rejected in August 1999 by the Law Commission.[90]

The government's determination to uphold law and order could be seen in its strong stand against the Jamaat-al-Muslimeen, when the government erected a fence delineating the boundary between the state's and the Jamaat's holdings.[91] Threats and displays of battle-readiness by Muslimeen spokesmen were met by Minister Joseph Theodore's strong words and decisive action, prompting at least two nationwide broadcasts by the Minister that week.[92]

The administration's resolve was, perhaps, nowhere better demonstrated than in the hanging of Dole Chadee and eight other men on June 4, 5, and 7, 1999. Laws were passed to introduce alternate jurors and the acceptance of evidence from dead witnesses; in July 1996, after a lack of success, due to jurors being rejected by the defence or seeking exemption from duty,[93] it was reported that persons in the vicinity of the court – a recreational and swimming area – were summoned to jury duty.[94] Finally on September 3, 1996, all nine men were sentenced to death. The US Drug Enforcement Agency described the conviction as a 'major achievement', identifying the group as 'primarily responsible for the majority of cocaine coming through Trinidad and the Eastern Caribbean'.[95] On May 29, 1998, the government announced Trinidad and Tobago's withdrawal from the optional protocol to the UN International Covenant on Civil and Political Rights (effective August 27, 1998) and from the Inter-American Commission on Human Rights (effective May 27, 1999), since those entities did not guarantee that petitions from murder convicts under sentence of death would be fully considered within 18 months.[96] The UNC had held regular public meetings since May 27, 1998, shoring up popular support for a constitutional amendment that it had planned to introduce to prevent prisoners under sentence of death from filing constitutional motions after their death warrants were read.[97] On September 21, 1998, the bill was defeated by a vote of 21 to 13.[98] On September 23, Panday called a special meeting of the PNM's members of parliament; however, no statement was issued after the meeting.[99] One week after the withdrawal from the Inter-American Commission took effect, the nine men were hanged in batches of three over the course of three days, after much protest from campaigners against capital punishment.[100] Nothing seemed able to stop the government's will. On June 4, 1999, the first day of the hanging, Panday announced that the local government elections would be held on July 12, 1999.

Related to this plank of their programme was the government's battle with the media, particularly the Caribbean Communications Network (CCN). The conflict centred around 'freedom of expression', 'democracy', and their limits, and grew increasingly hostile over the period. In May 1997, the government published a Green Paper on the reform of media law in order to 'open discussion' on the need to update and balance in the contemporary communications environment the responsibilities and rights of the public, government, and the media.[101] In particular, Ken Gordon objected to the suggestion in section 8.10 (2) in the proposed code of ethics that 'journalists and newspapers shall endeavour to highlight and promote activities of the State and the public which aim at national unity and solidarity, integrity of Trinidad and Tobago, and economic and social progress'.[102] The paper brought immediate criticism from Gordon who, in an address to the Publishers and Broadcasters Association, described the paper as 'deviously framed and offensive'. He called for the 'widest possible campaign' against it.

At an Indian Arrival Day celebration in Chandernagore (near Chaguanas) on May 29, 1997, Panday responded to Gordon by calling him a 'pseudo-racist' who used racism to promote his own interest, unlike a genuine racist who at least promoted his or her race.[103] On June 2, Gordon resigned from the chairmanship of state-run BWIA and from the Prime Minister's National Beautification Awards Committee, and instructed his legal advisers to take 'appropriate action' against Panday. Panday was unapologetic. He dismissed the well-publicised resignation and replaced Gordon with CEO of CL Financial, Lawrence Duprey, a close associate.[104] Speaking at the El Dorado Shiv Mandir on June 8, 1997, Panday made the famous declaration,

> *Every time I speak without a prepared script I seem to say something that unsettles somebody .... I wish to assure you that no one will attack my government and remain unscathed (*applause*). The struggle has been too long and it has been too hard not only for me but for too many of you .... You must not delude yourself into believing that the fact that we are in government that change has come.*[105]

In a hostile interview with the *Guardian* on November 16, 1997, Panday declared,

> *The media's disposition to view and to represent me and my Government through the prism of race has been at the core of my disagreements with the media. There has as well, been political bias in certain areas of the media. I have never been afraid to call a spade a bloody shovel when I thought it to be warranted.*
>
> *[Responding to a question about his allegedly 'quite unstatesmanlike' statements:] ... I will say no more other than that I give you no promise that I will ever be disposed to take unfair and biased attacks on me and members of my government with the statesmanlike silence of a bobolee.*[106]
>
> *In any event I think the country wants an effective Prime Minister, not an imperial ruler and not a self-styled Father of the Nation.*[107]

The green paper was effectively halted, however. No resulting legislation was passed, and in November and December 1997, peace was made. However, in 1998 the fight started again through a number of events.

On April 30, 1998, the government refused a sixth renewal of the work permit (granted in 1993) of Barbadian journalist Julian Rogers, host of TV6's *Morning Edition*, on the grounds that CCN had not complied with the condition that an understudy for Rogers be trained.[108] Some regional pressure was placed on the Trinidad and Tobago government over the issue. Barbadian Prime Minister Owen Arthur claimed that while he and Panday were in Chile together he had reminded the Trinidad and Tobago Prime Minister that the expulsion of Rogers had contravened the CARICOM agreement on the free movement of skilled workers. Panday denied such a conversation ever took place and also noted that the agreement had not yet been made law in Trinidad and Tobago.[109] At the 19th CARICOM Summit in St Lucia in July 1998, the matter was raised again, and Panday responded, 'I am not afraid of the media . . . . They didn't put us in power, we are here despite them, they're not as powerful as they think they are.'[110] Rogers remained in Barbados.

On May 28, 1988 (two days before Indian Arrival Day), the *Express* ran a red-ink headline, 'Racism at Piarco', basing its lead story on unsubstantiated PSA allegations of 'rampant racism and victimisation' practised by the state-controlled Airports Authority at Piarco Airport against Africans. The *Guardian* on the following day published the fact that 85 per cent of the Airport Authority's workforce was of African descent, according to the Airports Authority Human Resource Manager, Calvin Bess. Led by the prime minister, a controversy over the professionalism and political bias of the daily press followed. After taking leave of absence, *Express* editor Lennox Grant (former editor of the small *Tapia* party newspaper in the late 1980s) resigned from his post on August 10, 1998, to join the *Trinidad Guardian* as its new editor-in-chief.[111]

Matters were further incited three months later when the *Express*, TV6, and the PNM alleged that the prime minister had arranged the 'mother of all sweetheart deals' for Namcaran Singh (Narine Singh), chairman of the UNC New York Party Group, and a friend of the prime minister for 20 years, in an agreement with a United States company, InnCogen, to build a US$100 million electricity generating plant in central Trinidad.[112] On November 8, at a rally celebrating the third anniversary of the UNC government, Panday accused the media houses of 'wanting to exercise political power without fighting elections'. He accused sections of the press of racism and being politically tied to the PNM, drug dealers, and insurrectionists. Panday declared, 'We must treat them as political opponents who are out to destroy us. If we do not, they will destroy us. We must do them first.' Some journalists covering the rally were jostled by UNC members, while others reportedly had beer thrown over them.[113] Following the events, the UNC criticised its supporters' behaviour and denied that the prime minister's speech was intended to cause violence. On November 20 MATT organised a broadly anti-government march in Port of Spain for 'Democracy, Human Rights and a Free Press'.[114] The rally, which concluded at Woodford Square at 1:15pm, 15 minutes before Parliament's afternoon sitting, was reported to have attracted support from the opposition PNM, the NAR, NGOs, religious activists, cultural activists, the PSA, the National Union of Government and Federated Workers (NUGFW), the OWTU, the Trinidad and Tobago Unified Teachers Association (TTUTA), political commentators, and 'blind persons'.[115]

Another of the UNC government's main efforts was to 'celebrate' diversity, and attempt to turn it into a strength.[116] However, such efforts were often greeted with hostility by those who suspected that though apparently promoting equality, the aim was to covertly usher in Indian hegemony, undermine the position of Afro-Trinidadians, or both.

In 1997, the government granted 30 acres of land at Orange Grove Estate in Maloney, eastern Trinidad, for the establishment of a spiritual centre for African religions which would house a cathedral, a library, a building for counselling services and the training of ministers, and a trade school for children living in depressed areas.[117] On Baptist Liberation Day 1998, Panday was proclaimed an honorary Baptist and he declared, 'Fellow Shouter Baptists, I must be the luckiest man in the world: I was born in the home of a Hindu, I went to a Christian college, I got married to a Muslim woman, and today I have been consecrated into the Baptist Shouter Faith.'[118] On July 30, 1999, the government passed the Orisa marriage bill (introduced on July 2), noting that no other country in the world recognised such marriages (including the Orisa homeland, Nigeria). Panday noted that this had been clear discrimination 'paradoxically' perpetrated by the PNM government.[119]

Prominent African and Afro-American personalities were invited to Trinidad and Tobago during this time, including Reverend Jesse Jackson (who gave the feature address on July 15, 1997 at CLICO's[120] Workers Convention); Flight Lieutenant Jerry Rawlins, President of the Republic of Ghana (as the feature speaker at Emancipation celebrations on August 5, 1997); Erica Williams-Connell (who opened the Eric Williams Collection at the UWI on March 22, 1998); Retired US General Colin Powell (who was the Keynote Speaker at CL Financial management conference on March 23, 1998); and Winnifred Madikizela Mandela (invited by the ESC on a three-day visit in June 1998 to launch Emancipation celebrations). Though none were invited by the government, they were each formally received in the office of the Prime Minister, who spoke alongside each them at their feature addresses, with the exception of Mandela.[121] Introducing President Rawlins, the first Ghanain head of state to visit Trinidad and Tobago,[122] Panday was booed after he repeated his assertion that despite his efforts to create 'a unified prosperous society in which each individual knows he or she has a stake . . . [he continued] to face opposition from those who seek personal gains from divisiveness in the society.'[123]

On August 4, 1998, Panday formally commissioned the Chief Olukun Igbaro African Library of Trinidad and Tobago (named after President Robinson's chiefly title). In October 1998, the government established a three-member committee – headed by ESC chairman Khafra Kambon, with Anglican Pastor Clive Griffith (Kwame Mohlabani) and historian Michael Anthony as its other two members – to examine the proposal, announced by Panday on Emancipation Day, 1998, that King George V Park (in the well-established, high income Port of Spain suburb of St Clair) be renamed 'Emancipation Park' and a monument to honour African slaves be built there.[124] The St Clair Residents' Association, with the support of the PNM, Port of Spain Mayor John Rahael, and the Chamber of Industry and Commerce, threatened legal action against the government over the issue. The proposal was withdrawn on July 23, 1999.[125]

On January 13, 1997, the Indian High Commissioner to Trinidad and Tobago presented Prime Minister Panday with the keys to the temporary headquarters for the Mahatma Gandhi Institute for Cultural Co-operation, the cultural centre that became one of the problems identified in the NAR's 1988 Nanga Report.[126] On February 8, 1998, Indian Prime Minister Atal Bihari Vajpayee paid a visit to Trinidad (the first since Indira Gandhi's visit in 1968) and officially opened the permanent two hectare (five acre) site at Mount Hope.[127]

Prime Minister Panday was the chief guest at the government of India's 50th Republic Day celebrations on January 26, 1997. The invitation to Panday was extended by India's President Shankar Dayal Sharma who had been an official guest of the government of Trinidad and Tobago for the 150th anniversary of Indian Arrival on May 30, 1995 (while Patrick Manning was Prime Minister). Panday left for India with a contingent of 98 business persons, cultural artists, press officers, and officials. A highlight of the trip was his emotional first-time visit to Lakshmanpur, the village from where his great-grandfather had come.[128]

Following Dharmacharaya Krishna Persad's rejection of the 1995 Trinity Cross, in October 1998, a National Awards Committee headed by Chief Justice Michael de la Bastide recommended that the name 'Trinity Cross' be changed to the 'Order of Trinidad and Tobago' since the Cross 'was seen as a Christian symbol' and Trinidad and Tobago was a multi-religious society.[129] At about the same time, a Scholarships Review Committee was reportedly established to investigate perceived injustices in the selection process, a grievance of Panday since his days in the NAR.[130]

Panday did not have an entirely smooth relationship with his Indian support base, however. The Sanatan Dharma Maha Sabha (SDMS), the largest Hindu group in the country, clashed with the Panday administration on a few occasions. In 1997, it complained about the allocations to Emancipation Day activities (which officially amounted to TT$416,000 in 1996) relative to funding for its own activities (which the SDMS claimed was TT$100,000);[131] in a series of newspaper columns in the *Express,* it articulated opposition to the government's commitment to abolish the 11-plus Common Entrance exam, arguing that academic excellence would be needlessly sacrificed for egalitarian ideology and that more administrative chaos and corruption would be introduced in the new continuous assessment programme;[132] and during Indian Arrival Day celebrations in 1999, the SDMS claimed that it would file a $2 billion class-action suit against the state for 'restitution' of the value of the land that the state reclaimed from Hindus before 1945, when Hindu marriages (and therefore inheritance) were not recognised. They noted, however, that they would wait until the Attorney-General Ramesh Lawrence Maharaj demitted office so that they could secure his 'unparalleled legal expertise'. When asked about the statements, Prime Minister Panday responded, 'Am I expected to reply to every foolish statement made in this country?'[133]

In a more direct challenge to Williams's anti-clerical, centralising nationalism, in June 1998 the Panday administration announced that it would establish a committee to review the 1960 Concordat between the church and state.[134] In an interview on September 20, 1998, Panday remarked,

> *I believe the Concordat was a mistake by Prime Minister Dr. Eric Williams, though he may have imposed it with good intentions . . . . He wrongly thought he could promote unity by destroying diversity and creating*

> *a monolithic society. But by removing the moralising influence of religion from the educational system, he created the generation of amoral youths which is today attacking the society with a viciousness hitherto unknown. He, probably innocently, sowed the wind. Today we are reaping the whirlwind of that miscalculation.*[135]

In keeping with the Creole nationalist idea of 'Trinidad and Tobago culture,' however, the government established the country's first National Steel Orchestra, launched on Independence Day 1998, with 30 members being paid a monthly salary of TT$2,500. It also pledged to establish a Carnival Institute.[136]

Panday tabled the Equal Opportunities Bill, which he had advocated since 1990 during the Hyatali Constitutional Reform Committee on March 13, 1998.[137] The bill proposed to outlaw discrimination on the basis of gender, race (including mixed race), religion, political affiliation, origin (including geographical origin), and disability in the fields of employment, education, accommodation, and the provision of goods and services. The bill – in particular, Section 7.1 which sought to 'prohibit offensive behaviour in public which offends or insults another person or group ... [or incites] racial and religious hatred' – was largely condemned in the press, which suspected, as Selwyn Ryan argued in the *Express* of May 22, 1998, that it was 'a Trojan horse to silence certain calypsonians, and that one of its unintended consequences would be to kill the traditional calypso as an artform'.[138]

Despite the UNC's gestures, ethnic grievances and suspicions by Africans were heightened during the period. Calypsonians Cro Cro in 1996 ('All Yuh Look For Dat') and Mystic Prowler 1998 ('A Vision of T&T in 2010') won the Calypso Monarch titles singing songs that were plainly hostile to the idea of Trinidad and Tobago being led by Indians.[139] Small African-oriented organisations had sprung up, including one led by Arthur Sanderson (former MP for Fyzabad and junior minister in the NAR administration dismissed from his post for allegedly slapping his secretary), who proclaimed, 'Thank God UNC win, because African people eyes now open',[140] and the National Association for the Empowerment of African People (NAEAP), formed in March 1998 by Trinidad-born Selwyn Cudjoe, Professor of Africana Studies, Wellesley College, Massachusetts, USA.[141] The *Express* became a prominent forum for the almost weekly broadcast and elaboration of ethnic grievances, notably, but not exclusively, by its columnists Selwyn Cudjoe and Theodore Lewis, on a pro-African side, and Kamal Persad, Anil Mahabir, the Maha Sabha, and Rajne Ramlakhan, on a pro-Indian side.[142]

During the period, there was an almost constant running feud between Tobago and Trinidad. Its character, however, was quite different from the Trinidadian ethnic questions of recognition and self-esteem as it more directly involved decentralisation, administration, and formal politics. On September 22, 1998, independent cabinet member Pamela Nicholson voted against an amendment to the contentious Squatter Regularisation bill.[143] After the vote, Panday had informed Nicholson that her position was 'untenable' and that he could not tolerate violation of the principle of Cabinet responsibility. On September 23, Nicholson held a press conference to announce her resignation from government. She did not join the PNM, but her action increased the number of opposition members to 16, and reduced the government side to 20.[144]

Nicholson's resignation came against the background of constant bickering between the THA and the central government, mostly regarding control over the raising, allocation, and spending of funds. In 1997 and 1998, Hochoy Charles used numerous opportunities to express his dissatisfaction with the THA's budgetary allocations from the central government and pressed for a measure of financial independence.[145] On the other hand, bolstered by the claims of the THA opposition (which, by 1998, comprised PNM minority leader, William McKenzie, independent assemblyman, Moore-Miggins, and two former NAR assemblymen who had declared themselves independents, Beverley Ramsey-Moore and Richard Alfred), the central government queried the THA's use of funds allocated to it. In October 1998, THA funding for the 1998–99 fiscal year was withheld by the Minister of Finance, as the Disputes Resolution Commission considered a matter concerning the supply of details of Tobago's 1997 expenditure.[146] On June 12–13, 1999, Hochoy Charles met with the Attorney-General Maharaj and the Ministers of Finance and of Tobago Affairs, Kuei Tung and Job, on June 12 and 13, 1999, to discuss measures that included amendments to empower the THA to borrow up to TT$1 billion, to collect revenue payable in Tobago, and to guarantee the THA a minimum share of the recurrent development budget of Trinidad and Tobago.[147] Charles emerged from the meeting criticising the 'non-performance' of Minister of Finance[148] and on June 17 presented the THA budget asserting that 'after this budget, Tobago is finished with that kind of mendicancy budgeting forever'.[149] Subsequently, Charles met with Chief Justice Michael de la Bastide, Patrick Manning, Nizam Mohammed, and addressed a retreat of the CARICOM Heads of Government in Tobago on July 6, 1999, criticising the relationship between

Tobago and Trinidad in the presence of Panday, then CARICOM chairman.[150] At a news conference on July 9, 1999, Charles called on the 'people of Trinidad not to vote for the party in power when they go to the polls to vote in the 1999 Local Government election [on July 12]'. The *Guardian* led the following day's paper with the red-ink headline, 'Don't vote UNC.' National Alliance for Reconstruction (NAR) MP Morgan Job, however, stood with the government and was later criticised by Charles at the April 30, 2000 NAR Conference.[151]

Perhaps above all else, the Panday administration prided itself on its measurable and visible achievements, which had received a good measure of international recognition from the IMF,[152] the *New York Times* on September 4, 1998, the *ACP-EU Courier* (May/June 1998), *Business Week* (August 10, 1998), including the *Washington Times* (May 26, 1999), *Site Selection* magazine (July 1999), the *Oil and Gas Journal, Revista Latinoamericana* in January 1997,[153] the 1999 UN Human Development Report,[154] and the front page of the *Wall Street Journal* (March 13, 2001). During the local government elections of 1999, Panday more aggressively restated his claim, 'Any jackass can promise anything. We have come this time to change the politics of Trinidad and Tobago. We say no manifesto. We ent come to promise. We come tell you how much we have delivered. We ask you to judge us by what we do. Talk is cheap. Manifesto is cheap. Promise is cheap. Judge us by what we have done'.[155] However, against the government's zeal to deliver came seemingly unending allegations by the press, the PNM, activists, commentators, NGOs, and community groups of a lack of transparency, corruption (racial and partisan), authoritarianism, and bellicosity.

Undoubtedly, the economic indicators during the UNC's period of government were strongly positive, almost in entirety (see Appendix D). Most notably, real GDP growth had been continuous since 1994. At the same time, a 15-year low in the unemployment rate was reached in 1998. This had been achieved while the labour force grew steadily from 467,700 in 1990 to 562,600 in 1999, at an average rate of 2 per cent per annum (CBTT 1993; 2000).[156] Moreover, this growth occurred in an environment of low and steady inflation, reaching a 26-year low in 1996, and a relatively stable US$:TT$ exchange rate.

This growth had been even more remarkable considering the 30.3 per cent drop in the average annual price of oil between 1997 and 1998,[157] the difficulties in the world economy occasioned by the Asian and Russian crises in 1999, and the softening of prices for ammonia, urea, methanol, and steel products (see Table 7.2).

***Table 7.2. Prices of Selected Commodities, 1994–9 (US$/tonne)***

| | Ammonia fob Caribbean | Urea fob Caribbean | Methanol fob Rotterdam | Billets fob Latin America | Wire Rods fob Latin America |
|---|---|---|---|---|---|
| 1994 | 169 | 148 | 269 | 223 | 277 |
| 1995 | 199 | 207 | 268 | 237 | 296 |
| 1996 | 188 | 195 | 153 | 222 | 276 |
| 1997 | 161 | 136 | 187 | 222 | 295 |
| 1998 | 118 | 105 | 139 | 221 | 264 |
| September 1999 | 97 | 85 | 116 | 190 | 228 |

*Source*: *EB* (November 1999: 4)

Total government expenditure seemed to have settled around 25 per cent of nominal GDP, in contrast to the period between 1976 and 1989 when the proportion was consistently above 30 per cent, peaking at 47.4 per cent in 1982.[158] Not only was government expenditure playing a smaller role in the economy, the proportion of its revenues from oil had been consistently dropping, reaching an all time low of 17.5 per cent in 1999.[159]

The most important driving force in the economy seems to have been foreign direct investment, which reached an all-time high of US$999.6 million in 1997.[160] Importantly, the degree of openness in 1997 returned to pre-1966 levels, before Finance Minister A.N.R. Robinson introduced the restrictive Finance Act. Finance Minister Kuei Tung boasted in his 1998–99 budget speech that Trinidad and Tobago had become known to international investors as a place where 'the decision-making process on investment proposals . . . [was] completed with speed and aggressiveness'.[161]

The most important investments occurred in the energy sector (see Table 7.3), whose industries were mainly located at Point Lisas in Couva.[162]

***Table 7.3. Direct Foreign Investment in Private Sector Enterprises by Sector of Activity, 1991–7 (US$ million)***

| | 1991 | 1992 | 1993 | 1994 | 1995 | 1996 | 1997 |
|---|---|---|---|---|---|---|---|
| Petroleum Industries | 125.1 | 153.2 | 348.9 | 275.1 | 266 | 334.7 | 954.2 |
| Food Drink and Tobacco | 2.7 | -0.5 | 1.9 | 5.7 | 3.2 | 4.3 | 8.4 |
| Chemicals and Non-metallic Minerals | -0.5 | 0.3 | 0.1 | 128.7 | 1.7 | 2.3 | 2.3 |
| Assembly Type and Related Industries | 0.4 | 0.3 | -0.4 | -1.9 | -0.4 | 0.7 | -0.1 |
| Distribution | -0.3 | 1.6 | 4.2 | 1 | 6.2 | 4.4 | 3.1 |
| All Other Sectors | 16.7 | 16.1 | 17.9 | 112.4 | 19 | 9.9 | 31.7 |
| TOTAL | 144.1 | 171 | 372.6 | 521 | 295.7 | 356.3 | 999.6 |

*Sources: Balance of Payments* (1994, 1998)

By March 1998, Trinidad and Tobago had become the site of one natural-gas-processing facility (750 million cubic feet per day); four 'world scale' methanol plants (producing approximately 2.1 million tonnes per annum); eight ammonia plants (approximately 3.5 million tonnes per annum); and one urea plant (580,000 tonnes per annum); one iron and steel mill; and one iron carbide facility (300,000 tonnes per annum).[163] Between 1996 and 1998, two methanol plants (TTMC's second in May 1996, and Caribbean Methanol Company's second, Methanol IV, which started operations in March 1998) and three ammonia plants (PCS Nitrogen's[164] third, commissioned April 11, 1996, and its fourth, commissioned February 11, 1998; Farmland-Mississippi Chemicals' plant, commissioned on August 5, 1998) were opened.[165]

Unlike in oil,[166] Trinidad and Tobago held important positions in the ammonia and methanol industries: in 1998 it was the world's second leading exporter of ammonia (seeking to consolidate the leading position by 2002)[167] and the world's third largest exporter of methanol.[168] The PCS Nitrogen complex was the world's largest single producer of ammonia (producing approximately 1.75 million tonnes per annum) and the Farmland-Mississippi Chemicals plant was the largest single-train-ammonia facility in the world.[169]

On April 19, 1999, the US$1 billion Atlantic LNG (in Point Fortin, St Patrick) shipped its first exports, eight weeks ahead of schedule, making Trinidad and Tobago the world's 11th exporter of LNG and the eighth largest producer, with an output of three million tonnes a year.[170] The plant was the first to be built in the Western Hemisphere since 1969, and successfully reintroduced a cost-effective liquefaction system (Bechtel/Phillips) that had not been used since then.[171] In June 1998, before Atlantic came on stream, Amoco and Repsol announced their intention to quadruple their investment by building another 'train.'[172] Their partner, British Gas, remarked: 'Trinidad's strategic location and political stability gave it an advantage over its competitors such as Algeria and Nigeria'.[173]

Caribbean Ispat Ltd. (CIL) opened its 1.5 million tonnes per annum Midrex Direct Reduced Iron Plant, or DR3 Megamodule, the largest of its kind in the world in April 1999.[174] That same month, Phoenix Park Gas Processors, Ltd. completed a major expansion in April 1999 to process the natural-gas liquids from Atlantic LNG;[175] and on December 28, 1999, the 860,000 tonnes per annum, US$250 million Titan Methanol plant (the largest producer in the Northern Hemisphere) began production.[176] At the time of research, the energy sector was still in a dynamic phase, with agreements signed for the development of an ethylene project; a 500,000 tonnes per annum Iron Reduction Plant, by Cleveland Cliffs; and considerably more trains for the Atlantic LNG plant.[177] In October 1997, Energy Minister Finbar Ganga noted that the sector was in an 'unprecedented' period of expansion, 'possibly far in excess of the boom years' of the mid-1970s.[178]

Enabling the investments was the dramatic increase in hydrocarbon reserves, as exploration off the deep waters of the east coast[179] resulted in a series of major oil and gas discoveries, including Amoco's largest oil find in 25 years.[180] In 1992, proven reserves of crude oil were at a 23 year low of 466 million barrels. By 1999, reserves reached a 14-year high of 600 million barrels. Proven reserves of natural gas were at a 13-year low in 1993 of 8.5 trillion cubic feet. By 1999, it had more than doubled to an all-time high of 17.2 trillion cubic feet, with possible and probable reserves at 8.1 trillion cubic feet.[181]

At the 'Natural Gas in the Americas V' Conference, held in Trinidad and Tobago from June 20 to 23, 1999, Panday announced that Trinidad and Tobago expected to benefit from US$2 billion in direct foreign investment in 1999 and 2000, noting that (measured on a per capita basis) Trinidad and Tobago was the largest investment partner of the United States after Canada, with over 60 multinational corporations from the US operating in the country.[182]

The non-petroleum sector, however, had outstripped growth in the petroleum sector, revealing an apparent dynamism in the local economy that seemed to pervade all business in the country at the time – large and small, foreign and local, manufacturing and service, private and state-owned.[183] The country's balance of payments, foreign reserves, and non-oil exports appeared strong during this period, and the Panday government expressed its fullest support for Free Trade arrangements, whether bilaterally or through CARICOM.[184] Gross capital formation in 1997 was at a 15-year high, returning to pre-1982 levels.[185]

From this position the government embarked on a well-promoted social and infrastructural development programme, which Panday often linked to Trinidad and Tobago's economic success. For example, in an interview with *IBIS Magazine* in November 1997, Panday remarked, 'We've brought a tremendous amount of stability into the economic life of the country [now that the people in Trinidad feel more strongly that they belong]. That is shown by the enormous investments that are coming into the country. I think our coming to office has brought more social, political and economic stability.'[186] Supporting this notion, in 1996 there had been a net immigration into Trinidad and Tobago of 1,554 persons, as opposed to a net emigration of 10,265 in 1995. The only other time net immigration was recorded during the 1964–96 period was in 1982–83.[187]

The 1999 United Nations Human Development Report listed Trinidad and Tobago at the top of the 74 nations graded for medium human development.[188] Under the Public Sector Investment Programme in the 1999 budget, TT$394.78 million (the second highest allocation of the TT$1,222 million proposed expenditure) went towards social infrastructure.[189] Projects here included the establishment of a Centre for Socially Displaced Persons to deal with the problem of vagrancy, the first centre being opened in San Fernando on July 9, 1999;[190] a Community Development Fund to offer developmental assistance to and encourage participation of NGOs and community-based organisations;[191] a 'Drop-In Centres' programme of the Domestic Violence Unit based in 22 communities;[192] a Squatter Regularisation Programme in 1999, affecting 100,000 people in 25,000 homes;[193] and the raising of pensions from TT$420 a month in 1995 to TT$620 in 1998.

The government also aimed to provide 'Water for All' by the year 2000. The components of the plan included a TT$450 million programme to eliminate the water deficit in south Trinidad; the signing of an agreement on August 25, 1999 for the construction of a 24 million gallons per day desalination plant at Point Lisas at a cost of US$120 million;[194] and the construction of a TT$131 million Caroni Water Treatment plant commissioned in April 29, 2000.[195]

In addition, a Rural Electrification Programme had been embarked upon, and on February 25, 1999 New Zealand Post International signed an agreement to manage the new Trinidad and Tobago Postal Corporation for a period of five years.[196]

In its 1999 local government elections campaign, the UNC advertised that in its three and a half years over 400 kilometres of roads were rebuilt and resurfaced, and 30 completely new bridges were built in addition to the repair and the rebuilding of existing bridges. On June 21, 1999 the government launched its Rural Transport Services Project, which resulted in fares from Blanchisseuse to Port of Spain falling from TT$15 to TT$8. At the launch, Panday declared that he wanted to be remembered as 'a Prime Minister who loved all his people' and promised to end the exclusion of citizens of rural areas.[197]

The largest, and most controversial, infrastructural project was the US$105 million airport expansion. The project was begun by the Manning administration under the name Project Pride, but was halted due to charges of corruption. The Panday administration revived the project as essential to its vision of making Trinidad and Tobago a communications hub in the 21st century. On April 22, 1997, a report by retired Justice Lennox Deyalsingh found a 'measure of collusion' in the granting of the construction contract: Ishwar Galbaransingh had been a member of the committee that selected the management team who, in turn, granted the contract to the Northern-Yorke Construction-Coosal's consortium, in which Galbaransingh held a major interest. On April 25, Galbaransingh resigned from the chairmanship of TIDCO and on May 1 the Airports Authority chairman, Ameer Edoo, also resigned, together with two other government-appointed members. On July 31, 1997, the courts cleared Galbaransingh of charges due to unfair treatment in the inquiry, and on September 3, 1998, Galbaransingh received a new TT$207 million construction contract.[198] On June 22, 1999, Panday told a public meeting, 'I make one mistake with the airport contract . . . . I stopped the contract while the inquiry was going on. I should never have done that . . . . I am going to build that airport come hell or high water. They could do what they want, that airport coming.'[199] On June 8, 1999, Transparency International and seven construction industry associations (later supported by Roman Catholic Archbishop Anthony Pantin and Anglican Bishop Reverend Rawle Douglin) called on President Robinson to appoint a Commission of Inquiry to investigate the award of contracts for the airport project.[200] On July 28, President Robinson responded that an inquiry would be in the public interest, but that based on his own judgement he did not have the power to appoint such a Commission.[201]

Physical infrastructure wasn't the only area of concentration. The Panday administration embarked on major changes in the education system, amounting to what Panday called a 'revolution' in education.[202] The major aspect of the 'revolution' was the abolition of the Common Entrance exam, announced during the opening of the Eric Williams Collection on March 22, 1998, and effected in early 2000.[203] In May 1999, the IDB approved a loan of US$105 million, supplemented by the government's US$45 million injection, for a Secondary Education Modernisation Programme to construct 20 new secondary schools and improve the one hundred existing schools. The government's aim was to increase secondary education coverage from the existing level of 69 per cent 'to ensure there is universal secondary education for all by the year 2001'.[204] Other aspects of the government's reforms included curriculum reform, and the standardisation of textbooks, which antagonistically provoked the Textbook Evaluation Committee (headed by independent senator and UWI-based literary critic, Professor Ken Ramchand), TTUTA, and the Publishers' and Booksellers' Collective of Trinidad and Tobago to take a stance against the government.[205]

However, there were many problems with both the education and health systems, despite apparent attempts at reform and modernisation.[206] Seemingly constant throughout the period were protests by doctors, junior doctors, and nurses over poor conditions, shortages of supplies and staff, and administration problems with the relatively new Regional Health Authority system.[207] Also, in the education system, many schools were in extremely poor condition, sometimes unsanitary. This, too, provoked much protest by parents and teachers.[208]

Protests of a more diffuse nature were common as well. From August to September 1998, residents of the low-income area, John John, in East Port of Spain demanded that the relatively upscale 23-apartment John John Towers (whose construction began under the Manning administration) be given to residents of the area. The government resisted their protests and vandalism, and instituted a lottery system to distribute the housing.[209] In November 1998, there occurred simultaneously a sit-out at St Ann's Hospital, an impasse between the Tunapuna-Piarco Corporation and the Ministry of Local Government, and road blocks by community protesters in Maloney, La

Horqetta, and Mayaro/Guayaguyare.[210] Panday dismissed these as politically motivated (they all occurred in PNM-controlled areas, except for Mayaro, which only in 1995 came under UNC control). In June 1999, residents of East Port of Spain marched against crime, police harassment, unemployment, and racism[211] and, in July, residents of Tabaquite (the constituency of then Education Minister Adesh Nanan) mounted a series of protests and roadblocks, ending on July 19 when two protesters were arrested for littering and obstructing a free passage.[212] Referring to the protests, the *Guardian* accused the government of 'trumpeting their triumphs . . . [by] looking at the forest and failing to see the trees'.[213] At an election meeting in 1999, Panday (a veteran protester) contrasted himself to Manning, whom he accused of being a weak leader who was afraid to govern: 'Manning was afraid of protests. He did not understand that anything you going to do people are going to protest, but Manning was the kind of man who only know to back back from issues.'[214]

Controversy surrounded the state sector, particularly the National Flour Mills, BWIA, WASA/Severn Trent, National Petroleum, National Maintenance Training and Security Company, the URP, and the section of the Ministry of Education responsible for school textbooks.[215] Government and its opponents not uncommonly levelled charges of racism at each other. For instance, on January 16, 1997, Panday announced that he had requested a full report on the appointment in September 1996 of Ken Soodhoo as consultant with the National Petroleum Marketing Company. Soodhoo had been a member of the National Petroleum board and was also managing director of state-owned First Citizens Bank, from which he was dismissed in December 1996 under unclear circumstances. On January 26, Soodhoo resigned from National Petroleum but was asked to remain until mid-February to complete work in progress. Panday withheld publication of the Soodhoo report, however, claiming that it was libellous. He had also remarked that the concerns about Soodhoo's appointment were unfounded and that if Soodhoo's name were 'Voodoo' the opposition would not have made their allegations of bribery.[216]The *Express* voiced its indignation that dissent against the government was so regularly interpreted by Panday as having racial or partisan motivation, while the PNM regularly accused the UNC of being a government for 'themselves, their friends, and their families.'[217] In May 1999 the government introduced an Integrity in Public Life Bill but, despite its scope and sanctions, it had been dismissed by the opposition and media commentators.[218]

Despite the buoyancy of the economy, the lowest unemployment rate in 15 years, and the social programmes of the government, a section of the labour movement bitterly opposed the Panday administration, ostensibly for its programme of privatisation, retrenchment, encouragement of low-paying jobs, and reputedly 'anti-union' labour laws.[219] Perhaps most important in souring the relationship between Panday and the labour movement had been the bitter and largely unsuccessful TTUTA work to rule action from September 1996 to May 1997,[220] and the strike, led by the OWTU, by 700 non-academic staff at the UWI from March 31 to May 28, 1998.[221] As Labour Day (June 19) 1998 approached, Errol McLeod, president of NATUC and the OWTU, said that he would not be marching with 'certain people'. This exacerbated tensions within the movement, most vocally between the Communication Workers Union (CWU) and NUGFW.[222] Panday delivered a nationwide broadcast indicating that, for the first time in 30 years, he would not be taking part in Labour Day observances. He urged labour unity, a commitment to the welfare of workers in the contemporary environment, and defended his government's record with a lengthy list of achievements.[223] Panday also resigned his post as president of the ATS&GWTU. The following year the NATUC executive, by a vote of nine to four, invited both Panday and Manning to Labour Day celebrations, further pitting the NUGFW against the OWTU, TTUTA, PSA, and CWU, in particular. Manning had accepted NATUC's invitation, but on the eve of Labour Day celebrations Panday declined his invitation and once again urged labour unity. Manning then changed his mind.[224] In 1998 and 1999 the ATS&GWTU, the union most identified with Indians, did not participate in the Fyzabad observances. Other unions, on both sides of the dispute, did not attend. NUGFW members were booed off the platform at the traditional Fyzabad rally, and NUGFW subsequently passed a resolution asking for McLeod's resignation from NATUC.[225] The OWTU, PSA, TTUTA, and CWU formed themselves into a firm anti-government coalition and organised joint protests, including a rally in Port of Spain on September 10, 1999, demanding profit sharing and job protection in the National Flour Mills, TSTT, and Tringen, whose 51 per cent shareholdings the government had planned to divest.[226]

## 'JUDGE US BY OUR PERFORMANCE': FROM THE ELECTIONS OF 1999 TO 2000

The election campaign for the July 12, 1999 local government elections began a long series of campaigning which in the end resulted in a serious twist of fate for the Government. The 1999 local government election was fought aggressively by the UNC. Three years earlier, at the announcements of the results of the 1996 local government elections Panday had declared,

> *Most important I want to congratulate the strategists for the strategy they evolved in this election. If you notice how this election was fought. It was a pincer movement, a pincer movement where we moved from our strongholds and we were moving in to encircle and entrap the PNM and bring about victory on the citadel [i.e. Port of Spain] (*applause*).*
>
> *That is what the movement has begun from the east and is coming down. We are taking Sangre Grande and we are beginning to win seats in Tunapuna and so on and the strategy is to take from the East and to come down and to drive them into the Gulf of Paria on the West (*applause*). And from the South, move up and push them into the Atlantic Ocean in the North.*[227]

The UNC had been making such moves. On October 20, 1998, the party reportedly held its first meeting at the Queen's Park Savannah in Port of Spain;[228] in early 1999 it acquired an office at Piggot's Corner, Belmont, east Port of Spain, and the party had expressed intentions of acquiring the former office of PNM MP Kenneth Valley in Diego Martin. In 1999, the party delayed its campaign launch by one week to June 20 so that it could move from its regular Chaguanas Mid-Centre Mall venue to Macoya in the PNM-controlled Tunapuna/Piarco Regional Corporation. At that rally, the amount of Africans present surprised many observers. Panday declared in anticipated triumph, 'That Berlin Wall of division that the PNM constructed to keep the people apart has come tumbling down, never to be put back again.'[229] The UNC contested every seat in a local government election for the first time.

During its term in government, the UNC were able to attract an impressive list of former PNM and NAR members: Errol Mahabir (former PNM Deputy Leader, 1971–86, and Minister of Government, 1966–86) had been appointed chairman of ICN in January 1997, and member of the Task Force on State Boards on April 11, 1998;[230] former ULF MP and NAR

Minister Winston Dookeran was appointed Central Bank Governor on July 15, 1997;[231] former NAR minister Clive Pantin headed a 1997 Task Force to investigate errors in schoolbook texts;[232] Carson Charles (former NAR leader, 1992–93, and ONR member), along with 30 supporters, including members from his 1993 executive, joined the UNC in November 1997;[233] Muriel Donawa-McDavidson (PNM founding member and Minister of Government, 1981–86) in 1998 was appointed supervisor of National Days and Festivals activities, and deputised for Culture Minister Dr Daphne Phillips at the Sangre Grande Regional Corporation's Independence celebrations in 1998;[234] former NAR minister, Leader of Government Business in the House, and former MP for Toco/Manzanilla, Joseph Toney officially resigned from the NAR to join the UNC;[235] former PNM member and Speaker of the House (1991–95) Occah Seapaul was sworn in as a temporary government senator on September 3, 1998;[236] former ULF and UNC member Kelvin Ramnath was sworn in on December 15, 1998 as a temporary senator;[237] Desmond Cartey (former PNM minister, 1976–86, and MP for Laventille, 1981–86) was appointed manager of Social and Community Services on June 1, 1999;[238] and former PNM Attorney-General (1991–95) Keith Sobion was named adjudicator in the dispute over the settlement of the 1997 contract between the Northern-Yorke-Coosal consortium and the Airports Authority.[239]

For the elections, the UNC's media advertisements featured daily in the papers and almost hourly on radio.[240] Its television advertisements featured a surprising number of Africans, and the party had even purchased advertising on cable television during foreign programming. The majority of advertisements argued that no government had done as much in so little time. They provided impressive facts and details about what had already been achieved in the government's development, welfare, and infrastructure programmes.[241]

Most observers agreed that the PNM fought a much weaker campaign. Undermined by the October 1996 party elections and the defections of MPs Lasse and Griffith, in March 1997 a party constitution review committee was established, leading to the appointment of a Change Team in February 1998, and a Special Convention for the discussion of party reform on July 19, 1998. This did not stop dissatisfaction. On February 19, 1998, Opposition Chief Whip Ken Valley submitted a letter of resignation over the replacement of senator Penelope Beckles because of the support she had given to Keith Rowley in October 1996. Valley withdrew the resignation the following day after talks with Manning.[242] Members were further aggravated by Manning's frequent absences from the country from March to May 1998 and, in particular, his absence during the opening of the Eric Williams Collection on March 22, 1998. Manning called his critics 'doltish' and 'uninformed' as he claimed he had obligations in Venezuela. On May 11, however, Manning announced at a press conference that he had been undergoing heart treatment, culminating with surgery in Cuba on April 21 and 22. Manning did not even inform PNM executive party members, including Party Chairman Linda Baboolal and Deputy Leader Valley, explaining that he did not want to cause 'anxiety and trauma' in the country.[243] Manning was severely criticised by the press, who drew parallels with his government's phoney reports on Clint Huggins in October 1994. While Valley and Baboolal refrained from criticism, MP for Diego Martin East Colm Imbert indicated that some colleagues were not pleased.[244] In June 1998, PNM councillor Jaigobin Nanga (former NAR member) resigned as chairman of the PNM-controlled Tunapuna/Piarco Regional Corporation. In the elections for a new chairman, one PNM councillor voted for the UNC's candidate. This resulted in a six-six tie, even though the UNC only held five seats. The PNM's candidate, Jerry Narace, eventually won the chairmanship by the drawing of lots.[245] As the June 1998 convention approached, there was further public criticism of Manning by older members – in particular Kamaluddin Mohammed, Ferdi Ferreira, Overand Padmore, John Eckstein (former minister, 1981–86, 1991–95), and Cuthbert Joseph (former minister, 1971–86).[246] Panday often poked fun at Manning, telling a public meeting on November 23, 1997, for example, 'One man in politics appears incapable of learning from his mistakes . . . But I have to tell you, the truth is, I must confess, I like it. I like it so. Leave him right where he is because as long as he is there now, I will always be here now (*applause*) until 2015.'[247]

Manning consistently charged the UNC government of 'creeping dictatorship, "thiefing" and lies', referred to them as 'wicked, malicious, and vindictive', and warned, 'Look at Guyana and you will see what happens when the people feel an election was less than honest.'[248] Valid claims and concerns were mixed with wild accusations about 'diabolical plots' that the government wanted to place Manning under house arrest, or that the government staged protests against itself so that it could call a state of emergency and postpone elections.[249]

The PNM's 1999 campaign was noticeably less well financed than the UNC's,[250] and turned out significantly smaller crowds.[251] Valley said he would consider quitting politics if the UNC won the polls.[252] The campaign criticised the UNC as being 'united in corruption, dividing the country, nepotism, attacking our rights and freedoms, confrontation and scandal' and providing 'the worst [governance] we have ever experienced in the history of Trinidad and Tobago.'[253]

The PNM's case was strengthened by the frequent problems that its Regional and Municipal Corporations faced in the URP programme, and particularly with Minister of Local Government Dhanraj Singh, who in 1998 was given the nickname, 'The Sheriff'. Singh had been in trouble with the law on a number of occasions,[254] and on March 15, 1998 (the day before the URP was to newly begin operations under the Ministry of Local Government rather than the Ministry of Works) the prime minister announced that Singh was no longer allowed to carry his firearm.[255] The URP had been suspended by the government in December 1996 and January 1997.[256] The PNM corporations filed motions of no confidence against Singh in 1997 and in February 1999 refused to implement the URP in protest.[257] On the day of the elections, a High Court judge ruled in favour of the chairman, aldermen, councillors, and electors of the PNM-controlled Tunapuna/Piarco Regional Corporation against its CEO Raman Mahabir, who had breached the law by acting on the instructions, requests and directions from Singh on how, when and where road improvement works should take place within the Tunapuna/Piarco area. Chairman Jerry Narace remarked, 'My actions will ensure that local government will never be taken advantage of by a bully.'[258]

To the surprise of many observers, the UNC lost ground in the 1999 elections (see Appendix B). In terms of the control of corporations, the same result obtained in 1999 as did in 1996: the PNM held seven (Port of Spain, San Fernando, Arima, Point Fortin, Diego Martin, San Juan/Laventille, Tunapuna/Piarco), the UNC six (Chaguanas, Sangre Grande, Rio Claro/Mayaro, Couva/Tabaquite/Talparo, Penal/Debe, Princes Town), and the Siparia Corporation was tied. Despite the hyperbole surrounding the election, a lower proportion of voters, 38.7 per cent, turned out than in 1996, an overall decrease of 17,933 voters. Despite this, the UNC increased its share of the vote to 51.5 per cent in 1999 as opposed to 49.9 per cent in 1996. The PNM also increased its share to 46.3 per cent from 43.7 per cent. This was the result of the NAR's further loss of 19,900 votes.

Though once again polling fewer votes than the UNC, the PNM could better claim victory this time around as it increased its number of seats by four and secured 2,338 more votes than in 1996. The over-confident UNC lost four seats and received 2,062 less votes than in 1996. The seats that changed from UNC to PNM were Marabella South/Vistabella and Springvale/Paradise in the San Fernando Municipal Corporation; Malabar in the Arima Municipal Corporation; and most surprisingly, Enterprise South in the Chaguanas Municipal Corporation.

The UNC called for recounts in Apex/Fyzabad (in the tied Siparia Regional Corporation);[259] Marabella West and Cocoyea/Tarouba (in the San Fernando Municipal Corporation).[260] The Cocoyea/Tarouba recount took one week, with the results changing from 1425 (PNM)-1424 (UNC) on July 12; to 1428 (UNC) –1424 (PNM) on July 14; to the final 1453 (PNM) – 1446 (UNC) on July 19. The tie in Siparia had not been settled even after three weeks and after the UNC had contested the July 16 vote in which one UNC councillor submitted an invalid ballot, which would have resulted in control being given to the PNM.[261] Contrary to the expectations of some observers that Trinidad might explode like Guyana, there was no violence or popular demonstration at any time by either side during the contentious recounts and settling of the tie.

The election results provoked much commentary. The *Express* chastised the media- and information-obsessed UNC government that the election results showed that citizens were 'not *tabula rasas* to be written upon by what they see on TV or read in the newspapers.'[262] In a provocative analysis, Lloyd Best argued that the UNC had peaked in 1995–96 and that the pendulum was swinging back.[263] The UNC, however, noted that it received more votes in 1999 and claimed that if the results were superimposed on the 1995 electoral boundaries, the party would have captured 19 seats.[264] Nevertheless, on July 14, 1999 a specially convened caucus of the UNC was called to discuss its electoral performance.[265]

Almost immediately after the elections, the controversies that had previously engulfed the government re-emerged: protests in Tabaquite, opposition to the standardisation of textbooks;[266] government's defence of the death penalty,[267] residents' opposition to the Emancipation memorial;[268] building a police recreation complex adjacent to the Jamaat-al-Muslimeen lands;[269] attempts to persuade the President to call an inquiry into airport contracts, protests by the CWU, PSA, OWTU, and TTUTA;[270] and police corruption. The last matter was raised by a report implicating 13 policemen in the September 1998 prison escape of drug dealer Deochand Ramdhanie, prompting Panday and Manning to issue a joint statement agreeing to work together to investigate corruption within the police force. Three officers were subsequently charged in October.[271]

On October 20, 1999 Panday announced a major Cabinet re-shuffle. For the first time in his administration, Panday took responsibility for a ministry (Public Information and Communication); Kuei Tung acquired Planning and Development from Trevor Sudama, who was moved to Agriculture; Lasse (already in the Ministry of Finance, Planning and Development) was elevated to Cabinet rank,[272] while Job was also brought into that ministry while retaining his Tobago Ministry; Adesh Nanan was moved to the new Ministry of Tourism; and Kamla Persad-Bissessar moved to the troubled Ministry of Education. The most important addition was the addition as Minister in the Prime Minister's Office of 40-year old Lindsay Gillette, chairman of Gillette Technology Holdings (GTH), which owned Open Telecom, Computers and Controls Ltd, a cable television company, two radio stations (Power Radio 102 FM and Love 94 FM) as well as Gillette's Building Supplies. Gillette, appointed as a senator with Cabinet rank, was not a member of the UNC and his family were well-known supporters of the PNM. The Prime Minister described him as a 'trouble shooter' who would move 'from ministry to ministry, dynamiting the logjams, breaking the bottlenecks, unlocking the floodgates and so freeing up the system on a case-by-case basis'. Panday argued,

> *one of the major constraints to implementation has been the bureaucratic bottlenecks in a system that is patently outdated. Despite the best efforts of some of our public servants, they remain shackled by a dysfunctional system . . . . I am conscious of the fact that to effect a meaningful overhaul of the system would require constitutional changes, and at the present time we do not have the required majority to effect such changes. That time will come. We expect to have that majority in this House after the next elections. But in the meantime I must do something to speed up implementation of our plans and programmes. Since I cannot change the bureaucracy, I intend to pierce it and penetrate it. If I cannot remove the bureaucratic constraints then I must go over it, under it, through it or around it.*[273]

The first major accomplishment of Minister Gillette concerned the signing of the agreement for the second and third trains of the Atlantic LNG plant, which involved an estimated investment of US$7 billion, the largest single investment in the country's history. The government had intended to sign the 20-year agreement on January 31, 2000, but was opposed by the chairmen of NGC (Steve Ferguson) and the National Petroleum Marketing

Company (Carolyn Seepersad-Bachan), who were reportedly supported by Finance Minister Kuei Tung. They argued strongly against Clause 7 of the agreement, concerning the pricing of the gas supply, while Energy Minister Finbar Gangar was extremely vocal in his support. The Prime Minister and the Attorney-General apparently attempted to broker a deal satisfactory to all parties, causing lengthy postponement and wide debate, including opposition by the PNM, UWI economist Dennis Pantin, the OWTU, and TTUTA. On March 9, Panday left the country and appointed Gillette as acting Prime Minister. The fact that Gillette – recently appointed, unelected, and not a member of the UNC – was appointed over the usual choice of John Humphrey caused controversy itself. After returning on March 17, Panday remarked, 'I don't know what all the fuss is about. I left the country for one week and from what I was reading in the papers I thought the world was tumbling down ... What is it? Is it his race? He is Chinese. Is it his religion? He is a Catholic. Or is it his height? The fella is a little short.'[274] The deal was signed on March 13, 2000 by Finance Minister Kuei Tung, who was acting for Minister of Energy Gangar.[275]

Earlier, Panday made another significant appointment, on January 7, 2000, when the CARICOM ambassadorship (a post vacant for the previous three years) was conferred on Kamaluddin Mohammed who had served in a similar capacity to CARICOM's precursor, the Caribbean Free Trade Area.[276]

A month after the Cabinet re-shuffle, on November 21, 1999, at the fourth anniversary of the UNC government, Panday set a target for the UNC of between 24 and 26 seats which he said would come in less than a year, before the due date of January 2001. Panday criticised his party, its executive and his own role in the 1999 election results, promising to revitalise the party machinery to concentrate on elections rather than on government, advertisements, and crowds at public meetings. Panday declared, 'Citizens can be assured that the period between now and the elections will be the most exciting, dramatic, confused, desperate and traumatic period in this country since Independence.'[277] Panday embarked on a tour of all 36 constituencies, sometimes heavily criticising party members, executives, and constituency organisations, as in the borderline constituencies of Fyzabad and Tunapuna, which he called 'the worst constituency in the whole country' because of its internecine warfare.[278]

The UNC hired James Carville, senior political adviser to US President Bill Clinton, reportedly at a cost of more than TT$1.2 million. Carville made the first of several visits to the country on January 19, 2000.[279]

On February 3, Panday announced as enemies of the UNC President A.N.R. Robinson, Chief Justice Michael de la Bastide, CCN, the NAR, the PNM, Lloyd Best, and Selwyn Ryan.[280] Despite objections from the press, appeals by Selwyn Ryan for State protection, and a MATT-organised press conference at which Amnesty International criticised the Prime Minister, Panday remained unapologetic and continued to reiterate his list, even joking that he was protecting Ryan by telling people not to read his columns, since readers may want to smack him after reading his 'stupidness'.[281]

The attack against the president came in the middle of two stand-offs. The first occurred when, after the prime minister made a request on January 17, 2000, Robinson delayed replacing two government senators on the grounds that this violated the UNC-NAR Heads of Agreement. The two senators, Agnes Williams and Nathaniel Moore, were NAR appointees (via the prime minister, who is constitutionally empowered to appoint 16 senators). On December 15, 1999, they voted against the government's Tourism Development Bill. Panday had chosen two other Tobagonians, Winston John (a member of the NAR Tobago Island Council) and Jearlean John (CEO of the Public Transport Services Commission) to replace them. However, Robinson's delay was quite beyond the conventional interpretation of the President's constitutional sphere of discretion. Robinson and Panday engaged in an exchange of insults reminiscent of the 1987-8 period in the NAR Government, except reversed: Robinson accused Panday of not consulting him and speaking a 'blatant untruth' in claiming that Robinson requested to reduce the frequency of their meetings; Panday, on the other hand, referred to the constitutionality of his actions: as prime minister he was entitled to appoint and remove senators on his own discretion; the president was to act on his advice. The public dispute prompted the IRO to meet with the president on January 31, and Hochoy Charles also offered to mediate. Manning, however, supported Panday. Robinson finally acceded on February 2 via a press release, and the senators were sworn in on February 8.[282]

The second stand-off occurred immediately afterwards, when President Robinson, once again acting beyond the conventional interpretation of his constitutional powers, delayed the signing of the instruments to effect a Commission of Inquiry into the Administration of Justice. The initial request resulted from a speech given by Chief Justice Michael de la Bastide at the opening of the law term on September 16, 1999. De la Bastide criticised the Attorney-General for proposing to become the 'relevant minister' who must authorise the funding of the Judiciary and also a 1998 Constitutional Amendment which removed the protection given to the Judicial and Legal Service Commission from legal proceedings against it. The chief justice saw these moves as 'dangerous and unwarranted' threats to integrity of the judiciary.[283] After weeks of public exchange, during which time the Law Association appointed a one-man commission of inquiry, on December 16, 1999 the prime minister announced in a nationwide broadcast that the government would establish a Commission of Inquiry to investigate the claims, as it prioritised law and order in the development of the country. A similar announcement was made in Parliament on January 4, 2000.[284] Robinson, however, indicated by letter on December 18, that he would need to seek legal advice on the matter, since matters of a 'constitutional nature' may arise, i.e. the independence of the Judiciary (which has no representative in the Senate or in Cabinet) might have been compromised. On February 4, the formal request was sent to the president for signing. Robinson refused to sign the documents for more than three weeks, indicating that he was seeking advice. This caused further tension between Robinson and Panday. On February 29, Robinson signed the document, and the three-man Commission was launched on April 17, 2000, headed by Lord MacKay of Clashfern, former Lord Chancellor of the United Kingdom.[285] While Robinson yielded in these matters, he created a precedent that could not be reversed easily.

On February 25, 2000, Panday announced in the House of Representatives that, with the support of Manning, he had sent a letter on the previous day to the Commonwealth Secretariat at Marlborough House, requesting the presence of a Commonwealth Observer Group at the next general elections, in light of the unjustified claims by the opposition that the next elections would not be conducted fairly. Noting that this was the first time such observers were requested, Panday expressed the hope 'that the Opposition . . . [would] now desist from remarks which could impugn the integrity of our Electoral Processes.'[286]

During this time, too, a local government by-election was called for Rio Claro North after the murdered body of its councillor Hansraj Sumairsingh, chairman of the Rio Claro/Mayaro corporation, was found on December 31, 1999. His death was thought to be linked to his attempts to fight corruption in the URP, and police had questioned Dhanraj Singh on January 7, 2000.[287] On February 17, Panday gave an ultimatum to Singh to 'remove the criminal element' from the URP or face dismissal.[288] After being refused help from PNM Chairman Linda Baboolal, fellow Cabinet Minister Joseph

Theodore, and the local government corporations in what was widely considered an ill-defined task, on March 1 Singh handed in his report stating that he could not find any criminal elements. On March 4, Singh answered to reporters that he would not be contesting the next general elections, denying that he had been asked to step down by Panday.[289]

For the April 3 by-elections in Rio Claro North, Prime Minister Panday, Spiritual Baptist Archbishop Barbara Burke, former House Speaker Occah Seapaul, Works Minister Sadiq Baksh, Chaguanas Mayor Orlando Nagessar, and senior party officials of the UNC were present to support their candidate, Hazarie Ramdeen, while Port of Spain Mayor John Rahael, Mayor Elvin Edwards of Arima, Senator Joan Yuille-Williams (deputy Leader of the PNM), and Tunapuna/Piarco Regional Chairman Jerry Narace encouraged people to cast their votes for the PNM candidate, Roger Bholai. The UNC won the election by 1,588 votes to 655.[290] It was obviously another practice run for the general elections that were due later that year. The day after the Rio Claro North by-election, Panday enthusiastically declared, 'Manning is going to lead the PNM into two political defeats this year, later this year. That will be the Tobago House of Assembly elections, you can bet on that, and after that Mr. Manning will lead the PNM into yet another defeat in the mother of all battles, the next general election. That is also a bankable promise.'[291]

Although the country was expecting elections, Parliament was not dissolved at the end of the fifth session on October 6, 2000. Instead, the UNC Government proceeded with an unprecedented sixth session of Parliament on October 19. The UNC continued with its intensive programme of government. By the end of the term, a total of 247 laws had been passed, touching on many areas of life: integrity in public life, patents and industrial designs, copyright, equal opportunities, freedom of information, reform of parliamentary committees, public interest litigation, domestic violence, community mediation, legal aid and advice, international war crime tribunals, computer misuse, removing archaic laws discriminating against non-Christian practices, squatter regularisation, tax reform, and many others.

With regard to policy, after two years of tripartite discussion, the UNC concluded 'Compact 2000 and Beyond,' an 11-point agreement between employers, unions, and government to address economic and social issues. In education, the World Bank gave Trinidad and Tobago's education programme the highest rating in its review that year.[292] In a major administrative manoeuvre, an agreement was reached on October 20 in which, among other things, the Ministry of Education delinked teachers from the

Public Service so as to increase teachers' salaries by between 40 to 100 per cent.

In the conflict between the Chief Justice and the Attorney-General, the MacKay Commission submitted its 67-page report in October 2000. The Commission did not find that the Attorney-General had undermined the independence of the Judiciary. They cleared him of any wrongdoing and said he must continue being the conduit between the executive and the judiciary. In effect, the Chief Justice's allegations, they argued, were unfounded. This was notably different from the more equivocal conclusion of the one-man commission of Telford Georges, commissioned by the Law Association.[293]

Despite the impressiveness of the UNC's achievements, weaknesses were beginning to show. On August 25, 2000 Dhanraj Singh was not selected to contest his Pointe-à-Pierre seat and on October 12, Panday removed him from the Cabinet, without clear reason. Five days later, Singh left for New York, claiming that he was ill. However, in November Elliot Hippolyte, a member of the Jamaat-al-Muslimeen, was arrested and charged with the murder of Hansraj Sumairsingh.

In October 2000, Panday lost two cases brought against him by CCN and Ken Gordon. In the first case, it was decided that the Prime Minister (who was also Minister of Information and Communication) acted improperly by personally denying CCN a cellular telephone licence, because of his well-known, public antipathy toward the group. The second case found Panday guilty of defamation when he labelled Gordon a 'pseudo-racist' in 1997.[294] In that case, Panday was ordered to pay $696,854.40 to Gordon. Panday was threatened with bankruptcy proceedings, which if successful would disqualify him from contesting the next election. Panday effected a stay of execution on November 29.

The PNM had their own dynamics. They were buoyed by the 1999 local government elections results. As soon as the election results were announced, Manning summed up well the feeling later expressed by many as he proclaimed with satisfaction, 'There are some things that money just cannot buy.' He then demanded that general elections be called immediately. The day after, Manning confidently stated, 'You now understand all opposition talk – that the PNM cannot win under Manning – is just old talk.' The PNM published a full page 'Thank You' ad, and organised a two-day, two-hundred-car, island-wide motorcade for July 25 and 26.[295] The PNM's performance was seen by a number of persons as an African victory over a new Indian aggression. Selwyn Ryan described 'high fives', hugs, kisses, and 'body bumps,' and declared: 'Afro-Trinidadians have shown that they are not as gullible and venal as the UNC strategists [believed,] . . . with all the money and project work used to bribe the electorate. From the talks I've had over the last 24 hours, it appears that Afro-Trinidadians are no longer as defensive or apologetic as they were before the election . . . . They have gained the confidence in their capacity to resist the onslaught of the UNC.'[296] He later described the UNC's use of Africans in its advertising campaign as 'obnoxious'.[297]

However, the PNM experienced another departure from the prominent Mohammed family. On April 7, 2000, three months after his father, Kamaluddin Mohammed, accepted the post of CARICOM Ambassador, Alimudeen Mohammed resigned as chairman of PNM Party Group 12, as PRO of the San Juan/Barataria constituency, and as member of the PNM General Council, because his cousin, PNM Deputy Leader Senator Nafeesa Mohammed, was seeking nomination for the Barataria/San Juan constituency.[298] Nafeesa Mohammed's brother, Jamal (former chairman of Hulsie Bhaggan's MUP), also protested against her candidacy by a public letter and an appearance on a UNC platform. His grounds were the ill-treatment meted out to their father, Shamshuddin Mohammed, by Patrick Manning and the PNM. Adding to this problem, a majority of nominations for candidates were still to be filled by April 15, 2000, although the PNM had announced an Ash Wednesday (March 8) deadline.[299]

Of great importance was the PNM's declaration in the media and to the police on October 9 that the UNC planned to transfer 1,000 names from UNC stronghold constituencies to the residences of people with similar names in borderline seats such as Tunapuna and Ortoire/Mayaro. Two days later, an audio tape of two UNC activists allegedly planning to pad voting lists in the marginal constituencies was delivered to the *Sunday Express* and its transcript published. On October 13, the police requested assistance from the Elections and Boundaries Commission (EBC) in its investigations. That day police searched the home of former Minister of Local Government, Dhanraj Singh, who had been sacked on the previous day.

On October 19, the *Trinidad Guardian* carried details of the plan to pad the voters list, from information in a copy of an unsigned so-called 'special field operations report' upon which the police investigation was based.[300] On October 27, almost 80 Criminal Investigations Department police officers from the Port of Spain, San Fernando, and St James stations conducted searches into homes and businesses of UNC officials and supporters, including the home of Minister Sadiq Baksh, the home and office of Suzanne Seepersad (head of the Party Administrative Support Unit [PASU]), and the home and office of NGC Chairman and UNC supporter Steve Ferguson. Two computers and several diskettes were seized. The UNC condemned the searches and attributed the voter padding document to Richard Bickram, a former employee of PASU who was 'summarily terminated for cause, including the falsification of documents and the forging of signatures'. The UNC alleged that Bickram may have been a PNM plant, due to his previous association with that party. Another raid was carried out on November 1, at the home of the UNC activist immediately superior to Bickram. That day, Bickram, a protected witness assisting police in their investigations, had a series of writs filed against him in the San Fernando High Court for 19 bounced cheques totalling $33,900, made to UNC party activists.[301] The police continued to search the homes of UNC ministers, such as Harry Partap on November 3, and other party activists.

The NAR, meanwhile, seemed to increasingly shut itself out of Trinidad politics. After Nizam Mohammed was formally elected as NAR Leader on July 13, 1997, he declared that the party would seek to re-establish itself as an independent entity.[302] However, his stewardship was less than authoritative. Mohammed claimed that he had not been consulted about Job's appointment to the Cabinet in May 1997, and in May 1998 he refused to attend the elections to establish the NAR's Tobago Island Council out of the Tobago Steering Committee. Mohammed claimed that he was not properly informed.[303] Basdeo Panday ridiculed Mohammed's May 1998 statement in Barbados that it was 'time for a woman to be Prime Minister'. He wondered whether Mohammed disqualified himself or wanted to change his sex.[304] Beginning on June 17, 1999, Mohammed held unsuccessful talks with Patrick Manning about forming a coalition for the coming local government elections. In the aftermath, Mohammed publicly declared that Manning had to be removed as leader of the PNM. Manning dismissed the NAR as a 'two by four party', and NAR members including Robert Mayers and Lincoln Myers formed a party group distancing themselves from Mohammed, arguing that his actions and statements were never authorised by the NAR general council.[305] On October 24, 1999, the NAR national council appointed as interim leader Anthony Smart (former Attorney General, 1989–1991), with Mohammed claiming that he had been dismissed improperly. On April 30, 2000, Smart was elected NAR leader at its National and Special

Conference.[306] The party continued its decline, however, and many of its organisers and activists worked for either the PNM or UNC in the campaign.[307]

In Tobago, the Hochoy Charles administration was plagued with its own crises. In 1988, the THA was swindled out of US$2 million, which had been invested in a bogus Florida-based scheme. In another matter, on June 21, 2000, the THA granted a licence for cellular telephone service to a new, emerging company. The THA's actions were subsequently shown to be unconstitutional, and the licence was revoked by central government. In October 2000, the Attorney-General referred to the DPP the THA's unauthorised expenditure of $40 million on a Ringbang Millenium concert on December 31, 1999.[308] The concert was broadcast internationally and was seen as a promotional event for Tobago. On a brighter note, the first report of the Dispute Resolution Commission, submitted on September 14, 2000, vindicated the position of the THA that it was entitled to a greater, and consistent, share of the national budget, and that the THA be enabled to more effectively exercise its constitutionally prescribed autonomy (which was deemed to include borrowing its own money).[309]

Amidst the turmoil in Tobago, the NAR's dominance was met by a new opposition party composed of the three independents in the THA and supported by Pamela Nicholson. By 1999 they had formed the People's Empowerment Party (PEP) and in February 2000, PEP leader Moore-Miggins displaced the lone PNM member, William McKenzie, as the minority leader in the THA.[310] Meanwhile, the PNM established a Tobago Council to concentrate on its fortunes in that island.

At that news conference on November 2, 2000, Basdeo Panday announced that general elections would be held on December 11. It was the longest campaign that the country had ever experienced.[311]

The UNC used its position in government to the maximum. It produced a slick manifesto which emphasised with facts and figures its 'performance' in office, and presented a nine-point vision for Trinidad and Tobago to make it a 'developed country' by the year 2010. Individual candidates also distributed slick personal manifestos in the national press. The party's most memorable programme was the 'Dollar for Dollar' education programme, designed to reduce the cost of tertiary education by half. It continued its intensive media campaign, with a highlight that presented an innovative situation comedy series of television advertisements in which a husband and wife were politically divided.[312]

In addition, an elaborate inaugural ceremony to hand over the (as yet unfinished) Millenium Airport occurred on November 25. The cost of the airport, according to a Cabinet note dated August 10, amounted to $1.2 billion, up from the $662 million estimated five years earlier.[313] The capacity for expenditure was enabled by the huge investments in the oil and gas sector, that buoyed the Trinidad and Tobago economy. Sir John Browne, chief executive of BP, noted that his company invested on average 8 per cent of its annual exploration and production capital in Trinidad and Tobago 'over the past few years', amounting to roughly US$650 million.[314] Importantly, on December 7 (four days before the election), the government signed the final contracts with shareholders of Atlantic LNG for a two-train expansion of the LNG plant at Point Fortin. Unlike the agreement for the first train, the new trains would be subject to taxation. Government estimated that over the next 20 years it would receive from the business $1.5 billion in tax revenues, reliably providing for the entire period roughly 10 per cent of the annual national budget.[315] The government's ability to distribute largesse seemed assured.

The UNC team had suffered some personnel losses, however. Finance Minister Senator Brian Kuei Tung, Dhanraj Singh, and Reeza Mohammed (Minister of Agriculture and MP for Princes Town, whose loyalty to the party was publicly questioned through a tape recording made public by the Jamaat-al-Muslimeen) were no longer on the UNC team. Also, first-time candidate Reynold Baldeosingh withdrew his candidacy for the UNC in Arouca North the Friday before Nomination Day. He did so in support of his brother, Donald, who had been dismissed by the Cabinet from the chairmanship of PETROTRIN after refusing to comply with an order given to him by Prime Minister Panday.[316] But the UNC continued to attract a number of new persons, including calypsonian Winston 'Gypsy' Peters, activist Michael Als (in whose group 'Young Power' Patrick Manning was a member in 1969[317]), Roy Augustus from the ONR/NAR 'A-Team', Gillian Lucky (daughter of Justice Anthony Lucky), Gerard Yetming (former campaign manager with the ONR and NAR), Carlos John (a Director of CL Financial), and Muriel Donawa-McDavidson (former PNM MP [1966–61, 1986–91], Minister [1981–86] and foundation member, who became bedridden while preparing her candidacy for the UNC in San Fernando East against Patrick Manning[318]). In addition, CL Financial Chairman, Lawrence Duprey, openly appeared on the UNC platform, while former PNM community-level activists publicly proclaimed their new allegiance to the UNC. Notably, of the people mentioned, only Lucky was Indian. The others were Afro-Creole and Chinese. Notably, however, the UNC did not contest Tobago, yet again.

After elections were announced, Manning made an immediate gaffe by claiming that calling an election in the month of Ramadan was offensive to Muslims. He retracted his statement after a group of Muslim leaders accused Manning of using their holy month for 'political mileage'.[319] But the PNM's strength really came from its base in the calypso tents, comedy shows, the radio stations, and other fora for popular Afro-Trinidadian performance.

To an unprecedented degree, the election campaign was full of legal action and threat. On November 22, two days after Nomination Day, the *Trinidad Express* reported that Winston 'Gypsy' Peters (candidate for Ortoire/Mayaro) and William Chaitan (candidate for Pointe-à-Pierre) were not eligible to become members of the House of Representatives because of their dual citizenships. On November 23, PNM candidates for Ortoire/Mayaro and Pointe-à-Pierre, Franklin Khan and Farad Khan, wrote the EBC asking its commissioners to make a decision about the eligibility of Peters and Chaitan to contest the general election. In the meanwhile, on November 24 the DPP instructed the police to investigate whether Peters and Chaitan committed criminal offences when they filed their nomination papers. Peters and Chaitan were questioned by police on November 29 and 30. The PNM declared that it was 'payback time' for the two seats they lost in 1997, and called for their immediate arrest.[320] However, on December 1 the Election Boundaries Commission (EBC), on the advice of the Solicitor General, confirmed the nominations of Peters and Chaitan, stating that it did not have any authority to invalidate their candidacy.[321] On December 5, the PNM began the intensive circulation in the media of a notice that 'All Votes for William Chaitan are Wasted Votes'; a similar notice was made regarding Winston Peters. In addition, on Election Day, Peters was disqualified from voting by the EBC due to incorrect registration. As a counter-attack, on December 8, the UNC circulated a Notice of Objection in the daily press that 'all votes cast for Mr Patrick A.M. Manning in the Electoral District of San Fernando East would be considered wasted and thrown away' since on his nomination paper he listed his occupation as Member of Parliament. Technically, Manning's declaration was false, as Parliament was dissolved before Nomination Day. Panday, too, demanded on the campaign platform that Manning be arrested.[322] Similar notices were circulated regarding Eddie Hart in Tunapuna, and Eulalie James in Laventille West.

In the meantime, the 'voter padding' investigations continued. On November 18, the PNM alleged that the UNC planned to bring home hundreds of nationals living in Canada to vote in the election. On November 20, the EBC announced that it had rejected 252 out of 3,296 applications for a transfer of constituency into the five borderline seats of Tunapuna, Barataria/San Juan, St Joseph, Ortoire/Mayaro, and San Fernando West. All names were turned over to the police on November 10. The besieged UNC counter-attacked on November 23 by releasing a list of 120 'ghost voters' in San Fernando West. Later in the campaign, UNC MP for Barataria/San Juan Dr Fuad Khan accused PNM of voter padding. On November 24, the DPP ordered the arrests of 30 persons suspected of being part of the plot to pad the voters' list. Up to December 7, twenty-nine of them were arrested. At least 13 persons who were held allegedly in connection with voter padding were released by police with no charges laid against them. At least three filed constitutional motions that they were wrongfully detained and/or imprisoned.[323]

On December 7, the UNC held a press conference to 'counter [the] attempt [by the PNM] to intimidate voters into not exercising their right to vote'. They followed this with a series of full-page newspaper ads. The following day, recently appointed EBC Chairman Oswald Wilson delivered a public address to re-state the facts of the case in the face of wild public speculation.[324]

On December 3, the six-member Commonwealth Observer Team (composed of persons from Canada, Zambia, Australia, Belize, Sri Lanka, and Britain) arrived in Trinidad. Just before the election, on December 8, Selwyn Ryan predicted in the *Trinidad Express* that the PNM would win with 18 seats, while the UNC would receive 16 and the NAR 2. Given the close nature of the actual result, however, one cannot fault Professor Ryan for his projection. The almost equal number of votes received by each party suggested that the actual results might have been produced by stochastic movement. Unfortunately, he did not consider his margin of error.

Polling day proceeding relatively calmly, with no major incidents of note. Against the odds, arguably, the UNC emerged with a clear, but relatively vulnerable, mandate. They captured 19 seats and became the first administration since 1976 to win a second term of office. Manning's PNM, on the other hand, captured 16 seats; and the NAR, only one (see Appendices B and C). The voter turnout rate of 63.2 per cent, was virtually unchanged from the 63.1 per cent in 1995. However, the total number of persons who voted in 2000 increased by 68,307. The UNC gained a majority of the vote, winning 51.5 per cent of the votes cast, as compared to the PNM's 46.2 per cent. This was significant, as no party after the NAR in 1986 ever won over half of the ballot.

Another way to look at the UNC's increase is to consider that in 1995 the PNM secured 16,069 more votes than the UNC. It was only through alliance with the NAR that the PNM were outnumbered. In 2000, however, the UNC obtained 31,483 more votes than the PNM, without even contesting Tobago. The UNC were able to penetrate the East-West Corridor more significantly by capturing from the PNM the Tunapuna seat, while in the extreme south-east it displaced the PNM's control of Ortoire/Mayaro (won by Winston 'Gypsy' Peters).

Overall, the UNC made impressive increases in PNM strongholds. The party more than doubled its vote in Diego Martin West, Diego Martin East, and Port of Spain North/St Ann's West. In addition, it made gains of more than 50 per cent in St Ann's East, Laventille West, Arima, Port of Spain South, Laventille East/Morvant, and Diego Martin Central.

On the other hand the PNM was reduced to holding 15 seats in Trinidad. The PNM did increase its total vote by 8 per cent compared to 1995, but the UNC did so by 28.4 per cent. It was the PNM's capture of Tobago West that perhaps provided the greatest surprise, since the PNM had not won a Tobago seat in Parliament since 1971. The People's Empowerment Party (PEP) made no significant impact, except that its 720 votes in Tobago East could have tipped the balance toward the NAR (see Table 7.4). That seat was one of only three lost by less than 1,500 votes, and the only one won with a plurality.

***Table 7.4. Constituencies won with a margin of less than 1,500 votes in the December 11, 2000 elections***

| CONSTITUENCY | NAR | PEP | PNM | UNC | REJECTED BALLOTS | % VOTED | MARGIN OF VICTORY |
|---|---|---|---|---|---|---|---|
| Tobago East | 3,921 | 720 | 3,632 | - | 38 | 46.8% | 289 |
| Tunapuna | - | - | 8,726 | 9,062 | 197 | 68.5% | 336 |
| San Fernando West | - | - | 8,233 | 9,176 | 65 | 67.7% | 943 |

The Tobago vote showed a remarkable demobilisation, especially for the NAR. The NAR actually received 2,718 less votes in Tobago in 2000 than it did in 1995. This happened even though the electorate in Tobago increased by 3,716 (from 33,300 in 1995 to 37,016 in 2000). The decrease of the NAR vote in Tobago between the two elections was 36.7 per cent. The PNM, conversely, increased its vote in Tobago by 45.8 per cent.

## 'WHO WANT TO RESIGN, RESIGN!': THE ABORTED PARLIAMENT, 2001

Despite the comparatively clear mandate (as opposed to 1995), installing the second term of the UNC Government was fraught with problems. First was the contention that Winston Peters and Bill Chaitan (who both won their seats) were not eligible to sit in Parliament. The UNC sense of victory was thereby undermined as Patrick Manning declared at 11:45pm on election night that the PNM was not accepting the final result, and that they would go to the courts. Manning declared, 'The Constitution is about to be tested to the limit'.[325]

The day after the election, the President did not swear in Basdeo Panday as Prime Minister. Notably, the PNM wrote to President Robinson asking him to hold his hand on inviting anyone to form the next Government, until the outcome of a petition to the court challenging the nomination of Peters and Chaitan. Not only was the PNM contesting the results of those particular seats. The PNM argued against the legitimacy of the elections in general. On the day of the election, the Commonwealth Observer Team reached an 'interim conclusion . . . that up to the close of the polls the election was conducted in a manner which provided the people of Trinidad and Tobago with the opportunity to vote freely for the candidates of their choice. [The Observer Team members] were impressed by the orderliness, patience and good humour of the voters as they waited their turn.' On December 15, the Team submitted its report to Commonwealth Secretary General, Donald McKinnon.

That day, PNM Deputy Leader Ken Valley announced that it was 'inconceivable' that the level of alleged vote padding surrounding the election 'could have been implemented without the participation of the EBC'. Alleging a 'well-orchestrated programme' to steal the 2000 election, he accused the Commonwealth Observer Mission of simply being part of the 'sham'.[326] Some speculated that this line of attack was taken to divert pressure that would otherwise be directed toward getting Patrick Manning to step down from leadership of the PNM which he had promised to do if the PNM lost the elections. Accordingly, the recounts in Tunapuna and San Jan/Barataria were quite contentious, even if not escalating to violence.

However, the PNM's claims seemed supported by the irregularities surrounding the recount demanded by the PNM for the Tunapuna seat. The recount on December 16 affirmed the UNC's Mervyn Assam as winner. But the PNM objected to 13 unsealed envelopes which did not contain the signatures of the presiding officer and contained 2,577 votes for the UNC. The disqualification of those votes would have resulted in a PNM victory.

By this time, the president still had not appointed a new prime minister.[327] In the meanwhile, the PNM called for a Commission of Enquiry into the EBC. The Network of NGOs of Trinidad and Tobago for the Advancement of Women also asked President Robinson to appoint a Commission of Inquiry into the operations of the EBC, while the Trinidad and Tobago arm of Transparency International criticised EBC and suggested that it restructure itself and its electoral databases.

On December 13, Prime Minister Panday wrote to President Robinson to inquire why the president had not conformed to the established practice of appointing a prime minister within 48 hours of an election. The next day, the president returned the prime minister's letter stating 'there is no established practice regarding the time after a General Election within which the appointment or re-appointment of a Prime Minister takes place'. That day, the president sought advice from former presidents Sir Ellis Clarke and Noor Hassanali to discuss post-election issues.[328] Responding to public comment, EBC Chief Elections Office, Howard Cayenne, declared that the president did not have to wait for the recount in Tunapuna to appoint a prime minister. On the contrary, President Robinson declared, on December 15, he could not appoint a new prime minister until he received the certified results from the EBC. The EBC replied that although it was usual, the EBC was not required by any election rule to tell the President who has been elected. They were obliged to inform the speaker only.[329]

In the meantime, Panday publicly stated that the UNC would not be robbed of its electoral victory in the face of legal challenges by the PNM. He told his supporters to keep their UNC jerseys ready, hinting that he would not hesitate to call new elections. On December 16, the Solicitor-General, Lynette Stephenson, advised the president to appoint Panday as prime minister.[330] In the middle of the crisis, on December 18, the president delivered a televised national address, in which he insisted that he needed the official EBC report before he could declare the formation of a new government. Robinson declared that he would not yield to pressure and prematurely appoint a prime minister, and he criticised the Solicitor-General for offering advice on the appointment of a prime minister. Two days later, the PNM wrote to the president again, advising him not to appoint Panday as prime minister. That day, however, Robinson received the EBC report (one day after EBC Chairman Oswald Wilson mistakenly announced that the report was in Robinson's hands), and Panday was duly sworn in as Prime Minister on December 20, 2002. Robinson, aged 74, was hospitalised shortly after.[331]

On the day of Panday's appointment, Franklin Khan and Farad Khan were granted leave to file representation against Peters and Chaitan. Two days later, Peters and Chaitan filed, in defence, constitutional motions challenging the election petitions against them, arguing that their rights as citizens were being violated. They also applied to the court for a conservatory order suspending the hearing of the Khans' representation petitions. Importantly, because of Trinidad and Tobago's judicial system, if the appeals process were stretched to the limit, the PNM election petitions would have their final resolution in the Court of Appeal in Trinidad, while the constitutional motions would be finally determined by the Privy Council in London. Also in retaliation, UNC candidates for San Fernando East and Laventille East, Paul Phagoo and Princess Smart, filed election petitions on Christmas Day 2000 against elected members Patrick Manning and Eulalie James. The PNM described the UNC's Christmas Day application as 'frivolous and vexatious'. Basdeo Panday was obviously worried by the case. On December 29, he publicly declared that if Peters and Chaitan lost their court cases, he would be forced to call another election.

Meantime, a new source of anxiety had emerged. On December 22, President Robinson swore in only 15 of the 25 ministers that Panday advised, without explanation. Panday wrote to the president regarding the incomplete appointments. The next day, the president sought legal advice on whether or not he should swear in Peters and Chaitan and seven defeated UNC candidates whom Panday wanted as ministers.[332] Four days later, the prime minister and the president met to discuss the appointments and 'measures to ease the tension' arising from the impasse between them. On December 29, the government's first Cabinet meeting was held, amidst the uncertainty. Panday convened a press conference stating that he could find no legal or moral impediment to the senatorial appointment of persons who had been defeated at elections. He also expressed concern over the delay in the appointment of Roy Augustus (defeated candidate for Arouca North) as National Security Minister.[333] Thus began a series of public pronouncements involving not only the president and the prime minister, but prominent members of the legal fraternity, former presidents, a host of radio, television, and newspaper commentators, NGOs, civic associations and others. The prime pinister and the president's letters to each other were published in the daily press.

On December 31, 2000, Robinson agreed to swear in Peters and Chaitan. However, he believed that the problem involving the swearing in of the seven defeated candidates (Daphne Phillips, Michael Als, Dr Vincent Lasse, Dr Roodal Moonial, Stanley Ryan, Jennifer Jones-Kernahan, and Roy Augustus) was 'a particularly difficult one to resolve', as it was based on a principle which he found 'impossible to accept'.[334] Not only did people see it as a way to reward candidates whom constituencies rejected, it was seen as a way for Panday to undermine the elected (PNM) members of those constituencies (Diego Martin West, Toco/Manzanilla, Point Fortin, San Fernando East, La Brea, Diego Martin Central, and Arouca North, respectively), by offering ministries to at least some of them. However, the prime minister was not so restricted by the Constitution of the Republic of Trinidad and Tobago in his choice of senators. Again, Robinson's decision was outside the conventional interpretation of the president's sphere of discretion. The PNM supported the president's stand, as they did not in the senator controversy of January 2000. On January 2, 2001, the prime minister wrote to the president once more, requesting that the seven defeated candidates be appointed senators. The president rejected Panday's request. Panday announced that he was taking legal advice, stating, 'I'm always taken aback by violations of the Constitution.'[335]

On January 3, Peters, Chaitan, and Sudama were sworn in as Ministers. The PNM boycotted the ceremony, while the Council of the Law Association, and the heads of the South Trinidad, Greater Tunapuna, Greater Chaguanas, and the Penal/Debe Chambers of Industry and Commerce declared against President Robinson's position. The PNM and the NAR supported the president.[336] On January 4, President Robinson was invited to address the January 12 opening of Parliament. In the meanwhile, the IRO urged dialogue between president and prime minister, as tensions increased. The OWTU, CWU and PSA denounced the prime minister's proposed appointments as an abuse of power.[337]

On January 5, President Robinson addressed the nation, warning of a 'creeping dictatorship', and stating that he would not act like a 'rubber stamp . . . as though I do not have a brain.' He stated, 'I have heard it said that what the prime minister wants he must get. That is the road to absolutism. That is when dictatorship arises.'[338] Ramesh Lawrence Maharaj accused the president of seeking the former powers of the colonial governor.[339] In the meanwhile, NATUC advised the president to appoint the seven defeated candidates. On January 10, Robinson met for the second time with former Presidents Sir Ellis Clarke and Noor Hassanali, Caribbean jurist Telford Georges and Tajmool Hosein, QC. The outcome of the meeting was inconclusive.

At the opening of Parliament on January 12, President Robinson declined to read the 52-page speech presented to him by government, and delivered a short three-minute statement instead. Outside Parliament, President Robinson was presented with a petition containing more than 6,000 signatures from Professor Selwyn Cudjoe of NAEAP, which marched with other organisations in protest against Panday's proposed appointments. The march was conducted without receiving the required police permission, and Robinson's acceptance of the petition was looked at with apprehension by some.[340] The Senate, with only nine government senators, voted the prime minister's appointed Senator Ganesh Ramdial as senate president. On January 15, St Lucia Prime Minister Dr Kenny Anthony, CARICOM head with lead responsibility for justice and governance, arrived on the invitation of Prime Minister Panday for a 36-hour visit to Trinidad to obtain information about the political impasse in order to update the CARICOM heads of government. After the visit, the CARICOM heads of government gave their opinion that the constitution be followed, and that the prime minister's appointments be sworn in. On January 19, President Robinson met with Chief of Defence Staff, John Sandy, and (curiously) Acting Commission of Police, Everald Snaggs.

In the meanwhile, the UNC began a counter-attack. Attorney-General Ramesh Lawrence Maharaj sought legal opinions from Professor Anthony Bradley; Professor Sir William Wade from the UK and Sir Godfrey Les Quesne, QC; (the first two whom President Robinson quoted as authorities whose positions coincided with his own); and Justice P.N.M. Bhagwati and L.M. Singhvi from India. When approached, all of those solicited disagreed with President Robinson's position. A total of $131,860.30 was spent for the five opinions, and $76,008.33 on local advertisements to publish those opinions in the daily press.[341] More aggressively, on January 19 an interpretation summons was filed in the High Court registry on behalf of National Security Minister designate, Roy Augustus, seeking interpretation of those aspects of the Constitution that dealt with the appointment of senators and ministers. Roodal Moonilal filed a similar motion in San Fernando.

President Robinson, in the meanwhile, made a well publicised appearance in Tobago at the 183rd Conference of the South Caribbean District of the Methodist Church on January 21. On January 23, Panday announced in Parliament that forces opposed to his government were 'colluding to seize power, some by violent means'. He declared his intention to head the Ministry of National Security. Panday also objected to the president's direct communication with the CARICOM Heads of Government regarding the International Criminal Court and Treaty of Rome (of which Robinson was a prime mover, receiving a nomination for the Nobel Peace Prize for his achievement).[342] On January 25, Panday was sworn in as Minister of National Security. Despite Panday's concession, the UNC Government continued to pressure the president to follow the prime minister's advice. On January 26, Robinson, through a press statement, accused Panday and Maharaj of waging a 'campaign of harassment' against him in the hope of driving him out of office in disgust.[343] The next day, Maharaj held a press conference to argue that the President had no discretion in the appointment of the prime minister's senators. On January 29, President Robinson noted in a one-line statement to the press that he would 'reply when he considered it appropriate'.

During this conflict, Tobago was preparing for the Tobago House Assembly (THA) elections. During the general election campaign, on November 23, 2000, Hochoy Charles had successfully moved that the THA be dissolved. The elections were subsequently announced for January 29, 2001. Interestingly, not only the NAR and PNM contested, but two newcomers, the PEP and UNC, who were competing in THA elections for the first time.

The election results were surprising, as the arrangement of the past 21 years was undone (see Appendix B). The THA's new composition seemed to revert to the 1977 County Council arrangement, almost exactly: The PNM controlled eight seats and the NAR four. The loosening of the NAR's grip on the island was intimated in 1996 but by 2001 was a political fact. With the exception of Patience Hill/Bethel, the NAR were pushed back to the small DAC base in Tobago East again, Robinson's old parliamentary constituency. The urban-rooted PNM held Scarborough and the rest of the island, as it once did.

This breach was foreshadowed by a number of events, most notably the loss of Tobago West to the PNM in December 2000. Less effective, but still significant, was the entrance of the two parties coming out of or previously associated with the NAR – the PEP and the UNC. Interestingly, the UNC, though showing poorly, outperformed the Tobago-rooted PEP. Significantly, the NAR's steady, inexorable, sure decline after 1988 even placed its status as 'the Tobago party' in doubt. The political balance in Tobago was undergoing important re-alignment. The PNM's hold of Tobago would affect the fine national balance of forces.

The THA elections did not, of course, diminish concern over the senator controversy. Seventeen business leaders met with Prime Minister Panday on February 1 to discuss the crisis. That day, Justice Wendell Kangaloo warned against the apparent 'creeping dictatorship' in the society. Ramesh Maharaj sought advice on the judge's statement.[344] Also that day, Panday addressed the diplomatic corps in the country, stating that he 'simply [could not] . . . place the Constitution of our country and, by extension, other Caribbean and Commonwealth countries, at peril'.[345] The following day, the business leaders met with President Robinson. On February 12, the UNC decided to launch a series of regional assemblies on political issues. Two days later, on February 14, Robinson wrote to Panday that he was willing to appoint the seven defeated UNC candidates as senators and, if Panday insisted, he was prepared to appoint them as ministers. He wrote, 'My choice is clear, though not without reservations'.[346] On February 20, the seven senators were sworn in. The PNM boycotted the ceremony, and the interpretation summonses filed by Augustus and Moonilal were dropped.

Seemingly secure in Government, the UNC obviously intended to replicate its intensive and reforming first term of office. It creatively re-organised and consolidated government ministries, reducing the number from 24 to 18. The change ostensibly followed the 'Singapore model' by creating new 'synergisitcs modules with the aim of taking Trinidad and Tobago to developed country status in this decade.'[347] For example, Consumer Affairs was removed from Trade to the Ministry of Community Empowerment, Sport and Consumer Affairs, while the Foreign Affairs portfolio was merged with Trade and Enterprise Development. As Minister Carlos John argued, 'The age of diplomacy is really over . . . . Trinidad and Tobago's missions must now be business-driven and work to bring in foreign investors.'[348] One of the main planks of the government's new programme was to establish a 'Task Force 2010' team to spearhead the transformation of Trinidad and

Tobago into a 'developed country, a First World nation, in this decade'. The team emerged out of a Symposium on National Vision and Strategy held from May 29 to June 1, involving Cabinet ministers, industry chieftains from various sectors of the economy, key public officers, and leaders representing religion, labour and non-governmental organisations.[349] Keeping its manifest promise, the government launched the 'Dollar for Dollar' tertiary education programme on July 26, 2001. It was promoted as 'the largest single human development programme in the history of Trinidad and Tobago', aiming to triple tertiary enrolment by 2005, from 7 per cent to 21 per cent.[350] The government introduced a package of police reform bills in July, following the recommendations of a technical team headed by former President Sir Ellis Clarke. Panday continued to make overtures to Africans by promising, during Emancipation celebrations, to examine the possibility of including a representative, nominated by the ESC, on delegations representing Trinidad and Tobago at future Africa-Caribbean-Pacific and G77 conferences, and also to include African studies in school curricula.[351] In addition, 'Chutney music',[352] through the National Chutney Foundation, became State-funded for the first time in 2001, bringing its national status closer to the Creole musical arts of steelpan and calypso.

In June, Berlin-based Transparency International ranked Trinidad and Tobago as the 31st least corrupt country out of 91 in its 2001 Corruption Perceptions Index, with a score of 5.3 out of a clean score of 10. It tied with Hungary and Tunisia, was immediately above Solvenia and Uruguay, and immediately below Italy and Namibia.[353] Although the national media interpreted the ranking incorrectly (that is, with the exact opposite meaning), the result seemed to objectively vindicate the government. In addition, the government was able to divest a significant amount of its holdings and, at the same time, stimulate wide public shareholding through the newly formed National Enterprises Limited. This body was a holding company for TSTT, Trinidad Nitrogen Company, and National Flour Mills. In each company, the government owned a 51 per cent shareholding, and it offered the remaining available shares to the public.[354] In the energy sector, Ryder Scott, an independent auditor, submitted a report on the country's national gas resources in August 2001. The audit estimated the total proven, probable, and possible reserves of natural gas at 32.6 tcf, roughly 3 per cent less than the government's estimate. In addition to this was the identified and unidentified exploratory resources, which were estimated at 58.7 tcf. To place the figure in perspective, the proven gas reserves (19.7 tcf) were estimated to last 35 years at the current rate of gas consumption.[355] This allowed government to commission a Natural Gas Master Plan from Gaffney, Cline and Associates.

The UNC's second term, however, would be far less successful than the first. In terms of legislation, it introduced 43 bills in the Lower House and 31 in the Senate, passing only 14. This compares to an average of 60 bills, 62 bills, and 49 Acts per year, respectively, in the 1995–2000 term of office. The UNC were plagued with problems. In January 2001, Panday agreed to deposit $464,569.60 as security to obtain a stay of execution of an order to pay Ken Gordon damages for calling him a 'pseudo-racist.'[356] In addition, revelations about Ken Soodhoo were emerging, linking him to questionable, perhaps fraudulent, business transactions with the Gillette family.[357] The Gillettes unsuccessfully attempted to prevent the story from being published, and this itself became a news item. In regard to the Winston Peters case, a new matter arose. On February 12, the DPP issued a summons for Peters to answer the charge of making a false statement to the EBC for the purpose of being registered as an elector. However, on April 19, Peters was acquitted as there was insufficient evidence to find him guilty. In another disconcerting matter, on February 19 Dhanraj Singh was arrested for the murder of Hansraj Sumairsingh. It was the first time such a matter had ever been brought against a former minister of government, and it obviously aroused much interest and opinion. The case, the subsequent constitution motion filed by Singh, and a few dramatic twists would continue unresolved for the rest of the year. Also causing embarrassment, after the operational opening of the new Millenium Airport, the US Federal Aviation Administration in July 2001 downgraded Trinidad and Tobago from a Category 1 rating to a Category 2 for failing to comply with standards set by the International Civil Aviation Organisation.[358]

In the meanwhile, the cases deciding whether Peters and Chaitan were entitled to sit in Parliament were still dragging on. The High Court, on March 9, dismissed Peters' and Chaitan's constitutional motions, and also dismissed an application for a stay of the election petitions, so that the PNM matters could proceed. Two days later, Basdeo Panday and Ramesh Lawrence Maharaj made public statements against the ruling, denouncing the judge personally. On July 31, the last day of the 2000-01 law term, the Court of Appeal, in a two to one majority, dismissed Peters' and Chaitan's appeals, and ordered them to pay the costs of attorneys representing the defeated PNM candidates. On August 6, Peters and Chaitan were granted conditional leave to appeal to the Privy Council. However, the next day the Court of Appeal refused to grant a stay of the PNM's election petitions and decided that the matter would be heard on October 1. On August 18, Panday declared again that he would call a general election if the Privy Council were to rule against Peters and Chaitan.[359]

In yet another matter pending, the state appealed the October 2000 judgement in the constitutional motion brought against it by CCN regarding the granting of a cellular licence. The hearings for that case were ongoing, with no early resolution in sight. This was damaging not only for the allegations of impropriety: it continued to stall the government's plans to introduce competition in the cellular telephone market. Not only that, the Gillette family, once again, were found to have been involved. A company, with which the family was associated, had received the licence, instead, during the time that Lindsay Gillette was a member of Cabinet.[360] Adding to the government's problems, its well promoted promise of 'Water For All' by the year 2000 was also not delivered, due to delays in the US$120 million desalination project on the Point Lisas Industrial Estate.

In addition, the allegations against the Elecion and Boundaries Commission (EBC) were mounting in the press and on the political platform. In response, on February 8, the EBC decided to seek professional help from a public relations firm. Commissioner Raoul John, who had also recently been president of the Trinidad and Tobago Chamber of Commerce, was appointed as EBC spokesperson, and addressed the public on various matters. Stepping up their attack, on March 19 the PNM were granted leave by High Court judge to seek judicial review of the electoral list used in the December 11, 2000 general elections. On June 14, Arthur Sanderson's Communities United to Fight Underdevelopment staged a public protest against the prime minister's refusal to establish a Commission of Inquiry into irregularities in the same elections. On July 12, the police announced that the voter-padding probe had just ended, with a total of 125 persons interrogated, and 36 persons charged. Despite calls from interest groups, the prime minister refused to establish a Commission of Inquiry into the operations of the EBC, on the grounds that the government's involvement would compromise the EBC's independence. In the meanwhile, the EBC, published on August 19, the results of its Nationwide House to House Survey, enabled by a $10 million disbursement from the Ministry of Finance. According to the results of the survey, PNM Deputy Leader Keith Rowley had called for the immediate removal of the over 260,000 names on the voters list (constituting 29 per cent of the 955,198 listed names) that were found to be deceased, removed from their addresses, or to have migrated.[361]

The PNM were not in good shape themselves. On March 22, 2001, Patrick Manning held a press conference, calling on all persons, regardless of party 'who believe in democracy', to contribute to the PNM's Preservation of Democracy Fund, to help him meet his outstanding payments due to the Government following the loss of his appeal against Speaker Hector McLean in 1997. Manning stated that the Democracy Fund was at $194,000, and the state had increased pressure on him to pay the full sum, now reported at $1.5 million.[362] That same day, the PNM refused to participate in the three newly formed Joint Select Committees of Parliament which were responsible for monitoring the work of and reporting to the senate on all government ministries, municipal corporations, statutory bodies, and service commissions, with the exception of the Judicial and Legal Service Commission. The PNM, although supporting the relevant Constitutional Amendment in 1999, protested that these bodies would compromise the independence of many state bodies.

A new set of parliamentary troubles occurred when, in March 2001, PNM MP for Diego Martin Central, Kenneth Valley, accused the prime minister and Minister of National Security Basdeo Panday of interfering with hiring practices in the coastguard, so that more Indians could get positions. It was a heated issue that provoked Panday to accuse Valley of raising Afro-Trinidadian fears to gather support. Valley was brought before the Privileges Committee of Parliament for his statement. Valley counter-attacked by filing a motion to censure Panday for 'the incorrect, inaccurate and misleading information' Panday provided to the House on May 7 regarding the Coast Guard recruitment list.[363] Meanwhile, in the party, PNM MP for Diego Martin East, Keith Rowley, wrote a letter on April 2, 2001 suggesting that 'voter padding' had occurred in the PNM's internal elections of 1996 and that, as in national elections, PNM voting procedures should be reformed.[364] In Parliament, on May 24, Speaker of the House, former PNM MP Rupert Griffith, suspended Rowley for what the Speaker ruled as 'an insult to the Chair'. At that, PNM members walked out of the House and began a boycott of both Houses of Parliament. Keith Rowley, in the meanwhile, embarked on a round of private meetings with PNM members, aimed at 'reforming and reconstructing' the party.[365] The PNM halted their boycott on June 8, but that day the Speaker suspended PNM MP for Laventille East/Morvant, Fitzgerald Hinds, also for 'disrespect and disregard for the Speaker while he was on his feet'.[366] The PNM immediately resumed their boycott until discussions were held with the House Speaker. On June

29, the PNM and UNC reached an agreement which provided for Keith Rowley to return to Parliament on July 13 (the next sitting of Parliament), Ken Valley to drop his motion of censure against Panday, and the Privileges Committee to drop its action against Valley.[367] Keith Rowley, however, was not pleased with the arrangements made on his behalf and a ten-day war of words emerged between him and party officials.[368] During the crisis, on June 17, Robin Montano, brother of PNM Senator Danny Montano, son of PNM foundation member Gerard Montano, and prominent political commentator, resigned from the PNM, accusing the party members of making 'racist statements' to win support.[369] In the background was the awareness that the PNM leadership election had been scheduled for December 9, 2001.

At the same time, the UNC had started to show unexpected party cleavages, which would eventually prove fatal to its position in government. Panday had another angina attack in March 2001 and was advised to go to London for rest and further medical treatment. When he returned on April 8, Panday announced that ministers could contest the UNC internal Party Elections which were due on June 3.[370] By May 11, Nomination Day for Party Elections, Ramesh Lawrence Maharaj, Kamla Persad-Bissessar, and Carlos John had emerged as contestants for the post of Deputy Political Leader. Each had a slate of 11 supporting candidates. The battle became surprisingly hostile. Notably, Trevor Sudama withdrew his candidacy for Deputy Leadership position to support Maharaj. During the campaign, nine MPs, five senators, and three local government leaders supported Carlos John and his 'All-Inclusive Team', while three MPs and three Senators supported Maharaj and his 'Team Unity'.[371] Ramesh Maharaj, in fact, called on members of parliament supporting Carlos John to 'explain why'. He even challenged John to a public debate. Those on the Maharaj slate were accused of waging a race-conscious campaign that sought to elevate their long-standing status over the 'Johnnies-come-lately' to the party. Basdeo Panday chose to remain publicly neutral in the campaign. On July 3, Team Unity won ten of the 12 executive posts. Out of the 72,339 financial members of the UNC, only 26,344 members (38 per cent) voted. However, this was far more than the roughly 4,600 turnout of 1997. Maharaj won the Deputy Leadership with 10,983 votes (42 per cent) out of a total of 25,523 votes cast. Kamla Persad-Bissessar received 7,765 (30 per cent) votes and Carlos John, 6,775 (26 per cent).[372]

It was speculated that Panday was not pleased with the outcome of the UNC party elections, as Carlos John, being an Afro-Creole and a former director of the large local conglomerate CL Financial, would have supposedly widened the support base of the UNC. In the aftermath of the campaign, it was believed that Maharaj would now act as prime minister when Panday was absent. However, Panday declared that the deputy political leader was not constitutionally entitled to act as prime minister. Indeed, on June 12 John Humphrey was appointed to act as prime minister for a period of one week. Maharaj's supporters felt that this was an insult. Panday replied that since the prime minister and Attorney-General are the two required constituents of a Cabinet, Maharaj could not be named acting prime minister unless he was dismissed as Attorney-General and a new one appointed.[373] Surprisingly, on June 28, Panday announced a re-allocation of portfolios in cabinet. It did not affect the balance of responsibilities too greatly but, on balance, it seemed to favour ministers who were not part of Team Unity (Ramesh Lawrence Maharaj, Trevor Sudama, Ralph Maraj, and Sadiq Baksh).

During this time, allegations of corruption continued to accumulate. In the run-up to the 2000 elections, Maharaj had established an Anti-Corruption Squad to undertake a series of investigations, including the airport project, desalination plant, and the InnCogen deal, based on allegations made by the opposition. Maharaj hired Bob Lindquist, a Canadian forensic investigator who had been hired earlier by the NAR government to probe the John O'Halloran bribe scandal which led to the recovery of $29.6 million in 1991. The report was seen only by the prime minister, Maharaj, and the Assistant Commissioner of Police by May 2001. In the meanwhile, on June 29, a report by the Auditor-General on the North West Regional Health Authority (NWRHA) was laid in Parliament, revealing extensive fraud. Finance Minister Gerald Yetming subsequently commissioned a private investigation to review the operations of the authority, while also calling in the police services' Fraud Squad. These substantial allegations were compounded by other minor revelations such as that against Minister Ganga Singh and his guests who 'racked up a total bill of $180,000 at the VIP Liquor Bar during Carnival 2001' to be paid by taxpayers' money.[374]

As a counter-attack of sorts, the government-appointed chairman of the state-owned National Petroleum Marketing Company launched an investigation into questionable hiring practices, abuse of overtime and questionable donations in her company. Employees were accused of using company time to work for the PNM, and also using company money to fund the PNM. The investigation received the support of the prime minister.[375] Also, in July, Finance Minister Gerald Yetming filed a lawsuit against Patrick

Manning, for claiming that Yetming made available only doctored copies of the Auditor-General's Report, and that $1.7 billion was missing from the Treasury.

New evidence arose. On August 3, the Fraud Squad were given a copy of a controversial report by London-based Integrated Security Systems on the alleged widespread corruption at PETROTRIN, as intimated during the 2000 elections. The day before, however, Diego Martin West MP, Keith Rowley, read in Parliament excerpts of a leaked copy of the report, implicating at least one former minister. Excerpts were published in the press in July.[376] On August 9, Minister of Energy and Energy Industries, Lindsay Gillette and the DPP were given copies of the report. On September 7, PETROTRIN CEO Roderick Pariag tendered his resignation after less than one year in office. Maharaj requested a copy of the report, but was denied it by the prime minister.

On September 12, a forensic report into allegations of corruption at the NWRHA by Personnel Management Services Ltd. (of which a former Independent Senator was a prominent director) was sent to the DPP and the Fraud Squad. Two days later, four of the authority's managers were sent letters of termination.[377] On September 21, Keith Rowley in Parliament called on Basdeo Panday to explain the circumstances under which Panday received a cheque for $312,000 from 'something called the Northwest Liaison Office', headed by Dr Tim Gopeesingh, former chairman of the NWRHA. Another incident from the past was raised on September 28 as the government threatened legal action against the main company involved in InnCogen for outstanding payments due since 1998, and for its failure to develop the proposed paper and glass industries on the site.

On July 6, the PSA, joined by the CWU, the OWTU, Arthur Sanderson's Communities United to Fight Underdevelopment, and Fishermen and Friends of the Sea, protested against the government's refusal to pay arrears owed to PSA members since 1988. With gratuitous ethnic references the PSA president charged, 'We must make this place hotter than a chulha and we must all come out with our chinese chopper.'[378] On July 24, NAEAP and Communities United to Fight Underdevelopment organised a protest, 'Red Day of Resistance', against government corruption. The marchers did not receive the required police permission, and they obviously defied the authorities without penalty. Selwyn Cudjoe, The NAEAP leader, announced, 'This is the beginning of civil disobedience.'[379] The following day, the Public Service Association organised a candlelight vigil (which some protesters turned into an *obeah*[380] ceremony against Panday) to press for arrears, and to launch their 'own campaign against corruption'.[381] On July 27, the anniversary of the attempted coup, the police pre-empted other groups from protesting, by holding a parade (for the first time on that date) demonstrating their strength. On August 10, the NAEAP staged a 'Red Day of Resistance 2', calling for an end to the Peters and Chaitan court matters by December 11, 2001. On August 29, a protest organised by the Group of Independent Trade Unions (led by the OWTU, PSA, and CWU) saw eight trade unions, NAR and PNM representatives, unemployed people, schoolchildren, parents, pensioners, PNM mayor of San Fernando Gerard Ferreira, Fishermen and Friends of the Sea, and radical religious leaders marching five kilometres from Mount Hope to Woodford Square in Port of Spain to denounce the 'scourge of corruption now gripping the country'.[382]

In a television interview on July 30, Ralph Maraj stated that he was so concerned about the allegations of corruption that if he was not satisfied with the way that government handled the allegations, then he would have 'no choice but to resign' from Cabinet.[383] This, of course, upset many of his colleagues. Only Trevor Sudama openly supported Maraj. The following day, at a UNC rally in Port of Spain, after Panday defended the government's actions, he shouted with venom, 'Who want to resign, resign!'[384]

On August 11, Panday appointed Kamla Persad-Bissessar as acting prime minister while he was away. The next day, Maharaj made an unexpected grand entrance in the middle of a UNC Women's meeting which was being addressed by Persad-Bissessar. The act provoked Panday, on his return, to chastise an unnamed 'Judas' in the party, and to instruct party members to start looking for fresh candidates.[385] Panday re-shuffled Cabinet again on August 22, reducing the portfolios of Ramesh Maharaj, Trevor Sudama, and Ralph Maraj. That day, Ramesh Maharaj claimed that a hitman had been hired by an unnamed large local conglomerate to kill him. Battle lines were drawn between Team Unity, which controlled the UNC Executive, and Prime Minister Panday, who commanded the support of Parliament. Up to this point, however, neither side admitted to be in opposition to the other side, although it was obvious. Surprisingly, Nizam Mohammed, Raymond Pallackdharrysingh, and Kelvin Ramnath – all former colleagues of Panday who fell out with him at one time – publicly supported Panday in his row with Maharaj.[386] At a UNC Executive meeting on September 3, a major coup occurred when the Team Unity-controlled National Executive voted against Panday in favour of holding constituency elections, which were due in one week. The next day, UNC Parliamentarians and Cabinet members declared 'war' on the 'Gang of Four'. On September 6, the home of UNC Treasurer and Team Unity member, Unanan Persad, was raided by police, and his wife and daughter-in-law were body searched, ostensibly in a search for drugs. Nothing was found. Persad was in tears at a press conference, and publicly accused Panday, who was Minister of National Security, of trying to intimidate him. The cracks, about which everyone knew, were being openly acknowledged by the rivals. Team Unity began to speak against government corruption, proclaiming this as the source of the party conflict. On September 10, the UNC Constituency elections were held, with roughly 670 candidates contesting posts.[387] Both sides claimed victory as the result was equivocal. The next battle was the Budget Debate, as the fiscal year was to begin in October. There was abundant speculation as to what would occur. Surprisingly, on September 22, the UNC's 2001–02 Budget was passed. However, this was not done without Maharaj, Maraj, and Sudama severely criticising the budget and their own government.

On October 1, Basdeo Panday called a National Executive Meeting at 5:00pm. A massive crowd turned out to cheer Panday. Ramesh Maharaj did not attend. At that meeting, Ramesh Maharaj's appointment as Attorney-General was revoked. John Humphrey stated that had Ramesh Maharaj attended the meeting, he could have been 'lynched'.[388] At 11:00pm that evening, Ramesh Maharaj, Trevor Sudama, and Ralph Maraj sent letters to President Robinson withdrawing support for Basdeo Panday as prime minister.[389] The next day, Ralph Maraj resigned his Cabinet post, and Sudama announced his intention to resign. On October 3, however, Panday dismissed Sudama from Cabinet.

On October 2, the PNM General Council empowered Patrick Manning to make an alliance with the UNC dissidents, in an attempt to form a majority in Parliament. Interestingly, a few days earlier, on September 27, Patrick Manning had stated that the opposition had no intention of moving any motion of no confidence in the prime minister because that would have interfered with the elections petitions in the court, whose successful outcome the PNM hoped would have placed them in government. As the public speculation and anxiety grew, on October 4, former President Ellis Clarke, Tajmool Hosein, and the Law Association advised President Robinson that he could not remove Prime Minister Panday without a motion of no-confidence.[390] On October 5, the three dissident UNC MPs and Nathaniel Moore, NAR MP for Tobago East, three times voted with the Opposition against three simple bills brought by the government. Further contention arose at the end of the session when government moved to suspend the House to a date to be fixed, causing the opposition MPs to make an uproar, which the Speaker apparently ignored.[391]

On October 10, eight months after the last general elections, Prime Minister Panday advised the president to dissolve Parliament with immediate effect and to appoint December 10, 2001 as the time when a 'General Election of Members of the House of Representatives shall be held'. Panday explained that he had no choice but to call a snap election to forestall a 'palace coup' by the opposition PNM and the three ex-ministers.[392] The Parliament was the shortest in Trinidad and Tobago's history, and the campaign was the longest. It was as legally combative as the aborted term of office.

Before the campaign could get started, there was yet another obstacle in Panday's way. Again contravening conventional understanding of his constitutional powers, President Robinson did not immediately comply with the prime minister's advice. The same day Robinson received Panday's advice, he advised the prime minister to 'stay your advice to allow me to ascertain the position with respect to the preparation for Elections by the Elections and Boundaries Commission.' The same day, Panday indicated that he would not stay his advice. And again the same day, the president replied to Panday, refusing to follow the advice.[393] Robinson was supported by Patrick Manning, who also believed that the EBC was not ready to conduct new elections.

The President's difficulties with the EBC emerged in September. On September 7, Prime Minister Panday met with the EBC at the EBC's request. Three days later, the President summoned EBC Chairman Oswald Wilson for discussions. On the following day, September 11, the Office of the President accused EBC Commissioner Raoul John of causing further controversy with regards to the EBC, and suggested that John may have had an 'agenda' since he wore 'two hats', as EBC commissioner and president of the Trinidad and Tobago Chamber of Industry and Commerce. That day, Keith Rowley charged that Prime Minister Panday and the EBC were in collusion. The next day, President Robinson invited Raoul John to President's House, asking him to submit a letter of resignation from the EBC. John refused. On Friday, September 14, President Robinson revoked the appointment of John as EBC Commissioner. However, two of Robinson's former colleagues, Joseph Toney once NAR Minister of National Security, then NAR leader, and former Attorney-General, Anthony Smart, noted that the president had not acted in accordance with the constitution.[394] On

September 15, EBC Chairman Oswald Wilson was forced to deny a statement issued from the Office of the President, emphasising that he 'did not either in words or otherwise "denounce" any remarks made by Commissioner Raoul John'.[395] On the contrary, the EBC produced an advertisement defending Raoul John. In the meanwhile, John, refuted the statements issued from the Office of the President and defended his dual role as President of the Trinidad and Tobago Chamber of Commerce and EBC Commissioner. On Monday, September 17, in defiance of the President's orders, the EBC Commissioners met, with Raoul John present as usual. Defeated, the following day President Robinson withdrew Raoul John's letter of dismissal. However, on September 27, President Robinson twice held private talks with Prime Minister Panday and one with opposition leader, Manning, about the possibility of a constitutional amendment regarding the removal of EBC Commissioners. In their own defence, the EBC produced a newspaper advertisement on October 7 highlighting the Commonwealth Observer Team's favourable assessment of December 2000 election procedure.

The day after Panday advised Robinson to dissolve Cabinet, Oswald Wilson informed President Robinson that by the end of the month the EBC would be ready for a general election, since 'the field exercise in respect of the second phase of the [House to House] survey was completed on October 7, 2001.' Patrick Manning, however, declared that a general election could not be called in all 36 constituencies, because of the election petitions pending before the court with respect to four of those constituencies. Ramesh Maharaj, on the other hand, sent copies of the opinions of Professor Anthony Bradley and Geoffrey Robertson, QC, that the President could revoke the appointment of the sitting Prime Minister and appoint another person as Prime Minister in order to 'secure the maintenance of constitutional government in Trinidad and Tobago' as 'a last resort'. Maharaj, however, cautioned that the President must be slow in using his discretion. The opinion, however, did not accord with the conventional interpretation. Other Team Unity members, including the Tobago UNC leader, Mogril Polson, called on the President to reject the December 10 election date. This obviously gave hope to the PNM. On October 12, the PNM produced an advertisement claiming that 'there can be no free and fair elections!' and disputed the EBC's opinion that the Commonwealth Observer Team approved of the EBC's conduct in the December 2000 elections. On the contrary, CARICOM heads of government expressed support for Prime Minister Panday, stressing that it was 'incumbent upon' President Robinson to follow the advice of the prime minister on dissolving Parliament and holding an election.

President Robinson, meanwhile, charged that what EBC Chairman Oswald Wilson had told him conflicted with newspaper advertisements placed by the EBC from October 8 to10. The EBC informed the President that there was no conflict between the information given to the public in the print media and the information that the EBC gave to him. Meanwhile, on October 13, Karl Hudson-Phillips, Herbert Atwell, former NAR National Security Minister, Patrick Manning, and UNC Deputy Leader Ramesh Lawrence Maharaj privately met. That day, however, President Robinson dissolved Parliament.

The PNM debated its strategy regarding the EBC. On October 22, the PNM and EBC agreed to adjourn the judicial review of the December 11, 2000 electoral list in order to avoid an adverse effect on the current elections. The review was to be resumed on December 14, 2001. However, PNM allegations that the EBC were colluding with the UNC continued. The PNM seemed calmed, however, after a meeting with EBC officials on November 29 during which time the EBC reported on its activities in having the electoral lists 'cleaned'. PNM Deputy Leader Ken Valley declared that he was 'now satisfied that there . . . [would] be free and fair elections in Trinidad and Tobago', although he stated that reservations still existed. By this time, the controversy over Peters and Chaitan had become irrelevant and the PNM could not win the Pointe-à-Pierre and Mayaro seats by default as it had hoped. On October 17, the representation petitions against Manning and James were discontinued and the same happened to the election petitions against Peters and Chaitan on October 24.

During this time, Panday and Maharaj were fighting an intense battle, much of it through the national media (radio, newspapers, and television), for the legal control of the UNC. On the one hand, Panday was the political leader of the UNC, commanded the support of 16 Parliamentarians, and indisputably had the loyalty of most of the UNC membership. On the other hand, Maharaj was the Deputy Leader of the Party and controlled the party executive (elected by the party membership), along with small but significant groups of vocal supporters both inside and outside the party. The two groups conducted parallel meetings, waged campaigns against each other reaching the courts (following the pattern of the entire year), and attempted to expel each other from the party. Each claimed that they were the 'real UNC'. Panday based his claim on his leadership, while Maharaj based his claim on Panday's alleged betrayal of the UNC through government corruption and

Panday's thraldom to business interests. To ensure that each faction could contest the upcoming elections, on October 18 new party names were registered with the EBC. Panday and his supporters registered the name 'National Unity' and Maharaj registered the name 'Team Unity'. Interestingly, former PNM Minister of Finance, Wendell Mottley, registered the party name, 'Citizens' Alliance'.[396] On October 31, Maharaj met with the EBC seeking to convince the commission to recognise his faction as the UNC. The following day, Panday met with the EBC to do the same. On November 7, twelve days before Nomination Day, EBC decided to give the Basdeo Panday faction the right to use the UNC name and symbol, based on Panday's undisputed status as leader of the UNC. The EBC claimed that it could not constitute itself as a court of law to resolve other matters of contention in the party. Maharaj subsequently lost two appeals, clearing the way for Panday on November 16.

On November 19, Nomination Day, 110 candidates filed nomination papers – 36 UNC, 36 PNM, 30 Team Unity, 6 NAR, and 2 National Democratic Organisation. On November 21, UNC Chairman Wade Mark wrote letters to eight Team Unity members (Ramesh Maharaj, Ralph Maraj, Trevor Sudama, Garnet Mungalsingh, Barbara Gray-Burke, Saieed Mohammed, Muriel Armoroso, and Unanan Persad), all members of the UNC National Executive, to explain their registration under a banner other than the UNC's.

The results of the election were as dramatic and consequential as the year that preceded it. Trinidad and Tobago had an absolutely hung Parliament. The PNM and UNC received 18 seats each. The other three parties were shut out (see Appendix B). Emphasising the novelty of the situation was the fact that the Constitution did not anticipate such a predicament. The country was forced to face the fact of the stalemate, intimated by the slim majority of 1991, the snap election of 1995 (which was called, according to Prime Minister Manning, because he did not have enough seats), the 17-17-2 result of 1995, and the evenly split local government elections of 1996 and 1999. If the UNC anticipated that its spectacular rise would lead it to outstrip the PNM (as the PNM left behind the other parties in 1956), they were wrong. The UNC did not achieve much more than parity (which itself was an achievement, in the context of Trinidad and Tobago's political history).

In the elections of 2001, quite importantly, the PNM regained the borderline seat of Tunapuna from the UNC and took Tobago East (A.N.R. Robinson's old constituency) from the NAR. Significantly, the NAR seemed to finally die at the Parliamentary level. Also, Team Unity was soundly defeated, receiving only 2.5 per cent of the ballots cast. Their intervention did not make a difference in the results at all, as no seat was won with less than 50 per cent of the ballots cast. Together the PNM and UNC received 96 per cent of all votes cast. Both parties received more votes than they did in 1995, but not as many as they had received in 2000.

In analysing the results of the elections, it is important to note the lower number of voters in 2001 (560,778 ballots) as compared to 2000 (597,525 ballots), a difference of almost 37,000. It should be noted, however, that the amount was greater than the total number of voters in 1995 (see Appendix B). Each party mobilised fewer voters than it did in December 2000. In the 2000 elections, the UNC received an average of 12,381 votes in each of their 19 constituencies; the PNM won an average of 10,232 votes in each of their 16 constituencies; and the NAR won their single seat with 3,921 votes. In 2001, the UNC received an average of 11,460 votes in each of the 18 constituencies where they won, and the PNM an average of 9,347 in their 18. However, even though the number of voters decreased in 2001 compared to 2000 the voter turnout was higher (66.4 per cent) since the Elections and Boundaries Commission removed a net of 103,435 persons in the new list.

In contrast to 2000 when the UNC made its impressive gains, it lost 9.4 per cent of its overall support between 2000 and 2001. Losses occurred in every constituency, except Tobago where the UNC freshly contested. The party lost most of its support in the PNM 'core' constituencies and in Couva South, where Ramesh Lawrence Maharaj contested. The PNM lost support, too, 6.1 per cent overall, even though it made gains in Tobago East, Tobago West, Arouca North, Ortoire/Mayaro, Tunapuna, and Arouca South (in decreasing order of magnitude). Interestingly, Port of Spain, Laventille, Barataria/San Juan, and St Ann's were among the seats in which the PNM lost most support.

Only three seats were won with a margin of less than 1,500 votes. All were won with a majority. The three seats were Tunapuna (PNM), San Fernando West (UNC), and Ortoire/Mayaro (UNC). If we consider those constituencies which were won with a margin of 3,000 votes, we find that there were nine (see Table 7.5).

***Table 7.5. Constituencies won with a margin of less than 3,000 votes, December 10, 2001***

| CONSTITUENCY | UNC | PNM | TEAM UNITY | NAR | REJECTED BALLOTS | % VOTED | MARGIN OF VICTORY |
|---|---|---|---|---|---|---|---|
| Tunapuna | 8,543 | 8,819 | 184 | - | 57 | 75.8% | 276 |
| San Fernando West | 8,244 | 7,810 | 174 | - | 96 | 74.5% | 434 |
| Ortoire/Mayaro | 10,252 | 9,433 | 174 | - | 120 | 75.7% | 819 |
| Barataria/San Juan | 8,008 | 6,343 | 163 | - | 57 | 70.4% | 1,665 |
| St. Joseph | 8,824 | 6,793 | 242 | - | 18 | 72.4% | 2,031 |
| La Brea | 6,890 | 8,951 | 264 | - | 81 | 72.3% | 2,061 |
| Toco/Manzanilla | 7,509 | 9,787 | 224 | - | 89 | 67.6% | 2,278 |
| Tobago East | 2,384 | 4,866 | - | 2,384 | 68 | 49.6% | 2,482 |
| Point Fortin | 6,551 | 9,497 | 234 | - | 64 | 69.8% | 2,946 |

*Source*: Elections and Boundaries Commission, personal communication

The hung result has opened up a new set of questions for the country. An unambitious reading would see this as simply another election result. A more adventurous interpretation would argue that a climacteric point had been reached in the country's history. The reservations expressed in 1956 by Governor Edward Beetham were prescient, that a constitution which assumed the existence of political parties would result in 'either the emergence of parties inherently racial in outlook or make-up, or the development of an innately unstable government and legislature' due to the unlikelihood of the emergence of strong majorities.[397] Williams eventually instituted such a system of government, which depended on a strong legislative majority to hide its contradictions. The Panday governments, working with a threadbare majority, unexpectedly pushed the independence model of self-government to its extremes, raising questions about the division of powers and responsibilities, and limitations, of the president, the prime minister, the Courts and the Judiciary, the Tobago House of Assembly, and the constitution. Not even in the heightened points of Independence, Black Power, the constitutional reform period of the 1970s, or the early NAR years had these fundamental aspects of government been so visible, tangible, readily understandable, and alive. And, to top it off, the political forces have become evenly balanced, unlike in these other periods. What does this portend? Creative change?

Gridlock? Can the Williams model of self-government survive under these conditions? How will the parties and the citizenry evolve, adjust, or react?

The inconclusive end of our examination, with the political parties', indeed the country's, innocence regarding these fundamental questions — which are far more substantial than the contests for office with which they have been pre-occupied - highlights crucial aspects of the country's 'half-madeness'. The following years may very well be crucial, with future elections, possible constitution or legislative reforms, and political re-alignments — not to mention potential international political and economic developments — shaping the context in which Trinidadians and Tobagonians work out the ways by which they, perhaps, might grow.

# Conclusion

This study has sought to identify the main political challenges faced by the various governments of Trinidad and Tobago between 1956 and 2001. In chapter one, which covered the 1925–53 period of gradually increasing political responsibility, it was argued that the most notable aspect of political organisation was the absence of national parties. Instead there existed a diversity of interests and groups – regionally, ethnically, and labour based – while political aspirants contested seats as independents or as members of loosely-organised and short-lived parties. Up to 1955, there was no national organisation comparable to those which existed in Barbados and Jamaica, both ready to lead the country to self-government and independence. In chapter two we saw how Williams and the PNM – out of a combination of political shrewdness, determination, toughness, aggression, luck, and circumstance – had prevailed over the independent political tradition with their brand of party politics; vanquished the old politicians who had re-formed into the DLP; negotiated an agreement with the Americans on

Chaguaramas; reached a settlement on Independence with the British government and with the parliamentary opposition; and secured an unprecedented two-thirds majority in parliament. Chapter three described how the PNM maintained its two-thirds majority right up to Williams's death in 1981, despite the continuous extra-parliamentary radical trade union and Black Power opposition, the new generation of opposition parties that emerged in 1976, and the challenge posed in 1980–1 by the ONR.

Chapter four described how the Chambers administration could not sustain either the political or economic gains made during the Williams years. Despite the rhetoric about prudence and restraint, the Chambers administration did not act decisively enough to counter the recession. Chambers was seen to be an intellectual failure as well, with the many jokes made about his witlessness on the one hand, and the NAR's spectacular seizing of the political vanguard position on the other. Chapter five examined how the NAR, which had been popularly mandated with such enthusiasm in 1986, was a political failure. It could control neither its members nor the country, losing almost every significant battle it faced after the September 1987 local government elections, whether party indiscipline or social protest. The challenges of the period were exceptionally difficult – including economic downturn and being the first non-PNM government in office in thirty years – and the party was not up to the task, misjudging the commitment of its early supporters.

In Chapter six we saw how the PNM suffered its second loss in ten years, despite the general goodwill shown to the Manning administration at the beginning of its term in 1991. A combination of the UNC's and Panday's political skill, Manning's political blunders, a rise in Indian consciousness sparked by the 150th anniversary of Indian arrival, and perhaps a vague dissatisfaction with the economic and social situation (despite the objective improvements) served to dislodge the PNM. Chapter seven analysed the UNC's two administrations under the iconic Basdeo Panday. On the one hand, his administration was one of the country's most important, in terms of its reforming zeal and its ability to win a second term of office. On the other hand, the intense opposition against it eventually effected the unprecedented collapse of the government just eight months after resuming its second term in 2001. The UNC governments, with threadbare majorities, unexpectedly pushed the independence model of self-government to its extremes, highlighting the problems of legally constituted authority in Trinidad and Tobago: the division of powers and responsibilities of the president, the prime minister, the Courts and the Judiciary, the Tobago House of Assembly, and the constitution itself. A political and constitutional crisis was reached, the political forces reached parity, and the country was stalemated. Trinidad and Tobago was brought to an historic point.

The first subsidiary question of the study asked whether there were distinctive problems, programmes, goals, methods, and/or themes transcending particular governments and/or opposition. In the Trinidad and Tobago environment, political emergence and survival has been a significant task in itself, and seems to be a constant challenge. The initial establishment of the PNM and UNC governments with a plurality of votes against the expectations of the political observers and the political demise of the seriously-formed PDP, DLP, WFP, the Liberal Party, NJAC, DAC, Tapia, ONR, and NAR parties[1] testify to this historical fact.

While the challenges that each government faced were specific, one notes the constancy of intense yet diffuse and incoherent disputation in Trinidad and Tobago's politics, regardless of the economic strategy (broad five-year plans, state-led heavy industrialisation, private-sector led outward-orientation) or racial background (African-dominated, multi-racial coalition, Indian-dominated) of the various administrations. Arguably, the slow grinding to stalemate in 2001 was a manifestation of this.

The political problem identified by Eric Williams in his 'Case for Party Politics in Trinidad and Tobago'[2] remains to be solved in contemporary Trinidad and Tobago: that is, the creation of a system of disciplined, organised, durable, principled, national political parties.[3] Unfortunately, a considerable amount of political dissent in Trinidad and Tobago remains incoherent and undisciplined, seemingly averse to sustained organisation and/or expression through the existing formal institutions. This can be seen in the frequency of demonstrations and protestations against the government while there exists a comparatively high abstention rate in elections and other public exercises. Whether this can be remedied by constitutional re-organisation, or whether the problems are more deep-seated in habit, history, or social structure cannot be determined here, of course. This is properly the subject of another inquiry, quite different from the type undertaken in this book. The view of the author, however, is that formal constitutional reform is necessary to provide another context in which Trinidad and Tobago's politics can develop. However, the author is convinced that the most important reform can only result from the entrance of a new party (like the PNM in 1956) or the novel re-formation of the old ones (like the NAR in 1986). The potential challenges posed by the hung Parliament of 2001 put the country at a crossroads, with implications for both the formal and informal levels of politics. How the country evolves, adjusts, or reacts at this juncture is crucial.

Another subsidiary question was, how far have racial and ethnic concerns dominated politics in Trinidad and Tobago? Certainly racial and ethnic mobilisation has been important in politics since 1956, as is evidenced by the persistence of a core of PNM and PDP, DLP, and UNC seats in areas of high African and Indian concentrations respectively (except in 1971 and 1986). However, some important aspects of politics in Trinidad and Tobago should make one cautious about over-interpreting the role of ethnic competition, even in the face of stalemate.

For instance the argument that 'communalism' was dominant in Trinidad and Tobago's politics even before 1956[4] should be tempered by the fact that only the PDP in 1956 (which won five seats) could be reasonably counted as a communal organisation that successfully presented itself for political office. It should be noted that an explicitly 'racial' party like the African National Congress in 1961 and 1971, the strongly African-Christian focused Butler Party from 1946-66,[5] and the DLP's fairly open racial appeals to Indians in 1976 were electorally unsuccessful. In the 1956 elections, it should be remembered that the PNM polled a greater share of votes in the Indian-majority Caroni seats than it did in the Eastern counties and in St Patrick where Afro-Creoles were the majority. A straightforward racial argument is also contradicted by the fact that as the number and national proportion of Indians steadily grew in Trinidad and Tobago – from 195,747 (35.1 per cent) in 1946 to 429,187 (40.7 per cent) in 1980 – the Indian-led parties fared worse, with the DLP capturing 41.7 per cent of the vote and two-thirds of parliament in 1961, and the ULF capturing 15.1 per cent of the vote and less than one-quarter of the parliamentary seats in 1981.[6]

Apart from elections, too, interpretations of politics in the post-Independence era as primarily driven by African-Indian competition would not account for the anti-Williams Black Power movement that called for Africans and Indians to unite; NUFF's violent campaign against the Afro-Creole establishment; the loyalty displayed to A.N.R. Robinson's prime ministership by Indian Cabinet ministers Winston Dookeran, Bhoe Tewarie, Brinsley Samaroo and Sahadeo Basdeo; the opposition to him expressed by MPs Jensen Fox, Eden Shand, Arthur Sanderson, Ken Butcher, and Theodore Guerra; and the Muslimeen's demand in 1990 that Winston Dookeran replace A.N.R. Robinson as prime minister.

The danger in Trinidad and Tobago has never really been systematic, organised ethnic violence as much as malaise, dysfunction, apathy, and anomie. Changes of government have occurred in 1956, 1986, 1991, and 1995 with no threat of violence. Opportunities for violent conflict were quite abundant after the 2001 deadlock as well, yet no such confrontation occurred. On the other hand, serious crime, suicide, migration, and divorce did rise significantly in the 1980s, and continue to afflict social life.

The influence of race in politics is real, but the extent of its significance is questionable. The dominant theme among analysts of politics in Trinidad and Tobago seems to be that racial antagonism is the driving force of politics. Yet, despite this claim, none of the 'clashing' ethnic groups has any easily discernible ethnic goals. There are no significant 'supremacist' political movements among any of the ethnic groups, neither is there any notable separatist movement. The demands for more Indian programming on television, the reluctance to establish an Indian cultural centre, state funding for calypso and steelpan organisations, and so on, are hardly the stuff of latent violent ethnic conflict, but of constant frustration, petty-mindedness, and unproductive bickering. Indeed, there is not much of a sociological basis for strong ethnic separatist or supremacist movements in Trinidad and Tobago. There are no ancient, ancestral groups with strong claims to the land. (The 'Carib community' based in Arima are the only possible such group, and they have never made such claims in any serious way.) With regard to the two largest ethnic groups, the Africans are New World Africans, without connection to contemporary Africa. Indians, too, despite people's claims, are almost entirely ignorant of contemporary India. No ancestral languages are spoken (unlike in Mauritius, for example), everybody speaks the same Trinidad and Tobago English, all read the same newspapers and watch the same televised newscasts. There are no ethnic organisations with formal political powers (such as the Great Council of Chiefs in Fiji), and ethnicity does not legally determine access (positively or negatively) to housing, employment, or any other service (as in Singapore and Malaysia, for example). What analysts claim as 'racialist' politics in Trinidad and Tobago amounts to not much more than competition for office and demands for a share of government patronage in terms of jobs, business contracts, directorships, state funding, and so on. Indeed, if so much activity were not so dependent on such patronage, it is likely that the ethnic bases of parties would be of far less significance. This dependence is important to consider, but must be the topic of another study, of a different type from this one. To return to the point, the findings of the present study (particularly with the career of Dr Williams, the NAR, and the UNC) suggest the primary importance is of politics, not of race.

The last subsidiary questions asked were, how did Prime Minister Eric Williams survive in office for five terms? How did the three subsequent prime ministers fail to win a second term? How did Basdeo Panday break this trend? While others have argued that Williams was able to survive in office on the basis of racial appeals to Africans, the evidence presented in the study suggests that the answer to this question is more complex.

Williams's capture of power in 1956 was precarious and against the expectations of contemporary political observers who expected a coalition government. His establishment of a two-thirds majority in 1961 was the result of a tactical mix of aggressive confrontation, compromise, and a shrewd exploitation of luck and opportunity, while presenting to the electorate the best organised political party ever to have existed in the country. His achievement over his 25-year career as prime minister seemed to result from his undoubted political mastery of the Trinidad and Tobago psyche, particularly (but not only) among his Afro-Creole base, his determination and ability to face down his opposition, the consistency of his vision for the development of Trinidad and Tobago, the luck of the inflation of oil prices, and the disorganisation and weakness of the opposition.

Chambers, Robinson, and Manning, although burdened with severe economic challenges, were arguably political failures above all else. After Williams's death in 1981, the PNM lost its aggressive and forward-looking character, and no subsequent government had the political ability to secure a second term in office for almost 20 years. The PNM under Chambers did not institute the inevitably unpopular measures advocated by the Demas Report and instead increased expenditures to their highest ever levels. In addition, in the absence of Williams the opposition forces were able to band together, put the PNM on the defensive, and appear as the forward-looking element, espousing efficient and honest economic management and a new level of multi-racialism. The victory of the NAR was overwhelming, but despite the enthusiastic and unprecedented level of support, the NAR administration could not implement its programme because it could not hold up against the hostilities from without and within. Robinson failed to hold his party and the government together, and the attempted coup epitomised the level of political disorder and ineffectiveness. The 1991–95 Manning administration had fulfilled the structural adjustment begun in the 1980s and placed the country on a sustained path of economic growth in a liberalised environment. Manning's political blunders, the rising Indian consciousness stimulated by the 150th anniversary of Indian arrival, and the UNC's ability to capitalise on both were decisive in the PNM's defeat. One can only speculate, but it would be hard to imagine Eric Williams acting as weakly, indecisively, or inappropriately if he found himself in similar positions to those of Chambers, Robinson, and Manning.

Panday, on the other hand, achieved significant success but then brought on himself a devastating failure. As prime minister, Panday's audacity, aggressive determination, pragmatism, and perceptiveness in many ways resembled the political style of Williams. But that model was not flexible enough to be shifted effectively to Panday's situation in 1995–2001. For one example, Panday did not have a secure enough majority to act so blatantly as he pleased. By continuously upsetting his own party executive and his old political partners, his government was brought down prematurely. Hubris seemed to be at play here, for Panday did not see his limitations. His success in vanquishing Patrick Manning and the PNM also led him to frustrate the NAR, alienate A.N.R. Robinson, and scandalise the THA leader, Hochoy Charles. The UNC thereby lost the Tobago seats (which it needed), while Robinson, from his formidable position as Head of State, stepped in seemingly to lead the anti-Panday forces. On top of that, Panday estranged key party colleagues by too aggressively seeking expansion of the party base. It was their withdrawal of support that proved fatal for Panday.

The structural weaknesses of the party's support were not properly considered, for the UNC did not have a toehold anywhere in the capital city. This was a natural handicap for the party, as Port of Spain is socially and culturally central in Trinidad and Tobago. Finally, unlike Williams, Panday governed in a much more open environment, especially with regard to the multiform national media – in 1998 there were four daily newspapers, five weekly newspapers, three local television stations (apart from the 60 foreign television stations available through cable), and 14 radio stations – and to widespread personal communications technology. During Williams' time there was only one privately owned radio station – the other radio station, and the single television station were state-owned. In Trinidad and Tobago, the challenge of governing effectively for fully two terms remains to be fulfilled.

## IMPACT, IMPLICATIONS, AND RECOMMENDATIONS

The study has attempted to attend to detail, emphasise primary material, and to link the empirical material into a coherent whole, covering Trinidad and Tobago's politics in the twentieth century. The impact of this study in terms of what was learned is that the continuously developing context of Trinidad and Tobago politics and society must be centrally considered in future research. Attempts at detailed theory-building in such a continually changing environment should accordingly remain modest, unless a longer time-frame is analysed and a long-view developed. This is an important challenge for further research.

It is recommended that further research be conducted in the context of the findings presented above. Emerging from this study is a picture of Trinidad and Tobago that is fundamentally anarchic. This anarchy, perhaps, not only derives from its historical newness and heterogeneous antecedents, but also perhaps by its relatively insignificant position – economic, military, intellectual, and cultural – in the wider world, and its related 'purposelessness'. This bundle of attributes may be specific to Trinidad and Tobago or it may be found in other countries. Conceivably the 'half-made society' referred to by V.S. Naipaul might be a category of society which could be elaborated by thoughtful, comparative study. Perhaps study of other new, evolving societies such as those in Mauritius, Singapore, and Canada may temper, modify, or strengthen such understanding.

More specifically to research on Trinidad and Tobago, it should be recognised from the material presented in the study that formulaic understandings of race and ethnicity in the country's politics are insufficient. Subtler and empirically accurate analyses are needed to discern and evaluate the objective importance of ethnicity in politics.

Another area in which further inquiry may prove to be valuable is the study of political leadership, especially in societies of recent and/or diverse origins, and the question of succession. Perhaps a few more examples of leadership in different contexts may be needed to make such a study useful, however. These examples can be drawn from other societies (e.g. Sir Seewoosagur Ramgoolam and his successors Aneerood Jugnauth and Navin Ramgoolam in Mauritius, or Lee Kuan Yew and Goh Tok Chong in Singapore), or from Trinidad and Tobago itself after a few more persons have been elected prime minister.

Other questions for further research that may follow from this study are: is there a pattern to party stabilisation (1961–71, 1991–2000) and disorganisation (1925–61, 1971–91) in Trinidad and Tobago? Can generalisations be made about one-party dominance – such as that by the Partido Revolucionario Institucional in Mexico (1929–2000), the Indian National Congress (1947–1977), and the Liberal Democratic Party in Japan (1955–1993) – and the period following removal from office? Or in a wider context, are there important generalisable differences in the fundamental problems of politics between old societies (Iraq, India, Iran, Great Britain, and in a Caribbean context, Jamaica, Barbados) and new societies (Trinidad and Tobago, Canada, Mauritius, Singapore)? These questions seem well worth consideration.

This study has sought to provide a solid contribution to scholarship by providing new, useful, detailed information on the politics of Trinidad and Tobago, arranged in a coherent whole. In the process, it is hoped that a broad and sturdy base has been provided upon which future researchers can build and extend their own work – empirical, comparative, and theoretical.

## CONCLUSION: THE GHOST OF DR WILLIAMS

In many ways, this book has been about the improbable rise and unprepared fall of Dr Eric Williams and his particular vision and politics of nationalism in Trinidad and Tobago. His complete victory by the time of Independence arguably highlighted a fault in the society. The older politicians almost completely capitulated, both to Dr Williams and to Dr Capildeo. Substantial continuity with the past was broken, not for the first time in the country's historical development. Had the old politicians decisively joined the nationalist movement, or formed a strong conservative party, the foundations of a living tradition would have been built. Their withdrawal from political life, however, curiously allowed the country's idealised (or even caricatured) form of government and politics to re-establish itself, with Williams ruling the country almost as absolutely as the British governor would have, attempting to rule as benevolently as possible in what he perceived as the national interest. (Indeed, the wholly nominated Senate which Williams so strenuously advocated in 1955 – with its guaranteed government majority of one – revived the nearly forgotten nineteenth century fully-appointed Crown Colony Legislative Council, almost exactly, with its official majority of eleven over the ten unofficials, whose role was to express public opinion without having the responsibility or power to direct government.) Yet Dr Williams cannot be blamed for the withdrawal of once prominent figures – and the living traditions which they carried – from public life. Dr Williams had a valid and legitimate diagnosis of Trinidad and Tobago's problems, and with great force he applied his remedy – the creation of a strong, disciplined, nationalist party.

However flawed, incomplete, and antagonistic to his opponents as his vision and politics undoubtedly were, under his influence Trinidad and Tobago achieved the closest thing yet to a 'national will' or 'national interest'. Accounting for both its strengths and weaknesses were the particular conditions under which that nationalist focus developed: the local and international fashion of anti-colonialism, the opportunities and constraints of the Cold War, the politics of oil (both local and international), Williams's 'world historical'-minded political philosophy, his political abilities, and his limitations. Williams's nationalist politics, with all its limitations, has not been continued as a viable, living and evolving tradition by his own party, the PNM. The People's Charter (both original and revised) remains a rarely consulted archival document. His valuable collection of speeches, fully covering his 25 year career, has been out of print for years. PNM headquarters today sell none of his books or speeches. Williams's historic and independent nationalism has neither obviously influenced the subsequent NAR, PNM and UNC administrations, that arguably have not seen it necessary to move beyond the World Bank's generic and inoffensive triteness of 'adjustment', 'sustainable development', 'poverty reduction', 'empowerment', 'social inclusion' and other obvious aims promoted since the time of the Chambers Administration. On the whole, since Williams's reign, governments have not formed independent policies, rightward, leftward, or otherwise. The significance of Basdeo Panday, perhaps, lies in his flawed, yet almost successful, attempt to lead the country in the same manner as Dr Williams. This was both a strength and weakness. The possibility of governing Trinidad and Tobago effectively, outside Williams' model, has not yet fully emerged. To the detriment of Trinidad and Tobago, up to this point no viable national party has been secure enough, in government or otherwise, to develop a politics and vision of its own, without parroting or mimicry. A nation without a national interest, or a society without a social will, seems to perfectly illustrate what a 'half-made society' is.

# *Afterword*

## THE HUNG PARLIAMENT AND BEYOND

The hung Parliament of 2001-2 was the second of two consecutive short Parliaments, each lasting less than one year. Notably, these followed the long Parliament of 2000, with its unprecedented Six Sessions.

In a long-view, the hung Parliament can be seen as a crucial stage in the unfolding of a larger political and constitutional crisis. This began in 1999 when President Robinson expressed his reservations about appointing a Commission of Enquiry into the Administration of Justice, and later delayed in removing the Tobago Senators according to the Prime Minister's advice. In a narrower political sense, the hung Parliament was part of a piecemeal transfer of office from the UNC to the PNM, in what would have seemed like an unlikely situation just two years earlier.

Perhaps not surprisingly, the short view took precedence over the long. At the end of a stretched year, in which the country faced an inordinate number of formal constitutional and informal political challenges, the country seemed content with merely having a government in office, the deadlock apparently broken, leaving the fundamental questions untouched by conscious intervention.

The elections of December 10, 2001 gave both the incumbent UNC and the opposition PNM 18 seats each. The initial, sadly predictable reaction of each leader on election night was for the President to call on him to form the next Government. Lawyers, supporters, commentators, and leaders of smaller parties advocated on behalf of one leader or the other. On the other hand, other citizens, commentators, trade unions, NGOs, and presidential Senators argued that the tie provided an opportunity to address fundamental political and constitutional reform through a limited, interim joint government, which would have addressed fundamental, pressing issues agreed on beforehand by the political parties.

President Robinson asked to meet with the two leaders the following day, during which time the leaders agreed that they would 'initiate discussions between them in search of a resolution to the current crisis.'[1] Robinson referred to the 'fathers of the nation, Dr Eric Williams and Dr Rudranath Capildeo' who broke the impasse that existed during the Independence discussions in 1962, as examples.

Just before the meeting, Prime Minister Panday issued an official statement titled 'The Voters have set the stage for a Government of National Unity,' in which it was proposed that both he and Manning 'make partisan agendas secondary to the national interest, and that we work out an appropriate arrangement for sharing power in a government of national unity ... consider[ing] all the options ... including alternating leadership.'[2]

Ramesh Lawrence Maharaj argued that Panday's power-sharing proposal sought to cover up any genuine effort for investigation into corruption. Many PNM members, following the simple moral theme of their campaign, argued that it was impossible to work with the UNC as the two parties represented diametrically different principles, with the PNM representing 'good' (honesty and morality) and the UNC 'evil' (corruption). They also noted Panday's history of breaking working arrangements with the NAR in 1986-8 and 1995-6. Patrick Manning announced that under no circumstances would he share the Prime Ministership. Not only because of his scepticism as to the workability of Executive power-sharing, Manning rejected the idea on the grounds that an Opposition was necessary to the Westminster system of government (which he obviously assumed that Trinidad and Tobago operated).

On December 13-4, negotiating teams from the parties met at the Crowne Plaza Hotel. After some initial difficulty, the UNC and PNM reached an agreement that called for:

i. a Prime Minister to be appointed by the President in accordance with the provisions of the Constitution of the Republic of Trinidad and Tobago
ii. the parties to agree on a Speaker of the House of Representatives, who is to be identified before the appointment of a Prime Minister
iii. electoral reform including the removal of systemic and personnel constraints
iv. Constitution Reform relevant to a plural society so as to foster *inter alia* a collusive national community
v. the appointment of Commissions of Enquiry into twelve questionable Government projects, programmes, and activities undertaken during the period 1991-2000
vi. consensus building at the parliamentary level but not at the executive level
vii. giving effect to the 'Crossing of the Floor' Act and associated regulations
viii. fresh elections, but no agreement on time
ix. the establishment of Standing Parliamentary Committees on Energy Policy and Foreign Affairs
x. the referral of the Prevention of Corruption Bill to a Joint Select Committee of Parliament without prejudice to the PNM's proposal for the appointment of a special prosecutor[3]

There were four major areas (Power Sharing, Timing of Elections, Commission of Enquiry into the EBC, and Special Prosecutor) about which the two parties disagreed, with each party's stances included in the agreement. At the joint press announcement, when asked by the press what would prevent any party from breaking the agreement Panday responded, 'The electorate as you know is always the final arbiter in these matters and anyone who walks away from it will pay for it politically and pay dearly.' The agreement was presented to the President the next day.

Following through, Panday and Manning agreed to former UWI Principal, Professor Max Richards, as Speaker of the House. In the meanwhile, however, the UNC candidate had called for recounts of the ballots for the Tunapuna seats. Up to December 19, the second recount had not been completed. When the results finally confirmed the PNM's victory, the President called on Manning and Panday. He sought assurance from the two leaders that they had the support of all their respective MPs. In the meanwhile, the National Trade Union Centre, the Inter-Religious Organisation, and the Employers' Consultative Association made joint representation to Robinson, Panday, and Manning to discuss proposals for greater involvement of the population in the major decision-making processes once a new government was formed. On the other hand, Concerned Citizens of Trinidad and Tobago, led by Dr. Selwyn Cudjoe and Arthur Sanderson, met with the President to argue the case that Panday should not be re-appointed as Prime Minister.

On December 24, President Robinson decided to swear in Patrick Manning as Prime Minister. Addressing the nation afterward, the only explanation that the President gave for his choice was based on the reference to the constitutional preamble stating that 'men and society remain firm when society is based on moral and spiritual values and the rule of law.' Saying several times 'this is a burden I would prefer not to have' President Robinson then went on to call on his education at Oxford England, the oath of office of a minister, the constitution, and God to guide him in exercising his own judgement.[4]

Prime Minister Manning went on to appoint 30 ministers of government, including his wife as Education Minister; Foreign Affairs Minister Knowlston Gift, who served for a controversy-laden ten days in 1995; Public Administration Minister Lenny Saith, who was the centre of a financial controversy in the Manning Administration of 1991-4; and the curious choice of 36-year-old nightclub owner Howard Chin Lee as Minister of National Security. It was the largest Government ever in Trinidad's history, with the smallest number of Parliamentarians. Every single PNM MP was given a Ministerial position.

The UNC, on the other hand, were incensed and felt insulted by the President's insinuations. On December 29, a UNC special assembly passed a resolution to reject the President's choice of Prime Minister, to declare the ten-point plan null and void, to call for fresh elections immediately, and to take the issue international. The UNC argued that Oxford-based Professor Vernon Bogdanor, whom the President had referred to as an authority, had provided the UNC with the opinion that the President should have appointed the incumbent, Panday, as Prime Minister, to avoid the appearance of making a judgement that the UNC had lost the election and the Opposition had won it.[5] The party pledged to embark on a national mobilisation and 'civil disobedience' with the aim of forcing new elections. In response, Prime Minister Manning did not rule out a State of Emergency should law and order need to be maintained in the face of public opposition. However, despite the rhetoric, no such disturbances occurred.

Basdeo Panday, in addition, refused to accept the instruments appointing him as Leader of the Opposition, on the grounds that he did not lose the election. The post was left vacant. The UNC also withdrew support for Professor Max Richards as Speaker of the House, on the grounds that he allegedly appeared on a PNM platform in a previous election. Without an agreed Speaker of the House, the Parliament would not be able to function properly. Attorney-General Glenda Morean (with a background in marriage law and conveyancing), however, stated that the Government would be able to operate for a period of time without convening Parliament. This left the problem that the Ministers would not have taken their Parliamentary oaths. In addition, the Ministries were re-organised by Prime Minister Manning, who added such new Ministries as Ecclesiastical Affairs, significantly diverging from the heads of expenditure in the 2001 Budget. Such variations of appropriation should be approved by Parliament.

Interestingly, many, not only in government, did not view this as problematic. Professor Selwyn Ryan, for example, publicly supported the PNM against the UNC, arguing that Parliament was not an essential institution in Trinidad and Tobago. He contended, 'One has to be realistic rather than celebrate mere form. I believe that it is more important to make use of the opportunity presented by this hiatus to purge the system of the financial and administrative mess that was left behind by the UNC bunch who succeeded in violating every canon of good governance in our political book, all in the name of performance and self and group enrichment. The temporary loss of Parliament seems an acceptable price to pay for the opportunity given to cleanse the Temple of the money-changers. ... My own considered view is that the President's constitutional coup was providential and salvationist in that it gave the country the opportunity to have the UNC's crookery exposed.'[5]

The PNM Government did indeed embark on a crusade of investigations against the former UNC Government. It began with a Committee to determine the current state of the public finances of Trinidad and Tobago and continued with the bringing back of Bob Lindquist to continue his work on the airport probe, and the calling of Commissions of Enquiry into the Biche High School, the Airport Project, and the EBC. At the same time, the Director of Public Prosecutions, the Auditor-General, the Fraud Squad, and other legal arms conducted their own probes. The different types and levels of enquiry sometimes collided with each other, causing some problems. As a result, however, allegations appeared in the press almost daily against the former UNC Government, either at Ministerial level or at the level of state boards and appointees. Charges were plentiful, and quite scandalous. The party was unable to defend itself effectively.

If there was sufficient quantity, though, the quality of the evidence was sometimes lacking. This was most apparent in the Commission of Enquiry into the Functioning of the Elections and Boundaries Commission, chaired by retired Justice Lennox Deyalsingh, whose 1997 enquiry into the airport project was dismissed by the High Court because proper procedure was not followed. The Deyalsingh Commission heard many of the PNM's major allegations against the UNC fall flat, sometimes embarrassingly so, including the fiery 'voter padding' charges. In one instance, Health Minister Colm Imbert alleged that UNC supporters from outside of his constituency voted fraudulently by using the name of a constituent whom the Minister claimed was dead, and therefore should not have been on the voters list. The constituent, however, appeared in court the following day. He was asked by the lawyers at the enquiry whether he had ever been dead at any time before.

Despite the lack of evidence, the Commissioners of Enquiry recommended that the EBC Commissioners, who were never called to testify before the Commission of Enquiry, should resign. The EBC Commissioners refused, raising tensions with the PNM Government, who had long been openly critical of them.

The PNM also undertook a number of highly publicised projects in the 'social sector.' Manning was of the view that he had lost the government in 1995 because he did not pay enough attention to relief efforts, as opposed to the structural adjustment programme. He was determined not to make that mistake again.

According to the Constitution, Parliament was required to meet at least once every six months. Manning waited until almost the last possible day, April 5, 2002, four days before the deadline. The election of a Speaker was crucial because according to the Standing Orders of Parliament, the Speaker held a central place in the normal running of Parliament: election of a Speaker is the first order of business in a new Parliament (before members are even sworn in); it is the Speaker who must convene Parliament (on advice of the

Prime Minister); it is the Speaker who enforces the Standing Orders and, thereby, order in the House; and it is only the Speaker who can adjourn or suspend a sitting of Parliament. Without electing a Speaker, it was unclear how a sitting would end, or how a new meeting of Parliament would be called. Basdeo Panday informed the country that when Parliament sat, the UNC would not cooperate with the PNM in electing a Speaker, in order to pressure the 'selected' Prime Minister to dissolve Parliament and call fresh elections. The UNC planned to frustrate the election of a Speaker by making their own nominations and then voting against them. Perhaps with only half his tongue in cheek, Panday told reporters that he had 3,000 potential nominees. The PNM on the other hand confidently asserted that a Speaker would be elected, stating that 'there was more than one way to skin a cat.'

The sitting was sublimely absurd. The PNM's strategy was perplexing. Unusually, they spent two hours nominating and seconding their choice of Speaker. The UNC nominated another candidate. In so doing, separate votes were required for both candidates. The UNC voted against the PNM candidate (tying the vote at 18-18), and also voted against their own (making the vote 36 "noes"). The PNM objected and appealed to the Clerk of the House. The Clerk, however, was unable to make any ruling and simply asked the House, once again, to elect a Speaker. The exact process – a two hour nomination and seconding, the UNC nominating another candidate, a vote forced, a division called, the PNM protesting, the Clerk once again asking the House to elect a Speaker – occurred four times that evening, taking the sitting from 1:30pm to 12:30am. A long break was called and the House was to return from break at 1:30pm on April 6. On April 6, the same process occurred again until 5:30pm when another break was called. During the break, technically still during the first sitting, Patrick Manning announced that the President had been advised to prorogue the First Session of the Seventh Parliament.

This was quite unusual, as a Session of Parliament normally lasts for one year, and a Speaker was not elected in the first sitting of the First Session, as required. It was revealed later that the Prime Minister and President had discussed this course of action on April 4, the day before the first sitting. Manning decided to continue running Government without convening Parliament for an additional six months (October 6), or until the political dynamics changed in his favour (for example, if a UNC MP crossed the floor). This raised new questions. The first was that President Robinson's term of office had officially expired in February 2002. The Electoral College (that is, both Houses of Parliament) could not meet to elect a new President, so President Robinson (with his health badly deteriorating) continued in office. In addition, the life of the Local Government bodies was to expire in July 2002. Elections would have to be postponed. In the meanwhile, Local Government bodies were to be run by their Chairman only, with their councils dissolved. Finally, the 2001-2 Budget was to expire on September 30. Taking into account a grace period of one month, a Budget had to be approved by Parliament by October 31. The PNM used the time to continue its programme of investigating the previous UNC Government, and engaging in social expenditure.

The PNM's unconstitutional government went unnoticed as allegations against the UNC kept piling up. Basdeo Panday, who ironically was part of the NAR campaign of rooting out corruption in the PNM of 1986, used the same defence as Chambers and his colleagues: no one had been arrested. Yet that was not completely true. Not only was former Minister of Local Government Dhanraj Singh on trial for murder, former Minister of Finance Brian Kuei Tung, and well-known UNC financier and former chairman of the National Gas Company, Steve Ferguson, were arrested on charges related to corruption in the construction of the Millennium Airport. The UNC were definitely placed on the defensive. Allegations of a TT$10 million bank account held by Basdeo Panday in London, and another account held by Carlos John in which TT$52 million passed through in a roughly one year period were particularly devastating. The attempt to circumvent 'bureaucratic restraints' that Panday boasted about when he appointed Lindsay Gillette as a Minister in 1999, turned from being a sign of determination and innovation, into one of fraud and dishonesty. Much of the country was outraged, and the UNC seemingly decided not to address them.

A second sitting of Parliament (technically the first sitting of the Second Session) occurred on August 28. This time the PNM did not forward a two-hour nomination speech. The UNC, however, continued to nominate its own candidate, voting against both, in order to frustrate the election of a Speaker. Prime Minister Manning then moved to dissolve Parliament, announcing the election date as October 7, 2002. The UNC were pleased. Their campaign, strangely, was focused on the support that Abu Bakr of the Jamaat-al-Muslimeen had been lending to the PNM. Panday elaborated this theme incessantly. This tactic was used even though the UNC were able to attract former colleague Winston Dookeran to contest in St Augustine, since the PNM Government did not renew his tenure as Governor of the

Central Bank. Making the issue more puzzling was the fact that one UNC candidate in the elections, Dr Jennifer Jones-Kernahan, was a former NUFF rebel whose sister Beverly Jones was killed by police in a shootout; and another, Richard Thomas, was the brother of Andy Thomas, leading NUFF member and later an insurrectionist in the 1990 attempted coup. The PNM, on the other hand, continued the same campaign as it did from 1999: basically maintaining that the UNC was corrupt, that the PNM was honest.

The PNM election victory was historic, and deserves some analysis. It won 20 seats, and the UNC won 16 seats (see Table A.1).

***Table A.1.***
***Election Statistics, General Elections held on October 7, 2002***

| | Number of candidates | Number of seats won | Total Votes | % of Votes |
|---|---|---|---|---|
| **PNM** | 36 | 20 | 308,807 | 50.7% |
| **UNC** | 34 | 16 | 283,651 | 46.6% |
| **NAR** | 2 | 0 | 6,856 | 1.1% |
| **Citizens' Alliance** | 18 | 0 | 5,855 | 1.0% |
| **Democratic Party of Trinidad and Tobago** | 10 | 0 | 664 | 0.1% |
| **Rejected** | - | - | 2,697 | 0.4% |
| **Total Voted** | 100 | 36 | 608,530 | 100.0% |

Total Number of Electors on List: 875,360
Voter Turnout: 69.5%

*Source*: *TE*, October 9, 2002, p. 11 (with corrections made by the author); *TG* October 7, 2002, pp. 4-5

Firstly, there did not seem to be any 'election fatigue,' as many observers had conjectured. This idea of exhaustion had a basis in the 2001 results, when the total number of persons voting declined by almost 37,000 from the 2000 elections. In 2002, citizens voted in higher numbers than ever – almost 609,000. The voter turnout rate in 2002 of 69.5 per cent was the highest since 1961, when the voter turnout was 88.1 percent.

The great momentum in 2002 was on the side of the PNM, which polled a greater number in these elections than any party since the NAR in 1986, which polled 380,029 votes. The PNM's showing was truly impressive. Between 2001 and 2002, it increased its vote by almost 50,000. The UNC, while also increasing its vote from the previous year, was only able to do so by 5,000. For every extra vote the UNC brought out, the PNM brought out 10. Even more is revealed, however, when one attempts to locate from where these ballots came. The PNM increased its vote by almost 50,000 and the UNC by almost 5,000 (in total roughly 55,000). Yet the overall increase in voters was only 31,000 (whom it can be assumed were young voters). Even if all of the new voters voted for the PNM or UNC, that leaves at least 24,000 votes PNM votes unaccounted for. The figures show that in 2002, the "third party" vote (Citizen's Alliance, NAR, and DPTT) was down 7,000 from 2001 (when Team Unity, NAR, and the National Democratic Organisation contested). If it is assumed that all of these votes went to the PNM, this still leaves at least 12,000 extra votes for the PNM unaccounted. These extra votes, therefore, would have had to come from the UNC supporters of the year before. But there is more. Since 5,000 of the ballots from new voters and "third party" voters would have had to have gone to the UNC, the PNM could have taken up to 17,000 votes from the UNC. So the PNM increase in 2002 came from new voters, "third party" voters, and the UNC voters of 2001. This makes the PNM achievement more remarkable.

Indeed, in no constituency did the PNM lose votes. On the whole, taken in a proportional sense, the PNM gained 19 percent, compared to the UNC's 1.7 percent increase. What is most remarkable is that of the 18 constituencies which performed above the PNM average, 12 were in UNC strongholds. The PNM gain in Couva South, for example, was 76.1 percent. The PNM made headway into the UNC core. On the other hand, though gaining votes overall, the UNC lost voters in 16 seats (including Tobago, where it did not contest in 2002). In addition, the UNC's gains were made mainly in its strongholds, unlike in previous years. Finally, the UNC's highest relative gain (also in Couva South, at 17.1 percent) was lower than the PNM's average.

In addition, the 2002 election saw an increase in the number of seats won with a margin of less than 1,500 votes, from three to five. (See Table A.2)

***Table A.2.***
***Seats won with less than 1,500 votes, 2002***

| Constituency | PNM | UNC | Winner | 1st over 2nd |
|---|---|---|---|---|
| San Fernando West | 9,091 | 8,842 | PNM | 249 |
| Ortoire Mayaro | 11,025 | 10,707 | PNM | 318 |
| Tunapuna | 10,214 | 9,528 | PNM | 686 |
| Barataria San Juan | 7,486 | 8,391 | UNC | 905 |
| St Joseph | 8,124 | 9,352 | UNC | 1,228 |

*Source*: *TE*, October 9, 2002, p. 11 (with corrections made by the author); *TG* October 7, 2002, pp. 4-5

A new twist in long term voting trends occurred. Between 1991 and 2000, the UNC's votes were increasing rapidly, more than doubling from 151,000 in 1991 to 308,000 in 2000. The PNM's votes increased much more slowly over the same period, from 522,000 in 1991 to 598,000 in 2000. The UNC was clearly the party in ascendancy. However, in 2001, the number of votes for both parties fell, by 17,000 for the PNM and by 29,000 for the UNC. The UNC still had a majority of voter support, however. In 2002, however, both parties bounced back. But the PNM's bounce was much stronger than the UNC's. (See Table A.3)

The PNM's historic victory leads one to perhaps revise upwards an estimation of the political skills of Patrick Manning, the longest serving Parliamentarian in Trinidad and Tobago's history.

Despite the PNM's many strengths shown in these elections, however, there are some weakness and vulnerabilities that should be noted. For one, the voter turnout in the PNM seats (66.4 per cent) remained lower than in the UNC seats (72.8 per cent). In 2002, the PNM won its seats with an average of 10,251 votes; the UNC won its seats with 12,898 votes on average. In their own seats, then, the UNC won a slightly higher percentage of the total electorate on average (48.1 per cent) than the PNM (46.0 per cent). The gap lowered from the previous year, but it still existed. The lack of mobilisation in PNM core areas has been a problem that the party has faced for a very long time, indeed, since 1966. Also, focusing on Tobago, where the UNC did not contest at all this year, the PNM did increase its presence, gaining support relatively and absolutely. However, while the gap widened in Tobago West, it narrowed in Tobago East, to less than 2,000 votes.

*Table A.3.*
***Electoral trends, 1991-2002***

| Year | PNM Votes | % of ballots cast for PNM | % of eligible votes for PNM | UNC Votes | % of ballots for UNC | % of eligible votes for UNC | Total Voters | Total Electorate | Voter Turnout |
|---|---|---|---|---|---|---|---|---|---|
| **1991** | 233,950 | 44.8% | 29.4% | 151,046 | 28.9% | 19.0% | 522,472 | 794,486 | 65.8% |
| **1995** | 255,885 | 48.4% | 30.5% | 239,816 | 45.3% | 28.6% | 529,229 | 837,741 | 63.2% |
| **2000** | 276,324 | 46.2% | 29.2% | 307,807 | 51.5% | 32.5% | 597,525 | 947,689 | 63.1% |
| **2001** | 259,450 | 46.3% | 30.7% | 278,781 | 49.7% | 33.0% | 560,778 | 844,254 | 66.4% |
| **2002** | 308,807 | 50.7% | 35.3% | 283,651 | 46.6% | 32.4% | 608,530 | 875,360 | 69.5% |

*Source*: GORTT 1992b; 1996b; Elections and Boundaries Commission, personal communication; *TE*, October 9, 2002, p. 11 (with corrections made by the author); *TG* October 7, 2002, pp. 4-5

It is important to consider the importance of the 24,000 floating voters, that is, those who changed their votes from 2001 to 2002, in this case, from third parties or the UNC to the PNM. The level of float might seem minor in an electorate of 875,000. However, this is about the size of one full constituency. Most importantly, since 1991, elections have been won by very narrow margins. The difference in overall votes in 2002 between the PNM and UNC was only 25,000, and the difference in Ortoire/Mayaro and San Fernando West, which broke the deadlock, was only 567 votes.

Interestingly, the October 2002 Parliament is almost the opposite of what obtained just two years earlier in December 2000, when the UNC held 19 seats, the PNM 16, and the NAR 1. At that time the UNC was at its height, achieving its maximum number of seats. Conversely, the PNM was at another low point, with only 15 seats in Trinidad, and one seat in Tobago. (This contrasts with the PNM's height in 1981, when it held 26 seats in Trinidad, including Caroni East, Fyzabad, Princes Town, Nariva, and Pointe-à-Pierre.) By the election of 2001, the UNC still held the lead in Trinidad with 18 seats. The PNM's 16 seats in Trinidad were supplemented by its two seats in Tobago, won through a new relationship between the Tobago and Trinidad arms of the PNM. The hung Parliament resulted in a change of Government, with the PNM in control. By 2002, the PNM emerged with 18 seats in Trinidad, in addition to its two in Tobago, while the UNC were beaten down to 16 seats. The turnaround should perhaps primarily be seen as a fall of the UNC Government, and a spectacular one at that. The amazing fact is that in 2000, the PNM was virtually vanquished. The Rowley challenge of 1996, PNM Parliamentarians voting for Robinson in 1997, PNM councillors voting for a UNC Tunapuna chairman in 1997, the crossing the floor of Lasse and Griffith, Manning's unsuccessful court challenge and the resulting penalties, and the party's confinement to 15 seats in Trinidad in 2000, saw the PNM at its lowest point after 1986. However, just as Robinson's inability to conciliate Panday in 1987 strengthened the Indian community, giving it a strength and cohesion it did not have hitherto, Panday's arrogance revived the African base of the PNM, and outraged a large segment of others.

Panday declared in December 2001 that whoever broke the Crowne Plaza Agreement would have to pay the political price. It appears that he was right. Indeed, the tables have turned so completely that the PNM has thrown Panday's statement back at him, 'As long as you are there [in Opposition], I will be here [in Government].' Patrick Manning was able to win two consecutive terms of government, though his first term one was short. The challenge of governing Trinidad and Tobago for two full consecutive terms remains. At a period of crisis, and great opportunity, seemingly the entire country steadfastly tried to avoid the responsibility of tackling the fundamental questions raised by the political and constitutional crisis that began in 1999. After a brief flirtation with larger possibilities, the parties stuck to their narrow ends of office-seeking, by sometimes less than honourable means. A slow change of mandate did occur from 2000 to 2002, and the PNM were able to effect an impressive victory. However, the fundamental challenges remain. When President Robinson swore in Manning as Prime Minister on October 9, 2002, he commented, 'You have a second chance.' It remains to be seen how it will be used.

# Appendix A

## CHRONOLOGY OF POLITICAL EVENTS, 1921-2001

| | |
|---|---|
| **1921**<br>December 13<br>–February 14, 1922 | Wood Commission tours the West Indies |
| **1924** | Trinidad and Tobago Order-in-Council reconstituting the Legislative Council passed; elected members introduced for the first time, representing seven areas |
| **1925**<br>February 7 | First Legislative Council general elections in Trinidad and Tobago |
| **1928**<br>March 3 | Legislative Council general elections |
| **1931** | Divorce Bill generates sustained political controversy |
| **1933**<br>January 28 | Legislative Council general elections; elected members nominated to Executive Council for the first time |
| **1934**<br>August | A.A. Cipriani's Trinidad Workingmen's Association is tranformed into the Trinidad Labour Party |
| **1936**<br>July | Butler breaks with the Trinidad Labour Party to form British Empire Workers and Citizens Home Rule Party |

| | |
|---|---|
| **1937** | |
| June 19–July 6 | 'Butler riots'; two policemen and 12 civilians killed in the unrest; nine policemen and volunteers, and 50 civilians wounded |
| September 9 | Butler incarcerated |
| December 24 | Governor Sir Murchison Fletcher resigns officially on grounds of ill-health |
| **1938** | |
| | West India Royal Commission (Moyne Commission) tours the West Indies |
| January 4 | Legislative Council general elections |
| **1939** | |
| May | Butler released from jail |
| September | Butler re-arrested and detained as a security risk under the Defence Regulations |
| **1941** | |
| | Following the Report of the West India Royal Commission, the number of elected members in the Legislative Council is raised from seven to nine members; nine *ex-officio* members removed from the Legislative Council; Franchise Committee established Anglo-American Bases Agreement leads to establishment of US military bases in Trinidad |
| June 26 | Election held for additional Port of Spain seat |
| June 28 | Election held for additional Victoria seat |
| **1945** | Captain Cipriani dies; new Constitution established; Public Service Commission introduced; Centenary of Indian Arrival celebrated; Butler released from detention; County Council ordinance passed |
| July | Albert Gomes replaces Cipriani by winning the Port of Spain by-election |
| August 3 | Universal adult suffrage introduced; women allowed to become members of Legislative Council |
| **1946** | |
| April 18 | New County Council ordinance passed |
| July 1 | First Legislative Council general elections held under universal adult suffrage |
| October 28 | First County Council general elections held |

| | |
|---|---|
| **1947** | Twenty-member constitutional committee under the chairmanship of nominated member Sir Lennox O'Reilly appointed to recommend further constitutional reform |
| **1948** | Constitutional Reform Committee submits its Majority Report and four Minority Reports; Dr Eric Williams returns to Trinidad as Deputy Chairman of the Caribbean Research Council of the Anglo-American Caribbean Commission |
| **1949** | New Constitution passed |
| March 3 | The El Socorro Tackveeyatul Islamic Association Islamia school – the first state-funded, non-Christian denominational school – is opened |
| **1950** | Butler Party formed |
| April 20 | 1949 Trinidad and Tobago (Constitution) Order-in-Council comes into force; the new Legislative Council doubles the number of elective seats to 18 and reduces the number of nominated unofficials to five; the three *ex officio* members remain unchanged; the Executive Council has its role elevated from a purely advisory body to the 'chief instrument of policy', in which the governor only has a casting vote; all five elected members in the Executive Council granted limited Ministerial Responsibility, and each associated with the administrative work of particular Government Departments |
| August 30 | Legislative Council dissolved one year early to accommodate new Constitution |
| September 18 | Legislative Council general elections |
| **1952** | New Ordinance grants executive powers to County Councils |
| **1953** | County Council general elections held; Bhadase Maharaj forms the PDP |
| **1954** | |
| May 22 | Dr Williams placed on one year's probation with the Caribbean Commission |

| | |
|---|---|
| September – November | Williams gives public lectures; highlight is a debate with Dom Basil Matthews from November 5–17; Williams establishes a Committee for Education in Citizenship |
| November 24 | Williams writes to the Caribbean Commission telling them to promote him to Secretary-General or fire him |
| November 26 | Establishment of Select Committee on Constitutional Reform; Bhadase Maraj resigns his seat in protest at extension of Legislative Council |
| **1955** | Political Education Group formed |
| January 17 | Ashford Sinanan appointed to chair a 35-member Constitutional Reform Committee |
| January – May | Williams delivers public lecture series |
| May 26 | Williams informed that his contract would not be renewed; his employment with the Commission would cease on June 21, 1955 |
| June 13 | Bhadase Maraj wins Tunapuna by-election |
| June 21 - October 8 | Williams delivers five public speeches in Woodford Square and around the country; inaugurates 'The University of Woodford Square' on July 19 |
| August 30 | Elections set for September 26, 1956, one year after they were originally scheduled |
| October 6 | Williams presents Governor Beetham with a petition endorsing his proposals for Constitutional Reform |
| **1956** | |
| January 15 | The PNM holds its inaugural meeting |
| January 24 | PNM launched at Woodford Square |
| February | Negotiations on Federation of the West Indies |
| February 20 | County Council general elections |
| June 1 | New Constitution passed; provides for a Chief Minister, 24 elected members in the Legislative Council, and seven elected members in the Executive Council |
| July 14 | *PNM Weekly* launched |
| July 28–9 | PNM's first Annual Convention |
| September 24 | Legislative Council general elections; the PNM wins 13 seats in the 31–member Legislative Council |
| September 25 | Governor Beetham sends for Williams to discuss the formation of a government |
| October 26 | On the instructions of the Secretary of State for the Colonies, the Legislative Council sits with two nominated members chosen by the PNM, Eric Williams |

| | |
|---|---|
| | elected as Chief Minister, and all Ministerial positions won by PNM nominees |
| **1957** | |
| May 17 | Sir Alexander Bustamante visits Trinidad and Tobago; PNM demands that Chaguaramas (under American control) be made the capital of the West Indian Federation |
| May 23 | Trinidad unit of the federal DLP launched |
| July 18 | The PDP, TLP and POPPG dissolve themselves to form the DLP of Trinidad and Tobago |
| July 31 | West Indian Federal Constitution comes into effect |
| September 1 | Inaugural ceremony to launch the DLP |
| **1958** | Rudranath Capildeo invited by Williams to be principal of the Trinidad Polytechnic in St James |
| January 8 | Bhadase Maraj elected leader of DLP |
| March 25 | West Indian Federal Parliament elections; in Trinidad and Tobago, DLP wins six seats, PNM wins four |
| April | Williams delivers inflammatory speech, 'The Danger Facing Trinidad and the West Indian Nation' |
| April 22 | Opening of the Federal Parliament of the West Indies |
| December 6 | PNM launches *The Nation*, under the editorship of C.L.R. James |
| **1959** | |
| February 16 | County Council elections; DLP control five County Councils, PNM control two |
| July 8 | PNM wins UK Government approval for introduction of Cabinet system of government |
| **1960** | |
| March 29 | Dr Rudranath Capildeo succeeds Bhadase Maraj as leader of the DLP at a confused party convention |
| April–June | Gomes unsuccessfully challenges Capildeo for leadership of the DLP; Gomes leaves the DLP |
| April 22 | PNM March for Chaguaramas |
| June 7–19 | Secretary of State for the Colonies, Iain MacLeod, visits Trinidad; PNM Constitution for full internal self-government within the framework of the Federation of the West Indies approved by UK Government |
| September 28–December 9 | Conference on Chaguaramas held in Tobago; US agreed to renegotiate lease |
| October 2 | C.L.R. James expelled from the PNM |

| | |
|---|---|
| December 25 | Williams announces the Concordat between the Church and State regarding the education system |
| **1961** | |
| January 20 | Representation of the People Bill debated in the Legislature |
| October 15 | Capildeo calls on his supporters to arm themselves |
| November 22 | State of Emergency declared |
| December 4 | Parliamentary General Elections; PNM wins 20 seats, DLP ten |
| **1962** | |
| January 15 | PNM General Council rejects the proposed Federation of the Eastern Caribbean and resolves to pursue the national independence of Trinidad and Tobago, following Jamaica's withdrawal, after September 18, 1961 |
| February 19 | Draft Independence Constitution published |
| April 25–7 | Queen's Hall Conference |
| May 9–16 | Joint Select Committee of Parliament convened to consider comments from Queen's Hall Conference |
| February 20 | County Council elections postponed, and terms extended indefinitely |
| May 28–June 8 | Independence Conference at Marlborough House, London |
| June 25 | George Weekes elected to Presidency of the OWTU |
| August 31 | Trinidad and Tobago becomes an independent country in the Commonwealth |
| **1963** | |
| January | Dr Capildeo accepts a teaching post at the University of London, retains Leadership of the Opposition |
| December | Stephen Maharaj appointed Leader of Opposition in Parliament, while Capildeo retains leadership of the party |
| **1964** | |
| March 27 | Liberal Party formed after three DLP MPs resign on January 13 |
| **1965** | |
| March 9 | State of Emergency declared |
| March 18 | Industrial Stabilisation Bill introduced in Parliament; report of the Commission of Inquiry into subversive activities tabled |
| March 20 | ISA assented |

| | |
|---|---|
| March 22 | C.L.R. James placed under house arrest |
| August 8 | WFP formed after Stephen Maharaj leaves the DLP |
| **1966** | |
| November 7 | Parliamentary General Elections; PNM win 24 seats, DLP win 12 |
| **1967** | |
| June | *Trinidad Express* founded |
| December | Dr Capildeo refused leave; his Chaguanas seat declared vacant |
| **1968** | NJAC formed |
| January | Bhadase Maraj wins Chaguanas seat |
| June 24 | Local Government elections held for the first time since 1959 |
| November 14 | Tapia House Group founded |
| **1969** | |
| February 26 | NJAC stage protest in support of West Indian students at Sir George Williams University |
| May | TIWU Bus Strike in defiance of the ISA wins wide support |
| **1970** | |
| February 9–April 21 | 'Black Power' marches |
| April 13 | PNM Deputy Leader, A.N.R. Robinson, resigns from Cabinet |
| April 21 | State of Emergency declared |
| April 21–5 | Raffique Shah and Rex LaSalle lead army mutiny |
| May 10 | Williams announces a major Cabinet re-shuffle |
| August 7–September 13 | Draft National Security Act 1970 (Public Order Bill) introduced; widespread opposition to the bill is evoked; bill is withdrawn |
| September 20 | A.N.R. Robinson resigns from the PNM |
| November 19 | Another Cabinet shuffle is announced; State of Emergency lifted |
| November 27–9 | *PNM's Perspectives in the World of the Seventies* approved at a Special Convention |
| December 1 | DLP unsuccessfully move a motion of no-confidence; A.N.R. Robinson's ACDC merges with DLP |

| **1971** | |
|---|---|
| April 22 | Williams announces an early election |
| May 9 | A.N.R. Robinson announces that the ACDC-DLP would not contest the upcoming election, and instead would join the No-Vote Campaign |
| May 24 | Parliamentary General Elections; PNM win all 36 seats as major parties boycott election |
| June 18 | Constitutional Commission appointed under the chairmanship of Hugh Wooding |
| November 1 | Local Government Elections; PNM win 90 seats and control all municipal and county councils |
| September 11 | CPTU formed |
| October 19 | State of Emergency declared |
| **1972** | |
| June 14 | Industrial Relations Bill tabled; J.R.F. Richardson crosses the floor and makes a Parliamentary Opposition |
| **1973** | |
| September 12 | Attorney-General Karl Hudson-Phillips resigns from the Deputy Chairmanship of the PNM and from Cabinet |
| September 28 | Williams announces that he will not seek re-election as Political Leader of the PNM |
| December 2 | Williams changes his mind and accepts Leadership of the PNM |
| **1974** | First upward oil shock occurs |
| January 22 | Constitutional Commission reports to Parliament |
| December | Commission Report, Draft Constitution and Minority Report laid in the House of Representatives |
| December 13 & 17 | Williams rejects the Commission's report in Parliament |
| **1975** | |
| February 18 | ULF formed |
| March 18 | ULF march for 'Peace, Bread, and Justice' |
| June 16 | Joint Select Committee of Parliament established to draft a new constitution |
| **1976** | |
| February 20 | Majority and Minority Reports laid in Parliament |
| March 28 | ULF launched as a political party |
| August 1 | Republican Constitution proclaimed |
| September 13 | Parliamentary General Elections; PNM wins 24 seats, ULF ten, DAC two |

| | |
|---|---|
| September 24 | Trinidad and Tobago officially becomes a Republic |
| **1977** | |
| January | A.N.R. Robinson moves a resolution for internal self-government for Tobago |
| February 11 | A Joint Select Committee is established to consider the question |
| April 25 | Local Government elections |
| August 9 | Basdeo Panday removed as Leader of Opposition; replaced by Raffique Shah |
| **1978** | |
| | House Paper No. 6 of 1978 submitted and ratified, outlining Tobago's internal self-government |
| March 31 | Panday reinstated as Leader of Opposition; Minister of Works Hector McLean crosses the floor to the Opposition |
| September 26 | By-election in Siparia decides supremacy of Panday faction over Shah faction |
| **1980** | |
| March | Karl Hudson-Phillips and Ferdi Ferreira suspended from PNM |
| April 19 | ONR launched |
| April 21 | Local Government elections; PNM control all eleven municipal and county councils |
| September 12 | Tobago (Internal Self-Government) Bill debated; Robinson votes against it and walks out of the House; Bill passed, establishing the THA |
| November 24 | First THA elections held; DAC win eight seats, the PNM four; A.N.R. Robinson becomes first THA Chairman after withdrawing from national politics |
| November 30 | ONR launched as a political party |
| **1981** | |
| February 1 | ONR holds it inaugural meeting |
| March 1 | Tapia, DAC, and ULF forge Alliance |
| March 29 | Dr Eric Williams dies in a diabetic coma |
| March 30 | George Chambers sworn in as prime minister |
| May 9 | Chambers elected Political Leader of the PNM without opposition |
| November 9 | Parliamentary General Elections; PNM win 26 seats; ULF eight; DAC two |

| | |
|---|---|
| **1982** | |
| November 14 | NATT formed |
| **1983** | First downward oil shock occurs |
| February | NATT and the ONR form an 'Accommodation' |
| May 10 | Panday appoints Hudson-Phillips as Senator |
| August 8 | Local Government elections; Accommodation wins 66 seats, the PNM 54 |
| **1984** | |
| November 26 | THA elections; DAC win eleven seats, PNM win one |
| **1985** | |
| August 1 | Emancipation Day declared an annual national holiday |
| September 8 | NAR inaugurated |
| December | Lincoln Myers conducts 40-day fast to protest government's 'lack of accountability' |
| **1986** | |
| February 14 | Tapia House Movement, ULF, DAC, and the ONR dissolve themselves to form a unitary NAR |
| December 15 | Parliamentary General Elections; NAR win 33 seats, PNM three |
| December 31 | President Ellis Clarke appoints James Bain to the Public and Police Service Commissions |
| **1987** | |
| January 23 | NAR's first budget presentation; COLA withdrawn from public servants |
| February | Patrick Manning elected as Political Leader of the PNM after Chambers resigns |
| March 12 | *Wall Street Journal* publishes article on government corruption in Trinidad and Tobago regarding Tesoro deals |
| March 14 | President Ellis Clarke's term ends; appoints Cecil Kelsick to the Judicial and Legal Service Commission; Noor Hassanali elected President |
| March 27 | NAR introduces Constitutional (Amendment) Bill to revoke, retroactively Presidential appointments; it is later withdrawn due to public disapproval |
| April 11 | NAR adopts its unitary constitution; Prime Minister Robinson suggests that the President was 'fascist' because of the disrespect shown to the elected Head of Government |

| | |
|---|---|
| April 19 | *Trinidad Express* publishes article, 'The Indianisation of the Government', with its super-heading, 'Trinidadians Still Fear Take-over of the State by East Indians' |
| May 5 | Speaker Nizam Mohammed criticises Minister Carson Charles as being a 'Johnny-come-lately' |
| May 22–3 | Bishop Desmond Tutu visits Trinidad and Tobago, dubs it a 'Rainbow Country' |
| June 1 | Presidential Commission appointed to review the 1976 Republican Constitution |
| June 3 | Ministers Basdeo Panday and Kelvin Ramnath launch a public attack on the Government |
| September 14 | Local Government elections |
| November 21 | Panday and ULF colleagues again publicly attack the Government at the Sugar Industry Labour Welfare Committee awards ceremony |
| November 22 | NAR Parliamentarians call for the President to use his full powers to discipline the dissident Cabinet Ministers |
| November 26 | Robinson calls on entire Cabinet to submit resignations |
| November 29 | Cabinet shuffle announced; John Humphrey removed from Cabinet, Panday's and Ramnath's portfolios significantly reduced |
| December 15 | *Trinidad Express* published, 'The ULF Grab for Power' by 'Technocrat' |
| December 20 | NAR National Council appoints Jaigobin Nanga to head a committee to investigate the problems in the party |

**1988**

| | |
|---|---|
| January 31 | NAR dissidents organise another meeting denouncing the Government |
| February 8 | Panday, Ramnath, and Sudama expelled from Cabinet |
| March | Nanga Committee submits report |
| March 16 | Panday launches CLUB 88 as a pressure group within the NAR |
| March 17 | NAR National Council rejects reconciliation with dissidents |
| March 27 | NAR appoints a disciplinary tribunal to consider 31 charges against dissidents |
| April 29 | Panday brings motion of no-confidence against Robinson |
| May 15 | Panday, Ramnath, Humphrey, Sudama, and Pallackdharrysingh suspended from NAR |
| June | Minister Eden Shand suspended for unauthorised public statements |

| | |
|---|---|
| July | Industrial Court rules that the government re-instate COLA in addition to a salary increase of 2 per cent |
| July 5 | Government files a claim of TT$500 million in the Supreme Court of Ontario, Canada, against the estate of former PNM Minister John O'Halloran |
| August 29 | Port of Spain North constituency passes motion of no-confidence against Robinson |
| October 16 | CLUB 88 holds rally to launch itself as a political party |
| October 23 | NAR dissidents expelled from the party |
| November 16 | Government submits a letter of intent to the IMF requesting a 14-month stand-by arrangement in the amount of SDR 99 million |
| November 29 | THA elections; NAR wins eleven seats, PNM one |
| December 16 | Government refuses to abide by Industrial Court agreement, refuses to pay COLA, and reduces public servants' salaries by 10 per cent |
| **1989** | |
| March 6 | Unions organise a one-day 'general strike', the Day of Resistance |
| March 7 | Minister Pantin offers resignation; Robinson refuses |
| March 16 | UNC launched out of CLUB 88 |
| May 1 | UNC wins local government by-election in St Andrew/ St David county council |
| December | VAT introduced; 49 per cent of State-owned telephone company sold to Cable and Wireless |
| **1990** | |
| February 8 | SOPO formed |
| March 8 | President of the Senate, Michael Williams, resigns |
| March 14 | Government submits another letter of intent to the IMF requesting another 12-month stand-by arrangement |
| July 22 | UNC inaugurated; executive sworn-in after heated campaign |
| July 27–August 1 | Jamaat-al-Muslimeen stage attempted coup; initial government figures report 30 killed, 150 wounded, and TT$200 million damage to businesses: 102 business outlets affected by looting, 20 buildings destroyed by fire, and 27 severely damaged; State of Emergency called |
| September 5 | Life of the county and municipal councils extended for one year due to State of Emergency; at that time, the councils to be re-organised into regional corporations |
| September 10 | Panday appointed Leader of Opposition, with control of six seats |

| | |
|---|---|
| December 16 | Diego Martin Central by-election; PNM wins seat from NAR |
| **1991** | |
| March | TT$29.6 million (Cdn$8 million) awarded to the Trinidad and Tobago Government from the estate of John O'Halloran |
| July 21 | MP Eden Shand resigns from NAR |
| November 24 | UNC elect new executive after Panday and Ramnath split; Ramesh Lawrence Maharaj replaces Ramnath |
| December 16 | Parliamentary General Elections; PNM win 21 seats, UNC 13, NAR 2 |
| December 21 | Robinson resigns as leader of the NAR |
| **1992** | |
| September 28 | Local Government elections; PNM controls 10 of the 14 corporations, the UNC four |
| December 7 | THA elections; NAR win 11 seats, PNM win one |
| **1993** | Foreign exchange controls abolished, TT dollar floated |
| November | UNC MP Hulsie Bhaggan jailed for blocking the north-bound lane of the Uriah Butler Highway, with support of UNC MPs Kris Jurai and Mohammed Haniff; Panday disapproves |
| **1994** | |
| January | Minister Brian Kuei Tung resigns |
| May 30 | Pointe-à-Pierre by-election held; UNC wins seat from PNM |
| June 24 | Bhaggan supports the PNM Government's bill to amend the Corporal Punishment Act, which the UNC opposed |
| November 16 | Panday offers himself for arrest on charges of indecent assault and rape; Panday later warns of dirty tactics and a snap election |
| December 11 | Bhaggan founds MUP |
| December 13 | Two charges of indecent assault dismissed as 'substantially defective' |
| December 31 | Cabinet approves divestment, liquidation, and restructuring of 66 companies |
| **1995** | |
| January 24 | Panday re-arrested on two revised charges of indecent assault |

| | |
|---|---|
| March 10 | Two charges of indecent assault against Panday dismissed for the second time; their re-laying after being dismissed in December was ruled an abuse of process on the part of the DPP |
| March 26 | UNC adopts new constitution |
| April | Manning fires Alexander Lau by fax; Panday files a suit against the state for malicious prosecution |
| May 7 | Manning addresses the country as 'Father of the Nation'; fires Minister Ralph Maraj and replaces him with hitherto Permanent Secretary, Knowlston Gift |
| May 17 | Knowlston Gift resigns as a result of questioning about his past conduct |
| May 19 | Cabinet shuffle announced |
| May 30 | The 150th Anniversary of Indian Arrival celebrated |
| June | Attorney-General Keith Sobion introduces motion of no-confidence against the Speaker, Occah Seapaul; Seapaul rules the motion unconstitutional |
| June 14 | Panday presents a motion of no-confidence against Manning |
| July | Constitutional Amendment passed in Senate to permit the House of Representatives to remove the Speaker by a majority vote; initial shareholding agreement signed for Atlantic LNG project, a major landmark in the sustained growth of the natural gas sector and, through it, the rest of the economy |
| July 24 | Speaker adjourns sitting of Lower House, preventing the amendment from being debated |
| July 28 | Valley suspended for six months for shouting at Speaker, 'You can run, but you can't hide.' |
| August 3 | State of Emergency declared; Seapaul placed under house arrest |
| August 4 | House approves constitutional amendment; Ralph Maraj resigns from Cabinet |
| August 5 | Seapaul hands over duties to her deputy, Arima MP Rupert Griffith |
| August 7 | State of Emergency lifted |
| August 9 | San Fernando West constituency passes no-confidence motion in Maraj; Maraj appears on UNC platform |
| August 13 | Hulsie Bhaggan formally expelled from the UNC; Speaker refuses to declare her seat vacant |
| August 14 | Maraj sits in on Opposition benches |
| August 24 | Maraj resigns his seat and resigns from the PNM |
| October 6 | Manning announces date of general elections as November 6, after less than four years in office; Maraj |

| | |
|---|---|
| | announces his application to the UNC for membership |
| October 8 | A.N.R. Robinson accepts leadership of the NAR |
| October 9 | Minister of Finance, Wendell Mottley, announces that he will not stand for election |
| November 3 | Panday and Robinson appear on TV6's *Morning Edition* for the first time together since their break-up; Manning refuses invitation |
| November 6 | Parliamentary General Elections; PNM win 17 seats, UNC win 17, NAR win two |
| November 8 | Robinson and Panday agree to a coalition |
| November 9 | Panday appointed prime minister |
| November 11 | UNC and NAR sign nine-point Heads of Agreement; Robinson made Minister Extraordinaire |

**1996**

| | |
|---|---|
| January 5 | PNM's three Deputy Leaders – Wendell Mottley, Keith Rowley, and Augustus Ramrekersingh – resign from their posts after failing to persuade Manning to seek re-election as Party Leader |
| January 18 | *Trinidad Guardian* publishes 'Panday's Alarum' |
| January 22 | *Trinidad Guardian* publishes 'Chutney Rising – Panday' |
| January 26 | UNC government declare March 30 'Spiritual Baptist Liberation Day', a national holiday replacing Republic Day; 'Arrival Day' renamed 'Indian Arrival Day' |
| January 31 | Panday announces that the *Guardian* would no longer be invited to government functions |
| February | Ban of *Guardian* lifted; Press Complaints Commission to be established |
| February 11 | Manning's leadership re-affirmed by the PNM General Council, which also passes a resolution expressing full confidence in him |
| May | 20 *Guardian* staff leave and form the *Independent* |
| May 22 | bidding opened for production-sharing contracts on nine new blocks in the deep waters off the east coast; leads to major gas and oil discoveries |
| June 24 | Local Government elections; each party controls seven corporations |
| August | NAR executive accuses UNC of undermining it in the elections; declares that the party is not part of government |
| October 13 | PNM leadership elections; Manning's slate of candidates defeats challenge by Keith Rowley and his supporters; divisive campaign leaves scars |

| | |
|---|---|
| November | THA Act, No. 40 of 1996 passed, giving the THA Constitutional authority |
| December 9 | THA elections; NAR win ten seats, PNM one, and an Independent (former NAR Senator, Deborah Moore-Miggins) wins one |

**1997**

| | |
|---|---|
| February 12 | MP for Point Fortin Vincent Lasse crosses the floor to Government; made a Minister |
| February 14 | Presidential elections; the first time the post was contested; A.N.R. Robinson wins 46 votes and Justice Anthony Lucky received 18 |
| February 28 | MP for Arima Rupert Griffith crosses floor to Government; he is also made a Minister |
| March 7 | Speaker Hector McLean rejects Manning's application to have the Point Fortin and Arima seats declared vacant |
| April | Manning ordered to pay $1.2 million for legal costs in an unsuccessful suit against the Speaker's decision |
| April 14 | Pamela Nicholson resigns from the NAR; remains in Government as an Independent |
| April 22 | A report by retired Justice Lennox Deyalsingh finds a 'measure of collusion' in the granting of the construction contract for the Airport Project, particularly with reference to TIDCO chairman Ishwar Galbaransingh |
| May | Green Paper on reform of media law published; Ken Gordon opposes it |
| May 5 | Morgan Job wins the Tobago East by-election; defeats candidate supported by Pamela Nicholson and Moore-Miggins; Job later sworn in as Minister |
| May 29 | Panday calls Gordon a 'pseudo-racist' |
| July 31 | Court clears Galbaransingh of allegations made in Deyalsingh report |

**1998**

| | |
|---|---|
| March 22 | Panday opens Eric Williams Memorial Collection at the UWI; announces the impending abolition of the Common Entrance examination |
| June | Panday announces intention to review the Concordat of 1960 |
| June 19 | NATUC divided over opposition to Government; refuse to march together at Labour Day rally |
| September 22 | Minister Nicholson votes against Government's Squatter Regularisation Bill; she resigns from Government the following day |

**1999**

| | |
|---|---|
| July 12 | Local Government elections held; UNC and PNM each control seven corporations; PNM-controlled Tunapuna regional corporation win court case against UNC-appointed CEO for undermining its authority |
| October 20 | Panday announces Cabinet re-shuffle; Lindsay Gillette brought into Government as a 'trouble-shooter' |
| September 16 | Chief Justice Michael de la Bastide criticises Attorney-General and Government for compromising the independence of the judiciary |
| December 16 | Panday announces intention to establish a Commission of Inquiry into the administration of Justice |
| December 18 | President Robinson writes to Panday stating that he would need to seek legal advice on the matter, since matters of a 'constitutional nature' might arise |
| December 31 | The murdered body of Rio Claro/Mayaro councillor Hansraj Sumairsingh is found |

**2000**

| | |
|---|---|
| January 7 | Minister of Local Government Dhanraj Singh is questioned by police about the above murder |
| January 17 | Panday requests the replacement of two Tobago Senators; President Robinson refuses |
| February | PEP leader Moore-Miggins replaces PNM's William McKenzie as minority leader in the THA |
| February 2 | Robinson follows Panday's advice on the Senators |
| February 4 | Panday sends to President Robinson instruments to appoint a Commission of Inquiry into the Administration of Justice; Robinson refuses to appoint Commission |
| February 25 | Panday announces that, with the support of Manning, he had sent a letter to the Commonwealth Secretariat at Marlborough House requesting the presence of a Commonwealth Observer Group at the next general elections |
| February 29 | Robinson signs instruments for Commission of Inquiry |
| March 9 | Gillette appointed as acting prime minister |
| October | Commission of Inquiry into the Administration of Justice vindicates the Government; Panday loses two court cases filed by Ken Gordon and CCN; the first case ruled that Panday acted improperly by denying CCN a cellular telephone licence; the second case found Panday guilty of defamation when he called Gordon a |

| | |
|---|---|
| | 'pseudo-racist' in 1997; Panday ordered to pay $696,854.40 to Gordon, threatened with bankruptcy proceedings |
| October 6 | Fifth Session of Parliament ends |
| October 9 | PNM claims that UNC plan to transfer 1,000 names from UNC stronghold constituencies to the residences of people with similar names in borderline seats |
| October 12 | Dhanraj Singh removed from Cabinet |
| October 19 | Sixth Session of Parliament begins |
| October 27 | Almost 80 Criminal Investigations Department police officers conduct searches into homes and businesses of UNC officials and supporters |
| November 2 | Panday announces election date to be December 11 |
| November 22 | *Trinidad Express* reports that UNC candidates Winston 'Gypsy' Peters and William Chaitan are not eligible to become members of the House of Representatives because of their dual citizenships |
| November 23 | PNM writes EBC to contest the eligibility of Peters and Chaitan |
| November 24 | DPP orders investigations into Peters and Chaitan nominations; orders the arrests of 30 persons suspected of 'voter padding' |
| November 29 | Panday granted a stay of execution in the Ken Gordon judgment |
| December 1 | EBC confirms Peters and Chaitan nominations; PNM objects |
| December 3 | Commonwealth Observer Team arrive |
| December 8 | UNC objects to Manning, Eddie Hart, and Eulalie James nominations, due to their technically false declarations |
| December 11 | Parliamentary General Elections held; UNC win 19 seats, PNM win 16, NAR win one; Commonwealth Observer Team satisfied with poll; PNM declares that they will not accept the results |
| December 12 | PNM write to President Robinson asking him to hold his hand on inviting anyone to form the next government until the outcome of a petition to the court challenging the nomination of Peters and Chaitan |
| December 13 | Panday writes to Robinson inquiring why the President has not appointed a prime minister |
| December 14 | Robinson replies to Panday that 'there is no established practice' of appointing a prime minister within 48 hours; seeks advice of former presidents Sir Ellis Clarke and Noor Hassanali to discuss post-election issues |

| | |
|---|---|
| December 15 | President Robinson declares that he cannot appoint a new prime minister until he receives the certified results from the EBC; EBC disagree with the president's opinion; Commonwealth Observer Team submits report; PNM accuse the Team of being in collusion with the EBC and the UNC to 'steal' the election from the PNM; the PNM call for a Commission of Inquiry into the EBC; Panday tells supporters to remain prepared for another election |
| December 16 | Solicitor-General Lynette Stephenson advises president to appoint Panday as prime minister |
| December 18 | President delivers national address insisting on the EBC report, criticising the Solicitor-General |
| December 20 | PNM writes president again; president receives EBC report; Panday sworn in as prime minister; PNM files election petitions against Peters and Chaitan |
| December 22 | Peters and Chaitan file constitutional motions against the election petitions; President Robinson swears in 15 of 25 ministers |
| December 25 | UNC file election petitions against Patrick Manning and Eulalie James for signing false declarations |
| December 31 | Robinson agrees to appoint Peters and Chaitan, but not the seven defeated candidates |
| **2001** | |
| January 5 | President Robinson addresses the nation, warning of a 'creeping dictatorship' |
| January 12 | Parliament opens with seven empty seats in the Senate |
| January 15 | CARICOM head responsible for justice and governance visits Trinidad and Tobago; CARICOM sides with Panday |
| January 19 | An interpretation summons is filed in the High Court registry on behalf of National Security Minister designate, Roy Augustus, seeking interpretation of those aspects of the Constitution that deal with the appointment of senators and ministers; Roodal Moonilal files a similar motion in San Fernando. |
| January 23 | Panday announces intention to take responsibility for National Security |
| January 26 | Robinson accuses Panday and Ramesh Lawrence Maharaj of waging a 'campaign of harassment' against him |
| January 29 | THA elections held; PNM win eight seats, NAR win four |
| February 12 | DPP issues a summons for Winston Peters to answer |

| | |
|---|---|
| | the charge of making a false statement to the EBC for the purpose of being registered as an elector |
| February 14 | Robinson agrees to appoint the seven defeated UNC candidates as senators and, if Panday insisted, he was prepared to appoint them as ministers; he writes 'My choice is clear, though not without reservations' |
| February 19 | Former Minister Dhanraj Singh arrested for the murder of Hansraj Sumarisingh |
| February 20 | Seven senators sworn in; interpretation summonses dropped |
| March 9 | Peters and Chaitan constitutional motions dismissed; election petitions to be heard |
| March 19 | PNM granted leave by High Court judge to seek judicial review of the electoral list used in the December 11, 2000 general elections |
| April 8 | Panday announces that ministers can run in the next UNC internal party elections |
| April 19 | Peters acquitted on charges of making a false declaration as an elector |
| May | Valley files a motion to censure Panday |
| May 24 | Keith Rowley suspended from Lower House; PNM boycotts Parliament |
| June 8 | PNM halts boycott; Fitzgerald Hinds suspended; PNM resumes boycott |
| June 12 | John Humphrey appointed to act as prime minister |
| June 28 | Cabinet re-shuffle |
| June 29 | PNM and UNC reach agreement to wipe slate clean in Parliament |
| July 3 | Ramesh Lawrence Maharaj and his 'Team Unity' slate win ten of 12 executive positions; the campaign threatens to divide the party |
| July 31 | Peters and Chaitan appeals dismissed |
| August 11 | Minister Kamla Persad-Bissessar appointed to act as prime minister |
| August 22 | Cabinet re-shuffle reduces the portfolios of Ramesh Maharaj, Trevor Sudama, and Ralph Maraj, members of 'Team Unity' |
| September 3 | Panday outvoted by Team Unity-controlled UNC executive on the matter of holding constituency elections on September 10 |
| September 4 | UNC Parliamentarians declare 'war' on Team Unity |
| September 11 | The Office of the President accuses EBC Commissioner of having a hidden agenda |
| September 12 | President Robinson asks John to tender his resignation; John refuses |

| | |
|---|---|
| September 14 | Robinson revokes John's appointment |
| September 17 | EBC Commissioners meet with John present, in defiance of the president, who acted outside of his constitutional power |
| September 18 | John's letter of dismissal is withdrawn by the president |
| September 22 | UNC Budget passed, but Maharaj, Sudama, and Maraj openly criticise it |
| October 1 | Panday revokes Maharaj's appointment as Attorney-General; Maharaj, Maraj, and Sudama withdraw support for Panday as prime minister; they begin campaign to take control of the UNC |
| October 2 | Ralph Maraj resigns from Cabinet; PNM General Council empowers Patrick Manning to make an alliance with UNC dissidents, in an attempt to form a majority in Parliament |
| October 3 | Sudama fired from Cabinet position |
| October 5 | The three dissident UNC MPs and NAR MP for Tobago East Nathaniel Moore voted three times with the Opposition against three simple bills brought by the government |
| October 10 | Panday advises the president to dissolve Parliament with immediate effect and to appoint December 10, 2001 as the date of general elections; Robinson asks Panday to stay his advice so that he could ascertain the EBC's readiness; Panday does not stay his advice; Robinson ignores Panday's advice |
| October 11 | Maharaj provides advice that the President can appoint a new prime minister instead of calling a new election |
| October 12 | CARICOM issues statement that the president must follow the prime minister's advice |
| October 13 | Robinson follows Panday's advice and dissolves Parliament |
| October 17 | Election petitions against Manning and James discontinued |
| October 18 | Three new party names registered with the EBC: National Unity, Team Unity, and Citizens' Alliance |
| October 22 | PNM and EBC agree to adjourn the judicial review of the December 11, 2000 electoral list |
| October 24 | Election petitions against Peters and Chaitan discontinued |
| November 7 | The EBC decide to recognise Panday's list of candidates as the UNC list; Maharaj loses two subsequent appeals |
| December 10 | Parliamentary General Elections held; UNC win 18 seats, PNM win 18; Parliament absolutely hung |

# *Appendix B*

## SUMMARIES OF ELECTION RESULTS, 1925-2001

***Table 1. Election Statistics, General Elections held on February 7, 1925***

| | |
|---|---|
| Total Number of Seats Contested | 5 |
| Total Number of Candidates in Contested Seats | 11 |
| Total Voted | 6,832 |
| Total Electorate | 21,794 |
| Total Electorate in Contested Seats | 15,632 |
| Voter Turnout | 43.7% |

*Source*: *Blue Book* 1925: 118–121; *TG* February 8, 1925, p. 11; February 9, 1925, p. 9

---

***Table 2. Election Statistics, General Elections held on March 3, 1928***

| | |
|---|---|
| Total Number of Seats Contested | 3 |
| Total Number of Candidates in Contested Seats | 6 |
| Total Voted | 2,407 |
| Total Electorate | 22,020 |
| Total Electorate in Contested Seats | 5,844 |
| Voter Turnout | 41.2% |

*Source*: *Blue Book* 1928: 115–123; *TG* March 4 1928, p. 11

***Table 3. Election Statistics, General Elections held on January 28, 1933***

| | |
|---|---|
| Total Number of Seats Contested | 4 |
| Total Number of Candidates in Contested Seats | 9 |
| Total Voted | 4,828 |
| Total Electorate | 25,822 |
| Total Electorate in Contested Seats | 11,128 |
| Voter Turnout | 43.4% |

*Source*: *Blue Book* 1933: 101–9; *TG* January 29, 1933, p. 1

***Table 4. Election Statistics, General Elections held on January 4, 1938***

| | |
|---|---|
| Total Number of Seats Contested | 2 |
| Total Number of Candidates in Contested Seats | 4 |
| Total Voted | 3,592 |
| Total Electorate | 30,911 |
| Total Electorate in Contested Seats | 7,455 |
| Voter Turnout | 48.2% |

*Source*: *Blue Book* 1939: 122–131; *TG* January 5, 1938, p. 1

***Table 5. Election Statistics, General Elections held on July 1, 1946***

| | Number of Candidates | Number of Seats Won | Total Number of Votes | % of Votes |
|---|---|---|---|---|
| United Front | 7 | 3 | 29,835 | 21.7% |
| BECWHRP [a] | 5 | 3 | 32,479 | 23.7% |
| TUC and SP | 5 | 2 | 22,141 | 16.1% |
| TLP [a] | 3 | 1 | 16,091 | 11.7% |
| Progressive Democratic Party | 1 | 0 | 515 | 0.4% |
| Independents | 21 | 1 | 41,431 | 30.2% |
| Rejected | | | 8,408 | 6.1% |
| TOTALS [b] | 41 | 9 | 137,281 | 100.0% |

Total Electorate: 259,512
Voter Turnout: 52.9%

*Notes:* [a] = *Figures include votes secured by Timothy Roodal, who contested and won the St Patrick seat on both a BECWHRP and TLP ticket securing 13,619 votes*

[b] = *Figures count Timothy Roodal's candidacy and victory once only*

*Source*: COTT 1947b: 12–4; *TG* May 26, 1946, supp., p. 1

### *Table 6. Election Statistics, County Council General Elections held on October 28, 1946*

| | |
|---|---|
| Total Number of Seats Contested [a] | 62 |
| Total Number of Candidates in Contested Seats | 144 |
| Total Ballots Cast | 69,679 |
| Total Votes Cast [b] | 113,056 |
| Total Electorate | 189,351 |
| Voter Turnout | 36.8% |

*Notes:* [a] = Ten seats in five wards were uncontested. Ten candidates were returned unopposed.

[b] = *Each ballot included up to two votes each*

*Source*: COTT [1947a]: 5

---

### *Table 7. Election Statistics, General Elections held on September 18, 1950*

| | Number of Candidates | Number of Seats Won | Total Number of Votes | % of Votes |
|---|---|---|---|---|
| Butler Home Rule Party[a] | 18 | 7 | 46,458 | 23.4% |
| PPG | 2 | 2 | 6,507 | 3.3% |
| CSP[ab] | 13 | 2 | 24,595 | 12.4% |
| TLP | 12 | 2 | 15,193 | 7.7% |
| Trades Union Council | 6 | 0 | 9,025 | 4.5% |
| Independents | 91 | 6 | 92,717 | 46.7% |
| Rejected | | | 8,492 | 4.3% |
| TOTALS[c] | 141 | 18 | 198,458 | 100.0% |

Total Number of Electors on List: 283,150

Voter Turnout: 70.1%

*Notes:* [a] = *Figures include votes secured by APT James, who contested and won the Tobago seat on both a Butler Party and CSP ticket securing 4,529 votes*

[b] = *Two CSP candidates contested the seat of Port of Spain East*

[c] = *Figures count A.P.T. James's candidacy and victory once only*

*Source:* COTT [1951]; *TG* September 17, 1950, p. 22

**Table 8. Election Statistics, County Council Elections held on February 2, 1953**

| | |
|---|---|
| Total Number of Seats Contested | 72 |
| Total Number of Candidates in Contested Seats | 273 |
| Total Ballots Cast | 109,372 |
| Total Votes Cast [a] | 172,817 |
| Total Electorate | 231,359 |
| Voter Turnout | 47.3% |

*Notes:* [a] = *Each ballot included up to two votes each*
*Source*: COTT 1959a: 6; *TG* February 3, 1953

---

**Table 9. Election Statistics, County Council Elections held on February 20, 1956**

| | |
|---|---|
| Total Number of Seats Contested | 72 |
| Total Number of Candidates in Contested Seats | 231 |
| Total Ballots Cast | 129,360 |
| Total Votes Cast [a] | 192,555 |
| Total Electorate | 258,014 |
| Voter Turnout | 56.7% |

*Notes:* [a] = *Each ballot included up to two votes each*
*Source*: COTT 1959b: 5

**Table 10. Election Statistics, General Elections held on September 24, 1956**

| | Number of Candidates | Number of Seats Won | Total Number of Votes | % of Votes |
|---|---|---|---|---|
| People's National Movement | 24 | 13 | 105,153 | 38.7% |
| Butler Party | 20 | 2 | 31,071 | 11.4% |
| People's Democratic Party | 14 | 5 | 55,148 | 20.3% |
| Trinidad Labour Party-National Democratic Party | 12 | 2 | 13,692 | 5.0% |
| Party of Political Progress Groups | 9 | 0 | 14,019 | 5.2% |
| Caribbean National Labour Party | 8 | 0 | 3,864 | 1.4% |
| West Indian Independence Party | 1 | 0 | 446 | 0.2% |
| Caribbean People's Democratic Party | 1 | 0 | 627 | 0.2% |
| Independents | 39 | 2 | 40,523 | 14.9% |
| Rejected Ballots | | | 6,991 | 2.6% |
| TOTALS | 129 | 24 | 264,543 | 100.0% |

Total Electorate: 339,028

Voter Turnout: 80.1%

*Source:* COTT 1958

**Table 11. Election Statistics, Federal Elections held on March 25, 1958**

| | Number of Candidates | Number of Seats Won | Total Number of Votes | % of Votes |
|---|---|---|---|---|
| PNM | 10 | 4 | 117,445 | 47.4% |
| DLP | 10 | 6 | 117,409 | 47.4% |
| Butler Party | 1 | 0 | 12,235 | 4.9% |
| Independents | 2 | 0 | 558 | 0.2% |
| Rejected Ballots | | | 4,520 | 1.8% |
| TOTALS | 23 | 10 | 247,647 | 100% |

Total Number of Electors on List: 342,565

Voter Turnout: 72.3%

*Source*: COTT 1959a

**Table 12. Election Statistics, County Council Elections held on February 16, 1959**

| | Number of Candidates | Number of Seats Won | Total Number of Votes | % of Votes |
|---|---|---|---|---|
| PNM | 72 | 34 | 140,275 | 48.1% |
| DLP | 67 | 33 | 121,435 | 41.6% |
| Butler Party | 2 | 2 | 8,344 | 2.9% |
| Independents | 32 | 3 | 19,496 | 6.7% |
| Rejected Ballots | | | 2,336 | 0.8% |
| TOTALS | 306 | 72 | 291,886 | 100% |

Total Number of Electors on List: 280,341

Total Number of Ballots Cast: 156,516[a]

Voter Turnout: 55.8%

*Notes:* [a] = *Each ballot included up to two votes each*

*Source*: COTT 1959b: 11–5

**Table 13. Election Statistics, General Elections held on December 4, 1961**

| | Number of Candidates | Number of Seats Won | Total Number of Votes | % of Votes |
|---|---|---|---|---|
| PNM | 30 | 20 | 190,003 | 57.0% |
| DLP | 30 | 10 | 138,910 | 41.7% |
| Butler Party | 4 | 0 | 1,314 | 0.4% |
| African National Congress | 3 | 0 | 1,634 | 0.5% |
| Independents | 2 | 0 | 1,502 | 0.5% |
| Rejected Ballots | | | 149 | 0.0% |
| TOTALS | 69 | 30 | 333,512 | 100.0% |

Total Number of Electors on List: 378,511

Voter Turnout: 88.1%

*Source*: GOTT 1963c: 112

***Table 14. Election Statistics, General Elections held on November 7, 1966***

| | Number of Candidates | Number of Seats Won | Total Number of Votes | % of Votes |
|---|---|---|---|---|
| PNM | 36 | 24 | 158,573 | 52.4% |
| DLP | 36 | 12 | 102,792 | 34% |
| Liberal Party | 36 | 0 | 26,870 | 8.9% |
| WFP | 35 | 0 | 10,484 | 3.5% |
| PDP | 1 | 0 | 943 | 0.3% |
| Butler Party | 4 | 0 | 704 | 0.2% |
| Seukeran Independent Party | 2 | 0 | 569 | 0.2% |
| Independents | 4 | 0 | 1,467 | 0.5% |
| Rejected Ballots | | | 146 | 0.1% |
| TOTAL | 154 | 36 | 302,548 | 100% |

Total Number of Electors on List: 459,839

Voter Turnout: 65.8%

*Source*: GOTT 1967: 83

***Table 15. Election Statistics, Local Government Elections held on June 24, 1968***

| | Number of Candidates | Number of Seats Won | Total Number of Votes | % of Votes |
|---|---|---|---|---|
| PNM | 100 | 68 [a] | 63,538 | 49.9% |
| DLP | 82 | 28 | 51,011 | 40.0% |
| United Country Group, St Andrew-St David | 6 | 0 | 1,015 | 0.8% |
| Independents | 38 | 4 | 11,839 | 9.3% |
| Rejected Ballots | | | 46 | 0.0% |
| TOTAL | 226 | 100 | 127,449 | 100.0% |

Total Number of Electors on List: 437,279

Total Number of Electors in 86 Contested Seats: 365,603

Voter Turnout in 86 Contested Seats: 34.9%

*Note:* [a] *= This includes 14 uncontested seats in which no votes were counted*

*Source*: GOTT [1969]: 8–9

**Table 16. Election Statistics, General Elections held on May 24, 1971**

| | Number of Candidates | Number of Seats Won | Total Number of Votes | % of Votes |
|---|---|---|---|---|
| PNM | 36 | 36[a] | 99,723 | 84.1% |
| Democratic Liberation Party | 21 | 0 | 14,940 | 12.6% |
| African National Congress | 7 | 0 | 2,864 | 2.4% |
| Independents | 2 | 0 | 997 | 0.8% |
| Rejected Ballots | | | 73 | 0.1% |
| TOTAL | 66 | 36 | 118,597 | 100.0% |

Total Number of Electors on List: 454,541
Total Number of Electors in 18 Contested Seats: 357,568
Voter Turnout: 33.2%

*Note:* [a] = *This includes 18 uncontested seats in which no votes were counted*
*Source*: GOTT 1972b: 71

---

**Table 17. Election Statistics, Local Government Elections held on 1971**

| | Number of Candidates | Number of Seats Won | Total Number of Votes | % of Votes |
|---|---|---|---|---|
| PNM | 100 | 90[a] | 12,287 | 52.1% |
| National Progressive Party | 5 | 1 | 950 | 4.0% |
| Independents | 25 | 9 | 10,336 | 43.8% |
| Rejected Ballots | | | 1 | 0.0% |
| TOTAL | 226 | 100 | 23,574 | 100.0% |

Total Number of Electors on List: 438,298
Total Number of Electors in 26 Contested Seats: 86,672
Voter Turnout in 26 Contested Seats: 27.2%

*Note:* [a] = *This includes 74 uncontested seats in which no votes were counted*
*Source*: GOTT 1972a: 46–51

***Table 18. Election Statistics, General Elections held on September 13, 1976***

| | Number of Candidates | Number of Seats Won | Total Number of Votes | % of Votes |
|---|---|---|---|---|
| PNM | 36 | 24 | 169,194 | 53.6% |
| ULF | 26 | 10 | 84,870 | 26.9% |
| DAC | 36 | 2 | 25,586 | 8.1% |
| Tapia House | 29 | 0 | 12,021 | 3.8% |
| Democratic Liberation Party | 35 | 0 | 9,404 | 3.0% |
| Social Democratic Labour Party | 34 | 0 | 5,928 | 1.9% |
| Independents | 5 | 0 | 1,692 | 0.5% |
| West Indian National Party | 26 | 0 | 1,242 | 0.4% |
| Liberation Action Party | 19 | 0 | 872 | 0.3% |
| United Freedom Party | 21 | 0 | 1,047 | 0.3% |
| National Trinidad and Tobago Party | 1 | 0 | 115 | 0.0% |
| Young People's National Party | 1 | 0 | 104 | 0.0% |
| Rejected Ballots | | | 3,824 | 1.2% |
| TOTALS | 269 | 36 | 315,809 | 100.0% |

Total Number of Electors on List: 565,646

Voter Turnout: 55.8%

*Source*: GORTT 1977b: 149–51

***Table 19. Election Statistics, Local Government Elections held on April 25, 1977***

| | Number of Candidates | Number of Seats Won | Total Number of Votes | % of Votes |
|---|---|---|---|---|
| PNM | 100 | 69[a] | 64,725 | 51.1% |
| ULF | 56 | 27 | 47,899 | 37.8% |
| DAC | 28 | 4 | 8,304 | 6.6% |
| Independent | 11 | 0 | 2,987 | 2.4% |
| DLP | 5 | 0 | 1,456 | 1.2% |
| Tapia | 2 | 0 | 383 | 0.3% |
| Rejected | | | 879 | 0.7% |
| TOTALS | 202 | 100 | 126,634 | 100% |

Total Number of Electors on List: 587,403

Total Number of Electors in 75 Contested Seats: 441,089

Voter Turnout in 75 Contested Seats: 28.7%

*Note:* [a] = *This includes 25 uncontested seats in which no votes were counted*

*Source*: GORTT 1977a

***Table 20. Election Statistics, Local Government Elections held on April 21, 1980***

| | Number of Candidates | Number of Seats Won | Total Number of Votes | % of Votes Cast |
|---|---|---|---|---|
| PNM | 113 | 100[a] | 74,667 | 57.8% |
| ULF | 53 | 9 | 41,167 | 31.9% |
| Independent | 27 | 4 | 9,827 | 7.6% |
| Point Fortin Vigilante Welfare Group | 6 | 0 | 1,627 | 1.3% |
| Tapia | 2 | 0 | 528 | 0.4% |
| Rejected | | | 1,294 | 1.0% |
| TOTALS | 201 | 113 | 129,110 | 100.0% |

Total Number of Electors on List: 654,006

Total Number of Electors in 82 Contested Seats: 444,331

Voter Turnout in 82 Contested Seats: 29.1%

*Note:* [a] = *This includes 26 uncontested seats in which no votes were counted*

*Source*: GORTT [1980b]

***Table 21. Election Statistics, THA Elections held on November 24, 1980***

| | Number of Candidates | Number of Seats Won | Total Number of Votes | % of Votes |
|---|---|---|---|---|
| DAC | 12 | 8 | 8,447 | 52.8% |
| PNM | 12 | 4 | 7,097 | 44.4% |
| FHM | 7 | 0 | 351 | 2.2% |
| Rejected Ballots | | | 95 | 0.6% |
| TOTALS | 31 | 12 | 15,990 | 100.00% |

Total Number of Electors on List: 24,141
Voter Turnout: 66.2%

*Source*: GORTT 1987b

***Table 22. Election Statistics, General Elections held on November 9, 1981***

| | Number of Candidates | Number of Seats Won | Total Number of Votes | % of Votes |
|---|---|---|---|---|
| PNM | 36 | 26 | 218,557 | 52.6% |
| ULF | 12 | 8 | 62,781 | 15.1% |
| DAC | 8 | 2 | 15,390 | 3.7% |
| ONR | 34 | 0 | 91,704 | 22.1% |
| NJAC | 34 | 0 | 13,710 | 3.3% |
| Tapia House | 16 | 0 | 9,401 | 2.3% |
| National Freedom Party | 10 | 0 | 864 | 0.2% |
| Fargo House Movement | 1 | 0 | 143 | 0.0% |
| People's Republican Party | 1 | 0 | 25 | 0.0% |
| Trinidad Labour Party | 1 | 0 | 34 | 0.0% |
| West Indian Political Congress Movement | 1 | 0 | 130 | 0.0% |
| Independents | 2 | 0 | 39 | 0.0% |
| Rejected Ballots | | | 2,638 | 0.6% |
| TOTALS | 156 | 36 | 415,416 | 100.0% |

Total Number of Electors on List: 736,104
Voter Turnout: 56.4%

*Source*: GORTT 1982b: 202–3

***Table 23. Election Statistics, Local Government Elections held on August 8, 1983***

| | Number of Candidates | Number of Seats Won | Total Number of Votes | % of Votes |
|---|---|---|---|---|
| PNM | 120 | 54 | 95,426 | 39.1% |
| Alliance | 47 | 40 | 82,904 | 34.0% |
| ONR | 65 | 26 | 49,058 | 20.1% |
| NJAC | 103 | 0 | 13,013 | 5.3% |
| Curepe United People's Committee | 1 | 0 | 187 | 0.1% |
| Independent | 5 | 0 | 1,280 | 0.5% |
| Rejected Ballots | | | 2,157 | 0.9% |
| TOTALS | 341 | 120 | 244,025 | 100.0% |

Total Number of Electors: 742,400
Voter Turnout: 32.9%

*Source*: GORTT [1984b]: 284–91

***Table 24. Election Statistics, THA Elections held on November 26, 1984***

| | Number of Candidates | Number of Seats Won | Total Number of Votes | % of Votes |
|---|---|---|---|---|
| DAC | 12 | 11 | 11,189 | 56.6% |
| PNM | 12 | 1 | 8,200 | 41.4% |
| NJAC | 12 | 0 | 274 | 1.4% |
| Rejected Ballots | | | 123 | 0.6% |
| TOTALS | 36 | 12 | 19,786 | 100.0% |

Total Number of Electors on List: 28,220
Voter Turnout: 70.1%

*Source*: GORTT 1987a

***Table 25. Election Statistics, General Elections held on December 15, 1986***

| | Number of Candidates | Number of Seats Won | Total Number of Votes | % of Votes |
|---|---|---|---|---|
| NAR | 36 | 33 | 380,029 | 65.8% |
| PNM | 36 | 3 | 183,635 | 31.8% |
| NJAC | 36 | 0 | 8,592 | 1.5% |
| People's Popular Movement | 14 | 0 | 796 | 0.1% |
| Independents | 2 | 0 | 211 | 0.0% |
| Rejected Ballots | | | 4,037 | 0.7% |
| TOTALS | 124 | 36 | 577,300 | 100.0% |

Total Number of Electors on List: 882,029
Voter Turnout: 65.5%

*Source*: GORTT [1987c]: 202–3

***Table 26. Election Statistics, Local Government Elections held on September 14, 1987***

| | Number of Candidates | Number of Seats Won | Total Number of Votes | % of Votes |
|---|---|---|---|---|
| NAR | 125 | 79 | 250,055 | 58.5% |
| PNM | 125 | 46 | 137,754 | 39.3% |
| People's Popular Movement | 14 | 0 | 360 | 0.1% |
| Progressive Workers Democratic Movement | 3 | 0 | 90 | 0.0% |
| Independent | 13 | 0 | 5,584 | 1.6% |
| Rejected Ballots | | | 1,917 | 0.6% |
| TOTALS | 280 | 125 | 350,760 | 100.0% |

Total Number of Electors on List: 856,478
Voter Turnout: 41.0%

*Source*: GORTT [1988c]: 462–8

***Table 27. Election Statistics, THA Elections held on November 29, 1988***

| | Number of Candidates | Number of Seats Won | Total Number of Votes | % of Votes |
|---|---|---|---|---|
| NAR | 12 | 11 | 10,610 | 63.5% |
| PNM | 12 | 1 | 5,977 | 35.8% |
| Independents | 1 | 0 | 73 | 0.4% |
| Rejected Ballots | | | 60 | 0.4% |
| TOTALS | 25 | 12 | 16,720 | 100.0% |

Total Number of Electors on List: 31,224
Voter Turnout: 53.5%

*Source*: GORTT [1989]

---

***Table 28. Election Statistics, General Elections held on December 16, 1991***

| | Number of Candidates | Number of Seats Won | Total Number of Votes | % of Votes |
|---|---|---|---|---|
| PNM | 36 | 21 | 233,950 | 44.8% |
| UNC | 35 | 13 | 151,046 | 28.9% |
| NAR | 36 | 2 | 127,335 | 24.4% |
| NJAC | 29 | 0 | 5,743 | 1.1% |
| Independent | 5 | 0 | 1,623 | 0.3% |
| Rejects | | | 2,775 | 0.5% |
| TOTALS | 141 | 36 | 522,472 | 100.0% |

Total Number of Electors on List: 794,486
Voter Turnout: 65.8%

*Source*: GORTT 1992b: 286–95

### *Table 29. Election Statistics, Local Government Elections held on September 28, 1992*

| | Number of Candidates | Number of Seats Won | Total Number of Votes | % of Votes |
|---|---|---|---|---|
| PNM | 139 | 86 | 154,818 | 50.3% |
| UNC | 105 | 53 | 113,502 | 36.9% |
| NAR | 118 | 0 | 33,880 | 11.0% |
| Independent | 9 | 0 | 2,522 | 0.8% |
| Rejected Ballots | | | 3,072 | 1.0% |
| TOTALS | 371 | 139 | 307,945 | 100.0% |

Total Number of Electors on List: 774,223

Voter Turnout: 39.8%

*Source*: GORTT 1993a: 290–4

### *Table 30. Election Statistics, THA Elections held on December 7, 1992*

| | Number of Candidates | Number of Seats Won | Total Number of Votes | % of Votes |
|---|---|---|---|---|
| NAR | 12 | 11 | 10,401 | 58.24% |
| PNM | 12 | 1 | 6,562 | 36.74% |
| Independents | 3 | 0 | 757 | 4.24% |
| Rejected Ballots | | | 140 | 0.78% |
| TOTALS | 27 | 12 | 17,860 | 100.00% |

Total Number of Electors on List: 31,503

Voter Turnout: 56.7%

*Source*: GORTT 1993a

***Table 31. Election Statistics, General Elections held on November 6, 1995***

| | Number of Candidates | Number of Seats Won | Total Number of Votes | % of Votes |
|---|---|---|---|---|
| PNM | 36 | 17 | 256,159 | 48.8% |
| UNC | 34 | 17 | 240,372 | 45.8% |
| NAR | 19 | 2 | 24,983 | 4.8% |
| Natural Law Party | 17 | 0 | 1,590 | 0.3% |
| Movement for Unity and Progress | 5 | 0 | 2,123 | 0.4% |
| National Transformation Movement | 2 | 0 | 83 | 0.0% |
| The People's Voice | 1 | 0 | 16 | 0.0% |
| Rejected | | | 4,985 | 0.9% |
| TOTALS | 114 | 36 | 530,311 | 100% |

Total Number of Electors on List: 837,741

Voter Turnout: 63.3%

*Source*: GORTT 1996b

---

***Table 32. Election Statistics, Local Government Elections held on June 24, 1996***

| | Number of Candidates | Number of Seats Won | Total Number of Votes | % of Votes |
|---|---|---|---|---|
| PNM | 124 | 63 | 155,585 | 43.7% |
| UNC | 91 | 61 | 177,848 | 49.9% |
| NAR | 35 | 0 | 20,713 | 5.8% |
| Independent | 8 | 0 | 2,113 | 0.6% |
| Rejected Ballots | | | 2,761 | 0.8% |
| TOTALS | 258 | 124 | 359,020 | 100.0% |

Total Number of Electors on List: 816,809

Voter Turnout: 44.0%

*Source*: GORTT [1997b]: 291–5

***Table 33. Election Statistics, THA Elections held on December 9, 1996***

| | Number of Candidates | Number of Seats Won | Total Number of Votes | % of Votes |
|---|---|---|---|---|
| NAR | 12 | 11 | 8,973 | 59.68% |
| PNM | 12 | 1 | 5,023 | 33.41% |
| Independents | 3 | 0 | 935 | 6.22% |
| Rejected Ballots | | | 103 | 0.69% |
| TOTALS | 27 | 12 | 15,034 | 100.00% |

Total Number of Electors on List: 34,245
Voter Turnout: 43.9%

Source: GORTT 1997a

***Table 34. Election Statistics, Local Government Elections held on July 12, 1999***

| | Number of Candidates | Number of Seats Won | Total Number of Votes | % of Votes |
|---|---|---|---|---|
| PNM | 124 | 67 | 157,923 | 46.3% |
| UNC | 124 | 57 | 175,786 | 51.5% |
| NAR | 9 | 0 | 813 | 0.2% |
| PPM | 1 | 0 | 10 | 0.0% |
| Independent | 17 | 0 | 3,494 | 1.0% |
| Rejected Ballots | | | 3,061 | 0.9% |
| TOTALS | 275 | 124 | 341,087 | 100% |

Total Number of Electors on List: 881,766
Voter Turnout: 38.7%

*Source*: GORTT 1999a

***Table 35. Election Statistics, General Elections held on December 11, 2000***

| | Number of Candidates | Number of Seats Won | Total Number of Votes | % of Votes |
|---|---|---|---|---|
| PNM | 36 | 16 | 276,334 | 46.2% |
| UNC | 34 | 19 | 307,791 | 51.5% |
| NAR | 2 | 1 | 7,409 | 1.2% |
| People's Empowerment Party | 2 | 0 | 2,071 | 0.3% |
| The Mercy Society | 1 | 0 | 142 | 0.0% |
| Independent | 4 | 0 | 1,128 | 0.2% |
| Rejected | | | 2,650 | 0.4% |
| TOTALS | 79 | 36 | 597,525 | 100.0% |

Total Number of Electors on List: 947,689

Voter Turnout: 63.1%

*Source*: Elections and Boundaries Commission

***Table 36. Election Statistics (provisional figures), THA Elections held on January 29, 2001***

| | Number of Candidates | Number of Seats Won | Total Number of Votes | % of Votes |
|---|---|---|---|---|
| NAR | 12 | 11 | 8,647 | 38.4% |
| PNM | 12 | 1 | 10,509 | 46.7% |
| People's Empowerment Party | 12 | 0 | 1,589 | 7.1% |
| UNC | 11 | 0 | 1,764 | 7.8% |
| Rejected Ballots | | | n.a. | n.a. |
| TOTALS | 47 | 12 | 22,509 | 100% |

Total Number of Electors on List: n.a.

Voter Turnout: n.a.

Source: *TG* January 30, 2001, p. 1

| Number | Number | Total Number | % |
|---|---|---|---|

***Table 37. Election Statistics, General Elections held on December 10, 2001***

| | of Candidates | of Seats Won | of Votes | of Votes |
|---|---|---|---|---|
| PNM | 36 | 18 | 259,450 | 46.3% |
| UNC | 36 | 18 | 278,781 | 49.7% |
| NAR | 6 | 0 | 5,925 | 1.1% |
| Team Unity | 30 | 0 | 14,165 | 2.5% |
| National Democratic Organisation | 2 | 0 | 50 | 0.0% |
| Rejected | | | 2,407 | 0.4% |
| TOTALS | 110 | 36 | 560,778 | 100.0% |

Total Number of Electors on List: 844,254

Voter Turnout: 66.4%

*Source*: Elections and Boundaries Commission, personal communication

# *Appendix C*

## DISTRIBUTION OF CONSTITUENCIES BY PARTY, 1956-2001

**Figure 1. Distribution of Constituencies by Party, 1956 General Elections**

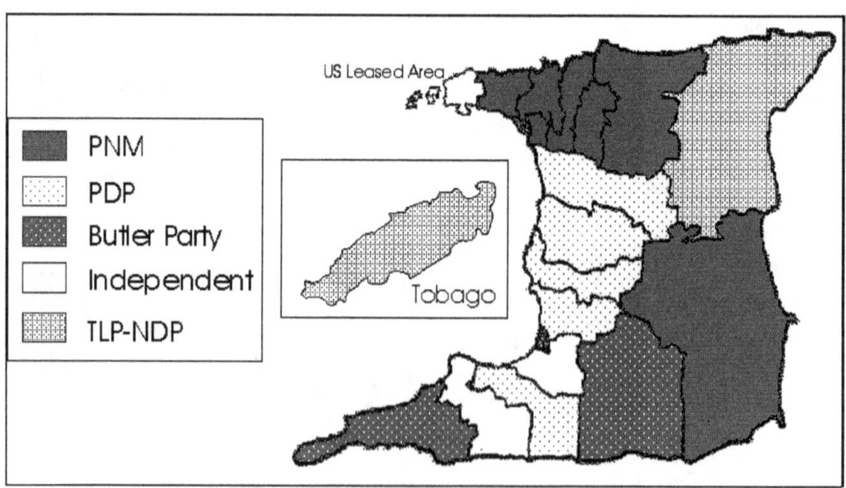


Created by the author from the *Trinidad Guardian* September 2, 1956, p. 9 and COTT 1958

**Figure 2. Distribution of Constituencies by Party, 1961 General Elections**

PNM
DLP
US Leased
Area
Port of Spain
Tobago
San Fernando

*Created by the author from Ryan 1972: 371 and GOTT 1965*

**Figure 3. Distribution of Constituencies by Party, 1966 General Elections**

PNM
DLP
US Leased
Area
Tobago

*Created by the author from Ryan 1972: 394 and GOTT 1967*

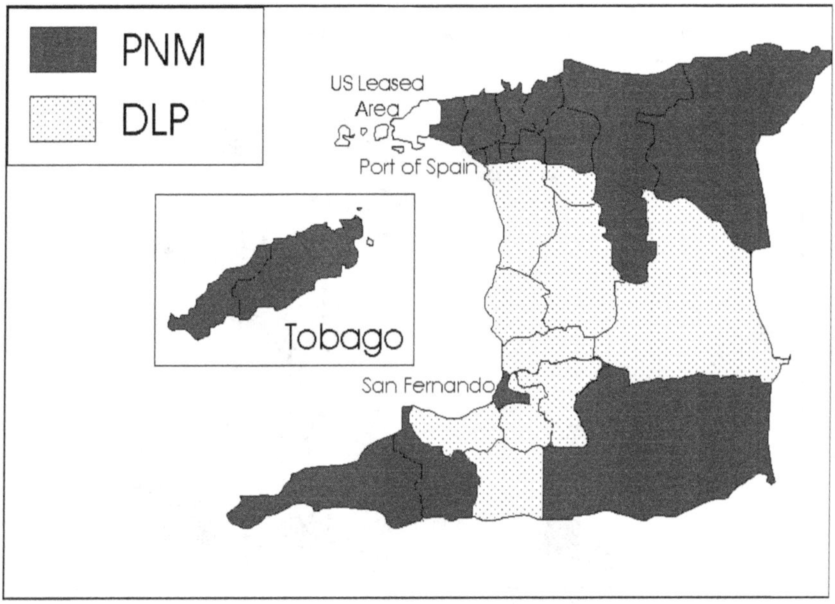

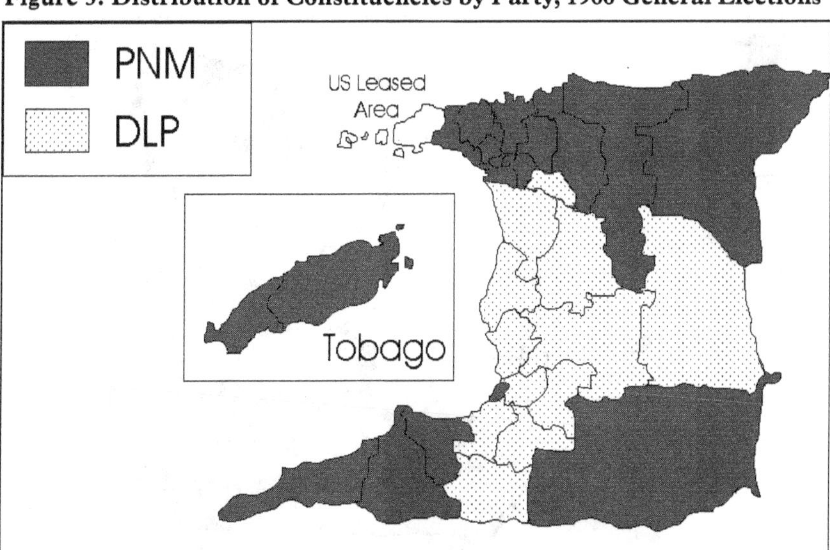

**Figure 4. Distribution of Constituencies by Party, 1971 General Elections**

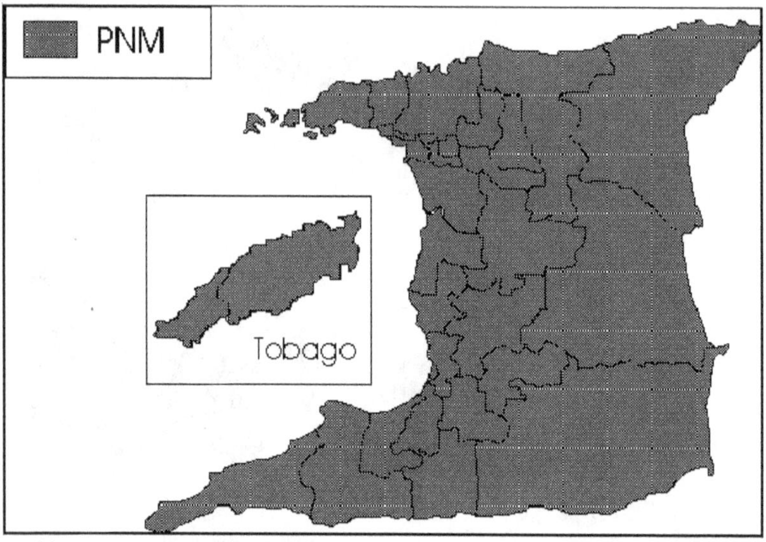

*Created by the author from GOTT 1972a*

**Figure 5. Distribution of Constituencies by Party, 1976 General Elections**

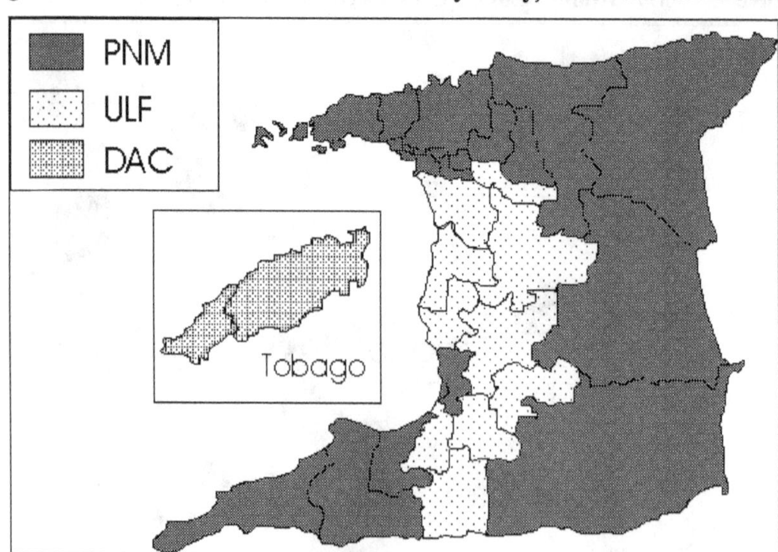


*Created by the author from GORTT 1977*

**Figure 6. Distribution of Constituencies by Party, 1981 General Elections**

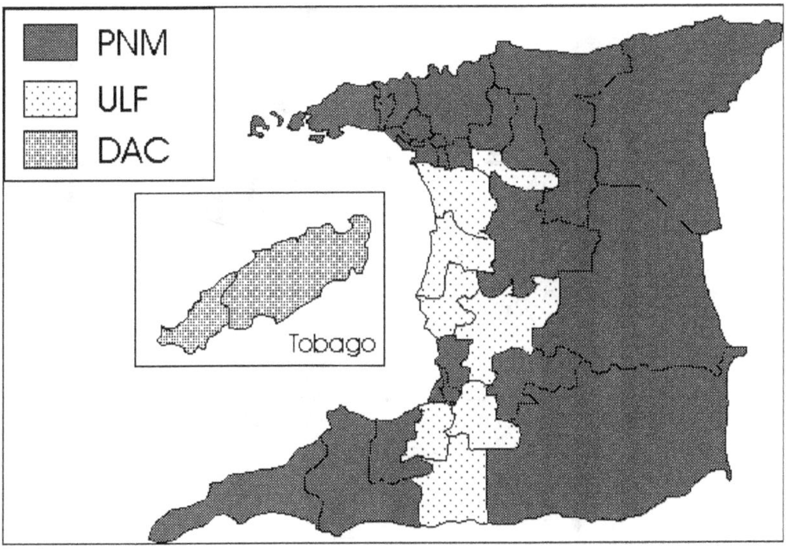

PNM
ULF
DAC
Tobago

*Created by author from GORTT 1982b*

**Figure 7. Distribution of Constituencies by Party, 1986 General Elections**

PNM
NAR
Tobago

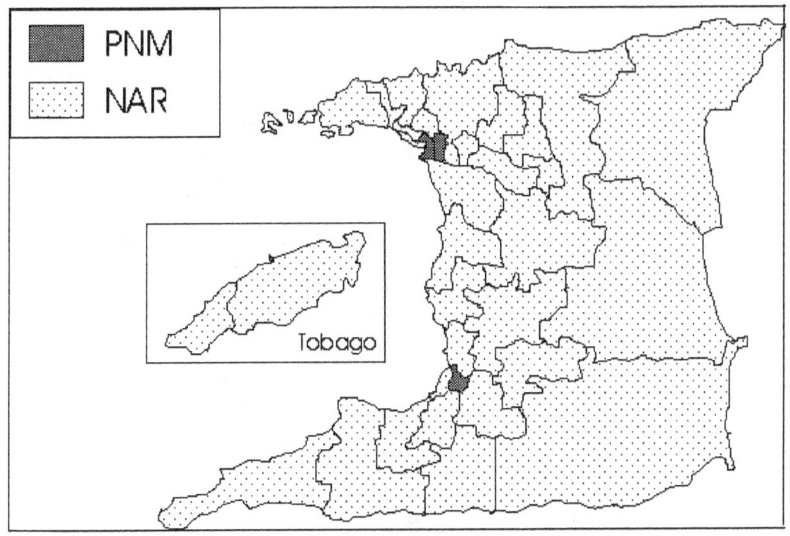

*Created by author from GORTT [1987]*

**Figure 8. Distribution of Constituencies by Party, 1991 General Elections**

PNM
UNC
NAR
Tobago

*Created by author from GORTT 1992b*

**Figure 9. Distribution of Constituencies by Party, 1995 General Elections**

PNM
UNC
NAR
Tobago

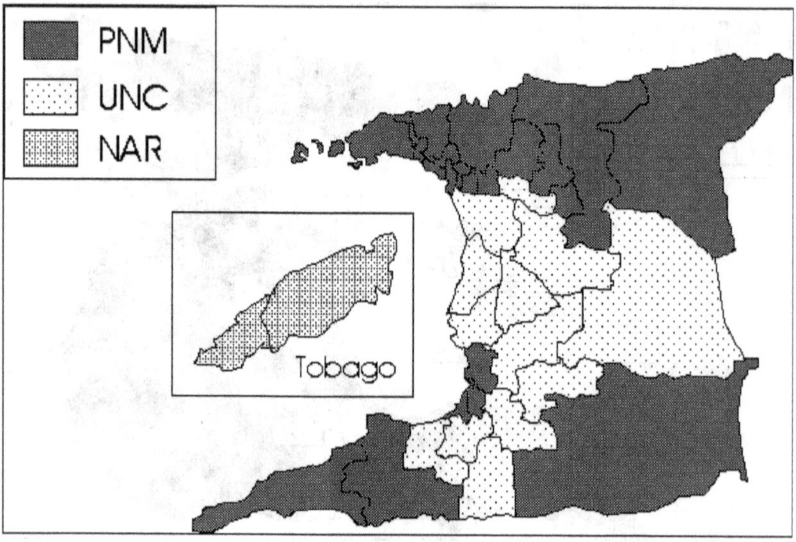

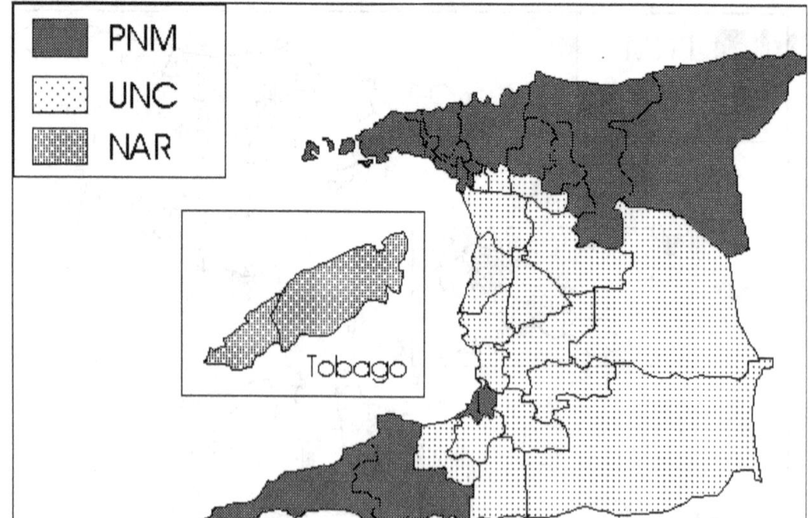

*Created by author from GORTT 1996b*

**Figure 10. Distribution of Constituencies by Party, 2000 General Elections**

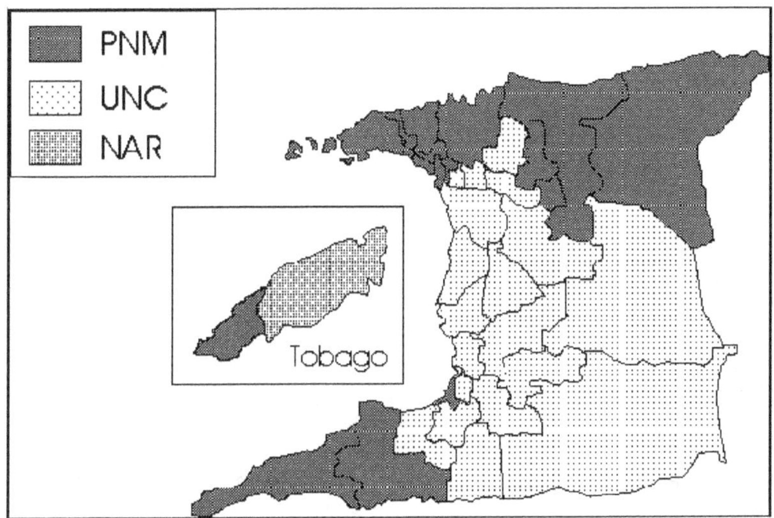


*Created by author from GORTT 2001*

**Figure 11. Distribution of Constituencies by Party, 2001 General Elections**

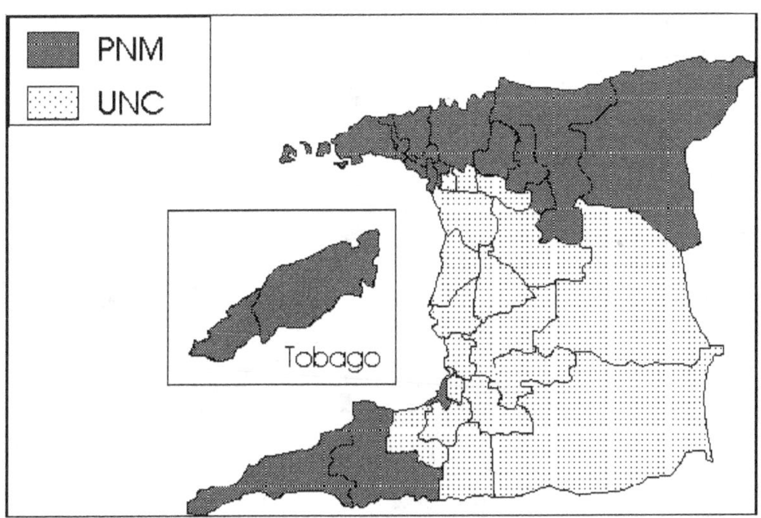


*Created by author from Elections and Boundaries Commission data*

# *Appendix D*

## SELECTED ECONOMIC INDICATORS, 1970-2000

***Table 1. Selected Economic Indicators, 1970-80***

| | **1970** | **1980** |
|---|---|---|
| Crude Oil Prices (US$/barrel) | $1.30 | $28.70 |
| Total Revenue (TT$ million) | $317.5 | $6,226.4 |
| Total Expenditure (TT$ million) | $390.1 | $5,446.3 |
| Capital Expenditure (as % of Total Expenditure) | 28.1% | 42.8% |
| GDP at Constant 1970 Prices (TT$ million) | $1,643.7 | $2,748.4 |
| Gross Capital Formation (as % of GDP at Constant 1970 Prices) | 25.9% | 64.6% |
| Government Expenditure (as % of GDP at Constant 1970 Prices) | 13.1% | 21.1% |
| Net Official Foreign Reserves (TT$ million) | $106.6 | $6,336.7 |
| Unemployment Rate | 12.8% | 9.9% |

*Source*: CBTT (1993)

## *Table 2. Selected Economic Indicators, 1981-6*

| | 1981 | 1982 | 1983 | 1984 | 1985 | 1986 |
|---|---|---|---|---|---|---|
| Crude Oil Prices (US$/barrel) | $32.50 | $33.50 | $29.30 | $28.50 | $28.00 | $15.00 |
| Crude Oil Production (thousands of barrels per day) | 189.3 | 177.0 | 159.8 | 169.5 | 176.1 | 168.9 |
| Current Oil Revenue (TT$ million) | $4,253.0 | $3,274.2 | $2,461.4 | $2,759.7 | $2,457.1 | $1,690.6 |
| Total Revenue (TT$ million) | $6,850.7 | $6,824.7 | $6,438.8 | $6,551.7 | $6,361.2 | $5,234.9 |
| Current Oil Revenue (% of Total Revenue) | 62.1% | 48.0% | 38.2% | 42.1% | 38.6% | 32.3% |
| Direct Taxes on Individuals (as % of Total Direct Taxes) | 16.9% | 30.5% | 36.7% | 33.6% | 34.8% | 39.1% |
| Indirect Taxes (as % of Current Revenue) | 11.9% | 13.9% | 17.3% | 17.6% | 21.2% | 23.1% |
| Total Expenditure (TT$ million) | $6,674.9 | $9,477.1 | $8,782.9 | $8,307.9 | $7,723.0 | $6,614.6 |
| Total Expenditure (as % of GDP at market prices) | 38.9% | 47.4% | 45.8% | 43.6% | 43.4% | 38.1% |
| Current Expenditure (as % of Total Expenditure) | 52.3% | 62.2% | 71.1% | 75.7% | 78.7% | 85.2% |
| Overall Surplus/Deficit (TT$ million) | $175.8 | -$2,652.4 | -$2,344.1 | -$1,756.2 | -$1,361.8 | -$1,379.7 |
| Overall Surplus/Deficit (as % of GDP at market prices) | 1% | -13.8% | -12.2% | -9.2% | -7.6% | -7.9% |
| Net Official Foreign Reserves (TT$ million) | $7,686.2 | $7,160.1 | $4,998.4 | $2,850.0 | $3,579.9 | $1,184.5 |
| Import Cover Ratio (months) | 19.5 | 12.9 | 9.9 | 7.4 | 11.5 | 2.9 |
| Total Debt to GDP Ratio | 10.2% | 10.7% | 13.9% | 16.7% | 27.8% | 37.0% |
| GDP growth at constant 1970 Prices | 4.0% | 3.8% | -10.3% | -5.8% | -4.1% | -3.3% |
| Unemployment Rate | 10.5% | 9.9% | 11.1% | 13.3% | 15.7% | 17.2% |

*Source*: CBTT (1993)

***Table 3. Selected Economic Indicators, 1987-91***

| | **1987** | **1991** |
|---|---|---|
| Crude Oil Prices (US$/barrel) | $17.30 | $17.50 |
| Crude Oil Production (thousands of barrels per day) | 155.2 | 144.1 |
| Current Oil Revenue (TT$ million) | $1,958.0 | $2,717.0 |
| Total Revenue (TT$ million) | $5,232.7 | $6,796.8 |
| Current Oil Revenue (% of Total Revenue) | 37.4% | 40.1% |
| Direct Taxes on Individuals (as % of Total Direct Taxes) | 33.7% | 26.0% |
| Indirect Taxes (as % of Current Revenue) | 22.2% | 33.0% |
| Total Expenditure (TT$ million) | $6,480.7 | $6,847.3 |
| Total Expenditure (as % of GDP at market prices) | 37.5% | 30.6% |
| Overall Surplus/Deficit (TT$ million) | -$1,248.0 | -$50.4 |
| Overall Surplus/Deficit (as % of GDP at market prices) | -7.2% | -0.2% |
| Current Expenditure (as % of Total Expenditure) | 86.9% | 89.1% |
| Gross Capital Formation as % of Real GDP | 14.2% | 13.0% |
| Overall Surplus/Deficit on the Balance of Payments (US$ million) | -$249.9 | -$332.2 |
| Other Exports (TT$ million) | $741.2 | $2,210.5 |
| Foreign Direct Investment (US$ million) | $33.1 | $144.1 |
| Net Official Foreign Reserves (TT$ million) | $284.9 | $3.4 |
| Import Cover Ratio (months) | 0.8 | – |
| Total Debt to GDP Ratio | 51.0% | 56.8% |
| GDP growth at constant 1970 prices | -4.6% | 3.1% |
| Unemployment Rate | 22.3% | 18.5% |

*Source*: CBTT (1993)

## *Table 4. Selected Economic Indicators, 1992-5*

| | 1992 | 1993 | 1994 | 1995 |
|---|---|---|---|---|
| GDP growth at constant 1985 prices | -1.1% | -2.6% | 5.0% | 3.2% |
| Crude Oil Prices (US$/barrel) | $20.57 | $18.45 | $17.19 | $18.44 |
| Crude Oil Production (thousands of barrels per day) | 135.8 | 123.9 | 131.0 | 130.7 |
| Gas Production (millions of cubic feet per day) | 722.0 | 684.7 | 744.0 | 773.6 |
| Total Revenue (TT$ million) | $6,233.5 | $6,743.5 | $7,564.7 | $8,511.8 |
| Current Oil Revenue (% of Total Revenue) | 29.2% | 26.7% | 25.1% | 29.8% |
| Total Expenditure (TT$ million) | $6,877.4 | $6,783.3 | $7,571 | $8,458.5 |
| Total Expenditure (as % of GDP at current prices) | 29.7% | 27.7% | 25.8% | 26.7% |
| Overall Surplus/Deficit (TT$ million) | -$644.0 | -$39.8 | -$6.3 | $53.3 |
| Overall Surplus/Deficit (as % of GDP at current prices) | -2.8% | -0.2% | 0.0% | 0.2% |
| Capital Expenditure (as % of Total Expenditure) | 6.3% | 4.4% | 6.2% | 7.4% |
| Gross Capital Formation (as % of Real GDP) | 8.6% | 9.0% | 12.5% | 10.5% |
| (Exports + Imports)/GDP at current prices | 76.1% | 82.6% | 78.7% | 93.0% |
| Foreign Direct Investment (US$ million) | $171.0 | $372.6 | $521.0 | $295.7 |
| Divestment Proceeds (TT$ million) | - | $5.9 | $522.2 | $610.1 |
| Exports excluding all mineral fuels (as % of all exports, excluding mineral fuels under processing agreement) | 39.6% | 42.4% | 51.9% | 52.2% |
| Overall Surplus/Deficit on the Balance of Payments (US$ million) | -$116.8 | $151.3 | $181.0 | $32.5 |
| Net Official Foreign Reserves (US$ million) | -$83.3 | $75.4 | $261.9 | $296.1 |
| Exchange rate, annual average (TT$:US$) | $4.25 | $5.35 | $5.92 | $5.95 |
| Total Debt to GDP Ratio | 50.1% | 60.4% | 53.5% | 51.1% |
| Unemployment Rate | 19.6% | 19.8% | 18.4% | 17.2% |
| Rate of Inflation | 6.5% | 10.1% | 8.8% | 5.3% |

*Sources*: *QEB* (December 1997), GORTT (1997c), *EIU* (1998a, 42), CBTT (1993), *AES* (1994; 1998)

## Table 5. Selected Economic Indicators, 1996–2000

| | 1996 | 1997 | 1998 | 1999 | 2000 |
|---|---|---|---|---|---|
| GDP growth at constant 1985 prices | 2.9% | 3.0% | 4.0% | 5.0% | 4.7% |
| Real GDP growth Petroleum Sector | 1.8% | -2.0% | 5.4% | 8.1% | 1.1% |
| Real GDP growth Non-Petroleum Sector | 3.3% | 4.5% | 3.6% | 4.1% | 5.8% |
| Crude Oil Prices (US$/barrel) | $22.16 | $20.16 | $14.37 | $19.3 | $30.29 |
| Crude Oil Production (thousands of barrels per day) | 129.2 | 125.8 | 123.0 | 125.2 | 119.7 |
| Gas Production (millions of cubic feet per day) | 689.6 | 884.0 | 996.0 | 1,281.0 | 1,498.0 |
| Total Revenue (TT$ million) | $9,542.5 | $9,953.7 | $9,658.4 | $9,714.0 | $13,036.5 |
| Current Oil Revenue (% of Total Revenue) | 32.1% | 20.8% | 17.7% | 20.6% | 34.3% |
| Total Expenditure (TT$ million) | $9,701.0 | $9,912.3 | $10,399.4 | $11,069.3 | $12,217.5 |
| Total Expenditure (as % of GDP at current prices) | 28.0% | 27.1% | 26.1% | 25.6% | 24.0% |
| Overall Surplus/Deficit (TT$ million) | -$158.5 | $41.4 | -$741.0 | -$1,355.3 | $819.0 |
| Overall Surplus/Deficit (as % of GDP at current prices) | -0.5% | 0.1% | -1.9% | -3.1% | 1.6% |
| Capital Expenditure (as % of Total Expenditure) | 6.0% | 11.5% | 8.3% | 4.8% | 10.0% |
| Gross Capital Formation (as % of GDP at current prices) | 24.3% | 36.1% | 27.0% | 20.9% | 17.5% |
| (Exports + Imports)/GDP at current prices (%) | 92.4% | 108.6% | 97.8% | 93.4% | 105.6% |
| Foreign Direct Investment (US$ million) | $356.3 | $999.6 | $731.9 | $379.2 | $654.3 |
| Divestment Proceeds (TT$ million) | $28.2 | - | $116.0 | $53.9 | $31.5 |
| Exports excluding all mineral fuel lubricants (as % of all visible exports) | 47.4% | 53.9% | 55.6% | 45.9% | 34.7% |
| Overall Surplus/Deficit on the Balance of Payments (US$ million) | $213.5 | $175.3 | $80.6 | $162.2 | $441.0 |
| Net Official Foreign Reserves (US$ million) | $509.0 | $684.9 | $765.5 | $949.8 | $1,388.0 |
| Exchange rate, annual average selling price (TT$:US$) | $6.0354 | $6.2846 | $6.2982 | $6.2997 | $6.2998 |
| Internal Debt / GDP (%) | 20.2% | 23.8% | 23.2% | 22.9% | 19.2% |
| External Debt / GDP (%) | 32.6% | 27.1% | 24.1% | 23.4% | 21.1% |
| Standard and Poor's Rating | BB+ | BB+ | BB+ | BBB- | BBB- |
| Moody's Rating | Ba1 | Ba1 | Ba1 | Ba1 | Baa3 |
| Unemployment Rate | 16.2% | 15.0% | 14.2% | 13.1% | 12.2% |
| Rate of Inflation | 3.3% | 3.7% | 5.6% | 3.4% | 3.6% |
| Composite Share Price Index | 167.4 | 352.3 | 436.3 | 417.5 | 441.5 |

*Sources*: *AES (1995; 1996; 1997; 1998; 1999; 2000; 2001)*

# *Appendix E*

## THE STRUCTURE OF GOVERNMENT

### *Table 1. Structure of Legislative and Executive Councils, 1925–1956*

| | **Legislative Council** | | | **Executive Council** | | |
|---|---|---|---|---|---|---|
| | *Official* | *Unofficial* | | *Official* | *Unofficial* | |
| | | Nominated | Elected | | Nominated | Elected |
| **1925** | 12 | 6 | 7 | 3 | Governor's discretion[a] | Governor's discretion |
| **1941** | 3 | 6 | 9 | 3 | Governor's discretion[a] | Governor's discretion |
| **1950** | 3 | 5 | 18 | 3 | 1 | 5 |
| **1956** | 2 | 5 | 24 | 2 | 0 | 7 |

*Note*: The Governor's position as President of both Councils is excluded from these figures, as is the Speaker, who presided over the Legislative Council from 1950.

[a] = *Up to 1931 the Governor normally appointed two nominated members only. From 1944, it was conventional to appoint one nominated and four elected members.*

***Table 2. The Structure of Parliament, 1961–1976***

| | **Lower House** | **Upper House** | | | |
|---|---|---|---|---|---|
| | Elected Members | Prime Minister's Appointees | Leader of Opposition's Appointees | Governor/Governor General/President's Appointees | Total Number of Senators |
| **1961** | 30 | 12 | 2 | 7[a] | 21 |
| **1962** | 30 | 13 | 4 | 7[b] | 24 |
| **1966** | 36 | 13 | 4 | 7 | 24 |
| **1976** | 36 | 16 | 6 | 9[c] | 31 |

[a] = *The Governor appointed these members in his discretion after consultation with such persons as he might wish to consult to represent special interests*

[b] =*The Governor-General appointed these members on the advice of the Prime Minister after the Prime Minister consulted those religious, economic or social bodies or associations from which the Prime Minister considered that such Senators should be selected*

[c] = *The President appointed Senators in his discretion from outstanding persons from economic or social or community organisations and other major fields of endeavour*

### *Table 3. Municipal and County Councils, 1946–68*

| | Number of Wards | Councillors per Ward | Total Number of Councillors | Election Procedures |
|---|---|---|---|---|
| **Municipal Councils** | | | | |
| City of Port of Spain | 5 | 3 | 15 | Each Councillor elected for a rotating three-year term; one Councillor in each Ward outgoing on Nov 3 annually |
| Borough of San Fernando | 4 | 3 | 12 | Each Councillor elected for a rotating three-year term; one Councillor in each Ward outgoing on Nov 3 annually |
| Borough of Arima | 1 | 6 | 6 | Each Councillor elected for a rotating three-year term; two Councillors outgoing on Nov 1 annually |
| **County Councils** | | | | |
| County of St George | 6 | 2 | 12 | All Councillors, outgoing at end of triennial period |
| County of Caroni | 4 | 2 | 8 | |
| County of Victoria | 5 | 2 | 10 | |
| County of St Patrick | 4 | 2 | 8 | |
| Counties of St Andrew/St David | 6 | 2 | 12 | |
| Counties of Nariva/Mayaro | 4 | 2 | 8 | |
| Ward of Tobago | 7 | 2 | 14 | |

*Source*: GORTT [1969]: 2–3

***Table 4. Municipal and County Councils, 1968–77***

| | 1968 | 1971–7 |
|---|---|---|
| Port of Spain City Council | 12 | 12 |
| Arima Borough Council | 6 | 6 |
| San Fernando Borough Council | 9 | 9 |
| St George County Council | 17 | 16 |
| Caroni County Council | 9 | 10 |
| Victoria County Council | 11 | 11 |
| St Patrick County Council | 10 | 10 |
| St Andrew-St. David County Council | 8 | 8 |
| Nariva-Mayaro County Council | 7 | 7 |
| Tobago County Council | 11 | 11 |
| **TOTAL** | **100** | **100** |

*Source*: Compiled by author from GORTT [1969]; 1972a; 1977a

***Table 5. Municipal and County Councils, 1980–7***

| | 1980 | 1983 | 1987 |
|---|---|---|---|
| Port of Spain City Council | 12 | 12 | 12 |
| Arima Borough Council | 7 | 7 | 7 |
| San Fernando Borough Council | 9 | 9 | 9 |
| Point Fortin Borough Council | 6 | 6 | 6 |
| St George West County Council | 17 | 19 | 20 |
| St George East County Council | 11 | 12 | 13 |
| Caroni County Council | 11 | 12 | 13 |
| Victoria County Council | 13 | 15 | 16 |
| St Patrick County Council | 11 | 11 | 12 |
| St Andrew/St. David County Council | 8 | 9 | 9 |
| Nariva/Mayaro County Council | 8 | 8 | 8 |
| **TOTAL** | **113** | **120** | **125** |

*Source*: Compiled by author from GORTT [1980b]; [1984b]; [1988c]

### *Table 6. Municipal and County Councils, 1992–1999*

| | 1992 | 1996–9 |
|---|---|---|
| Port of Spain Municipal Corporation | 12 | 12 |
| Arima Municipal Corporation | 7 | 7 |
| San Fernando Municipal Corporation | 9 | 9 |
| Point Fortin Municipal Corporation | 6 | 6 |
| Chaguanas Municipal Corporation | 8 | 8 |
| Diego Martin Regional Corporation | 9 | 9 |
| San Juan/Laventille Regional Corporation | 16 | 12 |
| Tunapuna/Piarco Regional Corporation | 16 | 12 |
| Sangre Grande Regional Corporation | 7 | 7 |
| Couva/Tabaquite/Talparo Regional Corporation | 15 | 11 |
| Mayaro/Rio Claro Regional Corporation | 10 | 6 |
| Princes Town Regional Corporation | 8 | 9 |
| Penal/Debe Regional Corporation | 8 | 8 |
| Siparia Regional Corporation | 8 | 8 |
| **TOTAL** | **139** | **124** |

*Source*: Compiled by author from GORTT [1993b]; GORTT [1997b]: 291–5; GORTT 1997a

**Number of seats in Tobago House of Assembly, 1980–2001**: 12 directly elected, 3 appointed by the Government of Trinidad and Tobago

# Appendix F

## REGIONAL DISTRIBUTION OF LEGISLATIVE COUNCIL AND PARLIAMENTARY SEATS, 1925-2001

| Region | 1925–38 | 1941 | 1946 | 1950 | 1956 | 1958[a] |
|---|---|---|---|---|---|---|
| North | Port of Spain; St George (2) | Port of Spain (2 members); St George (3) | North Port of Spain; South Port of Spain; St George (3) | St George West; Port of Spain North; Port of Spain South; Port of Spain East; Laventille; St Joseph; Tunapuna; St George East (8) | St George West; Port of Spain North; Port of Spain South; Port of Spain Southeast; Port of Spain Northeast; Laventille; San Juan; St Joseph; Tunapuna; St George East (10) | Port of Spain West/Diego Martin; Port of Spain East; St Ann's; St George East (4) |
| Central | Caroni (1) | Caroni (1) | Caroni (1) | Caroni North; Caroni South(2) | Caroni North; Caroni Central; Caroni South (3) | Caroni (1) |
| South | Victoria (1) | Victoria (2 Members)(2) | San Fernando; Victoria (2) | Pointe-à-Pierre; Naparima; San Fernando (3) | Pointe-à-Pierre; Naparima; San Fernando East; San Fernando West; Ortoire/ Moruga (5) | Naparima/ San Fernando; Victoria (2) |
| Deep South | St Patrick (1) | St Patrick (1) | St Patrick(1) | St Patrick West; St Patrick East(2) | St Patrick East; St Patrick Central; St Patrick West (3) | St Patrick (1) |
| East | St Andrew, St David, Nariva, and Mayaro (1) | St Andrew, St David, Nariva, and Mayaro (1) | St Andrew, St David, Nariva, and Mayaro (1) | Eastern Counties; Ortoire/ Mayaro (2) | St Andrew/St David; Nariva/ Mayaro (2) | Eastern Counties (1) |
| Tobago | Tobago (1) | Tobago (1) | Tobago (1) | Tobago (1) | Tobago (1) | Tobago (1) |
| **TOTAL** | **7** | **9** | **9** | **18** | **24** | **10** |

a = Parliament of the Federation of the West Indies

| Region | 1961 | 1966–71 | 1976 | 1981 | 1986 | 1991–2001 |
|---|---|---|---|---|---|---|
| **North** | Diego Martin; Maraval; Port of Spain North; Port of Spain South; Port of Spain East; Port of Spain West; Laventille; San Juan; Barataria; St Joseph; Tunapuna; Arima (12) | Diego Martin West; Diego Martin East; St Ann's; Port of Spain West; Port of Spain Central; Port of Spain South; Port of Spain East; Port of Spain Northeast; Laventille; Barataria; San Juan West; San Juan East; St Joseph; Tunapuna; Arima (15) | Diego Martin West; Diego Martin East; St Ann's; Port of Spain West; Port of Spain Central; Port of Spain South; Port of Spain East; Port of Spain Northeast; Laventille; Barataria; San Juan; St Joseph; Tunapuna; Arouca; Arima (15) | Diego Martin West; Diego Martin East; Diego Martin Central; St Ann's West; St Ann's East; Port of Spain North; Port of Spain South; Port of Spain East; Laventille; Barataria; San Juan; St Joseph; Tunapuna; Arouca; Arima (15) | Diego Martin West; Diego Martin East; Diego Martin Central; St Ann's West; St Ann's East; Port of Spain North; Port of Spain South; Port of Spain East; Laventille; Barataria/San Juan; St Joseph; Tunapuna; Arouca North; Arouca South; Arima (15) | Diego Martin West; Diego Martin East; Diego Martin Central; Port of Spain/St Ann's West; St Ann's East; Port of Spain South; Laventille West; Laventille East/ Morvant; Barataria/San Juan; St Joseph; Tunapuna; Arouca North; Arouca South; Arima (14) |
| **Central** | St Augustine; Caroni East; Chaguanas; Couva (4) | St Augustine; Caroni East; Chaguanas; Couva (4) | St Augustine; Caroni East; Chaguanas; Couva North; Couva South (5) | St Augustine; Caroni East; Chaguanas; Couva North; Couva South (5) | St Augustine; Caroni East; Chaguanas; Couva North; Couva South (5) | St Augustine; Caroni East; Caroni Central; Chaguanas; Couva North; Couva South (6) |
| **South** | Pointe-à-Pierre; Naparima; San Fernando East; San Fernando West; Princes Town (5) | Pointe-à-Pierre; Naparima North; Naparima South; San Fernando East; San Fernando West; Princes Town; Oropouche; Tabaquite (8) | Pointe-à-Pierre; Naparima; San Fernando East; San Fernando West; Princes Town; Oropouche; Tabaquite (7) | Pointe-à-Pierre; Naparima; San Fernando East; San Fernando West; Princes Town; Oropouche; Tabaquite (7) | Pointe-à-Pierre; Naparima; San Fernando East; San Fernando West; Princes Town; Oropouche; Tabaquite (7) | Pointe-à-Pierre; Naparima; San Fernando East; San Fernando West; Princes Town; Oropouche; Tabaquite (7) |
| **Deep South** | Point Fortin; La Brea; Fyzabad; Siparia (4) | Point Fortin; La Brea; Fyzabad; Siparia (4) | Point Fortin; La Brea; Fyzabad; Siparia (4) | Point Fortin; La Brea; Fyzabad; Siparia (4) | Point Fortin; La Brea; Fyzabad; Siparia (4) | Point Fortin; La Brea; Fyzabad; Siparia (4) |
| **East** | Toco/Manzanilla; Nariva; Ortoire/Mayaro (3) | Toco/Manzanilla; Nariva; Ortoire/Mayaro (3) | Toco/Manzanilla; Nariva; Ortoire/Mayaro (3) | Toco/Manzanilla; Nariva; Ortoire/Mayaro (3) | Toco/Manzanilla; Nariva; Ortoire/Mayaro (3) | Toco/Manzanilla; Nariva; Ortoire/Mayaro (3) |
| **Tobago** | Tobago West; Tobago East (2) | Tobago West; Tobago East (2) | Tobago West; Tobago East (2) | Tobago West; Tobago East (2) | Tobago West; Tobago East (2) | Tobago West; Tobago East (2) |
| **TOTAL** | **30** | **36** | **36** | **36** | **36** | **36** |

# *Appendix G*

## LIST OF INTERVIEWS

Lloyd Best, Leader of Tapia House Group, 1968–present; founder member of New World Group 1962–8. Series of interviews in June–September 1999.

Sheldon Daniel, Research Analyst, Government Affairs, BP Amoco, 1998–present; *Economist Intelligence Unit*, 1997–present. Series of interviews in June 1999.

Winston Dookeran, Governor, Central Bank of Trinidad and Tobago, 1997–present; Deputy Prime Minister 1988–91, Minister of Planning and Reconstruction, 1986–91. Interviewed on June 17, 1999.

Ken Gordon, Minister of Industry, Enterprise, and Tourism, NAR Government, 1986–1990; Managing Director, Trinidad Express Newspapers, Ltd. 1968–86; Executive Chairman, Caribbean Communications Network, 1991–present; Chairman Neal and Massey 1997–present. Interviewed on June 25, 1999.

Hansley Hanoomansingh, DLP Member of Parliament for Caroni East, 1966–71; National Council for Indian Culture Executive. Interviewed on June 27, 1999.

The Honourable John Humphrey, Deputy Prime Minister, Minister of Housing and Settlements, 1995–1999; Minister of Works and Transport, 1986–88. Interviewed on July 23, 1999.

Khafra Kambon, NJAC Executive, 1968–81; Chairman, Emancipation Support Committee 1993–present. Interviewed on August 18, 1999.

Dr. J. O'Neil Lewis, CMT, Ambassador to the United States, 1981–7; Ambassador to the EC, 1973–81; Acting Economic Advisor to the Government of Trinidad and Tobago, 1950–3; Public Service, 1958–65; Industrial Court, 1965–73; Deputy Chairman of the Integrity Commission of the Republic of Trinidad and Tobago, 1987–present. Interviewed on July 12, 1999.

Alloy Lequay, DLP Executive, 1960–76; NATT Executive; NAR Party Chairman. Interviewed on July 13, 1999.

Satnarine Maharaj, Secretary General, Sanathan Dharma Maha Sabha of Trinidad and Tobago, 1977–present. Interviewed on July 2, 1999.

The Honourable Patrick Manning, Prime Minister of Trinidad and Tobago, 1991–5; Leader of Opposition, 1995–present, 1987–91; Political Leader of the PNM, 1987– present. Interviewed on July 23, 27, August 3, 1999.

Kamaluddin Mohammed, Deputy Prime Minister, 1981–86; Minister of Government, 1956–86; Member of Parliament for Barataria, 1956–86. Interviewed on July 17, 1999.

Robin Moonan, Deputy Mayor of San Fernando, 1992–96; UNC candidate for Cocoyea/Tarouba, 1999 Local Government Elections. Interviewed on July 24, 1999.

Dr. Roodal Moonilal, Director, Policy Monitoring Unit, Office of the Prime Minister, 1998–present. Series of interviews in July–August 1999.

The Honourable Basdeo Panday, Prime Minister of Trinidad and Tobago, 1995–present; Deputy Prime Minister 1986–88; Leader of Opposition 1976–86, 1991–5; President General of ATS&GWTU 1974–98; founder member of WFP, ULF, NAR, UNC, NATUC. Interviewed on July 27, 1999.

His Grace The Archbishop Anthony Pantin, Archbishop of the Archdiocese of Port of Spain, 1968–2000. Interviewed on June 17, 1999.

His Excellency Arthur N.R. Robinson, President of Trinidad and Tobago, 1997–present; Prime Minister of Trinidad and Tobago, 1986–1991. Founding member of the PNM, DAC, NAR. Chief Secretary of the THA, 1980–6. Interviewed on August 16, 1999.

Dr Brinsley Samaroo, Minister of Decentralisation, 1988–91; Member of Parliament for Nariva, 1986–91; Leader of Opposition in the Senate, 1983–6. Series of interviews in July–September 1999.

Nicholas Simonette, PNM General Secretary, 1956–76; ONR Executive member. Interviewed on July 6, 1999.

# NOTES

1. UNDP 200
2. Ryan 1972
3. UNDP 2000; CBTT 2001; *EB* November 1999
4. For instance, in Ryan's pivotal text, his 'principal aim' was 'to explore the influence ... [of] cultural and ethnic diversity ... on the struggle for political and social reform and to suggest explanations for the failure of the programme of radical decolonization' (Ryan 1972: 3).
5. Manor 1991: 2–3
6. Manor 1991: 2, 6
7. Oxaal 1982; Lewis 1968
8. Oxaal 1982: xiv
9. Jerry Z. Muller, 'What is conservative social and political thought?' in *Conservatism: an anthology of social and political thought from David Hume to the present*, ed. Jerry Z. Muller, (Princeton: Princeton University Press, 1997) pp. 3–31.
10. Naipaul 1976: 271; Naipaul 1981: 207–8
11. For example, Barbados and Jamaica had been British colonies since 1627 and 1655, respectively. In contrast, Trinidad was captured by the British in 1797 and was formally ceded to Great Britain by Spain through the Treaty of Amiens in March 1802 at the end of the French Revolutionary Wars. British control of Tobago, which had been re-captured from the French in 1802, was confirmed and ratified in 1814 at the end of the Napoleonic Wars. cf. Lewis 1968: 197–8.
12. Reis 1929; Craig 1952
13. e.g., Wrong 1923; Craig 1952
14. e.g., *Developments* 1955; Ayearst 1960; Lewis 1968; Mordecai 1968
15. J. Edward Greene, 'A review of political science research in the English-speaking Caribbean: toward a methodology', *Social and Economic Studies*, 23:1 (March 1974) p. 1
16. The author was a lecturer in the Department of Sociology/Behavioural Sciences at the St. Augustine campus of the UWI from 1995–8.
17. e.g., see Munroe and Lewis 1971
18. L. Best, 'Outlines of a model of pure plantation economy', *Social and Economic Studies*, 17:3 (September 1968); Beckford 1972; Craig 1982b
19. e.g., Axline 1979; Payne 1980
20. Michael Manley was elected Prime Minister in 1972 and in 1974 declared his government's commitment to a new policy of Democratic Socialism.
21. Since its first elections under universal suffrage in 1953, Guyana had been governed by socialist and Marxist-oriented governments. Guyana gained independence in 1966, and in 1970 declared itself a Co-operative Socialist Republic.
22. The New Jewel Movement came to power through a revolutionary coup on 13 March 1979 after five years of independence.
23. e.g., Henry and Stone 1983; Payne and Sutton 1993

24. e.g., Domínguez et al. 1993; Edie 1994
25. Emmanuel 1993; LaGuerre 1997b
26. Ryan 1999b
27. Ryan 1972
28. Ryan 1972: 3
29. Ryan 1999a, 1999b, 1996, 1991, 1989a, 1989b, 1988, 1979, 1978
30. See Ryan et al. 1979; Ryan 1999a, 1999b, 1996, 1991, 1989a, 1989b
31. Ann Spackman, 'Constitutional development in Trinidad and Tobago', *Social and Economic Studies*, 4: 4 (December 1965); Ann Spackman, 'The senate of Trinidad and Tobago', *Social and Economic Studies*, 16:1 (March 1967); J.G. Verner, 'The recruitment of cabinet ministers in the former British Caribbean: a five-country study', *The Journal of Developing Areas*, 7:4 (July 1973); Hamid Ghany 'The 1995 general election and the appointment of a prime minister', In LaGuerre 1997a, 17–24; Hamid Ghany, 'Parliamentary crisis and the removal of the Speaker: the case of Trinidad and Tobago', *The Journal of Legislative Studies*, 3:2 (Summer 1997)
32. Ralph Premdas and Bishnu Ragoonath, 'Ethnicity, elections and democracy in Trinidad and Tobago: analysing the 1995 and 1996 elections', *Commonwealth and Comparative Politics*, 36:3 (November 1998); LaGuerre 1997a; John LaGuerre, 'General Elections of 1981', *Journal of Commonwealth and Comparative Politics*, 21: 2 (July 1983); John LaGuerre, 'The general elections of 1950', *Social and Economic Studies*, 29:4 (December 1980); Kevin Yelvington, 'Vote dem out: the demise of the PNM in Trinidad and Tobago', *Caribbean Review*, 15:4 (1987); Greene 'An analysis of the general elections in Trinidad and Tobago 1971', in Munroe and Lewis 1971: 136–144; Gordon Lewis, 'The Trinidad and Tobago general elections of 1961', in *The Aftermath of Sovereignty: West Indian perspectives*, ed. and introduced by David Lowenthal and Lambros Comitas, pp. 121–162
33. Deosaran 1993; Bishnu Ragoonath, 'The failure of the Abu Bakr coup: the plural society, cultural traditions and political development in Trinidad', *Journal of Commonwealth and Comparative Politics*, 31:2 (July 1993); Kathleen M. Collihan, and P. Danopoulos Constantine, 'Coup d'état attempt in Trinidad: its causes and failure', *Armed Forces and Society*, 19:3 (Spring 1993); *Caribbean Quarterly* 1991
34. Brian Meeks, 'The development of the 1970 revolution in Trinidad and Tobago', (unpublished M.Sc. thesis, University of the West Indies, Mona, Jamaica, 1976); Susan Craig, 'Background to the 1970 confrontation in Trinidad and Tobago' in Craig 1982b, vol. 2, 385–424; Oxaal 1982; Paul Sutton, 'Black Power in Trinidad and Tobago: the crisis of 1970', *The Journal of Commonwealth and Comparative Politics*, 21:2 (July 1983); Ryan and Stewart 1995
35. Kambon 1988; Ghany 1996
36. Kiely 1996
37. Malik 1971
38. Brian Meeks, 'NUFF at the cusp of an idea: grassroots guerrillas and the politics of the 1970s in Trinidad and Tobago', *Social Identities*, 5:4 (December 1999)
39. Canute Parris, 'Political dissidence in post-independence Jamaica and Trinidad: 1962–72', (unpublished Ph.D. dissertation, New School for Social Research 1976)
40. Reddock 1994
41. Carl Parris, 'Personalisation of power in an elected government: Eric Williams and Trinidad and Tobago, 1973–1981', *Journal of Inter-American Studies and World Affairs*, 25: 2 (May 1983); Carl Parris, 'Power and privilege in Trinidad and Tobago', *Social and Economic Studies*, 34:2 (June 1985); Carl Parris, 'Trinidad and Tobago 1956–86: has the political elite changed?', *The Round Table*, 314 (April 1990)

42. Craig 1974; FE Nunes, 'A ministry and its community: Tobago, a case study in participation', *Social and Economic Studies*, 23:2 (June 1974); Carl Parris, 'Chaguaramas revisited', in *The Caribbean yearbook of international relations 1975*, ed. Leslie F. Manigat, (Leyden: A.W. Sijthoff; St Augustine, Trinidad and Tobago: Institute of International Relations, 1975) ; 1976a; Carl Parris 'Size or class: factors affecting Trinidad and Tobago's foreign economic policy', In *Size, Self determination and International Relations: the Caribbean*, ed. Vaughn A. Lewis, (Mona, Jamaica: Institute of Social and Economic Research, 1976); Basil Ince, 'The media and foreign-policy formation in small states: Trinidad and Tobago', *International Journal*, 31:2 (1976); L.P. Fletcher 'Politics, public policy and Friendly Societies in Trinidad and Tobago', *Social and Economic Studies*, 39:3 (September 1990); S. Lloyd-Evans and R. Potter, 'Government response to informal sector retail trading: the People's Mall, Port of Spain, Trinidad', *Geography*, 78: 3 (1993); Ryan et al 1998
43. Ghany 1996
44. Malik 1971
45. Oxaal 1982 (originally published in 1968)
46. Bell 1967
47. Moskos 1967
48. Bell and Oxaal, 'Introduction', in Bell 1967: 1
49. Lewis 1968; Lewis, 'The Trinidad and Tobago general elections'
50. Magid 1988
51. e.g., Knight, 'Review of *urban nationalism: a study of political development in Trinidad*, by Alvin Magid', *The American Historical Review*, 95:2 (April 1990)
52. Eriksen 1992; Thomas Hylland Eriksen, 'Formal and informal nationalism', *Ethnic and Racial Studies*, 16:1 (January 1993)
53. Vera Rubin, 'Culture, politics and race relations', *Social and Economic Studies*, 11:4 (December 1962); Bahadoorsingh 1968; Malik 1971; LaGuerre 1982; Colin Clarke, 'Society and electoral politics in Trinidad and Tobago', In *Society and politics in the Caribbean*, ed. Colin Clarke, (St Antony's/Macmillan Series. Oxford: Macmillan Press, Ltd., 1991); Bishnu Ragoonath, 'Race and ethnic relations and the competition for political power in Trinidad', *Journal of Ethno Development*, 3:3 (1994); L. Dattoo, 'Ethnic conflict resolution in Trinidad and Tobago: the role of proportionality in representative bureaucracy', *Journal of Ethno Development*, 3:3 (1994); Ramesh Deosaran, 'Political management of conflict in a multicultural society', in *Choices and Change: reflections on the Caribbean*, ed. Winston C. Dookeran, (Washington, DC: Inter-American Development Bank. Distributed by Johns Hopkins University Press, Baltimore, 1996); Deryck Brown, 'Ethnic politics and public sector management in Trinidad and Guyana', *Public Administration and Development*, 19:4 (October 1999); Premdas and Ragoonath, 'Ethnicity, elections and democracy'; Ralph Premdas, 'Public policy and ethnic conflict regulation: Trinidad and Tobago', in *The Accommodation of Cultural Diversity*, ed. C. Young (London: Macmillan Press Ltd., 1999); Premdas 1996a; 1996b; Ralph Premdas, 'Public policy in a multi-ethnic state: the case of national service in Trinidad and Tobago', *Social and Economic Studies*, 45:1 (March 1996); Premdas 1993a; Ralph Premdas, 'Ethnic conflict in Trinidad and Tobago: domination and reconciliation', in *Trinidad ethnicity*, ed. Kevin Yelvington, (London: Macmillan Press Ltd., 1993); Ralph Premdas, 'Race, politics, and succession in Trinidad and Guyana' In *Modern Caribbean politics*, ed. Anthony Payne and Paul Sutton, (Baltimore: Johns Hopkins University Press, 1993)
54. One should mention here the scholarly and valuable historical-anthropological-sociological studies of Burton (1997) and Singh (1996) on the evolution of Africans and Indians, respectively, as political actors in Trinidad and Tobago.

55. Percy Hintzen, 'Trinidad and Tobago: democracy, nationalism, and the construction of racial identity', in Edie 1994: 59–74; Hintzen 1989; Percy Hintzen, 'Bases of elite support for a regime: race ideology and clientelism as bases for leaders in Guyana and Trinidad', *Comparative Political Studies*, 16: 3 (October 1983)
56. David Nicholls, 'East Indians and Black Power in Trinidad', *Race*, 12:4 (1971); Bishnu Ragoonath, 'Race and class in Caribbean politics', *Plural Societies*, 18:1 (July 1988); Ledgister 1988
57. Lloyd Best, 'Chaguaramas to slavery?' *New World Quarterly*, 2:1 (Dead Season 1965); Lloyd Best, 'The 'February revolution' in Trinidad and Tobago', In Munroe and Lewis 1971; Jose Sandoval, 'State capitalism in a petroleum based economy: the case of Trinidad and Tobago', in *Crisis in the Caribbean*, eds. Fitzroy Ambursley and Robin Cohen, (Kingston, Jamaica: Heinemann, 1983); Paul Sutton, 'Trinidad and Tobago: oil capitalism and the 'presidential power' of Eric Williams', in *Dependency under Challenge*, eds. Anthony Payne and Paul Sutton, (Manchester: Manchester University Press, 1984); Paul Sutton, 'External factors and political development in Trinidad and Tobago, 1962–1972' (unpublished Ph.D. dissertation, Victoria University of Manchester, 1979); Paul Ashley, 'The commonwealth Caribbean and the contemporary world order: the cases of Jamaica and Trinidad', in Henry and Stone 1983: 159–76; Carl Parris, 'Personalisation of power in an elected government: Eric Williams and Trinidad and Tobago, 1973–1981', *Journal of Inter-American Studies and World Affairs*, 25:2 (May 1983); Carl Parris, 'Resource ownership and prospects for democracy: the case of Trinidad and Tobago', in Henry and Stone 1983: 313–326; Dennis Pantin, 'Political crisis in Trinidad and Tobago: cause or coincidence?' *Caribbean Quarterly*, 37:2 and 3 (June–September 1991)
58. Maingot 1998
59. MacDonald 1986
60. MacDonald 1986: 1–2
61. Manor 1991: 8–9
62. Premdas, 'Ethnic conflict'
63. Williams 1969; 1981; Brassington [1975]; Gomes 1974; Mahabir 1978; Solomon 1981; Kambon 1988 (on George Weekes); Buhle 1988 (on C.L.R. James); Siewah and Moonilal 1991; Siewah and Arjoonsingh 1998 (on Basdeo Panday); Ghany 1996 (on Kamaluddin Mohammed)
64. In 1991 and 1994, a total of 57 trade union leaders, non-governmental organisation leaders, and academic-activists were interviewed on politics and development in Trinidad and Tobago (Kirk Meighoo, 'History, class, ideology, and empowerment: an examination of Servol and development in Trinidad and Tobago' [unpublished B.A. research paper, International Development Studies, University of Toronto, 1992]; Kirk Meighoo, 'Putting up a new resistance: towards an open, plural, and democratic left in Trinidad and Tobago', [unpublished M.Sc. research paper, Consortium Graduate School of Social Sciences, University of the West Indies, Mona, Jamaica, 1994]).

## CHAPTER 1

1. Central Bureau of Statistics. *West Indian Census 1946. A General Report on the Census Population.* (Kingston: Central Bureau of Statistics, [1950])
2. Brereton 1981: 16. In total, it has been estimated that 22,400 slaves were imported into Trinidad in its slaving history. This is well below the numbers imported into

Jamaica (747,500) and Barbados (387,000), for example, and represents only 1.3 per cent of slave imports into the British West Indies as a whole (1,665,000) (Yelvington 2000: 72).

3. An estimated 10,278 West Indian immigrants came to Trinidad between 1839 and 1849, while between 1871 and 1911 about 65,000 came. By 1897 there were about 14,000 Barbadians living on the island (Brereton 1981: 96–97).
4. Brereton 1981: 96–115
5. Armytage 1953: 6; also see K. Haraksingh, 'The rise and fall of Caribbean institutions', in *Violence, self and the Young Male*, ed. Arthur L. McShine, (Trinidad and Tobago: Lifeline, 1993) pp. 76–7.
6. Courlandish is a language which originated out of the Duchy of Courland (1561–1795). The Duchy of Courland is, today, incorporated in the modern states of Latvia and Lithuania.
7. Williams 1962a: 51–64, 139–166
8. *ASD* 1960; 1997
9. It should be noted that persons born in Trinidad of Indian parents were not considered as having a nationality of 'Trinidad'.
10. Brereton 1981; Williams 1962a: 65–85. A representative assembly known as the Cabildo existed in Trinidad under Spanish rule. Though it had little real powers, partly because of Spain's administrative weakness, there was a measure of local autonomy before Governor Chacon's reforms from 1786 (Williams 1962a: 17, 28–9, 46; Brereton 1981: 2–23, 73–4; Craig 1952: 77–8). In contrast, Tobago had elected representation in the Council and Assembly of Tobago for over a century, from 1763 to 1877, when the Crown Colony system was introduced there (Brereton 1981: 154–6).
11. In the 19th century, there were three municipal councils (the Port of Spain City Council, and the San Fernando and Arima Borough Councils, established in 1840, 1845, and 1888 respectively) established with a limited franchise (Craig 1952: 79). Brereton (1981: 142–157), Ryan (1972: 25–32), and Williams (1962a: 167–95) provide accounts of the 19th century reform movements and the Royal Commissions to which they made representations. The character of the movement, however, changed significantly in the early 20th century when the lower classes were brought into the agitation, through the 1903 Water Riots and the strike waves of 1919, turning many of the leading early reformers into supporters of Crown Colony government.
12. West Indies 1922: 3; McIntyre 1974: 240. T.A. Marryshow in Grenada had successfully petitioned the Secretary of State, Lord Milner, to re-introduce elective seats in the Grenadian Legislative Council after the war, encouraging numerous similar requests from the other colonies (West Indies 1922:5; Ayearst 1960: 33). In 1925, Major Wood was raised to the peerage as Baron Irwin, and was appointed viceroy of India that same year. While there, he pursued a generally liberal policy toward Indian nationalism. He returned to Britain in 1931 and in 1934 succeeded his father as 3rd Viscount Halifax. As foreign secretary (1938–40) under Neville Chamberlain, Halifax was generally associated with the policies of appeasement toward Nazi Germany.
13. West Indies 1922: 8.
14. Major Wood was not able to visit Tobago, and expressed concern that he was unable to receive the views of responsible opinion there (West Indies 1922: 25–6).
15. West Indies 1922: 22–3.
16. Interestingly, the Chamber of Commerce was at the forefront of the Trinidad constitutional reform movements in the 19th century (Williams 1962a: 216–7).

17. The deputation opposed any introduction of elected members, communal or otherwise, fearing that Indians, because of the disadvantage owing to their great undereducation, would lose their lone representative, Reverend C.D. Lalla, in the existing nominated Council (West Indies 1922: 24–5; Craig 1952: 31). The importation of indentured Indian labour ended only in 1917. Their fear was unwarranted, however, as since 1928 there were never less than two out of the seven elected members in the Legislative Council who were Indian. In 1946 four of the nine elected members were Indian, and in 1950 seven of the 18 elected members were Indian (Craig 1952: 85–6).
18. The TWA delivered the Address of Welcome to Major Wood upon his arrival in Trinidad on January 23, 1922. Major Wood stayed until February 2 and visited the island again on February 13–4 (West Indies 1922: 97).
19. West Indies 1922: 23–4
20. This was also recommended for the Windward Islands of St Vincent, St Lucia, and Dominica. Barbados, British Guiana. Jamaica already had representation, and Grenada's request had been approved. Elected representatives were not recommended for St Kitts and Antigua.
21. West Indies 1922: 26–7
22. Williams 1962a: 218; Ann Spackman, 'Constitutional development in Trinidad and Tobago', *Social and Economic Studies*, 14:4 (December 1965) p. 284
23. *Blue Book* 1925: 118–121. These posts (including the Protector of Immigrants, which oversaw the welfare of the Indians) were all in existence until 1941, when only the Attorney-General, Colonial Secretary, and Treasurer were retained (see Appendix F).
24. *Blue Book* 1925: 118–121.
25. Craig 1952: 43–5.
26. French patois had been the *lingua franca* among the rural and lower classes of the Creoles, while immigrants from the Middle East, Portugal, India, China, and Africa were often uncomfortable speaking English. For example, the local Magistracy officially employed Hindi, Creole-French, and Tamil interpreters in almost all districts. Among the income and property qualifications were an annual salary of £62 10s., or ownership of property of £12 10s. rateable value in a borough or £10 elsewhere (*Blue Book* 1925: 118–121).
27. Craig 1952: 68; Brereton 1981: 166; Spackman, 'Constitutional development', p. 284. Candidates had to own real estate to the value of £2,500 or derive £200 per annum therefrom; or must have had an income of over £400 per annum from any source. If they did not reside in the district for one year, they needed to own therein real estate of £5,000 in value or giving an income of £400 per annum (*Blue Book* 1925: 118–121).
28. Williams 1962a: 220; *Blue Book* 1925: 118–121. The two uncontested seats were Victoria and the Eastern Counties, which together contained 6,162 registered voters.
29. Singh (1994: 124–57) gives an excellent social history of the period, with a chapter ('Politics and Representation') focusing on the personalities, rivalries, and campaigns the period 1925–45.
30. Craig 1952: 66.
31. Eric Williams argued with regard to the 1950 elections that choices were made on the basis of 'personal attainments, charitable donations, racial origin' (quoted in Samaroo 2000: 6). Naipaul's (1969) fictionalised account of the 1950 General Elections, in which his uncle, Simbhoonath Capildeo, was a candidate for Patrick Solomon's Caribbean Socialist Party (CSP), provides an excellent, even if satirical,

insight into this type of local politicking. A brief account of the elections of 1933 and 1938 is provided by LaGuerre (1982: 19–30), which corroborates Naipaul's burlesque. Craig (1952: 67–91, 107–41) illustrates the absence of organised 'sides' in proceedings of the Council.

32. Naipaul 1995a: 83–4.
33. Craig 1952: 69–79.
34. Craig 1952: 69–79. Cipriani was Mayor in 1929–31, 1933–5, and 1938–9. In the borough and city councils, elections were held annually on November 1 and 3, for rotating three year terms. His impact on the development of Trinidadian nationalism is discussed in Lewis (1968: 203–7), Brereton (1981: 164–72), Oxaal (1982: 53–5), Ryan (1972: 28–43) and Williams (1962a: 222–3). In 1932 a political biography of Cipriani written by C.L.R. James, now out of print, was published in England with the financial assistance of Learie Constantine (Buhle 1988: 41; James 1932). A collection of his speeches was published soon after his death (Cipriani [1945]).
35. Craig 1952: 67–91; Brinsley Samaroo, 'The Trinidad Workingmen's Association and the origins of popular protest in a Crown Colony', *Social and Economic Studies*, 21:2 (June 1972) p. 205. Since 1925, Teelucksingh continuously held his Caroni seat, the only seat to be contested in all four elections of the period. Roodal held his seat continuously from 1928.
36. Craig 1952: 107–41.
37. While not large figures by international standards, it remains one of the most violent events in Trinidad and Tobago's history. Brereton (1981: 180) and Singh (1987: 62–7) provide good accounts of the disturbances. The Forster Commission of 1937, too, had investigated the events in Trinidad with a narrower focus on industrial relations (Johnson 1987: 277). A contemporary and sympathetic account was provided by a British observer, titled *Glory Dead* (Calder-Marshall 1939). A later publication is Jacobs (1976).
38. Craig-James 1987: 119–22
39. *West India* 1945: xiii. The Report did not place priority on political solutions and saw the problems as social, economic, and, above all, agricultural (*West India* 1945: 422). Although the Report was released to the public in June 1945, a summary was published in February 1940, apparently as a confidential document in the Colonial Office (Colonial Office 1947: 1; Samaroo 1973: 13).
40. *Annual Report* 1958: 127.
41. *TTYB* 1946: 146.
42. *Annual Report* 1958: 127; Ayearst 1960: 82; Craig 1952: 146–8; Samaroo 1973: 10, 13; Brereton 1981: 193.
43. Craig 1952: 153.
44. COTT 1947b. Universal adult franchise without an English literacy test was pushed through by the Colonial Office in London, contravening the 33-member Franchise Committee's Majority Report which had been supported by the Legislative Council, the Executive Council, and the Governor. Many Indians had opposed the Majority Report's recommendation of an English literacy test, claiming that it would have disproportionately disenfranchised their group (Samaroo 1973: 20–35).
45. COTT 1947b: 41–2.
46. Samaroo, 'The making of the 1946 Constitution', pp. 13–20. Samaroo provides an excellent overview of the debates and positions surrounding the reforms.
47. Brereton (1981: 175–6, 223–7), Gomes (1974: 17–9, *passim*) and Lewis (1968: 222–3) give good accounts of the social and cultural developments of the period. Cipriani

and the TLP condemned the Butler riots, dissociated themselves from the strikers, and advised the protesters to adopt constitutional measures (Brereton 1981: 181). Gordon Lewis (1968: 207) laments the decline of Cipriani's influence, describing the period 1938–56 as 'the nadir of Trinidadian life'.

48. Susan Craig-James, 'Smiles and blood: The ruling class response to the workers' rebellion of 1937 in Trinidad and Tobago', in Thomas 1987: 88. Though racial aspects of the 1937 disturbance are commonly acknowledged, Naipaul (1995b: 69–102) suggests that the riots were fundamentally racial, and provoked passions accordingly.
49. Beryl McBurnie in dance and Albert Gomes, C.L.R. James, Ralph deBoissière, and Alfred Mendes in literature were among the most notable.
50. James 1994.
51. Malik 1971: 9–10, 23; Ghany 1996: 11–46. The El Socorro Tackveeyatul Islamic Association, Islamia school – the first state-funded, non-Christian denominational school in Trinidad and Tobago – was opened on March 3, 1949.
52. Brereton 1981: 191–2. Indeed, future Hindu Indian leader Bhadase Maraj – shoeless country Indian turned millionaire by the age of 28 – had amassed his wealth through entrepreneurship in connection with the bases (*Master and Servant* 1991: 18–21)
53. COTT 1947b: 5–8. The Supervisor of Elections attributed the low turnout to unusually heavy and continuous rainfall.
54. COTT 1947b: 5; John LaGuerre, 'The general elections of 1946 in Trinidad and Tobago', *Social and Economic Studies*, 21: 2 (June 1972) p. 197; *TG* May 26, 1946, supp., p. 1. Dr E. de Verteuil of the Progressive Democratic Party withdrew from the Butler-Gomes contest in North Port of Spain.
55. *TG* May 26, 1946, supp., p. 1. The TUC and SP was a southern-based alliance between the Trades Union Council and the Oilfield Workers' Trade Union. The UF was an urban-based coalition of Patrick Solomon's West Indian National Party, Albert Gomes's Federated Workers Trade Union, the Negro Welfare, Cultural and Social Association, and the Indian National Council (Craig 1952: 154).
56. *TG* May 26, 1946, supp., p. 1.
57. COTT 1947b.
58. COTT 1947b; *TG* May 26, 1946, supp., p. 1.
59. After losing the election for the extra Port of Spain seat in 1941, Gomes won the Port of Spain by-election after Cipriani's death in 1945 (*TTYB* 1947: 146). In 1946, Butler moved out of his area of influence in St Patrick to contest the Port of Spain seat. He lost to Gomes by 5,212 votes to 1,984.
60. COTT [1947a]: 5; *Annual Report* 1956: 130; *Blue Book* 1933: 101–9.
61. COTT [1947a]: 5.
62. *TG* October 29, 1946, p. 1.
63. Craig 1952: 154–5.
64. Appointed to the Executive Council were Albert Gomes and Roy Joseph from the UF, C.C. Abidh of the TUC and SP, and Timothy Roodal of the Butler Party/TLP. Members not appointed were Patrick Solomon (UF member for South Port of Spain), Chanka Maharaj (BECWHRP member for St. George, and a popular wrestler), Ranjit Kumar, Victor Bryan (TUC and SP member for Eastern Counties), and APT James (BECWHRP member for Tobago).
65. Brereton 1981: 196–7; Ryan 1972: 158; Craig 1952: 155–6.
66. Quoted in LaGuerre, 'The general elections of 1946', p. 189.
67. LaGuerre, 'The general elections of 1946', p. 189.
68. Quoted in Ryan 1972: 79.

69. Gomes was a popular politician well known for his support of local writers, the Spiritual Baptists, the steelband movement, calypsonians, and trade unions. In 1945 he won the Port of Spain seat left vacant by Cipriani's death (Gomes 1974).
70. Quoted in Ryan 1972: 77–8.
71. Quoted in Craig 1952: 67–8.
72. See Williams (1955c), Solomon (1981: 32), Ryan (1972: 84), Brereton (1981: 196). However, it must be noted that Barbados and Jamaica had developed national party-based politics under similar constitutional constraints.
73. *Annual Report* 1958: 128.
74. The Secretary of State for the Colonies reduced the nominated element in contradiction to the recommendations of the Reform Committee's Majority Report, which recommended that the number remain the same (Craig 1952: 159).
75. In 1946, for example, St George had an electorate of 65,351 while Tobago had an electorate of 11,509 (COTT 1947b: 13–4).
76. *Annual Report* 1958: 128; *TTYB* 1952: 163; Spackman, 'Constitutional development', p. 285; Brereton 1981: 196, 198; Ryan 1972: 79–85. Spackman (1965: 285–7), Williams (1962a: 237–41) Craig (1952:160) and Ryan (1972: 79–89) give good accounts of the Majority Report, the Minority Report by Dr. Patrick Solomon, who called for greater responsibility, and that of Ranjit Kumar, who called for a balance between responsibility and the protection of minorities through the nomination system and proportional representation. According to a letter by Dr David T. Pitt, former President of the West Indian National Party, published in *The Economist* of February 26, 1949, the majority report of the Constitutional Reform Committee was 'considered unacceptable to the mass of Trinidadians. This is borne out by the fact that all of the municipalities, 5 of the 7 county councils, the Trades Union Council, and all the trade unions individually, and the people at mass meetings in all the large centres of population, passed resolutions calling for responsible government along the lines of the Solomon minority report.'
77. COTT [1951].
78. Under the new constitution, restrictions on membership were relaxed slightly, as it was no longer necessary for a member to be registered as a voter. Also, members were no longer required to write English, but to speak and 'read the English language with a degree of proficiency sufficient to enable him to take an active part in the proceedings of the Legislative Council' (COTT [1951]: 73).
79. *TG* September 17, 1950, p. 22.
80. Gomes was returned to Port of Spain North on a PPG ticket, James to Tobago on a Butler Party-CSP ticket, Roy Joseph (formerly of the UF) as an independent to San Fernando, Chanka Maharaj (former member for St George) to St Joseph on a Butler Party ticket, Ranjit Kumar (former member for Victoria) to Caroni North as an independent, and Victor Bryan (formerly of the TUC and SP) to the Eastern Counties on a CSP ticket. Patrick Solomon lost his former Port of Spain South seat to Norman Tang. C.C. Abidh and Legislative Council member since 1928 Timothy Roodal also lost their seats. John LaGuerre, 'The general elections of 1950', *Social and Economic Studies*, 29: 4 (December 1980) analyses the 1950 elections, noting that apart from constitutional issues, the candidates' appeals were localised. In these localised contexts, in the absence of strong parties, race, ideology, leadership, organisation, financial resources, academic qualifications, and kin relations were all important considerations in electoral success.
81. *TG* September 19, 1950, p.1. If a candidate received less than one-eighth of the votes cast, he lost his deposit.

82. Craig 1952: 167. James vacillated quite a bit. After his election victory, he denied that he was a member of Butler's Party. He argued, 'It is my fervent belief that insofar as Tobago is concerned, the member for Tobago should remain unobligated to any specific party. I am a member of the Tobago Political and Economic Party and my policy will be to support progressive legislation regardless of any party politics' (*TG* September 21, 1950, p. 7). In the 1953 County Council elections, he headed the Tobago Citizens' Political and Economic Party, which won only five of the 14 Tobago seats (*TG* February 3, 1953, p. 1).
83. They were appointed Ministers of Education and Social Services; Health and Local Government; Communications and Works; Labour, Industry, and Commerce; and Agriculture and Lands, respectively.
84. In 1953 in British Guiana, the People's Progressive Party (PPP), led by Guyanese Indian, trade union leader and Marxist, Cheddi Jagan, had won the first elections under mass suffrage in that colony. It would have been surprising if this development had not spurred the organisation of the PDP.
85. *Annual Report* 1958: 130
86. COTT 1959b
87. *TG* February 3, 1953, p. 1
88. Ayearst 1960: 41, 89; Lewis 1968: 181–6, 234–48

## CHAPTER 2

1. Ghany 1996: 80–3; Spackman, 'Constitutional development', p. 287; COTT 1958.
2. Spackman, 'Constitutional development', pp. 287–8. Pope Wilberforce McLean, T.U.B. Butler, A.P.T. James, Stephen C. Maharaj, and Bhadase Maraj voted against the extension.
3. Ghany 1996: 83
4. Ryan 1972: 99–101; Ghany 1996: 82. The suspension of the constitution in British Guiana in 1953, six months after the victory of the People's Progressive Party (PPP), led by the trade union leader, Marxist, and ethnic Indian, Cheddi Jagan, on the grounds that the PPP government had sought to establish a communist government in the colony, perhaps also provided a background for the alleged British apprehension of the PDP's potential ascension to power. Indeed, under the PPP Government, Guyana decided not to join the emerging Federation of the West Indies. Some observers blame the PPP's rejection of Federation on Indian apprehension of Negro domination.
5. Ayearst 1960: 234. Two members of the Butler Party also voted against the motion.
6. Williams 1969; Sutton 1981
7. Williams 1969:105
8. Williams 1969: 106–11; Mahabir 1978: 17–9, Oxaal 1982: 101, 106; Ghany 1996: 69–70, 101, 106
9. Oxaal 1982: 103
10. Williams 1968: v
11. Williams 1969: 86–92, 107, 113
12. These talks seem to have been sponsored by Albert Gomes (Samaroo 2000: 6).
13. Williams 1969: 113–4
14. Oxaal (1982: 104–5) gives a wonderfully vivid account revealing the prejudices, fears, hopes and tumult surrounding the debates.
15. quoted in Oxaal 1982: 104–5

16. Oxaal 1982: 106
17. In which he declared, 'I have become the centre of a lively and encouraging movement for an enlightened democracy ... and an active programme of community education,' specifically referring to the formation of the Committee on Education for Citizenship.
18. Williams 1969: 118–126
19. Ghany 1996: 81. That year, Williams had written draft manifestos for three still-born political parties: the Independent Labour Party, the United People's Movement, and the National Party. Important ideas in these manifestos emerged almost word for word in the PNM's People's Charter in 1956 (Samaroo 2000: 9, 16–7).
20. Oxaal 1982: 108. For an excellent account of the specific work undertaken by the PEG, see Samaroo (2000: 14–6), who has used materials only recently made publicly available in the Eric Williams Collection at the St Augustine Campus of the University of the West Indies, opened on March 22, 1998.
21. Williams 1969: 114–5
22. Ghany 1996: 81; Ayearst 1960: 86
23. Williams 1969: 127, 131; Oxaal 1982: 108; Mahabir 1978: 18–9
24. Williams 1981: 269–80
25. The word is used quite regularly in Trinidad to describe the boisterous, argumentative, and slight manner in which matters are habitually conducted.
26. Williams 1969: 141
27. Oxaal 1982: 112–3
28. In his August-September report to the Secretary of State, Governor Beetham had estimated an average peak attendance of 619 in the eight lectures since September (in Ghany 1996: 84).
29. Williams 1955a; 1955b; 1955c; 1955d; 1955e
30. Williams 1981: 108
31. Williams 1955b: 1
32. Williams 1955b
33. Ghany 1996: 75, 80
34. Oxaal 1968: 114; Williams 1969: 136.
35. Quoted in Ghany 1996: 80
36. Ghany 1996: 81–4
37. On October 8 he left for Geneva to attend an International Confederation of Free Trade Unions Conference on Plantation Labour, where he squared off with Albert Gomes, who had been an official delegate (Williams 1969: 141; Oxaal 1982:114–5).
38. Quoted in Malik 1971: 92
39. Williams 1969: 141–4
40. Williams 1962a: 242; PNM 1966a: 1–15
41. PNM 1966a: 1–4, 13–4
42. PNM 1966a: 21–40
43. Williams 1969: 148
44. Williams 1969: 149–50.
45. *TG* February 22, 1956, p. 1. The Butler Party won three seats in St Patrick County and one in Victoria. Maraj entered 20 candidates, with the winners taking five seats in Caroni, four in St George, two in St. Andrew/St David, two in Victoria, and one in St Patrick.
46. COTT 1959a: 6
47. Williams 1969: 152–61; PNM 1966a: 43–52
48. *PNM Weekly* July 2, 1956: 7

49. *Annual Report* 1958: 129; *TTYB* 1957: 163; Ayearst 1960: 86; Spackman 1965: 288; COTT 1958: 5
50. Spackman 1965: 288–9; Ryan 1972: 99
51. Williams 1969: 159
52. Ghany 1996: 87–8
53. The possible exception is the Butler Party's contesting of all 18 seats in the 1950 general elections. But A.P.T. contested on both a CSP and Butler Party ticket, and denied that he belonged to either party after he was elected. Solomon (1981: 130) argues that the Butler candidates were only loosely affiliated to the party, and so could not be counted as a national movement in the same way as the PNM. In any case, it is notable that up to the time of writing the PNM has remained the only party in Trinidad and Tobago to consistently contest every seat in every election since its founding.
54. Williams 1962a: 237
55. Oxaal 1982: 115. The fact that the two were medical doctors, however, highlighted Williams's distinction even among Island Scholars.
56. Ghany 1996: 32–3, 53. Started in 1947, this programme had been of great significance as it was the first Indian radio broadcast in Trinidad and Tobago, and Mohammed steadfastly had used it to promote Hindu-Muslim unity.
57. Williams 1969: 161
58. Ryan (1972: 128–62) describes the election campaigns of the other parties as well.
59. Before the PNM's existence, for example, Craig (1952: 167–8) wrote, 'The Indian community in Trinidad appears to be, at the time of writing, the most united political force in the colony . . . . Nationalist feeling among the coloured population is of more recent origin, lacking the intensity of Indian nationalist sentiment, and the racial unity of the negro has not yet found equally effective expression in political form.' Notably, 'The Rise of Creole Nationalism', is the major theme of Oxaal's (1982) seminal work, providing his book's subtitle.
60. Writing in 1953, Braithwaite (1975: 41–68) provides an excellent ethnography of this class.
61. Oxaal 1982: 100–1; Farquhar 1988: 28; Naipaul 1995b: 11–41; Gomes 1974: 173–7
62. Most scholars and participants, including Malik (1971: 93–4), Brassington ([1975]: 59–60) and PNM members Mohammed (1988) and Mahabir (1978: 30–6), have agreed that racialism, sometimes aggressive, had been noticeably heightened in the campaign of 1956. Ryan (1972: 128–62), Gomes (1974: 159–60, 173–5: 237), Farquhar (1988: 28) further contend that communalism was the most important aspect of the elections. Gomes (1974: 161–75), Solomon (1981: 75), LaGuerre (1982); Bahadoorsingh (1968); Oxaal (1982: 84–5) give accounts of the at least occasionally predominant influence of race in politics before 1956.
63. PNM 1966a: 17–52
64. Malik (1971: 51–68, 161) provides an excellent summary of Indian cultural and political attitudes, which included fear of miscegenation, and simple opposition to the PNM on parochial, racial grounds. The Catholic Church opposed the PNM on theological grounds, but were also fearful of a militant Negro ascension to power, no doubt. The hierarchy of the Catholic Church were mainly Irish expatriates at the time; only in 1968 did a Trinidad-born Archbishop come to lead the Archdiocese.
65. Gomes (1974: 182) had frankly noted, 'The less hermetic, more extrovert Negro was cherished as such by [the local whites] as the devil they knew'.

66. Williams 1969: 151; Ryan 1972: 129–132, 148; Malik 1971: 88; *TG* July 8, 1956, p. 8
67. *TG* July 3, 1956, p. 1
68. The instability following Cheddi Jagan and the People's Progressive Party's capture of government in British Guyana in 1953 probably provided a subtext to this warning.
69. *TG* July 4, 1956, p. 2
70. *TG* July 4, 1956, p. 1–2
71. *TG* July 11, 1956, p. 9
72. Famously, on the eve of the general elections, the *Sunday Guardian* (September 23, 1956, p. 22) published a centre spread with large head shots, side by side, of Eric Williams and Adolf Hitler, under the headline, 'Heil Williams?' On the same page ran another headline, 'PNM Constitution Denies God: Party Policy Urges Ultra-Nationalism.' The PNM organised a rally that evening denouncing the piece (Williams 1969, 163).
73. *TG* July 1, 1956, p. 5; July 8, 1956, pp. 9, 13; September 2, 1956, p. 14; September 18, 1956, p. 2
74. Ryan 1972:149–55, 235; Williams 1969:163; Ghany 1996: 86–7
75. TG September 2, 1956, p. 14
76. Ryan 1972: 132–8
77. TG July 8, 1956, p. 9
78. TG September 2, 1956, p. 1
79. TG July 15, 1956, p. 9
80. *TG* July 22, 1956, p. 10
81. Free speech in Woodford Square, the article reported, had been one of his motions in the City Council, and on one spectacular occasion seven policemen had to drag him out of the Council Chamber on account of his protests. On another occasion, he and others were charged in court for defying orders not to speak in the Square, and won the case in the Privy Council.
82. *TG* September 1, 1956, p. 1
83. Cf. Naipaul's (1995a: 48–56) brilliant analysis of Trinidadians' characteristic alertness to new fads as central to their own brand of 'modernity'.
84. *TG* September 2, 1956, p. 9
85. *TG* September 16, 1956, p. 9
86. Founded on June 14, 1956, following the February 1956 Federal Conference in London (Ayearst 1960: 223).
87. At that point, Trinidad and Tobago had been the only territory in the West Indies which was not represented in the WIFLP.
88. *TG* September 4, 1956, p. 1
89. Quoted in Ghany 1996: 89
90. Ghany 1996: 89–90
91. Williams (1969: 163) boasted that on the eve of the election, after the large Woodford Square meeting called to denounce the equation of Hitler with himself in that day's *Sunday Guardian*, he was astonished at the large crowd's swift and unquestioning compliance with his advice to 'go home right away and stay off the streets on election day after voting'.
92. The other three defeated were Aubrey James in Port of Spain Southeast (who changed affiliation from the TLP to the Butler Party), Raymond Quevedo (the calypsonian 'Atilla the Hun') in Laventille, and Chanka Maharaj in St Joseph (who changed from the Butler Party to contest as an independent).

93. Williams 1969: 165
94. COTT 1958: 23
95. Interestingly, this provides a counterpoint for scholars such as Ryan (1972) and Bahadoorsingh (1968) who argue that the main contest had been between Negroes, represented by the PNM, and Indians, represented by the PDP. The electoral data show that the PNM polled a respectable 39.8 per cent of the votes in the three Caroni constituencies of central Trinidad, the sugar-belt and Hindu heartland. Indeed, it was in St Patrick Central and St Patrick East where the PNM seemed to have special difficulty securing candidates, declaring them sometime after August 14 (Ghany 1996: 87–8). According to the 1946 Census, the proportion of Indians was 68.2 per cent in Caroni, 42.4 per cent in St. Patrick, and 50.4 per cent in the Eastern Counties (Central Bureau of Statistics 1949).
96. Ghany 1996: 99–100; Constitution Commission 1991: 11
97. Spackman, 'Constitutional development', pp. 290–1
98. Ghany 1996: 95–6
99. Williams 1969: 167
100. Williams 1969: 168
101. Solomon 1981: 50. First hand accounts of this term from the ex-Cabinet members (and Island Scholars) Williams (1969: 168–288), Mahabir (1978: 43–220), and Solomon (1981: 147–202), from opposition party members Gomes (1974: 191–223) and Brassington ([1975]: 1–124), a retold account from Cabinet Minister Mohammed (Ghany 1996: 95–160), and evaluations from Ryan (1972: 171–336) and Malik (1971: 128–141), allow an exceptionally full and many-sided view of the period.
102. Williams 1969: 168
103. Mahabir 1978: 45; Solomon 1981: 150–7
104. Mahabir 1978: 45–6, 93–8; Solomon 1981: 150–7; Ryan 1972: 174
105. T.U.B. Butler (St Patrick West) and AC Alexis (St Patrick Central) were the two that did not join (Solomon 1981, 124). Alexis later joined the PNM, and Butler started to give Williams vocal support, expressed on more than a few occasions with an anti-Indian sentiment (Ryan 1972, 182, Malik 1971, 100).
106. The West Indian Federal Constitution had come into effect on July 31, 1957 by an Act of the British Parliament, following the original Order in Council passed on August 2, 1956 (Ayearst 1960: 237).
107. Malik 1971: 98–9
108. Solomon 1981: 174–5; Brassington [1975]: 32, 46. The existence of the PNM seems to have consolidated the opposition. Even in the 1956 elections, the average number of contestants per seat declined from eight per seat in 1950 to five in 1956, and the ratio of independents to party candidates was 39 to 90 in 1956, as opposed to 90 independents to 51 party candidates in 1950. At least 71 candidates lost their deposits in 1956.
109. For instance, the DLP had issued no special policy pronouncements at their inaugural Conference (Malik 1971: 98).
110. Malik 1971: 98–9; Brassington [1975]: 52–6. More than a few persons were of the view that the PNM stimulated Negro chauvinism. Stephen Maharaj, from the Butler Party, had described regular racial harassment of opposition members by government supporters in the public areas of the Legislative Council after the PNM victory (quoted in Malik 1971: 96).
111. Brassington ([1975]: 46–56), Malik (1971: 129, 134) and Ryan (1972: 176–9) provide examples of the party's productive interventions in the Council in the matters of

public utility management, constitutional provision of minority safeguards, financial and administrative impropriety, and the threatening, intolerant attitudes sometimes expressed by Williams.

112. The most important early attempts to destabilise the PNM Government included the 'Car Loans' crisis started on May 31, 1957 by DLP member Ashford Sinanan who had accused Cabinet members Patrick Solomon and Donald Granado of financial impropriety, leading to an embarrassing, dishonourable and extended court action only resolved in 1961, in the PNM's favour. C.L.R. James in an early 1958 speech (*PNM Weekly* May 19, 1958, 1) dismissed the DLP, noting that the hostility that the industrialists and commercialists had shown to the development of nationalism prevented the emergence of a true right-wing, conservative party.
113. Williams 1969: 214–5, 252–9; Malik 1971: 128–159; Mahabir 1978: 93–98, Ryan 1972: 174–9, 183
114. Williams (1969: 204–245) provides an excellent, though perhaps biased, overview of the issue and its developments. Sir John Mordecai (1968: 107–23), former Deputy Governor-General of the Federation of the West Indies, also gives an inside account of the Chaguaramas affair.
115. Williams 1969: 213–25; Ghany 1996: 114
116. Williams 1969: 209
117. Williams 1969: 214–5; Ryan 1972: 176–9; Maraj 2001: 95–107. In the 1957 motion, the *ex-officio* members, Acting Colonial Secretary Ellis Clarke and Attorney-General Clifford de Lisle Inniss, along with T.U.B. Butler (St Patrick West) and A.C. Alexis (independent, St Patrick Central) voted with the PNM members, defeating the motion 18 to seven. In the 1958 motion, Colonial Secretary Solomon Hochoy, Butler, and Alexis voted with the PNM again, defeating the motion 17 to six.
118. The PNM won the Tobago seat, leaving it with only three seats in Trinidad: Port of Spain West/Diego Martin, Port of Spain East, and St Ann's. The DLP won all other seats, including St George East in which the borough of Arima was included. The PNM were affiliated to the WIFLP, which narrowly beat the federal DLP by 24 to 20, with the remaining seat going to the Barbados National Party. In Jamaica, the DLP also won more seats than the WIFLP, 11 to six (Ayearst 1960: 214–5).
119. It should be noted that Municipal elections were held annually in Port of Spain (five seats), San Fernando (four seats), and Arima (two seats) (Williams 1969: 274–6).
120. For example see the *PNM Weekly* (March 3, 1958, pp. 2, 4).
121. Brassington [1975]: 16, 20; Ghany 1996: 111–2. Butler contested the St Patrick constituency, but lost to the DLP candidate, M. Hussein Shah, who gained 14,947 votes compared to his 12,235. The PNM candidate, Dr Martin Sampath, received 7,944 votes.
122. One of the Jamaican PNP Government's two recommendations was also overruled (Ghany 1996: 106–111)
123. The DLP controlled St David/St Andrew, Nariva-Mayaro, Caroni, Victoria, and St Patrick. The PNM controlled St George and Tobago (COTT 1959b: 11–5). The Butler Party captured both seats in the ward of La Brea in St Patrick.
124. Brassington [1975]: 26–32; Malik 1971: 101; Williams 1969: 276
125. Brassington [1975]: 44. On his visit to Trinidad for the opening of the Federal Parliament on April 22, 1958, Minister of State for Colonial Affairs, John Profumo, had been briefed by Governor Beetham on the alleged exclusion of 'non-Negro Ministers' from the PNM's inner party discussions on constitutional reform. On April 24, both the Governor and the Minister of State raised the issue in discussions

with the Chief Minister (Ghany 1996: 112–4). Brassington ([1975]: 108–116) also tells of a CIA agent who had, in March–April 1960, allegedly offered half a million US dollars to fund the Gomes-Brassington faction of the DLP.

126. Williams 1969: 170–2; Solomon 1981: 158–66; Brassington [1975]: 43–6, 72–7. Attending those talks were Patrick Solomon, Ellis Clarke, C.A. Thomasos, W.W. Alexander, Albert Gomes, Simbhoonath Capildeo, Stephen Maharaj, Lionel Seukeran, and T.U.B. Butler. Learie Constantine joined at one meeting, and Sir Edward Beetham at a number (Colonial Office 1960: 10).
127. Solomon 1981: 166
128. Colonial Office 1960; Constitution Commission 1991: 11
129. For example, the borough of Arima was included in St George East, and San Fernando was combined with Naparima. However, on October 23, 1957 the PNM-dominated Legislative Council approved the regulations defining the ten constituencies, with no negative resolutions (COTT 1959: v).
130. *PNM Weekly* April 21, 1958
131. Mahabir 1978: 76–89
132. *TG* April 13, 1958, p. 2
133. *PNM Weekly* June 2, 1958, p. 6
134. Mahabir 1978: 79–80
135. PNM 1966a: 138–56
136. Williams 1969: 267
137. Williams 1960a: 19–21. James, however, was expelled from the party on October 2, 1960 on charges of mismanagement (Williams 1969, 267–8). James (1984) has written his side of his relations with the PNM, interpreting the split in political-philosophical terms.
138. Williams 1969: 225–235
139. McIntyre 1974: 212
140. Malik 1971, 132; Spackman, 'Constitutional development', pp. 294–8, 308; Mordecai 1968: 236–44; Constitution Commission 1991: 12. Attending those meetings were Patrick Solomon, Learie Constantine, Ellis Clarke, W. Alexander, Rudranath Capildeo, A.P.T. James, and J.P. Hutchison (Colonial Office 1960).
141. Williams 1969: 172
142. Williams 1969: 235–45. There was one other major development after the March for Independence and Chaguaramas. This was the emergence of a Concordat between the Church and State, announced on Christmas Day 1960, bringing the denominational schools under Government scrutiny in order to properly administer the introduction of free secondary school education and a Common Entrance Examination, originally announced on March 23 in the 1960 Budget (Williams 1960b: 11–2; Ryan 1972: 232–7).
143. Malik 1971: 98; Ryan 1972: 176, 183. Williams also did not contest the Federal Elections (Ayearst 1960: 224). This prevailing aloofness was partly a reaction to the limited jurisdiction and financial resources over which the West Indian Federation had authority, about which the *PNM Weekly* (March 3, 1958, p. 2) expressed extreme dissatisfaction.
144. Brassington [1975]: 13–4, 32–7
145. Malik 1971: 99
146. Brassington [1975]: 36–7, 61–4; Malik 1971: 105
147. Brassington [1975]: 32–40, 58–70
148. Brassington [1975]: 91; Malik 1971: 105

149. Malik 1971: 106
150. Malik 1971: 106
151. Dr Capildeo had made only small incursions into politics before – writing the 1953 PDP manifesto and giving public lectures on Hinduism (Brassington [1975]: 22, 81–2) – so he had a relatively unspoiled reputation. The comic phrase 'Doctor Politics' was apparently coined by DLP member Romalho Gomes to describe this strategy (Brassington ([1975]: 88).
152. Brassington [1975]: 88–98
153. Romalho Gomes was an unsuccessful candidate for the TLP-NDP in Port of Spain Northeast in 1956.
154. Brassington [1975]: 98–124
155. Williams 1960c: 8–9, 11
156. Malik 1971: 110–2; Solomon 1981: 182–94; Williams 1969: 253–4
157. GOTT 1963b: 6. Simbhoonath Capildeo's objections in Parliament are reprinted in Siewah 1994: 49.
158. Malik 1971: 114–20; Ghany 1996: 153. Indian Cabinet Ministers Mohammed (Ghany 1996: 153–4) and Mahabir (1978: 76–81, 138) recalled racism directed at them from within the PNM itself. Mahabir, it seems, retired from politics in 1961 partly because of the race issue (Mahabir 1978: 137–142).
159. Williams 1962b. On April 28, 1961, Williams (1969: 249) had also criticised the small Tobago Independence Movement as 'an attempt to maintain racial discrimination in Tobago'. On December 1, 1961 Williams (1969: 276) continued to maintain that the dominant issue of the election was 'the PNM versus the old Massa-dominated society of colonialism'.
160. As partial evidence, Malik (1971: 16) quotes a 1960 study by Arthur Niehoff which found that in St Patrick, with an Indian population of 43 per cent, only three out of 150 constables were Indian.
161. Malik 1971: 112, 117–8; Siewah 1994: 105–7; Ghany 1996: 152–7
162. For examples, see Malik (1971: 107–9), also Oxaal (1982: 159–73) who sympathetically reveals Capildeo's mental infirmity.
163. In Siewah 1994: 106
164. Singh 1993: 49; Malik 1971: 119–120; Solomon 1981: 181
165. The Tobago East and Toco/Manzanilla seats were won by two brothers, A.N.R. and Lionel Robinson, respectively..
166. Alexis had married into Dr Williams's family around the time he joined the PNM. However, important figures like Minister of Works, Communications, and Public Utilities, Learie Constantine; Minister of Health, Dr Winston Mahabir; and Parliamentary Secretary for Tobago Affairs, Ulric Lee, did not contest in the 1961 elections.
167. Solomon 1981: 179; Malik 1971: 123–7; Ghany 1996: 157
168. Only two Butlerites who ran in 1956 contested on the same ticket in 1961, Babooram Nathai (Ortoire/Mayaro) and Butler himself (La Brea). Stephen Maharaj (Princes Town), Leo Charles Mitchell (La Brea), Norman Alcantara (Port of Spain East), and Pope Wilberforce McLean (Laventille) contested on a DLP ticket. Sarran Sampath (Siparia) and Indar Persad (Caroni East) campaigned as PNM members.
169. See Ryan (1972: 238–91) and Bahadoorsingh (1968: 25–97) for greater elaboration of the racial aspects of these elections.
170. The vote was 256,261 (54.1 per cent) against Federation, and 217,319 (45.9 per cent) for it. There were 5,640 spoilt ballots and the turnout rate was 60.9 per cent (Mordecai 1968).

171. Williams 1969: 279
172. Williams 1969: 277–9; Ghany 1996: 130–51. Two days later, on 17 January, the Report of the Committee of the Legislature, which prepared proposals for a Constitution to take effect on Jamaica's Independence, was signed at Gordon House, Jamaica (Bell 1967). The date for independence was set for August 6, 1962.
173. Spackman, 'Constitutional development', pp. 295–320, provides a thorough examination of some of the major debates and issues surrounding the Independence Constitution. The Constitution was in fact drafted by Ellis Clarke, former Solicitor General (1954), Deputy Colonial Secretary (1956), and Attorney General.
174. A representative from the Association of County Councils of Trinidad and Tobago also followed them. The representative from the African National Congress, however, had been the first to object and leave (*Verbatim notes* 1962: 1–13; Spackman 1965: 318–9).
175. Malik 1971: 132–7; Spackman, ' Constitutional development', pp. 298–300; Ghany 1996: 152
176. GOTT [1969]: 2. After the bill was passed, the next local government elections would not occur until June 24, 1968.
177. Quoted in Spackman 1965: 303
178. See Singh (1993) for a collection of Indian Association pamphlets, including a 46-page document addressed to the Secretary of State for the Colonies, Reginald Maudling, dated May 16, 1962, outlining the case for proportional representation.
179. Malik 1971: 136–8
180. Williams 1969: 284–6; *Trinidad and Tobago* 1962. Peter Farquhar (1988: 28–9), a member of the DLP team at Marlborough House, insists that 'Williams' sole concern was that Bustamante might go to the Prime Minister's Conference and he might not be there,' an opinion supported by Williams's statements in his autobiography (Williams 1969: 284–6). Grenada had applied for consideration to join the Unitary State of Trinidad and Tobago, but its application had lapsed after the Trinidad and Tobago Government referred the application to the United Kingdom with a request for economic assistance to facilitate the merger (Williams 1969: 286; GOTT 1963b).
181. Malik 1971: 139–40; Spackman, 'Constitutional development', pp. 308, 320. Reflecting on the situation two years later in the British *New Society*, Albert Gomes ('Race and independence in Trinidad', *New Society*, 4: 100 (August 27, 1964), p. 16) expressed scepticism that the rapprochement between the racially-based political parties would 'outlast the honeymoon period of independence', giving a pessimistic view of Trinidad and Tobago's future.

## CHAPTER 3

1. Paul Sutton, 'Trinidad and Tobago: oil capitalism and the "presidential power" of Eric Williams', in *Dependency Under Challenge*, eds. Anthony Payne and Paul Sutton (Manchester: Manchester University Press, 1984), p. 44
2. GOTT 1963a
3. The Opposition claimed that the PNM was effectively undermining the authority of the Civil Service and his Government Ministers, creating a direct link between himself and the people. It might be seen as similar to the 'Oath of Salisbury', by which William the Conqueror secured the loyalty of the British population to himself, instead of to their local lords. In fact, a few years earlier, the calypsonian the Mighty Sparrow

famously dubbed Dr Williams, 'William the Conqueror'.

4. Williams 1969: 307–9, 318; Robinson 1986: 30–44; Robinson 1988: 57; Ryan 1972: 340; Paul Sutton, 'External factors and political development in Trinidad and Tobago, 1962–1972', (unpublished Ph.D. diss., Victoria University of Manchester, 1979), pp. 167–77. The expansion of educational opportunities under the PNM had been impressive, and transformed an entire generation. Between 1955 and 1964 there had been a 30 per cent increase in primary school enrolment and a 140 per cent increase in secondary school enrolment. In 1955, 204 children went to secondary school at Government expense; the number in 1962 was 3,291 and in 1964 was 3,750 (Williams 1969: 318).
5. Williams 1969: 324
6. Malik 1971: 141–4; Ghany 1996: 158–9
7. Malik 1971: 141–5; PNM 1966b
8. Ryan 1972: 256–9; Malik 1971: 118–9; Kambon 1988: 40–6
9. The OWTU was established on July 25, 1937 and registered on September 15, 1937 by Butler's assistant, Adrian Cola Rienzi (Krishna Deonarine) (Butler was incarcerated) (GORTT 1998: 63; Kiely 1996: 74).
10. Kambon 1988: 49
11. Kambon 1988: 67–9
12. Zin Henry, 'Industrial relations and the development process', in Ryan 1988: 48–9; Williams 1969: 318. This had followed the Honeyman Commission of 1962 which had investigated the disturbances in the sugar industry. The report, released near the end of March 1963, concluded that 'deliberate subversion' was at work there (Kambon 1988: 89).
13. Kiely 1996: 99
14. This union was also formed by Rienzi in the aftermath of the 1937 riots.
15. Malik 1971: 149–50; Kiely 1996: 99–102; Kambon 1988: 96–114
16. Walton Look Lai, 'C.L.R. James and Trinidad nationalism', in *C.L.R. James's Caribbean*, eds. Paget Henry and Paul Buhle (London: Macmillan Press, Ltd., 1992), pp. 197–8; Kiely 1996: 99; Williams 1969: 311. James, who had been mentioned in the Commission's report on subversive activities, tabled in parliament four days earlier, had been in the country only 18 hours, arriving as a cricket correspondent for the London *Times* and *Observer* (Look Lai, 'C.L.R. James', pp. 197–8).
17. Williams 1969: 311–4; Malik 1971: 150
18. Malik 1971: 150–1
19. Malik 1971: 148–157
20. Canute Parris, 'Political dissidence in post-independence Jamaica and Trinidad: 1962–72', (unpublished Ph.D. diss., New School for Social Research, 1976), p. 188
21. Williams (1969: 332) and PNM (1966b) describe the PNM's campaign, based on agrarian reform.
22. GOTT 1967: 83. Williams (1969: 332–7) gives a detailed account of the campaign, the most neglected by political observers. In the three best accounts of the period, Malik (1971: 157–8) gives it just over a page, Oxaal (1982: 182) devotes to it half of a paragraph, and Ryan (1972) omits it completely.
23. Butler contested the Point Fortin seat and received only 297 votes, losing to the PNM's minor candidate John R.F. Richardson. It was his last contest.
24. In 1961, the DLP won with a plurality of 49.35 per cent, and in 1966 the PNM won with a plurality of 49.96 per cent.
25. The PNM, too, had lost a significant number of its earlier prominent figures by this

time. In 1966, Dr Patrick Solomon was removed from his post as Deputy Leader due to his involvement in a police case regarding his future stepson, in addition to other difficulties with Williams (Solomon 1981: 234–47). This was popularly known as the Solomon Affair. He did not contest the 1966 elections. By this time, Williams had also fallen out with Sir Learie Constantine, who was knighted in 1962. In 1964 Sir Learie resigned from the PNM and in 1969 became the first black man raised to the peerage, sitting in the House of Lords.

26. Malik 1971: 158. Many people in the wider community, including the Government, had found the registration and voting arrangements during the elections to be unsatisfactory, and public criticism grew (Williams 1969, 336; Malik 1971, 158). By 1976 the voting machines had been replaced by ballot boxes.
27. Interview with Hans Hanoomansingh, 1999
28. Siewah 1994: 650. The book was published in 1968 in London by the Addison-Wesley Publishing Company.
29. The WFP invited the DLP and the Liberals to form the Tripartite Committee of the Trinidad and Tobago Opposition Parties (1968) to protest the use of voting machines.
30. Malik 1971: 158; Brassington [1975]: 129–74; Williams 1969: 337; Ryan 1972: 449. When Maraj made his re-entrance in parliament, Williams rose from his seat to cross the floor and shake Bhadase's hand. The shot became something of a standard 'flashback' for the local press (Brassington [1975], 149–50).
31. The elections procedures had been rationalised compared to the colonial period, with elections occurring in single-member constituencies, scheduled every three years.
32. Williams 1969: 337; GOTT [1969]. The division of votes, however, was less extreme, with the PNM winning 50 per cent and the DLP 40 per cent (GOTT [1969]).
33. Oxaal (1982: 195–305), Ghany (1996: 263–70) and Kambon (1988: 171–274) (a leader of the National Joint Action Committee [NJAC]), Shah (1971) (a leader of the army mutiny), Craig (1982a), Sutton (1983), and Meeks (1976) provide informative, detailed, and close-up accounts of the unrest. Also, Ryan and Stewart's collection (1996) gathers interesting retrospectives, 25 years later, from the major participants.
34. As a result of the ISA, in 1965 only four strikes were recorded, involving 7,610 workers. Officially, 1966 had been strike free (CBTT 1993; MacDonald 1986, 151).
35. Kambon 1988: 175–80; Kiely 1996: 112–3
36. Interview with Khafra Kambon, 1999; Kambon 1988: 193; Thomas and Riddell 1971: 4
37. The *Trinidad Chronicle* folded in 1959. This left the *Guardian* as the only national daily newspaper published during the 1961 and 1966 General Elections.
38. *TE* May 31, 1987, p. 2; Interview with Lloyd Best, 1999; Oxaal 1982: 214; Ryan 1972: 470; *TTR* March 2000, p. 26; Benn 1987: 84
39. DLP MPs Vernon Jamadar and Alloy Lequay were present at early planning meetings but did not join the action. Older politicians Peter Farquhar and Stephen Maharaj, however, did join and were incarcerated with the new, young activists (Kambon 1988: 179–82).
40. Kambon 1988: 171–80.
41. Interview with Khafra Kambon 1999.
42. Oxaal (1982, 214–6) provides an excellent, organised chronology of the myriad events of the time.
43. Williams 1970d: 6.
44. Williams 1970b: 9.

45. Ghany 1996: 264–6. See Robinson (1986: 119–28) for a similar speech delivered to that union's annual conference on August 29, 1970. Robinson replaced Patrick Solomon as Deputy Leader of the PNM, after Solomon's removal in 1966. In April 1967 Robinson was moved from the Ministry of Finance to the Ministry of External Affairs, and this was widely interpreted as a move by Williams to sideline Robinson after the controversy over the 1966 Finance Act (Sutton, 'External factors', pp. 171–2; Ghany 1996: 264–6). Robinson's official resignation from the party occurred with a statement issued to the General Council on September 20, 1970 (Robinson 1986: 129–30).
46. MacDonald 1986: 165–6; Oxaal 1982: 216; Shah 1971.
47. Williams 1970a, 1970b, 1970c.
48. Williams 1970c.
49. In the October 27, 1969 Speech from the Throne, a Joint Select Committee to consider constitutional change had been proposed, 'with particular reference to the introduction of a republican form of government' (Constitution Commission 1991: 15). The Committee met once only, most likely due to the unrest that followed.
50. Ghany 1996: 273.
51. Williams 1970b.
52. His father, Henry Hudson-Phillips, had been President of the POPPG (Ryan 1989b: 267).
53. Ryan 1972: 446–7, 465–7.
54. Ghany 1996: 272; MacDonald 1986: 168.
55. PNM 1970.
56. PNM 1970: 7. Williams was referring to the novel, *The Mimic Men*, by V.S. Naipaul, nephew of Simbhoonath and Dr Rudranath Capildeo.
57. Capildeo had argued that the DLP leadership should have been given to Bhadase Maraj. The following year, Dr Capildeo died in London in May 1970 (Siewah 1994: 677). On August 31, 1969, Dr Capildeo had been presented with the Trinity Cross, the highest honour in the newly instituted order of national awards.
58. Richardson had been dismissed from the PNM in the 1956–61 term, allegedly for 'fraternising with the enemy' (Mahabir 1978: 69; Brassington [1975]: 53).
59. MacDonald 1986: 169–70; Ryan 1972: 449–50. The division of votes was seven 'ayes' (including A.N.R. Robinson), 20 'noes', and 3 abstentions (Bhadase Maraj [Chaguanas], and DLP MPs R. Bhoolai [Nariva] and AM Baksh [Princes Town]).
60. GOTT 1972b; Ghany 1996: 274; MacDonald 1986: 170
61. Ryan 1972: 475–7; Ryan 1989b: 2; Ghany 1996: 275; Interview with A.N.R. Robinson, 1999.
62. Ghany 1996: 275; Ryan 1972: 453–70. Bhadase Maraj was able to bring eight other former DLP members (Ashton Fitzwilliam Chambers, Rampersad Bhoolai, Surujpat Mathura, Afraz Mohammed Baksh, Claudius Barclay, McVorran de Freitas, John Bharath, and Claudius Barclay), three former WFP members (Stephen Maharaj, M.A.S.A. Khan, and Ramdas Mahabir), and former independent Lionel Seukeran to contest the 1971 elections.
63. GOTT 1972b. The eight uncontested seats were St Ann's, Laventille, Barataria, Arima, Ortoire/Mayaro, San Fernando East, San Fernando West, and Tobago East. J. Edward Greene, 'An analysis of the general elections in Trinidad and Tobago 1971', in Munroe and Lewis 1971: 136–144, argues that Williams had become 'dictator by default', that the PNM were the country's only effective party, and noted the impotence of the opposition. There were two close contests, however. Bhadase Maraj lost the

Oropouche seat by only 224 votes, and his son-in-law, Satnarayan Maharaj, lost the St Augustine seat by only 335 votes.

64. GOTT 1972a: 46–8. The boycott was strongest in north Trinidad, San Fernando, and Tobago. Only one seat was contested in Port of Spain, two in Arima, and none in St George, San Fernando, and Tobago. On the other hand, there were six contested seats in Nariva-Mayaro, seven in Caroni, six in Victoria, four in St Patrick. In the 26 contested seats the PNM won only 12 seats and secured 52.1 per cent of the vote. The voter turnout in those seats was low, only 27.2 per cent.
65. See Meeks (1999) for an excellent insight into the group, including interviews with surviving members and details of key events.
66. Ryan (1989b: 7) quotes from one of their broadsheets, '[Death is] as meaningful as the oxygen in our lungs. We define death in our own terms and do not fear it.' Guy Harewood was killed by police on October 17, 1973 and NUFF's armed activities soon ceased (Meeks 1999; *Guardian* [London], October 20, 1973, p. 4).
67. CBTT 1993
68. MacDonald 1986: 172; Kambon 1988: 262, 271; CPTU 1991; Ryan 1989b: 5–7. In his televised announcement of the emergency, Williams cynically assured the population that there would be 'parang [Spanish-Trinidadian Christmas music] as usual . . . [and] Carnival as usual' (in Kambon 1988: 263).
69. In June 1971, for example, A.N.R. Robinson suggested that the Governor-General call a State of Emergency and install an interim government to implement electoral reform, with fresh elections to take place within one month (Ryan 1972: 485).
70. Quoted in Ryan 1972: 485.
71. On July 21, 1972, however, J.R.F. Richardson (brother of expelled PNM foundation member and DLP Deputy Leader Dr Elton C. Richardson), MP for Point Fortin and Parliamentary Secretary in the Ministry of Finance, had been appointed Leader of Opposition after he crossed the floor and formed the United People's Party. Richardson was soon followed by MP for Siparia, Dr Horace Charles (Ghany 1996: 276–80; Ryan 1989b: 96). This development had been interpreted by some as a cynical ploy by Dr Williams to give an air of normality to parliament (Ryan 1989b: 62; Siewah and Moonilal 1991: 124). The announcement that Richardson was an independent member was made on June 14, 1972, the same day that the Industrial Relations Bill was presented to the House.
72. Ghany 1996: 273, 278.
73. Williams 1972: 1.
74. in Ryan 1989b: 4.
75. Williams 1972: 13.
76. Williams 1972: 5.
77. PNM 1972: 40–1.
78. Ryan 1989b: 11–5. Hudson-Phillips aggressively campaigned for a re-invigoration of the PNM, with what some considered a lack of regard for the party elders. At one point, he brashly declared, 'who vex, vex' (Ryan 1989b: 12).
79. Williams 1973a: 1. At the September 1971 party convention, Williams had hinted that he might resign from the leadership of the party. The suggestion provoked some distress (Kambon 1988: 259; Ryan 1989b: 3–4). See Carl Parris, 'Trinidad and Tobago, September to December 1973', *Social and Economic Studies*, 30:3 (September 1981), pp. 42–62, for an analysis of events from September to December 1973.
80. Williams 1973a: 2.
81. Williams 1973a: 13–4.

82. Williams 1973a: 16, 30.
83. Williams 1973a: 17–20.
84. After the party's experience with previous Deputy Leaders Solomon and Robinson, three Deputy Leaders – Kamaluddin Mohammed, Errol Mahabir (cousin of Winston Mahabir), and George Chambers – were appointed at the Annual Convention of 1971 (Ghany 1996: 295).
85. Williams 1973a: 26.
86. Williams 1973a: 20–26, 29, 31. Susan Craig (1974) provides an excellent political sociological study of this phenomenon.
87. Williams 1973a: 33–4; Ryan 1989b: 9.
88. Williams 1973a: 34.
89. Ryan 1989b: 10.
90. After the appearance of the daily *Express* tabloid newspaper in May 1967, a popular weekly tabloid press flourished.
91. in Ryan 1989b: 9–10, 16–7; Ghany 1996: 300–3; Interview with Archbishop Anthony Pantin, 1999.
92. Quoted in Ryan 1989b: 16–7.
93. Ghany 1996: 300–4. At the same meeting, a resolution for the Party to form a delegation to visit Dr Williams and ask him to return was defeated with a vote of 34 against, 32 in favour, and 36 abstentions.
94. On November 7, the IRO, through an approach to the Governor-General, Sir Ellis Clarke, had succeeded in arranging a meeting with Dr Williams to ask him to reconsider his decision. At the December 2 PNM General Council meeting it seems as though the Party Chairman had led an orchestrated return of Williams (Ghany 1996: 302–3).
95. Ghany 1996: 300–4; Ryan 1989b: 21–5.
96. Williams 1973d: 2.
97. Sutton, 'Trinidad and Tobago', p. 50.
98. Williams 1974a, 1974c, 1974d, 1974e. In 1973, Trinidad and Tobago produced 8.5 million tons of oil, 0.3 per cent of world production (*BP statistical review* 1973: 6).
99. Williams 1974b: 39.
100. The Government of Trinidad and Tobago purchased the local assets of Shell on August 22, 1974 at a cost of TT$99.6 million (GOTT 1974).
101. Williams 1974b: 35.
102. Selwyn Ryan (1989b: 33–50), a member of the Commission, compares in detail the Independence Constitution, the Commission's proposals, and the final 1976 Republican Constitution.
103. Williams 1975a; Ghany 1996: 339; Siewah and Arjoonsingh 1998: 9; Ryan 1989b: 50, 55; Sutton, 'Trinidad and Tobago', p. 55
104. A new single chamber National House of Assembly was proposed, with 36 seats chosen by the first-past-the-post method, and another 36 appointed according to the overall proportion of votes received by each party.
105. Eric Williams, 'Proportional representation in Trinidad and Tobago: the case against', *The Round Table*, 250 (April 1973):, pp. 233–245; Williams 1973b
106. PNM 1973: 6.
107. Williams 1973a: 21.
108. Williams 1975a: 83.
109. Governor-General Sir Ellis Clarke, who replaced Sir Solomon Hochoy on January 31, 1973, automatically became the first President of Trinidad and Tobago on

September 24, 1976, by virtue of holding the post of Governor-General immediately prior. Though elected by Parliament, the President served a fixed term of office, and could only be removed under extraordinary circumstances, through ordinarily cumbersome means. This gave the President a degree of security not enjoyed by the previous Governor-General.

110. The removal of the voting machines resulted in a conspicuous increase in the number of rejected ballots, from 146 in 1966 to 3,824 in 1976 (see Appendix B).
111. Ryan 1989b: 42–50; Sutton, 'Trinidad and Tobago', pp. 55–6; Ghany 1996: 339; Constitution Commission 1991: 17. Foremost among these was the radical proposal to have a unicameral 72-seat National House of Assembly with a mixed first-past-the-post and proportional representation system.
112. reprinted in *TG* April 4, 1976, p. 12.
113. Williams 1975b: 13. Ryan (1989b: 56–137) extensively discusses the parties, programmes, strategies and debates in the 1976 campaign. Ryan, Greene, and Harewood (1979) and Ryan (1979) particularly note the confusion surrounding that year's elections.
114. Ryan 1989b: 107–9; Siewah 1994: 74.
115. The Tapia House Movement was the political party of the Tapia House Group.
116. Ryan 1989b: 57–8.
117. Ryan 1989b: 96. Basdeo Panday was granted leave of absence from the Senate on the day the Tapia members took their oaths.
118. *Crisis* (Baptiste 1976) provides a deep, multifaceted examination of the formation of the ULF.
119. CBTT 1993.
120. Baptiste 1976: 35.
121. Lending his support at the San Fernando-based march was T.U.B. Butler, who by then had been awarded the country's highest honour, the Trinity Cross, in 1970 (Baptiste 1976: 1, 31). In 1973, the Government declared June 19, the anniversary of the Butler riots, as Trinidad and Tobago's Labour Day. Butler died on February 20, 1977.
122. Shah and 17 other mutineers had been pardoned on July 27, 1972 as a result of a Court of Appeal judgement that the soldiers' court martials were defective. The Privy Council's refusal to grant leave to Attorney-General Karl Hudson-Phillips to appeal the decision led to the government's abandonment of the case (*TE* July 27, 1972, pp. 1, 14). On his release, Shah announced his intentions to get involved in radical politics, and on February 14, 1973 he assumed leadership of TICFA, amidst intense rivalry and opposition by many older union leaders (*TE* February 15, 1973, p. 1).
123. *Master and Servant* 1991: 48; Siewah and Moonilal 1991: xvi; Baptiste 1976: 195, 282–6; GOTT 1967: 89; Ghany 1996: 280. C.S. Espinet, Beulah Nelson, Basdeo Panday, and John Tyson were appointed Senators by Leader of Opposition Roy Richardson on September 15, 1972.
124. Ryan 1989b: 75
125. Ryan 1989b: 81–2
126. GOTT 1977: 167; Ryan 1989b: 79, 113, 139; Kiely 1996: 139–40
127. *TG* May 26, 1976, p. 8
128. *TG* May 26, 1976. The 'millstones' were Brinsley Barrow (Minister of State in the Ministry of Finance, Planning and Development, MP for Port of Spain Central), Shamshuddin Mohammed (Minister of State in the Ministry of Local Government,

MP for San Juan East, brother of Kamaluddin Mohammed, former Minister of Local Goverment), Carlton Gomes (Minister of Education and Culture, MP for San Juan West), Lionel Robinson (Minister of Agriculture, Lands and Fisheries, MP for Toco/Manzanilla, and brother of A.N.R. Robinson), and Victor Campbell (Minister of Works, MP for Ortoire/Mayaro)

129. Ghany 1996: 340–1; Ryan 1989b: 89–91. At the end of July, the Party waived disciplinary action against the three critics in light of the coming general elections.
130. Williams (1976: 38) had understood this as an unfortunately common global trend resulting from increased competition for the allegiances and interest of voters, who were increasingly endowed with shorter working weeks, more disposable income, and faced with the massive expansion of entertainment, sport, culture, and, most of all, television.
131. Both Selwyn Ryan (1989b: 121–2) and Lloyd Best (in Ryan 1989b, 122–5) argued that the ULF motorcade in north Trinidad two weeks before the elections changed the minds of Afro-Trinidadians at the last minute, inspiring racial voting for the PNM to keep the Indians in the ULF out of office.
132. *TG* September 26, 1976, p. 3
133. *TG* September 26, 1976, p. 4
134. GORTT 1977a; GORTT [1981]; Ryan 1989b: 166; Sutton, 'Trinidad and Tobago', p. 68. The local government elections, which were due in 1974, were postponed in order to accommodate constitutional reform.
135. In 1977, eight seats were uncontested in Port of Spain, nine in San Fernando, seven in St George, and one in Victoria. In 1980, with new councils, the numbers were 11 in Port of Spain, three in Arima, 14 in St George West, and three in St George East (see Appendix F).
136. Ryan 1989b: 204-5. Williams is widely alleged also to have boasted during the period, 'Money is no problem'. (MacDonald 1986: 191).
137. Williams 1974c: 7
138. GORTT 1980; NGC [1999]
139. CBTT 1993
140. GORTT 1983: 158; GORTT 1995: 7; K. Sargeant and P. Forde, 'The state sector and divestment in Trinidad and Tobago: some preliminary findings', (presented at the Annual Conference of the Regional Programme of Monetary Studies, mimeo, 1991), p. 8
141. Gocking 1998: 61–66; Sutton, 'Trinidad and Tobago', p. 64–5; Ryan 1989b: 228–9. Sutton, 'Trinidad and Tobago', pp. 57–8, described the situation as like a 'renaissance court' with everyone watching everybody else.
142. Ryan 1989b: 198–242
143. CBTT 1993
144. CBTT 1993
145. MacDonald 1986: 190–5. In 1960, however, Naipaul (1981: 1995a) noted the modern consumerism of Trinidadians as a fundamental national trait, while the account provided by Brereton (1981: 191–2, 219–20) of the 'American Occupation' in the 1940s, and the 8.5 per cent per annum growth in real GDP from 1951 to 1961 – both as a result of Trinidad's oil – suggests that Trinidad had developed these orientations at least 30 years before the boom of the 1970s.
146. MacDonald 1986: 197
147. Ryan 1989b: 166; Ghany 1996: 347–8; Siewah and Arjoonsingh 1998: 30–31. Ryan (1989b: 138–197; Ryan 1978: 242–364) provides detailed accounts of the extensive

and extreme ULF factionalism, with sections written by Richard Jacobs, UWI academic and unsuccessful ULF candidate for Arouca in the 1976 General Elections.

148. Ryan 1989b: 191
149. Ghany 1996: 347–8. McLean protested the increasing use of the police and heavy-handed tactics by the government to quell industrial and other discontent (Ryan 1988: 147).
150. Ghany 1996: 346–8; Ryan 1989b: 157–9
151. Many felt that this constituted a sort of overture to white Trinidadians and others who were offended by Black Stalin's conception of the 'Caribbean Man' as an Afro-Caribbean man.
152. Sutton 1984: 65, 68; Ryan 1989b: 247, MacDonald 1986: 204; Karl Hudson-Phillips, 'Address at the inauguration of the Organisation for National Reconstruction on Sunday 1st February, 1981, at the Chaguaramas Convention Centre' (Mimeo, 1981).
153. Ryan 1989b: 133–4
154. *TG* September 26, 1976, p. 10
155. Davidson (1979) provides the illuminating debates in the House on the issue.
156. Ghany 1996: 358–9; Davidson 1979: 176
157. GORTT [1978]
158. Paul Sutton, 'Trinidad-Tobago', (Mimeo, [1985?]), pp. 4–5; Ghany 1996: 358–9
159. MacDonald 1986: 196; Interview with Alloy Lequay 1999; Interview with Lloyd Best 1999; Siewah 1994: 476–7; Allan Harris, 'Report on a party of parties', (presented by Allan Harris to the Tapia Convention on 22 February 1981, in Best and Harris 1991), p. 42; Ryan 1989a: 42. The ONR, the Shah faction of the ULF, and NJAC declined to join the emerging coalition.
160. GORTT 1987b. The Tobago (Internal Self-Government) Act stipulated that members of the Senate and House of Representatives were barred from belonging to the THA (Sutton, 'Trinidad-Tobago', p. 5). The DAC splinter group, the Fargo House Movement, led by Winston Murray (the other MP elected to the House of Representatives on a DAC ticket) had campaigned for secession and lost its deposit (MacDonald 1986: 196–7). 'Fargo' was the nickname of A.P.T. James.
161. Quoted in Ryan 1989b: 192
162. Carl Parris, 'Personalisation of power in an elected government: Eric Williams and Trinidad and Tobago, 1973–1981', *Journal of Inter-American Studies and World Affairs*, 25: 2 (May 1983), p. 174. These were almost all concerned with administrative matters.
163. Parris, 'Personalisation of power', p. 187
164. Williams 1981: 2, 34

## CHAPTER 4

1. Ghany (1996: 376–401) and Ryan (1989b: 243–257) give accounts of the controversies surrounding the causes of Williams's death, the handling of the announcement, and the appointment of his successor. The most enduring controversy has surrounded whether President Clarke appointed on racial grounds the low-profile George Chambers over his senior and Leader of the House, Kamaluddin Mohammed. On November 20, 1995 (two weeks after the general elections that made Basdeo Panday the country's first Indian prime minister) until April 27, 1996, this issue was openly discussed for the first time in television, radio, and print media via interviews

with and statements by Clarke, Errol Mahabir, and Mohammed (Ghany 1996: 376–387). In the *Trinidad Guardian* (September 1, 1999, p. 5) in an Independence Day interview, Mohammed had been quoted, 'I should have been the Prime Minister after Williams died. Today this nation would not have been burdened with the racial situation as it is now.'

2. Ghany 1996: 403–4
3. A key figure in these scandals was John O'Halloran, local white businessman, one of the few persons close enough to Williams to be aware of his diabetic condition, and one of the three Ministers of Government who resigned in the aftermath of the Black Power marches. On May 5, four days before the PNM convention, O'Halloran had resigned as Chairman of the Trinidad and Tobago Racing Authority under contentious circumstances (Ghany 1996: 407–8).
4. Ghany 1996: 405–8
5. Ryan (1989b: 258–90), Ghany (1996: 408–11) and MacDonald (1986: 201–5) provide details of the campaign and its aftermath.
6. Ryan 1989b: 259–67
7. See Ghany 1996: 303
8. MacDonald 1986: 204
9. quoted in Ryan 1989b: 257
10. Ghany 1996: 410
11. In 1975 Best had declared an interest in forming a coalition of all the opposition parties along the lines of the Janata Dal party in India (Ryan 1989b: 257). It might be argued, however, that the 1957–60 DLP experience should have provided the model – its life cycle complete and its lessons cautionary – as opposed to the heady formative years of the Janata Dal.
12. quoted in Ryan 1978: 473–4
13. Lloyd Best, 'A foundation strategy', in Best and Harris 1991: 49–50. An earlier version of the theory was presented on January 13, 1980 as a paper for Tapia's 1979–80 General Assembly, identifying four constituent regions: north, central, and south Trinidad, and Tobago ('Measures for party reform', in Best and Harris 1991: 39).
14. Alloy Lequay, 'A ground floor: press release. From Alloy Lequay, convenor, tri-party talks, 7 March 1981', in Best and Harris 1991: 48
15. MacDonald 1986: 202–3; Ryan 1989b: 265
16. For example, the November 1981 issue of *People* magazine had devoted 20 pages and its cover to features and analyses of the ONR and its challenge to the PNM, compared to little more than one-third of a page of copy to the DAC, ONR, and ULF, and another third to three individual head shots of Best, Panday and Robinson.
17. Interestingly, Ranjit Kumar was a candidate for Naparima representing the Liberal Action Party in the 1976 elections. Another old personality that unsuccessfully resurfaced for the election was Stephen C. Maharaj, who contested Ortoire/Mayaro as a ULF candidate.
18. GORTT 1982b: 203, 213
19. Ryan 1989a: 42. John LaGuerre, 'General Elections of 1981', *Journal of Commonwealth and Comparative Politics*, 21: 2 (July 1983), p. 133, provides a gloomy reading of the elections arguing that 'owing to the diminishing influence of the race factor, Trinidad is moving inexorably towards one-party rule. ... The future shape of the party system in Trinidad and Tobago ... depends on the electoral future of the ONR.'
20. GORTT 1982b: 208–14
21. These seats were won by the ULF in 1976 with pluralities also, 46.5 per cent and 47.9 per cent, respectively.

22. Ryan 1989b: 279.
23. *TG* November 23, 1981, p. 1; Interview with Satnarine Maharaj, 1999.
24. Chambers 1982: 1, 5.
25. Chambers 1982: 1, 31.
26. GORTT 1970.
27. Chambers 1982: 20–2.
28. World Bank 1983: i.
29. GORTT 1984a: 3. As a proportion of real GDP, private consumption had risen from 60 per cent in 1970 to 73.4 per cent in 1981 (CBTT 1993).
30. Quoted in Chambers 1984: 4.
31. The average annual prices, it should be noted, may not represent the actual selling price of Trinidad and Tobago's oil on the international market.
32. Trinidad's first oil well was drilled in 1857, also at La Brea, by the Merrimac Oil Company of the USA. Much earlier, in 1595 Sir Walter Raleigh discovered the Pitch Lake in La Brea (Brereton 1981: 199).
33. CBTT 1993.
34. CBTT 1993.
35. CBTT 1993; MacDonald 1986: 206.
36. Lloyd Best, 'Alliance for reconstruction: the case. Address to the Alliance inaugural convention, Chaguaramas Convention Centre, 14 November 1982', in Best and Harris 1991, pp. 58–60. This amazingly re-states, quite independently, in different contexts, and 24 years later, the 13 groups which anthropologist Daniel Crowley identified in 1957 as constituting Trinidad and Tobago society (D. Crowley, 'Plural and differential acculturation in Trinidad', *American Anthropologist*, vol. 59 [1957], pp. 817–824).
37. Best, 'Alliance for reconstruction', p. 62.
38. Ryan 1989a: 4, 45; Siewah and Moonilal 1991: 404. Although only the ULF and DAC had won seats for the Alliance in 1981, Senators had been appointed by Leader of the Opposition Basdeo Panday from the three Alliance parties on November 27, 1981: Lloyd Best (as Leader of the Opposition in the Senate), Nuevo Diaz, Dr. Sahadeo Basdeo, Neville A. Hilton-Clarke, Maulana Dr Waffie Mohammed, and Dr Brinsley Samaroo (who became Senate Opposition Leader after Best had left in 1983 on a three-year Evaluation Mission in Central Africa for UNCTAD). Later appointments included former United DLP leader Alloy Lequay and Tapia member Lincoln Myers (Siewah and Moonilal 1991: 404; *TTR* June 19, 1987, p. 9; Ryan 1989a: 73).
39. Ryan 1989a: 42–3; GORTT [1984b]: 284–91; Siewah and Moonilal 1991: 404; MacDonald 1986: 208. It is notable that even with this arrangement of four parties, candidates were not put up for eight seats – two in Port of Spain, one in San Fernando, one in Point Fortin, three in St George West, and one in Victoria (GORTT [1984b]: 284–91).
40. GORTT [1984b]: 84; MacDonald 1986: 209
41. *TTR* December 18/23, 1986, p. 16; Ghany 1996: 70
42. Ryan (1989a: 40–65) provides an extended account of the debates and arguments, which included rivalries between ONR Deputy Leader Suruj Rambachan and ULF members Basdeo Panday and Trevor Sudama over leadership of Indians, Hindus, and the Oropouche constituency; between Panday and Hudson-Phillips over 'class ideology', and personal enmity during the Black Power marches; and between ex-PNM members Hudson-Phillips and Robinson, who were bitter enemies in the

debates over the Public Order Bill of 1970. Other issues included Creole apprehension of those who advocated Indian 'cultural autonomy' (on the surface meaning, quite tamely, little more than an enhanced media presence); Tobagonian 'nationhood' (meaning internal self-government and recognition of distinct status, but not independence); and recurring disputes over the allocation of constituencies to parties.

43. Sebastien 1985. From the ONR, only Mervyn Assam was listed as a participant.
44. GORTT 1987a; MacDonald 1986: 215
45. Ryan 1989a: 44–51; *TTR* December 18/23, 1986, p. 5
46. Robinson, however, displayed an apparent reluctance to re-enter the politics of Trinidad, which he had once described as a 'perishing society' with 'calaloo politics' (*TTR* December 18/23, 1986, p. 2; Ryan 1989a: 58). ('Calaloo' is an Afro-Creole Trinidadian dish made by thoroughly blending dasheen bush, hot peppers, crab meat, ochro, and coconut milk in one pot.) Problems with the coalition were seen in the August 1985 elections for county council chairmen, when National Alliance councillors had flouted party directives by attempting to block their Accommodation (ONR) colleagues (*TE* April 12, 1987, p. 9).
47. A.N.R. Robinson (1999), in an interview with the author, had claimed that some wanted to name the party the Alliance for National Reconstruction (ANR), but he rejected such encouragement of a 'cult of personality,' against which he claimed to have fought strongly in the PNM while he had been a member.
48. Ryan (1989a: 51) claims that the ONR leadership had been alone in seeking the views of its members regarding the formation of unitary party. However, it is obvious that Tapia regularly discussed the issue, and were sceptical (Best and Harris 1991; *TTR* October 31, 1986).
49. Ryan 1989a: 40-63; *TE* August 2, 1987, p. 1; *TTR* December 18/23, 1986, p. 2
50. Two weeks after the NAR had been launched as a unitary party, Best had written in the *Trinidad Express* (March 9, 1986, p. 15) his disagreement with the movement away from coalition towards a unitary party. He feared that this might effectively submerge the differing constituency interests.
51. 'Four Letters', in Best and Harris 1991
52. 'Four Letters', p. 71
53. *TG* September 21, 1986, pp. 5–7; *TTR* October 31, 1986, pp. 7–17
54. *TTR* October 31, 1986, p. 15. Hussein and Rampersad were unsuccessful in their bids.
55. Robinson had publicly refuted Best's claims, arguing in September that the NAR had given members of the party and the general public formal opportunities to comment on its draft *Platform for Change* (quoted in Ryan 1989a: 83). In October, Robinson pointed out that Best sought equal status with other party leaders, but that the NAR Deputy Leaders already represented the two parties dissolved to form the NAR: the NATT and the ONR (*TG* October 26, 1986, p. 1). If one were cynical, one could argue that Best's 'nine ethnic groups' theory was an elaborate attempt to justify for Tapia a role greater than its electoral performance would have warranted.
56. Ryan 1989a: 57–8, 62. The NAR apparently had brought in new party members and candidates, affiliated to none of the former parties, in order to 'balance' its slate (Ryan 1989a: 62).
57. Ghany 1996: 437–8; *NTT* March 27, 1985, pp. 1–2
58. *NTT* June 26, 1985, p. 10; Maingot 1998: 22; Kambon 1988: 325–6. Texaco had operated in Trinidad and Tobago since 1913 (GORTT 1998: 19).

59. Ryan 1989a: 257; Kiely 1996: 158
60. quoted in Ryan 1989a: 81.
61. Ryan 1989a: 81.
62. Ghany 1996: 443–9.
63. The Drug Report apparently was linked in the public mind to the escalating crime rate in the country. Between 1980 and 1985, the total number of crimes reported annually had risen from 35,036 to 53,998 (GORTT 1991). The government based its decision not to publish the report on the grounds that the commission had named magistrates and police officers based on testimony given by persons involved in the drug underworld, without allowing opportunities for the accused to respond to the charges (Ryan 1989a: 82).
64. Kevin Yelvington, 'Vote dem out: the demise of the PNM in Trinidad and Tobago', *Caribbean Review*, 15: 4 (1987), p. 29; *TTR* October 31, 1986, p. 15; Ryan 1989a: 71, 82.
65. *NTT* October 29, 1986, p. 13; Ghany 1996: 457; Yelvington, 'Vote dem out', p. 29; Ryan 1989a: 11.
66. 'EC-0' had been the name of the Central Bank form used to apply for foreign exchange in a system introduced by the Chambers administration in 1982 (Alvin Hilaire, 'Commercial policy in Trinidad and Tobago' [Port of Spain: Research Department, Central Bank of Trinidad and Tobago, Mimeo, 1992], p. 29; Penelope Forde et al., 'The evolution of the financial sector in Trinidad and Tobago [1970–1996]', in *The Financial Evolution of the Caribbean Community [1970–1996]*, ed. Laurence Clarke and Donna Danns, [St Augustine: Caribbean Centre for Monetary Studies, 1997], p. 433).
67. *TG* August 4, 1987, p. 1; Yelvington, 'Vote dem out', p. 29; Ghany 1996: 407–8; MacDonald 1986: 197; Ryan 1989a: 70, 81–2; *CI* July 1995, p. 2.
68. quoted in Ryan 1989a: 76.
69. Yelvington, 'Vote dem out', p. 30; Ryan 1989a: 71.
70. *TE* December 7, 1986, p. 8.
71. Yelvington, 'Vote dem out', p. 12; *TTR* December 18/23, 1986, p. 13; Ryan 1989a: 70. Best argues that the cruel jokes had circulated before the November 1981 elections, while Ryan suggests that they were heightened after the Chambers administration refused to support the 1983 US intervention in Grenada.
72. Yelvington, 'Vote dem out', p. 12.
73. Yelvington, 'Vote dem out', p. 29.
74. 'To pappyshow' means 'to make a mockery of'.
75. *TG* September 28, 1986, p. 3; Yelvington 'Vote dem out', p. 30.
76. Quoted in Ryan 1989a: 69, 72.
77. *TE* August 30, 1987, Independence magazine, p. 7; Ryan 1989a: 72.
78. Quoted in Ryan 1989a: 69; Ghany 1996: 464.
79. A study by W.C. Clarke noted that 13.5 per cent of newspaper articles devoted to the PNM was favourable, compared to the NAR's coverage, in which 80.8 per cent of the articles was favourable (Ryan 1989a: 81).
80. Ryan 1989a: 70, 81; Yelvington, 'Vote dem out', pp. 29–30; *TTR* December 1, 1986, p. 2; *TE* December 7, 1986, p. 19.
81. The eight were Desmond Cartey, Ronald Williams (whose brother Michael, an NAR activist, would become President of the Senate in the next parliament), Cuthbert Joseph, Ian Anthony, Winston Williams, Winston Hinds, and Hardeo Hardath. The first three were ministers, and Anthony was a Parliamentary Secretary. All were

generally low-profile, however.

82. Ghany 1996: 463; Ryan 1989a: 68
83. Yelvington, 'Vote dem out', p. 29; Ryan 1989a: 62–3
84. Ryan 1989a: 66–77; Yelvington, 'Vote dem out', pp. 29–31
85. Ryan 1989a: 77
86. *TG* November 30, 1986, suppl., pp. 3–27
87. *TG* November 30, 1986, suppl., p. 28
88. *TE* December 7, 1986, p. 8
89. Panday's later political party, the UNC, would form part of the Commonwealth delegation that monitored the South African elections on April 26–29, 1994 (Siewah and Arjoonsingh 1998: 55).
90. Siewah and Moonilal 1991: 240, 312, 314. Trinidad and Tobago was the first country to declare Emancipation Day a national holiday. NJAC had revived annual observations of Emancipation Day in 1973 (Interview with Khafra Kambon, 1999; *TG* July 22, 1999, p. 8).
91. Ghany 1996: 451–4; Patricia Mohammed, 'Reflections on the women's movement in Trinidad: calypsoes, changes, and sexual violence', *Feminist Review*, 38 (Summer 1991), p. 45; *Workingwoman* November 1991, p. 2
92. Quoted in Yelvington, 'Vote dem out', p. 30; Ryan 1989a: 77, 84
93. David Renwick (*TE* December 7, 1986, p. 8) believed that there was a possibility of a surprise showing by the PNM, as did Lloyd Best who feared a 'last resort to ... primal loyalty' (*TTR* 18/23 December 1996, p. 2).
94. Ghany 1996: 463–5; Ryan 1989a: 76–8, 84; Yelvington, 'Vote dem out', p. 31. As early as 1985, the PNM General Secretary lamented 'for all practical purposes the party is dead', (quoted in Ryan 1989a: 8).
95. *TE* December 7, 1986, p. 13
96. *TE* December 7, 1986, p. 1. Cynically anticipating this enthusiasm, the *Trinidad and Tobago Review* juxtaposed on the front page of its December 1, 1986 issue the almost indistinguishable pictures of the November 16 NAR meeting in Woodford Square and on Carnival Tuesday in February. It quipped, 'If ever there were elections that needed to be rigged it is these, for there can be only one satisfactory result on December 16th and that is: a slim margin for either major party – preferably the NAR – and, ideally, at least one seat for the National Joint Action Committee.'
97. *TG* December 14, 1986, p. 1
98. GORTT [1987c]: 9–15. Patrick Manning (1999) had opined to the author that had the elections been held only one week later the Port of Spain East seat, won by PNM Youth League leader Morris Marshall, would have been secured.
99. Morris Marshall's Port of Spain East and Overand Padmore's Port of Spain North were the exceptions (GORTT [1987c]).
100. The overall voter turnout had increased to 65.5 per cent (the highest rate since 1966), or an additional 161,884 electors.
101. GORTT 1982b: 202–3
102. Interview with Lloyd Best, 1999
103. *TTR* December 18/23, 1986, p. 1
104. *TTR* December 18/23, 1986, p. 1

## CHAPTER 5

1. *TG* December 22, 1986, p. 1; Yelvington, 'Vote dem out', p. 32; *NTT* January 28,

1987, p. 13.

2. *NTT* January 28, 1987, pp. 3–4, 9–10; Yelvington, 'Vote dem out', p. 32.
3. Siewah and Arjoonsingh 1998, vol. 1: 95; Carl Parris, 'Trinidad and Tobago 1956–86: has the political elite changed?', *The Round Table*, 314 (April 1990), pp. 147–156
4. *TE* April 19, 1987, p. 2.
5. PNM Ministers, magistrates, and police officials were supposedly named in the report, but in the public version published by Unique Services only police officers were systematically listed. None of the officers named were charged. However, the Ministry of National Security issued suspension notices of 53 police officers of varying ranks. Also suspended from duty were five magistrates whose names were supposed to have been mentioned in the Report. The most notable event in the wake of the report had been the resignation of Police Commissioner Randolph Burroughs (*Scott drug report* 1986; *NTT* February 25, 1987, pp. 6, 10; Ryan 1987: 82; Yelvington, 'Vote dem out', p. 32). Over two years later, on June 16, 1989, in an address carried on radio and television, Robinson had named five former PNM cabinet ministers who, he alleged, had been drug users and or dealers, quoting from a confidential letter sent to him by Louis Rodriguez, secretary of the Scott Commission. The *Trinidad Guardian* and the PNM expressed great concern at this 'brutal' abuse of privilege (*LRRCR* July 20, 1989, p. 3).
6. *NTT* January 28, 1987, p. 9; Ryan 1989a: 155, 319
7. *NTT* May 27, 1987, pp. 4–5
8. *NTT* February 25, 1987, p. 5. As with the publication of the Scott Drug Report, the Alexander Commission resulted in no significant action taken against anyone (Siewah and Moonilal 1991: 318).
9. *NTT* June 24, 1987, pp. 1–6; *TG* June 7, 1987, p. 6
10. Former United DLP leader, Alloy Lequay, was the NAR's General Secretary and appointed Leader of Government Business in the Senate.
11. In 1955 Noor Hassanali, then a magistrate in the San Fernando Magistracy, had hired Basdeo Panday as a Second Class Clerk, taking Panday away from his teaching job at St Clement's Vedic School (Siewah 1994: 531).
12. *NTT* January 28, 1987, pp. 1–2, 9; *NTT* March 25, 1987, p. 8; Ghany 1996: 412–4
13. Siewah and Samaroo 1991: 423. Two years later, on March 31, 1989 James died in London from respiratory failure. He was buried in Trinidad by the OWTU according to terms laid out in a will drafted in 1985. OWTU president Errol McLeod refused the government's offer of a state funeral, as Robinson was a Cabinet member in the PNM Government which had placed James under house arrest in 1965. Mention had also been made of Robinson's brother-in-law taking over editorship of the *Nation* after C.L.R. James was expelled from the PNM in 1960. Prime Minister Robinson did not attend James's funeral (Siewah and Moonilal 1991: 423).
14. Siewah and Arjoonsingh 1998, vol. 1: 393; Ryan 1972: 445
15. *NTT* January 28, 1987, p. 14; *NTT* April 29, 1987, p. 10. In 1989, during the proceedings of the Hyatali Constitution Commission, NAR chairman of the THA Jeff Davidson had argued that Tobago's right to secede should be included in the constitution. This did not find favour with most persons, in particular Prime Minister Robinson (*LARRCR* May 11, 1989, p. 6).
16. *NTT* April 29, 1987, p. 14; *TE* September 12, 1987, p. 5; Ryan 1989a: 160–1. External Affairs Minister Panday, who had been deeply involved in the matter, also reportedly had initiated a similar venture with the Government of Nigeria, but the arrangements did not similarly solidify (Siewah and Moonilal 1991: 315). Ralph Premdas, 'Ethnic

conflict in Trinidad and Tobago: domination and reconciliation', in *Trinidad Ethnicity*, ed. Kevin Yelvington (London: Macmillan Press Ltd. 1993), p. 154, reports that the Indian Government has made similar gifts to Guyana, Fiji, and Mauritius, three other small countries with large proportions of Indians (52 per cent, 59 per cent, and 70 per cent respectively [*Europa Yearbook* 1986]). According to the 1980 Census, 41 per cent of Trinidad and Tobago's population were Indians (*ASD* 1990).

17. *NTT* April 29, 1987, p. 3; *TE* April 12, 1987, p. 9; Ryan 1989a: 158–9. Former ONR Deputy Leader, Suruj Rambachan, had been one of the more prominent figures organising the event (*TTR* July 1987, p. 3).
18. *NTT* June 24, 1987, p. 11. The annual observation of Indian Arrival Day was begun in 1977, and in 1995 it became a national holiday (Siewah and Moonilal 1991: 287).
19. *TE* April 19, 1987, p. 9
20. Yelvington, 'Vote dem out', p. 32
21. Yelvington, 'Vote dem out', pp. 32–3, Ryan 1987: 157; Williams 1962a: 279
22. *TE* August 30, 1987, pp. 3, 46–7
23. *NTT* June 24, 1987, p. 6; *TE* August 30, 1987, sec. 3, p. 3
24. Quoted in Ryan 1989a: 118
25. *TG* April 19, 1987, p. 17. For over one year, the party did not have a constitution formally operationalising its unitary (as opposed to a 'federal' or coalition) status.
26. This was the government's labour-intensive make-work programme, known colloquially as 'ten days' because of its ten-day employment rotations, historically located in north Trinidad's 'East-West Corridor,' mainly Afro-Creole conurbation
27. *TTR* June 1987, pp. 3–4
28. *TE* April 12, 1987, p. 9; cf. Yelvington, 'Vote dem out', p. 33
29. *TE* March 8, 1987, p. 9
30. *TE* April 19, 1987, p. 9; *TG* March 15, 1988, pp. 15–6
31. The ATSEFWTU changed its name in 1978 to facilitate the organisation of workers in other sectors (Basdeo Panday, 'Trade unionism, politics and Indo-Caribbean leadership' [paper presented at ISER-NCIC Conference on Challenge and Change: the Indian Diaspora in its historical and contemporary contexts. University of the West Indies, St Augustine, Trinidad and Tobago, mimeo, 1995]).
32. *TTR* July 1987, pp. 11–13
33. *TG* June 7, 1987, p. 1. Robinson was reported to have remarked around this time that the ship of government was sailing through rough seas, because of an empty treasury, and it was to be expected that some of its crew would become seasick and 'vomit on each other'. Panday later rejoined that the nausea on the good ship NAR was the result of the stench coming from the ship's state rooms (*TE* February 14, 1988, p. 8).
34. *TG* July 27, 1987, p. 1
35. *TE* August 20, 1987, p. 48
36. Robinson 1987: 26
37. Robinson 1987: 20
38. On July 19, 1982 Labour Day celebrations were held jointly for the first time by the radical CPTU and the moderate Trinidad and Tobago Labour Congress (TTLC). In December 1983 the Joint Trade Union Grouping (later renamed Concerned Group of Trade Unions) had been formed with unions from both factions (Kiely 1996: 159–160).
39. Yelvington, 'Vote dem out', p. 32
40. *NTT* April 29, 1987, p. 15

41. *TE* March 8, 1987, p. 5; *NTT* March 25, 1987, p. 10
42. A similar complaint had been raised in at least one other instance when Minister of Energy Kelvin Ramnath had remarked that he only learned about the transfer of well-respected permanent secretary Trevor Boopsingh from his ministry through an announcement in the press (*TE* March 8, 1987, p. 9).
43. Constitution Commission 1991: 9; *NTT* January 28, 1987, p. 15; *TG* April 19, 1987, p. 1; Ryan 1989a: 108–14; Ryan 1999b: 190–1. Robinson even went so far as to suggest at the NAR Conference held on April 11 that Clarke was 'fascist' because of the disrespect shown to the elected Head of Government (*TG* April 19, 1987, p. 17).
44. *TG* March 13, 1987, p. 1; *TE* April 12, 1987, p. 25; *TTR* June 1987, p. 5; Ryan 1989a: 114–7.
45. *NTT* May 27, 1987, p. 11; *TG* April 19, 1987, p. 1; Ryan 1989a: 117. No constitutional reform resulted from the Report of the Hyatali Commission, which submitted its 39-page report (with 105 recommendations) to President Hassanali three years later on June 1, 1990. The committee included Dr Patrick Solomon, Dr Allan McKenzie, Mr Michael de la Bastide, Dr Selwyn Ryan, Dr John LaGuerre, and Dr Hamid Ghany (Constitution Commission 1991; Siewah and Moonilal 1991: 214; *LARRCR* July 26, 1990, p. 3).
46. Constitution Commission 1991: 10
47. *TE* May 31, 1987, sec. 2, pp. 6–13
48. e.g., *TTR* June 1987; July 1987
49. Ryan (1991: 84–122) provides a good account of the formation and growth of the Jamaat and, more generally, African conversion to Islam from the 1950s. Also see Nasser Mustapha, 'The influence of Indian Islam on fundamentalist trends in Trinidad and Tobago', *Sociological Bulletin*, 46: 2 (September 1997), pp. 245–65.
50. *TG* July 27, 1987, p. 1; *TE* August 8, 1987, p. 4; *TE* August 9, 1987, p. 5; *TE* August 13, 1987, p. 1; *TE* August 23, 1987, pp. 1, 3
51. The NAR had fully recognised the radical CPTU (with which Senator George Weekes was associated) as a legitimate trade union organisation, unlike the PNM regime which had only given the TTLC full recognition (CPTU 1991: 1, 42; Ryan 1989a: 342–3).
52. *TE* August 24, 1987, p. 1.
53. *TE* August 24, 1987, p. 5; *TE* February 3, 1996.
54. *TTR* June 1987, p. 3.
55. *NTT* January 28, 1987, pp. 8, 11.
56. *NTT* February 25, 1987, p. 10. Deputy Leader Kamaluddin Mohammed declared via a letter dated January 19, 1987 to the PNM General Secretary Alvin Quamina that he could not avail himself of nomination for leadership of the PNM, but that he would remain available to assist the party (Ghany 1996: 475–6). Dr Wills was at one time a close associate of A.N.R. Robinson. Dr Wills resigned from the PNM in September 1970 and was a founding member of the ACDC and later the DAC (*TE* July 29, 1974, p. 12; September 27, 1970, p. 5).
57. *TG* February 18, 1987, p. 9.
58. *TG* April 29, 1987, p. 1; *TG* March 23, 1987; *TE* May 29, 1988, p. 8. This included foundation member and one of the PNM's three Deputy Leaders since 1970, Kamaluddin Mohammed (Ghany 1996: 473–8).
59. *TE* May 4, 1987.
60. *TE* May 27, 1987, p. 8; *TG* February 19, 1987.

61. *TE* August 20, 1987, p. 8.
62. *TTR* August 1987, p. 2. This brings to mind Dr Williams 1955 Woodford Square speech, 'The Case for Party Politics in Trinidad and Tobago', where, after humorously ridiculing the existing state of politics, which was dominated by independent politicians and opportunistic, localised combinations, he declared, 'The first prerequisite of party politics in Trinidad and Tobago is the establishment of one good party'. (Williams 1981: 108).
63. Ryan (1989a: 127–78) gives a detailed account, focused on the racial dimension, of the many and convoluted arguments during this period.
64. *NTT* February 25, 1987, p. 3.
65. *TE* December 25, 1987, p. 1.
66. *TE* November 23, 1987, p. 1.
67. Siewah and Moonilal 1991: 417.
68. Ryan 1989a: 134.
69. Ryan 1989a: 140–2. Panday's Tourism portfolio had been added to Ken Gordon's Ministry of Enterprise and Industry. Panday had quipped that he was now a 'one-third minister' (Siewah and Arjoonsingh 1998, vol. 2: 186). Ramnath retorted that he should be called the Minister of Water, Telephones and Electricity since only '3 of the 14 public utilities were put under his control' (Ryan 1989a: 142).
70. Ryan 1989a: 143.
71. It should be noted, however, that opposed to the Panday faction were Indian Cabinet members and MPs Winston Dookeran (formerly of the ULF), Brinsley Samaroo (formerly of the DAC), and Beau Tewarie (formerly of Tapia). When the party eventually splintered, former ULF members and NAR MPs Emmanuel Hosein and Nizam Mohammed remained in the NAR. On the other hand, the ULF dissidents prominently included John Humphrey, a 'local white', although widely considered an eccentric.
72. Siewah and Arjoonsingh 1998, vol. 1: app., 12–8.
73. *TE* April 19, 1987, pp. 24–5.
74. Quoted in Ryan 1989a: 227; *Report* 1988.
75. *TE* February 14, 1988, p. 8. This included Dr Rampersad Parasaram, who later became an executive member in Panday's breakaway party.
76. Ryan 1989a: 179.
77. Siewah and Moonilal 1991: 45. Indeed, it was questioned why Senator Ken Gordon had 67 state companies under his charge, far more than any of the former ULF members.
78. *TG* March 30, 1988, p. 9. Karl Hudson-Phillips reportedly did not appear before the Nanga Committee, which academic commentator Ken Ramchand indicted as being too lightweight for such an important matter.
79. Ryan 1989a: 227–236; *TG* March 10, 11, 15, 1988.
80. reprinted in *TG* March 11, 1988, p. 13.
81. *TE* May 16, 1988, p. 3; Ryan 1989a: 239; Siewah and Moonilal 1991: 419–22.
82. *TG* April 3, 1988, p. 1.
83. *TG* May 17,1988, p. It was rumoured that CLUB 88 had planned a motion of censure at the forthcoming NAR Annual Conference (*TE* May 17, 1988, p. 8).
84. On May 8, 1988 Fox was reported in the press to have appealed to Hudson-Phillips to intervene in the impasse (Ryan 1989a: 242).
85. *TG* May 16, 1988, p. 1; *TE* May 17, 1988, pp. 1, 3; *TE* May 29, 1988. Some CLUB 88 supporters had questioned why Ministers Lincoln Myers, Pamela

Nicholson, Selwyn Richardson, and Albert Richards, who were also publicly critical, were not also disciplined (Siewah and Moonilal 1991: 188).

86. *TG* May 20, 1988, pp. 3, 18.
87. *TE* July 10, 1988, p. 21; *TTR* July 1988, p. 4.
88. Siewah and Moonilal 1991: 183.
89. Fox had also abstained in Panday's motion of no confidence against Prime Minister Robinson in the House of Representatives in April (*TE* September 11, 1988, p. 20).
90. *Trinidad and Tobago Mirror* September 9, 1988, pp. 1, 32; *TE* September 11, 1988, pp. 8, 20–1.
91. The NAR had called its Annual Conference for October 23, 1988, instead of February 1989 when it was due. The term of Political Leader was to officially end at the Conference (whenever it was held), and after elections the new Political Leader would appoint his two Deputies (*TG* July 10, 1988, p. 6).
92. Claims have varied from five to ten thousand (Ryan 1989a: 218) to 30,000 (Siewah and Moonilal 1991: 430).
93. Siewah and Moonilal 1991: 428–449; Ryan 1989a: 218.
94. Ryan 1989a: 220–3; Siewah and Moonilal 1991: 457.
95. Honorary Secretary of the DLP, FE Brassington [1975: 87–105], had made a similar point earlier, regretting his role in the displacement of Bhadase Maraj for Dr Capildeo as DLP leader.
96. Surendranath Capildeo, son of Simbhoonath and nephew of Dr Rudranath, also noted the similarity of the NAR and the DLP disputes, right down to the court case over the right to use the party symbol (*TE* May 21, 1988, p. 9). The same could have been said, as well, about Panday and Shah's court battles over the use of the ULF symbol (Samaroo and Arjoonsingh 1998: 31).
97. *TTR* August 1988, pp. 17–31.
98. A 'jammette' is an unruly, often lower-class, woman of loose morals and ill-repute.
99. *TE* September 11, 1988, p. 8.
100. *TE* June 26, 1988; July 10, 1988.
101. GORTT [1989]: 17; *LARRCR* December 8, 1988, p. 6.
102. *TG* May 1, 1988, p. 14; *TG* July 10, 1988, p. 14; Ryan 1989a: 261–3.
103. GORTT 1990b: i.
104. GORTT 1988b: 80, 85.
105. Siewah and Moonilal 1991: 183; *TTR* July 1988, p. 4.
106. Workingwoman were also the driving force behind the Sexual Offences Bill Action Committee.
107. *Workingwoman* July/August 1988, p. 1–4; *TG* July 10, 1988, p. 18; *TE* July 10, 1988, p. 8; *TE* June 26, 1988, p. 27; *TE* September 11, 1988, p. 15.
108. Ryan 1989a: 257–8.
109. *TE* September 11, 1988, p. 1; *TG* September 11, 1988, p. 1.
110. GORTT 1988a: 7. The approach to the IMF was made more controversial by the resignation on May 18, 1988 of Davison Boodhoo, a Grenadian national, who had been part of IMF teams that had visited Trinidad and Tobago in 1985, 1986, and 1987. Boodhoo's resignation was written in six parts, protesting the alleged 'high-handed manner in which the fund conducted its operations', the inordinately high level of conditionalities desired by the Fund, undue pressure placed on Trinidad and Tobago to enter formal stand-by arrangements, and, to achieve the Fund's ends, the deliberate exaggeration of key indicators, including the Relative Unit Labour Cost (RULC), the fiscal deficit, unpaid bills, decline in private sector bank deposits, and

government transfers to the public enterprises sector (*TE* July 10, 1988, pp. 2–9, 17–21).

111. This date was A.N.R. Robinson's birthday, about which he seemed to have a numerological attachment (Siewah and Moonilal 1991: 469). In addition to presenting the budget on this day, the 1986 NAR victory was won on the eve of his birthday (as was Eric Williams's victory in 1956), the 1990 Diego Martin by-election was called on December 17 (since December 16 was a Sunday), and the 1991 General Elections were scheduled on his birthday.
112. Between 1970 and 1983 Trinidad and Tobago provided TT$1,601.4 million to CARICOM governments and regional institutions (GORTT 1983: 86).
113. Robinson 1989: 11, 36–7, 39.
114. Interview with Ken Gordon, 1999; *TG* January 29, 1995, p. 1.
115. Calculated from Pantin 1988: 33.
116. EIU 1998a: 27.
117. Penelope Forde and Kelvin Sargeant, 'The state sector and divestment in Trinidad and Tobago: some preliminary findings' (presented at the Annual Conference of the Regional Programme of Monetary Studies, mimeo, 1991); GORTT 1995: 6.
118. Forde et al., 'The evolution of the financial sector', p. 435; Robinson 1986: 30. In Prime Minister Williams's 1967 Cabinet re-shuffle, Robinson, then Deputy Leader of the PNM, was removed from the Ministry of Finance. Many viewed this as a major reason for his resignation from the PNM in 1970 (Ghany 1996: 265–6). Robinson's 1970 resignation speech, protesting a meeting called to discuss disciplinary measures to be taken against him, is reprinted in *Caribbean Man* (Robinson 1986: 129–30).
119. EIU 1998a: 28.
120. GORTT 1990b: 77; GORTT 1993c.
121. GORTT 1990a: 4.
122. Alvin Hilaire, 'Commercial policy in Trinidad and Tobago' (Port of Spain: Research Department, Central Bank of Trinidad and Tobago, mimeo, 1992), p. 27; *LRRCR* July 26, 1990, p. 3. Another notable indication of Trinidad and Tobago's increasing acceptance of ties to other countries had been the amendment to the Citizenship Act, assented to on July 29, 1988, permitting dual citizenship for Trinidad and Tobago born or descended nationals (Siewah and Moonilal 1991: 175).
123. *TTR* July 1988, p. 4; GORTT 1988a: 7.
124. *TE* September 11, 1988, p. 31; *TG* September 11, 1988, p. 7; CPTU 1991: 43.
125. CPTU 1991: 30.
126. *TE* March 8, 1989, pp. 1–3; *TE* March 9, 1989, p. 3.
127. Later that day, Panday had been invited to speak in the poor, black, urban PNM stronghold of Laventille, the first time he had ever done so (Siewah and Moonilal 1991: 253–62).
128. CPTU 1991: 44; Siewah and Moonilal 1991: 367.
129. CPTU 1991: 18–21, 29–30.
130. CPTU 1991: 18, 41; MOTION 1989. Despite the radical activity, between 1987 and 1991 (inclusive), there were only 75 work stoppages resulting in 17,128 man-days of work lost. This is significantly less than the 148 work stoppages and 27,790 man-days lost between 1982 and 1986 (calculated from CBTT 1993).
131. Ryan 1996: 179–208.
132. Siewah and Moonilal 1991: 450, 453, 471; *TE* November 17, 1991, p. 10.
133. MOTION 1989.
134. CPTU 1991: 10, 45.

135. A mimeographed resolution, however, listed 32 organisations, including the UNC, PNM, Tapia, and Women Working for Social Progress (Summit 1990).
136. *SOPO* [1990].
137. Siewah and Moonilal 1991: 183–4.
138. The Government was unfortunately unable to capitalise on the intense nationalistic feeling induced by the football World Cup qualifying match on November 19, 1989 against the USA. It was the best placing that Trinidad and Tobago ever achieved, needing only one more victory to qualify. Trinidad and Tobago lost that match, however. That loss seemed to underscore a larger sense of unfulfilled promise.
139. Siewah 1994: 232–7, 295.
140. According to the 1980 census, 60 per cent of the population were under 25 years old (*ASD* 1990).
141. Ralph Premdas, 'Public policy in a multi-ethnic state: the case of national service in Trinidad and Tobago', *Social and Economic Studies*, 45: 1 (March 1996), pp. 86–7; Siewah 1994: 271.
142. *ASD* 1997. Around this time, many Indo-Trinidadians had claimed refugee status in Canada, allegedly on the grounds of racial persecution. The Canadian Government might have been open to such claims because of the racially motivated anti-Indian coups in Fiji in May and October 1987. Two papers were published by the Canadian Immigration and Refugee Board, in 1989 and 1993, to more closely examine the validity of refugee claims from Trinidad and Tobago.
143. quoted in Siewah 1994: 270.
144. A *dougla* is a person of mixed African and Indian descent. Statistics have not been kept on such mixtures since the 1946 census.
145. Premdas, 'Public policy', pp. 94–5, claims that Myers's marriage to an Indian woman became part of the background to the debates.
146. Premdas, 'Public policy', and Siewah (1994: 269–85) discuss the event in good detail.
147. *TG* July 10, 1988, pp. 1, 5.
148. Siewah and Moonilal 1991: 317.
149. *CI* July 1995, p. 2.
150. *Trinidad Under Siege* 1990: 4, 6, 22. July 27, 1990 was the first day of the Islamic year (Bloeser, 'Deprivation, rationality, and rebellion: the case of Trinidad and Tobago', *Caribbean Studies*, 25: 3–4 [July–December 1992], p. 294). *Trinidad Under Siege* (1990), put together by the *Trinidad Express*, collects 22 articles written at the time of the attempted coup, giving an excellent and broad view. Ryan (1991) provides a detailed account of the convoluted background to the insurrection.
151. Among the leaders of attack on TTT was Omowale Muhammed, a former National Union of Freedom Fighters (NUFF) member formerly known as Andy Thomas. As a NUFF 'guerrilla,' Thomas was convicted for the murder of a policeman but received a presidential pardon (Bloeser, 'Deprivation', p. 283; *TE* August 1, 2000).
152. *Trinidad Under Siege* 1990: 84.
153. Women not in the Cabinet and workers were allowed to leave. Attorney-General Anthony Smart had escaped when he was mistaken for one of these workers (*Trinidad Under Siege* 1990: 25).
154. Abu Bakr was a former police officer, born in an Anglican home, and originally named Lennox Phillips (Bishnu Ragoonath, 'The failure of the Abu Bakr coup: the plural society, cultural traditions and political development in Trinidad', *Journal of Commonwealth and Comparative Politics*, 31: 2 [July 1993], p. 33).

155. Incongruously, it was widely known that Miles was a lover of O'Halloran's as well.
156. *Trinidad Under Siege* 1990: 33–4.
157. Other members of parliament not at the Red House were Jensen Fox, government Senators Fyard Hosein and Alloy Lequay, Speaker of the House Nizam Mohammed, President Noor Hassanali, Basdeo Panday, and Patrick Manning. Ministers Brinsley Samaroo and Bhoe Tewarie returned to Trinidad on July 30 from trips abroad, while Minister of External Affairs and International Trade Sahadeo Basdeo stayed at the Eleventh CARICOM Summit in Jamaica to keep in contact with other regional heads of government (*Trinidad Under Siege* 1990: *passim*).
158. *Trinidad under siege* 1990: 48
159. Ironically, Feroze Shah,a younger brother of 1970 mutiny leader Raffique Shah,had been one of the Muslimeen's six Indian insurgents (Ryan 1991: 111–2). Also not without irony, three months before the coup attempt, Prime Minister Robinson, who had resigned from the PNM in 1970 in protest at its poor handling of the country's social and economic problems, declined an invitation to deliver the feature address at a conference on the '1970 Black Power Revolution: 20 Years Later' held on April 19–21, 1990 at the UWI (Denis Pantin, 'Political crisis in Trinidad and Tobago: cause or coincidence?' *Caribbean Quarterly*, 37: 2 and 3 [June–September 1991], pp. 64, 82).
160. *Trinidad Under Siege* 1990: 76–8. Robinson had apparently been shot and beaten by the Muslimeen after instructing the army, via a radio inside the Red House, to 'attack with full force' (*Trinidad under siege* 1990: 111–2).
161. *Trinidad under siege* 1990: 68–9. Although it was not mentioned in the list of demands, the motivation for the Muslimeen's actions has been widely understood as part of an ongoing land dispute with the government that can be traced back to 1966 (Ryan 1991: 84–122).
162. *Trinidad Under Siege* 1990: 82. Whether an agreement (and an amnesty) was in fact signed and how morally, even if not legally, binding such an agreement would be was raised by Selwyn Ryan (*Trinidad Under Siege* 1990: 69–72) and Basdeo Panday (Siewah and Moonilal 1991: 190) among others. Government officials had declared that the amnesty was invalid because it was signed under duress (*LARRCR* August 30, 1990, p. 2).
163. *LARRCR* August 30, 1990; October 4, 1990. Among those killed was MP Leo Des Vignes who died in Port of Spain General Hospital on August 1 from a gunshot wound in the ankle inflicted on July 27. Minister of Justice and National Security Selwyn Richardson was shot in the ankle but survived (*Trinidad Under Siege* 1990: 78).
164. *Trinidad Under Siege* 1990: 121–2. The youngest member charged was 14 years old. In 1991, *Caribbean Quarterly*, published out of the Mona, Jamaica campus of the UWI, put out a special double issue in broad sympathy with the attempted coup, titled 'The 1990 Muslimeen Insurrection in Trinidad and Tobago: Its Causes and a Measure of its Heroism.'
165. In a SARA poll conducted in September–October 1990, 75 per cent of the sample thought the Muslimeen were wrong to attempt to overthrow the government by force, although 60 per cent sympathised generally with the espoused social goals proclaimed by Bakr on TTT (Ryan 1991: 225).
166. Ryan 1991: 245, 322–332.
167. It has been widely claimed that when told about the coup, Panday responded, 'Wake me up when Abu Bakr finish' (Ryan 1991: 247). This flippant and lackadaisical

attitude had been condemned by the *Trinidad Express* (*Trinidad under siege* 1990) among others. Although the UNC did condemn the coup, up to 1999, neither the UNC nor the PNM commemorated with the NAR the anniversary of July 27. The UNC marked the yearly observance in 2000, the final year of its first term of office.

168. Siewah and Moonilal 1991: 187–95, 457. The six UNC MPs were Basdeo Panday (Couva North), Kelvin Ramnath (Couva South), Trevor Sudama (Oropouche), John Humphrey (St Augustine), Raymond Pallackdharrysingh (Naparima), and Govindra Roopnarine (Siparia).
169. *TE* September 12, 1990, p. 4. The UNC party executive, with Ramnath as its major figure, was apparently piqued at the fact that none of its members were appointed to the Senate (*TE* November 17, 1991, p. 10).
170. Siewah and Moonilal 1991: 189.
171. In the author's copies of the minutes of SOPO meetings, the last on record was September 12, 1990, at which UNC MP for St Augustine John Humphrey was present.
172. Interview in 1994 with Cecil Paul, CPTU, JTUM, OWTU, and MOTION executive member, conducted for the author's M.Sc. thesis (Kirk Meighoo, 'Putting up a new resistance', p. 46).
173. Siewah and Moonilal 1991: 458.
174. *LARRCR* January 24, 1991, p. 7.
175. Guerra was a prosecutor in the 1971 court martial proceedings against the army mutineers, and was the first person to be shot by the 'guerrilla' group, NUFF. (Brian Meeks, 'NUFF at the cusp of an idea: grassroots guerrillas and the politics of the 1970s in Trinidad and Tobago', *Social Identities*, 5: 4 [December 1999], pp. 415–439).
176. Siewah and Moonilal 1991: 459, 111; *LARRCR* January 24, 1991, p. 7; Ryan 1989a: 245–6.
177. Siewah and Moonilal 1991: 111.
178. *TE* June 22, 1991, p. 1.
179. Siewah and Moonilal 1991: 111–2.
180. *TG* August 2, 1991, p. 18.
181. In 1990 Sanderson had been freed from charges of assault against a woman, but the charges sullied his reputation (*Trinidad Under Siege* 1990: 28; *LARRCR* November 7, 1991, p. 2).
182. *LARRCR* November 7, 1991, p. 2.
183. *Workingwoman* November 1991, p. 8; Siewah and Arjoonsingh 1998, vol. 2: 53. In Nigeria, Robinson was bestowed the title Chief Olokun Igbaro of Ife.
184. GORTT 1990b.
185. Between February and December 1990, the government had signed eight debt re-scheduling agreements in order to avoid 'debt trap' (*LRRCR* January 25, 1990, p. 3).
186. Siewah and Moonilal 1991: 68–9.
187. CBTT 1993.
188. It should be noted that in 1990 the petroleum sector grew by 1.7 per cent in constant 1970 prices, while agriculture grew by 18.7 per cent. In 1991, the figures were 0.7 per cent and 6.8 per cent respectively. In 1991, the petroleum sector directly supplied 11 per cent of GDP at constant 1970 prices, while agriculture supplied 6 per cent (CBTT 1993). It should be noted that when contribution to GDP is measured using current prices, petroleum contributes a much larger share, and agriculture a much smaller share.

189. CBTT 1993.
190. Forde and Sargeant, 'The state sector', p. 8; GORTT 1995: 8. During this time, however, Total Government Expenditure decreased from TT$7,723 million in 1985 to 6,877.4 million in 1992 (CBTT 1993).
191. Robinson announced to the population that he had wanted an NAR victory as his birthday present (*LARRCR* December 12, 1991, p. 7).
192. Ryan 1996: 532–4; *LARRCR* December 12, 1991, p. 7.
193. *TG* March 24, 1991, p. 8; *TE* November 17, 1991, p. 10.
194. Ramesh Lawrence Maharaj appeared as a defence attorney in major criminal trials and against Government in several civil, constitutional and public law cases. He is the subject of a 1978 book titled, *Barrister Behind Bars*, by Marcel Berlins, then legal correspondent for the *Times* (London) writing on a landmark contempt of court case against Maharaj, which took place in 1975. Maharaj also served as president of the T&T Bureau on Human Rights, a non-governmental body.
195. *TE* November 24, 1991, p. 3; November 25, 1991, p. 2; Siewah and Moonilal 1991: 471; *LARRCR* May 16, 1991, p. 3.
196. Siewah and Arjoonsingh 1998, vol. 1: 70, 95.
197. In October 1991, Muriel Donawa-McDavidson, PNM MP for Laventille (and PNM Parliamentarian since 1961), declared herself an independent, claiming that the new PNM, which she called 'Patrick's National Movement', was not the party of 'lofty ideals' that she had helped to form (*LARRCR* November 7, 1991, p. 2). Besides Manning, who had been an MP since 1971, the only previous parliamentarians to contest the elections were former senators and ministers John Eckstein and Wendell Mottley (*LARRCR* January 23, 1992, p. 5). Unsuccessful PNM candidate for Tobago West in 1981, Dr Keith Rowley, contested Diego Martin West in 1991.
198. Patrick Manning, 'With the PNM there is hope: a major policy statement', (an address by the Honourable Patrick Manning, MP, political leader of the PNM, at the 28th annual convention of the PNM held at the Chaguaramas Convention Centre on Sunday 9 October, Mimeo, 1988).
199. As with the WFP in 1966, no UNC candidate contested Tobago West.
200. The PPM was led by Michael Als, a populist activist who started the 'Young Power' movement in San Fernando the late 1960s, that had as one of its members Patrick Manning (Interview with Patrick Manning 1999).
201. *TE* December 22, 1991.
202. *TG* March 22, 1992, p. 12.
203. *TTR* December 18/23, 1986, p. 2; Ryan 1989a: 58.
204. Best, 'Alliance', 59.
205. Joseph 1993: 259.

## CHAPTER 6

1. *LARRCR* January 23, 1992, p. 5. The Manning administration apparently did not ask for directors of state boards and statutory authorities to resign as the NAR did in 1987 (Ryan 1999b: 231).
2. Mottley 1992: 1, 21.
3. Mottley 1992: 6-13.
4. Mottley 1992: 12. In 1988, before de-graduation, the government had raised funds

for its adjustment programme through a private placement in the Japanese market (Robinson 1988: 11).

5. Mottley 1992: 21.
6. According to the 1990 census, San Fernando, the city from which Manning hails, had a population of 7,714 Indians (29.2 per cent), as opposed to 4,817 (11.3 per cent) in Port of Spain (home of Williams and Chambers), and 962 (2.1 per cent) in Tobago (home of Robinson). Moreover, Victoria county, in which San Fernando is located, had an Indian population of 122,918 (62.2 per cent) in 1990 (*ASD* 1997).
7. Ryan 1996: 225; *LARRCR* January 23, 1992, p. 5. Manning's alleged statement that he was 'looking for Indians' was regarded by many Indians as patronising. On the other hand, Ryan (1999b: 231–2) suggests that Afro-Trinidadians felt betrayed by Manning, seeing that the Speaker of the House, Occah Seapaul (sister of Minister Ralph Maraj, MP for San Fernando West), and President Noor Hassanali were Indian.
8. CES 1993.
9. CES 1994.
10. Ryan 1995. During this period, the UWI published a number of studies of Trinidad's ethnic groups, including 'Cocoa Panyols' (Venezuelans peons), Portuguese (Ferreira 1994), Indians (Ramesar 1994; Ramsaran 1993), Africans (Ryan and Barclay 1992; Ryan and Stewart 1994), and on ethnicity in general (Premdas 1993), often on their relationship to business. A book on the Chinese (Millette 1993) was also published by Inprint, owned by Owen Baptiste.
11. *TE* April 20, 1992, p. 5.
12. *LRRCR* May 14, 1992, p. 7. According to the author's calculations from the Parliamentary Bill Books, the Manning government presented an average of 39 bills per year in the Lower House between 1992 and 1995, the lowest annual average of any administration, during the shortest parliament in Trinidad and Tobago's political history.
13. In Ryan 1996: 290. Controversially, Maharaj was the lawyer for the Jamaat-al-Muslimeen, whose 114 jailed members were freed in July 1992 after high court judge Clebert Brooks declared that Acting President Carter's amnesty was legally binding and that the Muslimeen were 'unlawfully detained for twenty-two months'. The Muslimeen announced that it would seek damages in the vicinity of US$12 million, which in turn prompted counter actions from Margaret des Vignes (widow of Leo des Vignes), former NAR ministers Jennifer Johnson and Joseph Toney, and several TTT employees. Businessmen and the Attorney-General Keith Sobion also announced intentions to claim for damages (*LARRCR* August 27, 1992, pp. 2–3).
14. Siewah and Arjoonsingh 1998, vol. 1: 328.
15. Ramesh Lawrence Maharaj, 'The strategy employed by the United National Congress for the next general elections (1995)', in LaGuerre 1997a: 42–3.
16. *LARRCR* February 27, 1992, p. 2.
17. Siewah and Arjoonsingh 1998, vol. 1: 325. The PNM candidate received 2,837 votes.
18. *LARRCR* May 14, 1992, p. 7; Ryan 1989a: 129.
19. The UNC controlled the Chaguanas Municipal Corporation and the Couva/Tabaquite/Talparo, Princes Town, and Penal/Debe Regional Corporations.
20. *LARRCR* November 5, 1992, p. 6.
21. Three independents contested the THA elections as well.
22. GORTT 1993a.
23. GORTT 1992a.
24. GORTT 1992a: 6–9.

25. Renwick 1998: 65.
26. *CI* September 1995, p. 1.
27. *LARRCR* May 14, 1992, p. 7.
28. Forde et al., 'The evolution of the financial sector', p. 434
29. *CI* September 1995, p. 10
30. Central Bank researchers Forde et al., in 'The evolution of the financial sector', provide an excellent account of the changed roles of financial institutions and the legislative reorganisation that enabled the liberalisation process.
31. GORTT 1995. Note should be taken that the figures on divestment from the various sources (GORTT 1995; Maingot 1998; EIU 1998a; CBTT 1997; *Caribbean Insight*) do not always square.
32. CBTT 1997
33. *TG* May 2, 1993, p. 19. The PNM and the trade unions strongly opposed the NAR's attempt to introduce the scheme in 1991 (*TG* August 5, 1999, bus. sec., p. 1).
34. Siewah and Arjoonsingh 1998, vol. 1: 278
35. *CI* February 1995; March 1995
36. *CI* January 1995, p. 10. In 1994 the external debt was TT$10,106 million and the internal debt was TT$5,572.2 million (*QEB* December 1998).
37. According to the figures of the Central Bank, divestment proceeds accounted for TT$492.4 million of net external financing in 1994 and TT$589.3 million in 1995. Between 1991 and 1995, divestment proceeds accounted for TT$107.6 million of net domestic financing (*TTR* June/July 2001, p. 17).
38. GORTT 1995: 42–3
39. Maingot 1998: 21
40. The *Economist Intelligence Unit* (1998a, 26) has given yet another figure, US$175 million, as the amount raised from the sale of FERTRIN and TTUC to Arcadian in March 1993.
41. *CI* June 1995, p. 11
42. GORTT 1998: 40
43. EIU 1998a: 28
44. Maingot 1998: 22
45. EIU 1998a: 28
46. Maingot 1998: 24
47. Before the sale in 1993, Amoco had owned 49 per cent of FERTRIN, which started production in 1981 (EIU 1998a: 29; GORTT 1990b: 21).
48. EIU 1998a: 29
49. This was the among the first attempts at hydrocarbon exploration in Trinidad and Tobago's deep waters.
50. GORTT 1997e
51. *CI* May 1995, p. 10
52. In 1990 St Patrick had a population of 112,492 (10 per cent of the national population) as compared to 117,189 (12.6 per cent) in 1970 (*ASD* 1983; 1997). The *National Physical Development Plan* (GORTT 1982a) described it as a transitional zone of declining development.
53. *The Atlantic Story* [1999], p. 1; GORTT 1998: 2; *CI* August 1995, p. 11
54. The emergence of CL Financial was part of the change from the 'big four' conglomerates of the 1970s: Neal and Massey, McEnearney-Alstons, Geddes Grant, and Kirpilani's. Kirpilani's declared bankruptcy in 1986, Neal and Massey purchased Geddes Grant in 1992, and Middle Eastern-born businessman Anthony Sabga

purchased McEnearney-Alstons, renaming it Ansa-McAl (*TE* September 17, 1995, p. 5; Kiely 1996: 158).

55. EIU 1998a: 29–30; *CI* May 1995, p. 11; GORTT 1998: 31
56. *CI* July 1995, p. 10
57. *CI* January 1995, p. 10; GORTT 1998: 32
58. EIU 1998a: 27
59. GDP at constant 1970 prices peaked in 1982 at TT$2,983.4 million. In 1989, at the end of the seven-year recession, GDP at constant 1970 prices was TT$2,127 million, between the level of 1976 (TT$2,001.8 million) and 1977 (TT$2,184.4 million). In 1994, the author calculated that GDP at constant 1970 prices was between TT$2,225.5 million and TT$2,234.8 million, a level between that of 1977 and 1978 (TT$2,403.2) (CBTT 1993).
60. see Appendix D; CBTT 1993
61. Marshall was formerly leader of the PNM Youth League and was widely regarded as the most popular member of Government. Manning and Marshall did not have good relations, and in 1993 Manning issued an ultimatum to the ailing Marshall to deliver an action plan to deal with water problems in the country within a week. The public message was widely regarded as an act of spite.
62. Siewah 1994: 460
63. Siewah 1994: 460
64. Siewah 1994: 460–1
65. Siewah and Arjoonsingh 1998, vol. 1: 134, 145, 259
66. in Ryan 1996: 216
67. A popular daily tabloid newspaper started in 1995.
68. Siewah and Arjoonsingh 1998, vol. 1: 174
69. Ryan 1996: 216, 219, 223
70. Maharaj, 'The Strategy', p. 43
71. Siewah and Arjoonsingh 1998, vol. 1: 55
72. Maharaj, 'The Strategy', p. 43
73. *TG* November 23, 1993, p. 1. Around this time, on December 19, 1993, a SARA poll had indicated that, for the first time, Panday (by a slim margin) was the most popular political leader in the country.
74. One is reminded of Dr Williams's lament, 'Exactly what the PNM laughed at unmercifully and condemned at its birth in 1956, to the plaudits of the population, the same population is now demanding and advocating' (Williams 1973a: 20).
75. *TG* July 10, 1994, p. 10
76. *CI* January 1995, p. 10–1
77. *TG* October 1, 1995, p. 3
78. Then edited by Raffique Shah
79. Siewah and Arjoonsingh 1998, vol. 1: 151–68
80. *CI* January 1995; March 1995; April 1995; May 1995. On November 16, 1995, one week after Panday had been sworn in as prime minister, senior magistrate Anthony Mohipp dismissed the remaining three charges. Mohipp declared that there were 'grave discrepancies in the evidence, which appeared to have been fabricated'; there had been an abuse of process; one witness had 'clearly committed perjury'; and the prosecution evidence 'in its totality' was 'manifestly unreliable' (*CI* December 1995, p. 11; Siewah and Arjoonsingh 1998, vol. 1: 340–2, app. 42–6).
81. *TE* March 27, 1995, p. 1
82. Maharaj, 'The strategy', p. 43; *CI* August 1995, p. 4

83. Subsequently, Attorney-General Sobion discussed with the UNC amending the standing orders to comply with the Crossing of the Floor Act, introduced in 1978 (*CI* October 1995, p. 11; Ghany 1996: 346–8).
84. *CI* October 1995, p. 11; Siewah and Arjoonsingh 1998, vol. 1: 116
85. Ryan 1996: 291; Maharaj, 'The Strategy', p. 44
86. *TG* November 5, 1995, p. 11
87. *CI* December 1995, p. 4; Siewah and Arjoonsingh 1998, vol. 1: 98
88. *CI* June 1995, pp. 1, 12; Siewah and Arjoonsingh 1998, vol. 1: 172
89. *CI* July 1995, p. 2
90. *CI* August 1995, p. 11
91. On August 3, Seapaul filed an action claiming defamation of character against Attorney-General Sobion for statements made by him at two press conferences on July 3 and 5. On August 5, she filed a constitutional motion challenging the validity of the Constitution Amendment Act that created the procedure for the removal of the Speaker which was given Presidential assent on that day; and on August 21 she filed another constitutional motion challenging the validity of the proclamation of the State of Emergency and the Detention Order and claimed damages for unlawful arrest between August 4 and 7. The action against the Attorney-General was settled out of court in November 1995 after the general elections. It seems that the other matters have not been substantively heard in the High Court at the time of research (Hamid Ghany, 'Parliamentary crisis and the removal of the Speaker: the case of Trinidad and Tobago', *The Journal of Legislative Studies*, 3: 2 (Summer 1997), pp. 135–7; Siewah and Arjoonsingh 1998, vol. 1: 180).
92. While Public Utilities Minister, Maraj delivered the feature address at the 150th Anniversary Celebrations of Indian Arrival in Trinidad and Tobago, stating, 'I would be failing in my duty if I did not recognise the contribution that Panday has made in the country. Indeed he would go down in history as one who has struggled for the liberation, enlightenment and development of all the peoples of Trinidad and Tobago.' He was chastised by the May 27 *Express* editorial entitled, 'Now Really, Mr Maraj' (Siewah and Arjoonsingh 1998, vol. 1: 172). As early as May 8, in support of Ralph Maraj, Basdeo Panday publicly accused Manning of running a dictatorship.
93. *CI* September 1995, p. 4; Siewah and Arjoonsingh 1998, vol. 1: 180; Ghany, 'Parliamentary crisis', pp. 135–6.
94. *CI* January 1996, p. 10
95. The liberalisation of radio and television had been started under the NAR administration. Licences were granted to 26 radio and three television stations, but they did not start operating until the Manning administration assumed power (Interview with Ken Gordon, 1999).
96. *TE* July 12, 1998, supp., p. 1: *Media Trak* October 1993; March 1994; April 1998
97. Ryan 1996: 470; *ASD* 1997
98. Ghany 1996: 490–1. An appeal was subsequently filed, apparently without success.
99. The Shouters Prohibition Ordinance of 1917 outlawed the practice of the Shouter (Spiritual) Baptists, a Christian-Yoruba syncretic religion. The ordinance was repealed by the 'Gomes government' on March 30, 1951 (Siewah and Arjoonsingh 1998, vol. 1: 363). All forms of 'obeah' (West African-derived magic) had been banned in 1868 (Brereton 1981: 134).
100. There were 330,655 Catholics in Trinidad and Tobago in 1990 (29.4 per cent) as opposed to 331,733 in 1970 (35.6 per cent) (*ASD* 1983; 1997).
101. The issue of the denominational education seemed to be slowly returning to the

national agenda. On October 14, 1995, in apparent response to a White Paper put out by the government, 20 representatives of denominational schools held an 'urgent' meeting at St Joseph's Convent in Port of Spain to discuss 'the exclusion of any serious mention of the role of denominational boards in education' (*TE* October 15, 1995, p. 3).

102. Siewah and Arjoonsingh 1998, vol. 1: 171, 359–64. The two temporary senators, however, were vocal in support of Prime Minister Manning when Panday introduced his motion of no confidence on June 14, 1995.
103. Ryan 1996: 330
104. *TG* December 11, 1995, p. 1. The *mandir* was officially opened in December 1995.
105. The elections were to occur on the Hindu feast day of *Kartik*; in addition it was the Hindu Diwali season, with the Diwali Nagar in Chaguanas, inaugurated in 1985, as a major gathering point. The September 28, 1995 issue of *Nature* carried a report on the milk-drinking phenomenon. In India, reportedly, the Congress Party accused it of being a vote-getting ploy by the Bharata Janata Party (*TG* October 17, 1995). Some viewed it similarly in Trinidad (Wesley Gibbings, 'Journalism and the political process', in LaGuerre 1997: 53).
106. *ASD* 1997
107. 'Dole Chadee' was the alias of Namkissoon Boodram, named in the *Scott Drug Report* (1986: 15–26) as one of the most significant persons involved directly in the drug trade, with police allies going up to then Commissioner Randolph Burroughs.
108. *CI* March 1996, p. 11
109. *CI* April 1995; May 1995; July 1998; June 11, 1999
110. *CI* July 1995, p. 2
111. *CI* August 1995, p. 11. On January 15, 2001, the High Court ordered 58 members of the Jamaat-al-Muslimeen to pay roughly $20 million ($15 million plus 3 per cent interest compounded annually from 1990) to the State for damages relating to the attempted coup. The Jamaat appealed the decision. Previously, in August 2000 the Jamaat received from the State an interim payment of $1.5 million for damages to the Muslimeen's properties (*TE* January 16, 2001). Legal disputes over insurance claims, which amounted to over $200 million, also remained unresolved (*TG* March 23, 2001, p. 10).
112. *CI* May 1995; October 1995
113. *CI* September 1995, p. 11
114. *CI* September 1995; October 1995; November 1995
115. *CI* October 1995, p. 11
116. Ghany 1996: 482–3
117. These two were the only PNM Ministers, apart from Manning, who had had Governmental experience prior to 1991.
118. Siewah and Arjoonsingh 1998, vol. 1: 191; Ghany 1996: 483
119. *CI* November 1995, p. 3
120. Pierre was replaced in her constituency of Port of Spain South (Dr Williams's old seat) by a candidate also named Eric Williams.
121. Ryan 1996: 280–1
122. Siewah and Arjoonsingh 1998, vol. 1: 309
123. Siewah and Arjoonsingh 1998, vol. 1: 179. Siewah and Arjoonsingh (1998, vol. 1: 179–317) provide full transcripts of Panday's three key campaign speeches, one newspaper interview with *Newsday*, two television panel discussions, and Panday's paid political broadcast, during the period October 6 to November 4.

124. Manning had alleged in an interview with the author (1999) that Mottley had leaked the date to the UNC. Ryan (1996: 329) also reports the rumour that Mottley leaked the date to one of three prominent businessmen formerly supportive of the PNM – former Minister of Trade and Industry, Brian Kuei Tung, Ishwar Galbaransingh, and Steve Ferguson – who had publicly switched allegiance to the UNC three weeks before the election.
125. Siewah and Arjoonsingh 1998, vol. 1: 180–5
126. Siewah and Arjoonsingh 1998, vol. 1: 190–201; *CI* November 1995, p. 3
127. Siewah and Arjoonsingh 1998, vol. 1: 207–8, 272
128. Notably absent was UNC Senator Suren Capildeo – son of Simbhoonath, nephew of Dr Rudranath, and first cousin of Sir Vidia Naipaul – who lost the nomination for the Chaguanas seat to a relatively unknown customs officer, Manohar Ramsaran.
129. Siewah and Arjoonsingh 1998, vol. 1: 180–5, 190–1
130. The six who were not fielded were Raymond Pallackdharrysingh, Subhas Panday (Basdeo's brother), Krish Jurai, Mohammed Haniff, Sahid Hosein, and Carl Singh. Hulsie Bhaggan was expelled, and Sham Mohammed had died.
131. Ryan 1996: 310
132. Siewah and Arjoonsingh 1998, vol. 1: 191–2, 201–3; *CI* November 1995, p. 3
133. In the *Sunday Guardian* of November 5, 1995, Selwyn Ryan referred to the support given by Dookeran, Pantin, and Rambachan to the UNC as the 'grossest form of whoring' (quoted in Siewah and Arjoonsingh 1998, vol. 1: 335).
134. Siewah and Arjoonsingh 1998, vol. 1: 269, 277, 301, 307, app., 36; Bishnu Ragoonath, 'Indian arrival and political power in Trinidad and Tobago: the UNC's victory in the 1995 elections', in LaGuerre 1997: 40
135. Winston Dookeran and Selby Wilson declined offers to lead the party (*TG* October 9, 1995, p. 1).
136. Siewah and Arjoonsingh 1998, vol. 1: 191, 265; vol. 2: 21
137. The two UNC-controlled seats which the NAR contested were Nariva and St Augustine.
138. TV6 was owned by Caribbean Communications Network (CCN), formed in 1991 with former NAR Minister of Industry and Enterprise Ken Gordon as CEO. It became the country's second television station.
139. *CI* November 1995, pp. 2–3; Siewah and Arjoonsingh 1998, vol. 1: 257–300
140. Ryan 1996: 525
141. Siewah and Arjoonsingh 1998, vol. 1: 176, 263
142. Quoted in Siewah and Arjoonsingh 1998, vol. 1: 302–6
143. Siewah and Arjoonsingh 1998, vol. 1: 306
144. Siewah and Arjoonsingh 1998, vol. 1: 302–3, 313. After the elections, a report in the *Mirror* of November 17, 1995 suggested that 'the *Guardian* published a highly questionable conclusion in favour of the PNM . . . [which upon publication had] surprised market statisticians at MFO' (quoted in Siewah and Arjoonsingh 1998, vol. 1: 335).
145. An historical parallel which Panday reiterated right up to February 25, 2000 in the House of Representatives (GORTT 2000b).
146. *CI* November 1995, p. 3
147. Ryan's stubborn argument (1996: 276) that the elections were won by the UNC because the PNM did not sufficiently bring out its voters seems insupportable, except by rejection of the electoral data in favour of racial accounting and presumption of voting behaviour, or banal truism ('my own view is that the PNM would have

done better if more of its supporters had turned out to vote').

148. Siewah and Arjoonsingh 1998, vol. 1: 320; GORTT 2000b. See Ralph Premdas and Bishnu Ragoonath, 'Ethnicity, elections and democracy in Trinidad and Tobago: analysing the 1995 and 1996 elections', *Commonwealth and Comparative Politics*, 36: 3 (November 1998) and Ryan (1996, 1999a, 1999b) for ethnic interpretations of the 1995 and 1996 elections as Indian ascendance to power.
149. Siewah and Arjoonsingh 1998, vol. 1: 321
150. Siewah and Arjoonsingh 1998, vol. 1: 333

## CHAPTER 7

1. Indeed, Panday's vision expressed throughout his political career, which started in 1966, has been remarkably consistent. This is well documented in the collections of his speeches by Siewah and Moonilal (1991) and Siewah and Arjoonsingh (1998).
2. For a view of the UNC government as essentially a pro-Indian administration practising discrimination against Africans, see Ryan (1999b: 233–49).
3. For example, Selwyn Ryan, the *Independent*, PNM founding member Muriel Donawa-McDavidson, and long-time senior public servant Reginald Dumas (Siewah and Arjoonsingh 1998, vol. 2: 120, 278, 329; *TG* July 17, 1999, p. 8).
4. Following section 76(1b) of the Constitution of Trinidad and Tobago, the President had to be satisfied that the member appointed as Prime Minister commanded the support of a majority of members of Parliament. Members of government would then be chosen by the Prime Minister.
5. Ghany (1997) contrasts the actions of President Hassanali to the more passive role taken by Queen Elizabeth II after the British parliament was 'hung' by the February 28, 1974 general elections.
6. There may have been some resentment towards Manning by Tobagonians, as he met with the THA in 1995 regarding constitutional reform with respect to Tobago. However, the PNM did not bring the necessary legislation to Parliament.
7. Siewah and Arjoonsingh 1998, vol. 1: 336–7; Hamid Ghany, 'The 1995 general election and the appointment of a prime minister', in LaGuerre 1997a: 22–3; Interview with Ken Gordon, 1999; Ryan 1999b: 236
8. Siewah and Arjoonsingh 1998, vol. 1: 337–8
9. The *Express* of November 12, 1995 reported that the November 8 agreement contained six points (Siewah and Arjoonsingh 1998, vol. 1: 337).
10. in Ryan 1996: 344–5; Siewah and Arjoonsingh 1998, vol. 1: 396
11. *CI* January 1996, p. 10
12. On February 2, 1996, Persad-Bissessar was replaced by MP for Couva South, Ramesh Lawrence Maharaj, in what many interpreted as a planned strategy, due to the general hostility directed at Maharaj during the 1995 campaign. Persad-Bissessar was moved to the new Ministry of Legal Affairs, and the Cabinet was expanded to 22 persons.
13. *CI* December 1995, pp. 3–4
14. Siewah and Arjoonsingh 1998, vol. 1: 331–4
15. Siewah and Arjoonsingh 1998, vol. 1: 345
16. *EIU* 1998b: 12; Ryan 1996: 373; Siewah and Arjoonsingh 1998, vol. 1: 331
17. in Siewah and Arjoonsingh 1998, vol. 1: 333
18. *CI* January 1996, p. 10
19. NATUC was formed on June 12, 1991 as the single umbrella body representing all

of the country's trade unions, patching the split of 1965 (*Vanguard* June 19, 1991).

20. The PSA engaged in a two-day work stoppage on March 18–9, 1996 to press for final resolution of the payment, which had been owed to them through the tenure of two previous administrations. The final disbursement had amounted to TT$345 million in bonds and TT$470 million in cash (*CI* April 1996, p. 10; *Newsday* June 19, 1998, p. 13).
21. *CI* February 1996, p. 4. The projected surplus of TT$284 million became a deficit of TT$158.4 million, or 0.5 per cent of nominal GDP (CBTT 1999; *CI* February 1996, p. 4).
22. The original holiday to be replaced was Easter Monday, as announced in the House of Representatives (Siewah and Arjoonsingh 1998, vol. 1: 364). Easter Monday was kept after Tobagonians protested that the ending of the four-day Easter weekend would hurt its tourist industry. Interestingly, the UNC accepted the Tobagonians' arguments as opposed to the PNM's. The politics surrounding the granting of Liberation Day might be seen as constituting a significant change in philosophy and cultural hegemony, as sectional interests seem to have outweighed nationalist and previously-dominant established Christian ones, under a Hindu-led administration. For further elaboration see the author's 'Post-Modern Politics: Cyberprotest, Virtual Crises, and the Post-Creole' (*TTR* Labour Day 1997, pp. 20–3).
23. Siewah and Arjoonsingh 1998, vol. 1: 359–64; *TE* April 27, 1996, p. 2. In the first issue (June 1998) of its new party paper, *Magnum*, the PNM continued to assert that Arrival Day was the appropriate name for the holiday celebrated on May 30 (*TE* June 7, 1998, p. 33).
24. Siewah and Arjoonsingh 1998, vol. 2: app., 15; GORTT 1996c: 2
25. Khafra Kambon, chairman of the ESC (which Kambon helped found in 1992), was also a founding member of NJAC (which he left in 1983 on the eve of the local government elections). In May 1969, he and Basdeo Panday, then a lawyer for the OWTU, were jailed together after participating in the TIWU bus strike, protesting against the ISA and the Williams government (Kambon 1988: 180; Kambon 1999).
26. Siewah and Arjoonsingh 1998, vol. 1, 393, vol. 2, 11–2; Ryan 1999a, 224. Ture died of cancer in 1998.
27. Panday was also a founder member and First Vice-President of NATUC (*Vanguard* June 19, 1991).
28. Siewah and Arjoonsingh 1998, vol. 2: 338–40
29. Siewah and Arjoonsingh 1998, vol. 1: 383
30. *CI* February 1996, p. 4
31. in Siewah and Arjoonsingh 1998, vol. 2: app., 9–11
32. Both newspapers were associated with CCN.
33. *CI* March 1996, p. 10
34. David Cuffy who wrote the 'Chutney Rising' article stayed on and criticised his editors' attempts to 'gallery' for public attention through their resignations. Madeira was replaced by former editor of the *Express* Owen Baptiste. Those who left the *Guardian* founded the *Independent*, which started publication on May 10, 1996 and was financed by CL Financial. On August 21, 1998, the *Independent* was purchased by CCN, part of the Neal and Massey conglomerate, and managed by Ken Gordon (Siewah and Arjoonsingh 1998, vol. 1: 365–9; vol. 2: 132).
35. Siewah and Arjoonsingh 1998, vol. 1: 365–9; *CI* April 1996; May 1996; Ryan 1996: 392
36. Prominent persons such as *Express* editor Lennox Grant (*TE* June 9, 1996, p. 6),

Calypso Monarch Cro Cro (in Ryan 1996: 523–4), poet and artist LeRoi Clarke (in Ryan 1996: 347), NJAC leader Makandaal Daaga (formerly Geddes Granger) (in Siewah and Arjoonsingh 1998, vol. 1: 332), political scientist Selwyn Ryan (in Persad 1997: 3–4; *TE* April 23, 1996, p. 9), poet and author Wayne Brown (*Independent* May 28, 1996, p. 11; Persad 1997: 6–7), and journalist Gregory Stoute (*Newsday* June 19, 1996, p. 15) all expressed grave fears, sometimes verging on hysteria, about the implications of a UNC government such as the ending of liberal democracy or the emergence of an 'axis of three "East Indian" states (Trinidad, Guyana, Suriname)' marginalising Afro-Caribbean people.

37. Former chief executive George Charles from the National Flour Mills sued the government for TT$700,000, and NGC's former managing director Malcolm Jones was awarded TT$1.1 million in an out of court settlement, both for wrongful dismissal (*CI* July 1996, p. 11).
38. Ryan 1996: 358–61; *CI* March 1996; July 1996
39. GORTT 1996c: 30
40. PNM MP for Diego Martin East Colm Imbert in April 1996 complained in parliament that the new government started the 1996 URP Programme (on March 4, 1996) with a total of only six projects, as opposed to 20 which the PNM would normally allocate (Ryan 1996: 362). By the end of the year, the government recorded 650 infrastructural projects in nine sub-regions in Trinidad, with an incurred expenditure of TT$87 million, creating 87,883 employment opportunities and employing a total of 42,296 persons (GORTT 1996c: 31).
41. Ryan 1996: 361–4; Ryan 1999b: 232, 241–3
42. Siewah and Arjoonsingh 1998, vol. 1: 396–400; vol. 2: app., 17–21
43. *CI* December 1995, p. 10
44. *CI* February 1996; March 1996; May 1996
45. *CI* March 1996; July 1996. The government's determination to prosecute came against the background of the murder, on May 8, in New York, of the only state witness in the case relating to the shooting of Selwyn Richardson. The accused was set free, and that month the US State Department issued an advisory notice to prospective visitors noting that violent crime was on the rise (*CI* June 1996, p. 10).
46. Siewah and Arjoonsingh 1998, vol. 2: 22–7.
47. Both these seats were won by the PNM, with both the UNC and NAR losing their deposits in Chaguaramas/Glencoe, and the NAR losing its deposit in San Juan West/Caledonia (GORTT [1997b]: 291–5)
48. *CI* February 1996; March 1996
49. Ryan 1996: 361, 369
50. The PNM controlled Port of Spain, Arima, San Fernando, and Point Fortin Municipal Corporations, and the Diego Martin, San Juan/Laventille, and Tunapuna/Piarco Regional Corporations. The UNC controlled the Chaguanas Municipal Corporation and the Sangre Grande, Couva/Tabaquite/Talparo, Mayaro/Rio Claro, Princes Town, Penal/Debe, and Siparia Regional Corporations (see Appendix E).
51. The population of the Borough of Chaguanas (covering 23 square kilometres) according to the 1990 census was 57,311, compared to the population of Port of Spain (covering ten square kilometres) at 46,012 (*ASD* 1994/5,1). The increasing importance of the new borough is illustrated by anthropologist Daniel Miller of the University of London, who has used Chaguanas to understand Trinidad as a whole, in his work *Unwrapping Christmas* (1993), *Modernity* (1994), *Capitalism* (1997), and *The Internet* (Miller and Slater, 2000).

52. Ryan 1996: 378–9; Siewah and Arjoonsingh 1998, vol. 2: 43–6; Interview with Lloyd Best, 1999
53. *CI* September 1996, p. 11
54. *TG* October 13, 1996; October 14, 1996; October 20, 1996; *TE* October 20, 1996, pp. 10, 13; *CI* November 1996, p. 9; *EIU* 1998a: 11; Ghany 1996: 413
55. At the PNM Annual Convention of December 1997, Senator Nafeeza Mohammed, daughter of Shamshuddin Mohammed and niece of Kamaluddin Mohammed, was named the third deputy leader (*TG* December 28, 1997).
56. The challenges by A.N.R. Robinson in 1970 and Karl Hudson-Phillips in 1973 were the other instances of major dissent within the party. See Robinson (1986: 119–135), Ryan (1989b: 11–5), and Ghany (1996: 265–74, 300–4) for accounts.
57. *TE* October 20, 1997, p. 10
58. Ryan 1996: 377–80
59. GORTT 1996a; *CI* January 1997, p. 11; *TE* February 28, 2000
60. Moore-Miggins resigned on November 6, 1996, after abstaining on a proposal to reconvene the parliamentary select committee on the relationship between Tobago and Trinidad.
61. GORTT 1997a; Siewah and Arjoonsingh 1998, vol. 2: 42; *CI* December 1996, p. 11. Charles did not contest the 1988 elections and was therefore not a member in that term.
62. According to the 1976 Republican Constitution, the President is elected for a term of five years by an Electoral College composed of the Upper and Lower Houses of Parliament.
63. Reprinted in *TE* October 7, 2001, p. 11
64. *CI* March 1997, p. 4; *EIU* 1998a: 11
65. The government's members in the lower house totalled 18 (excluding Robinson and Lasse who did not vote), and in the senate totalled 16; the opposition had 16 seats in the lower house and five in the upper (as a newly appointed senator had not yet been sworn in); and there were nine independent senators.
66. *CI* March 1997, pp. 3–4. Panday claimed that two independent senators told him that they voted for Robinson.
67. Hector McLean, 'Proper procedures', *Parliamentarian*, 78:4 (October 1997), pp. 304–5; *CI* April 1997, p. 11. Ironically, that ruling had been made in September 1995 by Deputy Speaker Rupert Griffith, rejecting a request from the Opposition Leader Panday to have Huslie Bhaggan's Chaguanas seat declared vacant (*CI* October 1995, p. 11). It is also worth recalling that the resignation from the PNM on March 31, 1978 of Hector McLean (MP for Arouca and Minster of Works, Transport and Communication) prompted the Williams government, with the cooperation of Opposition Leader Panday, to introduce the Crossing of the Floor Act later that year (Ghany 1996: 346–8).
68. Not only had the Standing Orders not been amended as demanded by the 1978 legislation, Manning's referred to himself in his letter to the Speaker as Leader of the Opposition rather than Leader of the PNM, and 'a person other than the Leader of the Opposition and belonging to the same party had communicated with the Speaker styling himself "Leader of the Opposition (Party) in the House"' (McLean, 'Proper procedures', p. 305).
69. Siewah and Arjoonsingh 1998, vol. 2: 161; *CI* June 1997; December 1997; *TE* July 24, 1999, p. 9; *TG* May 7, 1999
70. See his *Think Again: Essays on Race and Political Economy* (1991) for his outspoken

opinions.

71. *TE* April 17, 1997, p. 1
72. On February 21, 1997, one week after Robinson was elected President, Tobago PNM treasurer Trevor Craig was reported to have likened Manning to an albatross around the PNM's neck (*CI* March 1997, p. 4).
73. In 1995, the NAR received 5,254 votes and the PNM 2,432 (GORTT 1996b).
74. Siewah and Arjoonsingh 1998, vol. 2: 165; *CI* May 1997; June 1997; February 1999; *TG* December 28, 1997; *TE* August 15, 1997, p. 14
75. Further reducing the PNM number in parliament was the effective withdrawal of PNM MP for Port of Spain North/St. Ann's West, Gordon Draper, after he became a consultant with the Commonwealth Secretariat in London. Draper's absence was similar to Dr Capildeo's in 1963–8.
76. Ryan (1999b: 244–6) provides a three-page list of specific grievances against the UNC government, with varying levels of legitimacy.
77. In the first half of 1998 over 2,300 exercises and 5,200 raids were carried out on drug blocks (GORTT 1998c: 26–7). In May 1998 alone, 1,046 persons had been detained for narcotic offences, 1,047 on outstanding warrants, and 48 persons for firearms and ammunition offences (Siewah and Arjoonsingh 1998, vol. 2: 312–3).
78. GORTT 1996c: 38–9; Siewah and Arjoonsingh 1998, vol. 1: 37, 200, 311–3; *CI* October 1997, p. 11; *TE* July 10, 1999, p. 26; *TG* July 30, 1999, p. 15
79. GORTT 1996c: 38–9. This included the charging of officers for the 1994 murder of Canadian visitors (*TG* September 26, 1998), and of others for crimes such as theft, conspiracy to kidnap, and rape (*TE* July 3, 1999, pp. 5, 7). On July 27, 1999 independent Senator Diana Mahabir Wyatt lauded that 'something finally is being done' to purge the police of its 'dissident' officers (*TG* July 29, 1999, p. 12).
80. The total number of justices of the peace was 120 at the time.
81. *CI* November 1997, p. 11; April 23, 1999; GORTT 1999c: 15; *TG* February 22, 2000
82. Up to 1998, two traffickers had been extradited to the US and three cases were pending (GORTT 1998b: 12; *CI* February 1998, p. 11).
83. GORTT 1996c: 39; GORTT 1998: 27; GORTT 1998b: 2, 11–2
84. Kuei Tung 1998, p. 4. According to the *Estimates of Expenditure* for 1998–9, the Ministry of Education received the largest allocation, and the Ministries of Finance and Health received the third and fourth largest, respectively.
85. Interview with Basdeo Panday, 1999; GORTT 1998c: 26; Siewah and Arjoonsingh 1998, vol. 2: 30–41, 184, 314–5, 325–6, 331.
86. Siewah and Arjoonsingh 1998, vol. 2: 311; *CI* December 1996, p. 4
87. *TG* February 18, 1997; May 4, 1997; May 9, 1997; May 16, 1997; May 18, 1997; *TE* November 3, 1996; February 19, 1997; May 15, 1997; May 17, 1997; May 21, 1997; May 30, 1997; *Newsday* March 6, 1997, p. 5; *CI* June 1997, pp. 1, 12; *TTR* Independence Day 1997, pp. 7–11; Ferguson 1997; Parris 1997; GORTT 1998b: 4
88. *TG* August 2, 1988, p. 8
89. *TG* June 23, 1999, p. 3
90. *TE* August 4, 1999, p. 5
91. After their previous attorney, Ramesh Lawrence Maharaj, had become Attorney-General, the Jamaat secured the representation of Subhas Panday, brother of the prime minister. In September 1996, the Muslimeen were ordered to pay the state TT$60 million in damages, and on March 11, 1997 they lost an appeal against a 1992 ruling that the organisation had no access to State land adjoining their mosque

in Mucurapo. In February 1998, the City Corporation issued a lease to the Jamaat to regularise the situation (Siewah and Arjoonsingh 1998, vol. 2: 53; *CI* October 1996, p. 11).

92. Siewah and Arjoonsingh 1998, vol. 2: app., 53; *TE* March 15, 1998
93. As of June 28, 1996, out of the 156 jurors originally empanelled, 75 sought exemption, of whom 31 were released from the pool (*CI* July 1996, p. 4).
94. Siewah and Arjoonsingh 1998, vol. 2: 42
95. *CI* September 1996; October 1996
96. *CI* July 1998, p. 12. The Judicial Committee of the Privy Council ruled in the case of Pratt and Morgan in November 1993 that the death penalty could not be executed after five years had elapsed, on the grounds that such delay constituted cruel and unusual punishment.
97. The UNC opposed a similar measure introduced by the PNM government in April 1995 (*CI* May 1995, p. 11).
98. A three-quarters majority (i.e., 27 votes) was required.
99. Siewah and Arjoonsingh 1998, vol. 2: 333, 347; *CI* October 1998, p. 10; *TE* September 6, 1998, p. 5
100. After the nine were hanged in 1999, the government announced that it would assist the two children who survived the 1994 murders (the younger one was 13 at the time) by rebuilding the family house, finding a job for one, supplying the other with school books and uniform grants, supplying household appliances, granting legal ownership of their father's property, and providing them each with public assistance of TT$171 per month (*TG* June 13, 1999, p. 1). This action presaged the Criminal Injuries Compensation Bill passed one month later, on July 19, 1999 (*TE* July 20, 1999, p. 5).
101. GORTT 1997d
102. GORTT 1997d: 26
103. The term was first used by Panday, when he was Leader of the Opposition, to describe then Speaker of the House, Occah Seapaul (Ryan 1999b: 231).
104. *CI* July 1997, p. 4
105. Siewah and Arjoonsingh 1998, vol. 2: 122
106. A 'bobolee' is an effigy traditionally beaten on Good Friday. It serves a symbolic function similar to the so-called 'scapegoat' in Yom Kippur.
107. Siewah and Arjoonsingh 1998, vol. 2: 154–6
108. Siewah and Arjoonsingh 1998, vol. 2: 192; *CI* May 1998, p. 11; *TE* May 13, 1998
109. *TE* May 8, 1998
110. *TG* July 5, 1998, p. 2
111. Siewah and Arjoonsingh 1998, vol. 2: 192–3, 264. Owen Baptiste had resigned from the *Guardian* on June 30, 1997, and was replaced by Carl Jacobs (*CI* July 1997, p. 4).
112. *TE* November 3, 1998
113. *CI* December 1998, pp. 1, 8
114. Selwyn Ryan marshalled comments from Jamaica's *Gleaner*, *Observer*, and *Herald* that were extremely critical of Panday ('outlandish' and 'unacceptable,' 'you [Panday] can't threaten us and get away with it,' 'the Jamaica press would eat Mr. Panday raw') (*TE* December 6, 1998).
115. *TG* November 21, 1998; *TE* November 21, 1998
116. Siewah and Arjoonsingh 1998, vol. 2: 142
117. The land grant effectively ended the two-year dispute among Baptist organisations,

dividing them into pro-PNM and pro-UNC factions, over whether a national holiday or a grant of land was more important (*Mirror* January 28, 1996, p. 9; Ryan 1996: 356–7).

118. Siewah and Arjoonsingh 1998, vol. 1: 361
119. *TE* July 31, 1999, p. 5; *TE* July 4, 1999, p. 6
120. CLICO (Caribbean Life Insurance Company) is the flagship company of CL Financial.
121. Siewah and Arjoonsingh 1998, vol. 1: 55–6; vol. 2: 124, 131–7, 274, 285, 351; *CI* August 1997, p. 11
122. C.L.R. James had been somewhat of a tutor to Kwame Nkrumah in the US from 1943–5, and Trinidad-born George Padmore, head of the International African Bureau in London, became a member of the Cabinet of Ghana in the immediate post-independence period. Padmore's ashes are buried in the Castle, Ghana's seat of government (Buhle 1988, 136–42; Siewah and Arjoonsingh 1998, vol. 2, 135).
123. Siewah and Arjoonsingh 1998, vol. 2: 131–7
124. Siewah and Arjoonsingh 1998, vol. 1: 361; vol. 2: 136; *TE* August 2, 1998, p. 3
125. *TG* June 3, 1999; July 19, 1999; July 24, 1999; July 27, 1999; July 29, 1999. The City of Port of Spain held the park's 199-year lease 'for a public walk, recreation ground or public park ... and for no other purpose whatsoever' granted in 1935 (the year marking the silver jubilee of the crowning of King George V). In addition, the Ordinance for Park and Recreation Grounds forbade the building of permanent structures in any of the nation's parks. There were at least three other instances, two in 1973 and one in 1986, when the government was prevented from building in the park a sporting or recreation complex.

    Interestingly, in May-June 1998 the PNM also supported the high income Diego Martin residents who opposed changing the name of 'Diamond Boulevard' to 'Wendy Fitzwilliam Boulevard' in honour of Miss Trinidad and Tobago's winning the 1998 Miss Universe title. Two days after the sign was erected it was blacked out with paint, bringing comment from Winnie Mandela who had been visiting Trinidad and Tobago at the time and hailed Fitzwilliam as an example of African beauty. Despite opposition, the government kept the new name (*Independent* June 19, 1998, p. 11; Siewah and Arjoonsingh 1998, vol. 1: 55–6).
126. *Report* 1988
127. *TE* February 9, 1999
128. Siewah and Arjoonsingh 1998, vol. 2: 93
129. *TE* October 15, 1998. According to the 1990 census, 29.6 per cent of the population were either Hindu or Muslim. If one added the categories 'None,' 'Other,' and 'Not Stated,' the proportion of non-Christians would be 39.6 per cent (*ASD* 1997).
130. *TE* October 16, 1998
131. *TG* May 24, 1997, p. 7
132. Siewah and Arjoonsingh 1998, vol. 2: 275; *TE* April 16, 1998; May 7, 1998; May 14, 1998
133. *TG* June 3, 1999, p. 6
134. *Independent* June 27, 1998, p. 14; *TG* July 5, 1998, p. 6
135. Siewah and Arjoonsingh 1998, vol. 2: 353
136. GORTT 1998c: 41; *TE* February 9, 1998; *TG* September 26, 1998
137. A Minority Report submitted by UWI political scientist John LaGuerre, one of the commissioners, recommended an Equal Opportunities Commission based on race and gender. On February 9, 1991 the UNC had established such a commission, of

symbolic value at most, in the Office of the Leader of the Opposition (Siewah and Arjoonsingh 1998, vol. 2: 263–4).

138. Siewah and Arjoonsingh 1998, vol. 2: 263–73
139. Full transcripts of the lyrics can be found in *Caribbean Dialogue* (October/December 1997: 120–1) and Ryan (1996: 523–4).
140. *TE* June 21, 1998
141. NAEAP 1998
142. Ryan's *The Jhandi and the Cross: the Clash of Cultures in Post-Creole Trinidad and Tobago* (1999) lists in depth many of the opposing ethnic views expressed in the contemporary climate.
143. The bill was originally passed in the Lower House on April 17, 1998, and had provoked protest from Morgan Job and Hochoy Charles over conflicts in THA/Central Government jurisdiction and the different implications of squatter regularisation in agricultural Tobago and in urban Trinidad (*TE* April 20, 1998; April 23, 1998; *TG* April 20, 1998).
144. *CI* October 1998; November 1998; *TE* September 24, 1988; September 25, 1998; *TG* September 25, 1998
145. *TG* December 27, 1997. For example, for the 1998 fiscal year, Charles requested TT$1 billion, but was allocated TT$300 million (*TE* February 5, 1998).
146. *CI* November 1998, p. 10. In 1998, the fiscal year had changed from January-December to October-September.
147. *TE* June 18, 1999, p. 11
148. *TG* June 14, 1999, p. 1
149. *TG* June 22, 1999, p. 3; *TE* June 23, 1999
150. *TE* June 18, 1999, p. 11; *TG* July 7, 1999; July 11, 1999
151. *TG* July 10, 1999, p. 1; *TE* May 1, 2000
152. *TG* February 7, 2000
153. In Maingot 1998: 24
154. *TE* July 24, 1999, p. 10
155. *TE* July 11, 1999, p. 7
156. On May 27, 1998, Panday declared that his goal was to bring unemployment down to less than ten per cent by the year 2000 (Siewah and Arjoonsingh 1998, vol. 2: 316). This had only ever been achieved in 1980 and 1982, when the figure was 9.9 per cent for both years (CBTT 1993).
157. In 1982–3, the average annual price of oil dropped 12.5 per cent, and in 1985–6 it dropped 46.4 per cent (CBTT 1993).
158. The low of 20.0 per cent in 1998 may not be comparable because of the change in the fiscal calendar that year.
159. In the period 1955–1991, the lowest proportion of current oil revenue to total revenue was 31.1 per cent, in 1988 during the recession. The highest ratio was 73.2 per cent, in 1975 (CBTT 1993).
160. For the entire 1974–82 oil boom period, direct investment totalled US$1,408.5 million, peaking at US$202.8 million in 1975 (CBTT 1993).
161. Kuei Tung 1998: 5
162. In February 1999, Neil Rolingson, Chief Executive Officer of the Point Lisas Port Development Company, had informed a visiting Canadian Trade Mission that Point Lisas had reached its saturation point with no more land available for development, but that 'two or three other sites' were being identified for heavy industrial use (*TG* February 23, 1999).

163. GORTT 1998a: 30. On January 23, 1999, the Nucor Iron Carbide plant (opened in 1994 as the first facility in the world to attempt to produce iron carbide commercially) suspended production on January 23, 1999 (*Gasco News* May 1999, p. 20; *EB* May 1999: 75). Most of the value of these plants were held by multinational companies, but local holdings were not insignificant. Government held 51 per cent equity in two ammonia plants (Tringen I and II), and through the NGC, 49 per cent in Phoenix Park Gas Processors, Ltd. and 10 per cent in Atlantic LNG. Local conglomerate CL Financial held equity in all four methanol plants: 26 per cent in TTMC I and II, 69 per cent in the Caribbean Methanol Company, and 70 per cent in the Methanol IV plant (GORTT 1998a, 30–4).
164. The Potash Corporation of Saskatchewan (PCS) Nitrogen company completed its purchase of the assets of Arcadian on March 6, 1997.
165. GORTT 1998a: 30–4; *CI* September 1998, p. 11
166. In 1999, Trinidad and Tobago held 0.1 per cent of the world's proven oil reserves, accounted for 0.2 per cent of world oil production, held 0.4 per cent of the world's proven natural gas reserves, and accounted for 0.5 per cent of world natural gas production (*BP Amoco* 2000).
167. *Caribbean Insight* (September 1998, p. 11) claimed that Trinidad and Tobago had already become the world's largest exporter of ammonia.
168. GORTT 1998a: 32; *Investment* 1999; *CI* July 2, 1999, p. 1
169. GORTT 1998a: 6; *CI* September 1998, p. 11
170. *TE* April 20, 1999; *CI* April 30, 1999, p. 2
171. *The Atlantic story* [1999], p. 2; *TE* November 3, 1998
172. *CI* July 1998, p. 10
173. *Latin American Monitor: Caribbean* May 1999, p. 7
174. *EB* May 1999; GORTT 1998a: 33
175. *Gasco News* May 1999, pp. 7–8
176. *TE* December 30, 1999
177. GORTT 1998a: 30–1. After the agreement had been signed in November 1998, plans were suspended in February 1999 (*CI* March 1999, 7)
178. *CI* November 1997, p. 10
179. Between April 22, 1996 and February 18, 1998, 13 production-sharing contracts, involving 16 international oil and gas companies operating through locally incorporated subsidiaries, were entered into with the government of Trinidad and Tobago (GORTT 1998a: 11).
180. *CI* September 1997; October 1997; November 1997; February 1998; June 1998; August 1998; November 1998.
181. GORTT 1997e; TIDCO 1999; CBTT 1993. In March 1998, the remaining life of natural gas reserves was estimated at 54 years at the current level of production. Since 1995 natural gas has outstripped crude oil production (GORTT 1998a: 36; *TG* August 31, 1998, p. 4).
182. *TE* June 22, 1999, p. 4; Maingot 1998: 3
183. *TE* July 9, 1999, p. 4; *TG* February 27, 1999; April 30, 1999; July 15, 1999
184. *ACP-EU Courier* May–June 1998, p. 14. This has included a bilateral agreement with Costa Rica and CARICOM agreements with Colombia, Dominican Republic, and Haiti. Also on the government's agenda has been plans for the Central American Common Market, the Andean Group, Argentina, and Mexico (GORTT 1998c: 3; TIDCO 1999: 42).
185. CBTT 1993. According to the author's calculations, real GDP levels in 1999 reached

a level found between 1980 and 1981, approaching the all-time peak level in 1982.

186. Siewah and Arjoonsingh 1998, vol. 2: 183
187. ASD 1997
188. *TE* July 24, 1999, p. 10
189. GORTT 1998c: 39
190. *TG* July 12, 1999, p. 16. It was estimated that there were 150 street dwellers in San Fernando.
191. *TG* July 9, 1999, p. 10
192. GORTT 1998c: 39
193. *TE* July 24, 1999, p. 10
194. *EB* November 1999: 67
195. GORTT 2000
196. *EB* May 1999: 75; GORTT 1988c: 35–7. It was reported that only 50 per cent of mail was delivered within 24 hours of posting, and many areas received infrequent deliveries or none at all. The parcel service was found to be so unreliable that according to a 1996 survey the average citizen mailed only one parcel in his or her lifetime (*CI* April 23, 1999, p. 3)
197. *TG* June 22, 1999, p. 3
198. *CI* April 1997; May 1997; June 1997; October 1998; *TE* April 16, 1998; August 8, 1999. The day the contract was signed, the media's attention was on the government's temporary appointment of Occah Seapaul to the Senate (*CI* October 1998, 11).
199. *TE* June 24, 1999, p. 5
200. *TG* July 27, 1999; August 11, 1999; *TG* July 25, 1999, p. 1
201. *TG* August 1, 1999, p. 1
202. GORTT 1998c: 2–3
203. Siewah and Arjoonsingh 1998, vol. 2: 274–84; *TE* April 8, 2000
204. *CI* June 4, 1999; July 2, 1999; *TE* June 23, 1999, p. 6; *TG* June 23, 1999, p. 19; *EB* November 1999: 67
205. *TE* July 17, 1999; July 20, 1999; July 21, 1999; *TG* July 7, 1999; July 16, 1999
206. The Economist Intelligence Unit (EIU 1998a: 21–2) identified the NAR's 1989 budget cuts as beginning the decay in the health and education sectors.
207. For example, *TE* August 5, 1999, pp. 2–3. The Regional Health Authority.
208. *TE* June 23, 1999, p. 8; *TG* June 17, 1999, p. 3; *TG* July 8, 1999, p. 3; *TG* June 14, 1999, p. 8
209. *TE* September 4, 1998, p. 10
210. *TG* November 19, 1998; *TE* November 18, 1998
211. *TE* June 6, 1999, p. 3
212. *TE* July 6, 1999, p. 3; *TG* July 15, 1999; July 16, 1999; July 20, 1999
213. *TG* November 19, 1998
214. *TE* June 26, 1999, p. 6
215. *CI* February 1998; March 1998, p. 3; *TE* May 27, 1998
216. *CI* February 1998, p. 4
217. *TE* May 27, 1998, p. 8; *TG* August 17, 1998, p. 1
218. Ryan 1999b: 247–8
219. *TE* June 16, 1999, p. 16
220. Panday had called the striking teachers 'criminals,' since they were barred from strike activity under the Industrial Relations Act. Their action was largely seen as a failure, as they settled for a 2 per cent pay increase for 1997, a 3 per cent increase in 1998, and none for 1996, after rejecting on May 21 an offer of a 5 per cent increase covering

1990–8 (Siewah and Arjoonsingh 1998, vol. 2: 339; *CI* October 1996; June 1997).

221. The strike action, in which occurred acts of sabotage including the throwing of two petrol bombs at the home of principal Compton Bourne, was taken to secure a 10 per cent pay claim for 1994–7. The strike, also considered a failure, was eventually settled through the Labour Minister, whose intervention the union had initially rejected, with a 7 per cent increase for 1996–9 (Siewah and Arjoonsingh 1998, vol. 2: 339; *CI* May 1998; June 1998).

222. *CI* July 1998, p. 11; *TE* June 19, 1998; June 20, 1998; *Newsday* June 19, 1998, p. 5

223. Panday's list included the introduction of the National Minimum Wage of $7 an hour; increasing the Old Age Pension from TT$420 to TT$520 a month; the introduction of the National Minimum Wage of $7 an hour; increasing the Old Age Pension; the commitment to provide a $300 million Tax-Free Housing Bond for the financing of low cost homes; the speedy determination of long overdue payment of money owed to public servants; the conclusion of three separate bi-lateral three-year Collective Agreements involving close to one hundred thousand public sector employees, resolving outstanding disputes dating as far back as the 1990-2 period, and the 1993-5 period; the regularisation of some five thousand daily, hourly and weekly paid workers with the Central Government from more than ten years, in some cases; the commitment to establish an Employee Stock Ownership Plan; and the support given to micro business and small business, particularly through the NGO Fund Aid, which was said to have generated over 25,000 jobs (Siewah and Arjoonsingh 1998, vol. 2: 338-44; *Newsday* June 19, 1998: 12-3).

224. *TG* June 19, 1999, p. 1; *TE* June 21, 1999, p. 3

225. *TG* June 20, 1999; July 5, 1999; July 25, 1999; *TE* June 20, 1999, p. 3

226. *TE* July 24, 1999, p. 8; *CI* September 24, 1999, p. 4; *TE* August 5, 1999, p. 7; *TG* August 1, 1999, p. 5

227. Siewah and Arjoonsingh 1998, vol. 2: 9

228. *TE* October 22, 1998

229. *TE* June 21, 1999, p. 3

230. Siewah and Arjoonsingh 1998, vol. 2: 252; *TG* December 28, 1997

231. *CI* August 1997, p. 11

232. *CI* October 1997, p. 11

233. *TG* December 28, 1997. After resigning from the leadership of the NAR in 1992, Charles formed the National Development Party. In 1993 he proposed that his party and the UNC form a coalition under Panday's leadership. Panday declined.

234. Siewah and Arjoonsingh 1998, vol. 2: 328–9; *TE* September 28, 1998

235. *TG* September 29, 1998

236. *CI* October 1998, p. 11

237. *TE* December 16, 1998

238. *TE* July 10, 1999, p. 3

239. *TE* June 16, 1999, p. 8

240. *TG* July 11, 1999, p. 21

241. The most famous advertisement, however, had no text and merely superimposed on the PNM's Balisier House headquarters the sign, 'Jurassic Park' (*TG* July 6, 1999, p. 12).

242. *CI* March 1998, p. 11

243. President Robinson had been on leave during the period February 10, 1998 to August 24, 1998 recovering from his own heart surgery, about which the nation was well-informed. Robinson's health was of national concern when he fainted during a

live television broadcast of the August 31, 1997 Independence Day parade at the Savannah opposite President's House. It was also public knowledge when Robinson was Prime Minister that he had undergone surgery in February 1988. Panday, too, underwent heart surgery on December 30, 1995, and six years earlier in December 1989, with the full knowledge of the country (Siewah and Arjoonsingh 1998, vol. 1: 350–1).

244. Siewah and Arjoonsingh 1998, vol. 1: 351–2; vol. 2: 279; *CI* June 1998, p. 11; *TG* May 13, 1998
245. Siewah and Arjoonsingh 1998, vol. 2: 5
246. *TE* October 20, 1996, p. 13; *TG* May 13, 1998; June 28, 1998, p. 8; July 5, 1998; July 19, 1998; *Independent* July 18, 1998, p. 7; *TE* July 19, 1998; Interview with Patrick Manning 1999.
247. Siewah and Arjoonsingh 1998, vol. 2: 174
248. *TG* August 17, 1998, p. 1
249. *TE* December 24, 1997; September 27, 1998; *CI* December 1996; February 1998; *TG* November 20, 1998; April 25, 1999
250. After the election, Manning claimed that the UNC spent over TT$7 million and the PNM under TT$1 million (*TG* July 27, 1999, p. 15).
251. The *Express* (July 11, 1999, p. 7) estimated 10,000 at the UNC's final rally at Macoya on July 10, and 3,000 at the PNM's in Woodford Square.
252. *TG* June 23, 1999, p. 3
253. *TG* July 4, 1999, p. 3; *TE* July 11, 1999, p. 7
254. In April 1997, Singh appeared before Chaguanas Magistrate Marcia Ayres-Caesar to answer various charges, including assaulting Assistant Traffic Commissioner Norton Regist, dangerous driving, driving without due consideration for other motorists, driving without insurance and failure to produce insurance on demand by a police officer. In March 1998, he was accused of brandishing a gun at URP workers. Referring to the workers, whom he charged were undisciplined, he told reporters, 'I am going to stick on them like hog love mud'. (*TE* February 21, 2000).
255. Siewah and Arjoonsingh 1998, vol. 2: 256
256. Siewah and Arjoonsingh 1998, vol. 2: 175
257. *TG* December 28, 1997; *TG* February 2, 1999
258. *TG* July 14, 1999, pp. 2–3
259. Won by the PNM's Arthur Sanderson (NAR MP for Fyzabad in 1986–91).
260. *TG* July 14, 1999, p. 1
261. *TG* July 31, 1999, p. 10; *TE* July 18, 1999, p. 5
262. *TE* July 14, 1999, p. 12
263. *TTR* August 1999, pp. 1–3
264. *TE* July 25, 1999, p. 11
265. *TE* July 16, 1999, p. 7
266. *TG* July 16, 1999; July 17, 1999; *TE* July 17, 1999; July 20, 1999; July 21, 1999
267. *TG* July 19, 1999, p. 3; *TE* July 27, 1999, p. 12
268. *TG* June 3, 1999; July 19, 1999; July 24, 1999; July 27, 1999; July 29, 1999
269. *TG* December 10, 1999; *CI* December 17, 1999, p. 4
270. *CI* November 12, 1999, p. 4; *TG* August 4, 1999; May 3, 2000; *TE* March 15, 2000; March 27, 2000; April 1, 2000
271. *CI* September 10, 1999; *CI* September 24, 1999; *CI* October 15, 1999, p. 4
272. Rupert Griffith had been brought into the Cabinet on May 28, 1998 as head of the new Ministry of Information, Communication, Training and Distance Learning

that, on October 20, 1999, Panday had reduced to Training and Distance Learning.
273. *TE* October 21, 1999
274. *TE* March 22, 2000; March 18, 2000. Gillette was appointed acting Prime Minister again on April 10, 2000. Panday later appointed Senator Dr Daphne Phillips, an Afro-Creole woman, as acting Prime Minister from November 11–3, 2000.
275. *TG* February 6–7, 2000; February 9, 2000; February 12, 2000; February 23, 2000; February 28, 2000; March 2–4, 2000; *TE* February 9–10, 2000; February 12, 2000; February 21, 2000; February 23, 2000; March 14, 2000
276. *TE* January 8, 2000; *CI* January 14, 2000, p. 3
277. *TG* November 22, 1999; *CI* November 26, 1999, p. 3
278. *TG* February 3, 2000; February 17, 2000; *TE* February 3, 2000
279. *TE* January 21, 2000
280. *TG* February 5, 2000
281. *TE* February 8, 2000; February 10, 2000; February 12, 2000
282. *TE* January 22, 2000; January 30, 2000; February 1, 2000; February 3, 2000; February 9, 2000
283. *CI* September 24, 1999, pp. 3–4
284. GORTT 2000a; 2000c
285. *TG* February 23, 2000; March 1, 2000. The other two Commissioners were Botswana court of Appeal Judge, Justice Austin Amissah, and one of India's most prominent Senior Counsels, Dr. L.M. Singhvi.
286. GORTT 2000
287. *TE* March 4, 2000
288. *TG* February 19, 2000
289. *TE* February 23, 2000; March 5, 2000; *TG* February 22–4, 2000; March 2, 2000
290. *TE* April 4–5, 2000. In 1999, the UNC received 1,377 votes and the PNM 400. No other candidates contested the seat (GORTT [1999a]).
291. *TE* April 6, 2000. According to the THA Act, however, unless the THA dissolves early, an election can be called by the President only between February 9 and March 9, 2001 (*TE* April 8, 2000).
292. *TG* November 18, 2000, p. 4
293. Georges was appointed on November 3, 1999 and submitted his report on February 16, 2000
294. Interestingly, the judge in that case was Peter Jamadar, son of Vernon Jamadar.
295. *TE* July 13–5, 1999; *TG* July 18, 1999; July 27, 1999
296. *TE* July 15, 1999, p. 18
297. *TE* July 18, 1999, p. 11. The 'backfiring' of the UNC's advertising campaign seems to parallel the effect of the media-intensive ONR general elections campaign of 1981 (Ryan 1989b: 282), both of which inadvertently strengthened the base support for the PNM.
298. *TE* April 11, 2000. In 1995, the UNC received 7,611 votes and the PNM 6,666 in Barataria/San Juan.
299. *TE* April 15, 2000
300. The report is reprinted in the *TnT Mirror* November 3, 2000, pp. 6–7.
301. *TE* November 3, 2000, p.12
302. *CI* August 1997, p. 11; *TG* December 28, 1997
303. *CI* May 1997; June 1997; *TG* December 28, 1997; *TE* August 15, 1997; May 14, 1988
304. Siewah and Arjoonsingh 1998, vol. 2: 320

305. *TE* June 24–5, 1999; *TG* June 25, 1999; July 2, 1999
306. *TE* May 1, 2000
307. The *Trinidad Guardian* (December 3, 2000, p. 9) provides an interesting list of former NAR activists working on various campaigns of the UNC and PNM.
308. *TG* October 3, 2000, p. 1
309. The report was reprinted in the *Trinidad Express* October 8, 2000, pp. 35–8.
310. *TE* February 8, 2000. In January 1999, before the PEP was founded, President Robinson refused Moore-Miggins's November 1998 request to be declared minority leader, despite receiving the backing of Beverly Ramsey-Moore and Richard Alfred, on the grounds that Moore-Miggins could not 'command' their support. PNM minority leader, William McKenzie (who had no other support), was tacitly supported by Hochoy Charles (*CI* February 1999, p. 7; *TE* December 16, 1998). Ironically, because then-President Clarke did not consider in 1978 that Raffique Shah could command the support of A.N.R. Robinson, Shah was refused leadership of the parliamentary opposition.
311. The Representation of the People Act was amended in 2001, to require five weeks notice for elections, instead of the previous three weeks.
312. To the embarrassment of the UNC, however, the female lead in the series appeared at the PNM's final pre-election rally on December 9.
313. A figure from the National Investment Properties Development Corporation provided a lower figure of $1 billion on August 25 (*TG* November 26, 2000, p. 15).
314. *TE* December 21, 2000, p. 4. On August 12, 1998 BP and Amoco merged into one company.
315. *TE* December 8, 2000
316. Four other Petrotrin directors – Errol McLeod (of the OWTU), Anthony Beaubrun, George de Verteuil, and Angus Khan – resigned less than one week after Baldeosingh's dismissal (*TE* November 21, 2000).
317. Interview with Patrick Manning, 1999.
318. Donawa-McDavidson died on January 15, 2001. After she withdrew from the election, she continued to give support to the replacement candidate, Dr Roodal Moonilal (*TE* January 16, 2001).
319. *TE December* 1, 2000
320. *TG* November 25, 2000, p. 3; December 1, 2000
321. *TG* December 2, 2000, p. 3
322. *TG* December 9, 2000, p. 3
323. *TE* December 8, 2000; *TG* December 9, 2000, p. 3
324. On December 2, adding to the sense of alarm, 83-year-old EBC Chairman, Sir Isaac Hyatali died from haemorrhaging associated with diverticular disease.
325. *TG* December 12, 2000, p. 3
326. *TG* December 16, 2000, p. 1
327. Until the appointment of a new Prime Minister, Panday legally held the position.
328. *TG* December 16, 2000, p. 3
329. *TE* December 16, 2000, p. 6
330. Her letter is reprinted in *TG* December 17, 2000, p. 8.
331. On Independence Day, 1998, President Robinson's ill health became a public concern, as he had collapsed in public on that occasion.
332. *TE* December 24, 2000, p. 5
333. *TG* December 30, 2000, p. 1
334. *TG* January 2, 2001, pp. 1, 8

335. *TE* January 3, 2001, p. 3
336. *TG* January 4, 2001, p. 1
337. *TE* January 7, 2001, p. 31
338. *TE* January 6, 2001
339. *TG* January 7, 2001, p. 1
340. Robinson later noted that, on April 22, 1960, he had presented a petition from the PNM to the Governor-General Lord Hailes at the very location where he received the petition as President in 2001 (*TE* January 27, 2001, p. 3).
341. *TG* June 12, 2001
342. *TE* January 24, 2001
343. *TG* January 27, 2001, p. 3
344. *TE* February 5, 2001
345. *TE* February 2, 2001
346. *TG* February 15, 2001, p. 14
347. *TG* December 23, 2000, p. 1
348. *TE* December 22, 2000
349. *TG* June 3, 2001, bus. sec., p. 6
350. *TE* July 27, 2001
351. *TE* August 3, 2001
352. 'Chutney' is the Trinidadian name for the popular local Indian music, whose roots are in Bhojpuri folk songs.
353. Transparency International 2001
354. The shares were offered in February 2001. The listing was oversubscribed, with shares bought by 6,581 investors of whom 6,278 were individual investors including employees (*TE* March 8, 2001, p. 21).
355. *TE* August 10, 2001; *TG* August 10, 2001
356. *TE* January 30, 2001, p. 5
357. *TE* January 7, 2001, p. 9; February 13, 2001, p. 5; February 18, 2001, pp. 10–11
358. *TG* July 7, 2001, p. 12
359. *TG* August 19, 2001, p. 3
360. *TE* June 3, 2001
361. *TG* August 19, 2001, bus. sec., p. 7
362. *TG* March 23, 2001, p. 1
363. *TG* June 12, 2001, p. 3
364. *TE* April 10, 2001
365. *TG* June 3, 2001, p. 6; June 10, 2001, p. 10
366. *TG* June 9, 2001, pp. 1, 3
367. *TG* June 30, 2001, pp. 1, 3
368. *TG* July 5, 2001
369. *TG* June 18, 2001, p. 3. Montano later joined the UNC to fight against Patrick Manning in San Fernando East.
370. *TE* April 10, 2001. In the June 13, 1997 internal party elections, Panday first made his announcement that Ministers of Government could not contest the 22 posts in the UNC. Ostensibly, this was to allow the Government to operate 'optimally and maximally' and at the same time allow the party to operate 'fully and optimally' to ensure that the UNC remain in power up to 2015 (*TE* July 14, 1997, p. 7). It resulted in unfitting political unknowns in top party positions.
371. *TG* May 13, 2001, p. 1
372. *TG* June 10, 2001, p. 11; *TE* June 10, 2001, p. 39

373. *TG* June 12, 2001, p. 1
374. *TG* July 3, 2001
375. *TE* July 18, 2001
376. for example, in *TG* July 15, 2001, p. 8
377. During the election campaign, the NWRHA scandal continued to unfold. On November 1, cost budget analyst at the NWRHA, Ranjit Sookdar, was arrested on charges of misbehaviour in public office and theft. On November 13, UNC Senator and former chairman of that Health Authority, Dr. Tim Gopeesingh, was arrested on nine charges of misbehaviour in public office.
378. *TG* July 7, 2001, p. 1. A *chulha* is a clay oven used by Indians, and a 'chinese chopper' is a type of cleaver. This obviously referred to the Indians in government and the Chinese Minister of Finance. The active PSA membership is overwhelmingly African.
379. TE July 25, 2001
380. *Obeah* is West African-derived religion and magic, with powers that are considered by many to be potent and fearsome.
381. TG July 26, 2001
382. TG August 30, 2001
383. TE July 31, 2001
384. TG August 1, 2001, p. 3
385. TE August 13, 2001
386. TG September 1, 2001, p. 5
387. TG September 9, 2001, p. 8
388. TG October 2, 2001, p. 4
389. The letters were reprinted in TE October 3, 2001, p. 7.
390. TG October 7, 2001, p. 1
391. On October 12, all PNM MPs, the three UNC dissidents and Nathaniel Moore petitioned to have the Speaker, Rupert Griffith, removed, according to the amendment passed in 1995 to remove as Speaker Occah Seapaul, Ralph Maraj's sister. Ironically, Rupert Griffith was Seapaul's replacement after her removal in 1995.
392. TG October 12, 2001, p. 9
393. The letters are reproduced in TE October 11, 2001, p. 11
394. TE September 15, 2001, p. 19
395. TE September 15, 2001, p. 13
396. TG October 19, 2001
397. Spackman 1965: 288–9; Ryan 1972: 99

## CONCLUSION

1. Despite the poor electoral performance of the Liberals, WFP, Tapia, and NJAC, the author sets them apart from such short-lived parties as the ANC, PPM, WINP, MOTION, and others.
2. Williams 1955a
3. It is of interest to note that the PNM remain the only party to have contested every seat in every general and local election. Technically, then, it is the only fully nationally organised party.
4. Most forcefully stated by LaGuerre (1982) but also stated in passing, or implied as a 'given' in Ralph Premdas, 'Public policy and ethnic conflict regulation: Trinidad

and Tobago', in *The Accommodation of Cultural Diversity*, ed. C. Young (London: Macmillan Press Ltd., 1999), pp. 103–26., Bahadoorsingh (1968), Malik (1971), and Ryan (1972).

5. However, the Butler Party effectively collapsed after its Indian members left in 1953 to join the PDP.
6. The combined NATT (ULF, DAC, and Tapia) vote amounted only to 20.8 per cent (GORTT 1982b: 202–3).

## AFTERWORD

1. *TG* December 12, 2001, p. 1
2. GORTT 2002, 'The voters have set the stage for a government of national unity,' Office of the Prime Minister, statement by the Prime Minister on the election results, Whitehall, December 11, 2001. Accessed on January 2, 2002.
3. *TG* December 16, 2001, p. 7
4. *TE* December 24, 2002 (Election Special), p. 7
5. *TG* December 30, 2001, p. 1
6. *TE* June 30, 2002

# *Bibliography*

## PRIMARY SOURCES


*AES*. *Annual Economic Survey* (Trinidad and Tobago: Ministry of Finance).

*ASD*. *Annual Statistical Digest* (Trinidad and Tobago: Central Statistical Office).

*Annual Report of Trinidad and Tobago for the Year 1956* (London: Her Majesty's Stationery Office, 1958).

*The Atlantic Story*. Trinidad and Tobago: NGC, 1999.

*Balance of Payments* (Port of Spain: Central Bank of Trinidad and Tobago/Central Statistical Office).

*Blue Book* (Port of Spain: Government Printer).

*BP Amoco Statistical Review of World Energy, 2000*. http://www.bp.com/worldenergy/oil/index.htm (July 28, 2000).

*BP Statistical Review of the World Oil Industry, 1973*. London: The British Petroleum Company Limited, 1973.

CBTT. Central Bank of Trinidad and Tobago. http://www.central-bank.org.tt (November 5, 2002).

________. Memorandum to file note, from L. Ramoutar, re: 'status of divestment', January 23 (mimeo, 1997).

________. Research Department, *Sunesis time series viewer* (diskette 1993).

CES. Centre for Ethnic Studies. *A Study of the Secondary School Population in Trinidad and Tobago: Placement Patterns and Practices, a Research Report*. St Augustine, Trinidad and Tobago: Centre for Ethnic Studies, 1994.

________. *Ethnicity and Employment Practices in the Public and Private Sectors in Trinidad and Tobago*. St Augustine, Trinidad and Tobago: Centre for Ethnic Studies, 1993.

COTT. The Colony of Trinidad and Tobago. *Report on the County Council General Elections 1959*. Prepared by the Supervisor of Elections, pursuant to section 59, subsection 5 of the County Councils Ordinance, Ch. 39, no. 15, Trinidad – M.13/62. Trinidad: Government Printing Office, 1962.

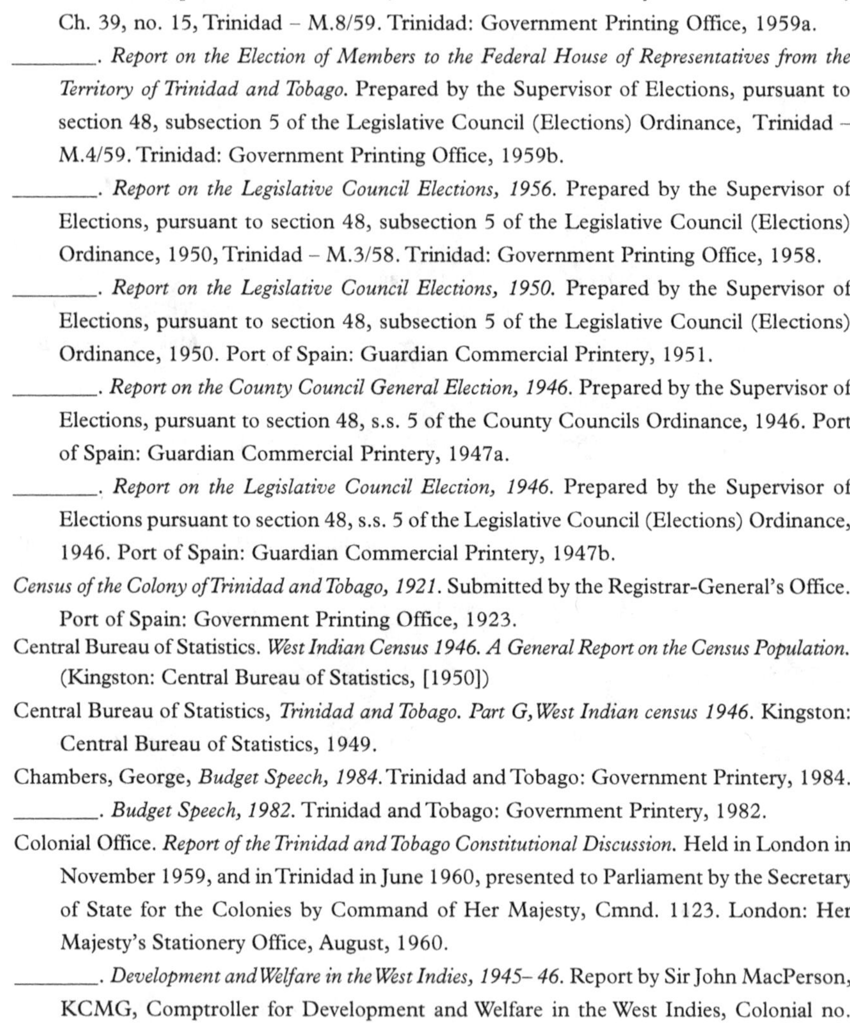

________. *Report on the County Council General Elections, 1956.* Prepared by the Supervisor of Elections, pursuant to section 59, subsection 5 of the County Councils Ordinance, Ch. 39, no. 15, Trinidad – M.8/59. Trinidad: Government Printing Office, 1959a.

________. *Report on the Election of Members to the Federal House of Representatives from the Territory of Trinidad and Tobago.* Prepared by the Supervisor of Elections, pursuant to section 48, subsection 5 of the Legislative Council (Elections) Ordinance, Trinidad – M.4/59. Trinidad: Government Printing Office, 1959b.

________. *Report on the Legislative Council Elections, 1956.* Prepared by the Supervisor of Elections, pursuant to section 48, subsection 5 of the Legislative Council (Elections) Ordinance, 1950, Trinidad – M.3/58. Trinidad: Government Printing Office, 1958.

________. *Report on the Legislative Council Elections, 1950.* Prepared by the Supervisor of Elections, pursuant to section 48, subsection 5 of the Legislative Council (Elections) Ordinance, 1950. Port of Spain: Guardian Commercial Printery, 1951.

________. *Report on the County Council General Election, 1946.* Prepared by the Supervisor of Elections, pursuant to section 48, s.s. 5 of the County Councils Ordinance, 1946. Port of Spain: Guardian Commercial Printery, 1947a.

________. *Report on the Legislative Council Election, 1946.* Prepared by the Supervisor of Elections pursuant to section 48, s.s. 5 of the Legislative Council (Elections) Ordinance, 1946. Port of Spain: Guardian Commercial Printery, 1947b.

*Census of the Colony of Trinidad and Tobago, 1921.* Submitted by the Registrar-General's Office. Port of Spain: Government Printing Office, 1923.

Central Bureau of Statistics. *West Indian Census 1946. A General Report on the Census Population.* (Kingston: Central Bureau of Statistics, [1950])

Central Bureau of Statistics, *Trinidad and Tobago. Part G, West Indian census 1946.* Kingston: Central Bureau of Statistics, 1949.

Chambers, George, *Budget Speech, 1984.* Trinidad and Tobago: Government Printery, 1984.

________. *Budget Speech, 1982.* Trinidad and Tobago: Government Printery, 1982.

Colonial Office. *Report of the Trinidad and Tobago Constitutional Discussion.* Held in London in November 1959, and in Trinidad in June 1960, presented to Parliament by the Secretary of State for the Colonies by Command of Her Majesty, Cmnd. 1123. London: Her Majesty's Stationery Office, August, 1960.

________. *Development and Welfare in the West Indies, 1945–46.* Report by Sir John MacPerson, KCMG, Comptroller for Development and Welfare in the West Indies, Colonial no. 212. London: His Majesty's Stationery Office, 1947.

Constitution Commission of the Republic of Trinidad and Tobago, *Report of the Constitutional Commission (1987).* Presented to His Excellency the President on June 1, 1990. Trinidad and Tobago: Government Printery, 1991.

CPTU. Council of Progressive Trade Unions. Grand Council Report 1st Jan. 1989 to 14th Sept. 1991 to Special Convention on the Dissolution of the Council of Progressive Trade Unions (CPTU). October 11 (mimeo, Port of Spain, 1991).

*EB. Economic Bulletin*. Port of Spain. May 1999–November 1999.

EIU. Economist Intelligence Unit. *Country Profile: Trinidad and Tobago, Suriname, Netherlands Antilles, Aruba, 1997– 8.* London: EIU, 1998a.

________. *Country Rreport: Trinidad and Tobago, Guyana, Suriname.* Second Quarter. London: EIU, 1998b.

*Gasco News*. Trinidad and Tobago: National Gas Company.

Gocking, C.V. *Democracy or oligarchy? Three essays 'Democracy or oligarchy?'* Tapia Booklet no. 1, Sunday, September 9. Tunapuna, Trinidad and Tobago: Tapia House Movement, 1973; 'Participatory Democracy'. Tapia Booklet, no. 8, Sunday March 16. Tunapuna, Trinidad and Tobago: Tapia House Movement, 1975; The Prime Minister and the Constitution. March. Tunapuna, Trinidad and Tobago: Tapia House Movement, 1976; Port of Spain: Trinidad and Tobago Institute of the West Indies, 1998.

GOTT. Government of Trinidad and Tobago, Office of the Prime Minister, Public Relations Division. Government to Purchase Shell, Press Release, August 22, no. 417, 1974.

________. Elections Commission. *Report on the Local Government Elections, 1971.* Port of Spain: Election and Boundaries Printing Section, 1972a.

________. Elections Commission. *Report on the Parliamentary General Elections, 1971.* Port of Spain: Election and Boundaries Printing Section, 1972b.

________. *Third Five-year Plan, 1969– 1973,* as approved by Parliament. Trinidad and Tobago: GOTT, 1970.

________. Elections Commission. 'Report on the Local Government Elections, 1968' (mimeo, 1969).

________. Elections Commission. *Report on the Parliamentary General Election, 1966.* Trinidad and Tobago: GOTT, 1967.

________. National Planning Commission. *Draft Second Five-year plan, 1964– 1968.* Port of Spain: GOTT, 1963a.

________. *Interim and Second Reports of the Legal and Constitutional Commission on the Question of Unitary Statehood of Grenada and Trinidad and Tobago.* Trinidad and Tobago: GOTT, 1963b.

________. Supervisor of Elections. *Report on the General Elections, 1961.* Trinidad and Tobago: GOTT, 1963c.

GORTT. Government of the Republic of Trinidad and Tobago, Elections and Boundaries Commission. 'The voters have set the stage for a government of National Unity.' December 11, 2002. *Report of the Elections and Boundaries Commission on the Parliamentary*

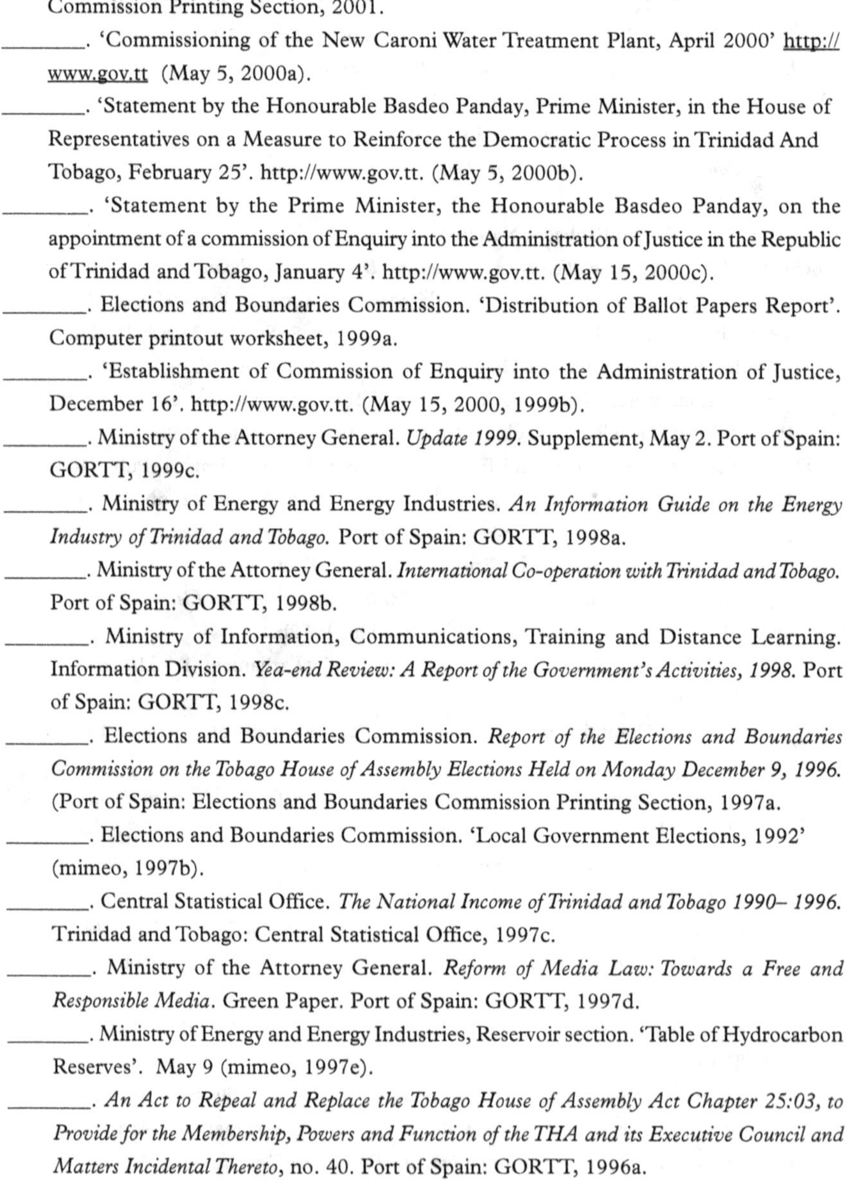

*Elections held on Monday 11th December, 2000.* Port of Spain: Elections and Boundaries Commission Printing Section, 2001.

________. 'Commissioning of the New Caroni Water Treatment Plant, April 2000' http://www.gov.tt (May 5, 2000a).

________. 'Statement by the Honourable Basdeo Panday, Prime Minister, in the House of Representatives on a Measure to Reinforce the Democratic Process in Trinidad And Tobago, February 25'. http://www.gov.tt. (May 5, 2000b).

________. 'Statement by the Prime Minister, the Honourable Basdeo Panday, on the appointment of a commission of Enquiry into the Administration of Justice in the Republic of Trinidad and Tobago, January 4'. http://www.gov.tt. (May 15, 2000c).

________. Elections and Boundaries Commission. 'Distribution of Ballot Papers Report'. Computer printout worksheet, 1999a.

________. 'Establishment of Commission of Enquiry into the Administration of Justice, December 16'. http://www.gov.tt. (May 15, 2000, 1999b).

________. Ministry of the Attorney General. *Update 1999.* Supplement, May 2. Port of Spain: GORTT, 1999c.

________. Ministry of Energy and Energy Industries. *An Information Guide on the Energy Industry of Trinidad and Tobago.* Port of Spain: GORTT, 1998a.

________. Ministry of the Attorney General. *International Co-operation with Trinidad and Tobago.* Port of Spain: GORTT, 1998b.

________. Ministry of Information, Communications, Training and Distance Learning. Information Division. *Yea-end Review: A Report of the Government's Activities, 1998.* Port of Spain: GORTT, 1998c.

________. Elections and Boundaries Commission. *Report of the Elections and Boundaries Commission on the Tobago House of Assembly Elections Held on Monday December 9, 1996.* (Port of Spain: Elections and Boundaries Commission Printing Section, 1997a.

________. Elections and Boundaries Commission. 'Local Government Elections, 1992' (mimeo, 1997b).

________. Central Statistical Office. *The National Income of Trinidad and Tobago 1990– 1996.* Trinidad and Tobago: Central Statistical Office, 1997c.

________. Ministry of the Attorney General. *Reform of Media Law: Towards a Free and Responsible Media.* Green Paper. Port of Spain: GORTT, 1997d.

________. Ministry of Energy and Energy Industries, Reservoir section. 'Table of Hydrocarbon Reserves'. May 9 (mimeo, 1997e).

________. *An Act to Repeal and Replace the Tobago House of Assembly Act Chapter 25:03, to Provide for the Membership, Powers and Function of the THA and its Executive Council and Matters Incidental Thereto,* no. 40. Port of Spain: GORTT, 1996a.

________. *Report of the Elections and Boundaries Commission on the Parliamentary Elections held on Monday, 6th November, 1995.* Port of Spain: Elections and Boundaries Commission Printing Section, 1996b.

________. Ministry of Public Administration and Information. Information Division. 1996b. *Year-end Review: A Report of the Government's Activities, 1996.* Port of Spain: GORTT, 1996b.

________. *Report on Public Participation in Industrial and Commercial Activities.* Trinidad and Tobago: Ministry of Finance, 1995.

________. Elections and Boundaries Commission. *Report of the Elections and Boundaries Commission on the Tobago House of Assembly Elections Held on Monday, December 7, 1992.* Port of Spain: Elections and Boundaries Commission Printing Section, 1993a.

________. Elections and Boundaries Commission. 'Local Government Elections, 1992' (mimeo, 1993b).

________. Central Statistical Office. *National Income of Trinidad and Tobago, 1981– 1991.* Port of Spain: GORTT, 1993c.

________. Central Statistical Office. *Population and Housing Census.* Volume 2: Demographic Report. Port of Spain: GORTT, 1993d.

________. Ministry of Trade, Industry and Tourism. 'Brief on the Trade Reform Programme' (mimeo, 1992a).

________. Elections and Boundaries Commission. *Report of the Elections and Boundaries Commission on the Parliamentary Elections held on Monday, 16th December, 1991.* Port of Spain: Elections and Boundaries Commission Printing Section, 1992b.

________. Elections and Boundaries Commission. 'Recommended Parliamentary Electoral District Boundaries of Trinidad and Tobago 1991' (mimeo, 1991).

________. Ministry of Finance. '2nd letter of intent'. March 14 (mimeo, 1990a).

________. National Planning Commission. *Restructuring for Economic Independence: Medium Term Macro Planning Framework, 1989– 1995.* September. Trinidad and Tobago: Central Statistical Office Printing Unit, 1990b.

________. Elections and Boundaries Commission. 'Elections to the Tobago House of Assembly, 1988' (mimeo, 1989).

________. Ministry of Finance and the Economy. '1st letter of Intent'. November 16. Ref: CB-G-330/8 (mimeo, 1988a).

________. National Planning Commission. *Draft Medium Term Macro Planning Framework 1989– 95.* Trinidad and Tobago: GORTT, July 1988b.

________. Elections and Boundaries Commission. 'Local Government Elections, 1987' (mimeo, 1988c).

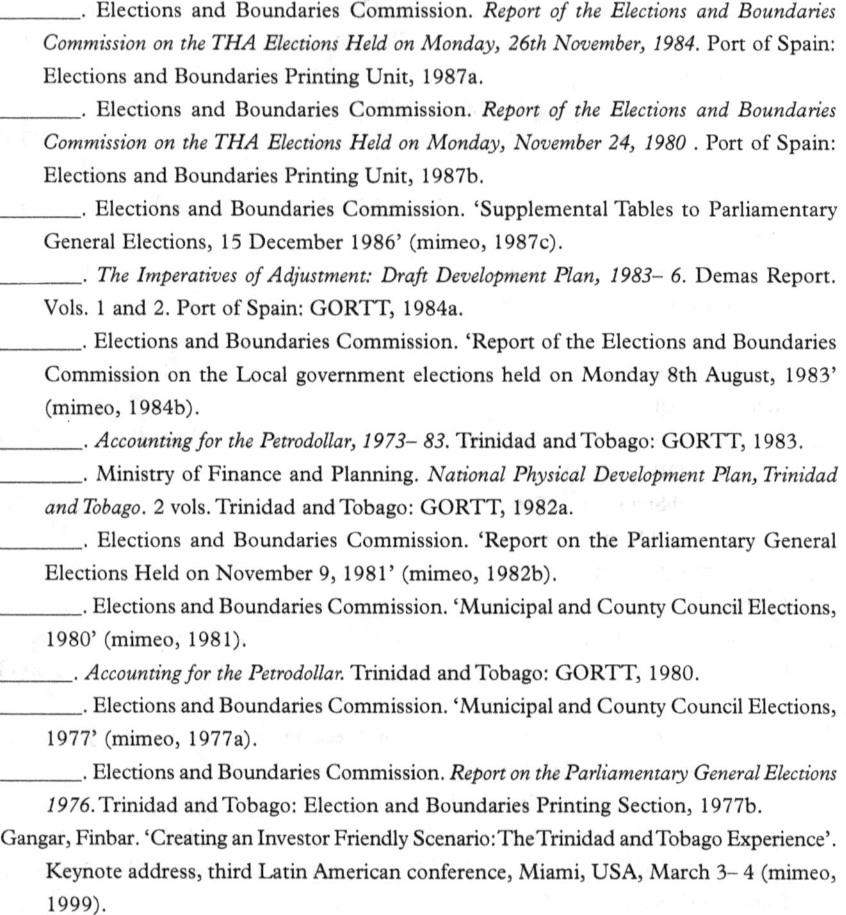

________. Elections and Boundaries Commission. *Report of the Elections and Boundaries Commission on the THA Elections Held on Monday, 26th November, 1984*. Port of Spain: Elections and Boundaries Printing Unit, 1987a.

________. Elections and Boundaries Commission. *Report of the Elections and Boundaries Commission on the THA Elections Held on Monday, November 24, 1980* . Port of Spain: Elections and Boundaries Printing Unit, 1987b.

________. Elections and Boundaries Commission. 'Supplemental Tables to Parliamentary General Elections, 15 December 1986' (mimeo, 1987c).

________. *The Imperatives of Adjustment: Draft Development Plan, 1983– 6*. Demas Report. Vols. 1 and 2. Port of Spain: GORTT, 1984a.

________. Elections and Boundaries Commission. 'Report of the Elections and Boundaries Commission on the Local government elections held on Monday 8th August, 1983' (mimeo, 1984b).

________. *Accounting for the Petrodollar, 1973– 83*. Trinidad and Tobago: GORTT, 1983.

________. Ministry of Finance and Planning. *National Physical Development Plan, Trinidad and Tobago*. 2 vols. Trinidad and Tobago: GORTT, 1982a.

________. Elections and Boundaries Commission. 'Report on the Parliamentary General Elections Held on November 9, 1981' (mimeo, 1982b).

________. Elections and Boundaries Commission. 'Municipal and County Council Elections, 1980' (mimeo, 1981).

________. *Accounting for the Petrodollar.* Trinidad and Tobago: GORTT, 1980.

________. Elections and Boundaries Commission. 'Municipal and County Council Elections, 1977' (mimeo, 1977a).

________. Elections and Boundaries Commission. *Report on the Parliamentary General Elections 1976*. Trinidad and Tobago: Election and Boundaries Printing Section, 1977b.

Gangar, Finbar. 'Creating an Investor Friendly Scenario: The Trinidad and Tobago Experience'. Keynote address, third Latin American conference, Miami, USA, March 3– 4 (mimeo, 1999).

Hudson-Phillips, Karl. Address at the Inauguration of the Organisation for National Reconstruction on Sunday 1st February, 1981, at the Chaguaramas Convention Centre (mimeo, 1981).

*IFS. International Financial Statistics.* Washington, D.C.: International Monetary Fund.

*Investment Opportunities in the Natural Gas Sector of Trinidad and Tobago.* Trinidad and Tobago: National Gas Company, 1999.

James, C.L.R. *Beyond a Boundary*, with an introduction by Robert Lipsyte. London: Stanley Paul, 1963; London: Serpent's Tail, 1994.

________. *Party Politics in the West Indies*, edited with an introduction by R.M. Walters. San Juan, Trinidad and Tobago: Vedic Enterprises, 1962; San Juan, Trinidad and Tobago: Inprint Caribbean, 1984.

________. *A Convention Appraisal: Dr Eric Williams*. Port of Spain: PNM Publishing, 1960.

Kuei Tung, Brian. *A Platform for Progress: Security for all. 1998–1999 Budget Statement*, October 5. Port of Spain: House of Representatives of Trinidad and Tobago, 1998.

Maharaj, Ramesh Lawrence. 'The Strategy Employed by the United National Congress for the Next General Elections (1995)', in LaGuerre 1997a: 42– 6.

Manning, Patrick. 'With the PNM there is Hope: A Major Policy Statement'. An address by the Honourable Patrick Manning, MP, political leader of the PNM, at the 28th annual convention of the PNM held at the Chaguaramas Convention Centre on Sunday, October 9 (mimeo, 1988).

McLean, Hector. 'Proper Procedures.' *Parliamentarian*. Vol. 78, no. 4 (October 1997): 304–5.

MOTION. Movement for Social Transformation. *Towards a New Democracy and the Road to Full Employment: Provisional Programme of the Movement for Social Transformation*. September 10. Trinidad and Tobago: Classline Publications, 1989.

Mottley, Wendell. *Budget Speech, 1992*. January 17. Trinidad and Tobago: House of Representatives, 1992.

NAEAP. National Association for the Empowerment of African People. Pamphlet. Tacarigua, Trinidad and Tobago, 1998.

NGC. National Gas Company. *Investment Opportunities in the Natural Gas Sector of Trinidad and Tobago*. Trinidad and Tobago: National Gas Company of Trinidad and Tobago, 1999.

PNM. People's National Movement. *The Chaguaramas Declaration: Perspectives for the New Society*. People's charter 1956, revised. Port of Spain: PNM Publishing, 1970.

________. *Highlights of the Trinidad and Tobago 1966 General Elections*. Port of Spain: PNM Publishing, 1966a.

________. *Major Party Documents*. Vol. 1. Port of Spain: PNM Publishing, 1966b.

*PNM Weekly*. Port of Spain: People's National Movement.

*QEB. Quarterly Economic Bulletin*. Port of Spain. December 1997–December 1998.

*Report of the Committee Appointed by the National Council of the National Alliance for Reconstruction to Investigate and Make Recommendations for Solving the Problems Affecting the Party and Government* (mimeo). Port of Spain: National Alliance for Reconstruction, 1988.

Robinson, Arthur N.R. *Budget Speech and Taxation Measures, 1989*. December 16. Trinidad and Tobago: House of Representatives of the Republic of Trinidad and Tobago, 1989.

________. *Caribbean Man: Selected Speeches from a Political Career, 1960– 1986*, ed., and introduced by Gregory Shaw. Port of Spain: Inprint Caribbean, 1986.

________. *Budget Speech, 1987.* January 23. Trinidad and Tobago: House of Representatives of the Republic of Trinidad and Tobago, 1987.

________. *The Mechanics of Independence: Patterns of Political and Economic Transformation in Trinidad and Tobago.* Cambridge, MA: The MIT Press, 1971.

*Scott Drug Report: Report of the Commission of Enquiry into the Extent of the Problem of Drug Abuse in Trinidad and Tobago and a Supplement with the Related Official Correspondence.* San Fernando, Trinidad and Tobago: Unique Services, 1986.

Sebastien, Raphael, ed. *Forging a New Democracy: Beyond the Post-colonial Era.* Trinidad and Tobago: Office of the Leader of the Opposition, 1985.

Shah, Lt. Raffique. 'The Military Crisis in Trinidad and Tobago During 1970', in Munroe and Lewis 1971: 215– 21.

*SOPO is Born!* Trinidad and Tobago: The Vanguard. Pamphlet, 1990.

Summit of National Leaders. 'Resolution'. February 8 (mimeo, 1990).

TIDCO. Tourism and Industrial Development Corporation. *Trinidad and Tobago Export Directory.* Port of Spain: TIDCO, 1999.

Transparency International. 'Press Release: New Index Highlights Worldwide Corruption Crisis, Says Transparency International'. http://www.transparency.org/documents/cpi/2001/cpi2001.html (June 28, 2001).

*Trinidad and Tobago: The Making of a Nation.* Central Office of Information Reference Pamphlet, no. 53. London: Her Majesty's Stationery Office, 1962.

Tripartite Committee of the Trinidad and Tobago Opposition Parties. *The Voting Machine Story.* January. San Fernando, Trinidad and Tobago: The Tripartite Committee, 1968.

UNDP. United Nations Development Programme. *Human Development Report, 2001.* New York: Oxford University Press, published for the UNDP, 2001.

________. *Human Development Report, 2000.* http://www.undp.org/hdr2000/english/HDR2000.html ( July 20, 2000).

*Vanguard: The Voice of Labour.* San Fernando, Trinidad and Tobago: OWTU.

*Verbatim Notes of Proceedings of Meeting on Draft Constitution Held at Queen's Hall, Port-of-Spain, 25th to 27th April, 1962.* (Port of Spain: Government Printing Office, 1962.

*West India Royal Commission Report.* Presented by the Secretary of State for the Colonies to Parliament by Command of His Majesty, June, Cmd. 6607. London: His Majesty's Stationery Office, 1945.

West Indies. *Report by the Honourable E.F.L. Wood, MP (Parliamentary Under Secretary of State for the Colonies) on His Visit to the West Indies and British Guiana.* December 1921– February 1922. Presented to Parliament by Command of His Majesty, June, Cmd. 1679. London: His Majesty's Stationery Office, 1922.

Williams, Eric. 'The PNM in the Next Five Years, 1976– 1981'. Address by the political leader, 18th annual convention. December 3 (mimeo, 1976).

________. *Constitution Reform.* Speech by the Prime Minister in the House of Representative, December 13 and 17, 1974. Trinidad and Tobago: Government Printery, 1975a.

________. '1976 and 1956'. Address to the PNM's 17th Annual Convention. October 3 (mimeo, 1975b).

________. Address by Dr The Honourable Eric Williams Prime Minister of Trinidad and Tobago over Radio and Television (mimeo, February 14, 1974a).

________. Address by the Political Leader, Dr Eric Williams, to PNM's 16th Annual Convention (mimeo, 1974b).

________ *The Energy Crisis, 1973– 4: Three Addresses by Dr Eric Williams, Prime Minister of Trinidad and Tobago.* Trinidad and Tobago: Office of the Prime Minister, 1974c.

________. Nationwide Radio and Television Broadcast by Dr Eric Williams, Prime Minister of Trinidad and Tobago on an Up-to-date Account of the Energy Situation, May 8 (mimeo, 1974d).

________. Prime Minister's Address to the Nation, June 27 (mimeo, 1974e).

________. *Fifteenth Annual Convention: Address by the Political Leader Dr Eric Williams.* Port of Spain: PNM Publishing, 1973a.

________. *PR: To Dissolve the Present PNM Majorities.* Port of Spain: PNM Publishing, 1973b.

________. 'Proportional Representation in Trinidad and Tobago: The Case Against'. *The Round Table*, no. 250 (April 1973c): 233–45.

________. 'Reply to the Convention Resolution Asking Dr Williams to Stay On' (mimeo, 1973d).

________. *Address by the Prime Minister of Trinidad and Tobago and Political Leader of the PNM: Fourteenth Annual Convention.* Port of Spain: PNM Publishing, 1972.

________. *Nationwide Broadcast* (June 30). Trinidad and Tobago: GOTT, 1970a.

________. *Nationwide Broadcast* (May 10). Trinidad and Tobago: GOTT, 1970b.

________. *Nationwide Broadcast* (May 3). Trinidad and Tobago: GOTT, 1970c.

________. *Nationwide Broadcast* (March 23). Trinidad and Tobago: GOTT, 1970d.

________. Fourth Budget Speech of the Honourable Dr Eric Williams, Minister of Finance to the Legislative Council of Trinidad and Tobago. March 23 (mimeo, 1960b).

________. *Education in the British West Indies.* With a foreword by John Dewey. Port of Spain: Teachers Educational and Cultural Association, 1951; New York: University Place Book Shop, 1968.

________. *History of the People of Trinidad and Tobago.* London: André Deutsch, 1962a.

________. *Massa Day Done: A Masterpiece of Political and Sociological Analysis.* Port of Spain: PNM Publishing, 1962b.

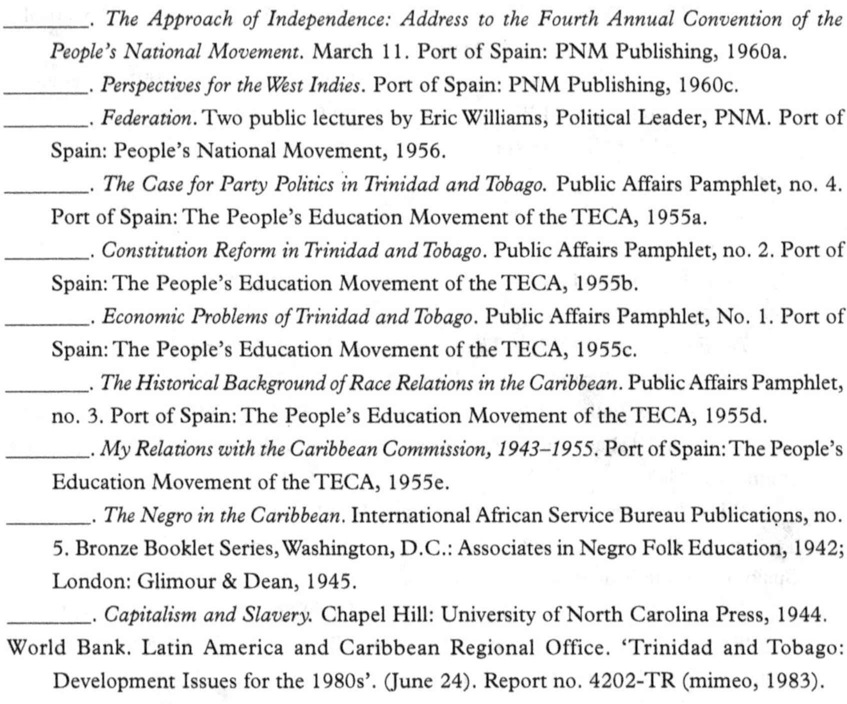

________. *The Approach of Independence: Address to the Fourth Annual Convention of the People's National Movement.* March 11. Port of Spain: PNM Publishing, 1960a.

________. *Perspectives for the West Indies.* Port of Spain: PNM Publishing, 1960c.

________. *Federation.* Two public lectures by Eric Williams, Political Leader, PNM. Port of Spain: People's National Movement, 1956.

________. *The Case for Party Politics in Trinidad and Tobago.* Public Affairs Pamphlet, no. 4. Port of Spain: The People's Education Movement of the TECA, 1955a.

________. *Constitution Reform in Trinidad and Tobago.* Public Affairs Pamphlet, no. 2. Port of Spain: The People's Education Movement of the TECA, 1955b.

________. *Economic Problems of Trinidad and Tobago.* Public Affairs Pamphlet, No. 1. Port of Spain: The People's Education Movement of the TECA, 1955c.

________. *The Historical Background of Race Relations in the Caribbean.* Public Affairs Pamphlet, no. 3. Port of Spain: The People's Education Movement of the TECA, 1955d.

________. *My Relations with the Caribbean Commission, 1943–1955.* Port of Spain: The People's Education Movement of the TECA, 1955e.

________. *The Negro in the Caribbean.* International African Service Bureau Publications, no. 5. Bronze Booklet Series, Washington, D.C.: Associates in Negro Folk Education, 1942; London: Glimour & Dean, 1945.

________. *Capitalism and Slavery.* Chapel Hill: University of North Carolina Press, 1944.

World Bank. Latin America and Caribbean Regional Office. 'Trinidad and Tobago: Development Issues for the 1980s'. (June 24). Report no. 4202-TR (mimeo, 1983).

## SECONDARY SOURCES

Abrams, Elliot. 'The Shiprider Solution: Policing the Caribbean'. *The National Interest* (Spring 1996); 85–92.

Anderson, W. and R. Grant. 'Political Socialisation Among Adolescents in School: A Comparative Study of Barbados, Guyana and Trinidad'. *Social and Economic Studies,* vol. 26, no. 2 (June 1977): 217–33.

Armytage, Frances. *The Free Port System in the British West Indies: A Study in Commercial Policy, 1766– 1822.* Imperial Study Series, gen. Ed.,Vincent T. Harlow. London: Longmans, Green and Co. Published for the Royal Empire Society, 1953.

Ashley, Paul W. 'The Commonwealth Caribbean and the Contemporary World Order: The Cases of Jamaica and Trinidad', in Henry and Stone 1983: 159–76.

Axline, W. Andrew. *Caribbean Integration: The Politics of Regionalism.* New York: Nichols Publishing, 1979.

Ayearst, Morley. *The British West Indies: The Search for Self-government*. London: George Allen & Unwin,1960.

Bahadoorsingh, Krishna. *Trinidad Electoral Politics: The Persistence of the Race Factor.* Institute of Race Relations Special Series 21. London: Institute of Race Relations, 1968.

Baptiste, Owen, ed. *Crisis*. Port of Spain: Inprint Caribbean, 1976.

Basdeo, Sahadeo and Graeme Mount. *The Foreign Relations of Trinidad and Tobago, 1962–2000*. San Juan, Trinidad and Tobago: Lexicon Trinidad, 2001.

Beckford, George. *Persistent Poverty: Underdevelopment of Plantation Economies of the Third World*. London: Oxford University Press, 1972.

Bell, Wendell, ed. *The Democratic Revolution in the West Indies: Studies in Nationalism, Leadership, and the Belief in Progress*. Cambridge, Massachusetts: Schenkman Publishing, 1967.

Benn, Denis. *The Growth and Development of Political Ideas in the Caribbean, 1774– 1983*. Mona, Jamaica: Institute of Social and Economic Research, 1987.

Best, Lloyd. 'Alliance for Reconstruction: The Case'. Address to the Alliance inaugural convention, Chaguaramas Convention Centre, November 14, 1982, in Best and Harris 1991:51–62.

________. 'A Foundation Strategy', in Best and Harris 1991: 49–50.

________. 'The "February Revolution" in Trinidad and Tobago', in Munroe and Lewis 1971: 210–4.

________. 'Outlines of a Model of Pure Plantation Economy. *Social and Economic Studies*, vol. 17, no. 3 (September 1968): 283–326.

________. 'Chaguaramas to Slavery?' *New World Quarterly*, vol. 2, no. 1 (1965): 43–70.

Best, Lloyd and Allan Harris, eds. *A Party Politics for Trinidad and Tobago: Flowering of an Idea*. Trinidad and Tobago: Tapia House, 1991.

Bloeser, Charles. 'Deprivation, Rationality, and Rebellion: The Case of Trinidad and Tobago'. *Caribbean Studies*, vol. 25 nos. 3–4 (July-December 1992): 277–304.

Boodhoo, Ken. *The Elusive Eric Williams*. Kingston, Jamaica: Ian Randle Publishers & Port of Spain: Prospect Press, 2002.

Braithwaite, Lloyd. *Social Stratification in Trinidad*. Mona, Jamaica: Institute of Social and Economic Research, 1975.

Brassington, Frank E. *The Politics of Opposition*. Diego Martin, Trinidad and Tobago: West Indian Sun Publishing, 1975.

Brereton, Bridget. *A history of Modern Trinidad, 1783– 1962*. (Kingston, Jamaica: Heinemann, 1981.

Brown, Deryck R. 'Ethnic Politics and Public Sector Management in Trinidad and Guyana'. *Public Administration and Development*, vol. 19, no. 4 (October 1999): 367– 79.

Buhle, Paul. *CLR James: The Artist as Revolutionary*. London: Verso, 1988.

Burton, Richard D.E. *Afro-Creole: Power, Opposition, and Play in the Caribbean*. Ithaca, NY: Cornell University Press, 1997.

Calder-Marshall, Arthur. *Glory Dead*. London: Michael Joseph, 1939.

Christopher, C. Auldwyn. *A New Era: A Pictorial Account of the Opening of the New Legislative Council of Trinidad and Tobago. A Who's Who in the New Government. Full results of General Elections*. Trinidad and Tobago: n.p., 1956.

________. *Historical Trinidad: Events and Other Records of the Island Outlined in Chronological Order from 1498– 1944*. Port of Spain: Guardian Commercial Printery, 1944.

Cipriani, A.A. *His Best Orations*. Port of Spain: Surprise Print Shop, 1945.

Clarke, Colin. 'Society and Electoral Politics in Trinidad and Tobago', in *Society and Politics in the Caribbean*. St Antony's/Macmillan Series, ed. Colin Clarke, 47–77. Oxford: Macmillan Press, 1991.

Collihan Kathleen M., and Constantine P. Danopoulos. 'Coup d'état Attempt in Trinidad: Its Causes and Failure'. *Armed Forces and Society*, vol. 19, no. 3 (Spring 1993): 435–50.

Craig, Hewan. *The Legislative Council of Trinidad and Tobago*. Studies in Colonial Legislatures, ed. Margery Perham, vol. vi. London: Faber & Faber, 1952.

Craig, Susan, ed. *Contemporary Caribbean: A Sociological Reader*. 2 vols. Trinidad and Tobago: Susan Craig, 1982.

________. *Community Development in Trinidad and Tobago: 1943– 1973: From Welfare to Patronage*. Working paper no. 4. Mona, Jamaica: Institute of Social and Economic Studies, 1974.

Craig, Susan. 'Background to the 1970 Confrontation in Trinidad and Tobago' in Craig 1982, vol. 2: 385– 424.

Craig-James, Susan. 'Smiles and Blood: The Ruling Class Response to the Workers' Rebellion of 1937 in Trinidad and Tobago', in Thomas 1987: 81–139.

Crowley, Daniel. 'Plural and Differential Acculturation in Trinidad'. *American Anthropologist*, vol. 59 (1957): 817–24.

Davidson, Jeffrey G. *Tobago versus PNM*. Port of Spain: Beacon Publishing, 1979.

Dattoo, L. 'Ethnic Conflict Resolution in Trinidad and Tobago: The Role of Proportionality in Representative Bureaucracy'. *Journal of Ethno Development*, vol. 3, no. 3 (1994).

Deosaran, Ramesh. 'Political Management of Conflict in a Multicultural Society,' in *Choices and Change: Reflections on the Caribbean*, ed. Winston C. Dookeran, 137–49. Washington, D.C.: Inter-American Development Bank, distributed by Johns Hopkins University Press, Baltimore, 1996.

Deosaran, Ramesh. *A Society Under Siege: A Study of Political Confusion and Legal Mysticism*. St Augustine, Trinidad and Tobago: Ansa-McAl Psychological Research Centre, University of the West Indies, 1993.

________. *Eric Williams: The Man, His Ideas, and His Politics (A Study of Political Power)*. Trinidad and Tobago: Signum Publishing, 1981.

*Developments Towards Self-government in the Caribbean*. The Hague: W. Van Hoeve, 1955.

Emmanuel, Patrick. *Governance and Democracy in the Commonwealth Caribbean: An Introduction*. Monograph Series No. 3. Cave Hill, Barbados: Institute of Social and Economic Research, 1993.

Domínguez, Jorge, Robert A. Pastor, and R. Delisle Worrell, eds. *Democracy in the Caribbean: Political, Economic, and Social Perspectives*. A World Peace Foundation Study. Baltimore: The Johns Hopkins University Press, 1993.

Edie, Carlene J., ed. *Democracy in the Caribbean: Myths and Realities*. Westport, Connecticut: Praeger, 1994.

Eriksen Thomas Hylland. 'Formal and Informal Nationalism'. *Ethnic and Racial Studies*, vol. 16, no. 1 (January 1993): 1–25.

Eriksen Thomas Hylland. *Us and Them in Modern Societies: Ethnicity and Nationalism in Mauritius, Trinidad and Beyond*. Oslo: Scandinavian University Press, 1992.

Farquhar, Peter, interview by Sunity Maharaj. *Trinidad and Tobago Review*, vol. 10, nos. 11 and 12 (Emancipation-Independence Anniversary, August 1988): 28–31.

Ferguson, Trevor. 'Sovereignty, Shiprider and Small States' (mimeo). University of the West Indies, St Augustine, Trinidad and Tobago, 1997.

Ferreira, Jo-Anne. *The Portuguese of Trinidad and Tobago: Portrait of an Ethnic Minority*. St Augustine, Trinidad and Tobago: Institute of Social and Economic Studies, 1994.

Fletcher LP. 'Politics, Public Policy and Friendly Societies in Trinidad and Tobago'. *Social and Economic Studies*, vol. 39, no. 3 (September 1990): 95–126.

Forde, Penelope, Anne Joseph et al. 'The Evolution of the Financial Sector in Trinidad and Tobago (1970– 1996)', in *The Financial Evolution of the Caribbean Community (1970–1996)*, ed. Laurence Clarke and Donna Danns, 407–82. St Augustine: Caribbean Centre for Monetary Studies, 1997.

Forde, Penelope and Kelvin Sargeant. 'The State Sector and Divestment in Trinidad and Tobago: Some Preliminary Findings', presented at the Annual Conference of the Regional Programme of Monetary Studies (mimeo, 1991).

Ghany, Hamid. 'The 1995 General Election and the Appointment of a Prime Minister', in LaGuerre 1997a: 17– 24.

________. 'Parliamentary Crisis and the Removal of the Speaker: The Case of Trinidad and Tobago'. *The Journal of Legislative Studies*, vol. 3, no. 2 (Summer 1997b): 112–38.

Ghany, Hamid. *Kamal: A Lifetime of Politics, Religion and Culture, a Biography*. San Juan, Trinidad and Tobago: Kamaluddin Mohammed, 1996.

Gibbings, Wesley. 'Journalism and the Political Process', in LaGuerre 1997a: 47–56.

Gomes, Albert. *Through a Maze of Colour*. Port of Spain: Key Caribbean Publications, 1974.

________. 'Race and Independence in Trinidad'. *New Society*, vol. 4, no. 100 (August 27, 1964): 15–6.

Greene, J. Edward. 'A Review of Political Science Research in the English-speaking Caribbean: Toward a Methodology'. *Social and Economic Studies*, vol. 23, no. 1 (March 1974): 1–47.

________. 'An Analysis of the General Elections in Trinidad and Tobago 1971', in Munroe and Lewis 1971: 136–44.

Haraksingh, Kusha. 'The Rise and Fall of Caribbean Institutions', in *Violence, Self and the Young Male*, ed. Arthur L. McShine, 74–8. Trinidad and Tobago: Lifeline, 1993.

Henry, Paget and Carl Stone, eds. *The Newer Caribbean: Decolonization, Democracy, and Developmen.* Inter-American Politics Series, sponsored by the Center for Inter-American Relations, New York, vol. 4. Philadelphia: Institute for the Study of Human Issues, 1983.

Henry, Zin. 'Industrial Relations and the Development Process', in Ryan 1988: 47–55.

Hilaire, Alvin. 'Commercial Policy in Trinidad and Tobago'. (mimeo). Port of Spain: Research Department, Central Bank of Trinidad and Tobago, 1992.

Hintzen, Percy. Trinidad and Tobago: Democracy, Nationalism, and the Construction of Racial Identity, in Edie 1994: 59–74.

________. *The Costs of Regime Survival: Racial Mobilization, Elite Domination and Control of the State in Guyana and Trinidad.* The Arnold and Caroline Rose Monograph Series of the American Sociological Association, ed. Ernest Q. Campbell. Cambridge: Cambridge University Press, 1989.

________. 'Bases of Elite Support for a Regime: Race Ideology and Clientelism as Bases for Leaders in Guyana and Trinidad'. *Comparative Political Studies*, vol. 16, no. 3 (October 1983): 363–91.

Inamete, Ufot. 'Politics and Governance in Trinidad and Tobago: Major Issues and Developments'. *Caribbean Studies*, vol. 25, nos. 3 and 4 (July-December 1992): 305–24.

Ince, Basil A. 'The Media and Foreign-policy Formation in Small States: Trinidad and Tobago'. *International Journal*, vol. 31, no. 2 (1976): 270–92.

Jacobs, W. Richard. *Butler Versus the King*. Port of Spain: Key Caribbean Publications, 1976.

James, C.L.R. *The Life of Captain Cipriani: An Account of British Government in the West Indies*. Nelson, Lancashire: Coulton & Co., 1932.

Job, Morgan. *Think Again: Essays on Race and Political Economy.* Trinidad and Tobago: Alkebu Industries, 1991.

Johnson, Howard. 'The Political Uses of Commissions of Enquiry: The Forster and Moyne Commissions', in Thomas 1987: 265–304.

Joseph, George 'Umbala'. *Diary of a Candidate.* Trinidad and Tobago: Umbala International Publishing, 1993.

Kambon, Khafra. *For Bread, Justice and Freedom: A Political Biography of George Weekes*. London: New Beacon Books, 1988.

Kiely, Ray. *The Politics of Labour and Development in Trinidad*. Kingston, Jamaica: The Press of the University of the West Indies, 1996.

Knight, Franklin W. 'Review of *Urban Nationalism: A Study of Political Development in Trinidad*, by Alvin Magid'. *The American Historical Review*, vol. 95, no. 2 (April 1990): 629–30.

LaGuerre, John Gaffar. *Politics, Society and Culture in the Commonwealth Caribbean*. St Augustine, Trinidad and Tobago: School of Continuing Studies, University of the West Indies, 1999.

________, ed. *The General Elections of 1995 in Trinidad and Tobago*. St Augustine, Trinidad and Tobago: School of Continuing Studies, University of the West Indies, 1997a.

________. *Issues in the Government and Politics of the West Indies: A Reader*. St Augustine, Trinidad and Tobago: School of Continuing Studies, University of the West Indies, 1997b.

________. 'General Elections of 1981'. *Journal of Commonwealth and Comparative Politics*, vol. 21, no. 2 (July 1983): 133–57.

________. *The Politics of Communalism: The Agony of the Left in Trinidad and Tobago, 1930–1955*. Trinidad: Pan-Caribbean Publications, 1982.

________. 'The General Elections of 1950'. *Social and Economic Studies*, vol. 29, no. 4 (December 1980): 321–35.

________. 'The General Elections of 1946 in Trinidad and Tobago'. *Social and Economic Studies*, vol. 21, no. 2 (June 1972): 184–204.

Ledgister, F.S.J. *Class Alliances and the Liberal Authoritarian State: The Roots of Post-colonial Democracy in Jamaica, Trinidad and Tobago, and Surinam*. Trenton, N.J.: Africa World Press, 1998.

Lequay, Alloy R, *Against the Tide: A Life Dedicated to Sports and Politics. Autobiography of Alloy R. Lequay, CMT.* 1992 Reprint. La Romain, Trinidad and Tobago: RPL, 2001.

Lewis, Gordon. *The Growth of the Modern West Indies*. London: MacGibbon and Key, 1968.

Lewis, Gordon. 'The Trinidad and Tobago General Elections of 1961'. *Caribbean Studies*, vol. 2, no. 2 (July 1962): 121–62.

Lloyd-Evans, S. and R. Potter. 'Government Response to Informal Sector Retail Trading: The People's Mall, Port of Spain, Trinidad'. *Geography*, vol. 78, no. 3 (1993): 315–18.

Look Lai, Walton. 'CLR James and Trinidad Nationalism', in *CLR James's Caribbean*, eds. Paget Henry and Paul Buhle, 315–18. London: Macmillan Press, 1992.

MacDonald, Scott B. *Trinidad and Tobago: Democracy and Development in the Caribbean*. Praeger Special Studies: Praeger Scientific. New York: Praeger, 1986.

Magid, Alvin. *Urban Nationalism: A Study of Political Development in Trinidad*. Gainesville: University of Florida Press, 1988.

Mahabir, Winston. *In and Out of Politics: Tales of the Government of Dr Eric Williams from the Notebooks of a Former Minister.* Port of Spain: Inprint Caribbean, 1978.

Maingot, Anthony. *Global Economics and Local Politics in Trinidad's Divestment Program.* North-south agenda papers, no. 34. Florida: Dante B. Fascell North-South Centre, December 1998.

Malik, Yogendra K. *East Indians in Trinidad: A Study in Minority Politics.* Published for the Institute of Race Relations. London: Oxford University Press, 1971.

Manor, James, ed. *Rethinking Third World Politics.* London: Longman, 1991.

Maraj, Bhadase Sagan, *Hostile and Recalcitrant.* Edited by Devant Maharaj et al. St Augustine, Trinidad and Tobago: SDMS of T&T, 2001.

*Master and Servant: Bhadase Sagan Maraj.* St Augustine, Trinidad and Tobago: SDMS of T&T, 1991.

McIntyre, W. David. *Colonies into Commonwealth.* Problems of History Paperbacks, Revised edition. London: Blandford Press, 1966; 1974.

Meeks, Brian. 'The Development of the 1970 Revolution in Trinidad and Tobago'. MSc thesis, University of the West Indies, Mona, Jamaica, 1976.

Meighoo, Kirk. 'Putting up a New Resistance: Towards an Open, Plural, and Democratic Left in Trinidad and Tobago'. MSc research paper, Consortium Graduate School of Social Sciences, University of the West Indies, Mona, Jamaica, 1994.

________. 'History, Class, Ideology, and Empowerment: An Examination of Servol and Development in Trinidad and Tobago'. BA research paper, International Development Studies, University of Toronto, 1992.

Miller, Daniel. *Capitalism: An Ethnographic Approach.* Explorations in Anthropology Series. Oxford: Berg, 1997.

________. *Modernity, an Ethnographic Approach: Dualism and Mass Consumption in Trinidad.* Explorations in Anthropology Series. Oxford: Berg, 1994.

________, ed. *Unwrapping Christmas.* Oxford Studies in Social and Cultural Anthropology. Oxford: Clarendon Press, 1993.

Miller, Daniel and Don Slater. *The Internet: An Ethnographic Approach.* Oxford: Berg, 2000.

Millette, Trevor. *The Chinese in Trinidad.* Port of Spain: Inprint Caribbean, 1993.

Mohammed, Kamaluddin, interview by Sunity Maharaj. *Trinidad and Tobago Review*, vol. 10, nos. 11 and 12 (Emancipation-Independence Anniversary, August 1988): 26.

Mohammed, Patricia. 'Reflections on the Women's Movement in Trinidad: Calypsoes, Changes, and Sexual violence'. *Feminist Review*, no 38 (Summer 1991): 33–47.

Mordecai, Sir John. *The West Indies: The Federal Negotiations.* London: George Allen and Unwin, 1968.

Moskos, Charles C., Jr. *The Sociology of Independence: A Study of Nationalist Attitudes Among West Indian Leaders*. Cambridge, Massachusetts: Schenkman Publishing, 1967.

Munroe, Trevor and Rupert Lewis. *Readings in Government and Politics of the West Indies*. Revised edition. Mona, Jamaica: Department of Government, University of the West Indies, 1971.

Mustapha, Nasser. 'The Influence of Indian Islam on Fundamentalist Trends in Trinidad and Tobago'. *Sociological Bulletin*, vol. 46, no. 2 (September 1997): 245–65.

Naipaul, V.S. *Conversations with V.S. Naipaul*. Ed. Feroza Jessawalla. Literary Conversation Series. general ed. Peggy Whitman Prenshaw. Jackson: University Press of Mississippi, 1997.

________. *The Middle Passage*. London: André Deutsch, 1962; London: McMillan.1995a.

________. *A Way in the World*. London: William Heinemann, 1994; London: Minerva, 1995b.

________. Introduction to *East Indians in the Caribbean: Colonialism and the Struggle for Identity*, eds, Bridget Brereton and Winston Dookeran, 1– 10. New York: Kraus International Publications, 1982.

________. *The Return of Eva Peron, With the Killings in Trinidad*. London: André Deutsch, 1980; London: Penguin Books, 1981.

________. *The Overcrowded Barracoon*. London: André Deutsch, 1972; London: Penguin Books, 1976.

________. *The Suffrage of Elvira*. London: André Deutsch, 1958; London: Penguin Books, 1969.

Nicholls, David G. 'East Indians and Black Power in Trinidad'. *Race*, vol 12, no 4 (1971): 443–59.

Nunes, F.E. 'A Ministry and its Community: Tobago, A Case Study in Participation'. *Social and Economic Studies*, vol. 23, no. 2 (June 1974): 176–85.

Oxaal, Ivar, *Black Intellectuals and the Dilemmas of Race and Class in Trinidad*. Cambridge, Massachusetts: Schenkman Publishing, 1971; 1982.

Panday, Basdeo. 'Trade Unionism, Politics and Indo-Caribbean Leadership'. Paper presented at ISER-NCIC Conference on Challenge and Change: The Indian Diaspora in its Historical and Contemporary Contexts (mimeo), university of the West Indies, St Augustine, Trinidad and Tobago, 1995.

Pantin, Dennis. 'Political Crisis in Trinidad and Tobago: Cause or Coincidence?' *Caribbean Quarterly*, vol. 37, nos. 2 and 3 (June-September 1991). 63–83.

________. 'Whither Point Lisas? Lessons for the Future', in Ryan 1988: 27–45.

Parris, Canute. 'Political Dissidence in Post-independence Jamaica and Trinidad: 1962–72' PhD diss., New School for Social Research, 1976.

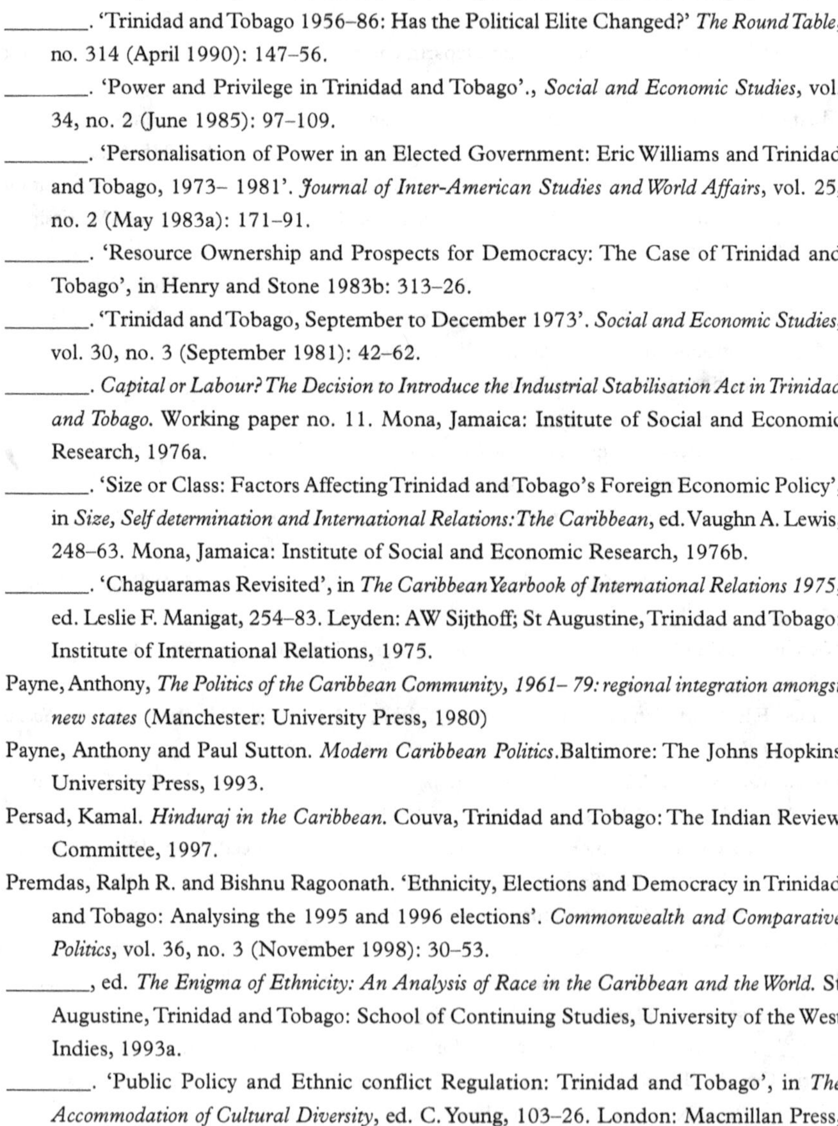

Parris, Carl D. 'A "limited sovereignty" for Caribbean States?' Institute of International Relations, University of the West Indies, St Augustine, Trinidad and Tobago, 1997.

________. 'Trinidad and Tobago 1956–86: Has the Political Elite Changed?' *The Round Table*, no. 314 (April 1990): 147–56.

________. 'Power and Privilege in Trinidad and Tobago'., *Social and Economic Studies*, vol. 34, no. 2 (June 1985): 97–109.

________. 'Personalisation of Power in an Elected Government: Eric Williams and Trinidad and Tobago, 1973– 1981'. *Journal of Inter-American Studies and World Affairs*, vol. 25, no. 2 (May 1983a): 171–91.

________. 'Resource Ownership and Prospects for Democracy: The Case of Trinidad and Tobago', in Henry and Stone 1983b: 313–26.

________. 'Trinidad and Tobago, September to December 1973'. *Social and Economic Studies*, vol. 30, no. 3 (September 1981): 42–62.

________. *Capital or Labour? The Decision to Introduce the Industrial Stabilisation Act in Trinidad and Tobago.* Working paper no. 11. Mona, Jamaica: Institute of Social and Economic Research, 1976a.

________. 'Size or Class: Factors Affecting Trinidad and Tobago's Foreign Economic Policy', in *Size, Self determination and International Relations: Tthe Caribbean*, ed. Vaughn A. Lewis, 248–63. Mona, Jamaica: Institute of Social and Economic Research, 1976b.

________. 'Chaguaramas Revisited', in *The Caribbean Yearbook of International Relations 1975*, ed. Leslie F. Manigat, 254–83. Leyden: AW Sijthoff; St Augustine, Trinidad and Tobago: Institute of International Relations, 1975.

Payne, Anthony, *The Politics of the Caribbean Community, 1961– 79: regional integration amongst new states* (Manchester: University Press, 1980)

Payne, Anthony and Paul Sutton. *Modern Caribbean Politics.*Baltimore: The Johns Hopkins University Press, 1993.

Persad, Kamal. *Hinduraj in the Caribbean.* Couva, Trinidad and Tobago: The Indian Review Committee, 1997.

Premdas, Ralph R. and Bishnu Ragoonath. 'Ethnicity, Elections and Democracy in Trinidad and Tobago: Analysing the 1995 and 1996 elections'. *Commonwealth and Comparative Politics*, vol. 36, no. 3 (November 1998): 30–53.

________, ed. *The Enigma of Ethnicity: An Analysis of Race in the Caribbean and the World.* St Augustine, Trinidad and Tobago: School of Continuing Studies, University of the West Indies, 1993a.

________. 'Public Policy and Ethnic conflict Regulation: Trinidad and Tobago', in *The Accommodation of Cultural Diversity*, ed. C. Young, 103–26. London: Macmillan Press, 1999.

________. 'Ethnicity and Elections in the Caribbean: A Radical Realignment of Power in Trinidad and the Threat of Communal Strife'. Working paper. Helen Kellogg Institute for International Studies, 1996a.

________. 'Ethnicity and Elections in Trinidad and Tobago: A Radical Re-alignment of Power in 1995' (mimeo). Department of Government, University of the West Indies, St Augustine, Trinidad and Tobago, 1996b.

________. 'Public Policy in a Multi-ethnic State: The Case of National Service in Trinidad and Tobago'. *Social and Economic Studies*, vol. 45, no. 1 (March 1996c): 79–102.

________. 'Ethnic Conflict in Trinidad and Tobago: Domination and Reconciliation', in *Trinidad ethnicity*, ed. Kevin Yelvington, 136–60. London: Macmillan Press, 1993b.

________. 'Race, Politics, and Succession in Trinidad and Guyana', in *Modern Caribbean Politics*, ed. Anthony Payne and Paul Sutton, 98–124. Baltimore: John Hopkins University Press, 1993c.

Ragoonath Bishnu. 'Race and Class in Caribbean Politics'. *Plural Societies*, vol. 18, no. 1 (July 1998): 71–101.

________. 'Indian Arrival and Political Power in Trinidad and Tobago: The UNC's Victory in the 1995 Elections', in LaGuerre 1997a: 25–41.

________. 'Race and Ethnic Relations and the Competition for Political Power in Trinidad'. *Journal of Ethno Development*, vol. 3, no. 3 (1994).

________. 'The Failure of the Abu Bakr Coup: The Plural Society, Cultural Traditions and Political Development in Trinidad'. *Journal of Commonwealth and Comparative Politics*, vol. 31, no. 2 (July 1993): 33–53.

Ramesar, Marianne. *Survivors of Another Crossing: A History of East Indians in Trinidad, 1880–1946.* St Augustine, Trinidad and Tobago: School of Continuing Studies, University of the West Indies, 1994.

Ramsaran, Dave. *Breaking the Bonds of Indentureship: Indo-Trinidadians in Business.* St Augustine, Trinidad and Tobago: Institute of Social and Economic Research, 1993.

Reddock, Rhoda. *Women, Labour, and Politics in Trinidad and Tobago: A History.*London: Zed, 1994.

Reis, Charles. *A History of the Constitution or Government of Trinidad.* Vol. 1, 2nd ed. Port of Spain: n.p., 1915; Trinidad: n.p., 1929.

Renwick, David. *Investing in Trinidad and Tobago.* Port of Spain: Media and Editorial Projects, 1998.

Robinson, Patricia. 'The Banking System: Twenty-five Years On', in Ryan 1988: 57–62.

Rubin, Vera. 'Culture, Politics and Race Relations'. *Social and Economic Studies*, vol. 11, no. 4 (December 1962), 433–55.

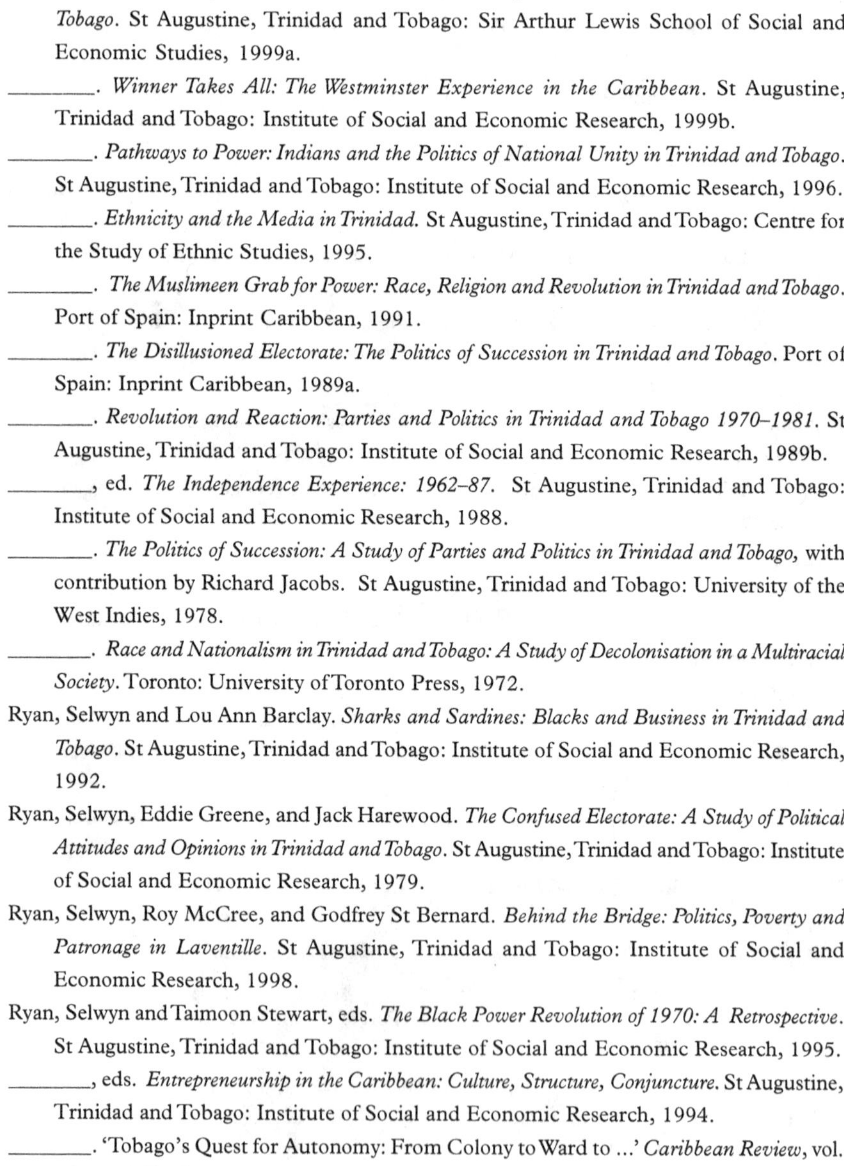


Ryan, Selwyn D. *The Jhandi and the Cross: The Clash of Cultures in Post-creole Trinidad and Tobago*. St Augustine, Trinidad and Tobago: Sir Arthur Lewis School of Social and Economic Studies, 1999a.

________. *Winner Takes All: The Westminster Experience in the Caribbean*. St Augustine, Trinidad and Tobago: Institute of Social and Economic Research, 1999b.

________. *Pathways to Power: Indians and the Politics of National Unity in Trinidad and Tobago*. St Augustine, Trinidad and Tobago: Institute of Social and Economic Research, 1996.

________. *Ethnicity and the Media in Trinidad.* St Augustine, Trinidad and Tobago: Centre for the Study of Ethnic Studies, 1995.

________. *The Muslimeen Grab for Power: Race, Religion and Revolution in Trinidad and Tobago*. Port of Spain: Inprint Caribbean, 1991.

________. *The Disillusioned Electorate: The Politics of Succession in Trinidad and Tobago*. Port of Spain: Inprint Caribbean, 1989a.

________. *Revolution and Reaction: Parties and Politics in Trinidad and Tobago 1970–1981*. St Augustine, Trinidad and Tobago: Institute of Social and Economic Research, 1989b.

________, ed. *The Independence Experience: 1962–87.* St Augustine, Trinidad and Tobago: Institute of Social and Economic Research, 1988.

________. *The Politics of Succession: A Study of Parties and Politics in Trinidad and Tobago,* with contribution by Richard Jacobs. St Augustine, Trinidad and Tobago: University of the West Indies, 1978.

________. *Race and Nationalism in Trinidad and Tobago: A Study of Decolonisation in a Multiracial Society*. Toronto: University of Toronto Press, 1972.

Ryan, Selwyn and Lou Ann Barclay. *Sharks and Sardines: Blacks and Business in Trinidad and Tobago*. St Augustine, Trinidad and Tobago: Institute of Social and Economic Research, 1992.

Ryan, Selwyn, Eddie Greene, and Jack Harewood. *The Confused Electorate: A Study of Political Attitudes and Opinions in Trinidad and Tobago*. St Augustine, Trinidad and Tobago: Institute of Social and Economic Research, 1979.

Ryan, Selwyn, Roy McCree, and Godfrey St Bernard. *Behind the Bridge: Politics, Poverty and Patronage in Laventille*. St Augustine, Trinidad and Tobago: Institute of Social and Economic Research, 1998.

Ryan, Selwyn and Taimoon Stewart, eds. *The Black Power Revolution of 1970: A Retrospective*. St Augustine, Trinidad and Tobago: Institute of Social and Economic Research, 1995.

________, eds. *Entrepreneurship in the Caribbean: Culture, Structure, Conjuncture.* St Augustine, Trinidad and Tobago: Institute of Social and Economic Research, 1994.

________. 'Tobago's Quest for Autonomy: From Colony to Ward to ...' *Caribbean Review*, vol. 14, no. 2 (Spring 1985): 7–40.

________. 'Trinidad and Tobago: The General Elections of 1976'. *Caribbean Studies*, vol. 19, nos. 1 and 2 (April-July 1979): 5–32.

Samaroo, Brinsley. 'Preparing for Politics: The Pre-PNM Years of Eric Williams'. Presented at the Conference on Eric Williams and the Pan-African Movement, Wellesley College, Massachusetts, April 7– 9, 2000.

________. 'The Making of the 1946 Constitution in Trinidad'. Fifth Conference of Caribbean Historians (mimeo). St Augustine, Trinidad and Tobago: University of the West Indies, 1973.

________. 'The Trinidad Workingmen's Association and the Origins of Popular Protest in a Crown Colony'. *Social and Economic Studies*, vol. 21, no. 2 (June 1972). 205–22.

________. 'Decolonisation in a Multi-racial Society: A Case Study of Trinidad and Tobago' PhD diss., York University, Toronto, 1967.

Sandoval, José Miguel. 'State Capitalism in a Petroleum Based Economy: The Case of Trinidad and Tobago', in *Crisis in the Caribbean*, eds. Fitzroy Ambursley and Robin Cohen, 247–68. Kingston, Jamaica: Heinemann, 1983.

Siewah, Samaroo, and Sattie Arjoonsingh, eds. and comps. *Basdeo Panday: The Making of a Prime Minister. Selected Speeches (1966–1998)*, 2 vols. Trinidad and Tobago: Chakra Publishing House [Caribbean], 1998.

Siewah, Samaroo, eds. And comps. *Lotus and the Dagger: The Capildeo Speeches (1957– 1994)*. Trinidad and Tobago: Chakra Publishing House [Caribbean], 1994.

Siewah, Samaroo, and Roodal Moonilal, eds. *Basdeo Panday: An Enigma Answered. A first Volume of Speeches*, with a foreword by Dr John LaGuerre. Trinidad and Tobago: Chakra Publishing House [Caribbean], 1991.

Singh, H.P. *The Indian Struggle for Justice and Equality Against Black Racism in Trinidad and Tobago, 1956– 1962*, compiled and introduced by Indian Review Press. Couva, Trinidad and Tobago: Indian Review Press, 1993.

Singh, Kelvin. 'Conflict and Collaboration: Tradition and Modernizing Indo-Trinidadian Elites (1917– 56)'. *New West Indian Guide*, vol. 70, nos. 3 and 4 (1996): 229–53.

________. *Race and Class Struggles in a Colonial State: Trinidad 1917–1945*. Kingston, Jamaica: The Press, University of the West Indies, 1994.

________. 'The June 1937 Disturbances in Trinidad', in Thomas 1987: 57–80. [which Thomas?]

Solomon, Patrick. *Solomon: An Autobiography*. Port of Spain: Inprint Caribbean, 1981.

Spackman, Ann. 'The Senate of Trinidad and Tobago'. *Social and Economic Studies*, vol. 16, no. 1 (March 1967): 77–100.

________. 'Constitutional development in Trinidad and Tobago'. *Social and Economic Studies*, vol. 14, no. 4 (December 1965): 283–320.

Sutton, Paul. 'Trinidad and Tobago: Oil Capitalism and the 'Presidential Power' of Eric Williams', in *Dependency Under Challenge*, eds. Anthony Payne and Paul Sutton, 43–76. Manchester: Manchester University Press, 1984.

________. 'Black Power in Trinidad and Tobago: The Crisis of 1970'. *The Journal of Commonwealth and Comparative Politics*, vol. 21, no. 2 (July 1983): 115–32.

________. 'Introduction to Williams' (1981) [journal/book and publishing details]

________. 'External Factors and Political Development in Trinidad and Tobago, 1962–1972' Ph.D. diss., Victoria University of Manchester, 1979.

Thomas, Roy, ed. *The Trinidad Labour Riots of 1937: Perspectives 50 Years Later*. St Augustine, Trinidad and Tobago: Extra-Mural Studies Unit, University of the West Indies.

Thomas, Tony and John Riddell. *Black Power in the Caribbean*. New York: Pathfinder Press, 1971.

*Trinidad under Siege: The Muslimeen Uprising, Six Days of Terror*. Port of Spain: Trinidad Express Newspapers, 1990.

*TTYB, Trinidad and Tobago Year Book*. Containing information obtained from official records and reliable sources. Port of Spain: Yuille's Printerie, 1946–1957.

Verner, JG. 'The Recruitment of Cabinet Ministers in the Former British Caribbean: A Five-country Study'. *The Journal of Developing Areas*, vol. 7, no. 4 (July 1973): 635–52.

Williams, Eric. *Forged from the Love of Liberty: Selected Speeches of Dr Eric Williams*, complied by Paul K. Sutton. Trinidad and Tobago: Longman Caribbean, 1981.

________. *Inward Hunger: The Education of a Prime Minister.* London: André Deutsch, 1969.

Wrong, Hume. *Government of the West Indies*. London: Oxford University Press, 1923.

Yelvington, Kevin. 'Caribbean Crucible: History, Culture, and Globalization'. *Social Education*, vol. 64, no. 2 (March 2000): 70–7.

________. 'Vote Dem Out: The Demise of the PNM in Trinidad and Tobago'. *Caribbean Review*, vol. 15, no. 4 (1987): 8–33.

## NEWSPAPERS

*Guardian*. London. October 20, 1973.

*Independent*. Port of Spain. May 28, 1996 – July 18, 1998.

*Newsday*. Port of Spain. March 6, 1997 – June 19, 1998.

*TE. Trinidad Express*. Port of Spain. July 27, 1972 – June 30, 2002

*TG. Trinidad Guardian*. Port of Spain. February 8, 1925 – December 30, 2001

*TTR.. Trinidad and Tobago Review*. Port of Spain. October 31, 1986 – June/July 2001.

*Trinidad and Tobago Mirror*. Port of Spain. September 9, 1988 – November 3, 2000.

*Vanguard*. San Fernando, Trinidad and Tobago. January 19, 1991.

## PERIODICALS

*ACP–EU Courier*. Brussels. May – June 1998.

*CI. Caribbean Insight*. London. January 1995.

*Caribbean Dialogue: A Journal of Contemporary Policy Issue*. St Augustine, Trinidad and Tobago. October/December 1997.

*Europa Yearbook 1986: A World Survey*, 2 vols. London.

*LARRCR.. Latin American Regional Reports: Caribbean Region*. London. May 11 – November 5, 1992.

*Latin American Monitor: Caribbean*. May 1999.

*Media Trak*. Port of Spain. October 1993 – April 1998.

*NTT. News from Trinidad and Tobago*. London. March 27, 1985 – June 24, 1987.

'The 1990 Muslimeen Insurrection in Trinidad and Tobago: Its Causes and a Measure of its Heroism'. *Caribbean Quarterly*, vol. 37, nos. 2 and 3, Special double issue (June-September 1991).

*People: The Caribbean Magazine*. Port of Spain. November 1981.

# Index

www.ingramcontent.com/pod-product-compliance
Lightning Source LLC
Chambersburg PA
CBHW050551270326
41926CB00012B/2008

* 9 7 8 9 7 6 6 3 7 0 7 9 4 *